# On This Date in Music

A Day to Day History of the Music that Inspires Us
and the Bands and Artists Who Create It

## by **Michael Walter**

On This Date In Music
By Michael Walter
Copyright 2018.

First Edition


For information about permission to reproduce selections of this book email Mike@EliteEntertainment.com or visit OnThisDateInMusic.com

ISBN-13: 978-0692179796 (Mike Walter Publishing)

Printed in the good old United States of America

# Introduction

I hope this book takes you a year to read. *no. missing alot of good surprises est*

Am I the first author ever to say that? Maybe. But seriously, I hope it does. Because then you've read this book like I always intended, one essay every day, instead of plowing through non-stop and trying to absorb all of these tales back-to-back-to-back. And you don't have to start that yearly trek on January 1st either. If you happen to pick this book up in the middle of the year, say on May 8th, you can start that day and read through till the following May 7th. There is no story arch that you need to follow. Every essay is a stand-alone piece, so you'll be fine.

I want to say a word about the selection process. As this project took shape there were a handful of stories that had to be told on specific dates. February 3rd and December 8th are the two most obvious (and tragic) examples. Other stories fell on specific dates by happenstance or luck. I could have done a piece on MTV pretty much any day, but placing it on August 1st, the day in 1981 it went on air, just made the most sense. U2 is a perfect example of luck (the luck of the Irish, you might say). I wanted to tell a story of an Irish artist on St. Patrick's Day. The musical Gods handed me a gift when I discovered that a young, unsigned, U2 won a talent contest on March 17th, 1978 which helped launch their career. That was a happy accident, just like Tom Petty recording "American Girl" on July 4th, 1976 or "White Christmas" sitting at #1 on December 25th, 1954. Most other stories though, could have been told on any given date. In fact, as I shuffled these essays around to make them all fit, some wound up landing on a half a dozen dates or more before I finally codified everything. I mention this to support my "start wherever you want and keep going" theory because the vast majority of these stories simply landed where they did by chance. The stories needed to be told (in my humble opinion). Which day they were told was rarely important.

As far as which songs, albums, bands and other stories got included in this project, I will readily admit that my biases show through. My biases and my background. I have been an avid reader of books about musicians my whole life so when I started this project, I naturally pulled from this knowledge first. Since I just happened to have read a number of books about the Beatles and the Stones I wound up with more stories about those British Invasion stalwarts than any other bands. I also enjoy disco and probably over-glorify the punk bands of the late seventies. Having completed this project and reworked or eliminated many of my initial essays, I stand by the selections that remain. I think they are all interesting and/or important which, in the end, were my only criteria. Bands and artists as far ranging as Rush and Jay-Z had to be covered because they are too important to modern music to be ignored. Stories like Willie Nelson, young and unknown, bumping into Patsy Cline's husband in a Nashville bar one day and handing him a demo of "Crazy," may not be as important but they sure are interesting. Others, like how Clapton wrote "Wonderful Tonight" or Michael Jackson came up with "Billie Jean" met both criteria. I think the songs are important enough that they had to be included, and the fact that their creation is so damn interesting just makes them better reads. Is every important and/or interesting musical story included in this book? Heck no! In fact I've already begun collecting stories for a follow-up so when you're through with this book, if you feel there's a glaring omission, reach out to me and let me know. I'll be sure to credit you in *On This Date in Music - Part Two*.

And finally I want to answer a criticism I may get before I even get it. And that is, Why me? Why am I qualified to write this book? I am not a music journalist or critic. I haven't interviewed any of the subjects of this book nor have I led a Forrest-Gump-like life that coincidentally put me at all of the events I write about. Heck, I don't even play a musical instrument nor, much to my frustration, can I hold a note. But as I said I'm an avid reader and as this project got underway I embraced this book with passion because it combines two things I love: music and storytelling. I've spent the better part of my adult life playing music for people as a DJ and the better part of my free time reading books and magazines and watching documentaries about artists and bands. When a song comes on the radio, I'm often the guy who goes, "You know how they came up with this?" and when whoever I'm with answers "no" I launch into another tale. They are stories I loved learning and enjoy sharing and that is my one and only expertise in this field.

I thank you for grabbing this book in whatever form you did. I hope you find these stories interesting and enlightening. But most importantly, I hope they lead you to the music. Whether or not you are already a fan of the band, album or song of the day, I hope you'll give it a spin. Find it on whatever platform you enjoy music these days and listen (or watch, if it's a video that is highlighted, especially Billy Squier's "Rock Me Tonight" - that one you have to watch!) I initially told many of these stories on Facebook and a good number of my friends would tell me I determined their playlist for the day. That was a great compliment to me because nothing brings us together like our love of music. It's one of the reasons I enjoy going to concerts where ten to fifty thousand strangers are all united by their love for a band. You sing along with people you've never met, or put your arm around their shoulders and sway, or hold up your lighter (nowadays your iPhone with the flashlight on) and illuminate a previously darkened arena, and for a brief moment, life is carefree. That's the magic of music. I've seen it first hand at the thousands of parties I have spun at through the years. The right song, the right note even, can make us forget our troubles and get lost in the sound. I hope you have had similar experiences in your life and that this book leads you to some more.

And now, unless it is New Year's Day, I invite you to flip to whatever date you're beginning this book on and start your year-long trek through the incredible soundtrack of our lives.

This book is dedicated to the artists, musicians and songwriters who create the music that becomes the soundtrack of our lives. From the bottom of my heart I thank you all for giving my life some rhythm and soul

"Music gives a soul to the universe, wings to the mind, flight to the imagination and life to everything."
Plato

## January 1st

On this date in 1970, as not only a new year began but a whole new decade dawned, Led Zeppelin's second LP, *Led Zeppelin II*, held a tenuous grasp of the top spot on the *Billboard* album chart. Just days before it had dislodged the Beatle's *Abbey Road* from that position but a week later *Abbey Road* would grab it back. After two weeks Led Zeppelin would reclaim the #1 spot but just for a week, when *Abbey Road* returned. Finally on January 31st of 1970 *Led Zeppelin II* would bump *Abbey Road* for a third time and then sit at the top of the album chart for 5 more weeks. It was as if the two albums and the two bands were wrestling to end one era and begin another. The sixties were over but they weren't going easily into the night. And the seventies had begun but the accouchement wasn't easy.  It was the shifting of tectonic plates, causing massive change to the landscape of rock and pop.  And there couldn't have been two more perfect bands to fight this fight as the decades flipped, for as influential as the Beatles had been to the sixties, Led Zeppelin would be their equal throughout the seventies.  One group created the whole paradigm for what a rock band could and should be. The other threw that paradigm out a hotel window, trashed the room, fucked some groupies and wrote songs about it all. The times had definitely changed.

Led Zeppelin emerged from the remnants of the Yardbirds. In fact for a short time they performed under the name the New Yardbirds before adopting Led Zeppelin. Everyone in the music scene in London knew guitarist Jimmy Page from his years of studio work and now here he was, finally helming a band worthy of his prodigious talents. Zeppelin released their self-titled debut in January of 1969 and began touring both sides of the Atlantic non-stop. That first album, and those early concerts, let the world know that there was a new, hard-rocking band to pay attention to. Wanting to strike while their reputation was growing, Led Zeppelin started to work up new songs for a follow-up while on the road. Many of the riffs and ideas that made up *Led Zeppelin II* came to the band spontaneously while playing live.  For example, they would often turn "Dazed and Confused" into a long and improvised jam session and Page would sometimes spontaneously play a riff or chord structure during this and think to himself, "There's the making of a new song." Zeppelin also started recording some of these new songs while on the road, working in whatever studio they could find. Singer Robert Plant has said: "It was crazy really. We were writing the numbers in hotel rooms and then we'd do a rhythm track in London, add the vocal in New York, overdub the harmonica in Vancouver and then come back to finish mixing at New York." The band's recording engineer, Eddie Kramer would add: "We did that album piece-meal. We cut some of the tracks in some of the most bizarre studios you can imagine, little holes in the wall. Cheap studios. But in the end it sounded bloody marvelous."

Marvelous indeed. There are few albums in the history of rock that can measure up.

*Led Zeppelin II* opens up with one of the most recognizable riffs in all of rock history. "Whole Lotta Love," with its immediately identifiable guitar lick, John Bonham's thunderous drumming and the most sexually urgent singing of Plant's career, is as good an album opener as there is in music history. And with that almost two minute breakdown, that seems to drag the listener to hell and back, the song is like nothing else recorded before or since. We take for granted how groundbreaking that song is because we live in a world where it exists. But prior to the release of *Led Zeppelin II* no one had ever recorded anything like "Whole Lotta Love." And that was just track one. From there we get the psychedelic trip of "What Is and What Should Never Be," the blues rock of "The Lemon Song" and the incredible love song that is "Thank You." Side Two opens with another classic riff as "Heartbreaker" gives Page yet another opportunity to show off his guitar skills. "Living Loving Maid (She's Just a Woman)" starts immediately after, as if the band didn't want the listener to catch a breath. "Ramble On" serves as a well-deserved respite after all that rocking and it also introduces some Tolkien imagery, name checking Mordor and Gollum. As a band, Led Zeppelin helped create heavy metal and, like "Ramble On," many songs from the genre traded in Middle-Earth and fantasy inspired themes. Next we hear one of the great drum riff intros as the instrumental rock jam, "Moby Dick," kicks off in John Bonham's capable hands. *Led Zeppelin II* raps up with a tribute to the band's real roots, dirty American blues, with a cover of Willie Dixon's "Bring It On Home." Of the nine tracks on the album, there's not a false note or missed opportunity to show the band's dedication to hard rock.

Along with hard rocking pioneers like Deep Purple and Black Sabbath, Zeppelin's sound would usher in heavy metal which would dominate the decade of the seventies. With electric guitars so far forward in the mix they were often distorted, thundering drums to drive the tempo, thick and dense bass work and vocals that were often screamed over that cacophony, heavy metal was music meant to be played loud. Very loud. Besides metal, Led Zeppelin also helped popularize album oriented rock stations (or AOR as they are popularly called). Prior to the early seventies almost every station played singles (and most, only Top 40 songs at that). But AOR introduced a much more progressive format, allowing DJs the freedom to spin songs that may not have been successful or even released as singles. Led Zeppelin's highest charted single was "Whole Lotta Love," which peaked at #4 in January of 1970. In fact, it's their only Top 10 song. Yet the band has sold over two-hundred million albums and they are staples on rock radio. They became one of the first über-successful bands that weren't beholden to sales of their singles for their popularity. Their albums flew off record store shelves and their concerts were always sold-out. So who cared if the Carpenters did better on the pop chart?

Similar to the Beatles, Led Zeppelin's recording career lasted about a decade. When John Bonham died in September of 1980 the band called it quits. They released a simple statement that read: "We wish it to be known that the loss of our dear friend, and the deep sense of undivided harmony felt by ourselves and our manager, have led us to decide that we could not continue as we were."

Repackaging of old albums, the occasional concert footage dusted off for a live release, and elaborate box sets have had to satisfy their still ardent fan base since then. Other than a couple of one-off reunion shows, Page and Plant have refused the financial temptations (and they are great) to reunite and tour once again. They seem content to let their legacy speak for itself. And oh, what a legacy it is.

If you own *Led Zeppelin II* you should crank it up today. If you don't, download it now. Take yourself back to New Year's Day, 1970 when the music world was irreparably changing. You'll thank me later.

## January 2nd

On this date in 1971, the Chicago Transit Authority's "Does Anybody Really Know What Time It Is?" peaked on the *Billboard* Hot 100 chart at #7, becoming their third consecutive Top 10 hit. The band from, you guessed it, Chicago, was on their way to becoming, according to *Billboard* magazine, the American band with the greatest singles chart success and album chart success.

The band that would eventually become Chicago started in the late sixties at DePaul University in the Windy City. Early on, they ambitiously called themselves the Big Thing but soon changed that to the Chicago Transit Authority. After relocating to Los Angeles, they started to gain a strong following and were soon signed to Columbia Records. Before their debut was even released Columbia secured some prominent opening slots for the band. The Chicago Transit Authority shared the stage with Jimi Hendrix and Janis Joplin. Hendrix would tell the band "Your horn players are like one set of lungs" and indeed if there is a defining sound for the band it is that impressive set of wind instruments. They have often been described as a "rock and roll band with horns."

As work got underway for their debut, it was obvious to all that it needed to be a double LP. But labels are usually reluctant to release double albums as they are often less successful. Record companies will sometimes acquiesce when it comes to established artists with proven track records but for a brand new band to release a double LP as a debut is fairly rare in the music industry. Columbia agreed only on the condition that the band would take a smaller royalty.

Their self-titled debut album was released in April of 1969 and it sold very well, eventually reaching #9 on the *Billboard* album chart and selling a million units in its first six months. But the album didn't initially produce any hit singles and they lost out on the Grammy for Best New Artist, which went to Crosby, Stills & Nash; Chicago Transit Authority was in good company though, with Led Zeppelin losing out that year as well. They were then threatened with legal action by Chicago's actual mass-transit company which is why they shortened their name to simply Chicago.

It's not often a band gets to release two eponymous albums (without repeating the title) but such was the case when the newly renamed Chicago released *Chicago* in early 1970. This too, was a double album with some epic suites clocking in at over 10 minutes each. One section of the "Ballet for a Girl in Buchannon" suite, "Make Me Smile," was released as the lead single and it is this happy and upbeat song that finally put Chicago high on the singles chart. "Make Me Smile" reached #9 and when its follow-up, "25 or 6 to 4" peaked at #4 Columbia wanted another single to release. But *Chicago* had been stripped clean of everything with hit potential (mainly because someone had decided to bury "Colour My World" as a B-side to "Make Me Smile") so they went back to the band's debut and released "Does Anybody Really Know What Time It Is?" as the band's next single. When that song cracked the Top 10, on this date in 1971, it was clear Chicago was well on their way to being a successful band.

With over 100 million albums sold and twenty Top 10 singles, Chicago is listed by *Billboard* magazine as the most successful American band in both categories. In 2016 the Rock and Roll Hall of Fame gave them a long-overdue induction. The "rock and roll band with horns" has proven that their original name, the Big Thing, was actually quite fitting.

## January 3rd

On this date in 1970, B.J. Thomas' "Raindrops Keep Fallin' on My Head" reached the top of the pop chart, becoming the first #1 single of the new decade. The song was written by two legendary composers specifically for a big budget movie, yet it was reportedly turned down by two even-more-legendary singers. When it finally fell to Thomas he scored the biggest hit of his career with it.

When production began on the 1969 film *Butch Cassidy and the Sundance Kid* and Paul Newman and Robert Redford were cast in the two lead roles, it was clear the movie was going to be big. Hal David and Burt Bacharach were brought in to score the film and were given the task of coming up with a song for the now legendary scene where Butch Cassidy (played by Paul Newman) rides a bicycle with Etta Place (played by Katherine Ross) on the handlebars. It's a light moment in an otherwise dramatic movie and the scene called for a similarly fun and whimsical song. As the duo got to work, Bacharach recommended the title "Raindrops Keep Fallin' on My Head" but his writing partner didn't love it. David tried to come up with something better but as they watched the scene over and over he realized Bacharach's original idea was perfect. They finished the song and though it has a playful feel to it the lyrics are profound, offering timeless advice about looking at the good things in life rather than focusing on the bad. There's great wisdom in the line "I'm never gonna stop the rain by complaining" that we could all be reminded of at times.

Once the song was composed, David and Bacharach set out to find a singer. They first approached country star Ray Stevens who showed up to watch the film and hear the song. He liked neither and decided not to sing "Raindrops Keep Fallin' on My Head." No doubt though, the song left a mark on him because there are obvious thematic similarities between "Raindrops" and "Everything Is Beautiful," a song Stevens would write and record just a year later. Legend has it Bob Dylan was also offered the song but he too turned it down. Which is when Dionne Warwick got involved. She'd already recorded a number of Bacharach/David compositions like "Don't Make Me Over" and "I Say A Little Prayer" so she knew both composers well. She was also labelmates with B.J. Thomas who was currently on the charts with his song "Hooked on a Feeling." Warwick recommended Thomas for the song and Bacharach, perhaps running out of options, gave his okay.

The day B.J. Thomas showed up in the studio to record "Raindrops" he had a cold and so in his first attempt at the song his voice was a little raspy. The movie producers loved it for the scene but Bacharach hated how he sounded so he had Thomas re-record his vocals once his throat was better. That's why the version used in the movie is different from the single.

"Raindrops Keep Fallin' on My Head" was released in mid-October of 1969 but didn't start moving up the charts until *Butch Cassidy and the Sundance Kid* came out later that month and started drawing big crowds. The movie was the highest grossing film of 1969. With over $100 million in box office receipts it more than doubled its closest competitor, *Midnight Cowboy*. Meanwhile "Raindrops" made a steady climb up the charts and reached #1 the first week of 1970. It would stay there for four straight weeks and would eventually take home the Oscar for Best Original Song, one of four golden statues earned by *Butch Cassidy*. "Raindrops" is B.J. Thomas' biggest hit although he did get back to the top of the chart a few years later with "(Hey Won't You Play) Another Somebody Done Somebody Wrong Song" which holds the distinction of being the #1 with the longest title. David and Bacharach had been commissioned to write a song to fit a scene but in doing so, they gave us an all-time optimistic classic. We'd all be better off remembering "It won't be long till happiness steps up to greet me."

## January 4th

On this date in 1982, Foreigner's very Un-Foreigner-like "Waiting for a Girl Like You" was stalled at #2 on the *Billboard* Hot 100 chart. It had been lodged at that spot for over a month and would spend the rest of January sitting right there, within spitting distance of the top. And although "Waiting" never did get to #1, it became Foreigner's biggest hit to date and showed the band the formula that would eventually take them to the top of the charts.

Foreigner came together in New York City in 1976 as a six-piece, hard-rocking band. Founder Mick Jones came up with the Foreigner moniker because the band was made up of three British musicians and three Americans, so no matter where they were, some of them would be foreigners. Their 1977 self-titled debut sold over four million copies and earned them an avid fan base with rockers like "Feels Like the First Time" and "Cold as Ice." They avoided a sophomore slump with their follow-up LP *Double Vision* which included the title track, "Hot Blooded" and "Blue Morning, Blue Day." Their third album, 1979's *Head Games* saw them take a slight step backwards in sales and so when they got together to record their next LP they were looking to score a hit.

For the album *4*, band leaders Mick Jones and Lou Gramm decided to work with producer Mutt Lange who was just emerging as a big name in the rock world, having produced back-to-back mega-hits for AC/DC, *Highway to Hell* and *Back in Black*. As they went over material for the new record, Jones and Gramm presented a ballad they'd co-written called "Waiting for a Girl Like You." Gramm, who wrote most of the lyrics, would explain later how effortlessly the song came to him, saying: "It's the kind of song that the pen does the writing, and you don't even know where it came from. ... Sometimes it's sort of mystical where these ideas come from." Despite the fact that Foreigner was better known for their up-tempo songs, and Lange had been hired for his hard rock pedigree, they quickly got to work on the ballad. Lange then made a curious call, recruiting a 19 year old musician named Thomas Dolby to record a synthesizer introduction to the song. Dolby would go on to worldwide success the next year with his hit "She Blinded Me with Science" and he credits the exposure he received from playing on "Waiting" for helping to launch his career.

Hoping to maintain their rocker image, Foreigner released "Urgent" as the lead single off *4*. "Urgent" made it all the way to #4 but their next single, "Juke Box Hero," stalled at just #26 on the chart. They then released "Waiting for a Girl Like You" in October of 1981 and their power ballad with the unique opener started climbing the charts, helped by a video that got steady play on MTV. The week of November 28th, "Waiting" made it to #2, behind Olivia Newton-John's "Physical" which had reached the top spot the week before. What often happens in situations like this is the #1 song will eventually drop and the #2 song will take its place. The following week there was no movement, with "Physical" staying at #1 and "Waiting" waiting at #2. In fact, all throughout the month of December, 1981 the top of the chart looked the same, with "Physical" lodged at #1 and "Waiting," well, waiting at #2. January came and still, "Physical" held firm. Finally, after "Waiting" sat at #2 for nine straight weeks there was movement, "Physical" dropped. But instead of Foreigner stepping into the top spot, Hall and Oates "I Can't Go For That" leapfrogged them both to take #1. "Waiting for a Girl Like You" spent a total of ten consecutive weeks at #2 before finally sliding down the charts.

The success of the song helped *4* become a #1 album, Foreigner's first and only, and the band would mine a similar vein a few years later with "I Want to Know What Love Is" which did finally land Foreigner a #1 hit.

On this date in 1991, Madonna's "Justify My Love" began a two week stay at #1 on the pop chart. It was Madonna's ninth chart-topper and one of her most controversial, from the video to the song's origins. But as usual, Madonna knew how to parlay controversy into sales, and in this case not just record sales, but into a record number of VHS sales.

Lenny Kravitz co-wrote "Justify My Love" along with Ingrid Chavez, a singer and Prince protégé, who had recently appeared with His Royal Badness in the movie *Graffiti Bridge*. The two created a demo with Chavez singing the lyrics with a whispered, almost heavy-breathing delivery. Kravitz then offered the song to Madonna who was preparing a greatest hits package to be called *The Immaculate Collection* and wanted to include two new songs on it to help promote sales. Madonna liked the song and Kravitz produced the recording session with Madonna using a very similar softly spoken delivery as Chavez had used on the demo.

The first controversy came with the video. To match the erotic vibe and lyrics of the song, Madonna worked with director Jean-Baptiste Mondino and the two put together a black and white clip of Madonna making love while another man watches. There are also some bizarre silhouetted dancers (who were spoofed brilliantly in *a Saturday Night Live Wayne's World* skit). The video contains images of sadomasochism, voyeurism, and bisexuality and maybe a bit of nudity (wait, is that nipple?) When MTV saw it, they banned it. But instead of lamenting that the biggest promotional vehicle in the world wasn't going to be playing her new video, she went on *Nightline* and gave an interview, casting herself as the misunderstood artist persecuted by a conservative culture. She then released the video on VHS tape (becoming the first artist to do so) just in time for the Christmas season. She sold over a million copies.

Controversy number two came once the song started climbing the charts. It turned out that Kravitz hadn't given Chavez songwriting credit. He claims to have had a previous agreement with her but she filed a suit which was settled out of court and she was quickly added as a songwriter. She was satisfied with the arrangement and when asked why, if both versions were so similar, Kravitz didn't just release the demo, Chavez replied realistically, "Because Madonna can make more money." But the copyright problems weren't over. The rap group Public Enemy then stepped up and said that the drum beat in "Justify" sounded eerily similar to their instrumental song, "Security of the First World." Hank Shocklee, Public Enemy's producer and the man who had created that particular rhythm track said, "I'm going on a rampage." But before they could file suit, it was brought up that "Security" sounded very much like the breakdown in James Brown's "Funky Drummer." Shocklee's response was that his beat was original but the comparison to Brown seemed to take the wind out of his sails. Instead of filing a suit he simply released an answer song, producing "To My Donna" (get it?) for the Young Black Teenagers. For his part, Kravitz denied borrowing or sampling the drum beat saying, "It's just one of those beats you find on the floor somewhere." His manager elaborated, saying, "There hasn't been any copyright infringement. From my recollection there never has been any copyright enforcement on a drumbeat. Otherwise half the songs of rock & roll would infringe on Chuck Berry." Neither Shocklee nor James Brown were given writing credits.

"Justify My Love" was such a huge hit for Madonna that she decided to continue to pursue the themes and sounds from the song. The following year she released *Sex*, a coffee table book containing explicit photographs of her, and *Erotica*, her fifth studio album in which she uses an alter-ego named Mistress Dita and taps into the same vibe of "Justify." She'd never matched the video sales success of "Justify My Love" though, in fact no one ever would. That video stands today as the highest selling music video of all time and since we live in a day and age where you can pull up any music video at any time on your smart phone, it's safe to say that's a record that'll never be broken.

### January 6th

On this date in 1973, "You're So Vain" by Carly Simon reached #1 on the *Billboard* Hot 100 chart by knocking Billy Paul's "Me and Mrs. Jones" from that spot. Simon would enjoy a three week run before Stevie Wonder's "Superstitious" climbed the pop chart summit. Three weeks at #1, millions of records sold and still the burning question remains, who exactly is she singing about?

Carly Simon was born in 1945 to a wealthy family. Her father, Richard Simon, is the co-founder of the publishing firm Simon & Schuster. Richard was also a classical pianist and so Simon's childhood home was always filled with music. She dropped out of college to pursue a career in music and in the early sixties formed the Simon Sisters along with her sister Lucy. They had a minor hit in 1964 called "Winkin', Blinkin' and Nod" but after a few albums and no other successes Lucy left to raise a family. In 1970 Elektra signed Carly Simon and her self-titled debut was released the following year. The album included "That's the Way I've Always Heard It Should Be" which became a Top 10 hit. Her follow-up LP *Anticipation* included the title track which also cracked the Top 10 (peaking at #3).

Besides the success and fame that came along with being a popular singer, Simon also moved in the right circles and dated, or was rumored to be linked with, many famous men before her 1972 marriage to singer James Taylor. "Anticipation," for example, was a song she wrote while waiting for singer Cat Stevens to pick her up for a night out. Mick Jagger, Warren Beatty and Kris Kristofferson are three of the more famous names on her list of possible paramours.

As Simon began preparing work for her third LP, (which would end up with the ironic title *No Secrets*) she started working on a song she was calling "Ballad of a Vain Man." She had the beginnings of the chorus with the line "You're so vain, you probably think this song is about you." Around this time she was speaking with a friend at a party when a guy walked in and her friend said, "Doesn't he look like he's just walked on to a yacht?" Simon loved that line and jotted it down in a notebook. It would eventually become the opening of the song she was working on. She was also on a flight about this time with her friend and musical collaborator Billy Mernit. Simon had the window seat and was sipping a cup of coffee. As they were chatting Mernit noticed the reflection of clouds in her cup and he said, "Look at the clouds in your coffee." Both songwriters, knowing a good line when they heard it, jotted that imagery down for future use. A few weeks later Simon called her friend and asked if she could use the line in a song. Mernit, to his credit, gave his permission.

Once the song was written, Simon set out to record it. She was working at Trident studios in London's Soho district and the day she was to record her vocals Mick Jagger showed up to watch her work. Harry Nillson was also there to sing backing vocals and the two invited Jagger to join. According to Simon, at one point Nillson stepped aside saying, "The two of you have a real blend - you should do it yourselves" and so, although it is uncredited, that's Mick Jagger singing along with Carly Simon during the chorus of the song (you can hear his distinctive voice during some of the "Don't you, don't you" parts).

"You're So Vain" was released in November of 1972 and rose quickly up the charts. It hit #1 on this date in 1973 and has gone on to be the most successful single of Simon's career. But the question remains, who is it that is so vain? David Bowie? Mick Jagger? Cat Stevens? Who is Simon singing about?

Warren Beatty has always been convinced the song is about him (which is pretty vain, when you think about it). Simon has been coy about the subject. Sometimes she has said it's an amalgamation of men and other times she has said there was one specific man she had in mind when she wrote the chorus. She started releasing letter clues at one point, saying the man had an A, an E and an R in his name (which eliminated a few of the suspects but didn't narrow it down completely). In 2003, Simon decided to use the mystery to help raise money for a charity. She auctioned off the secret to the highest bidder at the Martha Vineyard Possible Dreams charity with the caveat that the winner could not publicly reveal the name. Dick Ebersol, president of NBC Sports, won the auction with a $50,000 bid. He now claims to know the answer.

Like all great mysteries though, the unknown is probably more interesting than the actual truth. It's why wrapped presents hold so much anticipation. And why the right undergarments can be sexier than full nudity. "You're So Vain" is a great song, because it's a contradiction in terms. Simon is scolding the subject of the song because he thinks the song is about him when really, the whole song is about him. It's an ode to him. She is commenting on everything from the color of his scarf to his travel plans. She's clearly obsessed with him and so he has every right to be vain. It's a dichotomy set to music. But decades later we still don't know for sure who the song is about. And maybe that's for the best. Like the clouds in the coffee, it is a great image that is better left unexplained.

On this date in 1966, Simon and Garfunkel's "The Sound of Silence" spent its final day at #1 on the pop chart. The song's ascension to the top of the charts was an amazing surprise for the duo seeing how more than a year earlier their debut album had tanked so badly it caused them to split up. Now, they were internationally known singer/songwriters riding the wave of the burgeoning folk rock scene and they would go on to become two of the most important voices of a generation.

Paul Simon and Art Garfunkel grew up in the same neighborhood in Queens, New York. They shared a passion for music, specifically the harmonies created by the Everly Brothers and some of the doo-wop bands of the era, and they began singing together in their teens. They were signed to a record deal in 1956 when they were both 15, calling themselves Tom and Jerry and releasing an original song called "Hey School Girl" which they wrote one day when they couldn't remember the lyrics to the Everly Brothers' "Hey Doll Baby." The song earned them a spot on *American Bandstand* where they performed alongside Jerry Lee Lewis. But their career as teen doo-wop artists was short-lived and when their record label went bankrupt that was the end of Tom and Jerry. Both Garfunkel and Simon headed to college but kept music open as a career option. By the early sixties the folk scene was growing in lower Manhattan and the two became regulars as both patrons and occasional performers.

Paul Simon was the lyricist and main songwriter for the duo. One of his favorite places to compose songs was in the bathroom of his parent's house in Queens. The acoustics in a small, tiled bathroom can be incredible and Simon would sometimes turn the lights out to focus on his guitar playing. It was during one of these writing sessions, with the lights out in his parent's bathroom, that he spontaneously sang the line, "Hello darkness, my old friend." Over the course of the next six months Paul Simon would work on the song, delving deeper into the concept of loneliness and an inability to communicate with those around you. He reveals his New-York-City-centric upbringing in the classic line, "The words of the prophets are written on the subway walls and tenement halls." When he was finally happy with it, he and Garfunkel began playing "Silence" whenever they got up to perform in those downtown folk clubs where Bob Dylan was the reigning king of the genre. Was Simon influenced by Dylan? No folk writer of the era could deny they were and Simon certainly doesn't. He would say later: "I never would have wrote it were it not for Bob Dylan. Never, he was the first guy to come along in a serious way." The song was so heavy and serious though that some on the scene say it even became a joke. One folk singer from the era has said, "all you had to do was walk up to someone and say, 'hello darkness my old friend' and everyone would crack up."

While some may not have taken the song seriously, Simon certainly did. He had done some work in song publishing and understood the advantages of selling a song to an established artist, so he considered doing just that with his new composition. He presented "The Sound of Silence" to Tom Wilson, the producer at Columbia Records who was working directly with Dylan and other folk singers and groups. But when Simon and Garfunkel auditioned the song for him, instead of taking it for one of his already established artists, Wilson offered the two a contract and promised to produce them.

*Wednesday Morning, 3 A.M.*, Simon and Garfunkel's debut album, was recorded in early 1964 and released that October along with "The Sound of Silence" as a single. "Silence" had been recorded just as the duo always sang it, accompanied only with Simon's acoustic guitar. Both the album and the single were complete failures. Radio stations ignored them and their records collected dust in the few stores that even stocked them. Paul Simon and Art Garfunkel decided this duo-folk thing wasn't going to work out. Simon moved to England to start over as a solo artist and Garfunkel returned to college.

Then months later a curious thing happened. Some radio stations started playing "The Sound of Silence." There was no promotion behind the record, certainly no payola from Columbia Records as incentive. But this was back when radio DJs actually had a little say in the music they played, instead of some algorithm telling them what their demographic of listeners were predetermined to want to hear. Columbia Records saw an opportunity but they also knew the musical landscape had changed some. Dylan had gone electric that summer and, almost overnight, folk music had grown some muscle and was now being called folk rock. Tom Wilson was summoned to the studio and told to remix the original song. Instead of hunting down Paul Simon and Art Garfunkel he simply brought in the same musicians who had just worked on Bob Dylan's "Like a Rolling Stone." He overdubbed some electric instrumentation and drumming and Columbia re-released "The Sound of Silence" in September 1965. Neither Simon nor Garfunkel even knew their song had been tampered with, in fact legend has it Paul Simon hated the updated version when he first heard it.

But he soon learned to love it. The remixed version of "The Sound of Silence" started climbing the charts throughout the final months of 1965. Paul Simon returned from England and the duo got to work quickly on a follow-up album. The week after "Silence" vacated the top of the pop charts they released their second LP, cleverly titled, *Sounds of Silence*. The album contained the updated version of their hit single and would go on to establish Simon and Garfunkel as fresh new voices in the folk rock scene. The rest, as they say, is rock and roll history.

## January 8th

On this date in 2016, David Bowie released his 25th and final studio album, *Blackstar*. The LP dropped on Bowie's 69th birthday. It had been recorded slowly and gradually over the course of 2015 as Bowie's health deteriorated from liver cancer, a fact he kept hidden from just about everyone, including some of the musicians who played on the album. *Blackstar* would go on to become David

Bowie's first #1 album on the *Billboard* 200 chart, but he wouldn't live long enough to see it.

Throughout David Bowie's half a century long career in music, if he was known for any one thing, it was not being known for any one thing. Part chameleon, part trendsetter, and yes, part trend-follower, Bowie never stayed in one place, or played in one genre, for too long. The man single-handedly put glam rock on the map with his early seventies work and then just as quickly turned his attention to soul and early disco. And once he achieved his most commercial success dabbling in those genres he completely abandoned them for what has become known as his "Berlin Trilogy," the trio of albums he released between 1977 and 1979 in which he tested the limits of electronica and art rock. Then, by the mid-eighties he was back doing his most commercially accessible (and successful) work, becoming an MTV star with hits like "Let's Dance" and "Blue Jean." Bowie also enjoyed a respectable acting career both on stage (his role as the title character in Joseph Merrick's Broadway production *The Elephant Man* earned him high praise) and on screen (with memorable roles in *Labyrinth* and *The Last Temptation of Christ* as just a few examples).

By the turn of the millennium Bowie had done just about everything an artist can do and he seemed to step into a period of semi-retirement. He was rarely seen in public for a number of years and rumors swirled that he may be having health issues.

Then in 2013 Bowie released a new studio album which he'd recorded in relative secrecy. Though he didn't tour or give interviews to promote the LP, *The Next Day* sold fairly well in an age when album sales were down significantly. The album got to #2 in the U.S., making it the highest charting LP of his storied career.

The 2016 release of *Blackstar* was very similar. The music media had been given no notice, there was little indication that Bowie was even working on new material and then, poof, on his 69th birthday he released his 25th studio LP. And then two days later, he tragically succumbed to the liver cancer he'd been battling for eighteen months. David Bowie died on January 10th, 2016 at home in his New York City apartment.

Besides the obligatory, and incredibly deserved, tribute articles that appeared right after his death, the music media also focused on Bowie's final album, pulling back each onion layer looking for clues. Was this Bowie's last message to his fans? Was he telling us anything about mortality or trying to convey his belief in an afterlife?

To be sure, it's a unique position for an artist to knowingly work on his or her final project. Warren Zevon recorded the incredible LP *The Wind* in 2003 shortly after his doctors diagnosed him with inoperable pleural mesothelioma. The album came out two weeks before he passed away. But death, for most, sneaks up on us, and certainly in the annals of rock and roll history there are far more overdoses and plane crashes that take our heroes from us unexpectedly, than there are long, drawn out illnesses that put a writer in the unique position of composing songs that will almost certainly be their Final Statement. Viewed in that light, *Blackstar* is far less obvious than *The Wind*. Sure Bowie begins his song "Lazarus" with the line, "Look up here, I'm in heaven" (and the video for that song is filled with morbid imagery). But references to death or dying do not run rampant through the album.

So focus turned to the title *Blackstar* and there was no shortage of possible interpretations.

Sometimes cancerous lesions are called black stars for the way they appear on MRIs, but more often than not these are associated with breast cancer and not liver cancer. There is also chatter among apocalyptic conspiracy theorists of a planet sized object in the solar system (often called Nibiru) that is on course to hit Earth at some point in the not-too-distant future and maybe *Blackstar* was Bowie's way of reminded us of our impending demise. But the one explanation most focused on was the Elvis Presley connection. Bowie had always been a huge Elvis fan (and not just because they share the same birthday) and recently an unreleased Presley song had surfaced called "Black Star," in which the King of Rock and Roll sings about death ("When a man sees his black star, he knows his time has come"). Surely Bowie would have been aware of the song and, given his current medical prognosis, it would have meant something to him.

All conjecture aside, there is no doubt that *Blackstar* was David Bowie's final message to his fan base and the musical community, but he did it, as he did everything in his career, his own way. He left us with an album that is layered and nuanced and not something easily interpreted or even listened to. The opening title track alone is a ten minute opus that takes the listener through multiple tempo changes. The video for that song is also dark and somber, reflecting the song's mood. Bowie appears in the video blindfolded as he would in the video for "Lazarus." And incredibly, after a 50 year career that included such groundbreaking albums as *The Rise and Fall of Ziggy Stardust and The Spiders from Mars* and *Young Americans* and *Let's Dance*, posthumously, David Bowie reached the top of the U.S. Album chart for the very first time. He asked his fans to look up, that he was in heaven. They did so by purchasing his final LP and saying a fitting goodbye to the Thin White Duke.

### January 9th

On this date in 1969, Marvin Gaye's "I Heard It Through the Grapevine" was enjoying a seven week run at #1 on *Billboard*'s Hot 100 chart. It was a song that Motown's owner Berry Gordy didn't believe was good enough for Gaye yet it would become his first chart-topper and one of the most successful songs of his storied career. See, even a genius like Gordy can't be right all the time.

Barrett Strong was a Motown staff singer and songwriter who came up with the beginning of "I Heard It Through the Grapevine" in 1966 when he overheard people in Chicago using the term "heard it through the grapevine" to describe rumors and innuendo. He wrote some lyrics and the bass line but needed help finishing the song. He first brought it to Motown's most successful writing team of Lamont Dozier and brothers Brian and Eddie Holland (popularly known as Holland-Dozier-Holland) but they explained to Strong that they never shared writing credit. Unwilling to give his song up completely he then asked Motown producer Norman Whitfield for assistance. The two finished the song and then presented it at the next Friday morning meeting at Motown. These legendary meetings were an opportunity for the label's songwriters to present their latest compositions and propose which singers they hoped would front their songs. Gordy liked "Grapevine" but when Strong and Whitfield suggested Marvin Gaye as the singer, Gordy thought it was a bad fit. He chose instead to assign "Your Unchanging Love" to Gaye and have Smokey Robinson record "Grapevine." Robinson recorded the song but Berry was unimpressed and his version wasn't released till years later. The Isley Brothers then recorded it but their version met a similar fate and remains unreleased. Then in 1967 Gladys Knight and the Pips recorded a gospel-influenced version of the song that Gordy did like. Their version became a hit, getting all the way to #2. Gordy then gave his blessing to have Marvin Gaye record the song which he did with Norman Whitfield producing the session. It was Whitfield who made the decision to have Gaye sing the song slightly higher than his normal range. This gave Gaye's voice a strained feeling which perfectly matched the song's message of lamenting a lover's cheating. Gaye would say later, "I simply took direction . . Had I done it myself I would not have sung it at all like that." Despite the obvious passion in Gaye's version, Gordy still didn't think it had hit potential so he stuck it as an album track on Gaye's 1968 LP *In the Groove*.

It wasn't until E. Rodney Jones, a DJ on Chicago's WVON started playing Marvin Gaye's version of "I Heard It Through the Grapevine" from the album, and the song started getting phone-in requests and interest in record stores in the Windy City, that Gordy finally released it as a single. Gaye's "Grapevine" hit record stores on October 30th, 1968 and climbed the charts instantly. It hit #1 on December 14th and sat there through the holidays, finally relinquishing the top spot on February 1st, 1969. Gaye had already been a star at Motown but this was his first #1 and is the longest running #1 of his career. "I Heard It Through the Grapevine" then enjoyed renewed interest in the late eighties when California Raisins used it in a commercial that featured claymation raisins dancing to the track.

Berry Gordy got a lot right in his years running Motown but clearly he missed the mark on Marvin Gaye singing "I Heard It Through the Grapevine." He just didn't hear it as a hit while everyone else clearly did.

On this date in 1989, Metallica released the song "One." Though it would peak at just #35 on the *Billboard* Hot 100 chart, "One" has become a signature song for the band that virtually invented thrash metal and its video is on most of the Best Music Video lists.

As Metallica began to prepare their 1988 album *....And Justice For All,* death weighed heavily on their minds. In September of 1986, during a European tour their bus had overturned and bassist Cliff Burton was killed in the accident. For a while the remaining members were unsure if they should continue but eventually, with Burton's family's blessing, they decided he'd want them to carry on. It was during this time of uncertainty and mourning that James Hetfield, the band's lead vocalist and main songwriter, was given a copy of the book *Johnny Got His Gun*. The novel, published in 1938, is about an American soldier in World War I who is severely injured by an artillery shell. He wakes up in a hospital realizing that he has lost his arms, legs, and all of his face (including his eyes, ears, teeth, and tongue), but his mind is still functioning, leaving him a prisoner in his own body. Hetfield was moved by the book, especially coming on the heels of the bus accident, and he began to think of using both as an inspiration for a song. He was particularly intrigued by the random odds of death. The entire band had been on that bus yet only Burton had been killed. Similarly, the protagonist in *Johnny Got His Gun* writes about the same thing in one passage where he is dwelling on the odds of being so severely injured yet surviving: "It was like reading in the paper that someone has won a lottery and saying to yourself there's a guy who won a million to one shot. . . .Now he was just the reverse. He had lost a million to one shot. Yet if he read about himself in a newspaper he wouldn't be able to believe it even though he knew it was true. And he would never expect it to happen to him. Nobody expected it. But he could believe anything from now on out. A million to one ten million to one there was always the one. And he was it. He was the guy who had lost."

Hetfield, with help from the band's drummer Lars Ulrich, completed the song about being trapped in one's own body ("Darkness imprisoning me. All that I see, absolute horror. I cannot live, I cannot die. Trapped in myself, body my holding cell") and though they never touched on the randomness of our mortality they decided to call the song "One" as a reminder that even a million to one odds leaves one who may fall to fate. They also channeled the frustrations of death perfectly in the slow build of the song. It starts like a gentle ballad and ends in a furious wall of noise with guitarist Kirk Hammett wailing away, Ulrich thrashing the drums and Hetfeild screaming about his life in hell.

When the song was complete the band wanted to use portions of the 1971 movie *Johnny Got His Gun* in the music video. They began talks with the studio that owned the movie but licensing certain scenes was getting too complicated. Finally they just inquired about buying the rights to the movie and since this option was actually cheaper, Metallica bought the film. Clips from the movie are interspersed with shots of the band playing the song. It would be hard to find a more powerful video than Metallica's "One."

A little over a month after the song's release, the 31st Annual Grammy Awards took place at the Shrine Auditorium in Los Angeles. The Grammys introduced a brand new category that year called, Best Hard Rock/Metal Performance and since ....And Justice For All had been released in August of 1988 it was among the nominees, alongside other Hard Rock stalwarts like Iggy Pop and AC/DC. Metallica was asked to perform at the award ceremony that evening and they left the Shrine Auditorium completely drained with their live version of "One." Moments later, Alice Cooper and Lita Ford took the stage to announce the new metal award and everyone was shocked when they read "Jethro Tull." Ian Anderson apparently had been so sure his band wouldn't win the award he hadn't even bothered to show up that night.

Metallica has had higher charting songs but none as powerful and dramatic as "One," especially when you watch the video. In 2009 Metallica was inducted into the Rock and Roll Hall of Fame and Burton, the "one" who had perished, went in alongside his bandmates who had survived the crash.

## January 11th

On this date in 1971, Columbia released Janis Joplin's version of "Me and Bobby McGee." The song was completed just days before Joplin's death on October 4th, 1970 and it would go on to be her only chart-topper as well as her signature song. The lyrics spoke of letting go of a loved one and missing them so much you'd trade all your tomorrows for one more day with them. No doubt her fans felt similarly about the blues singer from Texas, another talented artist gone long before her time.

Janis Joplin was born in Port Arthur, Texas in early 1943. She loved music growing up, especially the blues, and was considered an outcast and "freak" by her classmates in high school because she read a lot, painted, sang and even hung out with some black students. She attended the University of Texas at Austin but dropped out before getting her degree and in 1963 moved to San Francisco because she'd heard so much about the burgeoning music scene there. Not only did she find her musical kin in the Bay Area but she discovered a whole new world of drugs as well. She'd been a drinker in Texas. Now she was exposed to heroin and hallucinogens and speed to go along with her copious Southern Comfort consumption.

In 1966 Joplin joined the psychedelic rock band Big Brother and the Holding Company and they released their eponymous debut album the following year. 1967 also saw the band perform at the Monterey Pop Festival and though that June weekend will forever be famous for Jimi Hendrix' breakthrough moment in the U.S., Big Brother's set was also eye-opening and gained them much attention. By 1968 Joplin had emerged as the star of the band and they were now using the cumbersome title: Janis Joplin and Big Brother and the Holding Company. They would release one more album together, 1968's *Cheap Thrills*, before going their separate ways. Joplin then released *I Got Dem Ol' Kozmic Blues Again Mama!* in 1969, the same year she performed at Woodstock. She was clearly inebriated at the show and her performance was marred by her unsteady voice. When the six sided LP, *Woodstock: Music from the Original Soundtrack and More* was released, none of the songs from her set were included.

She attempted to sober up after this and there was a period in 1970 where she wasn't drinking or doing drugs. Unfortunately, that wouldn't last and as she began work on her next LP, *Pearl*, she was off the wagon, drinking and shooting heroin as well.

Kris Kristofferson is a fellow Texan, born in 1936 in the Lone Star State. He moved to Nashville in the sixties and struggled for a while to make it as a singer and songwriter before being signed to Monument Records in 1969. Monument's owner Fred Foster called his newest artist one day and said, "I got a song title for you." He offered Kristofferson "Me and Bobbi McKee." Foster had a secretary with that name and he thought it was very musical so he told Kristofferson to use it and write a song about a couple that breaks up and breaks the singer's heart. Kristofferson would say later, "I thought there was no way I could ever write that because I can't write on assignment." He spent months avoiding his label chief for fear of admitting he hadn't done anything with the song title he'd been given. But it stayed stuck in his head and then one day he found himself on a long drive in a rain storm and the line "windshield wipers slappin' time" popped into his head. He then figured out the scenario that the singer and Bobby McGee (he'd misheard Foster when he gave him the name so he used McGee and not McKee) were hitchhikers picked up by a trucker. He had the song finished by the end of the drive. Roger Miller (of "King of the Road" fame) recorded and released the first version of "Me and Bobby McGee" in 1969. Then a year later Kristofferson included a version on his debut LP. Gordon Lightfoot also released a version of the song as did Kenny Rogers and The First Edition. But none of these versions became as iconic as Janis Joplin's.

Janis Joplin began work on new material for an album in September of 1970. She asked Paul Rothchild to produce the LP. Rothchild is best known for his work with the Doors and he called Joplin "a producer's dream" because she was so focused during her time in the studio. She'd heard Kristofferson sing "Me and Bobby McGee" and chose to include it on the album. Work on the song was completed on October 1st, 1970. Three days later Joplin was found dead of a heroin overdose at the tender age of 27.

The decision was made to release "Me and Bobby McGee" on this date in 1971. According to Kristofferson, he didn't even know Joplin had recorded the song till the day after she died. Now it was climbing the charts and would hit #1 in March, becoming just the second song ever to reach the top of the charts after an artist's death (Otis Redding's "(Sittin' On) The Dock of the Bay" had been the first a few years earlier). Joplin's final album *Pearl* also hit #1 on the *Billboard*

200 chart. No one can ever know if she would have achieved this level of success had she not passed away but what we do know is that by dying so young, Joplin joined that legendary group of artists who have all passed away at 27 years of age. One of the last things she'd done professionally was to sing the line "Freedom's just another word for nothin' left to lose." Joplin, who'd fought many demons in her short life, was now free from them all.

## January 12th

On this date in 1980, "Rapper's Delight" by the Sugarhill Gang peaked on the *Billboard* Hot 100 chart at #36. Most music historians do not claim that "Rapper's Delight" was the first rap song, nor is the Sugarhill Gang universally respected as hip hop pioneers (which is ironic, as we'll see). But for the vast majority of Americans, "Rapper's Delight" was the first song they ever heard that featured rapping. It was their introduction to this new genre that for most seemed like a passing fad. Fast-talking over a loop of someone else's song? How could this be the birth of a new genre?

The roots of rapping go back to West Africa where it was traditional for a griot, or storyteller, to deliver stories rhythmically, while drums played behind him. The practice came to America in the hull of slave ships and continued on the plantations and homesteads of the south. The emergence of the blues also contained some elements of early rapping. The 1950's song "Gotta Let You Go" by Joe Hill Louis is a good example of the amalgamation of both genres. Vaudeville and musical theater also incorporate rap-like techniques with "patter songs" where lyrics are spoken, usually very quickly over, a fast tempo. One listen to "Why Can't a Woman Be More Like a Man?" by Rex Harrison from *My Fair Lady* and you can hear the similarities to what would become rap music. In Jamaica they use a term called "toasting" which is similar to rapping where an MC talks or even chants over a beat.

From all these influences, rapping began to emerge at street parties in New York City. It began with the announcements that were made at these parties. The DJs who were spinning the music would hand a microphone to an MC who would announce where the next party was going to be. Each MC tried to outdo the other so they would make their announcements in more and more elaborate ways, attempting to rhyme and flow with the beat. Pretty soon the announcements became the attraction and the DJs who were spinning began looping the break of whatever song they were playing to give the MCs a consistent beat and rhythm to "rap" over. These DJs weren't equipped with the latest technology to do this looping so they simply had two copies of the same record and went back and forth from one to the other. One of the most popular records to do this with was Chic's "Good Times" because the beat is slow and easy to rap over and the long break on the 12" single was perfect for looping.

And for many years, that's where rap stayed, in the street parties and school halls of New York City where DJs set up their gear and people danced. There was little to no interest from record labels to sign any of these rappers, nor did any of them see commercial potential in their craft.

This is where Sylvia Robinson enters the story. Robinson was a singer and musician from New York City who had a few minor hits in the fifties. By the mid-sixties she'd settled in Engelwood, New Jersey where she and her husband started a record label that specialized in soul and R&B called All Platinum. She scored the biggest hit of her singing career on her own label, releasing "Pillow Talk" in 1973 which climbed all the way to #3. A few years later the couple opened Sugarhill Records (named after the Sugarhill section of Harlem) a subsidiary label they set up specifically to record and release the rap music that was becoming popular in New York City. Robinson then assembled a group of rappers all from the Engelwood area: Wonder Mike (Michael Wright), Big Bank Hank (Henry Jackson) and Master G (Guy O'Brien) to make a rap record. It's for this reason that most musical historians don't consider the Sugarhill Gang to be early pioneers of the genre - because none of the three were a huge part of that early street party scene. Although one, as we'll see, had ties that became entangled.

"Rapper's Delight" was recorded in the summer of 1979. They used "Good Times" for the backing track and each MC rapped a different section. The 12" single clocks in at over 14 minutes. The song was released in the fall of 1979 just months after "King Tim III (Personality Jock)" by the Fatback Band had been released (as a B-side) so historically that record is the first rap song ever released. But "Rapper's Delight" had far more success and it opened the floodgates for more rap artists to be signed and recorded. The song also gave the genre its other name. With the opening lyric of "I said a hip hop, hippie to the hippie the hip, hip hop . . ." many people started asking record stores for that new "hip hop song." Soon enough rap had a second name: hip hop.

And then, almost predictably, the controversies began. According to Niles Rodgers (he of Chic fame and cowriter of "Good Times") he was aware that "Good Times" was a popular song to be looped and rapped over. There's a legendary story of Blondie singer Debbie Harry inviting Rodgers to a street party where he heard MCs rapping over his track. He is said to have been flattered. And there's an equally legendary story of Rodgers partying in a club one night when he heard "Rapper's Delight" for the first time. He approached the DJ who was spinning and was shown the record with the DJ telling him he'd just bought it that day. Rodgers was no longer flattered. He immediately threatened a lawsuit and just as quickly he and "Good Times" cowriter Bernard Edwards were added as composers and given their share of royalties. Rodgers was initially turned off by "Rapper's Delight" but came around later (possibly after he started receiving royalty checks). "As innovative and important as 'Good Times' was," he said later, "'Rapper's Delight' was just as much, if not more so."

The other controversy came from an early rapper named MC Grandmaster Caz. Caz knew Big Bank Hank and, according to Caz, when Hank landed the gig with the Sugarhill Gang he called Caz and asked for a rap. Caz claims to have written the Superman section of Hank's rap and that Hank even stole the line "I'm the grandmaster with the three MCs" from a rap Caz would perform. Caz's crew consisted of himself and three MCs so the line makes more sense coming from Caz rather than Hank who only worked with two other rappers. In the end Caz did not sue for credit, though in 2000 he released a song called "MC Delight" which is a straight rip off of "Rapper's Delight" and in which he tells his side of the story.

The Sugarhill Gang scored two other minor hits, 1981's "8th Wonder" which peaked at #82 and 1982's "Apache" which made it to #53. Sugarhill Records also had some more success, signing legendary hip hop artists like Grandmaster Flash and the Furious Five, Funky Four Plus One, Crash Crew and Treacherous Three. Grandmaster Flash's 1982 song "The Message" is often credited as the first rap song to talk about more serious subjects than going "over a friend's house to eat." This opened the doors for more socially conscious rappers like Public Enemy and N.W.A. By 1986 the Sugarhill Gang had disbanded and the label had gone under but the genre they helped put on the map was only just gaining momentum.

Hip hop has not just affected the music we listen to but it has changed the language we speak, the clothes we wear and the topics we discuss. Whether or not Sylvia Robinson and the crew she assembled were pioneers or poseurs hoping to capitalize on a new trend is a discussion for another day. What no one can argue is that "Rapper's Delight" slammed opened the door for hip hop and musically, things would never be the same again.

## January 13th

On this date in 1968, Johnny Cash performed two shows at the Folsom State Prison in California. This wasn't the first time he'd played in a prison, in fact he was something of a hero among inmates, but it was a special day nonetheless and it would help turn Cash's career around. The resulting album, *At Folsom Prison*, is one of the greatest live LPs ever released and it helped show the industry that recording an artist in concert and releasing it as a packaged set could be a viable option. James Brown had famously done it a few years earlier, now Johnny Cash did it and pretty soon, the flood gates for live offerings were open.

Johnny Cash began his professional singing career at the age of 22 when he signed with Sun Records. Rock and roll legend has it that Cash auditioned for Sam Phillips by singing some gospel songs. Phillips wasn't interested in recording gospel music, he was all-in on the burgeoning rockabilly and rock and roll sound, but he heard promise in Cash's voice so he told the young man, "Go home and sin and come back with a song I can sell." Cash has denied those words ever came out of Phillips' mouth but they are too good not to repeat even with the caveat that they may not be true.

When Johnny Cash did sit down to write some music, he was inspired by the movie *Inside the Walls of Folsom Prison* he'd seen recently. He thought about the worst possible reason anyone could have for committing murder and that's when he wrote the line, "I shot a man in Reno, just to watch him die." He wrote the song focusing on the torture that prisoners must go through when they think of the freedom people outside the walls enjoy while they are locked away. Though he'd never served prison time, he must have nailed the emotion, because "Folsom Prison Blues" not only sold well, it made him a legend among the incarcerated. He started receiving letters from inmates all over the country thanking him for the song. Some even asked Cash to come perform for them. He first sang at a prison in 1957 at Texas' Huntsville State Prison. When that went well, he became a regular performer for inmates.

Associating with prisons and criminals helped Cash develop his outlaw image which was enhanced by his heavy drinking and drug use. For a while he was able to keep cranking out hits despite these addictions but eventually his behavior and production became too erratic and Cash started slipping in popularity. He cleaned up his act in 1967 and then attempted to get his career back on track. His big comeback idea was to record and release an album from a show he performed at a prison. Though his record company approved, they weren't exactly enthusiastic about the idea. Till this point, other than a few jazz albums and James Brown's career defining *Live at the Apollo*, the track record of live albums wasn't very good. The assumption was that the listening public preferred songs that were perfected in the studio and didn't want or need the feel of a live performance. Plus, recording equipment was still rudimentary so capturing a concert with good enough quality to release was a big challenge. But Columbia gave Cash its approval and arrangements were made for him to perform at Folsom State Prison on this date in 1968.

Cash decided to do two shows that day in case there were any problems recording the first one. He hit the stage about 9:30 in the morning beginning with his now signature, "Hello. I'm Johnny Cash." He then launched into the song he'd written so many years before, using that particular institution as an inspiration. It is this version of "Folsom Prison Blues," faster and more muscular than the original version he'd released over a decade before, that would reinvigorate Cash's career. The single and the album, despite very little promotion from Columbia, both became hits. In 1969 Cash followed up with another live recording from a prison, *At San Quentin*, which went all the way to #1 on the album chart. The Man in Black was back and his legend as one of the baddest outlaws in all of rock and roll history was sealed.

On this date in 1964, the Kingsmen were stuck at #2 on the *Billboard* Hot 100 chart with their version of "Louie Louie." It's a position they had arrived at in mid-December of 1963, sitting one slot behind "Dominique" by The Singing Nun. Somehow the combination of that song, which is about the founder of the Dominican Order and sung in French by a nun, and Bobby Vinton's overly sappy "There! I've Said it Again" kept "Louie Louie," even with all the controversy that surrounded it, from reaching #1. Here's the story:

The roots of "Louie Louie" go back to a song from the fifties called "El Loco Cha Cha." One night Richard Berry, a singer with an incredibly rich baritone voice, was waiting to take the stage in a Los Angeles nightclub, when the band playing before him launched into that song. Berry was struck by its simple yet catchy riff and before he performed that night he grabbed a brown paper bag and jotted down some lyrics to go with the tune. He said he was inspired by the first person angle of Frank Sinatra's "One For My Baby" in which Sinatra is speaking to a bartender named Joe. Berry named his bartender Louie and wrote a song about a guy telling his bartender how much he misses his "fine little girl" from Jamaica and is about to "sail the sea" to "tell her I'll never leave again." Berry uses some odd wording in the lyrics like, "It won't be long me see me love" and, most famously, "Me gotta go." But every word in his version is understandable to the listener. And though he straight up stole the riff and melody from "El Loco Cha Cha," he is listed as the only songwriter. Berry recorded and released "Louie Louie" in 1957 and though it sold a respectable 40,000 copies it never charted nationally. He was planning a wedding a few years later and to help pay for it, he sold the publishing rights to many of his compositions. He got $750 for "Louie Louie."

A few years later, a singer from Tacoma, Washington named Rockin' Robin Roberts released the first cover version of "Louie Louie." Along with his band the Wailers (not Bob Marley's backing band) they reinterpreted the song, using a saxophone to play the catchy opening riff and changing the time signature to make the song less calypso and more rock and roll. Roberts scored a regional hit with his version of "Louie Louie" which pretty much meant every bar band in the Great Northwest had to incorporate the song into their setlist.

The Kingsmen were one of those bands. They hailed from Portland, Oregon and by the early sixties they had developed an avid following. "Louie Louie" was a highlight of their sets and pretty soon they booked some studio time to record their own version of the song. Legend has it that the night before they were set to record, they played a 90 minute version of "Louie Louie" in order to have the beat and melody down cold (for unsigned bands, studio time is precious so it is best to go in totally prepared). One listen to their version and that legend falls apart. "Well rehearsed" isn't exactly how anyone would describe it.

On April 6th, 1963, the Kingsmen headed into studio to record "Louie Louie," as well as a B-side for the single. Jack Ely, the band's lead singer, was surprised to see that the microphone in the studio was suspended from the ceiling and way too high for him. He was forced to stand on his toes, strain his neck back and yell, instead of sing, which helps explain his almost unintelligible delivery of the lyrics. At about a minute into the song the band's drummer, Lynn Easton, broke a drum stick and yelled something out (it, like Ely's singing, is indiscernible but Easton would claim later he yelled "fuck!") Then, as the band came out of the guitar solo, Ely started the third verse too soon. He stopped, after singing just "me see," then let the band finish the break before starting the verse over again. You can hear that error at about the two minute mark.

Despite all this, everyone deemed their first attempt at "Louie Louie" acceptable. And since the song was not being multi-tracked none of the mistakes could be fixed in post production. The band moved on to record the B-side, "Haunted House," and then called it a day. The entire session cost $50, a sum the band members split amongst themselves.

The Kingsmen's version of "Louie Louie" came out just a month after it was recorded and by the end of the summer, 1963, it had sold a mere 600 copies. By this point, Easton had told the band he was sick of being behind the kit and he wanted to become their frontman. Offered the job of drumming, Jack Ely quit the band. It was around this time that a Boston DJ named Arnie Ginsburg played the Kingsmen's version of "Louie Louie" on his radio show and pronounced it the "Worst Record of the Week." His listeners apparently disagreed though and they began calling in and requesting the song. From there "Louie Louie" began getting requests outside of the Boston market and then a little fortuitous rumor helped spur its sales. Since Ely's delivery is so unclear some people started claiming the lyrics were salacious. Alternative lyrics began popping up in various places claiming to be the actual words that Ely was singing. And they were vulgar. Pretty soon Indiana governor Matthew Welsh declared the song "pornographic" and the F.B.I. opened a case to study the lyrics. Yes, you read that correctly, the United States' Federal Bureau of Investigations looked into "Louie Louie." And after almost three years (yes you read that correctly as well, the case remained open for 31 months) they released a statement saying, "it was not possible to determine whether this recording is obscene." Your tax dollars hard at work!

Of course, the negative publicity and bans from certain radio stations only spurred record sales. As the song began to move up the charts in late 1963, Jack Ely approached his old band about getting back in. They turned him down which meant that Lynn Easton had to lip-sync Ely's original singing on all the television appearances the band was now getting. Ely would attempt to capitalize on the song's success by releasing future recordings like "Love That Louie" and "Louie Louie '66." Apparently he sang the lyrics on those songs too clearly because they were not shrouded in mystery or controversy. Nor did they sell very well.

For many people, the appeal of rock and roll is its primitiveness. There is a universality in its simplicity. It's best when it's raw and stripped down and gives the impression that maybe anybody could do it. That is the true appeal of the

Kingsmen's slapdash version of "Louie Louie." Ely's delivery, while slurred and incoherent, is also laced with urgency. When he belts out "Let's go!" at the end of the song, the listener may have no idea where he wants to take them, but they go nonetheless. How can you not with such a passionate delivery? There have been over 1,600 cover versions of Richard Berry's original song, which remember he stole the riff for, then sold for less than a thousand dollars, but none have the same makeshift, ingenuous feel as the Kingsmen's. It's worth cranking it up sometime today, just to hear what rock and roll at its most fundamental level can sound like.

## January 15th

On this date in 1965, the Who released "I Can't Explain." It was the first recording for the band using their new name and though it wouldn't sell well in the U.S., the song helped broaden their fan base in England. Pete Townshend, who wrote the song and played most of the guitar work on it, readily admits to copying another British band's style but soon enough the Who would blow by that band in popularity and record sales. Something that, like the singer of the song, you can't explain.

Pete Townshend, Roger Daltrey and John Entwistle all grew up in the same area in London, part of the post-World War II generation. Townshend and Entwistle shared a love of music and started playing together as teenagers. Entwistle started out trying to play guitar but when he struggled due to his large fingers, he switched to bass. Roger Daltrey, who was a year ahead of the other two, had a rough go of it in school. He was expelled at 15 for gang violence. He began to do construction work before discovering his own love of rock and roll. In 1959 Daltrey formed a band he called the Detours and found work doing weddings and other social events. Then, on one of those days that has taken on mythic importance in the annals of rock history, Roger Daltrey happened to pass John Entwistle playing bass on the street. Daltrey was impressed and recruited Entwistle who, of course, recommended his friend Pete as a guitarist. The Detours were three-quarters of the way to becoming the Who.

The band would go through a few more personnel and name changes before finally becoming the Who. The last piece of the puzzle was the day they found Keith Moon. They were in search of a drummer at the time and Moon, who was playing with another local band, sat in with them for one of their shows. Rock legend has it that Moon played so furiously with the Who that he broke a bass drum pedal and tore a drum skin. Daltrey, who was still the de facto leader of the band at this point, knew he'd found his drummer.

Early on, the Who played straight ahead covers of soul and R&B songs, in fact they promoted themselves as a "Maximum R&B" band. Roger Daltrey seemed uninterested in writing and playing original songs. Perhaps it was his inability to do so or maybe it had to do with playing so many weddings and social functions where bands are expected to cover songs everyone already knows. Daltrey has been quoted as saying, "It never seemed a necessity in those days to have your own stuff because there was this wealth of untapped music that we could get hold of from America." So it was Pete Townshend who emerged as the band's composer and in 1964 he presented the others with a song he'd written called "I Can't Explain." The Kinks were huge on the London scene at the time and Townshend makes no apologies about being inspired by their use of a catchy opening guitar riff and power chords to carry a song. One listen to "You Really Got Me" or "All Day and All of the Night" and you can hear the clear similarities to "I Can't Explain." Townshend would say later, "It can't be beat for straightforward Kink copying." Of the lyrics of the song, Townshend sees his immaturity as a writer: "There is little to say about how I wrote this. It came out of the top of my head when I was 18 and a half." Sometimes he'll also admit that the "dizzy in the head" and "feeling hot and cold" lines aren't just about being love sick, saying the song is about a guy "who can't tell his girlfriend he loves her because he's taken too many Dexedrine tablets."

"I Can't Explain" helped the band get signed to a record deal and it was the first song they recorded as the Who. Jimmy Page, a session player at the time, may or may not appear on the final recording. There is no doubt he was in the studio that day as Shel Talmy who was producing the session admitted to having him there as a backup, and the members of the Who saw him (Daltrey would say later they were thrown by the fact that their new producer didn't trust them) but it's unclear whether his contributions actually made the final mix.

The song was released on this date in 1965 which became a breakout year for the Who in their homeland. The three singles they released that year, "I Can't Explain", "Anyway Anyhow Anywhere" and "My Generation" all hit the Top 10 in England. Two weeks after the release of their first single they made their debut appearance on the British television show *Ready Steady Go!* Pretty soon the band was ready to explode and they became a driving force in what we now call the British Invasion. And to this day, the Who open almost every concert with that Kinks-inspired riff before launching into their first release, "I Can't Explain."

### January 16th

On this date in 1996, a small plane was fired upon as it sat off the beach of Negril. Jamaican authorities thought the plane was filled with drug smugglers but it actually contained two internationally known music stars and an iconic record label owner. No one was injured but of course the incident was immortalized in a song. You can't nearly kill a songwriter and expect him not to write about it.

Jimmy Buffett's career began in Nashville in the late sixties but it was a fateful trip to Key West in 1971 that changed everything for the singer/songwriter. He went to the tiny island in Florida to earn some money busking (singing on the streets for loose change) and fell in love with the area. Soon enough he'd move to the Keys and his songwriting started to become infused with a laid back, island sound. His 1977 song "Margaritaville" reached #8 on the pop chart and established Buffett as a singular voice in country music with a tropical feel. Buffett has made a cottage industry from this, with legions of fans called Parrotheads who see him when he tours, eat at one of his restaurants and read his books. Buffett learned to fly in the eighties and he owns a number of small planes that he uses to get around the Keys and even the Caribbean islands. He truly lives the "island life" 365 days a year.

Chris Blackwell was born in 1937 to an English father and a Costa Rican mother. He spent much of his childhood in Jamaica as his father was often there on business. One day as a young man his boat ran aground on a coral reef off the Jamaican coast. He swam to shore and was rescued and nurtured back to health by some Rastafarians. He became extremely interested in the Rasta culture and music after this experience and soon he borrowed $10,000 from his parents to start a record label he fittingly called Island. Blackwell's greatest achievement may well be helping to bring Bob Marley's music to the rest of the world but Island's stable of talent wasn't just limited to Jamaican reggae artists. They've released music from artists ranging from the Spencer Davis Group to Jethro Tull to U2.

The U2 connection is how Blackwell and Bono became friends. Island signed the band in 1980 and released their first album in October of that year. U2 has spent their entire career on Island. The label has actually changed hands, being sold to PolyGram and then folded into the Universal Music Group, but U2 has stayed loyal to the label that first signed them.

All this explains how Bono and his family happened to be visiting Blackwell at his Jamaican estate in January of 1996 when Jimmy Buffett paid a visit. Though Buffett never recorded for Island he and Blackwell, both avid island-hoppers and tropical lovers, knew each other well. At some point during their time together, Buffett convinced the rest of the group that the best jerk chicken on the island was to be found at a place in Negril. Jamaican roads are famously horrible so Buffett offered to fly the group in his Grumman HU-16 Albatross flying boat, which he'd nicknamed Hemisphere Dancer, to the opposite side of the island. Blackwell, Bono and Bono's wife Ali and their two children all climbed aboard and took off. The flight was smooth and soon enough Buffett was landing his plane just off the beach in Negril.

That's when all hell broke loose.

Someone had tipped off Jamaican authorities that drug runners would be landing at about the same time and, as the Hemisphere Dancer nestled into the warm waters off the coast, shots were fired. Buffett attempted to radio for help and explain who they were but the firing continued, with one bullet even puncturing the plane's windshield. Finally Buffett took off and returned to Blackwell's estate on the north side of the island. Nobody was injured though Bono would say later, "it was absolutely terrifying. I was convinced we'd all be killed." Jamaican police were surprised by the incident as well, with one high-ranking official telling reporters it wasn't "regular" for his policemen to simply open fire on a suspicious aircraft, adding, "We're not clear why it would have been necessary to shoot." Bono and his family left the island immediately and weeks later he was telling anyone who'd listen about his near-death experience. Buffett chose the more artistic way to cathartically talk about the incident. He wrote a song about it. Using a Reggae beat and the title "Jamaica Mistaica," Jimmy Buffett tells the story of that day. In the chorus, Buffett sarcastically sings, "Come back to Jamaica . . . we promise not to shoot you out of the sky." All these years later and the Jamaican tourist board still hasn't adopted the song in an ad campaign.


## January 17th

On this date in 1981, bassist Nikki Sixx left the Los Angeles based band London and began rehearsing with drummer Tommy Lee and vocalist/guitarist Greg Leon (who had played together in a band called Suite 19). The trio rehearsed together for a while, underwent some personnel changes and finally came up with a name, all before becoming one of the defining bands of the 1980s glam metal movement.

Sixx, Leon and Lee rehearsed for a while before Leon left the still unnamed band. Sixx and Lee then turned to a local classified publication named *Recycler* where musicians often posted their availability. They read an ad that said: "Loud, rude and aggressive guitar player available." They liked what they read and in no time Bob Deal, better known as Mick Mars, was added to the lineup. Lee then remembered a singer he'd known years before named Vince Neil who was currently playing in a Cheap Trick cover band. Lee asked Neil to join the band but he initially declined. It was around this time that the trio decided they needed a name. Sixx suggested Christmas but the others hated it. Then Mars recounted a story from years ago when he was in a different band and somebody said to them they looked like a motley crew. He'd written it down because he liked how it sounded but he didn't spell it correctly so he'd written, "Mottley Cru." He brought this up and the others liked what they heard but decided the name needed umlauts, those odd markings over certain vowels that many bands like Blue Öyster Cult, Queensrÿche and Motörhead were already using. But one umlaut wasn't enough for this crew. Inspired by their favorite beer, Löwenbräu, they decided to use two, and thus, Mötley Crüe was born.

Neil eventually came into the fold and in May of 1981 they self-released their first single, "Stick to Your Guns/Toast of the Town." They'd created their own imprint to release the song before they had an actual record contract, naming it Leathür Records because in metal you can never have too many umlauts. This single is extremely rare and today it is highly coveted. If you own a copy, you're probably sitting on at least a $1,500 seven inch single. In November of that year the band released their debut album, *Too Fast For Love* on their own imprint but then the band was signed to Elektra Records and their debut was remixed and re-released. Their first album was a moderate seller and wouldn't break the band but they toured relentlessly to support it and it was on one of these trips that the band had an early, defining moment. During the Crüesing Through Canada Tour '82 they were arrested while passing through customs for wearing their spiked stage attire. The Canadian authorities considered these "dangerous weapons" and when they searched the band they discovered a carry-on bag filled with pornography. The band admitted later that both of these incidences were publicity stunts. And they worked. The band was labeled as the new Bad Boys of Hard Rock and though their debut was largely ignored their second album became highly anticipated.

That album, as it turned out, became the LP to break them. *Shout at the Devil*, which included the title track, "Looks That Kill" and "Too Young to Fall in Love" established Mötley Crüe as the hardest band in the new glam metal field, the prettiest band in the heavy metal field and the loudest and rowdiest new band in all of music. They'd go on to produce such hard rock anthems as "Girls, Girls, Girls" , "Dr. Feelgood" and "Kick Start My Heart." Bands like Ratt and Poison and Bon Jovi would follow in their wake but none of them were as hedonistic and outrageous as Mötley Crüe, the band that on this date in 1981 took their first steps towards becoming a crew.

## January 18th

On this date in 1986, "That's What Friends Are For" began a four week run at #1 on the *Billboard* Hot 100 chart. It bumped Lionel Richie's "Say You Say Me" from the top spot and would remain at #1 till February 15th when Whitney Houston's "How Will I Know" took its place. The song was part of a popular trend in the mid-eighties. It was a collaboration by various artists who produced a song to raise money for a charity. Not only would "That's What Friends Are For" raise millions for AIDS research but the song helped bring early awareness to the disease when some people, including the then-current President, refused to even talk about it.

"That's What Friends Are For" is a song written by Burt Bacharach and Carole Bayer Sager for the 1982 movie *Night Shift*. Rod Stewart sang the song originally and it played over the closing credits of the movie. This version appears on the film's soundtrack but was never released as a single.

A few years later Dionne Warwick was preparing material for an upcoming album. She'd sung other Bacharach compositions previously ("I Say a Little Prayer", "Walk On By" and "Wishin' and Hopin'" just to name a few) so it was natural she'd peruse his material before deciding what to record. When she saw "That's What Friends Are For" she loved it and envisioned it as a duet, preferably with Stevie Wonder. When Wonder agreed a recording date was set up for some time in the fall of 1985.

The day Stevie Wonder arrived to record his parts for "That's What Friends Are For" Elizabeth Taylor and Neil Simon happened to be in the studio. Taylor was an early advocate for AIDS research and awareness and when the artists got to talking about the growing epidemic, it was suggested that maybe the song they were working on could become a charitable release. This was less than a year since the song "Do They Know It's Christmas?" raised so much money and awareness for the Ethiopian famine and since then the flood gates had been opened, with "We Are the World" coming out in March of 1985 and the Live Aid benefit concert taking place that summer. Warwick was intrigued and once she decided to make the record a benefit for American Foundation for AIDS Research, she knew they had to add a few more singers. Warwick reached out to Gladys Knight and then Clive Davis recommended Elton John and he too was added to the song. Because of the piecemeal way this was brought together each singer sang their parts separately and Sager, who produced the song along with Burt Bacharach, has said that putting it together was like doing a jigsaw puzzle. The four singers did eventually come together for the video shoot which has been described as a "very emotional evening in which a lot of tears were shed."

AIDS had first been clinically observed in the U.S. in 1981. Because of its propensity to infect gay men, early on the disease was called G.R.I.D., which stood for gay-related immune deficiency. By late 1982 scientists realized the disease wasn't confined to the gay community and it was clear their initial acronym was misleading. They changed it then to AIDS (acquired immune deficiency syndrome). Congress allocated funding for AIDS research in May, 1983 but for years the scientific community, as well as the gay community, felt research was underfunded and awareness campaigns needed to be more prevalent. It became obvious early on that one of the ways the disease could be spread was through unprotected sex (straight or gay) and so the word needed to get out about the importance of practicing safe sex. Ronald Reagan, president from 1980 to 1988, is criticized by some for being slow to react. In 1986 he proposed a federal budget that actually called for an eleven percent reduction in AIDS spending (from $95 million in 1985, down to $85.5 million in 1986) and he wouldn't speak publicly about the epidemic till May of 1987.

With so little federal assistance for AIDS research, "That's What Friends Are For" certainly made a difference. Sales of the single raised over 3 million dollars but probably more importantly, the song brought awareness to the growing epidemic. How many lives were saved because people practiced safe sex after hearing about AIDS for the first time through promotion of the song could never be calculated. But what we do know is that Elizabeth Taylor stopping into a studio in 1985 and talking about the disease got Dionne Warwick thinking about doing something that could make a difference. She recruited some friends in the industry who were willing to help. And their song did just that. The song sings of the love and support you get from true friendship and the artists involved in the project offered that and more to an untold number of people.

On this date in 1975, Barry Manilow's "Mandy" was sitting pretty at #1 on the *Billboard* Hot 100 chart. Though Manilow is a prolific songwriter and composer, "Mandy" is not his own composition. It was a cover version, with a name change, of a song that had been a hit a few years earlier in the U.K. Now here it was, catapulting this virtual unknown into stardom and launching one of the great, easy-listening careers in pop music history.

Manilow was born Barry Alan Pincus in Brooklyn in 1943. At his bar mitzvah he took his mother's maiden name of Manilow. He studied music at the New York College of Music and at Juilliard. He also worked at CBS while going to school which is where he got his first minor break. CBS director Bro Herrod asked a then 21 year old Manilow to arrange some songs for a musical version of *The Drunkard*. Manilow accepted the assignment then went a step further and wrote an entire original score that Herrod loved. The musical ran Off Broadway for eight years.

After college Manilow found steady work as a writer and performer of commercial jingles. He was responsible for such earworms as "Like a good neighbor State Farm is there" , "I am stuck on Band-Aid brand, 'cause Band-Aid's stuck on me!" and McDonald's "You deserve a break today." His commercial credits also included Kentucky Fried Chicken, Pepsi, Dr Pepper and Tab and he won two Clio Awards for creative excellence in advertising. His connections at CBS also helped him land a job as the musical director for the television series *Callback*. He also worked with Bette Midler at the famed Continental Baths in New York City. She loved working with him so much she asked him to co-produce and arrange her first two albums.

In the early seventies Manilow released three songs with a few other studio musicians as the group Featherbed (which was produced by Tony Orlando). The songs went nowhere. Bell Records (a subsidiary of Columbia Pictures), which had released the Featherbed singles, then decided to give Manilow a shot at an album which became his debut release in 1973. Like the Featherbed recordings, this initial offering did not make much of a splash. Shortly after this release, Clive Davis (who had just been fired by CBS Records) was hired by Columbia Pictures (not affiliated with Columbia Records) as a consultant. Within months he would fold their various labels into his own new entity, Arista Records. Davis began firing many of the old acts on these labels, a fate that Manilow might have met had Davis not happened to see Manilow playing live one night. Davis was impressed and he assured Manilow he would not be let go.

As Manilow began putting together material for his second LP he used a combination of songs he'd written or cowritten, as well as songs brought to him by others. One of those was a song called "Brandy" which had been a Top #10 hit in England for Scott English in 1971. Clive Davis recommended it to Manilow who liked the song but knew he had to change the title. In 1972 Looking Glass had had a #1 hit with a song called "Brandy (You're a Fine Girl)" so they changed the title to "Mandy" to avoid any confusion.

Arista released *Manilow II* and "Mandy" in October of 1974 and both began to sell much better than anything Manilow had previously released. The single got to #1 on the pop chart in January of 1975 and the LP went to #9 on the album chart. Davis' faith in Manilow paid off.

There have long been rumors about the genesis of the name "Brandy." Scott English once told a reporter it was his dog's name but he later recanted that, saying the reporter had called him early one morning to get the scoop and he just said that to get off the phone. He has also used an off-color joke to explain it, saying he always liked the English expression, "Brandy goes down fine after dinner, doesn't she?" More than likely the name Brandy was used for the same reason so many songwriters have used a particular name in their lyrics: meter. The lyrics call for a two syllable name and since Brandy is never at the end of a line it doesn't have to rhyme with anything else. So while we'll never know why English used "Brandy" we do know his opinion of Manilow's version. He initially hated it because Manilow had omitted two of his lines and moved others to the bridge. But when the royalty checks starting rolling in, he rethought his original opinion.

Throughout Barry Manilow's career he would often compile songs for his LPs using the same mix of his own compositions and songs written by others. This was never more famous, and confusing, then Manilow's next #1 hit, "I Write the Songs." Once again Clive Davis brought this song to Manilow's attention and recommend he cover it. The song had been written by former Beach Boy, Bruce Johnston, and had already been released by Captain & Tennille and David Cassidy. But after Davis' persuasion Manilow recorded a version that became his second #1 hit. It was sort of confusing in 1975 to hear Barry Manilow on almost every radio station singing that he writes the songs and then find out he hadn't written that one!

Barry Manilow has sold over 80 million albums worldwide and in 1978 he accomplished a feat only done by a few other artists when he had five of his LPs on the *Billboard* album chart simultaneously. He's had fifteen Top 10 albums and eleven Top 10 singles including three #1 records. And whether you call yourself a "Fanilow" or not, you've probably got a Manilow song or two as a guilty pleasure. C'mon, admit it.

### January 20th

On this date in 1982, during an Ozzie Osbourne show in Des Moines, Iowa, an object was thrown from the audience and landed on stage. Osbourne looked down and saw a bat and figured it was a fake, rubber one. Always the crowd-pleaser, Osbourne picked it up, put it in his mouth and began to bite its head off. When he felt the bat bite back he realized it was no fake. Ozzie Osbourne was already considered one of the wildest madmen in all of rock. Biting the head off a live bat would just make him that much more legendary.

In 1979 the other members of Black Sabbath broke the news to Ozzie Osbourne that he was fired from the band he'd helped form. They blamed their decision on his increasingly erratic behavior, fueled by his excessive substance abuse. Osbourne contested that he was no worse off than the rest of the band but nonetheless, he was ousted and forced to go it alone. His resulting solo career began with the 1980 album *Blizzard of Ozz* which featured Osbourne's now signature song, "Crazy Train." His follow-up solo LP *Diary of a Madman* solidified Osbourne's place in the world of heavy metal. He was a true hard rock superstar and his persona, both on and off the stage, was that of an unpredictable wild man. It was on the Diary of a Madman tour on this date in 1982 that Osbourne made headlines by biting the head off a live bat. Since the bat bit back, Osbourne was forced to get a rabies shot after the show. In the pre-internet and social media days it was much harder for a news story to go viral but this one certainly did. And it added to Osbourne's now mythological status as rock's most unpredictable performer.

This wasn't the first time Osbourne had bit the head off a creature. About a year before this incident, he'd been in a meeting with CBS executives at which he planned to compliment everyone on their efforts in promoting his debut album and then release three doves into the room as a sign of peace. That was the plan anyway. What no one had factored in was how much brandy Osbourne would drink prior to the meeting and how a drunken Ozzie would decide to alter that plan at the last minute. At one point Osbourne interrupted a female PR executive's speech by asking her if she liked animals. When she replied "Yes" Osbourne bit the head off of one of the doves, in his words, "Just to shut her up." When everyone in the room reacted as you'd imagine, Osbourne took a second dove and repeated the stunt. The third dove, somehow survived the meeting.

A month after the bat incident, Osbourne would make news again when he and his band were in San Antonio. As that story goes, Osbourne's wife Sharon had hidden his clothes because he was drunker than usual (which is saying a lot) and she figured if he couldn't find his clothes he wouldn't leave his hotel room and get into any trouble. Silly woman. Osbourne simply donned one of his wife's dresses and hit the streets of the Texas town. When he found the need to urinate he looked around for a spot. Finding a large concrete structure, he hiked up the dress and relieved himself. Turns out Osbourne wasn't just in some random section of San Antonio but he'd stumbled into Alamo Plaza and that large concrete structure was actually the statue, known as the Alamo Cenotaph or the Spirit of Sacrifice, commemorating the Battle of the Alamo. So while Osbourne didn't pee on the Alamo Wall (as rock legend remembers it) he did choose the next best (or worse) spot and he was promptly arrested by the San Antonio police. Though the fine he received was a mere slap on the wrist San Antonio took the extra step of banning Osbourne from their city for the next ten years.

Ozzie Osbourne's antics shouldn't detract from the music he's given to the world. Both during his time in Black Sabbath, where he helped invent the genre we now call heavy metal, and on his own as a solo artist, Osbourne has produced some of the most unapologetically brash songs in the rock canon. He's often called "The Godfather of Heavy Metal" and if anything, that nickname under-emphasizes his importance to the genre.

## January 21st

On this date in 1978, the *Saturday Night Fever* soundtrack climbed to #1 on the album chart where it would reside for an incredible 24 straight weeks, finally relinquishing that spot in July. Disco had been growing in popularity for a few years and 1978 would be the year it broke out completely, with the *Saturday Night Fever* movie and soundtrack leading the way. Pretty soon polyester suits and platform shoes were all the rage, the entire world was dancing under mirrored balls and all anyone wanted to do was strut. Disco would have a short shelf life of dominance but for one year at least, it ruled the world, turning everything glamorous and glitzy.

The seeds for what would become *Saturday Night Fever* were planted in 1976 when New York magazine ran an article by British journalist Nik Cohn entitled "Tribal Rites of the New Saturday Night." At the time Cohn claimed to have infiltrated the club scene in Brooklyn, getting to know some of the regulars there and writing the article based on his observations. Years later he'd admit that he only visited the club 2001 Odyssey in Brooklyn a few times and his article was mainly based on some guys he knew in the mod scene in London.

Be that as it may, the article did capture some of the traits of the disco culture and it grabbed the attention of Robert Stigwood. Stigwood owned a production company called Robert Stigwood Organization (RSO). He saw the commercial potential of disco early on and had already helped salvage the career of one of the bands on his label by getting the Bee Gees to start recording dance music and soulful ballads. Plus he'd already had some success with movie musicals (RSO had produced the screen adaptation of *Jesus Christ Superstar* in 1973 and the Who's *Tommy* in 1975). And finally, Stigwood needed something to shoot because he'd just signed John Travolta to a three picture deal with the intent of having him star in *Grease* but the owners of that musical insisted production be put off till 1978 because the play was still doing so well on Broadway. So when he read Cohn's article he saw the makings of disco-themed movie and purchased the rights to it.

The film was well into production before the Bees Gees were brought in to record some music for it. They were already working on songs for a new album but when Stigwood contacted them to describe the plot and the scenes he needed songs for they got right to work. They wrote and recorded "If I Can't Have You", "Stayin' Alive", "Night Fever", "How Deep Is Your Love" and "More Than a Woman" over the course of a long weekend. "If I Can't Have You" would be re-recorded by singer Yvonne Elliman and included on the soundtrack. The other four all appeared in the movie and on the record as well as two older Bee Gees songs, "Jive Talkin'" and "You Should Be Dancing." "You Should Be Dancing" had been released in 1976 and it was the song Travolta used to practice his dance routines to. In fact, it was Travolta who recommended it be used in the film. The producers wanted to use "Night Fever" for its obvious tie in to the title of the film in the big dance scene early in the movie where Travolta takes over the floor of the club, but Travolta's suggestion was ultimately used and was obviously the better choice. Besides the Bee Gees' contribution, the double LP soundtrack included songs from other dance music stalwarts like KC and the Sunshine Band, the Trammps and Kool and the Gang.

The soundtrack was released in November of 1977, a few weeks ahead of the film. The movie did well at the box office but it was the soundtrack that broke all kinds of records. It stayed on the *Billboard* Top 200 album chart for 120 weeks and became, at the time, the highest selling soundtrack of all time (*Bodyguard* would top it in 1993). It also became the first soundtrack to win the Grammy for Best Album.

1978 will always be remembered as disco's shining moment. Dance clubs opened on seemingly every corner and fashions everywhere resembled those seen in the movie (just how many white suits were sold that year is probably incalculable). And though it didn't last (nothing that popular ever does) dance music has never completely gone away either. The word "disco" was verboten for a while so we used terms like "club" or "house" but in the end, it's all the same: music that is made to make you move. The *Saturday Night Fever* soundtrack is filled with songs like that. It's impossible to play that album front to back and not find yourself wanting to hit the dance floor and be as young and glorious and confident as John Travolta in his shining white suit. The Bee Gees sang loudly and proudly in their song that opens the movie, "got the wings of heaven on my shoes." When disco is played loud and proud, it's a feeling we all have.


### January 22nd

On this date in 1983, the Clash's "Rock the Casbah" peaked at #8 on the pop chart. The song had a peculiar path from inception to fruition and then it would take a while before it gained the attention of radio and MTV. Once it did, "Rock the Casbah" went into heavy rotation on both and eventually became the Clash's highest charting song.

The Clash began in London as part of the early punk scene. When they signed a record deal in the beginning of 1977 some claimed it spelled the end of punk music because they had "sold-out." Their first single, "White Riot" had all the punk elements: it was fast and loud and angry and clocked in at under two minutes. Their self-titled debut album came out in April of 1977 and is considered one of the greatest LPs in the brief and incendiary history of punk rock. But the Clash were always more than just punk rockers and pretty soon they were introducing other elements into their straight ahead wall-of-noise rock sound. Their 1979 LP, *London Calling* shows them toying with reggae, R&B and even pop which was a good thing because the punk movement had already imploded by this point so those early bands either evolved (like the Ramones) or dissolved (like the Sex Pistols). The Clash evolved and by the early eighties nobody knew what to expect every time they released a new album.

In 1981 they started working on new material for an LP and they decided to do some work in New York City. Topper Headon, the band's drummer, admitted later that he loved New York City but it offered too many distractions to the band. They were already growing apart and trying to record in the Big Apple made things almost impossible. Headon would say: "We'd lost that unity and had stopped hanging out together as friends, and would all turn up at the studio at different times, writing stuff as and when it came up. The sessions were supposed to start at two in the afternoon, though by the time everyone turned up it was seven. I got there early, and what else was I going to do except put down an idea?"

Headon is referring to one day specifically when he found himself alone in the studio with a song idea in his head. This was a rarity with the Clash as Mick Jones and Joe Strummer were the main songwriters in the band. Headon did the first thing any drummer would do. He laid down his percussion track. When he found he was still alone, he went back and added a piano portion. Then he played the bass track. By the time the rest of the band showed up he had the entire song laid out and when he played it for them they were impressed. Till he added his lyrics.

Headon had recently broken up with a woman and he'd written a nasty, break-up song to go with his instrumental track. It was downright pornographic. Strummer asked to see the lyrics and when Headon handed them to him he crumpled the paper up, tossed it in the trash and said, "how incredibly interesting." Strummer had a much better idea that had come from something their manager Bernie Rhodes had just said to them recently. The band had taken to jamming out on songs and were finishing with five or six minute pieces as opposed to the shorter, harder tracks they produced in their early days. One day Rhodes had stopped by the studio to listen to their work and after hearing a few of these longer songs he'd commented, "does everything have to be as long as a raga?" (referring to a style of Indian music that is known for being long and having a lot of melody changes). Shortly after, Strummer had written the line, "The King told the boogie men you gotta let that raga drop." Then he started developing a song based on a story he'd heard about Iran banning disco records. The song hadn't yet taken shape (other than the opening line and concept) but when Strummer heard Headon's instrumental track that day he knew the two were meant to go together. Strummer excused himself, went into the bathroom of the studio and completed the lyrics in no time. He told the story of an Arabian king (Shareef) who wants to ban music ("He don't like it") but even his jet fighters, once dispatched, can't help turning on their cockpit radios and, well, rocking the Casbah.

As work was completed on what would become the Clash's 1982 LP *Combat Rock*, MTV was already becoming something of a force in the industry. The Clash shot a video for the song in Texas, playing their track in front of a pump jack in an oil field. In the video, Topper Headon is not the one playing drums. After contributing the instrumental track for the song, the band fired him for his increasing drug use and replaced him with their original drummer Terry Chimes.

The song was released as a single in June of 1982. The Clash released both "Should I Stay or Should I Go" and "Rock the Casbah" the same week and this glut confused the marketplace. "Should I Stay" climbed the charts first, peaking just outside the Top 40 in September of '82. Once it started to decline, MTV and radio picked up "Rock the Casbah" and the song began its ascent, peaking at #8 on this date in 1983. A decade later the song was chosen by Armed Forces Radio as the first song played to begin Operation Desert Storm. A decade after that, in the days following September 11th, 2001, "Rock the Casbah" was one of the songs listed by Clear Channel Radio in a memo that went out to its 1,200 stations as "inappropriate to play" following the terrorist attack. With that ban lifted, "Rock the Casbah" enjoys frequent spins on eighties and rock radio as a fun song that tells a silly story of music winning out over a tyrant's orders.

## January 23rd

On this date in 1986, the Rock and Roll Hall of Fame held its first induction dinner, giving the honor of being one of the first inductees to fifteen men, each of whom played a huge role in shaping rock and roll and helping it become so popular. The star-studded dinner was hosted at the Waldorf Astoria in New York City as it would be for next few years. Induction dinners like this went on for years before the Rock and Roll Hall of Fame even had a physical location at which to honor these musical legends. But no matter, that first induction class is as iconic as the Baseball Hall of Fame's first class, a veritable Mount Rushmore of rock and roll luminaries.

The Rock and Roll Hall of Fame was originally conceived in 1983 by Atlantic Records founder and chairman Ahmet Ertegun. He felt rock and roll was important enough to deserve a place where its history could be archived and its superstars celebrated. He set up a committee that included *Rolling Stone* magazine's founder Jann Wenner, attorney Allen Grubman (who has been called "the most powerful lawyer in the music business") and record executives like Seymour Stein, Bob Krasnow, and Noreen Woods. They had two goals early on, first to find a location for the permanent home for the hall, and second to decide on an induction process and choose the first class of inductees. By 1986 the location committee was still at work, considering spots in New York City, Philadelphia, Memphis and Cleveland. Of the cities, Cleveland was lobbying the hardest and at the first induction dinner supporters of the Plum City made their voices heard. It was decided early on in codifying the induction process that artists would be eligible 25 years after the release of their first record. Each year over 500 musical historians and experts vote on eligible performers based on their influence and the significance of their contributions to the development and perpetuation of rock and roll. The hall would also recognize non-performers as well as early influencers.

When the Baseball Hall of Fame opened in 1936 the first five men inducted make up a legendary class: Ty Cobb, Walter Johnson, Christy Mathewson, Honus Wagner, and Babe Ruth. The Rock and Roll Hall of Fame's first inductees are just as seminal. There were ten artists: James Brown, Little Richard, Elvis Presley, Fats Domino, Ray Charles, Chuck Berry, Sam Cooke, the Everly Brothers, Buddy Holly and Jerry Lee Lewis. Robert Johnson, Jimmie Rodgers and Jimmy Yancey were recognized as early influencers. Alan Freed (who coined the term "rock and roll") and Sam Phillips (he of Sun Studio fame) were the first two non-performers inducted. And John Hammond, the legendary talent scout who discovered and signed some of the most famous names in rock and roll history was given the first Lifetime Achievement in the Non-Performer Category induction.

The first induction dinner had a very informal feel to it. Nowadays the dinner is a huge production but if you can find some clips of the very first one (they are prevalent on YouTube) you'll see what feels like a very unceremonious ceremony. Ahmet Ertegun served as the MC that first night. He offered quick biographies of each inductee then brought up another artist to officially induct that person. Those speeches have become more and more elaborate (and often memorable) through the years but at the first dinner they were often abbreviated and off-the-cuff. Keith Richards, inducting Chuck Berry, laughed when he admitted, "I lifted every lick he ever played" before getting more serious and saying: "this is the fellow who started it all." John Fogerty, inducting Buddy Holly, talked about how everyone from himself to the Beatles were inspired by Holly and the Crickets. Billy Joel thanked Fats Domino for, as Joel said, being: "the man who proved the piano was a rock and roll instrument." Roberta Flack, inducting Little Richard, gave a shout out to Tina Turner, Laverne Baker and Janis Joplin then said, "Maybe next year will be the year for women." (the next year Aretha Franklin would become the first woman inducted). And Hank Williams inducting Jerry Lee Lewis, seeking to answer the unspoken question about why a country guy was there, said, "I respect music for how good it is not what label it has on it."

The evening ended with an all-star jam session which featured some of Chuck Berry's most famous songs like "Reelin' and a Rockin'" and "Roll Over Beethoven." Everyone jammed: John Fogerty, Billy Joel, Jerry Lee Lewis, Keith Richards, Neil Young, Steve Winwood and of course Chuck Berry himself. The night seemed to belong to him above all the other inductees.

In 1995 the actual hall, officially called the Rock and Roll Hall of Fame and Museum, opened in Cleveland. The city had made the best offer to land the museum and there is certainly great historical significance for the city, being the place where Alan Freed became famous with his "Moondog House" radio show and thrust the term rock and roll into the lexicon. Any music lover should make this a bucket list location. It is well worth the trip to Cleveland just like the Sun Studio tour is well worth the trip to Memphis.

The Rock and Roll Hall of Fame has not been above criticism since its inception. Like any hall of fame, there will always be questions about why certain inductees aren't in. And there are certain genres (like prog-rock and heavy metal) that don't seem to get the recognition that others do. Some question the inclusion of artists outside what most would consider "rock and roll," like some of the rappers or disco artists who have made it in. And even some of the inductees have taken their share of pot shots. Maureen Tucker, the Velvet Underground's drummer, has called it "the Hall of Lame" and the surviving members of the Sex Pistols refused to attend when they were inducted in 2006, instead sending a note that called the Hall of Fame "a piss stain." And the gender issue that Roberta Flack mentioned at the first induction dinner hasn't been fixed either. Less than 10% of the inductees are women, although the flip side of that argument is that the music industry does tend to be, as James Brown sang, "a man's world."

Criticism aside, most music fans eagerly await the annual list of inductees (if for no other reason than to debate them) and the induction dinner, while much more polished than those early years, is still required viewing and often promises a surprise or two. Ahmet Ertegun's dream has certainly been realized. The Rock and Roll Hall of Fame has truly become the place where rock's history is preserved and its superstars celebrated.

## January 24th

On this date in 1987, Billy Vera and the Beaters' searingly heartbreaking "At This Moment" made it to #1 on the pop chart when it bumped Gregory Abbott's "Shake You Down" from the top spot. The song would enjoy a two week stay at the top before giving way to "Open Your Heart" by Madonna. "At This Moment" is about a real woman who broke Billy Vera's heart but it would take a fictional television couple's break-up to turn the song into a hit. Later, the actors who played that fictional couple got married in real-life and the song, though it is a break-up song, followed them for years. Here's the story:

Billy Vera began his recording and songwriting career as a teenager in the early sixties. He had more success early on selling songs to the likes of Fats Domino, Ricky Nelson and Dolly Parton. But he was a singer and performer at heart and in the late seventies he found himself living in New York playing in clubs with his band. He met a young woman at about this time and when they started dating she told him about her last boyfriend and how depressed he was when she broke up with him. She described his anguish over the end of the relationship so vividly that Vera was moved to write a song about it. He got about two-thirds of the way through "At This Moment" but then couldn't complete it. For months he sat on the unfinished song. Then, the woman broke up with him. Now, Vera shared the same emotions that he'd heard so much about and he was able to complete the song, writing the now famous "if you'd stay I'd subtract twenty years from my life" line.

Vera signed a record deal about this time and released a live album titled *Billy Vera and the Beaters*. "At This Moment" was released as a single but it barely broke the Hot 100 chart in late 1981. Their record label folded and the band moved to Los Angeles where they again found themselves playing regularly on the nightclub circuit.

It was in one of those Los Angeles clubs that Billy Vera got his big break. He was playing one night and a producer from the hit television show *Family Ties* happened to be in the audience. The show's breakout star Michael J Fox's character Alex was involved in a relationship with Ellen (played by Tracy Pollan) and the producer was looking for a song with just the right amount of emotion and schmaltz to use in an upcoming episode. He heard Vera sing "At This Moment" with its soaring middle section and painfully drawn out ending and he knew the song was perfect. The only problem was, at the time, only the live version existed. The television show had Vera and the Beaters re-record bits of the song in a studio, figuring the audience noise from the live version could be distracting on television. Because they were only going to use segments of the song they didn't need a complete studio recording. The song appeared in a few episodes and suddenly everyone wanted a copy of it. Rhino Records rereleased Vera's live album as well as the single and this time, with the incredible promotional power of Alex Keaton crying while standing in front of a jukebox while Vera sang about his own broken heart, the song went to #1 five years after its initial release.

Though their characters broke up, Michael J Fox and Tracy Pollan became a couple and they eventually wed in 1988. Not only had they helped launch "At This Moment" but the song became synonymous with them as a couple. Fox would say later, "Tracy and I couldn't get on the dance floor anywhere in the world for like ten years without them playing 'what would you think...'" (the opening lines of "At This Moment.") Fox and Pollan are still married and have had four children. In 1998 he publicly announced that he is battling Parkinson's disease and he has since became a very vocal advocate for research about the disease. Vera has never matched the success he had with "At This Moment" but he has had a long and productive career as a composer and singer. As for the woman who broke so many hearts, Vera hasn't ever named her, although he does admit to staying in touch with her for a while after their breakup until he realized she was just the type of woman who likes to have men "mooning over her." Once he realized he was one of those men, he stopped. Safe to say he would no longer subtract twenty years of his life just to have her back.

On this date in 1972, one of the most enigmatic songs in the history of rock and roll, Don McLean's "American Pie," was in the middle of a four week run at #1 on the pop chart. Most people know McLean's signature song was inspired by the plane crash that killed Buddy Holly, Ritchie Valens, and J. P. "The Big Bopper" Richardson, the infamous "Day the Music Died," but what else he is singing about in that eight and a half minute opus that is filled with odd imagery and poetic symbolism is mostly anybody's guess because McLean, for the most part, has been reluctant to explain anything about "American Pie."

Here's what we do know. Don McLean was a 13 year boy with a paper route on February 3rd, 1959. He learned of Buddy Holly's death when he cut into his stack of morning papers to deliver them. He already had an appreciation for Buddy Holly and the early rock and rollers so it was a seminal moment for the young boy and it stayed with him forever. Years later, as the American zeitgeist was changing so rapidly throughout the sixties, McLean kept flashing back to that morning and thinking about the loss of innocence and how the world was changing. And in his opinion, not in a good way. He felt like things were headed in the wrong direction and becoming, in his words, "less idyllic." And so he sat down with the goal to write "a big song about America and about politics" but to use symbolism to convey his feelings. He wanted the song to be esoteric and not preachy. As he focused on that morning and seeing the headline about the crash the opening words of the song came to him, "a long long time ago . . ." The second verse, in which he mentions delivering papers and "bad news on the doorstep," is as lyrically straightforward as McLean would get. From there, the imagery gets more and more vague.

It would take McLean months to finish "American Pie." He worked on it from time to time and in various places, drawing, presumably on events from the sixties. We can only presume since McLean has been so tight-lipped about everything. When he's pressed for a meaning he'll often say, with a smirk, that the song "means I don't ever have to work again." In 2015 he sold the original manuscript of the song (fetching over a million dollars and confirming that the song does indeed mean he doesn't have to work anymore). At the time he confirmed some of the things that had always been guessed at: the king is indeed Elvis and the jester who steals his crown is Bob Dylan. And the stanzas that begin with "jack be nimble, jack be quick" do refer to the death of Meredith Hunter at the Altamont Free Concert, which many people feel was the symbolic end of the sixties. But there is still so much that is open to interpretation and McLean would just as soon leave it that way. He has said, "people ask me if I left the lyrics open to ambiguity. Of course I did. I wanted to make a whole series of complex statements. The lyrics had to do with the state of society at the time."

And again, that state, in McLean's opinion at least, was not good. "American Pie" has a clear sense of brooding and unease throughout the song which is why, when the manuscript was sold, it was interesting to see the stanza McLean chose not to include in his final work. Those words lend a bit more optimism to the song and may well have changed the entire tone, which could be why he omitted them:

> And there I stood alone and afraid
> I dropped to my knees and there I prayed
> And I promised him everything I could give
> If only he would make the music live
> And he promised it would live once more
> But this time one would equal four
> And in five years four had come to mourn
> and the music was reborn.

At the turn of the millennium the Recording Industry Association of America (RIAA) released its list of the "Songs of the Century." They placed "American Pie" fifth, behind Judy Garland's "Over the Rainbow", "White Christmas" by Bing Crosby, Woody Guthrie's "This Land Is Your Land" , and "Respect" by Aretha Franklin. The song that McLean himself calls "an indescribable photograph of America" is one of the most memorable and iconic songs ever written. And like any good art, it probably means different things to different people which is what makes it so unforgettable.

## January 26th

On this date in 1985, Madonna's "Like a Virgin" began its sixth and final week at #1 on the *Billboard* Hot 100 chart. It had arrived there on December 22nd of 1984 when it knocked Hall and Oates' "Out of Touch" from the top spot and it would stay at #1 for one more week before giving way to "I Want To Know What Love Is" by Foreigner. "Like a Virgin" was the first of Madonna's dozen career chart-toppers and it has become one of her signature songs. Pretty impressive for a song that wasn't written for her specifically and for a track her famous producer wasn't that wild about.

"Like a Virgin" was the original brainchild of songwriter Billy Steinberg. Steinberg had originally tried to make it in music as a musician but his band Billy Thermal broke up in the late seventies and he found himself working back at his father's vineyard in Thermal, California. But then Linda Ronstadt decided to record "How Do I Make You," a song he'd written and recorded with Billy Thermal and when her version hit the Top 10 in 1980, he realized there was just as much money to be made writing songs as there could be performing them. Pat Benatar would then record his compositions "I'm Gonna Follow You" and "Precious Time." Through working with Benatar he met Tom Kelly who co-wrote her song "Fire and Ice" and the two decided to try collaborating.

Steinberg was still helping out his dad and he can vividly recall the day he was driving a pickup around the dusty vineyard when "Like a Virgin" came to him. He'd been through a bad relationship but had just met someone new and had that giddy, new love feeling. The opening lines "I made it through the wilderness" came to him first and then he thought up the chorus. Of his use of the word "virgin" Steinberg has since said: "I wasn't just trying to get that racy word virgin in a lyric. I was saying ... that I may not really be a virgin — I've been battered romantically and emotionally like many people — but I'm starting a new relationship and it just feels so good, it's healing all the wounds and making me feel like I've never done this before." He then brought the lyrics to his new cowriter and they attempted to set them to music. He and Kelly both envisioned a sensitive ballad and so Kelly sat down at his piano and started playing notes. The opening verse sounded good but then when they got to the chorus they stopped and realized it would never work. Steinberg would say later: "How can you write a tender ballad called 'Like a Virgin'? It just sounded ridiculous." Kelly was ready to give up on the song but Steinberg urged him to keep trying and finally, almost out of frustration Kelly started slapping his bass guitar at a faster tempo and singing the lyrics in a high, almost mocking, falsetto. Steinberg screamed "that's it!" and the two quickly laid down the song as a demo using Kelly's vocals and the faster tempo.

Steinberg and Kelly had a meeting set up with Warner Brothers' Mo Ostin where they played him a number of their demos. Ostin liked "Virgin" and thought it would be perfect for Madonna who was signed to the Warner subsidiary label Sire Records. Madonna's debut album had put her on the map and Warner was hoping for a strong sophomore showing from her. Ostin has since said, "When I played it for Madonna she went crazy, and knew instantly it was a song for her and that she could make a great record out of it." Her opinion of the song, however, was not shared by everyone. Niles Rodgers had been tabbed to work with Madonna on her second album and as they were going through potential material he was unimpressed with "Virgin." He thought the song was silly and the chorus had no hook. But then as they started working on other things, he realized he couldn't get it out of his head. Days later he was singing it to himself and as he'd admit later, "if it's so catchy that it stayed in my head for four days, it must be something." Madonna was thrilled when she heard he'd changed his mind and the two worked on the song, staying incredibly close to the original demo. As work finished up for Madonna's second album they felt it was the strongest song and the title not a little provocative, so they made it the title track. A release date was set for the second half of 1984 but then a problem arose. Songs from Madonna's debut were still selling. Warner pushed the release date of "Like a Virgin" back a few times to let that album's final single, "Lucky Star" run its course.

Because of the delayed release, as the first ever MTV Video Music Award Show neared, it was unclear what song Madonna would perform. Everyone knew her hits from her debut so singing "Holiday" or "Borderline" would have been perfect. And since the new album and single were more than a month away from hitting the streets it could be a wasted promotional opportunity to unveil "Virgin." But Madonna saw the potential in a performance that everyone would be talking about the next day and she rehearsed her now iconic performance of the song and readied it for television. She appeared in a wedding gown that night, starting out on a huge wedding cake before working the crowd then getting down on her knees, simulating sex and masturbation and showing off a rather sexy white garter belt under that wedding dress. The performance was titillating and erotic and people were not only talking about it the next day but for weeks and weeks to come.

"Like a Virgin" was released on Halloween in 1984 and it shot up the charts. Her album had to wait till *Purple Rain* and *Born in the U.S.A.* (the two dominant LPs of 1984) had run their course but it too eventually got to #1.

The MTV Video Music Awards (VMAs for short) have become the place to go for shocking moments. It has showcased everything from Lady Gaga's meat dress to Diana Ross jiggling Lil Kim's breasts to Howard Stern's Fartman appearance and to Miley Cyrus doing whatever it was she was doing during Robin Thicke's "Blurred Lines." But Madonna's performance of "Like a Virgin" still makes the top of everyone's list of shocking moments at the VMAs, if, for no other reason than shocking an audience at an award show was still, well, virgin territory. Nowadays it seems like it's everyone's goal but when Madonna did it, no one expected it. As for Steinberg and Kelly they have gone on to collaborate on many other classic songs including "True Colors" by Cyndi Lauper, "Eternal Flame" by the Bangles, "I Touch Myself" by Divinyls, "I'll Stand By You" by the Pretenders and "So Emotional" by Whitney Houston. And as for Madonna, well, you probably know what she's done over the course of her career. "Like a Virgin" simply solidified her as a true international superstar and proved her debut LP was not a fluke. She's gone on to sell 300 million records in her career and is recognized as the most successful female recording artist ever. She's also the highest grossing solo touring artist of all time (male or female) and though she doesn't don the wedding dress much anymore, "Like a Virgin" is always in her setlist.

## January 27th

On this date in 1970, Van Morrison released his third solo LP, *Moondance*. He had written and produced the album with a more commercial sound hoping to win back some fans he'd lost with his previous release. Not only would he achieve that goal but *Moondance* is recognized today almost universally as Morrison's career masterpiece and one of the most flawless albums of all time.

George Ivan Morrison was born in August of 1945 in Belfast, Northern Ireland. His father's first name was George as well so early on, he was given the nickname Van. His father also owned one of the largest record collections in all of Ireland so the young Van grew up exposed to everything from Muddy Waters to Ray Charles and from Charlie Parker to Solomon Burke. Morrison would say years later: "If it weren't for guys like Ray and Solomon, I wouldn't be where I am today. Those guys were the inspiration that got me going." But the elder

Morrison wasn't done pointing his son in the direction of a career in music. When Van turned 11 his father bought him an acoustic guitar and just a year later, the young boy formed his first band. At 17, he was touring Europe with the Irish show band, the International Monarchs. In 1964, Morrison formed the band Them. They released two albums and ten singles in their two years together but it was the B-side of their song "Baby, Please Don't Go" that they'll always be remembered for. That song, "Gloria," has gone on to be a garage band classic and has been covered by the likes of Jimi Hendrix and the Doors. The Doors probably heard that song for the first time when they opened for Them during a two week residency at LA's Whiskey a Go-Go. It is said that Jim Morrison was very impressed by Van during these shows and studied his namesake's stagecraft. After Them broke up, Van decided to try a solo career. One of his first solo recordings, "Brown Eyed Girl" became a Top 10 hit in 1967. Perhaps as a way of distancing himself from the obvious pop accessibility of "Brown Eyed Girl," Van then produced *Astral Weeks*. Today, that album is appreciated for its ethereal beauty and almost stream-of-consciousness lyrics but when it was released towards the end of 1968 it was largely ignored by both critics and music fans. In all fairness Van Morrison was competing with some heavy hitters in late 1968. Everything from the Beatles' *White Album* to Hendrix' *Electric Ladyland* LP were dominating the airwaves at the time, but *Astral Weeks*' dismal sales left the young singer wondering whether or not he would make it as a musician.

In an interview years later, Morrison would talk about his philosophy as he prepared the material for what would become *Moondance*. "I make albums primarily to sell them," he said, "and if I get too far out a lot of people can't relate to it. I had to forget about the artistic thing because it didn't make sense on a practical level. One has to live." Morrison had recently married his American girlfriend Janet Planet (some say so he could remain in the U.S.) and the two moved into a home near Woodstock, New York, an area known for its thriving artist community. There, in the summer of 1969, with the Woodstock Festival taking place just miles away, Morrison began writing songs for his next album. He abandoned the abstract sounds of *Astral Weeks* and aimed for a more upbeat, R&B driven sound. It's impossible to hear "Everyone" or "Caravan" or the title track and not tap a foot or snap a finger. And for the album's slower songs like "Into the Mystic" or "Crazy Love" he still found a melody that would hook the listener. His lyrics were no less poetic and beautiful but the overall sound of *Moondance*, especially compared to its predecessor, was much more melodious and memorable.

Van Morrison did most of the production for *Moondance* because, as he would say later, "No one knew what I was looking for except me, so I just did it." The album was released on this date in 1970 and it was immediately received well by the critics with Robert Christgau, perhaps summing up everyone's opinion when he wrote in the *Village Voice*, "Forget *Astral Weeks*--this is a brilliant, catchy, poetic, and completely successful LP." Spin magazine has since called it "the great white soul album." Morrison has gone on to a long and successful career as a singer/songwriter so it's hard to imagine a time when he was one more unsuccessful album away from being out of the business but that was very likely the case in 1969. He focused all his energies and skills and from the opening line of the album's first song "And It Stoned Me," ("Half a mile from the county fair...") to the album's optimistic and infectious closer ("Glad Tidings") he produced an unforgettable collection of songs. Sometimes it's amazing what happens when a true artist feels a little pressure to produce a successful work. The great ones always deliver.

### January 28th

On this date in 1985, the American Music Awards took place in Los Angeles, California. Instead of attending the usual post-award-show parties though, most of the musicians who were in town for the show headed to a late night recording session. The resulting song, "We Are the World," would sell more than 20 million copies and the entire project would raise over $75 million for famine relief in Africa.

In December of 1984 a number of English musicians got together and recorded a song called "Do They Know It's Christmas?" with the intent of raising money for famine relief in Ethiopia. Shortly after that song made international headlines (and raised tons of money), Harry Belafonte began gathering support for American artists to follow suit. Belafonte's first phone call was to Ken Kragen, a philanthropist as well as a very successful entertainment manager and Kragen immediately contacted his two most famous clients: Kenny Rogers and Lionel Richie. They agreed to help immediately and then they enlisted two more high profile names in the industry: Stevie Wonder and Michael Jackson.

The date for the recording session was set in place quickly for the obvious reason that so many of the country's most successful artists would be in town for the American Music Awards. Kragen continued working the phones, setting a goal to recruit two artists to the project every day. He says today that the turning point was when he got Bruce Springsteen to agree to attend. That seemed to persuade some of the more rock oriented performers that this wasn't just going to be a soul and R&B thing. The roster was building but as the day approached, they still needed a song.

Lionel Richie and Michael Jackson got to work. They met a number of times at Hayvenhurst, the Jackson family home in Encino, California and came up with the framework for the song. Their goal was to write an anthem, something catchy enough and powerful enough to be sung by some of the nation's top performers. La Toya Jackson got to witness some of the writing sessions and she would say later, "I'd go into the room while they were writing and it would be very quiet, which is odd, since Michael's usually very cheery when he works. It was very emotional for them." From those emotional sessions came most of "We Are the World" and on January 22nd an initial recording session was planned to lay down the basic track and guide vocal of the song. On January 24th, Quincy Jones, who had been recruited to produce the session, shipped cassette tapes to the performers who had already signed on to the project -- over 40 total musicians. The cassette tapes included the backing track and vocal guide and a note from Jones that read, in part: "In the years to come, when your children ask, 'What did mommy and daddy do for the war against world famine?', you can say proudly, this was your contribution."

The 12th annual American Music Awards was hosted by Lionel Richie and dominated by Prince and the Revolution. When the show was over so many musicians headed to the A&M Recording Studios in Hollywood that a reported 50 had to be turned away (46 participated). Prince however was not among them. He'd said from the beginning he wasn't interested in recording the song but everyone else involved still held out hope that he'd change his mind at the last minute and get caught up in the spirit of the moment. And even though Prince contributed an original song to the *We Are the World* album, his absence caused him a lot of negative publicity, especially when one of his bodyguards got into an altercation that same evening with some paparazzi. The media feasted on the fact that Prince was out partying while his peers in the industry were in the studio working for a worthy cause.

Those that did arrive, and were famous enough to gain entrance, were greeted with a sign that read, "Please check your egos at the door." Stevie Wonder was also telling everyone that if the song wasn't completed in one take, he and Ray Charles were going to drive everyone home that night.

By all accounts the recording went fairly smoothly. There was one minor disagreement about what key the song was in (Billy Joel at one point went to the piano, played a note and said, "see, it's in E." He then added, "I hate E.") Stevie Wonder caused a little confusion when he started insisting that one line should be changed to Swahili (he eventually lost the argument). And Willie Nelson caused some grumbling when he interrupted his whiskey drinking with Waylon Jennings to say (loud enough for everyone to hear) that the project was great but wouldn't it be better if they all did something for people in their own country. (Nelson would heed his own advice just months later when he helped organize the first Farm Aid benefit concert.) And there were lighter moments as well, like when Cyndi Lauper was told she had to remove some of her jewelry because she was moving around and the microphone was picking up the jangling of her earrings and bracelets. After one take Lauper can be heard asking, "Am I still clicking?" And when Ray Charles announced between takes, seemingly out of nowhere, that he hadn't had "no good lovin'" since January (the fact that it was still January brought some levity to the room).

Recording wrapped about 8am and Quincy Jones didn't get to work on piecing everything together till later the next day. When he did, he felt he didn't have enough for the big finish he wanted. He loved what he'd gotten out of Bruce Springsteen passionately singing the chorus but he didn't have a counter-melody so he summoned Stevie Wonder back into the studio and had him record a sort of call and response to Springsteen. For the video, Springsteen and Wonder are blended together into one shot and Wonder is wearing a different shirt than he had been the night before.

Jones completed the single and it was prepared for release. The song dropped on March 7th and became an instant huge seller, hitting #1 on April 13th where it sat for a month. An album of the same name was released on April 23rd which included the Prince donated song, "4 the Tears In Your Eyes" as well as "Tears Are Not Enough" which was recorded by a number of Canadian artists for famine relief under the name Northern Lights. The album also sold well, hitting #1 on LP chart the week after its release. All totaled the project raised approximately $75 million and helped feed and clothe many people in Africa. Bruce Springsteen, who had shown up to the recording session driving a pickup truck (unlike everyone else who arrived via limousine) would sum up all the artists' feelings about the recording session when he said, "Anytime somebody asks you to take one night of your time to stop people starving to death, it's pretty hard — you can't say no." Springsteen and almost 50 other artists didn't say "No" on this night in 1985 and from their efforts came an iconic anthem that helped save so many lives.


### January 29th

On this date in 2003, Eminem's motivational anthem "Lose Yourself" was finishing up its incredible 12 week run at #1 on the *Billboard* Hot 100 chart. Way back in early November of 2002 it had bumped Nelly's "Dilemma" from the top spot and it would stay through the end of January, finally relinquishing the #1 position to "Bump, Bump, Bump" by B2k & P Diddy. A song that Eminem wrote on the set of his movie *8 Mile* became the biggest seller of his career and a song so many have since used to pump themselves up for a big moment in their lives.

Eminem burst onto the hip hop scene in the mid-nineties, earning a reputation as a rapper with a unique and forceful flow and a creative writing style that incorporated his sharp sense of humor. His 2000 single "The Real Slim Shady" put him on the map nationally and he was soon looking for a vehicle to launch him from stardom to super stardom. Like Prince did with *Purple Rain*, he found that vehicle in a movie. He was cast to play a young Caucasian rapper named Jimmy "B-Rabbit" Smith Jr., who, like Eminem himself, is living just outside of Detroit and looking to make it in the hip hop world dominated by African-Americans. Just like Prince's character The Kid in *Purple Rain*, B-Rabbit is not exactly autobiographical but there are many similarities to Eminem's actual upbringing.

When shooting started Eminem had a portable recording studio set up near the set because he wanted to continue producing music for the movie. During any downtime, Eminem was either writing lyrics or in the studio recording. He began to formulate the idea for "Lose Yourself," writing in character as B-Rabbit and would carry around a sheet of paper all the time where he would jot down lines for the song. That actual piece of paper makes an appearance in the movie and ultimately the video for "Lose Yourself." Finally one day towards the end of production, he summoned some musicians to the studio-in-a-trailer and had them lay down the track and power chords that he would rap over. Channeling B-Rabbit's one and only moment to shine in the rap battle near the end of the film, Eminem nailed his entire rap in one take.

"Lose Yourself" was so last minute that the initial movie preview that was released to theaters used his song "Cleanin' Out My Closet." But once the studio heard "Lose Yourself" the trailer was reedited and served as the perfect preview for the movie. *8 Mile* opened at #1 and ultimately broke the $100 million mark in domestic box office receipts. The official soundtrack, *Music from and Inspired by the Motion Picture 8 Mile*, which featured songs from Eminem as well as other rappers like 50 Cent and Nas, opened up at #1 as well. But "Lose Yourself" was the huge success of the project, spending three months at #1 and becoming Eminem's signature song.

"Lose Yourself" was nominated for an Oscar but when Eminem found out the producers of the Academy Awards wanted him to sing a family friendly version (rather than bleep certain words on the fly), he decided not to perform it at the show. He wasn't even in attendance. Going in to the award show, the odds-on favorite to win Best Original Song was U2, whose "Hands That Built America" was featured in *The Gangs of New York*. When Barbra Streisand opened the envelope to announce the winner that night she even let out a surprising "Whoa!" and raised her eyebrows before announcing "The Oscar goes to Eminem." Luis Resto, one of the song's producers, accepted the award. "Lose Yourself" thus became the first song to win Best Original Song and not be performed live at the ceremony since they began televising the Oscars.

People listen to music for many reasons. To chill, to cheer up, to reminisce. Sometimes, someone needs a song to kick them in the ass and inspire them to reach for new heights. There are a lot of songs that can do that, but none more effectively than "Lose Yourself," especially the non-family-friendly version. When Eminem raps, "Success is my only mother fuckin' option, failures not," before launching into that chorus that'll make you wanna run through a brick wall, it's as big and powerful a message as has ever been recorded. Eminem may have channeled his character, B-Rabbit, to write the lyrics but his message is as universal as time itself. There are times in life when you have one shot, one opportunity, and you better never let it go.

# January 30th

On this date in 1969, the Beatles played a 42 minute, surprise concert on the rooftop of the building they owned in London. It would be the last time the four Beatles ever played together in front of an audience of any kind.

By 1968 things were rapidly unraveling for the band that had dominated the decade. The four Beatles were each involved in their own projects and affairs and the future of the group was very much in doubt. Paul McCartney, probably the only one of the four who was eager and enthusiastic about keeping the band going, had come up with the bright idea of filming the recording sessions for their next album for a documentary to coincide with that album's release (because nothing alleviates internal stress like a bunch of cameras in your face). The band hired Michael Lindsay-Hogg, whom they'd worked with on short promotional films (early music videos) for "Paperback Writer", "Hey Jude", and "Revolution" to direct the movie. As work progressed on the record and the film, it was decided that they needed a big finish and shooting a Beatles concert would be it. The Beatles, though, had stopped touring years ago and their only recent public performances had been in television studios for "All You Need Is Love" and "Hey Jude." So the band was going to have to do a one-off show somewhere. Numerous locations were proposed from the near (London's Palladium) to the far (the Sahara desert) to the far out (a 2,000-year-old Roman amphitheater in Tunisia). As the band started thinking about the logistics involved they decided to just keep it simple. In December of 1968 the Jefferson Airplane had played a surprise "concert" on a rooftop in New York City (they got one song in before the NYPD shut them down) and the Beatles thought this idea not only sounded unique but much easier than traipsing themselves, their gear and this film crew out to God-knows where. Later in the year when the band was back to work on a different album they'd make a similar decision. There was talk of calling that album Everest and flying the band to the Himalayas to take a cover shot on the mountain but finally they all just said fuck it, named the album *Abbey Road* and took a picture of the four them walking across the street in front of their studio. Apathy had certainly set in among the Fab Four.

January 30th, 1969 was a bitterly cold and windy day in London. Starting first thing in the morning, gear began being assembled on the rooftop of the Apple Records building. Alan Parsons, who was a sound engineer working with the band at the time and would go on to greatness both as a band leader and famously engineering Pink Floyd's *Dark Side of the Moon*, was dispatched to get some pantyhose to serve as windscreens for the microphones. He walked to a nearby store and asked for three pairs of pantyhose, any size. He'd say later, "They thought I was either a bank robber or a cross-dresser." To fight off the bitter cold John Lennon wore one of Yoko Ono's fur coats and Ringo Starr borrowed his wife's raincoat for an extra layer of warmth. A team of handlers kept cigarettes lit the whole time which George Harrison would cup between songs in an effort to keep circulation going in his fingers. Only McCartney braved the temperatures in a suit jacket and dress shirt. Besides the four

Beatles, keyboardist Billy Preston also performed. Preston had been working with the band and Harrison specifically wanted him there because he felt they all got along better when an outside, professional musician was present.

Beginning about noon the band launched into "Get Back." People in the surrounding area were taking their lunch breaks and many of them filed into the streets to see where the loud music was coming from. The Beatles had told no one about this show, not even the local police whose station was just down the street. The first version of "Get Back" was more of a sound check and when it was over, they launched right back into the same song. They then jammed a mash up of "Get Back", "I Want You" and "Don't Let Me Down" before doing a full version of "Don't Let Me Down." The band then played "I Got a Feeling" and "One After 909." "One After 909" is one of the oldest songs John Lennon and Paul McCartney ever wrote together. McCartney has said he has vivid memories of working on the song as a 17 year old with his new friend John Lennon. "It's not a great song," McCartney has said, "but it's a great favorite of mine because it has great memories for me of John and I trying to write a bluesy freight-train song." The band had attempted to record it back in 1963 but it had sat on the shelf till they brushed it off for this latest project, perhaps out of sentimentality because both Lennon and McCartney knew things were nearing an end.

By this point, about a half hour into their playing, the crowd out front had grown to the point that traffic was blocked on the streets and most of the adjoining rooftops were filled with on-lookers. The local police were nice enough to call over and say they'd be there in ten minutes. An Apple employee, discussing how the advanced notice gave everyone a chance to dispose of their drugs, was quoted afterwards saying, "When the police raided the building, there was a whole chorus of toilets being flushed." When the police arrived they made their way to the rooftop but were again very respectful. They could have cut the band off mid-song and started hauling people away but they simply gave the instruction that the show needed to come to an end.

The last song the Beatles played, with the bobbies looking on was another take of "Get Back." Mal Evans, the band's road manager, switched off the guitar amps at the beginning of the song in an attempt to appease the police but Harrison promptly switched them back on. During the ending of the song McCartney ad-libbed: "You've been playing on the roofs again, and that's no good, and you know your Mummy doesn't like that ... she gets angry ... she's gonna have you arrested! Get back!" When the song was over John Lennon said, "I'd like to say thank you on behalf of the group and ourselves and I hope we've passed the audition." Though the version of "Get Back" that would make the record wasn't from the rooftop concert, Lennon's final words were added to it.

The four Beatles would never play before an audience together again. After working on the songs that would become *Let It Be* and then handing the tapes off to Phil Spector to produce them, the band recorded the songs that would make up *Abbey Road*. That album would be released on September 26th 1969 and *Let It Be* wouldn't see the light of day till May of 1970, a few weeks after the band announced their break-up. So Beatles' fans are always left arguing what is the last thing we'll ever hear from the band. Some argue it should be the end of *Abbey Road* since that's the last album the band ever worked on together. And since that album ends with "And in the end, the love you take is equal to the love you make" (before the "hidden track" called "Her Majesty," that is) that's a pretty impressive coda to a great career. Those who go with *Let It Be*, since it was the last album the band released, are left with the final lyric "Get back to where you once belonged" before Lennon's snarky closing about passing the audition. Either way, it seems like a great finale for a band that literally changed the world.

## January 31st

On this date in 1999, Britney Spears had just claimed the #1 spot on the *Billboard* Hot 100 chart with her debut single "...Baby One More Time." The song had bumped off Brandy's "Have You Ever?" the day before and it would enjoy a two week stay at the top before giving way to "Angel of Mine" by Monica. Spears was still a teenager at the time and she rode the wave of young pop artists who would dominate the charts at the turn of the millennium.

Britney Jean Spears was born on December 2nd, 1981 in McComb, Mississippi. Early on she showed her aptitude as a performer, singing a song at her kindergarten graduation and earning a solo dance number at her first dance recital. She won many talent shows growing up and her parents encouraged her as a performer. When she was eight, her mom brought her to an audition for the revival of the Mickey Mouse Club but she was rejected for being too young. However at the audition Nancy Carson, a New York City talent agent, saw her and was very impressed. She recommended Spears enroll at New York City's Professional Performing Arts School, and Spears' mom took the advice. Pretty soon the two were living in New York and Spears was hired as the understudy for the lead role of Tina Denmark in the Off-Broadway musical *Ruthless!*. When she turned 11 she was old enough for the Mickey Mouse Club and she joined a cast that included Christina Aguilera, Justin Timberlake, Ryan Gosling, and Keri Russell.

When Spears was still 16 years old she started shopping a demo looking for a record contract. Jeff Fenster at Jive Records was very impressed and he signed her to a deal. He'd say later: "It's very rare to hear someone that age who can deliver emotional content and commercial appeal. For any artist, the motivation—the 'eye of the tiger'— is extremely important. And Britney had that." Jive sent her to Sweden to work with songwriters and producers like Max Martin, Denniz Pop and Rami Yacoub, among others. Martin offered Spears a song called "Hit Me Baby One More Time" that he'd written and that had previously been rejected by the Backstreet Boys and TLC. Spears loved it but

Jive was concerned that the "Hit me" in the title might condone domestic violence so they shortened the title to just "...Baby One More Time."

In October of 1998 Britney Spears' debut single " . . . Baby One More Time" was released along with a video that fulfills just about every school girl fantasy any guy has ever had. Spears began a shopping mall tour (a la Tiffany) but very quickly outgrew that and before long she was opening for NSYNC. Pop music was exploding at the time with boy bands and pop singers fighting for chart dominance and radio play. "...Baby One More Time" kept climbing the charts and its video kept getting MTV play (yes, MTV was still playing videos at the time although their influence was waning and they'd soon become a reality TV channel). Spears' debut album (also called ...Baby One More Time because you can never have enough ellipses...) debuted at #1 on the LP chart, the same week her single went to #1. In doing so, Spears broke several records. She became the first new female artist to have a #1 single on the *Billboard* Hot 100 and #1 album on the *Billboard* 200 at the same time. She also became the first new artist (male or female) to have a single go to the #1 spot the same week that the album debuted at #1 as well as the first new female artist to have the first single and first album at #1 the same week. And finally, Spears is also the youngest female in *Billboard* history to have a single and album at #1 in the same week.

Spears would enjoy many years of success before the pop craze finally dried up. Today she is enjoying renewed interest in her music and that entire genre. Max Martin has gone on to much success as a songwriter and producer. He has written or cowritten, as of this publication date, an incredible 22 #1 singles including "California Gurls" by Katy Perry and Snoop Dogg, "Blank Space" by Taylor Swift and "Can't Stop the Feeling!" by Justin Timberlake. Songs he's written or cowritten have sold over 150 million units and enjoyed countless streams online.

# FEBRUARY

## February 1st

On this date in 2004, Janet Jackson was the featured entertainer at halftime of Super Bowl XXXVIII. The wardrobe malfunction that took place at the end of her twelve minute performance (sometimes referred to as "Nipplegate") would become the most searched moment ever on the internet and would change things for Super Bowl halftimes, award shows and Miss Jackson herself for years to come. Whether it was a mistake or a publicity stunt we'll probably never really know. But what we do know is Janet Jackson's jewelry adorned right nipple, exposed for less than a second, caused more controversy than any body part since Adam and Eve put on the fig leaves.

The first Super Bowl wasn't even called the Super Bowl. The game was played on January 15th, 1967 and it was called the NFL-AFL Championship Game. It was Kansas City Chief's owner Lamar Hunt, when he overheard his grandchildren ask for a toy named a Super Ball, who got the bright idea to call it the Super Bowl. The earliest Super Bowls featured college marching bands as halftime entertainment and Up With People had the honor of performing a number of times from the mid-seventies to the mid-eighties. But as ratings for the Super Bowl grew, and the game started becoming a national event, more and more focus started being placed on the halftime entertainment. Chubby Checker, in 1988, became the first big name performer to grab that spot and then in 1991, New Kids On the Block became the first big contemporary act to fill the halftime entertainment. After that, the halftime show started becoming a coveted position as artists started to realize the promotional opportunity of performing in front of the largest annual television audience. Gloria Estefan performed in 1992, then Michael Jackson took the halftime show to a whole new level in 1993.

Janet Jackson had been approached about performing at the 2002 Super Bowl (following the 2001 season) but after the September 11th terrorist attack, a few NFL executives had gone to see U2 perform and they thought the Irish rock band would be perfect for the first big game following that tragic day. Jackson was bumped and asked to perform at Super Bowl XXXVIII, two years later. She had struck up a friendship with Justin Timberlake years earlier when she had his band NSYNC open during her Velvet Rope World Tour and so she asked him if he'd join her during her performance. Though Janet Jackson was the featured entertainer, there would be other performers besides Timberlake. P. Diddy, Nelly and Kid Rock were all tabbed to appear. Once the setlist was in place, rehearsals got underway and at some point it was decided that at the very end of the show, when Timberlake sang the final line of his song "Rock Your Body" ("I'm gonna have you naked by the end of this song") he would tear away the top of Jackson's wardrobe to reveal her red bra underneath. Timberlake was on tour at the time and only able to attend one rehearsal so this plan could not have been worked out too far in advance or practiced to perfection.

Even prior to the Nipple-Seen-Round-the-World, the twelve minute show wasn't exactly the classiest thing ever put on stage. Being an election year the theme was "Choose or Lose" and after a pre-taped opening that urged viewers to "choose to vote," Jessica Simpson, in hot pants and a sequined bustier, erased that solid civic message by yelling "choose to party!" When Janet Jackson first appeared it was to perform her hit song "All For You" and she was surrounded by shirtless male dancers. Then the rappers took the stage and as rappers are wont to do, both Diddy and Nelly spent a fair amount of time touching their crotches. During Nelly's "Hot in Herre" his backups dancers, in a sign of things to come, tore off their cheerleader skirts at the "I will take my clothes off" line, revealing short-shorts. It would be pointed out later when parents made an uproar about their children seeing Janet Jackson's nipple, that at some point before that, good parenting might have kicked in and, for junior's sake, the channel could have been changed. It's not like the first 11 minutes and 59 seconds were an Elmo sing-along.

Kid Rock then performed wearing an American Flag as a poncho. A slit had been cut in the middle of the flag so it could be worn over his head which has to be against some written or unwritten rule somewhere about how to treat the flag.

After Kid Rock, Janet Jackson returned to sing "Rhythm Nation." The choreography with her and her backup dancers was excellent during this portion and when that segment ended, with Jackson shouting out things like "ignorance," "bigotry" and "illiteracy" with the callback after each being an emphatic "No!" it was easily the highlight of the halftime show. One can only wonder what may have become of Janet Jackson if things had just ended right then and there.

But of course, they didn't. Justin Timberlake then emerged from beneath the stage beat-boxing before launching into his hit song "Rock Your Body." He and Jackson did a fair amount of bumping and grinding during this song and at one point Timberlake simulated smacking her ass. Timberlake and Jackson made their way to center stage by the end of the song, even switching sides so he would be on her left. As Timberlake sings the "naked" line he reaches his left hand across his body and Jackson's and grabs her right breast. On "song" he yanks and exposes her breast which, on close inspection features a nipple that is pierced and adorned with a star-shaped piece of jewelry called a nipple shield. Jackson looks down at her breast, perhaps in amazement that 150 million people are now seeing her half-topless and after a half a second the television broadcast jumps to an overhead shot of the stadium.

Half a second.

Most of the viewing audience at home were left wondering, "did we just see . . . ?" Salli Frattini, the executive producer for MTV, who had planned the entire performance, was in a truck outside of the stadium. She and her crew began celebrating the end of the 12-minute halftime performance, which she thought was a complete success. It wasn't until she received a phone call from a superior who was watching at home and was angered at what they'd seen that she rewound the tape. Her heart sank as she mumbled, "Oh shit, did that just happen?"

The fallout was quick and decisive. First came the hand wringing and apologizing. CBS, the network broadcasting the game, released a statement that said: "The moment did not conform to CBS broadcast standards and we would like to apologize to anyone who was offended." NFL Commissioner Paul Tagliabue said the show fell far short of the "tasteful, first-class entertainment" the league expected. And MTV, which had produced the show, said: "The tearing of Janet Jackson's costume was unrehearsed, unplanned, completely unintentional and was inconsistent with assurances we had about the content of the performance. MTV regrets this incident occurred and we apologize to anyone who was offended by it." Janet Jackson released a video apology (where she looks like someone is pointing a gun at her just off camera) in which she took full responsibility, saying: "My decision to change the Super Bowl performance was made after the final rehearsal. MTV, CBS, the NFL, had no knowledge whatsoever and unfortunately the whole thing went wrong in the end. I am really sorry if I offended anyone, that was not my intention."

The Federal Communications Commission (the FCC) fined CBS $550,000 which CBS would appeal and eventually have dropped. The FCC then increased the fine for each incident of indecency from $27,500 to $325,000.

The NFL announced that it would never allow MTV to produce a halftime show again. Both Viacom (which owned CBS) and MTV blacklisted Janet Jackson. Other media outlets that had nothing to do with the incident, but apparently found Jackson's bare nipple too much to bear, followed suit. Jackson was scheduled to appear at the Grammy Awards being held the following week, but her invitation was withdrawn (while Timberlake's was not). "Janet Jackson" became the most searched term on the internet and YouTube co-founder Jawed Karim has claimed that the public's desire to see the video again and again was part of the impetus to launching the video hosting site. TiVo orders also spiked after the event because those who had the device were able to rewind and see if they saw what they thought they saw.

Janet Jackson's career has never been the same. And true, you can't just blame this one incident, many artists find their fan base dwindling at a certain point, but being blacklisted by the top media companies in the country has certainly taken its toll on her popularity. Justin Timberlake, on the other hand, has gone on to unprecedented success both in music and movies. Television, too, changed drastically after the incident. Daytime soap operas, which had begun pushing the envelope to the point of showing rear male nudity during sex scenes cleaned up their act after the FCC said they'd be monitoring them closer than ever. The use of delays on live broadcasts has increased and expanded (a delay would have allowed for the nipple to be skipped over). And for the next seven years there wouldn't be a newer act, or a female act, to perform at the halftime show. In 2011, the NFL must have felt safe again from the fear of female nudity when they allowed the Black Eyed Peas, with their female lead singer Fergie, to take that still coveted slot.

Many felt the uproar over Janet Jackson's nipple was a diversionary tactic. It was an election year and some on the right would rather not have had the focus on the war in Iraq and the failure at that point to find weapons of mass destruction or, for that matter, to capture or kill Osama Bin Laden. Many also pointed to the growing amount of violence on television and how there was no one trying to monitor that. Indeed there is some irony in the fact that a football game is basically three hours of men colliding with each other at full speed and the hardest hits are the ones we celebrate and re-watch over and over. Yet a half second nip slip is all anyone wanted to talk about for weeks after. If we in America didn't see the foolishness in that, those outside the country certainly did. Headlines around the world pointed out the U.S.'s continuing sexual conservatism, with some of those international newspapers actually showing a picture of the nipple (and to date no one has been harmed by seeing it). Years later it is still a seminal moment in pop culture history. We all know where we were when it happened. And whether we were shocked or not probably says a lot about how we view sexuality (or jewelry). And if you were in the kitchen grabbing a beer when it happened, it probably says a lot about how much you care about halftime shows. Either way, they'll never be the same again.


## February 2nd

On this date in 1984, Yes' "Owner of a Lonely Heart" was wrapping up its two week stay at the top of the pop chart. The song had arrived there on January 21st, knocking the Michael Jackson and Paul McCartney duet "Say Say Say" from the top and it would remain till February 4th when it gave way to Culture Club's "Karma Chameleon." There are many examples in modern music of a band tweaking or even changing its style and sound in a blatant attempt to score a hit; probably none more obvious than "Owner of a Lonely Heart." The band that had helped create a genre which came to be known as progressive rock (prog rock to its friends) that renounces any and all pop accessibility and celebrates long, winding songs that are the complete antitheses of Top 40, pop radio; the band that had once put out a double album (*Tales from Topographic Oceans*) containing just four songs, that band, now had a #1 hit and a song as catchy as anything on the radio or MTV at the time.

Yes came together in London in the late sixties. Their fourth studio album, *Fragile*, is the LP that broke them in the U.S. and is often considered their masterwork. Keyboardist Rick Wakeman had just joined the band and he helped create their signature sound, an almost classical-like virtuosity combined with mystical and cosmic imagery in their lyrics and gentle yet powerful vocals. "Fragile" contains what many consider to be Yes' signature song, "Roundabout" which got as high as #13 on pop chart in 1972. "Roundabout" has all the elements of a quintessential Yes song, and indeed a prog-rock song in general: it's long (8 and a half minutes), it contains fantastic, if enigmatic imagery ("Your silhouette will charge the view" may not be easy to understand but wow, what a line!), it is masterfully played and it has a ton of tempo changes. If "Roundabout" set the template for Yes songs, they certainly continued to deliver them over the next few years, with songs and whole albums that were more opus' than pop songs. Yes went for the grandiose and in the process, rejected the easy accessibility of pop music.

That is, until they went through a major line-up change in 1980 over differences of opinion about their musical direction. Essentially, vocalist Jon Anderson and Wakeman wanted the band to continue producing their signature sound, while the others in the band wanted to start rocking out a little more and moving slightly towards a more mainstream sound. Things came to a head and Anderson and Wakeman both left the band. Shortly thereafter, the remaining members of Yes were working out new material and the Buggles (of "Video Killed the Radio Star" fame) just happened to be in the same studio. The Buggles were a duo consisting of keyboardist Geoff Downes and singer Trevor Horn, both of whom, as it turned out, were huge Yes fans. When they heard their idols were working up new material they offered them a song. Chris Squire, who'd been a founding member of Yes and with the departure of Anderson was now their de facto leader, invited the two to join the band. They both accepted and contributed to Yes' 1980 LP *Drama*.

Following the tour to support that album, depending on who you speak to, the band either broke up or took a hiatus. For the next few years the only "new" Yes releases were old Yes material. A live album, *Yesshows*, was put out at the end of 1980 and then a greatest hits compilation, *Classic Yes,* came out in 1981.

In 1982 Chris Squire met a singer named Trevor Rabin and the two started a band called Cinema. Squire brought in a few of his old Yes bandmates. He approached Horn about joining but he said he'd rather produce. As Cinema took shape it turned out four of the five people in the band were ex-Yes members (including John Anderson who was back by this point) and pretty soon their record label was urging the band to just call themselves Yes which they eventually decided to do (although some fans will always call this line-up "Yes West" to distinguish it from the original). With the addition of the two Trevors (Horn producing and Rabin playing and singing) the new Yes sound and approach was far different from the classic seventies Yes sound.

And the results were far different as well. "Owner of a Lonely Heart" which was written by Trevor Rabin, Jon Anderson, Chris Squire and Trevor Horn and produced by Horn became the lead single when it was released on October 8th, 1983. The song would hit #1 in the winter of 1984, becoming the band's first and, to date, only chart-topper. Two other singles, "Leave It" and "It Can Happen," charted as well, reaching # 24 and # 57 respectively. "Owner of a Lonely Heart" also earned the band a nomination for Best Pop Performance, meaning they'd come a long way since *Tales from Topographic Oceans*. There's a lyric in "Owner of a Lonely Heart" that goes: "You are the steps you take. You and you and that's the only way." No one could argue Yes had become a pop band. The band had taken those steps. Of course, some of their original fans begrudged them this success, but isn't that always the way? When a band jumps from one genre to the next, they will often find new fans as well as lose some old ones. For every lover of 18 minute songs that meander their way through an aural tapestry, there's another music fan that wants to clap and sing and be done with a song in four and half minutes, tops. There's a saying about that (you can't please all the people . . .) and Yes certainly found out it was true.

## February 3rd

On this date in 1959, just after midnight, three young musicians boarded a plane in Clear Lake, Iowa. The next morning, the man who owned the plane set out to find them. He only flew a few miles before he spotted the plane's wreck. All three musicians, and the pilot who would ultimately be blamed for the crash, had died on impact.

In the summer of 1958, Buddy Holly broke up his band, the Crickets and moved to New York City to do some recording. He married Maria Elena Holly (nee Santiago) in August of that year and the two settled into an apartment in Greenwich Village. He returned to Texas in September where he met with a DJ in Lubbock named Waylon Jennings. Jennings expressed interest in becoming a recording artist and Holly produced a few songs for him. Upon his return to New York, in October of 1958, Holly entered a studio for what would be his last time. He recorded a number of songs including the beautiful ballad, "True Love Ways."

Holly, like so many recording artists through the years, had signed some bad contracts early on and around this time he found himself near bankruptcy. The easiest way for him to make money was to perform live. He played a number of shows towards the end of 1958 with his wife Maria accompanying him. After the holidays, he decided to set out again but this time Maria was not able to join. She was pregnant and stayed home to rest.

Holly put together what he called the Winter Dance Party tour and assembled a band consisting of Waylon Jennings on bass, Tommy Allsup on guitar and Carl Bunch on drums. It was an ambitious endeavor, especially considering the time of year. The tour was slated to perform at 24 locations in the Midwest in as many days. Even the most famous artists in the fifties appeared as part of a package tour (even Elvis) so Holly was joined by fellow early rock and roll pioneers Dion DiMucci (Dion and the Belmonts), Richie Valens and J. P. Richardson, better known as "The Big Bopper." The tour began on January 23rd, 1959 in Milwaukee, Wisconsin. From the outset it was plagued by trouble. First of all the logistics were horrible as the group of musicians and their handlers were forced to travel hours and hours between shows. And the tour bus was a nightmare, breaking down repeatedly and losing its heating system from time to time. Within the first week almost every musician was sick with something and Bunch, Holly's drummer, even came down with frostbite and was forced off the tour. For a few shows Valens would fill in on drums for Holly's sets.

February 2nd was originally scheduled as a day off on the tour but a week in the promoters sought to fill in the off day and offered the musicians a little more cash. Everyone was tired and fatigued and sick but they all agreed to pick up an extra date so calls were made and the Surf Ballroom in Clear Lake, Iowa was secured. Despite the fact that it was a Monday night and the weather was bitterly cold with a light snow, over a thousand people showed up. It truly was a winter dance party!

When the show was over, everyone was looking at a six hour drive to their next destination, Moorhead, Minnesota. Holly was at the end of his rope. He needed to get some laundry done. He decided to charter a flight for him and his bandmates and let the other performers tough it out on the frigid tour bus. The manager of the Surf Ballroom, Carroll Anderson told Holly he knew a guy and he put him in touch with Hubert Dwyer who owned Dwyer Flying Service. For $36 per passenger, Dwyer agreed to fly three of them to Fargo, North Dakota (the closest airport to Moorhead).

After the show, Richardson played the "I've got the flu" card, along with the "I'm a headliner on this tour" card. Holly had originally intended to treat his two other bandmates to the flight but soon he caught wind that Jennings had offered his seat to Richardson. Holly chided him, saying, "I hope your old bus freezes over" to which Jennings responded, "I hope your old plane crashes." Jennings has said those words still haunt him to this day. After hearing that Richardson had secured a seat from Jennings, Valens got to work on Holly's other bandmate, Tommy Allsup. Allsup wasn't as generous though. He held out for a while before offering a coin toss to decide who got to go. He made the offer to the two remaining headliners but Dion, after hearing the cost was $36, said he wanted no part of it. That was the amount his parents paid every month for rent and he just couldn't justify spending that much for a flight when the bus, frigid as it was, would get him there in due time. So it came down to Allsup and Valens. Bob Hale, who'd been the MC for that night's show, had the honor of tossing the coin. He threw a coin in the air and Valens called heads. Heads it was. Valens won the flight; Allsup, the rest of his life. Years later Allsup would open a bar. He named it Heads Up.

When Holly, Richardson and Valens arrived at the airport they found out that Hubert Dwyer was not going to be their pilot. That duty fell to 21 year old pilot Roger Peterson who was not yet certified for "instrument flying" (when visual is out of the question and a pilot has to rely solely on referencing instruments like a gyroscope which tells a pilot which direction they are flying). Peterson was also given weather information that failed to mention an oncoming blizzard. Dwyer arrived to the airport about 12:50 AM, just in time to see the plane off. He watched as the Beechcraft Bonanza (which was not, as legend has it, named American Pie) took off into the snowy night and turned left in a northerly position. Satisfied that his charges were on their way, Dwyer then headed home.

It wasn't until early the next morning that Dwyer became worried. Peterson had not checked in by radio which he should have after landing in Fargo. When Dwyer arrived at the airport that morning, he saw that his plane wasn't back yet either. Now he was really worried. He took off in another one of his planes and attempted to retrace the original flight pattern. He didn't have to go far. Just miles from the airport he saw the wreckage in the field. He alerted the sheriff's office which had a difficult time getting to the site due to the previous night's heavy snowfall. When they finally got there, only Peterson was still inside the wrecked fuselage. Holly, Richardson and Valens had all been thrown from the plane when it made impact and cartwheeled along the frozen ground for a few hundred feet. All four passengers were killed instantly upon impact.

Maria Holly would first hear about her young husband's death on television. She went into such shock she miscarried their baby. After this incident it became an unwritten rule that news agencies do not report deaths until the next of kin have been notified. Later, obviously still burdened with guilt, she would say: "I blame myself. I was not feeling well when he left. I was two weeks pregnant, and I wanted Buddy to stay with me, but he had scheduled that tour. It was the only time I wasn't with him. And I blame myself because I know that, if only I had gone along, Buddy never would have gotten into that airplane."

A subsequent investigation would determine that the crash was caused by pilot error. Peterson, suffering from vertigo in the blinding dark of night and snow, thought he was ascending when he was really descending. And maybe that's the perfect analogy for Buddy Holly. He had arguably the shortest career of any rock and roll legend, lasting a little under two years between the time of his first release, "Love Me" in April of 1956, and his untimely death. Yet his reach is felt with so many of the Rock Gods that would come along in the sixties and therefore the musicians who would be inspired by them. Some people call February 3rd, 1959, The Day the Music Died, but we all know that's inaccurate. The lives of Richardson and Valens and Holly were tragically cut short, and who knows what future work they took to their graves. But the music didn't die. If anything, their tragic deaths left them as figurative immortals, filled with untold potential that could now only be imagined.

It says something about us as a society that on the very same day that that Beechcraft Bonanza crashed and killed its four occupants, an American Airlines flight from Chicago crashed into the East River while trying to land at Laguardia Airport in New York City. 65 people died in that tragic accident. But other than their nearest kin, everyone in America thinks of February 3rd, 1959 as the day we lost Buddy Holly. It says something about how we value celebrity and rockstars and people who speak to us on an almost universal level. Holly's "True Love Ways" would finally be released posthumously, as part of a greatest hits compilation called The Buddy Holly Story Volume 2. Some have argued it's the most played "first dance" song at weddings. Whether that's true or not, there's no doubting the song's intimacy speaks to people on a completely different level than anything any of the early rock and rollers had yet to produce. If "True Love Ways" was a precursor to what Buddy Holly was set to produce in the next decade it makes his passing even more tragic (if that's possible). He was a man of boundless potential and it all disappeared on this day in 1959.

## February 4th

On this date in 1977, Fleetwood Mac released *Rumours*. The album is one of the most complete works in all of rock history, without a filler track on it, and it would go on to be the band's most successful work as well as one of the biggest sellers in music history. The entire album was written and recorded during multiple breakups within the band and drama that was only multiplied by abundant alcohol and drug use. Stevie Nicks would look back on the creation of this album and say, "Devastation leads to writing really good things." If anything, she undersold the point.

The first lineup to call itself Fleetwood Mac formed in London in the mid-sixties as a blues band. They gathered quite the following throughout Europe but made nary an inroad in the U.S. They were an all male outfit until 1970 when Christine McVie, who'd recently married bassist John McVie, joined the band. They continued to undergo lineup changes and then, in 1974, drummer Mick Fleetwood heard a track by the Los Angeles based band Buckingham Nicks. Fleetwood loved Lindsey Buckingham's guitar playing and promptly asked him to join the band. Buckingham agreed but under one condition: his bandmate and girlfriend Stevie Nicks had to join as well. Buckingham said they were a package deal, take it or leave it. The other members of Fleetwood Mac agreed and the quintet that would go on to worldwide success was now in place, featuring a married couple (John and Christine McVie) a couple who were dating (Buckingham and Nicks) and a drummer who was married to someone not in the band.

In 1975 this new lineup released a self-titled album that would finally break them in the U.S. The album sold five million copies and included three Top 20 hits: "Over My Head", "Rhiannon" and "Say You Love Me." After a lengthy tour, during which some of the relationships started to fray at the seams, the band convened at the famous Record Plant studios in Sausalito, California to work on new material. The band hoped to build on their growing fame but in their wildest dreams they couldn't have predicted the success their next album would bring them. Nor the drama.

By the time recording got underway everyone in the band was going through a breakup. The emotions involved informed almost every song. The McVies divorced while the record was being recorded and then Christine took up with the band's lighting technician. She showed up in the studio one day with a song she'd just written called "You Make Loving Fun," inspired by this new relationship. John happily played his part on the record with Mick Fleetwood explaining later, "Knowing John, he probably thought it was about one of her dogs." Other songs spoke directly about the break-ups, like Stevie Nicks' remarkably haunting "Dreams" in which she sings "Listen carefully to the sound of your loneliness like a heartbeat drives you mad. In the stillness of remembering what you had, and what you lost." "Dreams" hit #1 in June of 1977 becoming the band's first chart-topper and helping to keep *Rumours* flying off record store shelves. Buckingham answered "Dreams" with a few of his own songs, like "Second Hand News" which was chosen to open the album (and in which he admits, "I know there's nothing to say, someone has taken my place.") "Second Hand News" began life as a much mellower track but when Buckingham heard the Bee Gees' "Jive Talkin'" he gave the song a similar feel. Listen to the two back-to-back and you can hear the obvious similarities. Buckingham also wrote "Go Your Own Way" in which he sings, "Loving you isn't the right thing to do" before adding, "Shacking up is all you wanna do." Nicks has denied the "shacking up" accusation by the way, claiming she never cheated on Buckingham. Another Christine McVie contribution, "Don't Stop," had a more optimistic outlook on break-ups, reminding the listener over and over that "yesterday's gone" and so we should focus on tomorrow.

Anyone who has ever been involved in a breakup knows how difficult it is to see the other person when things are falling apart and emotions are running high. The members of Fleetwood Mac not only saw each other almost everyday during the recording process but they had to collaborate together, sometimes helping to shape songs that were obviously about them (and not complimentary either). Imagine singing a line like "Players only love you when they're playing" and knowing your ex-lover wrote it about you. Or playing bass while your ex-wife sings "You make loving fun, and I don't have to tell you but you're the only one" about some other guy. Every member of the band has described the writing and recording process as tense and difficult and full of drama. But from all that friction and even, at times, hostility, came an amazing collection of songs. Songs that spoke right to the hearts and minds of everyone listening.

*Rumours* was released on this date in 1977 and it would first climb to #1 on the album chart in early April. All totaled the album would spend 31 non-consecutive weeks at the top and produce four Top 10 singles. And as if recording the album hadn't been enough of a strain on everyone's emotions, the band then spent most of 1977 on the road, promoting the album and playing to sold-out crowds everywhere. The album stands up all these years later. It's well worth listening to all the way through, first song to last in one sitting. In fact, if you have 40 minutes free today I'd highly recommend it. Let that familiar strumming of the opening song "Second Hand News" come to life in your headphones and follow Fleetwood Mac's journey over the next ten songs. And even though you'll probably be listening digitally, after "Songbird" get up and mimic turning a record over. Because back in the day, artists put a lot of thought into the song that would kick off side two of an LP. "The Chain" is the only song on the entire album that is credited to all five band members and indeed it is a true collaborative effort, with everyone singing passionately the "If you don't love me now you will never love me again" sections and of course the soaring finale of the song: "chain, keep us together." Somehow this amazing quintet of musicians and broken-hearted artists found the chain that kept them together and in doing so they created a timeless masterpiece. Listen to it all the way through, culminating with Stevie Nicks singing about break-ups and cocaine in her elegiac "Gold Dust Woman." You'll be glad you did.


## February 5th

On this date in 1980, Pink Floyd's *The Wall* was sitting at the top of album chart, a position it would enjoy for an incredible 15 straight weeks. The double LP had arrived at #1 on January 19th, 1980 and it would not relinquish the spot until May 2nd. It's an album that began because of Roger Waters' frustrations at his band's über-success, and ironically it would thrust Pink Floyd even further into the public spotlight. Waters created the ultimate concept album, and the project has had a number of different incarnations since its inception. And it all began with spit.

Pink Floyd's popularity grew exponentially throughout the seventies. They began the decade as an obscure psychedelic band prone to long, experimental songs. But their 1973 album *Dark Side of the Moon* changed all that and they soon became international superstars. Their next two albums, *Wish You Were* Here and *Animals* solidified their place as prog rock gods and their tours became epic extravaganzas. By 1977, for their Animals tour (also called the In the Flesh Tour) the band had moved from arenas to large stadiums and this frustrated Roger Waters, who by this point was the band's chief songwriter and visionary. He grew increasingly irritated during this tour and often had fall outs with his bandmates and sometimes even berated the audience if they wouldn't quiet down during some of the show's mellower numbers. Things came to a head at the very last show of that tour in Montreal. Waters was at a breaking point and when a group of rowdy fans in front of the stage refused to settle down during a quiet moment Waters spat at them. Guitarist David Gilmour also left the stage out of frustration and it was left up to the band's backup guitarist to play the final few songs. When the show ended there was a small riot in front of the stage.

The band went into a hiatus following the tour, but Waters was deeply affected by the experience, and started thinking of his next project. He was always a writer who dove into his own personal experience to search for material but now he swam even deeper. He developed a character, a rock star, named Pink, who was an amalgamation of his own experience as well as Pink Floyd founder Syd Barrett. Barrett had left the band in 1968 after becoming depressed and withdrawn, possibly from a bad acid experience. Pink would also withdraw from society and become increasingly angry and paranoid and Waters thought of a wall as a metaphorical symbol for the man's isolation. Every experience in his life would be another brick in that wall, from his father dying in World War II (which had happened to Waters) to his overbearing mother to his tyrannical teachers. And bricks weren't restricted to just youthful experiences. As Pink matured, his own infidelities, his drug use, his success, all of these and more were bricks in Pink's wall, isolating him from society.

Roger Waters presented his concept to the rest of the band when they got together about a year after the Animals tour had ended. Besides the album he proposed a tour in which the band would slowly be blocked from the audience as bricks were added to the front of the stage throughout the show. The visual would be amazing but there was a practical reason for this as well. Waters and the others hated playing in big stadiums and felt they couldn't connect with the audiences of that size. With a wall between them, they'd no longer even have to try.

One of the techniques Waters employed on *The Wall* was something he'd done before on previous Pink Floyd albums, and that is the concept of everything coming full circle. Though an album has a first and last track, if the end of the final song is somehow connected to the opening of the first song, the album can be thought of as one long loop and the beginning no longer needs to be track one. This is actually a lot easier to do today in our digital age than it was in the seventies when albums or cassettes had to be flipped. *Dark Side of the Moon*, for example begins and ends with the same heartbeat. *Animals* opens with the song "Pigs on the Wing 1" and closes with "Pigs on the Wing 2." With *The Wall*, you have to listen very closely, but before the opening power cords of the first song, "In the Flesh" (an obvious nod to the tour that had given Waters the original idea for the album) there's a faint voice that says "we came in" followed by some flute playing. At the very end of the album, the last track "Outside the Wall" ends with the very same flute and then you can faintly hear "isn't this where." Played together in a loop, the listener will hear, "Isn't this where we came in?"

Waters wrote the bulk of the album with Gilmour co-writing a few of the songs. Recording took almost a year, from the end of 1978 right up until the album's release in November of 1979. The band worked with two different producers (James Guthrie and Bob Ezrin) in a myriad of locations (Paris, New York and Los Angeles). It was Ezrin who suggested the disco beat for the song "Another Brick in the Wall Part II" as well as having children scream the "We don't need no education" part. Ezrin had suggested something similar to Alice Cooper years earlier for his hit song "School's Out." "Another Brick in the Wall Part II" became Pink Floyd's only chart-topping single and its ubiquitous radio play throughout the winter of 1980 helped promote the album and keep it at the top of the charts.

The resulting tour was a financial disaster as the logistics of building the wall and showing video footage on it were extremely expensive. The band played 31 total shows and actually lost money on them. In 1982 the movie *Pink Floyd – The Wall* was released featuring a mix of live action and animation to tell Pink's story (with Bob Geldof playing the lead character). In 1990 after the fall of the Berlin Wall, Roger Waters (who'd left the band by this point) organized a one-off show, featuring special guests, to commemorate East Germany's freedom. That show was recorded and released as a live album. And from 2010 to 2013 Waters played the entire album in concert featuring the wall being built on the stage and videos projected on it. It's estimated that tour brought in over $450 million, so it's safe to say Waters recouped whatever losses he incurred from the first Wall tour.

*The Wall* is a brilliant album because, although it deals with one specific character's feelings of isolation and despair, its themes are universal. We all have experiences, both in our childhood as well as our adult years, that shape who we become. And we all build walls to protect our most vulnerable and sensitive sides. Most of us don't take these to the extreme like Syd Barrett or the fictional Pink, but it is certainly something we can all relate to. And isn't that what great art really is? A single piece, whether it's a painting or a play or, in this case, an entire album, that tells a story that hits home to those who experience it. We share many common emotions and the great artist can connect all of us by speaking to one or more of these feelings, reminding us how similar we all are. *The Wall*, with its 20 million albums sold and resulting movie and hundreds of live performances, has obviously done that as well as any album in the rock era.

### February 6th

On this date in 1965, the quintessential Wall of Sound record "You've Lost That Lovin' Feelin'" by the Righteous Brothers began a two week stay atop the pop chart. It bumped off Petula Clark's "Downtown" and would give way to "This Diamond Ring" by Gary Lewis & the Playboys on February 20th. Though its two week stay doesn't exactly make it a mega hit the song has taken on legendary status for its production and incredible vocal performance.

Bill Medley and Bobby Hatfield first sang together in a band in Santa Ana, California called the Paramours. Their lone single, "There She Goes (She's Walking Away)," was released in December of 1962 and when it failed to make a dent on the charts the band broke up. Medley and Hatfield then began singing together as a duo and when they performed at the El Toro Marine base some black marines called them "righteous brothers." They soon adopted it as their name. They signed to Moonglow Records, the same label that had released their Paramours song, where they scored moderate hits like "Little Latin Lupe Lu" (#49) and "My Babe" (#75) in 1963. Their reputation continued to grow in 1964 when they opened for both the Beatles and the Rolling Stones in some of their first U.S. shows and then played on the first episode of the new music television show *Shindig!* Their paths crossed with Phil Spector at a show at the Cow Palace in San Francisco in October of 1964. The Righteous Brothers were on the bill along with Spector's group, the Ronettes. Spector loved their sound and approached Moonglow about allowing them to record and release some songs on his Philles label. Moonglow gave their permission.

Phil Spector was born in 1940 in the Bronx, New York. His father committed suicide when he was just 9 years old and a few years later his mother moved them to Los Angeles. He was a musical prodigy from an early age, learning to play guitar and performing in talent shows as a kid. As a teenager he was a member of a band called the Teddy Bears. He wrote, recorded and released a song for the band called "To Know Him Is To Love Him," taking the title from the inscription on his father's tombstone. The song got all the way to #1 in 1958, the first year of *Billboard's* Hot 100 chart. The band's success was short-lived though and by 1959 they'd broken up. Spector moved back to New York City then and threw himself into studio work, learning everything he could about producing records. Alongside his mentor Jerry Leiber, he co-wrote and co-produced "Spanish Harlem" for Ben E. King, a Top 10 hit in 1960. The following year he started his own label, Philles Records, and scored his first #1 hit in 1963 with "He's a Rebel" by the Crystals. He had great success during this time spearheading the "girl group" sound producing the Ronettes and Darlene Love. When he met the Righteous Brothers in 1964 he'd only ever signed black artists to his label but he loved their "blue-eyed soul" sound and was eager to work with them and take them to the next level of success.

Spector flew the husband and wife songwriting team of Barry Mann and Cynthia Weil from New York to Los Angeles to write something for his new singers. Mann had written a song a few years earlier called "I Love How You Love Me" which Phil Spector had produced for the Paris Sisters. That song opens with the line "I love how your eyes close whenever you kiss me." Mann and Weil decided to flip that line around, and write a song about a relationship ending, and the singer lamenting that his partner no longer closes their eyes. The opening line thus became "You never close your eyes any more when I kiss your lips," and the song took shape from there. They recorded a demo using their vocals which are in a much higher range than Medley and Hatfield's. When the duo heard it they said it sounded like it would make a great song, for the Everly Brothers. But Spector loved it and convinced them they could lower it to their range. They then got to work on the song and spent an incredible eight hours laboring over the vocals. Neither Medley nor Hatfield had ever spent that much time on one song. They were used to banging out their vocal track in about a half hour, but they respected Spector's meticulousness in the studio and believed in his ability. Hatfield however did become annoyed when Spector told him that Medley would sing the entire first verse and that he, Hatfield, wouldn't come in till the chorus. When Hatfield asked Spector what he was supposed to do while Medley was singing solo, Spector replied: "You can go directly to the bank."

In Spector's previous productions he had begun to use a dense aural technique, layering and echoing instrumentation to create a wall of sound. "I was looking for a sound so strong," Spector would explain: "If the material was not the greatest, the sound would carry the record." Despite the strength of Mann and Well's lyrics and the passion of Medley and Hatfield's singing, Spector still employed his wall of sound philosophy producing "You've Lost That Lovin'

Feelin.'" The song was so deep and slow and dense that when he first played it for the song's writers, they thought he had it at the wrong speed.

When the song was done Spector realized he had one big problem. The song clocked in at three minutes and forty-five seconds. Almost four minutes. meaning a full minute longer than pop radio desired. He refused to trim the song so he did the next best thing. He lied. He had the time printed on the label as 3:05. It took a while, and a bunch of confused station programmers who kept wondering why their playlists were running long, before everyone caught on. By that point the song was a hit and stations just continued to play the song in its entirety. Billy Joel, who was a huge Righteous Brothers fan and would induct them into the Rock and Roll Hall of Fame in 2003, referenced this in his song "The Entertainer" with the lyric, "If you're gonna have a hit you gotta make it fit, so they cut it down to 3:05."

Andrew Oldham, who was then the manager of the Rolling Stones and a friend of Spector, got to hear the song before it was released. In his autobiography Oldham described the experience: "The room was filled with this amazing sound, I had no idea what it was, but it was the most incredible thing I'd ever heard. I'd never heard a recorded track so emotionally giving or empowering." It was Oldham who coined the term "wall of sound" which Spector would later trademark.

"You've Lost That Lovin' Feelin'" was released in November of 1964 and it climbed to #1 on this date in 1965, becoming, at the time, the longest song to hit the top spot. There have been numerous cover versions through the years but there is really only one true version of the song, the one that matches Spector's amazing and innovative production with Medley and Hatfield's righteous vocals. Take three minutes today, okay, three minutes and forty-five seconds, and crank up the song and appreciate it for what it is: a heartbreaking lyric of a lost love, one of the best examples of Phil Spector's production style and two vocalists at the very top of their game.

### February 7th

On this date in 1981, Kool & the Gang's "Celebration" knocked "The Tide Is High" by Blondie from the top of the pop chart. The song would enjoy a two week stay before giving way to "9 to 5" by Dolly Parton. Though it's the bane of most Mobile DJs' existence because for years it was almost required playing at any party, the song still enjoys a strong shelf life as one of those happy and upbeat tracks that just makes people want to, well, celebrate. It's a call for everyone around the world to come together and celebrate good times which is surely something we all could use right now.

Kool & the Gang came together in the late sixties when five high school friends in Jersey City, New Jersey formed an instrumental band called the Jazziacs.

They changed their name to Kool & the Flames in 1967, then Kool & the Gang a few years later to avoid confusion with James Brown's Famous Flames. In 1969 they signed a contract with a brand new record label called De-Lite Records and released their self-titled debut that same year. The album produced two mild hits and sold well enough to earn the band a follow-up. Their early stuff was very funky, with successful songs like "Jungle Boogie" (which peaked at #4 in 1973), and "Hollywood Swinging" (#6 in 1974) becoming indicative of their sound: all around 110 beats per minutes and driven by a heavy funk sound, thunderous bass and vibrant horns.

In 1978, former school teacher James "J.T." Taylor joined the band and they began working with a new producer, Eumir Deodato, who would encourage them to take a more mainstream approach to their sound. The first album that Deodato produced for Kool & the Gang was 1980's *Ladies Night*. That LP instantly became their most successful to date, peaking at #13 on the album chart, and producing two Top 10 hits: the title track which went to #8 and "Too Hot" which peaked at #5.

When the band convened to work on their next album they wanted to continue to pursue the smoother, more pop sensible sound of "Ladies Night." The extended version of that song had included the line "come on let's all celebrate" and the band used that line to start working on a new song. According to saxophonist Ronald Bell, who had converted from Christianity to Islam, he wrote the basic chords and the line, "everyone around the world, come on, let's celebrate" after reading the creation story in the Quran about how the angels celebrated. When the song was completed, Taylor played it for his mother and she predicted its success, telling her son to get ready, "you're going to be singing that song for the rest of your life."

Kool & the Gang released their twelfth studio album, *Celebrate,* in September of 1980. The lead single was "Celebration" and both the album and the song began assaulting the charts. *Celebrate* would peak at #10 a month after its release but "Celebration" just kept climbing. The week of January 17th, 1981 the song had climbed to #14. Then, three days later, on the day Ronald Reagan was sworn into office as the 40th U.S. President, the Iranian hostage crisis came to an end. The hostages were welcomed home with Kool & the Gang's "Celebration" playing as they deplaned. The extra exposure of the song and the euphoria America was feeling at the moment, helped propel "Celebration" to #1 on this date in 1981.

"Celebration" is certainly a song that suffers from overexposure. The common lexicon calls it "played out." It's a song that is so perfect for parties, with a danceable beat, lyrics about celebrating and those easy to sing along "yahoo's," that it got played at almost every wedding and private party for years and years. And for some (especially DJs who spin at weddings every weekend), that overexposure means they'd rather hear nails on a chalkboard than "Celebration" one more time. And that's fair. But what can't be argued is Kool & the Gang produced one of the first, great, post-disco dance songs. The lyrics aren't deep (despite Bell's inspiration there are no religious undertones) and the music is just straightforward R&B laced pop. But the song is timeless and its message universal. Bring your good times. And your laughter too. C'mon, let's celebrate. It's all right!

## February 8th

On this date in 1986, in the first chart week following Super Bowl XX, "The Super Bowl Shuffle" by a group calling itself the Chicago Bears Shufflin' Crew, peaked on the *Billboard* Hot 100 chart at #41. The Chicago Bears had not only completed one of the most dominant seasons in NFL history but they became the first, and so far only sports team to record a "hit" song.

The Chicago Bears had won their division in 1984 and gotten all the way to the NFC Championship Game where they lost to the San Francisco 49ers, the eventual Super Bowl champions. That season the 49ers released a song called "We Are the 49ers" that included profound lyrics like "We don't take no stuff, everyone knows we're too tough" but made no mention of the Super Bowl. Outside of the Bay Area, the song went largely, and rightfully, ignored. In the offseason the Bears made some key moves to improve an already dominant roster, including drafting mammoth defensive lineman William "The Refrigerator" Perry.

As the 1985 campaign got underway it was clear this could be a special season for the Chicago Bears. The team hadn't been to a Super Bowl yet in their history and hadn't won an NFL Championship since 1963, but this collection of talent was not only great on the field, they were a lot of fun off the field as well. They were loud and brash and funny with characters like their outspoken quarterback Jim McMahon and the rookie Perry who was already doing commercials and developing a name for himself as the lovable big guy. The Bears won their first few games in dominant fashion, and their defense, which was led by coordinator Buddy Ryan, was proving to be unstoppable. In week six, when they went to San Francisco and beat the defending champions 26-10, the hype around the team reached a fever pitch and most of the players soaked it in. Instead of deflecting the attention and being humble, this was a group of men who knew how good they were and had no problem telling you, because on Sunday, they were going to back up their words. Which is why, at midseason, when the idea was floated to make a rap song promoting their possible upcoming appearance in the Super Bowl, so many of them signed on.

It was wide receiver Willie Gault who started recruiting his teammates to the concept. Gault already aspired to a career in acting after his playing days were over. He'd landed a Hollywood agent who got him his first on-camera action, appearing as one of the dancing firemen in the music video for Linda Clifford's "The Heat in Me." That song was produced by Red Label Records which is how Gault met Red Label owner Dick Meyers. Meyers had an old demo laying around called "The Kingfish Shuffle" and he had some songwriters tweak it to become "The Super Bowl Shuffle." Gault said he'd get as many teammates as he could to take part. Veteran running back Walter Payton signed on quickly. He was not as outspoken as some of his younger teammates but he loved music and even played the piano and didn't want to miss the chance to be on the song. Perry was also quick to agree to take part, as he was looking for any opportunity to further his brand. Some of the other defensive players also hopped on. Free Safety Gary Fencik was courted hard because, as Gault said, "He's like the white guy in the group that's really cool, and he's been around for a while and he's a really good-looking guy." It took some persuasion but Fencik finally agreed. But Gault was unsuccessful getting all the high profile players. Defensive end Dan Hampton (he of the awesome nickname "Danimal") refused, saying, "I thought it was presumptuous to say, 'Oh yeah, we're going to the Super Bowl' when the franchise had never been in one." As each player signed on, Gault would notify Meyers and he would put together a rap for them.

After week eight, a 27-9 shellacking of the Vikings, those participating went to Meyers' basement studio to record their individual raps. Cornerback Mike Richardson showed up just to check out the recording process but Meyers convinced him to get involved. The record executive asked him a few questions. When Richardson told him he was from Los Angeles Meyers wrote a rap that included the line, "L.A. Mike" which became Richardson's permanent nickname. Richardson marveled at Meyers' ability to write him in, saying, "I thought the guy was a phenomenal writer for him to just write me in the way he did, and some of the other guys, the way he tailor-made their parts, it was magical." The Bears continued winning and work progressed on the song. On November 17th, 1985, the day the Bears beat the Cowboys 44-0, the song was finished. The Bears were 11 and 0 at this point. They weren't just beating opponents, they were mauling them, and the sports world was marveling at their dominance. And then, the song was unveiled.

Neither head coach Mike Ditka, nor anyone in the Bears' front office had any idea about the project till they heard it on the radio. Ditka was an old school player, more workman-like than most of his charges, but he brushed it off, saying later: "We had a fun group of guys, and I never discouraged them from having fun. . . Did I think it was inappropriate? No. If you don't think you're going to win, then you're not going to win, that's why I thought it was pretty much a symbol of the fact that they thought they were going to win." The Bears PR man Ken Valdiserri hated the presumptive nature of singing about going to the Super Bowl long before they were there ("it could make us look foolish" was his quote) but he decided to just go along with it rather than creating internal strife over a silly song. In the game after the song was released the Bears shut out the Lions 36-0 so if there was a jinx attached to the song, it didn't strike immediately.

A video shoot was set up for the following Tuesday. The Bears were traveling to Miami to play the Dolphins in a Monday night match-up so that Tuesday would be an off-day for the club. But that night the Bears suffered their first loss of the season and on the flight home, a few of the players talked about not making the shoot. To complicate things, the Bears had worn their dark, home jerseys in Miami, (the NFL allows the home team to decide whether they want to wear light or dark uniforms and since Miami had chosen their home whites the Bears had to counter with their black jerseys) so the equipment crew had to get the uniforms laundered overnight for anyone who wanted to participate in the shoot. But the next day, a fair amount of the team showed up, enough to record most of the video and though the mood was somber, things worked out. Players who didn't have individual rap parts were either placed in the chorus, or given musical instruments and told to feign playing them. Jim McMahon and Walter Payton didn't make it to the video shoot so their portions were shot later in the week using an early version of green screen technology.

The video was completed in time for Christmas and the VHS tape became a big seller in Illinois.

The team won their final three games to finish 15 and 1. Expectations were high as the team began its playoff run, especially with the song getting plenty of radio play and the video in steady rotation on MTV, but if their opponents had any extra motivation to knock off the Bears it didn't show. The Bears shut out the Giants 21-0 in the first round of the playoffs then beat the Rams 24-0 to earn the franchise's first ever trip to the Super Bowl.

Super Bowl XX was held in New Orleans. There wasn't a bar on Bourbon Street that week that wasn't cranking "The Super Bowl Shuffle" almost nonstop. The team that at mid-season had put out the song was now in the big game and they put their money where their mouth was by demolishing the New England Patriots 46-10 on January 26th 1986. The song would peak in the first chart week following the game just outside of the Top 40.

"The Super Bowl Shuffle" was nominated for the Best R&B Vocal Performance Grammy. A few of the players attended the award show that night but they ultimately lost to Prince's "Kiss." Willie Gault would say later, "It's hard to fight a little guy with heels on."

When the team had been approached to participate they were promised that a "substantial portion" of the proceeds for the record would be donated to Chicago charities. Walter Payton even mentions it in his rap section ("We're not doing this because we're greedy. The Bears are doing it to feed the needy.") But Red Label initially donated just 15% of the proceeds to local charities and soon the media made an issue out of that. Since the players barely made any money from it, the question became, where was all the money going? Eventually Red Label wound up donating close to $300,000 but many involved felt that was nowhere near enough. In 2014 some of the players involved sued to make sure proceeds had gone where they were supposed to.

The success of "The Super Bowl Shuffle" opened the floodgates and pretty soon teams from every sport, whether they had champion-caliber rosters or not, were lining up to record a song. A quick search of Youtube will uncover embarrassments like Seattle Seahawks' "Locker Room Rock," the San Francisco 49ers' "Team of the '80s," the Oakland Raiders' "Silver and Black Attack" and the Los Angeles Rams' "Ram It." Yet there will only ever be one "Super Bowl Shuffle." It took a team of superior talent and a roster of outgoing personalities to put it together and capture a magical moment.

## February 9th

On this date in 1974, the Love Unlimited Orchestra's "Love's Theme" knocked Barbra Streisand's "The Way We Were" from the #1 spot on *Billboard*'s Hot 100 chart. It would stay at the top for just one week before "The Way We Were" reclaimed that spot but it was still a surprising triumph for a song that had been given up on by its label and broken in a very new and unique way.

Barry White grew up South Central Los Angeles in the fifties. As a teenager, he spent seven months in juvenile detention for theft. During this period, he heard Elvis Presley's "It's Now or Never" and he felt the song was a message, telling him to turn his life around. Now. According to White, that moment single-handedly changed his life. When he was free, he dedicated himself to making it in the music industry.

White had already developed the rich, deep baritone voice that would become his trademark and he began singing in a band, as well as writing and producing for other artists. He discovered a girl group named Love Unlimited and in 1972 he wrote and produced their debut LP, *From a Girl's Point of View We Give to You... Love Unlimited.* The album sold a million units and produced the classic soul ballad "Walkin' in the Rain with the One I Love", which made it to #14 on the pop chart. He next decided to work with a male singer and he put a few demos together of songs he'd written in an effort to entice someone to sing with him. When others heard his distinctive voice on the demos they convinced him he should release the songs himself. He released his debut solo album in early 1973, titled *I've Got So Much to Give,* which included the #3 hit song, "I'm Gonna Love You Just a Little More Baby." He followed that LP quickly with his second album, *Stone Gon'* which contained the #7 hit song, "Never, Never Gonna Give Ya Up." Around this time White also put together the Love Unlimited Orchestra, a 40-piece orchestra that he intended to use as the backing band for his own work as well as another Love Unlimited LP.

One of the first projects he worked on with his new orchestra was something he was calling "Love's Theme." He composed the melody then composer Gene Page arranged the strings. White's intention was to write lyrics for the song and offer it to his girl group, but when he heard the final instrumental track he decided it didn't need anything else and that lyrics would only detract from the melody and groove of the song. He released the lush and beautiful song as an instrumental under the band name the Love Unlimited Orchestra. The song was released in November of 1973 and initially it failed to make an impact. This was still a few years before dance music had emerged from the nightclub scene and no radio stations were playing anything like this. It was a brand new sound. R&B was usually grittier and not filled with lush violins and pop music didn't have this infectious of a dance beat. So the song was ignored and seemed destined for obscurity.

Till it started getting spins in the night clubs of New York City.

20th Century promotions man Billy Smith was one of the few people at his label (which distributed Barry White) who heard the hit potential in "Love's Theme." And he suspected there was a way to bypass radio and get the song heard. He knew the club scene in and around New York City was exploding so he got the song to some of the most popular DJs on the circuit. Guys like Nick Siano, Bobby Guttadaro (better known as Bobby DJ) and David Rodriguez started spinning the instrumental track and the song started selling. It wasn't till then that radio picked up on it. Siano recalls being in the back of a cab listening to WBLS when the DJ said he was premiering a new song called "Love's Theme" and Siano screamed at the radio. Premier!? He had been playing it in his night clubs sets for weeks.

"Love's Theme" began getting radio play and selling and it would hit #1 on this date in 1974. In recognition of his help in breaking the song. Bobby Guttardaro was presented with a gold record, becoming the first primarily club DJ to receive such an honor.

After the song became a hit White decided to add lyrics and allow his girl group Love Unlimited to release the song as well. Who did he hire to write the lyrics? Aaron Schroeder, the man who'd written the lyrics to "It's Now or Never" the song that had helped White see that his life was at a turning point and it was up to him to set things straight. The version with lyrics was included on Love Unlimited's 1974 LP *In Heat*.

Disco was still in its nascent phase and "Love's Theme" is credited for adding a rich and lush element to the funk and R&B stew that would eventually develop into the sound that became known as disco. "Love's Theme" wasn't the first disco song but it was among the first to crawl from the clubs and achieve chart dominance. In April of 1974, "TSOP (The Sound of Philadelphia)" by MFSB featuring the Three Degrees would climb to #1 as well and that song is also recognized as being an early and influential disco track. Then in the summer of 1974 the charts would be "rocked" with back to back #1 disco songs, the Hues Corporation's "Rock the Boat" and "Rock Your Baby" by George McCrae. All of these songs benefited from frequent club play before radio stations began spinning them and pretty soon the labels were understanding the promotional value of club DJ spins. 1975 thus saw the creation of the first "Music Pool" in which labels would give free, promotional records to club DJs in exchange for their feedback (and hopefully peak hour spins). So much of this can be traced back to "Love's Theme," a melody so beautiful it didn't need words, and a track so powerful it helped change the way dance music would be promoted for decades to come.

On this date in 1979, Earth, Wind & Fire's infectiously happy sing-along song "September" peaked at #8 on the *Billboard* Hot 100 chart. EWF had higher charting songs, including their lone #1, "Shining Star," but no one would argue that "September" isn't a signature song for the funk band from Chicago as they took a brief foray into the world of disco.

Maurice White began his career in music as a session drummer for the R&B label Chess Records. That's him drumming on Fontella Bass's "Rescue Me" and Billy Stewart's "Summertime." He also played for legends like Muddy Waters and Etta James. White then put together a band called the Salty Peppers and scored a moderate hit with 1969's "La La La." When their follow-up single, "Uh Huh Yeah" failed to chart White moved to Los Angeles where he put together a new band. White's astrological sign is Sagittarius which has a primary elemental quality of Fire and seasonal qualities of Earth and Air and so White named this new outfit Earth, Wind & Fire as an homage to his zodiac sign.

Earth, Wind & Fire released their eponymous debut in 1971 and Lester Bangs, the renowned Rolling Stones critic, noted its similarities to Sly and the Family Stone. He also criticized the lyrics for being "a bit too preachy." The band underwent some lineup changes in the first half of the seventies but Maurice White was the consistent leader and visionary. If his lyrics were a bit preachy it's because he believed in viewing the world through rose colored glasses and he had no problem sharing his views through his music. He has said: "Lyrically, you need to talk about what you know to be true. I have always attempted to share my studies and philosophy in my lyrics."

The band built their reputation slowly. This was back in a time when record labels allowed artists to produce music and find their audience in due time. Overnight successes were a nice treat for the industry but never expected. Columbia Records, which signed EWF after their first two albums, hung in there with the band and their patience was eventually rewarded. Their first Columbia release, 1972's *Last Days and Time* peaked at #87 on the album chart. In 1973 *Head to Sky* made it to #27. A year later *Open Our Eyes* got to #15. And then in 1975, the band broke through to the big time, releasing *That's the Way of the World* which went to #1 on the album chart and included the aforementioned chart-topper "Shining Star." Other hits followed, "Sing a Song" and "Getaway" and "Serpentine Fire." The band had softened their hard funk sound through the years and with the popularity of disco, added a faster tempo to some of their offerings.

By 1978 Columbia wanted to put a greatest hits compilation together and since adding a few new songs to a package like this is a great way to get a band's ardent fans to buy it, the band set out to write and record a new song for the optimistically titled *The Best of Earth, Wind & Fire, Vol. 1*. They decided to try and bring in a lyricist to help with the song and that's how the eccentric artist Allee Willis got involved.

Willis received a phone call one day from Maurice White asking if she'd be interested in writing some material with the band. She showed up the next day in the studio and as she walked in she heard them playing an infectious opening riff. She said to herself, "Dear God, let this be what they want me to write for." It turns out it was. Guitarist Al McKay had come up with the melody and White and Willis had written a few lyrics, conjuring happy images like soul singing and stars stealing the night away. White says he'd written the opening line, "Do you remember, the 21st of September" in a Washington, D.C. hotel room while there were riots going on in the streets. It wasn't September 21st and he has no idea where that particular date came from. Willis would say later, "I do remember us experimenting with other dates, but 21st just sang phonetically fantastic."

Willis questioned the "ba dee ya" chant going into the chorus. She initially saw this is as a lyrical placeholder but when she pressed White about coming up with actual words for it, he told her "no." He'd never been shy about leaving nonsensical sounds in the middle of his songs in lieu of actual lyrics (his first hit was "La La La" after all) and he felt "ba dee ya" expressed his feelings perfectly. Willis explains: "When it was obvious that he was not going to do it, I just said, 'What the fuck does 'ba-dee-ya' mean?' And he essentially said, 'Who fucking cares?'" She ends the story by adding, "I learned my greatest lesson ever in songwriting from him, which was never let the lyric get in the way of the groove."

And what a groove it is. No one who has ever heard "September" can easily get it out of their head. It's infectious and it just begs to be sung along to. The song was released in November of 1978, disco's biggest year, and it joined the millions of dance songs fighting for radio space. "September" eventually peaked at #8 on this date in 1979 but it has never left the playlist of millions of DJs who spin it consistently at weddings and private parties. Some people sing "party on" during the "be dee ya" part, others belt out White's original, nonsensical lyrics, but no matter what they sing, it's at the top of their lungs. And they feel good. And when a song can do that, it's a pretty triumphant thing.

On this date in 1963, the Beatles spent an entire day at Abbey Road studios, recording the bulk of their first album, *Please Please Me*. The band that would become famous just a few years later for being studio rats, taking hours to get a single note right and spending days on end experimenting with different sounds and new techniques, the band that once asked their producer if he could plug a microphone directly into one of their vocal cords just to see what kind of sound it would produce, that band, finished ten songs in one day.

The Beatles signed with EMI's Parlophone Records in 1962 and on October 5th they released their debut single in the U.K., the Lennon-McCartney penned "Love Me Do." The B-side of the single was another Lennon-McCartney original, "P.S. I Love You." The single performed well, peaking at #17 which was high enough that Parlophone asked for another song. That next single, "Please Please Me" (backed with "Ask Me Why") was released on January 11th, 1963 (again, in the U.K. only). "Please Please Me" shot up the U.K. charts, helped by the Beatles' appearance on the British television show *Thank Your Lucky Stars*. Suddenly, Parlophone felt they had a hot commodity on their hands and they wanted to release a full album before things cooled off. At the time most British albums contained fourteen songs so the band needed to record ten more to add to the four they had already released (two A sides and two B sides). George Martin, who had produced the band to that point at Abbey Road Studios, booked them for this date in 1963. Typically, Abbey Road Studios scheduled three daily recording sessions: 10am - 1pm, 2:30-5:30pm and 7:00-10:00pm. Martin reserved all three for the Beatles that day.

The boys rolled in like true professionals, and got started straight away. John Lennon was already complaining of a sore throat but he didn't seem too bothered by it early on. The first session was not overly productive. No doubt, the four young musicians weren't even used to being awake at that hour, not to mention expecting to perform. They did nine frustrating takes of "There's a Place" before finally getting the tenth one down. When the band said they'd move on to "Seventeen" next, Martin can be heard on the studio tapes mumbling, "I think it ought to have a different title." The band apparently agreed and the song would later be renamed "Saw Her Standing There." They took nine attempts at this one, with many of them interrupted halfway through by Paul McCartney who kept complaining that Ringo Starr was playing the song "too fast." Eventually it was deemed their first recording of the song was their best but Martin loved McCartney's count in on the last one (his now famous "one, two, three, FAW"), which was clearly the result of his frustration, so that count in was spliced in front of the first take.

And then it was time for lunch.

The studio techs headed out to a local pub for a pie and a pint but the band stayed behind to rehearse for the afternoon sessions. Richard Langham, the tape operator for that day's sessions, would say later: "when we came back they'd been playing right through. We couldn't believe it. We had never seen a group work right through their lunch break before."

The afternoon session was more fruitful. The band completed "A Taste of Honey" and "Do You Want To Know a Secret." Then it was time for Lennon to sing, as he and McCartney split the vocal duties on "Misery." He handled it all right and then the afternoon session was over and the band took their first break of the day.

The evening session began with thirteen fruitless takes of "Hold Me Tight." Finally the band shelved the song and moved on (they'd finally complete it for their second LP *With the Beatles*). By now they were watching the clock and cognizant that they still had to bang out five songs. They started to work on some of the covers they typically played live. Lennon, his sore throat getting more and more aggravated, took three tries to sing lead on "Anna (Go To Him)." Then, with Ringo Starr drumming and singing simultaneously, they nailed "Boys" in one take. George Harrison sang "Chains" which they recorded four times before deciding the first one had been their best. Then Lennon took the lead vocal for the Shirelles' "Baby It's You." They completed the song in three takes with Lennon's voice showing clear signs of deteriorating.

It was 10pm. The band had finished nine songs in three, three hour sessions. They seemed satisfied and the studio crew began cleaning up. Langham would say later: "Sessions never normally over-ran past 10pm. At 10:05 you'd meet half the musicians on the platform of St John's Wood station, going home." But then the band started asking if they could do one more. When a studio employee complained about staying late, Brian Epstein, the Beatles' manager told him he'd drive him home. Martin asked the band if they wanted to lay down "Twist and Shout." It was a favorite of the band's and usually their show closer and they had envisioned it as the final song of their album. But Lennon sang the lead and the song called for him to really belt it out. The others looked over at John Lennon with hopeful eyes. He reached for some Zubes (lozenges), gargled some milk and then, for some reason, stripped off his shirt. The band launched into a song they'd played hundreds of times before. From Liverpool to Hamburg to London, they'd rocked "Twist and Shout" at the end of so many shows, tired, sweaty and fatigued. Lennon, on his last vocal cords, screeched his heart out. He told *Rolling Stone* years later: "I couldn't sing the damn thing – I was just screaming." McCartney concurred, but also added, "It was a pretty cool performance." Indeed it was. Lennon's raspy delivery fit the song perfectly. There was a grittiness to it that set it apart from anything else on their debut. The band began to play the song again, figuring a second take might be even better, but when Lennon opened his mouth nothing came out. He'd given his all and it would take weeks for him to get his voice back to normal. Looking back years later, Lennon would say: "The last song nearly killed me. My voice wasn't the same for a long time after; every time I swallowed it was like sandpaper. I was always bitterly ashamed of it, because I could sing it better than that; but now it doesn't bother me. You can hear that I'm just a frantic guy doing his best."

The whole band had done their best. They were young and the future was wide open and, unlike the meticulous notes taken in the studio that day (which is how we know how many takes it took to complete each song), no one made note of what the band did after they left Abbey Road that night. One can only imagine that the four boys headed out for a pint and probably joked about how Lennon sounded like an old man now or made Ringo pick up the tab because he was so new to the band. The Beatles would go on to become the most famous rock stars ever, probably four of the most famous people in the whole world, but on this night in 1963 they were just four young musicians, spent after a long day in the studio and hoping their hard work would pay off.

## February 12th

On this date in 1981, Rush released their eighth studio album, *Moving Pictures*. The prog rock power trio from north of the border continued their recent trend of moving ever so slightly towards a more commercially accessible sound and it worked like a charm. *Moving Pictures* went on to become the band's highest selling LP in the U.S. and produced some of their most recognizable songs. They didn't leave their ardent fan base in the dust, but they did bring a whole new group of admirers under their tent.

Rush came together in Toronto in the late sixties. After some early line-up changes the trio of guitarist Alex Lifeson, singer and bassist Geddy Lee and drummer John Rutsey was set and they began to hit the bar and high school dance circuit. They independently released their first single in 1973, a cover of Buddy Holly's "Not Fade Away." When they couldn't find a label to sign them, they decided to take things into their own hands and form their own record label, Moon Records. They released their debut, self-titled album in 1974. Rush underwent one last lineup change after this, when Rutsey left due to health issues and was replaced by Neil Peart. Peart's first appearance with the band was on August 14th, 1974 when Rush opened for Uriah Heep. There were 11,000 people in attendance. Peart, besides being one of the most interesting drummers in rock and roll history, known for using some of the most varied and complex time signatures, is also an excellent lyricist and he took over songwriting duties for the band right away, allowing Lifeson and Lee to focus on the instrumental aspect of Rush. Beginning with their second LP, *Fly By Night*, the band moved away from the straight rock sound of their debut (which many compared to Led Zeppelin) towards the more complex sounds of what was becoming known as progressive rock (or prog rock for short). *Fly By Night* included the band's first song that was also an epic mini-tale "By-Tor and the Snow Dog", with complex arrangements and mythological imagery. The band had found the sound they would settle into for the next few years and it was very much the quintessential prog rock formula of long and winding songs with intricate instrumentation and lyrics that strayed into the fantasy or sci-fi realm.

Their fourth album, *2112*, featured the title track that was 20 minutes long. And in concert, they'd really open it up.

Rush developed a passionate fan base and to call them all geeked out intellectuals who spent their afternoons playing Dungeons and Dragons would be a generalization. Surely some of them played D&D at night.

As the seventies came to an end, Rush made a conscious effort to move slightly closer to the mainstream. Their first album of the eighties, *Permanent Waves*, didn't have one song over 10 minutes long, and included some songs like "The Spirit of Radio" and "Freewill" that were actually rock radio friendly. And as radio play increased, so too did sales figures. For the first time the band had a legitimate hit album (*Permanent Waves* peaked at #4 in March of 1980) and when they went to work on their next LP, they clearly wanted more.

The band got together in late 1980 to record material for what would become *Moving Pictures*. The second song they worked on was a poem that Pye Dubois of the band Max Webster had written called "Louis the Lawyer." Peart, who was always using classic literature as inspiration for his lyrics, changed the title character to Tom Sawyer and then Lee and Lifeson helped him put the poem to music, using an incredible growling effect from Lee's synthesizer, intricate drum patterns from Peart and a soaring guitar solo from Lifeson. "Tom Sawyer" is a signature song for Rush and a concert highlight. It, like most of *Moving Pictures*, is a song made for rock radio and made to be cranked up. *Moving Pictures* also includes their song about the pitfalls of celebrity, "Limelight" and "Red Barchetta" which has also become an AOR (album oriented rock) favorite. But Rush, who hadn't left their prog rock roots completely, included an instrumental track called "YYZ" (the code for Rush's hometown airport, Toronto International) figuring, what the heck, one last eleven minute song for old times' sake.

In typical Rush sense of humor, the cover art for *Moving Pictures* contains a visual pun. The photo on the front shows workers carrying paintings. They are, of course, moving pictures. And the people who are watching the workers are crying. They are, of course, emotionally "moved" by the pictures. But wait, there's more. The back cover reveals that the front cover is part of a film shoot, one more "moving picture" reference.

The Rock and Roll Hall of Fame has long been criticized for neglecting the prog rock genre. For some reason it doesn't reach their standards of rock and roll (while somehow Donna Summer does). Rush's ardent fan base campaigned hard for their band's induction and finally, in 2013, 15 years after they'd been eligible, the band got in. During his induction speech the Foo Fighters' David Grohl, asked the intriguing question, "When the fuck did Rush become cool?" Indeed, they've long been recognized for their prodigious musicianship, complex compositions and science fiction infused themes. But it took their move to the mainstream, perfected with *Moving Pictures* which was released on this date in 1981, to show the larger rock and roll world just how cool they are.

On this date in 1996, 2Pac released his double LP *All Eyez On Me*. It would be the last LP during his short yet brilliant career and many consider it not only his masterwork but the high-water mark for nineties hip hop.

Lesane Parish Crooks was born in June of 1971 in the East Harlem section of New York City. He was born into a family of activists, with both parents members of the Black Panthers, and other family members involved in the Black Liberation Army and when he was just one he was renamed after the 18th century Incan emperor Túpac Amaru II (who was executed after leading an indigenous uprising against Spanish rule). Growing up, however, Tupac demonstrated more interest in entertainment than agitation. At twelve, Shakur enrolled in Harlem's 127th Street Repertory Ensemble and was cast as the Travis Younger character in the play *A Raisin in the Sun*, which was performed at the Apollo Theater. When his family moved to Baltimore he attended the Baltimore School for the Arts, where he studied acting, poetry, jazz, and ballet. He also began demonstrating his rapping skills about this time, and those who went to high school with him remember him as a talented and driven young man. One of those students was Jada Pinkett (later Jada Pinkett Smith) with whom he developed a lifelong friendship.

Shakur's family then relocated to Marin County, California where, in 1990, Shakur broke into the music business as a roadie and backup dancer with the hip hop group Digital Underground. The band immediately recognized his skills and had him contribute to the track "Same Song" which appeared in the film *Nothing But Trouble* and on the soundtrack for the movie. Shakur's roadie-ing days were over.

By the end of 1991 he released his first LP, *2Pacalypse Now* in which Shakur confronts issues such as racism, police brutality, poverty, black on black crime, and teenage pregnancy. His debut showed the hip hop world there was a new and innovative voice on the scene and there were no issues too controversial for him to rap about. Two years later Shakur released his second studio album, *Strictly 4 My N.I.G.G.A.Z...* in which he continued emphasizing his political and social views.

Shakur's life was not without controversy. He rapped about, and even celebrated, the "thug life" and he lived it as well. In 1992 a gun he owned was involved in the accidental shooting of a six year old boy. Though no charges were filed the accepted story by most is that Shakur was involved in a confrontation in which he drew his legally registered Colt Mustang but then dropped it. When a member of his entourage picked up the weapon it accidentally discharged and the young boy, Qa'id Walker-Teal, was hit in the head and killed. The boy's family sued Shakur for wrongful death; the case was settled with Shakur paying a reported half a million dollars. The following year he pleaded guilty to a misdemeanor charge of assault when he struck a fellow rapper with a baseball bat. He served ten days in prison for that offense. Then in November of 1993 Shakur and some in his entourage were charged with sexually assaulting a woman in a hotel room. Shakur was convicted of first-degree sexual abuse and sentenced to 1½–4½ years in prison. After serving nine months his case went to appeal but Shakur couldn't afford the $1.4 million bail which would get him out of jail. Suge Knight, the CEO of Death Row Records, posted the bail in exchange for Shakur releasing three albums under the Death Row label.

The first two of those three albums became the double LP *All Eyez on Me* which was released on this date in 1996. With all the controversy surrounding him, Shakur was determined to deliver an epic album. And he did. Instead of lamenting the gangster life that had cost him his freedom, he celebrates it over most of the 27 tracks that make up *All Eyez On Me*. There are amazing guest appearances from Snoop Dog, Nate Dogg and most notably Dr Dre on the #1 hit "California Love." The album sold over half a million copies in its first week and has moved over five million units since its release.

On September 7th, 1996, Shakur was in Las Vegas for the Bruce Seldon-Mike Tyson fight. He was gunned down in the famously unsolved drive-by shooting. He was just 25 years old. In many of Shakur's songs, he celebrated gangster life but also predicted it would bring him to an early end. In one of his songs he asked "How long will they mourn me?" and in another he rapped "Death is for a son to stay free. I'm thugged out." And in two of his songs, "I Wonder If Heaven Got A Ghetto" and "Changes" he rapped "I wake up in the morning and I ask myself is life worth living should I blast myself?"

Shakur was hard at work before his death and he left multiple albums worth of material, most of which has been released posthumously. Still, music lovers will always be left to wonder how his art would have evolved with maturity and what social observations he would have made over the decades since his murder. Like any artist who dies before their time, we mourn the loss as well as their future contributions that we'll never benefit from. 2Pac Shakur will always be remembered as a poet of the street, an unapologetic thug, and a hip hop icon gone long before his time.


### February 14th

On this date in 1976, Heart released their debut album *Dreamboat Annie* in the United States which contained the Top 10 single "Magic Man." The band that had fled north of the border were, almost overnight, huge names in the States and would become favorites on rock radio for decades to come.

The earliest lineup of Heart (called White Heart for a while) came together just outside Seattle, Washington in the early seventies. One of the early members, Roger Fisher, had a brother named Mike who had fled to Canada to avoid being drafted and serving in the Vietnam War. One day he slipped back over the border to see his little brother play and instantly fell in love with Roger's bandmate Ann Wilson. The feeling was mutual and Ann decided she would follow Mike back across the border. The rest of the band already knew how integral Ann was to their chemistry (and thus, chances of success), so they followed her north. After a while, Ann's sister Nancy did too. Nancy would then become involved with Roger at which point she joined the band.

Ann and Nancy Wilson became the focus of Heart. They were the lead singers, the main lyricists and it didn't hurt that they were both beautiful. Rock was still mostly a male dominated industry in the seventies and sure, there'd been Janis Joplin and Grace Slick but the exceptions were so few and far between that Heart, with not just one female lead but two, stood out. Heart played the bar and club scene in and around their new home of Vancouver and developed quite the following. They soon started putting together original material for a debut album and that's when Ann, with the help of her sister, wrote "Magic Man" about Mike Fisher. The line "'Come on home, girl' mama cried on the phone," is about how their mother used to urge them to come back to the States. And the line "He's a magic man, oh, he's got the magic hands" is about, well, you can probably figure that part out. Mike Fisher also inspired "Crazy On You" which makes Mike Fisher one of the great male muses in rock history.

*Dreamboat Annie* was released in August of 1975 in Canada but it didn't make an initial splash. The band was still stuck playing the club circuit until they got a call from Rod Stewart's people asking them to open for him in Montreal. When they played that night they were shocked by the reaction of the crowd which seemed to know every word to every one of their songs. It turned out a local radio station had been playing their debut album and they had developed quite the following in the City of Saints. The album was finally released in the U.S. on this date in 1976 and it caught on like it did in Montreal. Both "Crazy on You" and "Magic Man" would soon become rock radio mainstays and the album sold over a million copies.

Heart has their first record label, Mushroom Records, to thank for the inspiration behind their next big song. To celebrate the album going platinum (selling over a million units) Mushroom placed an ad in a number of trade publications with a picture of Ann and Nancy standing back to back and bare shouldered with the caption "Heart's Wilson Sisters Confess 'It Was Only Our First Time!'" According to Ann she wasn't even aware of the ad till a promoter asked her about her lover and when she started answering about Mike he said, "no, your sister." Ann and Nancy and the whole band were furious about the ad and they channeled that anger into a song called "Barracuda," with lyrics like "you lying so low in the weeds, bet you gonna ambush me." Heart broke their contract with Mushroom after this, signing with CBS subsidiary Portrait Records, which released the band's second LP, *Little Queen*. That album proved the band was no one-hit wonder and their angry anthem "Barracuda" became another rock radio staple.

Neither Nancy nor Ann wound up marrying their respective Fisher boyfriends and when those relationships ended in the late seventies it certainly caused some friction in the band. Since then, Heart has had its ups and downs but mostly they've enjoyed a long and successful career, drifting from their hard rock sound to a more pop friendly vibe in the eighties when they scored their biggest commercial successes with Top 10 singles like "What About Love?", "Never," "These Dreams" and "Nothin' At All." The band has sold more than 30 millions albums and in 2013 they were inducted into the Rock and Roll Hall of Fame.

## February 15th

On this date in 1968, the Beatles began a very important trip to India to study under the Maharishi Mahesh Yogi. It would prove to be a very productive and creative time for the band and would bring a lot of worldwide exposure to Eastern religions and philosophies. But it would also end in disillusionment from the band towards a man they had previously revered. Here's the story:

George Harrison was the first of the four Beatles to get turned on to Eastern philosophies and his gateway, naturally, was music. In 1966 he spent six weeks in India studying the sitar under Ravi Shankar where he was first exposed to Transcendental Meditation (TM). In August of 1967 he and the rest of the band attended a lecture by the Maharishi in London. They were so enthralled they decided to attend a ten day retreat the Maharishi was offering in Wales but just a day into that retreat their manager, Brian Epstein, died. The Maharishi consoled them by saying that Epstein's spirit was still with them and their good thoughts would help him "to have an easy passage to his evolution."

As 1968 began the band carved out some time between projects to fly to India to study under the Maharishi. On this date John Lennon and his wife Cynthia, Harrison and his wife Patti, and Patti's sister Jenny Boyd landed in Delhi and were driven to the International Academy of Meditation in Rishikesh (the "yoga capital of the world"). Four days later Paul McCartney and his girlfriend Jane Asher and Ringo Starr and his wife Maureen arrived. There were already some celebrities at the academy when the Fab Four arrived; among them were Mia Farrow (along with her sister Prudence), the singer Donovan and Beach Boy Mike Love. John Lennon was respectful of the Maharishi but as always, couldn't resist a joke or two. During their first group talk together he patted the Maharishi on the head and said, "There's a good little guru" which caused the room to erupt in laughter. Lennon also joked about Harrison at one point (Harrison took this stuff way more seriously than the others) saying, "The way George is going, he'll be flying a magic carpet by the time he's forty." But Harrison had his lighter moments too. He happened to celebrate his 25th birthday while in India and the Maharishi gave him an upside down globe to commemorate the occasion, saying, "The globe I am giving you symbolizes the world today. I hope you will help us all in the task of putting it right." Harrison immediately turned the globe over, and exclaimed, "I've done it!"

The band initially intended to stay in India for two months but Starr and McCartney wound up leaving early. Ringo Starr hated the food and his wife hated the accommodations, especially the number of flies. When Starr complained to the Maharishi he replied, "For people traveling in the realm of pure consciousness, flies no longer matter very much." The Starrs were unmoved. McCartney blamed work as his reason for leaving early. He was, by this point, the de facto leader of the band and the only one making real decisions about their future so this was probably a legitimate reason. Meanwhile Harrison and Lennon stayed the duration.

The Beatles were incredibly creative during their time in India (hours and hours of meditation will do that to you). Some of the most notable songs to emerge from the trip appear on the *White Album*. Mia Farrow's sister Prudence threw herself so deeply into meditation she became a recluse. Lennon would say later she was "trying to reach God quicker than anybody else." He wrote "Dear Prudence" for her. Another came about when Mia Farrow confided in John Lennon that the Maharishi had made a sexual advance towards her. Lennon was already starting to grow disillusioned by the end of his stay in India, specifically by the constant mention of how much money the Beatles should be donating, and when he heard Mia's story he went off and wrote a scathing song with the title "Maharishi." When it came time to record it the rest of the band urged him to change the title to avoid a libel suit so he chose something with the same number of syllables and came up with "Sexy Sadie." Lennon also wrote "Revolution" in India, taking the lyric "It's gonna be all right" from his studies with the Maharishi. Paul McCartney was also busy. After seeing two monkeys having sex outside he wrote the rocker "Why Don't We Do It in the Road" and spending time with Mike Love in Rishikesh, inspired him to use the Beach Boys' "California Girls" as a springboard to write "Back in the U.S.S.R." In fact, a large portion of the *White Album*, which wound up being a double LP because of how much material they had, was either written in India or inspired by the trip. And the Beatles weren't the only ones being productive. Donovan left India having written "Hurdy Gurdy Man."

On April 11th, Lennon and Harrison both decided it was time to go. When the Maharishi confronted them and asked them why, Lennon sarcastically replied, "If you're so cosmic, you'll know why." He'd clearly had enough of the holy man. However when the cars driving them back to Delhi broke down, the group had to wonder if the Maharishi had placed a curse on them.

Disillusionment aside, the Beatles' trip to India brought a lot of awareness to Eastern philosophies and to Transcendental Meditation specifically. Today, it's estimated over 6 million people worldwide practice TM daily and the list of celebrities who swear by it is endless. The Maharishi is quoted as saying: "Being happy is of the utmost importance. Success in anything is through happiness." And that's something you don't have to spend two months in India to understand.

On this day in 1973, Elton John was enjoying his first visit to the top of the U.S. pop chart with his hit song "Crocodile Rock." The song had arrived at #1 on February 3rd when it dislodged Stevie Wonder's "Superstition" from that spot and it would remain through February 23rd when it surrendered the crown to "Killing Me Softly With His Song" by Roberta Flack. John and lyricist Bernie Taupin intended the song to be a throwback to all the things they enjoyed growing up, but for one songwriter they got a little too close to his original song. "Crocodile Rock," like so many songs before and since, became the subject of a copyright suit.

Elton John toured Australia in 1972 which is where he first heard of the band Daddy Cool and their song "Eagle Rock" which was the most successful Australian single of the early seventies. The song celebrates doing a dance called the Eagle Rock. John and Taupin set out to write something similar and, inspired by Bill Haley's "See You Later Alligator," created a fictitious dance called the Crocodile Rock. They wanted the song to sound like a classic fifties jitterbug, in the mold of "At the Hop" or "Rock Around the Clock." Taupin even name checks that Bill Haley classic with the line, "While the other kids were rocking round the clock, we were hopping and bopping to the Crocodile Rock." Years later Taupin would reflect back and call the song a dichotomy because, "I don't mind having created it, but it's not something I would listen to."

"Crocodile Rock" was released just before Thanksgiving of 1972 and it quickly began climbing the charts, becoming John's first #1 a few months later. But with success came scrutiny. The first to publicly question the song was Don McLean who mentioned its similarities to "American Pie." Indeed, both look back longingly on growing up in the fifties and lament the death of rock (or music in McLean's case). And both feature a Chevy. But McLean only mentioned the parallels and left it at that. Buddy Kaye, who had composed the song "Speedy Gonzalez" which Pat Boone had a hit with in 1961, decided to file suit. In a 1974 lawsuit, he claimed Elton John and Bernie Taupin illegally incorporated chords from "Speedy Gonzales." If you listen to both you can definitely hear Kaye's point, especially the way Boone sings the "la la la's" in the chorus. The parties settled quickly out of court and later John would dismiss the criticism by saying: "I wanted it to be a record about all the things I grew up with. Of course it's a rip-off, it's derivative in every sense of the word."

Looking back, John and Taupin both appreciate "Crocodile Rock" for helping establish them as young stars in the business, but they are also glad they went on to bigger and better things, artistically at least. John has said: "It was just a one-off thing. It became a huge hit record, and in the long run, it became a negative for me." Taupin is even tougher on it, saying: "I don't want people to remember me for 'Crocodile Rock.' I'd much rather they remember me for songs like 'Candle in the Wind' and 'Empty Garden,' songs that convey a message. . . there are things like 'Crocodile Rock,' which was fun at the time, but it was pop fluff. It was like, 'Okay, that was fun for now, throw it away, and here's the next one.' So there's a certain element of our music that is disposable, but I think you'll find that in anybody's catalog."

Disposable and fun. Two ways to describe bubblegum pop and you can understand why a songwriter would rather be known for their "deeper" stuff. Still, "Crocodile Rock" had an infectious energy and a profound reminiscence that captured the music listening public, so much so that it became the first of Elton John's nine career #1 hits.

## February 17th

On this date in 1979, the Village People's "Y.M.C.A." began its third consecutive week at #2 on the *Billboard* Hot 100 chart. The group would never score a #1 so their song about how a Y.M.C.A is a great place for gay men to meet other gay men, was their most successful song. But the theme of "Y.M.C.A." was no exception for the Village People. Everything about the band and most of their songs is, well, gay.

The Village People were a creation of the French composer Jacques Morali. He'd already had success in the disco world with a band he created called the Ritchie Family and their two Top 20 songs, 1975's "Brazil" (#11) and 1976's "The Best Disco in Town" (#17) so he was often given demo tapes from hopeful singers. When he heard the one Victor Willis handed him he just knew they had to work together. In fact Morali told Willis, "I had a dream that you sang lead on my album and it went very, very big." Morali wrote and produced a couple of songs, Willis sang on them and Morali released them under the name the Village People (named for the Greenwich Village neighborhood of New York City which is known for its large gay population). One of those early songs was "San Francisco (You've Got Me)" which, with lines like "It's a city known for its freedom . . .Inhibitions, no, you don't need them" celebrates the gay culture in San Francisco. When that song started getting attention suddenly Morali needed a band to go with Willis' voice. He placed an ad in a trade publication that read: "Macho Types Wanted: Must Dance And Have A Mustache." He then created a group and dressed them using stereotypical gay men fantasy personae (construction worker, leather-clad motorcycle rider, cowboy etc).

The Village People were invited on Dick Clark's *American Bandstand* and their reputation continued to grow. They released "Macho Man" in early 1978 and the song climbed to #25. "Macho Man" celebrates, well, macho men. The lyrics don't go much deeper than that. The word "macho" appears over 50 times which is nothing compared to the word "body" which is sung over a hundred times. For a follow-up Morali and Willis wrote "Y.M.C.A." (in about 20 minutes) and it became the band's biggest hit. At first the Young Men's Christian Association was none-too-pleased with the song and they threatened to sue the band over trademark infringement but the parties eventually settled.

The Village People were able to score one more hit before the door was slammed shut on the disco era. They released "In the Navy" in January of 1979 and the song peaked at #3 in May. When the Navy heard it they asked the band if they could use it for recruitment. The band agreed and even offered the song for free, in exchange for allowing them to shoot a video on a naval ship. The Village People got their video but ultimately the Navy decided not to use the song. Perhaps they finally caught on that the band wasn't just singing the praises of joining the Navy but that it too, like the Y.M.C.A., was a great place for gay men to find other gay men.

The death of disco put a lot of bands out of business, none more so than the Village People. The final nail in their coffin came when the band starred in the 1980 movie *Can't Stop the Music* which was so God-awfully bad it inspired the creation of the Golden Raspberry Awards (the Razzie's for short). *Can't Stop the Music* has the "honor" of becoming the very first winner of the Golden Raspberry Award for Worst Picture. Their motion picture, along with the demise of disco, was the death knell for the band, at least for the next few decades, till it started becoming safe to use the word "disco" again and bands that had ruled the nighttime world in the seventies were packaged and able to get back on the road. But the "Y.M.C.A." never quite left the playlist of some event DJs, egged on by the group dance in which all four letters are spelled out with hand gestures. While some DJs would never be caught dead playing the Village People's biggest song, others have kept it alive all these years with crowds who sing (and spell) along to the chorus.

### February 18th

On this date in 1978, Billy Joel's *The Stranger* got to #2 on the album chart. It sat there for a frustrating six consecutive weeks, blocked by the tour-de-force that was the *Saturday Night Fever* soundtrack. Though it failed to reach #1 *The Stranger* was Joel's breakthrough LP and would establish him as one of the great artists of his era.

Billy Joel was signed to Columbia Records in 1972 and released *Piano Man*, his first LP for them, in 1973. He'd previously released an album called *Cold Spring Harbor* with a smaller label named Family Productions but as a Columbia artist he was now with one of the big labels, the home of Bob Dylan and Simon & Garfunkel just to name a few, and his career was off and running. *Piano Man* peaked at #27 on the album chart, impressive for a debut, but his next two LPs underperformed (*Streetlife Serenade* which peaked at #35 in 1975 and *Turnstiles* which stalled at just #122 the following year) and Joel was at the risk of becoming a one album wonder.

Before beginning work for his next album Joel took a bold step. Like so many of his generation, he'd always admired the Beatles and so he reached out to George Martin and asked him to produce his next release. Martin considered it. He respected Joel's writing and piano work immensely, but he wasn't a fan of Joel's touring band and Joel was not willing to work with studio musicians as Martin requested. Eventually the two decided that it was not meant to be and Joel turned to legendary producer Phil Ramone. When Ramone listened to Joel and his band he loved their energy. Then Joel played him a few of the songs he'd already written for the project and the producer signed on immediately. Joel would describe working with Ramone as a blast and the results certainly speak for themselves.

While working on the title track for *The Stranger* Joel whistled a section for Ramone and then asked his producer to find an instrument to play that part. Ramone said, "No, that's 'The Stranger,' the whistling." While working in the studio Joel also realized he had a few bits of songs that weren't completed. One was about a couple named Brenda and Eddie and another about hanging out at bar called the Village Green (with the awesomely reminiscent line "Cold beer, hot lights, my sweet romantic teenage nights.") He had another section he'd written after dining out one night when his waiter asked if he wanted "a bottle of white, a bottle of red, or perhaps a bottle of rose instead." Joel had jotted the line down at the time, appreciating its rhyme and knowing he could use it in a song someday. Joel decided to take a page from George Martin's playbook and he wove these snippets together like the Beatles had done with the medley on side two of *Abbey Road*, thus producing the epic "Scenes From An Italian Restaurant." *The Stranger* also included the beautiful ballad, "Just the Way You Are" which became a huge hit for Joel and also earned him the 1979 Grammys for Record of the Year and Song of the Year.

Besides the album going to #2, *The Stranger* produced four Top 40 singles and it eventually overtook Simon and Garfunkel's *Bridge over Troubled Water* to become the best-selling album on Columbia Records. But among all the accolades and awards showered on Billy Joel for *The Stranger*, perhaps the most significant was a handwritten note he received after the album's success. It read: "You were right; I was wrong. I should have considered working with your band. Congratulations." And it was signed, George Martin.

### February 19th

On this date in 1878, the U.S. Patent office awarded Thomas Edison patent #200,521 for, as he had filed, a Phonograph or Speaking Machine. Edison had stumbled on his creation in his race to invent the telephone, and though he'd lose out on that invention to his fiercest competitor Alexander Graham Bell, he'd win the race for inventing a machine that could both record, as well as playback, sound waves. Like so many groundbreaking inventions, it is no overstatement to say the world would never be the same again.

Thomas Alva Edison was a born tinkerer as well as entrepreneur. In his lifetime he would found fourteen companies including General Electric which today is one of the largest publicly traded companies. He was also awarded over a thousand patents in his lifetime. One of the first, and the one that earned him the nickname "The Wizard of Menlo Park," was the phonograph. His laboratory was located in Menlo Park, New Jersey, an area that has since been renamed Edison, in his honor.

Edison was working on improving the telegraph and trying to figure out a system for relaying, not just dots and dashes, but the actual human voice, when he discovered a way to capture sound onto a spool of paper by transferring the vibrations of a diaphragm (vibrations that are produced by sound) onto an embossing point like a needle, and then capturing those onto some kind of impressionable medium. He used paraffin paper at first before trying a tinfoil wrapped cylinder which could then be spun. On Christmas Eve, 1877, Edison filed his patent application which stated: "the object of this invention is to record in permanent characters the human voice and other sounds, from which characters such sounds may be reproduced and rendered audible again at a future time." He had also showed his invention to the editorial staff at *Scientific American* which reported, in their December 22nd, 1877 issue, "Mr. Thomas A. Edison recently came into this office, placed a little machine on our desk, turned a crank, and the machine inquired as to our health, asked how we liked the phonograph, informed us that it was very well, and bid us a cordial good night."

It was Alexander Graham Bell who came up with the next big innovation in sound reproduction, by using a wax-coated cardboard cylinder to capture the sound vibrations. In 1890, German inventor Emile Berliner initiated the transition from cylinders to flat discs using a spiral groove running from the periphery to the center, thus inventing the earliest form of records as we know them. It was the Victor Talking Machine Company, founded in 1901, that helped get these inventions into people's homes. Their windup phonographs, called Victrolas, became the earliest mass produced "record players." By the 1920s, many of these were being built in the same cabinet with a radio and marketed as "radio-phonographs." In the late twenties the first "Jukebox" was produced. It was big and bulky because it contained eight separate record players mounted on a Ferris Wheel type device allowing customers to chose one of eight songs. As automation improved (and jukeboxes could contain just one player) these devices became ubiquitous in bars and clubs.

Of course, no record player is useful unless there are discs to play on them. With the advent and increasing popularity of players, came the demand for content which created the first musical stars. Ferruccio Giannini and Enrico Caruso, both opera singers, became two of the first "recording artists" to become popular. The 300 member Mormon Tabernacle Choir also became an early big seller and by the 1920s jazz and blues artists like Mamie Smith, Duke Ellington and Louis Armstrong were becoming stars. Bing Crosby and Frank Sinatra then ushered in the age of the crooner and before long an artist could reach hundreds of thousands of homes without ever leaving a studio. Records created stars which drove demand which led to ever improved technology. But it all goes back to this day in 1878 when Thomas Edison was granted one of his first patents.

The man who would go on to invent the light bulb and motion pictures made perhaps his biggest (and certainly loudest) impact on society with his "Phonograph or Speaking Machine." The world would never sound the same again.

## February 20th

On this date in 1982, at sunset on a beautiful beach in Maui two young musicians exchanged wedding vows. Their relationship has not only stood the test of time, succeeding in an industry where so many marriages fail, but throughout the eighties they produced an incredible string of hits.

Patricia Mae Andrzejewski was born in the Greenpoint section of Brooklyn, New York, in 1953. By eight she was already singing in school plays and taking vocal lessons. She dropped out of college after just one year to marry her high school sweetheart Dennis Benatar, something she would say later she knew was a mistake the day of the wedding. After Dennis' stint in the army the couple settled down in New York City and the young singer, now going by Pat Benatar pursued a singing career. She was dabbling in two fields for a while, trying to make it in musical theater as well as singing rock songs. Soon enough she was signed to Chrysalis Records and began assembling a band and working on material for a debut album. It was 1979 and at 26 years old Benatar was a star on the rise with a marriage on the rocks. She'd soon divorce her first husband just as her career was taking off.

Which is why, according to Benatar, the last thing she was looking for when she started auditioning musicians for her band, was a boyfriend. Still, when a young guitarist named Neil Giraldo walked in to the studio for an audition, her heart skipped a beat. She thought he was, "the most drop-dead gorgeous man I had ever seen in my life" and in her 2010 autobiography, she would write that she immediately said to herself, "girl, you have just seen the father of your children." But Giraldo was in a relationship himself, dating *Exorcist* actress Linda Blair and so when he landed a spot in her band, it was simply a working, platonic relationship. In the beginning.

In August of 1979 Benatar released her debut LP, *In the Heat of the Night*, which included her breakthrough single, "Heartbreaker." The album also included a song Giraldo had contributed to called, "We Live for Love" which includes the prescient lyrics "Is there a place where we can go? Where time stands still for those who know? Till eternity we'll fulfill our desires."

Benatar and her band hit the road to support her debut. One night she and Giraldo were out having a drink after a show and Giraldo broke down and told Benatar he thought Blair was cheating on him. Benatar would write later that while she was sympathetic on the outside, deep down, she was overjoyed. "This is a done deal," she remembers thinking. "You. Are. Mine." And she was right. With her marriage over and Giraldo and Blair splitting up, the two became a couple. Pretty soon they were bandmates, lovers and collaborators. She has commented on that, saying "it's kind of an incestuous relationship. There isn't any part of our lives that isn't intertwined." Giraldo has said, "It was a partnership from the very beginning. We were just two missing pieces that found each other." Their collaboration led to songs like "Promises in the Dark" and "Hell is for Children" just to name a few. Benatar's second album *Crimes of Passion* would continue her rise to fame, including her first Top 10 single "Hit Me With Your Best Shot." On August 1st, 1981, when the brand new music video channel MTV launched it was Benatar's video for her song "You Better Run" which had the honor of being the second video ever played on the channel.

By early 1982 Benatar was a bonafide rock star and so when she and Giraldo thought about getting married they both had one goal: privacy. They flew to Hawaii, found a judge who would marry them and then walked along the beach and literally asked two strangers to be their witnesses. As the sun set behind them, Benatar and Giraldo exchanged wedding vows. Their marriage has lasted through the turbulent ride of rock star fame and fortune and it hasn't always been easy. Both face temptations on the road. In her memoir Benatar recalls a show where a woman in the front of the stage kept yelling at her husband and opening her blouse to show him her breasts. At one point the woman put her hands on the stage and Benatar casually made her way over and stepped on them. That shut her up (and closed her blouse).

The couple still tours together to this day. They have two beautiful daughters and a gorgeous home in Los Angeles. When *Rolling Stone* asked her what advice she'd give to a young female singer she said with a laugh, "Marry your guitar player." It's a plan that might not work for everyone but for Pat Benatar and Neil Giraldo it's been a winning formula both personally and professionally for over 35 years. How many rock and roll couples can say that?

## February 21st

On this date in 1973, Steely Dan's first big single, "Do It Again" was peaked at #6 on the *Billboard* Hot 100 chart. It was a pretty solid early success that would bode well for the band's future.

Steely Dan is a duo consisting of Walter Becker and Donald Fagen. They met attending Bard College, in Annandale-on-Hudson, in upstate New York when Fagen passed a cafe that Becker was playing in. Fagen introduced himself and then he asked that simple yet fateful question that has been the impetus for so many great groups through the years: "Do you want to be in a band?"

Fagen and Becker started playing together immediately, in a number of different incarnations and under a few different band names like the Don Fagen Jazz Trio, the Bad Rock Group and the Leather Canary. At one point their drummer was a young Chevy Chase who would make his fame in comedy rather than behind the kit. Though other musicians came and went it was Fagen and Becker who had forged the bond that would take them to the highest heights of the music industry. They had similar musical tastes and a commonality that no one else could match: they were always the smartest guys in the room. And they know it too. From their earliest meeting to the songs they began to compose together, Fagen and Becker saw life, and music, as boring if they weren't challenging. Their music has always had a complexity to it, a whimsical-sarcasm, an inside-joke-for-the-cerebral crowd that makes their fan base feel like they are in the know.

Their quick-witted nature and love of obscure references began as early as naming the band. When ABC Records signed them in 1972 they asked the two for a name. Fagen and Becker replied, Steely Dan. It's doubtful anyone at their record company got the über-obscure reference. It's doubtful most people would. You'd have to have read the Beat Generation classic *Naked Lunch*, written by William S. Burroughs and remembered that the steam-powered dildo he wrote about was called a "Steely Dan III from Yokohama." Yeah, that obscure.

After coming up with the name, Fagen and Becker got to work on their debut album. As they would with all of their future work they brought in musicians: guest musicians and session musicians. And then, some extra musicians just to be safe. They actually completed their debut album, *Can't Buy a Thrill*, in pretty reasonable time, especially compared to some of their future LPs. "Do It Again," which had the honor of being the first track on the album as well as the lead single is, like so many Steely Dan songs, hard to understand in a literal sense. It's more about the mood created, and in the case of their first release, that mood was hope and optimism. You don't try to understand Steely Dan songs. You let their lyrics, and their jazz-fusion-meets-soft-rock sound wash over you and feel the vibe they are trying to send out.

After "Do It Again" announced to the world that there was a new band on the scene, Steely Dan followed up with "Reelin' in the Years" which got as high as #11. With their debut album they'd earn a solid fan base which eagerly awaited where this band would take them. And with their initial success, Fagen and Becker became more and more ambitious in the studio. By the time they got to recording their eighth LP, 1980's *Gaucho*, their obsessive perfectionism would cause them to spend over a year working on its seven songs while using 42 different musicians. When their loyal fans heard that album's classics like "Babylon Sister" and "Hey Nineteen" they felt it was worth the wait.

Steely Dan was one of those bands that were hard to compartmentalize. People called their sound jazz rock or smart rock. *Rolling Stone* described them as: "the perfect musical antiheroes for the seventies." But attempts to define them or label them were fruitless. They were an ever-changing duo, bored in one place and always searching for the next muse. And they were always the smartest guys in the room.

On this date in 1997, the Spice Girls' debut single "Wannabe" began a four week run at #1 on the *Billboard* Hot 100 chart. The song introduced the world to this brand new, all-female band and their "girl power" message and it took all that girl power just to get their record company to release the song as their lead single. When the song became a worldwide success their record executives had to admit these five women with little-to-no experience in the industry knew better than they did.

In 1994 Heart Management, which consisted of the father-and-son team Bob and Chris Herbert, placed an ad in the British entertainment weekly, *The Stage*, that read: "Are you street smart, extrovert, ambitious, and able to sing and dance?" From the more than 400 hundred women who replied, five became the Spice Girls. After months of rehearsals and choreography classes, Heart Management set up a showcase in front of some industry insiders. Producer Richard Stannard was in attendance and he fell in love with the band immediately. He called his songwriting partner, Matt Rowe, and said he had found the pop group of their dreams. When Rowe met the Spice Girls he had a similar reaction, saying later, "I loved them immediately. They were like no one I'd met before." In her autobiography, Mel B (Scary Spice) wrote that the duo instinctively understood the group's point of view and knew how to incorporate "the spirit of five loud girls into great pop music." Heart management asked Stannard and Rowe to work with their band and see what they could come up with.

The first song they all worked on together was a slow R&B number that didn't make their debut album. After this the group suggested doing something more upbeat and Rowe created a beat on his drum machine that, he would say later, reminded him of the song from *Grease* "You're the One That I Want." Within thirty minutes they had all written "Wannabe" together, with contributions coming from the two songwriters as well as all five singers. The band came up with the nonsensical "zigazig-ha" lyric, as Melanie Chisholm (Sporty Spice) would explain later: "You know when you're in a gang and you're having a laugh and you make up silly words? Well we were having a giggle and we made up this silly word, zigazig-ha. And we were in the studio and it all came together in this song."

Before the band even signed their first record deal they became frustrated with Heart Management's unwillingness to listen to their ideas and they left the two men who had placed the ad that brought them together. They signed with Simon Fuller's 19 Entertainment who helped them land a recording contract with Virgin Records. Virgin listened to the work that had already been done for their debut and decided "Say You'll Be There" or "Love Thing" should be the band's debut single. The five Spice Girls thought it should be "Wannabe." Virgin felt the song, with its rapping, wouldn't appeal to everyone like their other choices and they stood their ground. But the band stood firmer, channeling the "girl power" ethos in "Wannabe" they told Virgin it was "non-negotiable." Geri Halliwell

(Ginger Spice) would say later, "'Wannabe' was either a hit or a miss, love or hate. It would either do everything or nothing. We felt, well, if nobody likes it then we have got other songs up our sleeves, but that was the one we wanted to release." Virgin finally relented.

"Wannabe" was released in England in July of 1996 and it made a steady climb to #1 in the band's homeland. It wasn't until January of 1997 that the song was released in the U.S. and it climbed the charts even faster than it had in the U.K. In fact, the song would end up #1 in 37 different countries and its worldwide sales figures of over seven million makes it the best-selling single ever by an all female group. Its message of female empowerment resonated with fans everywhere who also enjoyed singing along with the "zigazig-ha" parts. The Spice Girls never did match the success of their debut but for one shining moment they had produced a song that will forever exemplify the pop movement of the nineties.

## February 23rd

On this date in 1940, in a hotel room in New York City, 28 year old folk singer Woody Guthrie, who'd already been across the United States and back, sat down and wrote the lyrics that eventually became what some consider our alternative national anthem, "This Land Is Your Land." But Guthrie's intentions weren't as patriotic as one might think and his original lyrics were even tweaked a few times to make the song a little less caustic and even, some would say, socialist. Still, it stands today as a true American classic.

Woodrow Wilson Guthrie was born in 1912 in Oklahoma. He loved music and by his teen years he was busking, playing songs for loose change or food. He was also an avid reader although, with no parental supervision (his mother was institutionalized and his father had left Oklahoma to find work in Texas) he dropped out of high school and never did earn a degree. Eventually he joined his father in Texas and then, during the famous Dust Bowl or Dirty Thirties, he migrated to California to find work. He lived a pauper's life during these years, like so many, scraping by to find work and subsistence. This experience informed his songwriting throughout his life.

But his love of music helped him and by the end of the thirties he was not only writing and playing his owns songs, he had made a name for himself as a radio DJ. He worked at a station that was owned by a populist-minded New Deal Democrat, Frank W. Burke, and he met many socialists and communists in Southern California during this time. In the late thirties with war raging again in Europe, America went through a period of intense patriotism and Kate Smith's version of "God Bless America" became a ubiquitous anthem for the times. Guthrie, who was not a fan of the blind loyalty the song promotes as well as the holier-than-thou attitude of God blessing a specific land, grew tired of hearing the song everywhere he turned.

Guthrie's radio career came to an end in California and he made his way east to pursue a singing career. When he arrived in New York City he checked into a hotel and on one of his first days in the big city, he heard "God Bless America" for the umpteenth time and it set him off. Guthrie was a big fan of the folk/religious group the Carter Family and he just took the melody of their song "When the World's On Fire" and used it to fit new lyrics to. He wrote a song he called "God Blessed America" which included the line after each stanza "God blessed America for me." The second line of the song documents his recent journey, "from California to the New York island" and on the surface the song mostly celebrates the beauty of America, especially the wonderful visual, "As I was walking that ribbon of highway, I saw above me that endless skyway." But two of the stanzas that eventually got left out when the song was initially recorded reveal Guthrie's feelings about capitalism. The first went:

> Was a high wall there that tried to stop me
> A sign was painted said: Private Property,
> But on the back side it didn't say nothing
> God Blessed America for me.

and the second went:

> One bright sunny morning in the shadow of the steeple
> By the Relief Office I saw my people —
> As they stood hungry, I stood there wondering if
> God Blessed America for me.

Then, for some reason, Guthrie stashed the song away for four years. During this time the U.S. was dragged into World War II and the patriotism that had existed in the late thirties was ratcheted even higher. By the time Guthrie recorded the song, he realized that taking a sarcastic swipe at "God Bless America" during a time of war was not such a great idea. So he changed the end of each stanza to the much more politically correct "this land was made for you and me" and he left out the two controversial stanzas. A recording from 1944 of Guthrie singing the song with the "private property" part included surfaced a few years ago which shows he recorded it but since it didn't make his initial release of the song he must have reconsidered it.

"This Land Is Your Land" has thus had an interesting history. It is taught to many school children as an alternative anthem that celebrates the beauty of the U.S.A. (leaving out the two controversial sections) but it has also enjoyed a rich history as a protest song. Guthrie had a productive and influential (albeit shortened) career as a folk singer before his passing at just 55 years old. Perhaps fittingly there was a mistake with the copyright for "This Land Is Your Land," (the publishers didn't renew their claim to the song in time) and so it is now considered in the public domain. Guthrie, with his lifelong leaning towards socialism, probably wouldn't mind that. In the late 1930's when he was asked to print some of his lyrics in a songbook that was made available to listeners of his radio show, he included the note: "This song is Copyrighted in U.S., under Seal of Copyright #154085, for a period of 28 years, and anybody caught singin' it without our permission, will be mighty good friends of ourn, cause we don't give a dern. Publish it. Write it. Sing it. Swing to it. Yodel it. We wrote it, that's all we wanted to do."

Whether you see "This Land Is Your Land" as a plea for social justice, a sarcastic answer to another patriotic song or a beautiful ode to a great nation is your personal choice. What's undeniable is that it's one of the greatest songs ever composed about America and it was written on this date in 1940 by a young man who'd just traveled that "ribbon of highway" across America. He believed this land was made for everyone and he wrote a timeless classic to prove it.

## February 24th

On this date in 1980, Air Supply had just released their single "All Out of Love" in the U.S. The band that had been unable to break into the American market, despite success in their homeland of Australia, suddenly had back-to-back hits on the *Billboard* Hot 100 chart. They have a record company icon to thank for that, in more ways than one, and they are quick to give him credit.

Russell Hitchcock and Graham Russell met in 1975 while both were appearing in an Australian production of the musical *Jesus Christ Superstar*. The two decided to work together and they called their band Air Supply because Russell had seen that name in a dream years before. While there were other musicians in and out of the band for a while, Air Supply has always been about these two men and their unique talents, specifically Russell's writing ability and Hitchcock's soaring, almost ethereal, voice. Their first Australian single, "Love and Other Bruises" climbed to #6 on the Kent Music Report chart (the Australian equivalent of *Billboard*) in early 1977. Though they built a reputation and solid fan base in Australia over the next few years their songs weren't even available in the States. In 1979 they released their fourth album, *Life Support* which contained a five-and-a-half-minute version of "Lost in Love", which Russell claims to have written in 15 minutes. It's that song that caught the attention of Clive Davis who was running Arista at the time. He purchased the international rights to the song, edited it to make it fit pop radio's format and released it in the U.S. According to Russell he wasn't even aware of any of this till he saw a notice in Cash Box magazine saying Arista had just released "Lost in Love" and it was destined to be a Top 5 hit. The magazine was correct as "Lost in Love" peaked at #3.

When Russell and Hitchcock finally met with Davis he asked them what else they had. They played him a song they had worked on called "All Out of Love" which Davis loved just as much as "Lost in Love" except for one line. Originally the chorus went, "I'm all out of love, I want to arrest you" and when Davis inquired about that Russell said, "It means to get your attention." Davis, never one to mince words said, "It's too weird. In America they won't understand that." It was Clive Davis who came up with "I'm so lost without you" and he received a co-writing credit for contributing those five words. Russell would say later, "we'll never know if it would have worked the other way. And I doubt it, to be honest. Because Clive is usually right." "All Out of Love" went to #2 in 1980, giving Air Supply back-to-back mega-hits in the U.S. and setting them up for a very successful run of soft rock greatness in the early eighties.

Air Supply has had eleven Top 40 hits in the U.S. (five of which have the word "love" in the title) and though their popularity waned after the first half of the eighties they continue to tour to this day with a rabid fan base that comes to hear all those love songs, and Hitchcock's incredible, one might even say arresting, voice.

## February 25th

On this date in 1984, "Jump" by Van Halen began a five week run at #1 on the *Billboard* Hot 100 chart. Sound-wise, the song was a bit of a departure from the guitar-driven music Van Halen was known for. It caused tensions within the band when some perceived it as them selling out just to have a hit and ultimately it was one more step towards their lead singer leaving the band. But before all that, the song was a monster hit and its video helped introduce Van Halen to a whole new audience.

Brothers Eddie and Alex Van Halen were born in the Netherlands but their family relocated to California when they were still children. They formed a number of different bands in the early seventies and as their popularity grew they found themselves needing more and more sound equipment for their ever-growing gigs. They started renting gear from David Lee Roth who was in another local band but eventually they got sick of the extra expense so they just asked Roth to join their band. He accepted and made the suggestion that they change their band name to their last name, Van Halen, because he thought it showed strength.

Van Halen's self-titled debut album was released in 1978 and instantly earned the band a rabid fan base that loved their heavy, guitar-driven sound. Eddie was singled out for his gifted guitar work and Roth for his wild, frontman persona.

Though Eddie was a master on guitar he was also a multi-instrumentalist and he often tinkered around with a synthesizer. Sometime in the early eighties he wrote the introduction for what would become "Jump." But when he played it for the band they didn't love it. Sometime after this Eddie set-up his own home studio which enabled him to work independently from the band and he fleshed out the synthesizer riff and came up with an entire musical bed. Once again he brought it to the band and this time Roth said he'd take a crack at writing lyrics for it. According to Roth, the band's roadie Larry Hostler was driving him around one day and they popped in the tape and listened to it a few times. Roth mentioned a news report he'd seen about a man who was threatening to commit suicide by jumping off a high building. Roth said if he were in the crowd of people looking on, he would have shouted, "might as well jump." Hostler encouraged Roth by telling him the line had potential. Then Roth figured out that "jump" could be about committing to love (instead of suicide) and soon enough he had the lyrics all worked out. Roth later told *Musician* magazine that Hostler was "probably the most responsible for how it came out" although he wasn't given a writing credit - such is the life of a roadie.

With a song that had hit potential the band needed a great video. With Roth directing they filmed the band performing the song and also got shots of them playing up to the camera. When MTV put the video into heavy rotation it became a template for how inexpensive "performance videos" could be done.

The success of "Jump" and their LP, *1984*, brought the band tons of new fans. But it also highlighted the growing tensions between Roth and Eddie. Roth released an EP called *Crazy From the Heat* while he was still officially the lead singer for Van Halen and when his cover version of the Beach Boys' hit "California Girls" peaked at #3, it all but spelled the end. There are a number of reasons given for Roth leaving Van Halen and they vary based on who you speak to and what day you speak to them. But the bottom line is, before they parted ways, the band created some amazing albums and songs that established them as one of the great American rock bands. And after Roth's departure they had even more success with Sammy Hagar as their lead singer. So looking back, maybe "Jump" wasn't about suicide or committing to love, maybe when Roth came up with "go ahead, jump!" he was convincing himself to leave the band and go out on his own.

### February 26th

On this date in 1965, Gary Lewis & the Playboys were sitting at #1 on the *Billboard* Hot 100 chart with their version of "This Diamond Ring." The song wound up being sandwiched between two all-time classic recordings as it had knocked off "Unchained Melody" by the Righteous Brothers on February 20th and would stay at the top for two weeks before giving way to the Temptations' "My Girl." That's a pretty good legacy for a version of a song that one of its writers claimed to be "revolted by."

Bob Brass, Irwin Levine and Al Kooper wrote the song "This Diamond Ring" while they were selling songs as a way to break into the music business (which Kooper, of course, would do most successfully, working with Bob Dylan when he went electric and then forming the band Blood, Sweat and Tears). The lyrics lament a break-up, with the singer asking who will buy a diamond ring now that his love has left him (hey, at least she gave the ring back!) and they intended the song to be a soulful, almost bluesy, number to fit the lyrics. They offered it first to the Drifters and when they turned it down they approached Bobby Vee about recording it but he didn't like the song so he passed. Finally, two lesser known artists decided to record it, soul singer Sammy Ambrose and the pop/rock band Gary Lewis & the Playboys. Both versions were released in January of 1965. The Ambrose version failed to gain chart traction while Gary Lewis' became the hit.

Lewis used studio musicians to record his version and wound up with a pretty prestigious backing band, including drummer Hal Blaine, bassist Joe Osborn and Leon Russell who not only played keyboards but arranged the music as well. The arrangement is a fairly uptempo, pop-sound which gives the song what is commonly called lyrical dissonance, when the feel of the song (in this case, happy) doesn't match the words (in this case, sad). Gary Lewis has said that people approach him all the time saying they got married because of "This Diamond Ring" and he always thinks to himself, "Really? It's a break up song!"

In his 2008 memoir, *Backstage Passes and Backstabbing Bastards*, Al Kooper said that he and his fellow songwriters were "revolted" by the Playboy's version because it removed all the soul from what should have been an R&B number. He says they, "made a teenage milkshake out of it."

That teenage milkshake not only hit the top of the charts just a month after its release, it opened the door for Gary Lewis & the Playboys who released a string of hits in the next few years. "Count Me In" made it to #2 as did "Save Your Heart for Me." "Everybody Loves a Clown" peaked at #4 and then "She's Just My Style" made it to #3. And those are just their 1965 hits. By the end of that year Gary Lewis would be named *Cash Box* magazine's "Male Vocalist of the Year," (beating nominees Elvis Presley and Frank Sinatra). At a time when the British Invasion was leaving very little chart room for anyone else, Gary Lewis & the Playboys proved a lot of people like milkshake.

### February 27th

On this date in 1966, Nancy Sinatra's single "These Boots Are Made For Walkin'" was enjoying the view from the top of the pop chart. The song had arrived at #1 the day before, knocking Lou Christie's "Lightnin' Strikes" from that spot, and it would remain there for one week, relinquishing the spot to "The Ballad of the Green Berets" by Barry Sadler. With the hit, Frank Sinatra's daughter not only salvaged her career but, in her father's words, she could write her own contract with Reprise (the label they both shared) because she was now selling more records than her old man at the time.

It has to be a mixed blessing to have a parent who is an incredibly successful musician. Sure, your last name will always open doors and offer you more opportunities than some no-name artist looking for a break. However, you'll always be compared to your parent, and it's often impossible to measure up. For every Miley Cyrus (who blew past her father Billy Ray in the music industry) there are scores of Julian Lennons and Dweezil Zappas. Some children of stars will avoid their parent's profession for just that reason. For Nancy Sinatra though, music always seemed to be the career path she'd take. When she was just 20 she made her professional debut on her father's television special, *The Frank Sinatra Timex Show: Welcome Home Elvis*, celebrating the return of Elvis Presley from the Army. Nancy and her father danced and sang a duet, "You Make Me Feel So Young/Old" and very soon after, her dad's record label, Reprise, signed her to a contract.

Nancy Sinatra's first few singles were not hits and Reprise started weighing whether or not to keep her on the roster. Surely they didn't want to do anything to upset Frank Sinatra, who, though he was going through a little career slump at the time, was still their highest profile artist. But business is business (even show business) and Reprise had to be wondering what to do with Nancy Sinatra. They decided to try and team her up with singer, songwriter and producer Lee Hazelwood.

As the two began to work on material, Hazelwood showed Sinatra a demo of a song he'd written called "These Boots Are Made For Walkin'" Hazelwood had been in a bar in Texas when he overheard some patrons teasing an older guy because his young girlfriend was controlling him. The man had responded by putting his feet up on a bar stool and saying: "I know what you think - that she might be the boss. But I am the boss of my house, and these boots will walk all over her the day that I'm not." Hazelwood liked the imagery of boots walking all over someone and he fleshed out a song from that overheard comment. It was a song he intended to sing himself but when Nancy Sinatra heard it she wanted it. And she made a convincing argument to get it. She pointed out to Hazelwood that if a man sings that line it sounds cruel and maybe even abusive. But when a woman sings it, it sounds more empowering. The songwriter was convinced and a recording session was scheduled with Hazelwood producing.

Hazelwood wanted Nancy Sinatra to sell her sexual side hard for the record. In the studio, he told her to sing like she was "a young girl who fucks truck drivers." Whether or not she channeled that exact persona, her vocals certainly got everyone's attention. The backing track was exemplary as well, especially the bass line which Hazelwood wanted to sound like someone walking. Mission accomplished. It's a great sound to go along with Sinatra's incredible delivery.

"These Boots Are Made For Walkin'" went on to become Nancy Sinatra's signature song. Though she'd never match its success she did have a string of hits afterwards and Reprise no longer needed to worry about the fallout if they should let her go. When her record contract was up for renewal she consulted with her father who told her to re-sign with Reprise but under whatever terms she wanted. She could write the contract now, he told her, because she was outselling even her famous father.

On this date in 1970, Simon And Garfunkel's soaring, Gospel-inspired ballad, "Bridge Over Troubled Water" began an incredible six week run at #1 on the *Billboard* Hot 100 chart. The song would be the last #1 for the famous duo and it would go on to be the biggest song of the year.

Paul Simon readily admits to listening to the gospel group the Swan Silvertones often in the late sixties so there is no doubt that he would have heard their version of the old negro spiritual song "Oh, Mary Don't You Weep" which contains an improvised lyric: "I'll be your bridge over deep water if you trust in me." That line must have sat in Simon's subconscious because according to him he wrote the first two verses and the chorus of "Bridge Over Troubled Water" so quickly that he marveled at it. Simon would say later: "I have no idea where it came from. It came all of a sudden. It was one of the most shocking moments in my songwriting career. I remember thinking, 'This is considerably better than I usually write.'" "Oh, Mary Don't You Weep" also contains the lyric "Now listen if I could right now I wanna tell you that I surely would" which sound similar to Paul Simon's lyric in "El Cóndor Pasa (If I Could)" (which he wrote around the same time).

Wherever his inspiration came from, Simon composed the song on guitar before realizing it would sound better on piano because it would emphasize the song's gospel feel. He played a demo version for his partner, Art Garfunkel, and asked him to sing it. At first Garfunkel refused, saying he liked Simon's falsetto on the demo. They eventually let their producer Roy Halee decide and Halee agreed with Simon, Garfunkel's "white choir boy voice" would suit the song better. It's a decision Simon long regretted, admitting later, "There were many times on a stage, when I'd be sitting off to the side and Larry Knechtel would be playing the piano and Artie would be singing 'Bridge', people would stomp and cheer when it was over, and I would think, 'That's my song, man.'"

Halee was also the one who suggested the song needed a third verse. They were already working on the song in the studio at the time when Halee made the suggestion, and Simon scribbled another stanza as quickly as he'd written the rest. He was dating Peggy Harper at the time (she would soon become his first wife) and she had just recently noticed her first grey hairs. So Simon began this extra verse with the line, "sail on silver girl" as a nod to her. As they produced the song, Halee suggested they mimic Phil Spector's recent production of "Old Man River" by the Righteous Brothers. That song starts simple, with a piano and Medley singing in his deep rich baritone. Halee felt "Bridge" would benefit from the same treatment, starting with just Garfunkel singing over a simple piano before building to a powerful crescendo. Halee's instincts proved to be correct, it's one of the reasons the song stands out, that it goes from so intimate to so grandiose in five epic minutes. "Bridge" also shared radio air space that winter with the Beatles' "Let It Be" which has a similar, building production (which, of course, was done by Spector).

When the duo submitted their fifth studio album to their record label, Columbia chief Clive Davis heard "Bridge Over Troubled Water" and predicted immediately that it would be a monster hit. And as usual, Davis was right. The single would sell 6 million copies and be the highest seller of the year. Their album of the same name also topped the charts and ended 1970 as the biggest selling LP. "Bridge Over Troubled Water" has been covered countless times but it was the version done by Elvis Presley (a childhood idol of Paul Simon's) that meant the most to the song's composer.

Simon and Garfunkel broke up after this album and Paul Simon went on to a very successful solo career. He's sung "Bridge" plenty of times throughout his career but the version Art Garfunkel sang will always be the quintessential rendition of the song, even if Simon regrets his own decision to have him do it. Paul Simon wrote a timeless classic about supporting someone you love, being there for them when times are rough and when darkness comes. The song is uplifting and there's probably no singer who could have brought Simon's masterpiece to life like Garfunkel had done.

### February 29th

On this date in 1968, at the 10th annual Grammy Awards, the Beatles were big winners, taking home the Grammy for Album of the Year for their masterwork *Sgt. Pepper's Lonely Hearts Club Band* as well as the Grammy Award for Best Recording Package for the same album. As iconic and groundbreaking as the music on *Sgt. Pepper's* proved to be, the cover art is still something people talk about to this day and some musicologists consider it to be the greatest album cover ever.

The entire *Sgt. Pepper's* project was Paul McCartney's brainchild. The band was fatigued from touring and felt restricted by their insane level of fame and so it was McCartney who came up with the idea that they should create a fictitious band as an alter ego that would allow them to experiment musically. None of the other Beatles objected so McCartney took the reigns and steered this project from inception to fruition. And this included the album's artwork.

McCartney sketched out his original concept of having the band photographed surrounded by an eclectic mix of celebrities. He presented it to the band and allowed them each to suggest some people who should be included. A list was made and letters were sent asking for permission to use that person's likeness. Most people gave their permission while some declined. Mae West initially refused saying she didn't like the idea of being associated with a "Lonely Hearts Club." She acquiesced after all four Beatles wrote her letters to implore her to change her mind. Once the list was complete art work was commissioned. Most of those shown would be cardboard cutouts while nine of them were wax figures. The final list of 66 people ranges from the most famous (like Marlon Brando, Bob

Dylan and Marilyn Monroe) to the fairly obscure (like the guru Mahavatar Babaji [Harrison's choice] and painter Larry Bell). On March 30th, 1967, the day the photo shoot took place, there were some last minute discussions and a few cutouts that had been created were left out of the shot to avoid possible controversy, most notably, Jesus Christ and Adolf Hitler (no surprise, both had been Lennon's suggestions). Besides the people represented, the set was peppered (pun intended) with some interesting props that included a statue Lennon had brought from his house, a hookah pipe and a brass instrument called a euphonium. And of course the band's name was spelled out in red flowers at the forefront. The Beatles themselves were dressed in their colorful, Sgt.-Pepper's-era uniforms while posing just next to wax figures of their younger selves. Photographer Michael Cooper got to take the now historic picture. Months later when the Rolling Stones felt the world needed their take on psychedelia they too chose Cooper to take the cover shot for *Their Satanic Majesties Request.* When people criticize that album for being derivative of the psychedelic movement and for copying *Pepper's,* they mean it, down to the photographer shooting the cover.

The cover shot of *Sgt. Pepper's Lonely Hearts Club Band* is only one thing that stands out about the album's packaging. *Pepper's* was distributed in a gatefold format and the inside is taken up with just one dramatic photo of the four Beatles in their *Pepper's*-era attire, staring sincerely into the camera. McCartney would say later that their intention when taking this shot was to "look into this camera and really say I love you! Really try and feel love; really give love through this!" Mission accomplished. The album's lyrics were then printed on the back cover which was a first for a rock album. Original printings also included a sheet of cardboard cut-outs, a fake mustache, two sets of sergeant stripes, two lapel badges and a stand-up cut-out of the Beatles in their *Pepper's* uniforms. When it was all put together the album artwork was the most expensive to date, costing over 3,000 British pounds at a time when the average album cover cost about 50 pounds.

*Sgt. Pepper's Lonely Hearts Club Band* is recognized by many as the Beatles' greatest album and the high-water mark for the psychedelic era of rock. Music aside, the album was also groundbreaking for its creative cover art that so many music lovers stared at endlessly in an attempt to figure out who all these people were posing with their musical heroes. It's an iconic album and album cover and both were recognized with Grammy Awards on this date in 1968.

# MARCH

On this date in 1969, one of the most famous (or infamous) concert incidents ever took place. It has also led to one of the great unsolved mysteries in the history of rock and roll. The Doors performed at the Dinner Key Auditorium in Miami and a clearly inebriated Jim Morrison attempted to start a riot and maybe showed the audience his penis. Or maybe he didn't. After hundreds of pictures were entered into evidence at a trial (yes, there was a trial over whether he exposed himself) the truth of the matter remained a mystery. And then Morrison took the answer to the grave so we'll never really know. But what we do know is that the Miami Incident (as it became known among Doors' fans) helped expedite the end for the band and Morrison's legal troubles were a big reason for him to relocate to Paris. Here's the story:

Jim Morrison was always fascinated by tension. He saw live performances as an opportunity to test his audience. He once said, "I like people who shake other people up and make them feel uncomfortable." From the Doors' earliest days this manifested itself onstage with Morrison pushing his audience to the brink. The spoken word section of their song "The End" was often where Morrison tested the limits of his audience's tolerance. On record Morrison taps into the classic Oedipus complex but live, he would often dwell on the sordid details till the audience reacted. He was a master of this, bringing a crowd to the brink before steering them back to sanity. He knew how to build the tension to a fever pitch before releasing it. But as the Doors became more and more famous and Morrison more and more inebriated, the line was harder and harder to balance. And by 1969 he had begun to rebel against his own fame and his sex symbol status. He hated the fact that the Doors had gone from an underground band respected by the avant-garde, to rock stars who were covered like pop stars. Morrison wanted to be taken seriously as a poet and shaman when meanwhile all many fans wanted was the celebrity Jim Morrison.

In early 1969 Morrison attended a few performances of the Living Theater. The troupe presented various beatnik plays and experimental shows and were known for their obscenity, nudity and even anarchy. Morrison attended four shows in a row at USC in late February and was clearly affected by them. He was inspired by the shock-provoking performances and the way the audience reacted to them. After the last show, just before he was to leave for a concert in Miami, Morrison and his friend Tom Baker spent the rest of the night discussing how he could incorporate something similar into a rock and roll show. He wanted to create a reaction; maybe even a riot.

So on this date in 1969 Morrison and his longtime girlfriend Pamela Courson were set to fly to Miami. There, the Doors would perform a show, then the next day they were scheduled to fly to Jamaica for a vacation. But Morrison and Courson got into a huge fight and it was decided she wouldn't make the trip. Morrison then missed his flight and had to connect through New Orleans where he spent way too much time in the airport bar. When he finally arrived in Miami, he was probably too drunk to perform. The Doors manager Bill Siddons said later: "I noticed Jim's facial muscles had slackened, the only way I could tell how drunk he was. So I knew he was real drunk." But since the band had already been paid their $25,000 performance fee, there was no way they were going to cancel. Plus, the arena was full, in fact over-full since the promoter had had seats removed in order to squeeze in more fans (and of course sell more tickets). The theater that normally sat about seven thousand was packed to almost twice that. And the band was warned before they went on that the stage was poorly built and could collapse during their show. And with no air-conditioning, the temperature in the building was climbing rapidly. If Morrison dreamed of creating chaos, he already had the perfect environment.

When the Doors finally hit the stage they began playing "Break On Through" but Morrison wasn't in a singing mood just yet. Instead he launched into his first diatribe of the evening, saying to the crowd: "I'm not talking about no revolution. And I'm not talking about no demonstration. I'm talking about having a good time." The band then launched into "Back Door Man" with Morrison extolling them to play louder. He sang this one for a bit before going off on a tangent of incomprehensible moaning and screaming. He then made his first plea to the audience for some love, asking, "Isn't anyone gonna love my ass?" Audio from the show reveals the crowd was enjoying things to this point. "Five to One" was next and Morrison again strayed from the lyrics before too long, this time getting confrontational, telling the crowd that they were, "all a bunch of fucking idiots." He antagonized them even further, "letting people tell you what you're gonna do. Letting people push you around. How long do you think it's gonna last? How long are you gonna let it go on? How long are you gonna let them push you around?" As the crowd silenced, Morrison continued: "Maybe you love it. Maybe you like being pushed around. Maybe you love getting your face stuck in the shit." He then repeated, "You're all a bunch of slaves" a few times before asking them, "What are you gonna do about it?" over and over.

The show continued in similar fashion. Songs were started and sung about halfway through before Morrison either lost interest or went off on another tangent. During "Love Me Two Times" Morrison knelt in front of Robby Krieger while he played guitar. Whether Morrison was paying homage or simulating oral sex is just one of the great mysteries from the night. During a long and drawn out version of "When the Music's Over" the crowd sounds as if it's beginning to turn, grumbling and even booing at times.

Then, during what turned out to be the show's finale, "Light My Fire," Jim Morrison started prompting the audience yet again. He told them there were no rules. Whatever they wanted to do, do it. Morrison was handed a lamb at this point and he held it for a bit before saying, "I'd fuck her but she's too young." He then started inviting people to join the band on the rickety stage. When the police, who were acting as security, tried to put a stop to this he traded hats with one of them before tossing the police hat into the crowd. He then encouraged everyone to shed their clothes, saying, "Let's get naked" and, "Take your clothes off and love each other." He said he knew they didn't come for the music. They came for something else. He let that hang in the air for awhile like he was so apt to do before finally saying, "You want to see my cock, don't you?" Morrison was grabbing his crotch and fiddling with his zipper at this point. He'd taken off his shirt and was using it to cover his crotch while he fumbled with it. The audience was now in a frenzy. His bandmates were telling him not to do it. At this point the promoter rushed on stage to calm things down but Morrison kept screaming, "We're not leaving till everyone gets their rocks off." He pulled his shirt away for an instant then covered back up. "Did you see it?" he asked. Morrison either jumped off the stage or was pushed at this point. Concert goers followed him around the floor of the arena in a drunken conga line. With more and more people jumping on stage it began to teeter and the rest of the band made a hasty exit. Morrison was able to free himself from the maelstrom and actually wound up in a balcony, proudly surveying the mayhem he'd created.

After the show, backstage, there was no talk of legal issues. Morrison and the band signed autographs for some policemen and the next morning they all got on their scheduled flights to Jamaica.

*The Miami Herald* reviewed the concert writing: "The hypnotically erotic Morrison, flaunting the laws of obscenity, indecent exposure and incitement to riot, could only stir a minor mob scene toward the end of his Saturday night performance. . . Morrison appeared to masturbate in full view of his audience, screamed obscenities and exposed himself." By all accounts it was the *Herald* article that embarrassed the police and Miami officials into action. When the national media picked up the story the FBI got involved. On March 5th the Dade County Sheriff's Office issued an arrest warrant for Morrison, charging him with a single felony count and three misdemeanors. They would later add an additional charge, simulated oral copulation, for his stunt with Krieger. Morrison was told of the news while lying on the beach and he thought it was a practical joke. Once he was convinced of the veracity of the charges he took the defensive stand that art shouldn't be governed by normal rules of indecency. He turned himself in on April 3rd and was released on $5,000 bail. Morrison told a few people during this time that he had, in fact, exposed himself. When Pam asked him why he said, "I wanted to see what it looked like in the spotlight." He told another friend he thought he might have, "fished it out." Meanwhile, most of the band's upcoming shows were cancelled and radio, for the most part, stopped playing Doors' songs. There will always be speculation that the negative publicity from the Miami Incident cost them a spot at Woodstock.

Before the trial was set, Morrison was offered a plea bargain. If the Doors would play a free concert in Miami the charges would be dropped. Morrison turned down the deal and a trial took place in September of 1970. Despite the fact that no photographs clearly show Morrison's penis, and no witness could say definitively that they'd seen it, Morrison was convicted of two misdemeanor counts: indecent exposure and open profanity. He was sentenced to six months in prison. He appealed his sentence and the case was still awaiting a decision when he moved to Paris in March of 1971. When he died on July 3rd of that year, the case was still unresolved. Florida issued a posthumous pardon to Jim Morrison in 2011.

Whether or not Jim Morrison showed his penis to a concert audience on this date in 1969 will never be definitively known. What we do know is that throughout his short, incendiary career, Jim Morrison always pushed the boundaries as a frontman, redefining the role of lead singer forever. But his actions in Miami didn't just push the boundaries. They obliterated them. Morrison, with inspiration from an avant-garde theater group and one too many pre-show cocktails created a near riot in Miami and set in motion one of the great rock and roll mysteries.

## March 2nd

On this date in 1897, the Italian inventor Guglielmo Marconi filed a British patent under the title Improvements in Transmitting Electrical Impulses and Signals and in Apparatus There-for. Though many other inventors had been involved in the creation of "wireless telegraphy" Marconi's patent, and the work he and his team did in the subsequent years, would lead eventually to the birth of the radio as we know it.

There was a great deal of interest in radio waves in the physics community in the late 19th century. Heinrich Hertz proved that electric waves could be transmitted and received wirelessly (which is why radio frequencies are measured in hertz) and Nikola Tesla invented, among other things, an induction coil, which became known as the Tesla coil, and was widely used in early radios. While these and other scientists were fascinated by the physics involved, it seems no one understood the commercial significance of radio like Guglielmo Marconi. Whether or not he foresaw a day when 50,000 watt stations could broadcast to entire countries is debatable, but there is no doubt he saw radio as the next major step in communication and in doing so, his name will always be associated with the device. In 1912, for example, he opened the world's first factory for mass producing radios and was integral in making this technology more accessible to everyday people.

In 1920 the Westinghouse Electric Corporation, located in Pittsburgh, had the realization that they'd sell more radios if someone was broadcasting content worth listening to. They were the recipients of the first radio license in the U.S. with which they established KDKA. Their very first broadcast was November 2nd, 1920 during which they announced the results of the Harding-Cox presidential election (spoiler alert: Harding won in a landslide). Soon the airwaves were filled with news broadcasts, religious services, sporting events. and of course, music, sweet music. In 1922, WEAF, broadcasting out of Albany, New York, became the first station to sell air time to advertisers. They charged $9 for a 30 second spot. By the mid-twenties with the commercial potential of this new medium being realized, some stations combined to form networks and thus the creation of the National Broadcasting Company (NBC) which began regular broadcasting in 1926, with telephone links between New York and other

Eastern cities. Congress then passed the Radio Act of 1927 which created the Federal Radio Commission (the precursor to the Federal Communications Commission or FCC) in an attempt to regulate, and of course tax, this new form of communication.

The earliest music played on radio was often called "wireless concerts." Broadcasters would play a record on a phonograph (an invention also still in its infancy) and stick a microphone near its speaker. It was rudimentary but surely it worked, especially during the Great Depression. When some people can barely afford to feed their families, very few had the disposable income to purchase a record; but if you already owned a radio, you could tune in a station and listen to music. What started as mostly free-form broadcasts, soon became organized as stations became known for specific genres. If you liked country music or classical or jazz, you knew where to tune to in your market. And in the fifties, these stations helped popularize rock and roll music. A parent was probably able to stop their child from buying certain records, but when little junior sneaks a transistor radio (first sold in 1954) into their bedroom and listens late at night, who knows what devil music they'll be exposed to? There are countless stories of musicians who say they knew they wanted to play music the first time they heard Little Richard or Elvis Presley or Buddy Holly coming through the tiny little speaker of their transistor radio. One generation begot the next and isn't that always the way?

When television became the next big medium many people predicted it would lead to radio's demise. But of course it hasn't. Just like video didn't kill the radio star in the eighties. There is something magical about the portability of radio that will keep it alive forever, even if we receive our signals differently nowadays, with Wi-Fi and satellite replacing old fashioned radio waves in many modern instances. Music lovers will always be drawn to radio and most will react positively when one of their favorite songs comes on (even if they happen to own that song and could have played it anytime they wanted). There's something communal about the radio experience; while you listen alone, you also know there are thousands, maybe even millions tuned in to the same broadcast. Who among us hasn't caught themselves singing along to a song while sitting in traffic, only to look and see the driver one car over singing the same song? That's the magic of what we call broadcasting, where one sender connects with so many others. Marconi may not have envisioned Alan Freed or Wolfman Jack or Howard Stern but he did see the commercial potential of "transmitting electrical impulses and signals" and by filing his patent, on this day in 1897, he took a major step towards connecting so many people with similar tastes and passions.

On this date in 1951, Ike Turner's Kings of Rhythm, using the name Jackie Brenston and his Delta Cats, recorded a song called "Rocket 88." Musical historians have for years tried to trace the evolution of rock and roll and discover the Holy Grail, the First Rock and Roll Song. It's probably an impossible task but if you're going to roll up your sleeves and try to do it, "Rocket 88" has to at least be in the conversation.

Evolution is an inexact science. Whether it's complex living creatures, scientific discoveries or musical genres, nothing is ever created in a vacuum. There are small, incremental steps that finally evolve into what we see (or in this care, hear) today. It's why scientists will tell you, despite the Genesis story, there isn't really an Adam or Eve. And it's also why the debate can rage on forever about what song was the first rock and roll song. Musicians didn't just wake up one day and say, "Let's start a new musical genre." No, what became known as rock and roll developed from elements of the blues and country music (specifically rockabilly) and R&B and jazz and even gospel. Certainly the electric guitar (invented in 1931 but becoming more prevalent with musicians throughout the forties) helped and the accidental effect used in "Rocket 88" lent a new sound that would become popular. The rock and roll beat became a defining factor as well. It was slightly different from R&B with an accentuated back beat, or as Chuck Berry would sing, "It's got a back beat you can't lose it." All these elements combined and some cynics would say some elements had to be stripped away, namely the African American artist, for rock and roll to finally emerge. And when it did, as we all know, the world would never be the same again.

So let's head back to this date in 1951. Ike Turner, a musician from Mississippi, had formed a band called the Rhythm Kings which played covers of popular jukebox hits. He and the band stopped in to see B.B. King play in a club one night and they convinced him to let them take the stage with him for a bit (King's memory is that it was only Turner who joined him on stage). Impressed by what he heard, King recommended the band to Sam Phillips who, just the year before, had opened a recording studio and record label called Sun. Phillips invited the band up to Memphis for a recording session and they jumped at the chance.

The problem was, they didn't have an original song. They were a cover band. On the drive to Memphis, the band's saxophonist, Jackie Brenston, suggested a song about the new Oldsmobile 88. The car had come out in 1949 and was one of the first "muscle cars." Oldsmobile advertised it as having a V-8 "Rocket" engine, using the slogan, "Make a Date with a Rocket 88." Brenston composed the song on the drive, finishing before they all arrived at Sun Studios (Turner would say later he helped with the lyrics although he is uncredited) and since Brenston was going to sing lead as well, Turner agreed to switch their name for the recording session to Jackie Brenton & His Delta Cats.

And then, their amp fell off the back of their vehicle. Or maybe it didn't. Maybe it just got wet and the cone was damaged. There are differing reports probably because it wasn't that important at the time. Ask any musician, gear gets damaged all the time. And every incident isn't recorded for all perpetuity because it's going to introduce a brand new sound. One doesn't know the impact something like this is going to have till after the fact. So all we know today is their amp got damaged somehow and it's one of the reasons "Rocket 88" is considered so monumental in the evolution of rock and roll. When they arrived at Sun Studios on this day in 1951, they attempted to repair the cone by stuffing newspaper behind it to support it. When the band's guitarist Willie Kizart tried it out, his electric guitar had a distorted sound to it. One might call it fuzzy. Sam Phillips said he liked the sound and the band went ahead and recorded their brand new song. "Rocket 88" was released the following month and it went to #1 on the R&B chart. Brenston was presented with a brand new Oldsmobile 88 by General Motors to thank him for the publicity the song generated.

So is "Rocket 88" an early example of rock and roll or just an R&B song with a broken amp? Well, it certainly has some elements (some intentional and some not) that would put it in the rock and roll category. Besides the distorted guitar sound there's the song's theme. It's about a car (a popular subject of rock and roll songs) but there's also a double entendre which may or may not have been intentional, especially in the lyric: "Takin' my rocket on a long, hot run. Ooh, goin' out, oozin' and cruisin' and havin' fun."

The aftermath of the song is very "rock and roll" as well. Turner claims he made only $40 from it, having been cheated by, "some dude at the record company." In 1991, when the Rock and Roll Hall of Fame named "Rocket 88" as the first rock and roll song, Turner was in jail for cocaine possession so he couldn't accept the award. Brenston was no longer alive. He, like so many rock stars after him, fell victim to his own success. He blew through whatever money he made in the business, became an alcoholic and eventually passed away in 1979 at just 51 years of age.

Turner has said he doesn't think "Rocket 88" is even rock and roll, but that it paved the way for the new genre. His opinion is based on race and it's shared by many. Turner has said: "Sam Phillips got Dewey Phillips to play 'Rocket 88' on his program – and this is like the first black record to be played on a white radio station – and, man, all the white kids broke out to the record shops to buy it. So that's when Sam Phillips got the idea, 'Well, man, if I get me a white boy to sound like a black boy, then I got me a gold mine,' which is the truth. So, that's when he got Elvis and he got Jerry Lee Lewis and a bunch of other guys and so they named it rock and roll rather than R&B and so this is the reason I think rock and roll exists – not that 'Rocket 88' was the first one, but that was what caused the first one." Certainly the fact that Bill Haley recorded his own version of "Rocket 88" later in 1951 and some people point to this version as the first rock and roll song, lends some credence to Turner's argument. And the fact that Sam Phillips is on record as saying, "If I could find a white man who had the negro sound and the negro feel, I could make a billion dollars."

Whether or not it was the beginning of a whole new genre of music, or just one step along the path, and whether or not that amp fell from the car or just got wet, are arguments with no resolutions. All that aside, "Rocket 88" is an impressive song for having been written on the way to a band's first big recording session. It jumps, it swings, it rocks. And it celebrates a car (and maybe something else). So, heck yeah, it's rock and roll!

## March 4th

On this date in 1984, *This is Spinal Tap*, or as it was written in some places *This Is Spinal Tap*, had just been released to theaters. The movie, which is categorized as both a rockumentary and a mockumentary, was not very successful in its initial theatrical run but it received a second life on home video and cable and today is considered a cult classic and by far the funniest satirical look at rock bands ever produced.

In the late seventies, following the underground success of *Saturday Night Live*, a number of sketch comedy shows were attempted on network television. One of these was called *The T.V. Show* which was set to star Rob Reiner who at that point was known mostly for his role as Michael Stivic or "Meathead" on *All in the Family*. The show never got past the pilot stage but one of the skits that had been created for the pilot did. It was a performance video of a fictional hard rock band called Spinal Tap singing a song called "Rock and Roll Nightmare." Band members included Michael McKean, Christopher Guest and Harry Shearer who would go on to star in the movie. Reiner was going to be in the band but, as the story goes, he looked horrible in spandex so he was nixed from the scene. From the sidelines, he got to watch how the comedians stayed in character and ad-libbed while they were on the set and he knew this had some comedic potential. When his show wasn't picked up, he thought he'd take a stab at fleshing out the fictional band into a feature length film. And even though he'd yet to direct a movie by this point, he was able to secure some financing to write a script for the movie. Instead, he shot a twenty minute short utilizing the actors' improvisational skills and with that, he was able to land a movie deal.

*This is Spinal Tap* was shot the same way. Instead of a script, Reiner presented the cast with scenarios for each scene and encouraged them to ad-lib. Reiner, who played the documentarian, named his character Marty because he based it on Martin Scorsese in *The Last Waltz*, the movie that captured the Band's final concert. One of Reiner's keen hires was Peter Smokler, a veteran cinematographer who'd already shot a number of documentaries. Smokler's camera work gave *This is Spinal Tap* a real-life feel and though some complained about the "shaky camera work" most complimented the movie's home-made style or what the French call cinéma vérité. The French can make anything sound cool!

When all was said and done it took Reiner weeks to edit the hundreds of hours of film he'd captured. He claims to have had a seven hour version of the movie edited at one point, but was eventually able to whittle it down to the final, 82 minute version. Through the years, longer "director's cuts" have been released on home video but that seven hour version has yet to see the light of day. And because almost every bit of dialogue is improvised, Reiner wanted the entire cast to be listed as screenplay writers. The Writers' Guild opposed this though so only Reiner, McKean, Guest and Shearer got writing credit.

*This is Spinal Tap* was released on March 2nd, 1984 and initially, the movie failed to find its audience. Part of the problem was that the film was not promoted as a hoax. It seemed obvious to most, but some people were actually bewildered by it and Reiner says he was often asked why he would make a documentary about a band nobody had heard of. Ozzy Osbourne admits to being one of those who was fooled, although he'd say later he should have realized it was a spoof because, "They seemed quite tame compared to what we got up to." But other musicians loved it, mainly because the movie struck so close to home for them. Rock stars as far ranging as Eddie Van Halen, Robert Plant, Eddie Vedder, and Dee Snider have all said they love the movie and they watched it incessantly on their tour buses. Glenn Danzig has said when he saw the movie he commented, "This is my old band!" And Sting once told Rob Reiner: "I've seen the movie 50 times. I don't know whether to laugh or cry." Tom Waits didn't have that dilemma, he claims to have cried the first time he saw the movie because of its realism. U2's The Edge had a similar reaction. He has said, "The first time I ever saw it, I didn't laugh. I wept. I wept because I recognized so much and so many of those scenes." The Edge also claims the movie shows, "how easy it is to parody what we all do." And in the rock world, the movie is often used as a description. In 1992, Lars Ulrich was speaking about the Metallica/Guns 'N' Roses tour and he called it, "so Spinal Tap." And if you're in a band and someone says, "You're funnier than *Spinal Tap*," it's time to check your ego. "Shit sandwich," which, in the movie is used as a two-word review of Spinal Tap's *Shark Sandwich* LP, has also entered the lexicon as a phrase for something undesirable.

*This is Spinal Tap* is one of those movies many people have seen multiple times and have their favorite scenes. It might be the eighteen inch Stonehenge, or when the band gets lost trying to find the stage or when they get stopped at airport security. But whichever ones you pick, know that you're not alone. Besides just about every rock star in the world, critics have come around to the movie and view it all these decades later as a brilliant send-up of the rock world that places it in the upper echelons of all-time great comedies. In fact, *Time Out London* calls it the "best comedy film of all time." And many critics who use a one through ten numbered system to rank movies, have given *This is Spinal Tap* an eleven as an homage to the amplifier scene. If you haven't seen the movie recently (or ever) it's worth tracking down a copy today. Just remember, it's all a goof and shouldn't be taken seriously, even when the drummers spontaneously combust.

On this date in 1971, at Belfast's Ulster Hall, Led Zeppelin unveiled a new song that they'd been working on for the past few months. The song was long and featured numerous tempo changes and bassist John Paul Jones remembers the crowd being, "bored to tears." Fortunately this didn't deter the band from completing the song and including it on their next LP, *Led Zeppelin IV*, because today that song, "Stairway to Heaven," is considered by most music fans to be one of the most epic compositions in the annals of rock history. And it all began with very humble origins, in a tiny, remote cottage in the woods in Wales.

Led Zeppelin spent most of 1970 on the road, playing everywhere from Reykjavík, Iceland to Honolulu, Hawaii. At most of their live shows "Dazed and Confused" would become a long, improvised number featuring various solos including Jimmy Page playing his electric guitar with a violin bow. The song would begin even slower than on the record and slowly build, sometimes over the course of 45 minutes to a fast and ferocious ending.

When the band finally came off the road, Page and Robert Plant retired to a Welsh cottage called Bron-Yr-Aur for some well-deserved rest and relaxation. The cottage had no running water or electricity so it was the perfect place to escape for the Rock Gods who had taken over the world by this point. Page was so impressed with the place and its bucolic beauty he wrote an instrumental piece and named it "Bron-Yr-Aur." The song appeared on their sixth studio album *Physical Graffiti*.

While whiling away the time, the two musicians couldn't help but get started on new material. One of their early goals was to replace "Dazed and Confused" in their live shows. They wanted to compose a suite that would naturally incorporate multiple tempo changes. Page already had a number of guitar parts written and recorded on cassette tape and Plant got started composing lyrics. He has said the opening came to him one day in a flash, and he just started writing: "I was holding a pencil and paper, and for some reason I was in a very bad mood. Then all of a sudden my hand was writing out the words, 'There's a lady who's sure all that glitters is gold. And she's buying a stairway to heaven.' I just sat there and looked at the words and then I almost leapt out of my seat." Many of the images in the song came from where the two were staying, with references to rings of smoke through the trees and forests echoing with laughter (does anybody remember laughter?), as well as what Plant was reading at the time (namely Lewis Spence's *The Magic Arts in Celtic Britain*). The two presented the song to Jones and drummer John Bonham and the band began recording sections of it in late 1970. Jones has said: "Page and Plant would come back from the Welsh mountains with the guitar intro and verse. I literally heard it in front of a roaring fire in a country manor house! I picked up a bass recorder and played a run-down riff which gave us an intro, then I moved onto a piano for the next section, dubbing on the guitars." By November of 1970 Page was mentioning the song in interviews. He told one journalist: "You know how 'Dazed and Confused' and songs like that were broken into sections? Well, we want to try something new with the organ and acoustic guitar building up and building up, and then the electric part starts.... It might be a fifteen-minute track."

On this date in 1971, the song made its first appearance in a live Zeppelin show. If Jones' recollection is correct and that first crowd was unimpressed they were alone in their opinions. Even before the song was released, it started growing on crowds. After a show in Los Angeles, Page talked about the crowd's reaction to the song: "I'm not saying the whole audience gave us a standing ovation, but there was this sizable standing ovation there. And I thought: 'This is incredible, because no one's heard this number yet. This is the first time they're hearing it!' It obviously touched them, you know."

As *Led Zeppelin IV* neared completion the band knew how important "Stairway To Heaven" was going to be. They placed the song at the end of side one and printed the lyrics to "Stairway" (but no other song from the LP) on the inside sleeve. The song was too long to release as a single and the band refused to allow an edit so it never charted, but it did help drive album sales since anyone who wanted a copy had to buy the whole LP. *Zeppelin IV*, which not only contains "Stairway" but other Zeppelin classics like "Black Dog", "Rock and Roll" and "Going to California", and has sold almost 40 million copies worldwide. Page has said that for him: "'Stairway to Heaven' crystallized the essence of the band. It had everything there and showed the band at its best... as a band, as a unit. Not talking about solos or anything, it had everything there. ... It was a milestone for us. Every musician wants to do something of lasting quality, something which will hold up for a long time and I guess we did it with 'Stairway.'"

He needn't guess. "Stairway To Heaven" holds up all these years later as an epic rock song, filled with thrilling tempo changes, enchanted lyrics and just enough mysticism to make you, well, make you wonder, of course.


### March 6th

On this date in 1982, *Beauty and the Beat*, the debut album by the Go-Go's, climbed to the very top of the *Billboard* album chart. The band that no record label wanted to sign were now queens of the music world and though they were only looking to sell some records, they unwittingly helped create an entirely new genre of music. One that would dominate the decade of the eighties.

The Go-Go's came together in Los Angeles in the post-punk era of the late seventies and they were often viewed as a bit of a novelty act because of their all-female lineup. Their early musicianship didn't help the case. They weren't exactly maestros. But they forged their sound through gig after gig, improving their skills and forcing their audiences to take them seriously. A big step forward was when they brought in Gina Schock as their drummer. She not only gave the band a much more focused and powerful percussion sound but Schock's insistence that the band rehearse regularly helped them become a more cohesive unit. In 1980, the British ska band Madness invited the Go-Go's to England for a three-month tour. While there, the band recorded their first single "We Got the Beat" for British punk label Stiff Records (home of Elvis Costello and Devo). The song became a minor hit in some of the London and U.S. clubs that were changing format to what was being called new wave and when the Go-Go's returned home they figured their first single would help them land a record deal.

They were dead wrong. All girl groups, especially those doing harder rock or punk (as opposed to pop), were considered a novelty and there was no track record of success that labels could point to. The Runaways were probably the best comparison and while they are viewed in hindsight as being a groundbreaking and door-opening band, their lack of chart success didn't exactly have executives scouring the clubs for the next female punk band. In her memoir, the band's lead singer, Belinda Carlisle, wrote: "All the labels knew about us, and I am positive we would have been signed right away if we had had a guy or two in the band. Joe Smith, the head of Capitol Records at the time, personally told us that even though he adored us, he couldn't sign the Go-Go's because no female band had a track record worth investing in." Finally, the band signed with IRS Records which was sort of a consolation prize. In their *Rolling Stone* cover story of 1982 it was pointed out that, "IRS was where you went if you couldn't get a deal with a real label."

The label assigned veteran girl-group producers Richard Gottehrer and Rob Freeman to work with the band. Gottehrer had produced "My Boyfriend's Back" in 1963 for the Angels and had recently worked with Blondie. The band was flown to New York to record their debut but instead they hit the clubs. Hard. Though they completed their album in three weeks, Carlisle and the others remember that time for the partying and drinking they did. While the band's aim was to record a punk album (and they certainly adopted the right, we-don't-give-a-fuck attitude while in the Big Apple), Gottehrer and Freeman, with instructions from IRS, attempted to make them pop friendlier. The results made the executives at IRS extremely happy but the band was horrified when they heard the master tapes. Their punk edginess had been glossed over. Their anger and angst, all but gone. After a band meeting they decided to ask for the album to be remixed but IRS refused. When *Beauty and the Beat* was released to decent reviews and solid sales, the band changed their tune. Carlisle would say later, "As a wider audience responded positively to the album, all of us began to change our opinion and think, 'Oh, it's not that bad.'" The band's guitarist and main songwriter Charlotte Caffey admits, "Had we done it the way we originally wanted, I don't think we'd have the career we've had so far."

The sound that had been created for their debut, the push and pull between the rawness of punk and the smoothness of pop, the in-your-face attitude versus radio-friendly accessibility would become a defining feature of new wave. Other bands were certainly defining the genre around the same time as The Go Go's, or even earlier, from the Talking Heads to the aforementioned Blondie to the Cars, but no one could deny that the band's success, with an album that topped the charts for six weeks and produced two hit songs, helped pave the way for new wave to dominate the MTV generation.

On this date in 1987, the Beastie Boys' "(You Gotta) Fight for Your Right (to Party!)" peaked on the pop chart at #7. The song and its accompanying video are send-ups to a stereotype, that of the stupid, drunken, frat boy, but pretty soon the Beastie Boys became synonymous with that group. It's a reputation they fought hard to shake and they eventually did, going on to be one of the most successful hip hop bands ever.

Michael Diamond is a musician from New York City. His most successful early endeavor was a punk rock outfit called the Young Aborigines. That band went through some line-up changes, a name change to the Beastie Boys and then, an entire genre change as they shifted their focus from hard rock to hip hop. That shift came when the band produced a hip hop song called "Cooky Puss" which is based on a prank call they made to a Carvel store. When they played the song live they got a great response and they realized that musical tastes were changing. This was the early eighties and the door had been closed on the punk rock scene. Meanwhile rap was emerging and becoming more popular and the Beastie Boys experienced that first hand when they incorporated "Cooky Puss" into their setlist. They decided to start focusing more on rap and having a DJ on stage with them when they performed. One of the DJs they hired around this time was a young man named Rick Rubin.

Rubin, similar to the Beastie Boys, was a punk rock kid who was becoming more and more interested in hip hop. He not only DJed for the Beastie Boys but he was beginning to get into production as well. He founded a record label in 1983 from his dorm room at NYU that he called Def Jam Records. Russell Simmons soon joined up with him and the two began releasing some of the most important, early hip hop recordings. The Beastie Boys were still unsigned and so Rubin made them an offer and soon enough they were working on their debut album for Def Jam.

As work got underway for what would become *Licensed to Ill*, the Beastie Boys kept in touch with their hard rock past adding plenty of guitar work to their songs. Some called their debut "rap rock" and that's a fair title. The Beastie Boys stood out from many of the early hip hop acts because they weren't sampling dance or R&B songs as much as playing guitar licks and harder drums for their tracks. They even brought in glam rocker Kerry King, he of Slayer fame, to play guitar on "No Sleep till Brooklyn."

When they came up with "(You Gotta) Fight for Your Right (to Party!)" they were tapping back into "Cooky Puss," a song that was really a joke. "Fight" was similar. It was such an over-the-top goof that surely everyone would hear it as a send up, right? No one could possibly listen to the song and think, "This is the Beastie Boys." If that's what the Boys thought they couldn't have been more wrong. As the song raced up the charts, and its accompanying video got tons of plays on MTV, the reputation of the Beastie Boys became synonymous with "those guys." They were the rude, drunken partying dudes from the video, spiking the punch and starting the food fight. And as Mike D has lamented, "There were tons of guys singing along to 'Fight for Your Right' who were oblivious to the fact it was a total goof on them."

Goof or not, the song blew up. And rightfully so. From it's opening guitar chord and "kick it!" to it's scream-alongable chorus, "Fight for Your Right" is every bit an eighties classic party song. Whether or not the public got the joke, they got the song. Big time. After four singles that failed to crack the Top 40, "(You Gotta) Fight for Your Right (to Party!)" made it all the way to #7 on this date in 1987. This same chart week *Licensed to Ill* became the first hip hop album to hit #1 on the LP chart.

The Beastie Boys were always going to have a tough time establishing credibility. They were, after all, three white guys trying to make it in rap. And it was important to them not to be seen as poseurs or just another white act committing cultural appropriation. With the success of "Fight," that battle got even tougher. But the Beastie Boys proved themselves over their long and successful career that they weren't just three frat boys singing about partying. They were groundbreaking artists who just happened to choose hip hop as their genre of choice.


## March 8th

On this date in 1993, a previously unknown artist named Beck released his second single on the independent record label, Bong Load Custom Records. Unlike his first single "MTV Makes Me Want To Smoke Crack" (released on the same label) "Loser" began getting radio play on some college and modern rock stations which was amazing considering that Bong Load had no promotional arm to speak of. The song's popularity grew to the point that Beck was offered a record deal (with Geffen Records-subsidiary DGC Records). "Loser" was re-released almost a year later and pretty soon this unknown singer was the reluctant voice for the new "slacker generation."

Bek David Campbell was born in 1970 in Los Angeles, California to pretty eclectic parents; his father is a musician and his mother, a visual artist and former Andy Warhol superstar. His parents separated when he was just 10 and he stayed in L.A. with his mom. He credits the City of Angels for exposing him to such a diverse musical upbringing. He heard everything from rock to hip hop and pop to Latin and all of these elements and more would find their way into his future work. He got his first guitar at 16 and started playing folk tunes and country music in coffee houses and on city buses. He became used to playing to indifferent audiences and, in an effort to get noticed, he would often break into a spontaneous rap or make up ridiculous lyrics just to see if anyone was paying attention. He dropped out of high school and caught a cross-country bus, landing in New York City still shy of his 20th birthday. He fell in with the East

Village "anti-folk" crowd where his spontaneous and experimental lyrics were only encouraged and he became emboldened to push the envelope even more, writing surrealistic songs about pizza and how MTV made him smoke crack. He slept on friends' couches and the occasional street corner and though he never caught a break, he grew bolder artistically during his time in New York. When he returned to L.A. in 1991 (to avoid a second cold winter on the New York streets) he continued with his off-beat brand of entertainment, appearing on-stage at times in a Star Wars storm trooper mask or something equally unpredictable.

Tom Rothrock, who co-owned an independent record label named Bong Load Custom Records, saw Beck one night and became intrigued. He released "MTV Makes Me Want to Smoke Crack" and then introduced the young singer to Karl Stephenson, a record producer for Rap-A-Lot Records, telling Beck, "I know this guy who does hip hop beats and stuff."

The very first night Beck and Stephenson got together, "Loser" was created. Beck started off by playing some folk stuff which left Stephenson completely unimpressed. Stephenson then laid down a drum loop and broke out a sitar and sampled a few chords. He created the music bed while Beck scribbled some lyrics. At first Beck tried rapping but when Stephenson played it back Beck exclaimed that he was the worst rapper in the world and a loser. This led to Beck singing, "I'm a loser baby, so why don't you kill me." Stephenson and Beck looked at each other with raised eyebrows. They may have stumbled onto something. Six hours, and plenty of pizza and Doritos later, the two had a complete song. Beck has admitted that, though the lyrics came out of him spontaneously, he did tap into some imagery he'd used in the past. He'd say later: "I don't think I would have been able to go in and do 'Loser' in a six-hour shot without having been somewhat prepared. It was accidental, but it was something that I'd been working toward for a long time." Those lyrics, whether spontaneous or not, are brilliantly vague and artistically indistinct. While "with the plastic eyeballs, spray paint the vegetables, dog food stalls with the beefcake pantyhose" might not make any literal sense, when Beck raps them they somehow come to life. He created images (like a maggot on a sleeve) made statements about his place in life ("In the time of chimpanzees I was a monkey") and asked questions (like "Who's chokin' on the splinters?") that spoke to a generation just coming of age and wondering where their place was.

Bong Load released "Loser" on this date in 1993 with less than zero expectations. They pressed 500 copies on 12" vinyl and Beck went back to playing coffee houses. Then, some old fashioned word-of-mouth started to get the song played on college stations and modern rock radio. Stations in Seattle started playing it and when a station in New York requested a copy Bong Load told them they were sold-out. Beck, still bouncing between friends' couches and, at times, living in a storage shed, suddenly started getting offers from record labels. DGC signed him and "Loser" was re-released in January of 1994. It peaked at #10 in April and in no time the song became an anthem for Generation X which was becoming known as the slacker generation. It's a role Beck didn't want and rejected out of hand. "Slacker my ass," he would say later,

"I never had any slack. I was working a $4-an-hour job trying to stay alive. I mean, that slacker kind of stuff is for people who have the time to be depressed about everything."

To this day "Loser" stands as Beck's highest charting single but that doesn't mean he's been a one-hit wonder. He's continued to push the boundaries and defy any genre-definitions with each of his albums and his lyrics continue to make little literal sense, while creating unforgettable imagery. "Loser" introduced Beck to the world (and got him out of storage sheds) but in some ways, he'll always be the young kid eating pizza and scribbling lyrics just as many of his fans will always feel like monkeys in the time of chimpanzees.

## March 9th

On this date in 1997, Christopher Wallace, aka The Notorious B.I.G., was gunned down after leaving a party in Los Angeles. The shooting took place less than six months after Tupac Shakur's murder and though both crimes remain unsolved, they will forever be linked in the hearts and minds of music fans as the culmination of the senseless East Coast–West Coast hip hop rivalry. We may never know why both men were killed or who committed the murders, but we do know two incredibly talented artists were taken way too early.

Christoper Wallace was born in 1972 in Brooklyn, New York and raised by a single mom from the age of two. She worked two jobs to keep a roof over their heads and food on the table which left Wallace with a lot of unparented time. He was dealing drugs by 12 years old and his teenage rap sheet is littered with arrests for possession and weapons charges. But he also started rapping at a young age, entertaining people on the streets and performing with local groups. He started going by the name Biggie Smalls, a reference to a character in the 1975 film Let's Do It Again as well as his ballooning weight. He attended George Westinghouse Career and Technical Education High School in downtown Brooklyn at the same time future rap superstars DMX, Jay-Z and Busta Rhymes were all enrolled there. In 1992, he made a demo tape that found its way to Uptown Records A&R man (and record producer) Sean Combs who signed Wallace immediately. Soon after his signing Combs was fired from Uptown and established his own label, Bad Boy Records, with Wallace as one of his first artists.

Wallace changed his name yet again, this time to The Notorious B.I.G. and he gained his first national exposure in 1993 when he appeared on a remix of Mary J. Blige's "Real Love." The following year his debut single, "Juicy" became a big seller, hitting #3 on the rap chart, #14 on the R&B chart and getting as high as #27 on the pop chart. His debut LP, ominously titled Ready to Die, dropped in September of 1994 and it too rose quickly up the charts. Suddenly there was a new voice in hip hop and the music world loved his loose and easy flow as well as his brutally honest lyrics about his life and struggles. B.I.G. admitted openly in his songs to selling drugs and robbing and talked about the struggles of hustling on the streets of Brooklyn.

Wallace became friends with Tupac Shakur around the time he was exploding on the scene. The two were often compared by the music press and since Shakur had been around longer some accused Wallace of stealing his style. But initially at least, the two got along well and Wallace spent a significant amount of time on the West Coast hanging with Shakur and his crew.

Then suddenly, almost out of nowhere, a rivalry sprung up between rappers on the West Coast and rappers on the East Coast. In November of 1994, Shakur was recording in New York City and was robbed and shot five times in the lobby of the studio. Shakur accused Combs and Wallace which was the hip hop equivalent of throwing gasoline on a fire. Suddenly the rivalry became a feud and it would have a violent and deadly outcome. Shakur fanned the flames of the dispute with his 1996 song "Hit 'Em Up" in which he claimed to have slept with Wallace's wife ("That's why I fucked your bitch, you fat motherfucker") and called Wallace and his crew "bitches." Shakur became the victim of a drive-by shooting in September of 1996, just months after "Hit 'Em Up" was released. He lasted six days in a coma before finally passing away on September 13th, 1996. Though Wallace and his producers claimed he was in New York at the time of the shooting, there will always be speculation that he was involved somehow in Shakur's murder if not the actual gunman.

On March 7th, 1997, Wallace was in Los Angeles for the Soul Train Awards. When he appeared on stage he was met with a mixed reaction including some boos. The following night he attended a party and after he left, just after midnight on March 9th, he was gunned down in the streets of Los Angeles, eerily similar to the way Shakur had been killed not six months before.

Two weeks after his death, Wallace's second album, *Life After Death*, was released. The LP hit #1 on the album chart and its lead single, "Hypnotize," hit #1 on the pop chart, making Wallace the fifth artist to top the chart posthumously. "Mo Money Mo Problems," also from *Life After Death*, went to #1 as well.

Tupac Shakur and The Notorious B.I.G. will be forever linked. They were the dominant rappers of the nineties even though their lives and careers were cut senselessly short. Their murders, though committed brazenly out in the public, remain unsolved. And anytime an artist dies so young they will always be remembered for the lost potential of their future work. We'll never know what music either of them would have produced in the future but we will always be allowed to dream of it. And of course, each left the music world with a treasure trove of recordings to enjoy in perpetuity. In his first single Wallace told us his success was all a dream. A dream cut too short as far as hip hop fans were concerned. Way too short.

On this date in 1979, Gloria Gaynor's empowerment anthem "I Will Survive" hit #1 on the *Billboard* Hot 100 chart. The song knocked Rod Stewart's "Da Ya Think I'm Sexy" from the top and would enjoy a two week stay before surrendering to the Bee Gees' "Tragedy" only to regain the top spot for one more week in early April. Such was the state of pop music in 1979, disco's last year of chart dominance.

Gloria Gaynor was actually one of disco's first breakthrough stars when her 1974 version of "Never Can Say Goodbye" not only became the first #1 song on *Billboard*'s brand new dance chart but also climbed to #9 on the pop chart in January of 1975. At the time, a dance song hitting the Top 10 was still enough of an aberration that record people stood up and made note. "Never Can Say Goodbye" is often credited as being one of the first songs to "break" based on club exposure rather than radio plays which would quickly lead to the labels working with club DJs, setting up record pools and encouraging their feedback on what was getting people dancing. This was a seismic shift in the way music was promoted and it was a sign that the disco era would not just be a passing phase. Unfortunately for Gaynor that was her last hit for a number of years so, while disco was dominating the charts, she largely missed out on the wild ride.

Meanwhile, Dino Fekaris was a staff songwriter at Motown Records for seven years before being unceremoniously fired from the label. He was contemplating his fate one day, wondering if he still had a future in the music business when one of the songs he'd written for the band Rare Earth came on the television. That moment inspired him. He took it as a sign and he found himself jumping up and down on his bed screaming: "I'm going to make it. I'm going to be a songwriter. I will survive!"

Fekaris hooked up with another former Motown staffer named Freddie Perren and the two began composing songs. They wrote a song called "Reunited" and placed it with the duo Peaches and Herb. Then Fekaris told Perren his story about jumping up and down on his bed and the two knew instinctually that "I will survive" had great lyrical potential. They sat down and co-wrote the song, shifting the focus from surviving a job termination to a break-up, and when they were done, they both agreed it could be a hit. They then decided to let fate decide who'd record it. They'd offer the song to the next female singer they ran into. Soon after, Perren got a phone call from Polydor Records looking for someone to produce a record for Gloria Gaynor. Perren agreed to work with the singer on a cover version of "Substitute" which the Righteous Brothers had recorded a few years earlier. Before the session, Perren played Gaynor the demo he and Fekaris had put together for "I Will Survive" and she too heard the song's hit potential. They wound up recording both "Substitute" and "I Will Survive" in the same session.

Everyone involved knew in their hearts that "I Will Survive" was the better song so it was a shock to all parties when Polydor insisted on releasing "Substitute" as the A-side and "I Will Survive" as the B-side. The single was released and

"Substitute" peaked at just #107 on the pop chart in October on 1978. Then, a radio DJ in Boston named Jack King flipped the record and started playing "I Will Survive." King said later, "I couldn't believe they were burying this monster hit on the B-side. I played it and played it and my listeners went nuts!" Soon enough Polydor corrected their error and re-released the single with "I Will Survive" as the A-side. It made a steady climb up the chart and hit #1 on this date in 1979.

"I Will Survive" has survived for its universal message of endurance and empowerment. The song began with a man who was contemplating his future and became emboldened to push on. When it took shape, it became a song about overcoming a bad break-up. But it's become an anthem for women and the gay community as well, a paean, really, for anyone who wants to sing along and tell the world that they too grew strong and learned how to get along. It's the perfect song for any survivor.

## March 11th

On this date in 1972, Paul Simon's "Mother and Child Reunion," his first solo recording after breaking up the duo Simon and Garfunkel, was creeping up the charts. The song would make it as high as #4 on the pop chart and would show the world that, though the duo were through, Simon would continue producing fresh news sounds for decades to come. Just as importantly, the song introduced most of America to a musical genre they'd never heard before, unless they'd vacationed in Jamaica.

Paul Simon and Art Garfunkel grew up as grade school friends and, with their 1965 #1 hit "The Sound of Silence," became important and influential figures in the sixties' folk rock scene. 1970 was their most successful year, with the duo scoring the #1 album and the #1 song of the year (*Bridge Over Troubled Water*.) According to Paul Simon that über-success was one of the reasons he felt he had to go solo. In a 1972 *Rolling Stone* interview he admitted that creating a follow-up to that album would have been a daunting task. He told Jon Landau, "I'm delighted I didn't have to write a Simon and Garfunkel follow-up to *Bridge Over Troubled Water* which I think would have been an inevitable let down for people." He also wanted to spread his wings artistically, admitting to Landau, "I wanted to sing other types of songs that Simon and Garfunkel wouldn't do."

His first foray into a different sound came in Jamaica working with some reggae artists including Jimmy Cliff's band. They laid down the rhythm track for a song that Simon hadn't written lyrics for yet, which was odd for Simon; he usually wrote lyrics along with rhythm. When he returned to New York he did so with Jimmy Cliff's 1969 song "Vietnam" which is a tragic anti-war song in which a soldier writes a letter home saying he'll be home soon, only to die in battle before making it there. The man's mother receives a telegram telling her the news.

Simon thought of writing a song with similar emotions but with a less obvious setting. Around this time he went to a Chinese restaurant and saw a chicken and egg dish on the menu called A Mother and Child Reunion. He had his theme and he had his title and he was off and running.

For many Americans, "Mother and Child Reunion" was their first introduction to reggae music. A few months later Johnny Nash, another American who spent time in Jamaica and became influenced by the island's rhythms, produced a #1 hit with the reggae infused "I Can See Clearly Now." In the next few years Eric Clapton would cover Bob Marley's "I Shot the Sheriff" and soon Marley and others would spread their sound around the world. And of course for Simon, dipping his toes into the musical waters of Jamaica was only the beginning. If Paul Simon's solo career is marked by anything it's the diverse genres that he dabbles in and is influenced by. Whether it was the latin dance sound of 1980's "Late in the Evening," the South African Mbaqanga vibes on his incredible 1986 *Graceland* album or the Afro-Brazilian influences on his 1990 LP *The Rhythm of the Saints*, Simon has always sought to expand his musical horizons and challenge himself and his listeners to travel along. On this date in 1972, "Mother and Child Reunion" was climbing the charts and if you've followed Simon's career, he's literally guided you around the aural world. And it's been quite the ride.

## March 12th

On this date in 1988, an unknown singer named Rick Astley climbed to the top of the *Billboard* Hot 100 chart with his debut single "Never Gonna Give You Up." The song replaced "Father Figure" by George Michael and it would enjoy a two week stay before giving way to Michael Jackson's "Man in the Mirror." Most music fans, if they heard the song before seeing its video, would not have guessed that the owner of that powerful and rich baritone voice was a skinny, red-headed, white guy. In fact, even Astley's record company didn't believe it.

Astley started his career in the music business playing drums for a London-based band called FBI. When the band lost their lead singer Astley volunteered to take over that role. He was quickly discovered and signed by the production team of Stock Aitken Waterman (Mike Stock, Matt Aitken and Pete Waterman) who began working with the then 19 year old singer, grooming him to be a recording artist. Astley was living with Waterman during that time and one day Waterman had a long phone call with a woman he was dating. When he hung up the phone Astley said, "You're never gonna give her up." The line stuck with Waterman and the next time he sat down to write lyrics he used that phrase to build a song around.

The team initially recorded Astley singing "Never Gonna Give You Up" with some background harmonies. When they were done they weren't happy with the results so they scrapped the backing vocals and had Astley sing the song with a more urgent delivery. They liked this version and brought it to RCA Records where executives, too, were impressed. But when the producers showed them a photo of Astley, no one believed it. On tape, Astley, with his soulful voice and deep baritone sounded like a cross between Barry White and Luther Vandross, so how could he look like a cross between Ron Howard and Howdy Doody? Astley had to sing live for the executives before they were convinced.

"Never Gonna Give You Up" was released in late 1987 and began a slow and steady climb up the charts, hitting #1 on this date in 1988. Though it was Astley's only career chart-topper, he had a nice stretch of Top 10 hits over the next few years including "When I Fall in Love" and "Together Forever." But by the early nineties Astley had fallen from chart relativity and for all intents and purposes his significance as a pop star was through.

Until Rickrolling became a thing.

In 2007, an internet prank began spreading where people were tricked into clicking on a link they thought was something else, only to be sent to Youtube to see Rick Astley singing "Never Gonna Give You Up." The bait and switch prank stunt, which became known as Rickrolling, got so popular various clips of the video have hundreds of millions of views. And on April 1st, 2008, YouTube got in on the joke, replacing every featured clip on its front page to a Rickroll. Astley saw the humor in the joke, calling it, "bizarre and funny" and he even participated in it, making a surprise appearance, or what they called a Live Rickroll, at the Macy's Thanksgiving Day Parade in November of 2008.

Though the song today is viewed as a humorous goof, it was a very popular and serious song in the late eighties with Astley's voice booming from so many radios and TVs. Whether the look matches the voice or not doesn't matter. "Never Gonna Give You Up" is a soulful, timeless hit.

## March 13th

On this date in 1976, the Four Seasons' "December, 1963 (Oh, What a Night)" took over the #1 position on the *Billboard* Hot 100 chart, becoming the band's fourth and final chart-topper and giving them a rather historic distinction. While most other American bands had been relegated to the sidelines by the British Invasion of the sixties, the Four Seasons stayed relevant and successful. They are the only U.S. band that had #1 hits before the Beatles arrived in America, during the Fab Four's career and after they disbanded. That's an impressive feat for a band that, a decade earlier, couldn't land a gig at a bowling alley.

Francesco Stephen Castelluccio was born in Newark, New Jersey in 1934. As a teenager his amazingly powerful falsetto voice caught people's attention and he soon changed his name to Frankie Valli and began performing as a solo artist and in various bands. With the Four Lovers he released "You're the Apple of My

Eye" which made it to #62. Robert John Gaudio was born in the Bronx, New York in 1942 and raised in Bergenfield, New Jersey. He was just fifteen when, as a member of the Royal Teens, he wrote a song called "Short Shorts" which made it to #3 in 1958. Then came a fateful day when the Four Lovers shared a bill with the Royal Teens. Gaudio was amazed at the Four Lovers' lead singer and his incredible voice. Gaudio envisioned himself more of a songwriter than a performer anyway and here was a singer he desperately wanted to write for. Bob Gaudio soon left the Royal Teens to join forces with Frankie Valli. It's a partnership that would take the two to unprecedented levels of success.

Just not right away. With Gaudio in the fold the new lineup went looking for some work. One day they auditioned at a bowling alley lounge in New Jersey called Four Seasons. When they failed to land the job they figured they'd get something out of the experience so they changed their name to that of the lounge.

But it wasn't long before the combination of Gaudio's writing skills and Valli's voice struck gold. In the summer of 1962 the Four Seasons released their first single, "Sherry," which shot to #1 for five straight weeks. Their second single, "Big Girls Don't Cry" hit #1 in November of 1962, matching its predecessor's five weeks at the top. 1963's "Walk Like a Man" hit #1 as did 1964's "Rag Doll." Throughout the sixties the Four Season would be mainstays on the charts as well as pop radio with Top 10 hits like "Working My Way Back to You" and "Can't Take My Eyes Off of You."

By the mid-seventies the routine was pretty set for the band. When it was time to make a record Gaudio would present his compositions, they'd work them up in the studio and then, with Gaudio producing, they'd record the material. In 1975, when the band was working on material for their upcoming LP, *Who Loves You*, Gaudio presented them with a song called "December 5th, 1933" which basically celebrated the end of prohibition. Valli loved the melody but hated the lyrics so Gaudio rewrote the song from a man's perspective looking back on his first sexual experience. This being the mid-seventies, details had to be alluded to and left mysteriously vague so, "I was never gonna be the same, what a lady, what a night" is as graphic as the song gets (unless you consider, "I felt a rush like a rollin' ball of thunder, spinnin' my head around and taking my body under" to be ribald.) This, again, being the mid-seventies, with disco permeating the airwaves, Gaudio gave the song a very dance-floor-friendly vibe. While the Four Seasons were working on "Oh, What A Night," the Bee Gees were climbing the charts with their #1 hit "Jive Talkin.'" If Gaudio modeled his song after anything contemporaneously, surely it was "Jive Talkin'." Both songs share an almost identical tempo and their melody is driven by a single, dominant instrument (in "Jive's" case the guitar, in "Night's" case the piano). Vocal duties for "Oh, What a Night" were divvied up between drummer Gerry Polci, bassist Don Ciccone and Valli who just sings the bridge and chorus. The song was released in late December of 1975 and made a quick and steady climb up the charts. On this date in 1976, it became the band's fourth #1 single.

Bob Gaudio, who'd fallen in love with Frankie Valli's voice the moment he'd heard it, has written scores of hits for the man, both with the Four Seasons as well as after the band broke up and Valli pursued a solo career. Their story has been immortalized in the musical *Jersey Boys* which is an entertaining and historic look at this incredibly successful band. In 1990, the Four Seasons were inducted into the Rock and Roll Hall of Fame. Eight years later the bowling alley where they couldn't land a gig, but did find a name, was finally knocked down.

## March 14th

On this date in 1972, "Bang a Gong (Get It On)" by T. Rex was sitting at #10, its peak position on the *Billboard* Hot 100 chart. Though the band had plenty of hits in the U.K., "Bang a Gong" was their one and only Top 40 single in the U.S. and is widely considered not only their signature song, but one of the greatest contributions in the sub-genre of music that became known as glam rock.

Marc Feld was born in post-war London and like so many his age he grew up idolizing American rock and roll. He was given a guitar as an adolescent and became so engrossed in the instrument his grades suffered and eventually he was thrown out of school at just 15 years of age. A good looking young man, he attempted to make a living as a model for a while before throwing his full attention to his real passion, music. He changed his name a few times, once to Toby Tyler, then, using Bob Dylan as an inspiration, he came up with the surname Bolan ("Bo" for the beginning of Bob and "lan" for the end of Dylan). He admired the folk singer so much one of his first solo efforts was a cover of "Blowin' in the Wind." When Bolan's solo career failed to take off he decided to form a band, giving it the grandiose name of Tyrannosaurus Rex. They developed a strong following in the London area, including another struggling musician named David Bowie and, fortuitously, the Radio 1 DJ, John Peel. It was Peel who would help break the band locally by airing everything they released in heavy rotation.

Tyrannosaurus Rex had a great rock sound but they were incredible to look at as well. Bolan, with his delicate, almost effeminate, features, became a star of the underground music scene and when the local music press started focusing on his looks, he was motivated to emphasize them more and more. He started playing with the concept of androgyny in a time when rock stars were supposed to be über-masculine. He took to wearing feather boas on stage and then emphasizing those cheek bones that everyone was talking about with glitter. When his fans started showing up to shows dressed in similar fashion, the age of glam rock was underway. When their 1970 song, "Ride a White Swan," reached #2 in the U.K., they burst from the underground scene to national prominence as did their fashion sense.

When Bolan sat down to write "(Get It On) Bang a Gong" he had two inspirations: Chuck Berry's song "Little Queenie" and sex. Bolan wanted to channel Berry's song (which is a rocker about a young girl) and write one for himself about a "dirty, sweet" young girl. He claims his riff was taken from "Little Queenie" (although the two don't sound much alike) and he included Berry's line, "Meanwhile, I'm still thinking" in the coda. Whether or not he mimicked "Little Queenie," Bolan did create a song that oozes with sexuality, from its grinding beat to Bolan's breathy, one might say post-coital, delivery. And though the lyrics border on the obscure, with images of hubcap diamond star halos and teeth of the Hydra, there's little doubt what Bolan means when he sighs, "You're built like a car oh yeah." When Bolan first played the song for Peel he was shocked to find out the radio DJ didn't like it. Their disagreement over the song ended their once solid friendship and the two would never speak again.

The song was released as "(Get It On) Bang a Gong" in the U.K. but in the States, where a song by the jazz band Chase called "Get It On" had just been released, the title was flipped to "Bang a Gong (Get It On)." "Gong" was released in the U.S. in the summer of 1971 and made a slow climb up the charts, getting picked up by radio station after radio station. T-Rex (they had shortened their name by this point) was a relatively unknown band on this side of the pond so the song grew the old-fashioned way, through word of mouth and radio call-in requests. "Gong" peaked at #10 this week in 1972.

When most people in the U.S. think of glam rock they think of Bowie and the New York Dolls. Both are great examples of this flashy, fashion-forward genre which blurs the line between genders. But history tells us Bolan was the first to push the boundaries of what was acceptable for a frontman. And while glam rock may have been gone in about the same time it takes to vacuum up all that glitter, it left an indelible mark. Where before the only real paradigm for a rock singer was the black leather clad macho man, Bolan and his ilk helped create a world where Jagger was free to prance around the stage in tight football pants and KISS could make themselves up like cartoon heroes. America may only know Bolan and T. Rex for "Bang a Gong" but we'd be witnessing the ripple effects of his boa and glitter forever.

Unfortunately for Marc Bolan he wasn't around to witness much of that. He met an early, and some might say ironic, death. Marc Bolan had grown up with an irrational fear of car accidents. And though many of his songs features images of automobiles, he had never even learned to drive. He just didn't trust himself behind the wheel. On September 16th, 1977, two weeks shy of his 30th birthday, his girlfriend Gloria Jones was driving him home after a night out. She lost control of the car, struck a fence and Bolan was killed instantly. The site of the crash remains a memorial to this day where fans will often visit and leave flowers. Whatever a "hubcap diamond star halo" is, those fans probably envision Bolan wearing one for eternity.

On this date in 2004, the Rock and Roll Hall of Fame held their 18th annual induction dinner at the Waldorf Astoria Hotel in New York City. It was a star-studded night for the music industry with an inductee list that included bands like Traffic, ZZ Top and the Dells as well as solo artists George Harrison, Jackson Brown, Bob Seger and Prince. And while the Hall of Fame dinners have become known for their all-star jam session finales this one may be the most famous of all time because it featured a guitar solo by a performer who is not well known as an all-time great ax man. That is, before this night. By the end of the dinner, as he strutted triumphantly off stage, no one would ever question his guitar skills again.

The format for the Rock and Roll Hall of Fame induction dinner has been solidified since the earliest years. In 1986 when the Hall inducted their first class they ended the ceremony with a jam session, allowing all the musicians in the room to get up and play. That first year it was a very spontaneous moment. Paul Shaffer was the musical director that night and he brought along plenty of extra instruments not knowing what would happen. As he said later, "We didn't want people to feel as if they had to sing for their supper, but we had brought in instruments just in case." As it turned out, asking musicians to jam isn't usually a burden, in fact keeping them from the stage is probably a harder task. In the next few years the jam session finale became an annual event to the point where it started to be planned and even rehearsed.

Such was the case as the Hall of Fame prepared for its 2004 induction dinner. Joel Gallen, who was producing that year's event, wanted to end the night with a tribute to George Harrison, who'd passed away a few years earlier, by playing his iconic song "While My Guitar Gently Weeps." Gallen said later, "My dream right from the start was, imagine if I can get everybody up onstage at the end of the night to do 'While My Guitar Gently Weeps,' and Prince comes out and does the guitar solos." He reached out to Prince who said he'd consider it. He wanted to listen to the song a few times and see if he could contribute. Prince's people followed up with Gallen a few weeks after to say that Prince was interested but he had concerns about who would own the footage of the performance. Prince had always been very controlling of his image and during his lifetime was famous for blocking videos of himself on the internet. Gallen assured him the footage was the property of the Hall of Fame and wouldn't be used without his consent. Prince was assured and agreed to participate.

The night before the induction ceremony a rehearsal was held. Gallen asked Prince to attend but he never got a firm commitment that he would. As the band convened on stage, suddenly Prince appeared with guitar in hand ready to rehearse. He said hello to Tom Petty and Jeff Lynne who were going to be part of the finale and then Steve Ferrone, Petty's drummer went over to introduce himself to Prince. Prince told him he knew who he was which delighted Ferrone. He thought it was probably because he had played on Chaka Kahn's version of "I Feel For You" but then as he walked away Prince started playing a solo from an

Average White Band song that Ferrone had written. He was impressed with Prince's knowledge and proudly thought, "He knows who I am!" The band eventually launched into a rehearsal of the song and as the first solo approached Marc Mann, who was a member of Lynn's Electric Light Orchestra and part of the band, started to play. Prince seemed ready to take the solo but he strummed along during Mann's solo instead. The same thing happened with the solo at the end of the song so for a while it seemed superfluous to have Prince involved. When they were finished with the run through Gallen directed the band to have Prince take the second solo. By this point it was late and Prince was ready to split. He assured the director that he was fine but they never did a full rehearsal to see what Prince could do with that second solo. Gallen simply trusted that Prince could pull it off.

The next night, things went as they usually do at the induction dinners. There were speeches and remembrances and each artist getting into the hall had a chance to play some of their music. All, except Harrison of course. He had passed away in 2001 so his son Dhani Harrison was there to accept his induction. Then it came time for the finale and the band launched into "While My Guitar Gently Weeps." As they'd done in rehearsal, Mann took the first solo and he played it perfectly. Virtually note for note in fact from what Eric Clapton had recorded for the song.

Then it was time for Prince's solo. On camera you can see Dhani look over smiling as if he's anxious to hear what Prince will play. Prince starts with a few long, soaring notes. There's nothing particularly skillful here yet but he was clearly just warming up. About 30 seconds into playing, while Petty continues to sing "Look at you all," Prince starts to wail. And his fingers start dancing. Gallen wisely has multiple cameras trained on Prince so we can see his solo from various angles. And in the cutaways we see the expressions on the other musicians' faces. Prince turns directly to face Petty at one point and the two make eye contact. We can't see Prince's expression but Petty smiles quickly while Dhani is grinning ear to ear, clearly loving the moment. Prince then falls backwards off the stage while still playing, a moment that Ferrone admits was startling, saying later, "everybody in the band freaked out, like, 'Oh my God, he's falling off the stage!'" But Prince had a handler standing by to catch his fall and push him back on stage. He never stops playing a note during this. It was a common move for Prince when playing live, stolen directly from the James Brown book of stage moves. Then, when Prince finishes his solo, before the band even starts the song's ending, he tosses his guitar in the air and struts off stage.

If Prince had set out to prove that night that he belonged with the guitar greats he did just that. Craig Inciardi, curator at the Rock and Roll Hall of Fame Museum, would say later: "I've seen every induction performance from '92 to the present. . . on a purely musical level, a technical level as far as musicianship, that performance seems like the most impressive one." Gallen would add, "As a rock guitar player, (Prince) can go toe to toe with anybody." Petty would summarize it saying: "He just burned it up. You could feel the electricity of 'Something really big's going down here.'"

During Prince's lifetime, the video was hard to find. It would pop up on Youtube from time to time but then just as quickly be shut down. Prince very famously employed a team of people to scour the internet looking for clips of him and his lawyers would quickly fire off cease and desist letters whenever something was discovered. But since Prince's untimely death in 2016, his estate has been a lot more lax about his image. These days if you search Youtube for "Prince in concert" you could spend the rest of the day watching footage of him. And of course, his Rock and Roll Hall of Fame performance is much more readily available. It's worth watching sometime to see how a true musical genius shows off his skills. No one but his biggest fans respected his guitar skills before this night in 2004. Afterwards, it was hard to find anyone that wouldn't put Prince on the Mount Rushmore of great guitarists.

## March 16th

On this date in 1968, Otis Redding's "(Sittin' On) The Dock of the Bay" began a bittersweet, four week run at #1 on the *Billboard* Hot 100 chart. Redding had toiled in the music business for a decade by this point, his opportunities often limited by his skin color. Yet he'd finally broken through to mainstream success and recorded his first chart-topper, only to have his life cut tragically short before the song was even finalized. "(Sittin' On) The Dock of the Bay" thus has the dubious distinction of being the first ever posthumous #1 song.

Otis Ray Redding, Jr. was born in 1941, the son of a sharecropper in still racially segregated Georgia. He left school at 15 to help his family financially, finding work as a well digger and gas station attendant. But a passion for music coursed through his veins and he idolized both Little Richard and Sam Cooke, hoping to someday achieve even a modicum of their success. While he was still a teenager, a Macon, Georgia DJ by the name of Hamp Swain organized a regular talent contest with a $5 weekly prize. The first time Redding entered he won. He came back the next week and won again. He'd go on to win the contest fifteen consecutive weeks and the local exposure helped him land singing jobs in various bands. He was soon writing his own songs and began touring what was known as the Chitlin' Circuit, a string of venues that were open to black entertainers during the era of racial segregation. It wasn't exactly the big time but Redding was making a living doing what he loved.

Redding's big break came when a friend of his was given the opportunity to audition for Stax Records. The friend didn't drive so Redding drove him to Memphis, Tennessee where the friend got to sing with Stax' house band, Booker T & the M.G.s. The audition proved fruitless and they wrapped up early but since there was still time in the session someone asked Redding if he'd like to give it a shot. He belted out a song he'd written called "These Arms of Mine" and he, not his friend, left that day with a recording contract.

Redding became known for his soulful, passionate, sometimes even somber delivery. A radio DJ dubbed him "Mr. Pitiful" which Redding promptly turned into a song. Though he certainly could turn up the tempo -- listen to his cover of the Rolling Stones' "(I Can't Get No) Satisfaction" or "I Can't Turn You Loose" if you doubt that -- and he could produce R&B that made you want to move -- he wrote "Respect" and had a Top 40 hit with it before Aretha Franklin turned it into a Female Anthem -- he is at his best when he is tapping into his fervent side and channeling all the sadness and despair of his upbringing. Redding's vocals are often as raw as an open wound.

In 1967 Redding was invited to California to play at the Monterrey Pop Festival and though history remembers these three days for Jimi Hendrix and Janis Joplin's breakout performances, Redding, too, made quite the impression and expanded his audience exponentially. After the festival he had a chance to play at the famous Fillmore in San Francisco and so for a while he was living on a houseboat across the bay in Sausalito. It's here that he came up with the melody for "(Sittin' On) The Dock of the Bay" as well as the lines about watching the ships roll in and leaving Georgia for the "Frisco Bay."

Back in Memphis towards the end of 1967, Redding started recording sessions for his next album. He showed the beginnings of "(Sittin' On) The Dock of the Bay" to his guitarist and producer Steve Cropper and they finished the chorus, two verses and a bridge. They recorded the song intending to add a third verse so Redding just whistled the melody in its place. On December 7th, 1967 Redding worked on the song in Memphis then took off for some appearances and shows. He headed to Cleveland on December 8th and 9th then flew from Cleveland to Madison, Wisconsin for a show the next day. But he wouldn't make it. The plane he was in crashed into a lake just outside of Madison and all but one occupant was killed. Redding was just 26 years old.

Cropper would finish producing the album, determined that his friend's final work would be released. When he got to "(Sittin' On) The Dock of the Bay" he considered fading out before the whistling but he decided to leave it in. He felt it fit the come-what-may attitude of the song. There's some irony in the fact that the last thing Otis Redding, a man who was so famous for his vocal delivery and lyrics, ever recorded was whistling.

"(Sittin' On) The Dock of the Bay" was released on January 8th, 1968, and, perhaps fueled by the tragedy of his untimely death, the song became a huge crossover hit. It went to #1 on this date in 1968 and would remain there for four consecutive weeks. The song is a beautiful ode to the healing powers of sitting around and relaxing (or chillaxing in today's lexicon.) Redding had spent his entire life moving, working, striving to achieve. But in his limited time in California he'd had the chance to relax, to sit and watch the ships. One can only hope he felt great pride in how far he'd come to that point and great hope in his future prospects. It's the type of introspective calm that can come over someone when they are, "Watching the tide roll away." Thankfully, for all of us, he immortalized the moment in song. And yeah, the whistling is a perfect ending to an incredible, albeit truncated, career.

On this date in 1978, in Limerick, Ireland, the Harp Lager Talent Contest took place with a grand prize of £500 (about $850) and an opportunity to record a demo for the record label CBS Ireland. Four teenagers who had just recently changed their name from the Hype to U2 took the top prize which not only provided them with their first studio experience but affirmed their talents and inspired them to keep rehearsing because maybe, just maybe, they had a future in the music industry.

In the fall of 1976 in Dublin, Ireland, a 14 year old named Larry Mullen posted a note on his school's bulletin board looking for musicians to join a band. Mullen chose the date and the location (his mum's kitchen) so technically he'd be the leader of the band. That is until a 15 year old named Paul Hewson showed up. Hewson, who would change his name later to Bono, was a year older and already had that frontman swagger. As Mullen would say later, "It was the Larry Mullen Band for about ten minutes. Then Bono walked in and blew any chance I had of being in charge."

The band started rehearsing covers and chose the name Feedback because it was the only technical term they knew (and they produced a lot it every time they turned on their amps). They started as a seven piece outfit but after three young men dropped out the lineup was down to four: Bono singing, Mullen on drums, David Evans on guitar (he would soon change his name to the Edge) and Adam Clayton on bass. They changed their name again to the Hype and began rehearsing every weekend and some days after school as well as playing the occasional school dance or bar gig, even though they weren't yet old enough to legally drink (yes, Ireland has a minimum drinking age). They'd change their name yet again to U2 because, as the story goes, when a friend proposed a few different names it was the one they disliked the least. Punk was all the rage in England in 1977 and U2 was inspired and even encouraged by bands like the Clash and the Buzzcocks. Those bands proved that musical proficiency was not exactly a prerequisite to making it big and U2 were among the scores of young bands on both sides of the pond who saw this as permission to bang away on their instruments and create music. Passion was more important than prowess, anger trumped ability, and U2, before they developed the aptitude, certainly channeled the right energy.

Limerick is on the opposite side of Ireland from Dublin, a few hours car ride away, but when the boys heard about the talent contest they knew they had to give it a shot. 36 different bands performed on March 16th, 1978 throughout different venues in Limerick. From those, eight were chosen as finalists to compete the following evening at the Savoy Cinema. U2 made it as a finalist, then on this date in 1978 they played a three song set and were voted the winners. One young musician from a competing band said, "We were all dumbfounded when they won, because truly, they were awful!" His band had played all cover songs while U2 had done three originals and he felt that made the difference. Whatever the reason, U2 were named the winners and the Edge would say later: "We couldn't believe it. I was completely shocked. We weren't of an age to go out partying as such but I don't think anyone slept that night." He would add, "It was just a great affirmation to win that competition."

The band worked with CBS Ireland and put out a three song EP (released solely in Ireland). Only a thousand copies were initially pressed and though it's been rereleased a few times the original vinyl is still a rarity and collector's piece. The band was touring Ireland regularly at this point, building a following pub-by-pub, playing an unapologetically brash mix of originals and covers. After circling the Emerald Isle a few times they returned to their home city of Dublin in February of 1980 where they played a sold-out show at a 2,000 seat arena. It was testament to how far they'd come in such a short time and it was also their next big break. An A&R man from Island Records was in attendance that night, having been sent over from England by the label to see what all the hype was about with this young Irish band. Within a month, U2 were signed to Island and by the fall of that year, just four years after Mullen had placed that sign on his school's bulletin board, U2's first international release, *Boy*, appeared in record stores.

The rest, as they say, is rock and roll history.

## March 18ᵗʰ

On this date 1979, Sister Sledge released "We Are Family." The song would peak at #2 on the *Billboard* Hot 100 chart, blocked for two consecutive weeks in June by Donna Summers' "Hot Stuff." It would go on to be one of the most iconic songs of the late disco era and it's still played at weddings and private parties -- wherever families are brought together to celebrate and get their share of the world's delights.

Sister Sledge was made up of four sisters: Debbie, Joni, Kim and Kathy Sledge, from Philadelphia, Pennsylvania. They began playing together in the early seventies, releasing their first single "Time Will Tell" in 1971 on a local music label called Money Back. They were then signed to ATCO (a subsidiary of Atlantic Records) and released their first LP, *Circle of Love*, in 1975. That album failed to chart in the U.S. but they found an audience in Europe with their debut and also their follow-up, *Together*. Atlantic Records believed in their hit potential so they hung on to the band and commissioned a third LP. They just knew they needed to find the sisters some better songs and a producer who could capitalize on their dance sound.

Meanwhile, Chic was scoring huge disco hits for Atlantic Records. "Dance, Dance, Dance (Yowsah, Yowsah, Yowsah)" had gone to #6 in 1977 and "Le Freak" had been a chart-topper the following year. Atlantic Records brought Nile Rodgers and Bernard Edwards, the creative duo behind Chic's success, in for a meeting and asked the two to write and produce some music for other bands on their label. Rodgers and Edwards were intrigued until the label executives started throwing out names like the Rolling Stones and Bette Midler. The two men were intimidated to say the least. Plus they saw it as a no-win situation. If they wrote and produced a song for an established act and it failed, they'd be seen as the kiss of death. Conversely, if the song became a hit, the band would probably get all the credit. So Rodgers and Edwards made a different suggestion. They proposed the label give them an unknown, struggling act. This way they could prove themselves and if the band broke, they'd get the credit. Atlantic Records President Jerry L. Greenberg liked the idea and suggested Sister Sledge. Rodgers and Edwards asked about their background. Greenberg described them as four sisters who were like birds of a feather. As he went on and on about them, Rodgers and Edwards took some notes. They then went back to the studio to write a song. They basically turned their notes into lyrics and before even meeting the band, based largely on Greenberg's description of the four sisters, Rodgers and Edwards penned "We Are Family."

When it came time to record the song, Rodgers and Edwards took a unique approach in an attempt to get some spontaneity from the singers. Kathy Sledge was chosen to sing lead and they didn't give her the lyrics ahead of time. Instead they gave her the next line in her headphones just before she was to sing it. The plan worked perfectly and after just one take everyone felt they'd nailed the song. "We Are Family" is probably one of the most famous songs sung in just one take.

Rodgers and Edwards were commissioned to write and produce an entire album for Sister Sledge. Of the eight songs on the LP, though "We Are Family" was the title track, "He's the Greatest Dancer" was chosen as the lead single. The song did well, hitting #1 on the R&B and Dance chart and #9 on the pop chart. "We Are Family" was then released on this date in 1979. It would peak at #2 in June, the same time the album was peaking at #3 on the LP chart. Months after the song had slid down the charts it remained in the forefront of pop culture as it became the theme song for that year's World Series champion Pittsburgh Pirates. For the team, the song represented their diverse backgrounds and how they'd come together, as a family, to play championship baseball. For others, the song has become an anthem that can be sung proudly about any similarity, whether it's familial or cultural or preferential. "We Are Family" has been sung millions of times by like groups and it always makes people feel connected and closer. It's an amazing paean for the ages and with it, Rodgers and Edwards did exactly what they'd hoped to do. They'd proven they could write and produce a hit for an unknown band.

On this date in 1962, Columbia Records released the self-titled debut album of a 21 year old artist they'd signed a few months earlier. Of the album's 13 tracks only two were originals. The album was mostly ignored by critics and the record buying public although years later, once he'd become the Voice Of A Generation, Bob Dylan's first album has been revisited by both parties and held in high regard. But at the time, in the halls of Columbia Records, the album, which the legendary John Hammond had spearheaded and produced was being whispered about as "Hammond's Folly."

Robert Allen Zimmerman was born on May 24th, 1941 in Duluth, Minnesota. His family moved to Hibbing, Minnesota when he was six which is where he'd spend the rest of his childhood. He fell in love with music early on and listened to everything: country, R&B and of course the earliest offerings of rock and roll. While attending Hibbing High School he formed a band called the Golden Chords which competed in a talent contest at the school one day. The principal was so disgusted at their rendition of Danny & the Juniors' "Rock and Roll Is Here to Stay" that he cut off their microphones. In 1959, using the name Elston Gunn, he performed with Bobby Vee. After graduating high school, he moved to Minneapolis to attend the University of Minnesota and this is where his focus turned from rock and roll to folk music. Looking back years later he would say that, with rock and roll, "the songs weren't serious or didn't reflect life in a realistic way. I knew that when I got into folk music, it was more of a serious type of thing. The songs are filled with more despair, more sadness, more triumph, more faith in the supernatural, much deeper feelings." He started performing in coffee houses around this time and introducing himself as Bob Dylan after reading some poetry by Dylan Thomas.

After just three semesters in college, Dylan dropped out, packed up his acoustic guitar and headed east. His musical idol, Woody Guthrie, was hospitalized in New York City around this time and Dylan was determined to meet him. Speaking about Guthrie later, Dylan called him "the true voice of the American spirit." Whether he suspected it or not, in just a few years people would be saying the same about the young man from the Mid-West.

Dylan arrived in New York City in the winter of 1961 and he did indeed get to visit with Guthrie a number of times, even bringing his guitar to the hospital and playing some of Guthrie's songs to the ailing artist. It's the folk music equivalent of Plato studying at the feet of Socrates or the single season when Joe DiMaggio and Mickey Mantle played together for the Yankees. To make these meetings even more poignant, Dylan played Guthrie some of his own originals in that hospital room, including a song he'd written for his idol, "Song To Woody," which name checked Guthrie's classic "Hard Travelin'" song with the final lines, "the very last thing that I'd want to do, is to say I've been hitting some hard traveling too." We don't know much about these meetings between the two but one piece of advice from teacher to student has been passed down through rock and roll legend. Guthrie reportedly told Dylan, "kid, don't worry about writing songs; work on your singing."

Besides visiting with Guthrie, Dylan fell in with the downtown folk scene and very quickly began to gain a following. In September of 1961, the New York Times printed an article by Robert Shelton titled, "Bob Dylan: A Distinctive Stylist" which called Dylan, among other things, "a bright new face in folk music," and, "both comedian and tragedian." Apparently Dylan hadn't heeded Guthrie's advice though because the article also says his "voice is anything but pretty." But the article helped Dylan gain attention and he was soon asked to play harmonica on an album folk singer Carolyn Hester was recording for Columbia Records. John Hammond, the resident folk guru at Columbia Records heard Dylan's work for Hester and soon encouraged the label to sign him. Bob Dylan's debut LP was released a little over a year from the time he first arrived in New York.

And it flopped. Or more accurately, it was ignored. Critics paid no attention nor did radio or the record buying public. To be sure, folk music wasn't exactly the most commercial genre to begin with, but Dylan's debut sold so poorly the joke around Columbia, playing off the old description of Alaska as "Seward's Folly" was that the album was "Hammond's Folly." Dylan and Hammond ignored the jibes and got quickly to work on a follow-up. It was that album, *The Freewheelin' Bob Dylan*, released in May of 1963, that put Dylan on the map. The album opens with "Blowin' in the Wind" and contains thirteen tracks, twelve of which were written or cowritten by Bob Dylan. Like his mentor, he was already taking on big issues like civil rights and the threat of war. Soon he was being called the Spokesman of a Generation and though he hated the title he never shirked from the responsibility that came along with it. Even when he "went electric" a few years later, Dylan never sang about the mundane things that turned him off about early rock and roll. In his paradigm, a song was meant to make a difference. His lyrics challenge and threaten and defy. And so what if he never did work on that singing. He became the Voice Of A Generation nonetheless.

**March 20ᵗʰ**

On this date in 1982, Joan Jett's "I Love Rock 'N Roll" climbed to #1 on the *Billboard* Hot 100 chart, ending the J. Geils Band's six week run at the top with their first and only #1, "Centerfold." "I Love Rock 'N Roll" would enjoy an incredible seven week stay at the top before relinquishing that spot to the "Theme from Chariots of Fire." "I Love Rock 'N Roll" had taken a long and arduous path to the top of the charts but once it got there it'll always be considered Jett's signature song and an unforgettable ode to the power of putting "another dime in the jukebox, baby."

"I Love Rock 'N Roll" was originally written in 1975 by Alan Merrill and Jake Hooker of the British band the Arrows. According to Merrill he had heard the

Rolling Stones' "It's Only Rock 'n Roll" and felt like Mick Jagger was almost apologizing for rock and roll. He wrote "I Love Rock 'N Roll" as a "knee-jerk" reaction to the Stones' song and his band recorded the track but their label didn't love it so it was released initially as a B-side. It wasn't till the wife of the owner of their record label heard the song and thought it was great that the single was re-released with the sides flipped. But it made no difference. Without an enthusiastic promotional effort behind the song it went nowhere. However, the Arrows did perform the song when they appeared on the U.K. television show *Pop 45* which landed them their own TV show that ran for fourteen weeks in England.

As fate would have it, the all female punk band, the Runaways, was touring England and their guitarist and singer Joan Jett happened to see the Arrows perform "I Love Rock 'N Roll" on their television show one day. She loved the song and encouraged her bandmates to record it but she was met with nothing but resistance. Still, her enthusiasm for the song never waned and as the Runaways dissolved in 1979 she recorded her own version of the song using ex-Sex Pistols' Paul Cook and Steve Jones as backing musicians. Jett had yet to land a major record label deal at this point so her first go at "I Love Rock 'N Roll" was released on Vertigo Records, landing again as a B-side where it was destined to remain in obscurity till a few rock radio stations started playing it. Suddenly Jett and her management were getting requests to release the song as a single but she felt she could record a better version of the song so she set out to re-record it.

Joan Jett placed an ad in the *LA Weekly* looking for, "three good men" for her backing band. She formed the Blackhearts and recorded an album (which did not include a re-recorded version of "I Love Rock 'N Roll") but since she still didn't have a record deal she self-released the album under the name Joan Jett and sold copies after her live appearances. Finally, through word of mouth, her song "Bad Reputation" started getting airplay and Jett was signed to a deal with Boardwalk Records, the label Neil Bogart established after selling Casablanca. Her first album was re-released using the name *Bad Reputation* and Jett was told to record a follow-up. This time around she included a new version of "I Love Rock 'N Roll" and the song was released as the lead single to the album of the same name. The single dropped on January 20th, 1982 and rose quickly up the charts, hitting #1 on this date that same year.

"I Love Rock 'N Roll" is an ode to the timeless simplicity of rock and roll with images of jukeboxes and "singing that same old song." The song had twice been relegated to B-side-status and now, after an incredible seven year journey during which the song kept defying the odds, it was one of the biggest songs of the year.

On this date in 1965, the Beatles were enjoying the view from the top of the charts with their song "Eight Days a Week." It was a view the Fab Four were used to by this point. "Eight Days a Week" was their eighth U.S. #1 and it would be their first of four trips to the top of the charts in 1965.

The songwriting combination of John Lennon and Paul McCartney is legendary for their artistry as well as their success. And while both men are seen as important voices throughout the sixties, they often approached the craft of composing songs with workmanlike discipline and pushed themselves for practical, as well as creative reasons, especially by 1964, when the band had already tasted success and their lifestyles had expanded to include some of the finer things in life. McCartney admits to this readily and with no shame. He has said, "John would be getting an extension on his house or something, and the joke used to be, 'Okay! Today let's write a swimming pool.' It was great motivation." The two would schedule time together and sit with their ideas to flesh out songs. Often one would have an opening line or title and the other would contribute a verse or the bridge.

It was on the way to such a songwriting appointment that McCartney came up with the idea for "Eight Days A Week." Or at least that's one of the stories he's told about the song. The other credits Ringo Starr as the impetus to "Eight Days A Week." In one tale, McCartney is on his way to Lennon's for a writing session, sitting in the back of a limousine (again, the boys have come far in just a few years) and just to while away the time and make conversation he asks the chauffeur if he's been busy. When the driver replied that he's been working eight days a week, McCartney knew he had his next song. The other story is that "eight days a week" is just another of Ringo Starr's malapropisms. The Beatles' drummer was famous for saying odd, quirky things that kept the band in stitches (especially during their marijuana phase) and sometimes found their way in to their songs. "A hard day's night" is a perfect example. Starr would say that after a long show and it eventually became, not only a hit song, but the title of their first film. "Tomorrow Never Knows" is another example of what became known as Ringoisms that inspired Beatles' songs.

Whichever story you believe, McCartney and Lennon wrote the lyrics together (with McCartney contributing most of them) and then they brought the composition in to the studio to flesh it out. This is another sign of the band's burgeoning success. Studio time is expensive so when bands are starting out they work up songs completely (usually from playing them live for a while) before laying them down in a studio. But by 1964, the Beatles, like so many successful bands after them, were known to bring song ideas into the studio and work them up into full recordings. And because George Martin and his staff at Abbey Road were meticulous notetakers and documented every session, we know the band worked on "Eight Days A Week" on October 6th, 1964. They didn't have an opening riff for the song or even an introduction idea so they played with a few, including an a cappella opening. They finally scrapped that idea and came up with an opening guitar introduction then decided to do something unique, a fade-in to the beginning of the tune. This is the version that got released and would become famous for the introduction. The song is also unique for the Beatles because usually, whoever wrote the bulk of the song (Lennon or McCartney) would then sing lead on it. But though most of the lyrics are Paul's, John sings lead on "Eight Days A Week." And it's a song Lennon doesn't love. He would look back years later and say, "Eight Days A Week' was never a good song. We struggled to record it and struggled to make it into a song. It was [Paul's] initial effort, but I think we both worked on it. I'm not sure. But, it was lousy anyway." The Beatles were still touring at this point but curiously they never played the song live. Perhaps Lennon's lack of the enthusiasm kept it off their set lists.

But one man's lousy is another man's hit song and that's what "Eight Days a Week" became. It enjoyed a two week stay at #1, sandwiched between two classic Motown hits: "My Girl" by the Temptations and "Stop! In the Name of Love" by the Supremes.

1965 would be the last year of the Beatles' "love period." Almost every song they recorded in their early years, especially those that were released as singles, had something to do with a boy and a girl. There's a young innocence in songs like "She Loves You" and "I Want to Hold Your Hand" and "Eight Days a Week" but as the boys were maturing and becoming more worldly, so too was their songwriting. By the end of 1965 the band released *Rubber Soul* and already the themes of their songs were changing. Some Beatles' fans lament the change while others appreciate their later, more serious work. "Eight Days a Week" stands as one of their last songs during this early phase and even though John Lennon might not have appreciated it, millions of record buyers did.


**March 22ⁿᵈ**

On this date in 1980, Pink Floyd's "Another Brick in the Wall (Part II)" climbed to #1 on the *Billboard* Hot 100 chart. The song ended Queen's four week run at the top with their song "Crazy Little Thing Called Love" and it would enjoy its own four week stay before bowing out to Blondie's "Call Me." The song was a huge departure for Pink Floyd as the band spent most of their first decade seemingly avoiding any pop success and yet here they were with a hit song that had an undeniable disco beat to it. The band had even been loath to release singles, feeling their music was better appreciated by listening to their full albums, yet here was a single track from a quintessential concept album, sitting at the top of the charts. And they have the song's producer to thank for it.

When Pink Floyd convened in 1978 to start working on material for a new album, Roger Waters, who was the main creative force of the band by this point, presented the band with two themes for their next album. One was called *The Pros and Cons of Hitchhiking* and the other *Bricks In The Wall*. Waters played some demos he'd already worked on for each idea and the band selected the latter (*The Pros and Cons of Hitch Hiking* would become Waters' first solo album after leaving Pink Floyd a few years later).

As *Bricks In The Wall* took shape the title was shortened to simply *The Wall* and the band choose to work with a few producers in a number of different locations to complete the album. Bob Ezrin was one of those producers and when he heard the demo for "Another Brick in the Wall (Part II)" he knew it had hit potential if Waters would only write a second verse. Waters intended the song simply to be part of a medley including "Another Brick in the Wall (Part I)" and "The Happiest Days of Our Lives" so he'd only written an opening verse (with the hilarious double negative "we don't need no education") and a chorus that consisted of just one line ("all in all, you're just another brick in the wall.") Ezrin added the disco beat behind the song first, inspired by something he'd heard the band Chic playing, and when he did, he became even more convinced the song was a winner. He pleaded with Waters to write a second verse and bridge. According to Ezrin's memory, the band refused, saying, "well you're not bloody getting them. We don't do singles, so fuck you."

Ezrin didn't argue. But he went behind the band's back and tinkered with the song. He took one of Nick Mason's drum fills that had already been recorded and moved it to the chorus so he could repeat that one line a number of times. Then he took a page from his old playbook. A few years earlier, Ezrin had been working with Alice Cooper on his song "School's Out" and it was Ezrin's suggestion to add the choir of school children singing the chorus, which helped make it Cooper's highest charting song. Ezrin figured since "Brick" was already about children, it wouldn't be a stretch to try that trick again. He waited till the band flew to the U.S. to continue working on other parts of the album to record kids singing the one verse he had. He sent sound engineer Nick Griffiths to a school near Islington, England with the instruction to "get 24 tracks of kids singing this thing." Ezrin then added: "I want Cockney!"

Ezrin put the song together as he envisioned it and then played it for the band. When they heard it, they had to agree with their producer. Waters would say later, "It wasn't until I heard the 24-track tape he sent while we were working at Producer's Workshop in Los Angeles that I went, 'Wow, this is now a single.' Talk about shivers down the spine."

*The Wall* was released in November of 1979 and the band released "Another Brick in The Wall (Part II)" as a single a few weeks later. It was Pink Floyd's first single since 1975's "Have a Cigar." Both the album and the single started climbing their respective charts. The album went to #1 in January where it would sit into May. And on this date in 1980 "Brick" became the band's first (and to date only) chart-topper.

When the song broke big it was revealed that the choir of kids hadn't been paid for their contribution and it upset the teachers at the school that the children had sung an anti-education song. The band offered the choir free recording time and gave the school a monetary reward as well as a platinum record. All in all, this seemed to assuage everyone.

Despite the song's success, Waters hopes everyone knows the message is satirical. He is very pro-education but has horrible memories from his own time in school in the fifties, much of which is the topic of *The Wall*, and he meant "Brick" to be "a rebellion against errant government, against people who have power over you, who are wrong. Then it absolutely demanded that you rebel against that." Whether or not that's rewriting history is subjective but the thing we do know is Pink Floyd's song, especially once Ezrin put his creative spin on it, is an unforgettable slice of rock/disco that helped the band reach the top of the charts.

## March 23rd

On this date in 1990, "Just A Friend" by Biz Markie was sitting at #9 on the pop chart. It was the highest the song would get and the only time the rapper would crack the Top 40. But if you're going to be a One Hit Wonder, let it be as memorable as "Just A Friend," a song that, to this day, brings a smile to the face of just about anyone listening.

Marcel Theo Hall was born in 1964 in Little Egg Harbor, New Jersey. At some point his family moved to Long Island which is where he began rapping as a teenager. In 1988, using the stage name Biz Markie, he released his debut album *Goin' Off* which featured the underground rap hit "Pickin' Boogers." It's fair to say, even early on, Markie viewed rap as a vehicle for entertainment and even humor. This was a prominent philosophy among many early rappers, even going back to the genre's first hit, "Rapper's Delight," which deals with the very important topic of going "over a friend's house to eat." Sure, there were more serious rappers early on and that branch of the genre would evolve in the next few years with conscious hip hop and gangsta rap, but there were, are, and always will be, rappers who use the medium for pure entertainment purposes. One listen to Markie's earliest offerings like "Make the Music with Your Mouth, Biz" and "Pickin' Boogers" and it's obvious which side of the rap fence Markie was proudly on.

For his follow-up album, *The Biz Never Sleeps,* Markie came up with the song "Just A Friend" using Freddie Scott's 1968 song "(You) Got What I Need" as a basis. Markie didn't sample the song, as many rappers did and continue to do, but rather he interpolated it, meaning he took the same chord structure used in Scott's song and had it played as the melody for "Just a Friend." He also sings the same hook as Scott, "You got what I need," albeit in a comically awful way. Famed Philadelphia songwriters and producers Kenny Gamble and Leon Hoff wrote the original "(You) Got What I Need" but when "Just A Friend" was released neither asked for credit so Marcel Hall is listed as the sole songwriter.

With the melody laid down and the chorus established, Markie then filled in the rest with a humorous rap about trying to pick up a female fan after a show who tells him she's got someone else but he's "just a friend." It's not till the end of the song when Markie sees her kissing her "friend" that he realizes his pursuit has been in vain. It's not earth-shattering, world-changing content, but the combination of Markie's flow, his funny storytelling and of course, that God-awful singing helped make the song a novelty hit. It peaked at #9 this week in 1990 and though Markie has never come close to matching the song's success he has parlayed an entire career from the recognition he received from his one hit.

Though Gamble and Hoff never made an issue about their song being "borrowed" by Markie, Gilbert O'Sullivan did. When Markie released his third LP which included the "Just a Friend" follow-up "Alone Again" he again helped himself to an existing song, this time using O'Sullivan's "Alone Again (Naturally.)" O'Sullivan filed a lawsuit and it's actually this case that set the precedent for all future rap songs to give credit for using samples or interpolations. Some people believe it's Vanilla Ice's issue with Queen and Bowie that straightened the matter out but remember, that case never went to trial because Ice simply added them as songwriters to avoid a legal case. The landmark ruling in the Grand Upright Music Ltd v Warner Bros Records Inc case stated that every sample needed to be cleared by, and credited to, the original artist. This meant that not only did rap artists need to share writing credit, they also had to seek prior permission before sampling an original work not in the public domain. Markie pulled his third LP and reissued it without "Alone Again" but sales were disappointing at best. His next album, the appropriately titled, *All Samples Cleared!* LP, continued Markie's downward trend in popularity. He was well on his way to being a One Hit Wonder.

But oh, that one hit. It's helped maintain a fairly successful career for the rapper. He's appeared in music videos, television shows and even in the movie *Men in Black II* where he plays an alien version of himself. Chris Rock had Biz Markie open for him on a comedy tour in 2008 and his one hit makes sporadic appearances in television shows and movies where again, he enjoys the full financial benefit since he is still listed as the sole songwriter.

Can you turn a single joke into an entire career? You can if it's as good as "Just A Friend." A song and an accompanying video that is self-effacing and memorably humorous enough to keep its creator working for decades to come. Give it a spin today. If it doesn't bring a smile to your face, as Markie would say, "Oh snap!"

On this date in 1977, Andreas Pavel filed a U.S. patent for a device he was calling a, "portable high-fidelity stereophonic reproduction system" with the nickname of "A Stereobelt." With today's technology we take portable audio (and even video) for granted, yet prior to Pavel's intention, and what controversially followed it (specifically, Sony's Walkman) the only way to make music portable was through a big boom box, therefore sharing it with everyone around you, or a tiny transistor which not only lacked audio quality, it only allowed you to listen to radio stations. What Pavel envisioned was a much more intimate experience, with the listener wearing headphones and, as his patent stated, experiencing, "a sensation of being surrounded by a three-dimensional field of lifelike sound events." It was a heady and trippy description for portable music but about what you'd expect from a German philosopher.

Pavel was born in Germany right after World War II and he studied philosophy in Berlin. He was a music lover and would often sit around with friends, listening to everything from Bach to Janis Joplin. He would often yearn to be able to take his stereo with him on his walks so he began tinkering with a cassette player to make it more portable and battery operated. He clearly remembers the day in February of 1972 when he'd completed the prototype of what he'd call the Stereobelt. He and his girlfriend were in Switzerland and they went for a walk, both wearing headphones, and he popped in a cassette with the song "Push Push" on it (a collaboration between the jazz flutist Herbie Mann and the blues-rock guitarist Duane Allman.) "I was in the woods in St. Moritz, in the mountains," he recalls. "Snow was falling down. I pressed the button, and suddenly we were floating. It was an incredible feeling, to realize that I now had the means to multiply the aesthetic potential of any situation." Very philosophical!

Obviously blown away by his invention's potential for enhancing people's lives, Pavel began approaching electronics companies. He was met with nothing but rejections. Grundig, Philips, Yamaha, ITT, they all turned him down. The way Pavel remembers it: "They all said they didn't think people would be so crazy as to run around with headphones; that this is just a gadget, a useless gadget of a crazy nut." Finally, Pavel wrote his own business plan and blueprint, ambitiously calling it "The Coming Audio Revolution." He filed patents in multiple countries, including the U..S. on this date in 1977. But with no funding behind him, Pavel lacked the means to mass produce his creation and find out for himself whether it was a useless gadget or the beginning of an audio revolution.

A year later, the co-founder of Sony, Maseru Ibuka, approached his R&D department and asked them to build him a portable, battery operated cassette player so he could listen to his operas on the trans-Pacific flights he often took. It didn't take many flights for Ibuka to realize his idea would be accepted by the mass-market and soon Sony was cranking out its first line of what they called

"The Walkman." On July 1st, 1979, the first Walkmans were sold in Japan and in June of 1980 they were introduced in the U.S.

That's when Pavel and Sony began a head-to-head legal battle that would drag on for decades. Pavel sought immediate relief. Whether Sony had copied his invention, or whether it truly was Ibuka's independent idea, has never been decided. But what is undeniable is that Pavel had the earliest patents and the Walkman was arguably close enough to his Stereo Belt to have stepped on some legal toes. At first Sony agreed to pay Pavel royalties, but only for certain units and only those sold in Germany. After a few years of negotiations and mounting legal bills, Pavel received a check for 150,000 Deutsche Mark (about $80,000) which represented about 1% of Sony's profits from sales in Germany. Meanwhile, the Walkman was being sold in record numbers around the world, and was being credited for changing the way consumers listened to music. It was, to steal Pavel's words, An Audio Revolution.

At the end of the eighties Pavel filed another lawsuit, this time in Great Britain, a country that had granted him a Stereo Belt patent and where Sony had been selling versions of its Walkman for almost a decade. Sony, as big corporations often do in these situations, counter-sued and bled Pavel dry with legal fees. By 1996, the case was dropped in England and Pavel owed more than $3 million to lawyers. The philosopher who had experienced the "sensation of being surrounded by a three-dimensional field of lifelike sound events" and who had wanted to share that experience with the world, was on the brink of bankruptcy. He took one last legal gamble, threatening Sony with lawsuits in every country he'd filed his initial patent, which of course included the U.S. Finally, in 2003, Sony blinked and they reached an out-of-court settlement. Though both parties agreed to confidentiality, rumors are the payment was over $10,000,000. By then though, the Walkman had faded from popularity, replaced, of course, by the iPod and other MP3 players. Friends of Pavel's encouraged him to seek similar recourse with Apple but he was finally done with the legal system, saying, rather philosophically, "Somebody becomes a lawsuit, he loses all interest in other things and deals only with the lawsuit." But Pavel denies that the legal battles consumed him completely. "Nobody ever said I was obsessed," he would explain. "I kept my other interests alive, in philosophy and music and literature. So, no, I'm not interested anymore in patents or legal fights or anything like that. I don't want to be reduced to the label of being the inventor of the Walkman."

It's a cruel twist of fate, when you think about it. An invention that began so idealistically, with snow falling in the woods and its creator listening to high-fidelity music while feeling he now "had the means to multiply the aesthetic potential of any situation" and something that has brought so much joy and escapism to so many millions, by allowing them to enjoy their own music while traveling or working or exercising, was fraught with so many legal wranglings for so many years. But in the end, the world got its freedom to listen on the go, and its inventor, though he waited years for it, became a rich man. And now you know who to thank the next time you stick your earbuds in and enjoy your favorite band. It's not Steve Jobs or Sony or anyone else. It was a German philosopher named Andreas Pavel who first dreamed of portable music and the ability to listen anywhere and anytime.

## March 25th

On this date in 1972, Deep Purple released one of the most iconic and influential albums in the annals of hard rock history, their sixth studio LP, *Machine Head*, which included their signature song, and one of the most recognizable riffs of all time, "Smoke on the Water." The song documents an amazing moment that the band witnessed, retelling the experience almost as a medieval minstrel would, which may not be coincidental considering how steeped in renaissance culture the band's guitarist (and creator of that iconic riff) was. Here's the legendary story of "Smoke on the Water":

Guitarist Ritchie Blackmore was a founding member of Deep Purple. He gave the band its name, which he came up with because the depression era jazz number "Deep Purple" was his grandmother's favorite song. The band released their debut album, *Shades of Deep Purple*, in July of 1968. Their cover version of Joe South's "Hush" brought the band instant success, reaching #4 on the *Billboard* Hot 100 chart and helping push their debut album to #24. An opening slot on Cream's final tour didn't hurt their exposure among hard rock fans. Over the next few years they built their reputation slowly and by releasing so much material in such a short time (six studio albums in their first three and a half years) they kept their growing fan base always expecting something new.

In December of 1971 Deep Purple found themselves in Switzerland with plans to record their next album at the Montreux Casino, which sits on Lake Geneva. Frank Zappa and his band the Mothers of Invention were playing a show at the casino and the next day Deep Purple was scheduled to record. But at the Zappa show, a fan shot a flare gun that started a fire. The casino had to be quickly evacuated and Deep Purple watched from their hotel across the street as the iconic building erupted in flames. They also noticed a layer of smoke settling over the lake. The band was relocated to the Grand Hotel where they used the Rolling Stones' mobile recording studio to complete their album.

Then, Ritchie Blackmore came up with a riff. It was a riff that has since become one of the most famous in rock history. He says he was inspired by a BBC program called Wives of Henry VIII. "The riff is done in fourths and fifths," he explained, "a medieval modal scale. It makes it appear more dark and foreboding. Not like today's pop music thirds." Blackmore is a fan of all things medieval so it's no surprise he'd be inspired by the era.

With the memorable opening done, the rest of the band wrote lyrics basically retelling the story of the fire and how they recorded the album using the Rolling Stones' mobile studio (calling it "the Rolling truck Stones thing" in the lyrics.)

Within no time they had completed what would become their signature song, "Smoke on the Water." The lyrics mention it all: Frank Zappa, some stupid kid with a flare gun burning the place to the ground and ending up at the Grand Hotel. And of course they included the visuals of smoke on the water (of Lake Geneva) and fire in the sky. The band set the events to lyrics using incredible imagery and they memorialized it forever.

When the song was done they played it for Claude Nob who is the founder of the Montreux Jazz Festival and was in attendance at the Zappa concert. Nob is credited with saving so many kids' lives that night by helping evacuate them (he's the "Funky Claude" mentioned in the lyrics, "running in and out, pulling kids out the ground.") When the band played the song for Nob they still weren't sure about including it on their upcoming album. Nob told them they were crazy and predicted it would be huge. They included "Smoke on the Water" on *Machine Head* mainly because of Nob's encouragement.

*Machine Head* made it all the way to #7 on the *Billboard* album chart and "Smoke on the Water" to #4 on the pop chart. Hard Rock was coming into its own in the early seventies and Deep Purple, along with early stalwarts like Led Zeppelin and Black Sabbath were helping to create a new genre that would soon become known as heavy metal. That "dark and foreboding" riff that Blackmore came up with would not only become one of the most identifiable openings to any rock song, but an early characteristic of heavy metal, a sub-genre of rock that often delved into dark and mysterious places. "Smoke on the Water," a song that literally helped launch a new genre of music, has a stupid kid with a flare gun to thank for its inception.

### March 26th

On this date in 1977, Hall & Oates' "Rich Girl" knocked Barbara Streisand's "Evergreen (Love Theme From A Star Is Born)" from the top of the *Billboard* Hot 100 chart. It was the duo's first of six career trips to the top of the charts. They'd enjoy a two week stay before bowing to ABBA's "Dancing Queen."

Darryl Hall and John Oates met under the most stressful of circumstances. In 1967 they both found themselves at the Adelphi Ballroom in Philadelphia, members of separate musical groups, competing in a band competition. But shots were fired in the ballroom and everyone fled for protection. A 21 year old Darryl Hall and a 19 year old John Oates found themselves hiding in the same service elevator. When things settled down and the two got to talking they discovered they had a common passion for soul and R&B music and when they sang together they immediately recognized the magic in their harmonies. The two moved into an apartment together and began singing as a duo. On the mailbox of their shared apartment they had written "Hall & Oates" and that soon became their moniker. They were signed to Atlantic Records and released their debut LP, *Whole Oates* in 1972. They first appeared on the U.S. charts the following year when their single "She's Gone" peaked at #60. In 1976 they had their biggest hit to date when "Sara Smile" cracked the Top 10.

Around this time Darryl Hall was dating a woman named Sara Allen (whose smile inspired their previous hit) who was still friends with an ex-boyfriend named Victor Walker. Walker's father was a wealthy man (owning multiple pancake houses and Kentucky Fried Chicken franchises) and Allen's stories of how spoiled Walker would act, knowing his father would always bail him out of trouble, amused Hall. One day he even witnessed it first hand. Walker visited Allen and Hall and was acting very strange, throwing, what one might call a hissy fit. The experience inspired Hall to sit down and write a song called "Rich Guy" with the chorus, "He can rely on his old man's money, he's a rich guy." But as he put the song together, Hall realized it would sound strange coming from a male singer so he changed the gender of the song's title character.

Scotty Edwards, whose bass playing provided the groove for many a disco hit around this time ("Hot Stuff", "Shake Your Groove Thing" and "I Will Survive") provided the bottom end for "Rich Girl" and, as usual, Hall and Oates' harmonies gave the song an undeniable hook. "Rich Girl" was released on January 22nd, 1977 and on this date it rose to #1.

Some years later, David Berkowitz, New York City's infamous mass murderer nicknamed The Son of Sam, claimed that "Rich Girl" inspired his murdering rampage. The claim cannot possibly be true seeing how his killing spree started before the song was released, but Darryl Hall was devastated by the news. Eventually, when Berkowitz's claim was disproven the duo was relieved and they used the experience as inspiration for a song called "Diddy Doo Wop (I Hear the Voices)" which includes the line "Charlie liked the Beatles. Sammy liked Rich Girl" (referring to Charles Manson's love of the Beatles' song "Helter Skelter").

By all accounts Victor Walker got over his spoiled brat phase. Along with his brother he went on to manage his family's restaurants after his dad retired. As for Hall & Oates, "Rich Girl" was just the start of their huge chart success. They've accumulated 29 Top 40 hits in their illustrious career, including 16 Top 10 singles and six #1s, making them one of the most successful duos of all time. And yet you have to wonder if they'd even gotten together had it not been for the shooting at that band competition all these years ago. Amazing how such a disharmonious event could bring the world such beautiful harmonies.

## March 27th

On this date in 1984, Billy Idol's "Rebel Yell" was sitting just outside the Top 40 at #46 on the *Billboard* Hot 100 chart. It was the highest the song would get although it's gone on to be one of Idol's signature songs and a highlight in his live shows.

When Billy Idol's London based punk band Generation X broke up, Idol moved to New York City to try to make it as a solo artist. He began working with Bill Aucoin, who had previously managed KISS and formed a musical partnership with guitarist Steve Stevens. He released an EP called *Don't Stop* in 1981 and then his eponymous debut album in the summer of 1982. Idol was very much in the right place at the right time as his punk rock fashion and shock of bleach blond hair were perfect eye-candy in the early days of MTV. Videos for his songs like "White Wedding" and "Mony Mony" were often in heavy rotation on the nascent music channel and he was a figurehead in what has becoming known as the "Second British Invasion" which was spurred on by so many artists and bands from England being played on MTV.

As work was about to get underway for his second LP, Idol found himself at a birthday party at Ronnie Wood's brownstone in New York City. Mick Jagger and Keith Richards were also in attendance. They were all swigging from bottles of whiskey and Idol found himself admiring the Confederate cavalry officer on the label and the name of the whiskey: Rebel Yell. He asked if they'd had the bottles custom made because he'd never heard of the brand but they told him no, it was just a Southern mash bourbon that they all enjoyed. Idol was so impressed by the name he asked them if they ever thought they'd use it for a song, explaining that he thought it would make a great title and he may even name his next album Rebel Yell. As Idol wrote in his autobiography *Dancing with Myself*: "I'm sure they couldn't have cared the slightest but up until that point I had no idea what I wanted to name the album we were about to record. Here, right in front of me, in the public domain at the very mouth of the Stones, I had my answer. Thanks lads. Now all I had to do was write the song."

Though he always had an interest in the U.S. Civil War, Idol realized straight away that the "rebel yell" in his song had to be a cry for love. As he explained in his autobiography, "ladies are the most powerful creatures in this world, and this would be an anthem to love between a man and a woman." He worked out lyrics about, "a little dancer that came dancin' to my door" and brought them to the studio where he and Stevens completed the song. Stevens then came up with the unique, ray-gun sounding guitar effect heard in the song and Idol soon had a title track and lead single for his next album.

With MTV such a valuable promotional vehicle for Idol, he had to make a killer video for "Rebel Yell." The clip he put together ticked off all the boxes. It's a performance video where Idol and Stevens and the rest of Idol's band are seen playing the song. Idol is in all his eighties post-punk glory, with a sleeveless, unbuttoned shirt to show off his biceps and abs, his blond hair spiked to the heavens and one leather-gloved hand. He sings, he snarls, he raises his fist to the camera. Meanwhile Stevens can be seen firing off his ray-gun guitar bursts through the heavy cloud from the obligatory smoke machines. Jeff Stein, who directed the video out in New Jersey, talked about the crowd of fans he'd had bussed out saying, "We had lots of beer and wine on the busses, which nowadays you could not do. Everyone was well soused. I put the hot looking girls with the big tits up front." MTV grabbed the video gluttonously and started playing it in heavy rotation.

Though "Rebel Yell" didn't quite crack the Top 40, the album's second single, "Eyes Without a Face" (another MTV favorite) made it to #4 and helped propel *Rebel Yell* to #6 on the album chart. Idol is just one of the artists who were omnipresent on MTV in its earliest years but nobody did it with more attitude than Billy Idol.

## March 28th

On this date in 1967, at A & R Studios in New York City, Van Morrison recorded "Brown Eyed Girl." Though it's a song he's not very fond of, many people consider it his signature song and it's only one of two Top 10 hits the Irish singer-songwriter has ever produced (1971's "Domino" is the other). And despite the chart success, according to Morrison, he's never seen a penny from "Brown Eyed Girl."

Van Morrison was a founding member of the Northern Irish rock band Them who are known for their garage rock classic "Gloria." After the band's breakup Morrison flew to New York at the urging of Bert Berns who owned Bangs Records and had produced a number of Them songs. Berns convinced Morrison that he could manage him to a huge solo career and Morrison hastily signed a contract with Berns. The deal would prove onerous and one-sided (like so many contracts between musicians and managers) and Morrison would spend years trying to get out from under it. But before things soured, Berns booked Morrison into the famed A & R Studios in Midtown Manhattan for a marathon two-day session in which Morrison was able to complete eight songs.

One of those songs was a composition that began as a song about an interracial couple named "Brown Skinned Girl." Berns thought the song had great commercial potential but its topic and title would get it banned from radio and therefore the song would never sell. Morrison agreed and after 22 takes, on this date in 1967, he completed "Brown Eyed Girl." Though they'd changed the title, Morrison's song still met with some resistance from most radio stations, until he edited the line in the third verse, "making love in the green grass" to a repeat of the line "laughin, and a-runnin," from the first verse to make it more radio-friendly. Imagine that for one second and put it in context to what is heard today on radio. "Making love in the green grass" was too risqué for radio at one point. Amazing!

With the help of the edit and the solid radio play that followed, "Brown Eyed Girl" became a hit throughout 1967's famous Summer of Love. The song eventually peaked at #10 in September of that year. In an attempt to capitalize on the song's popularity, Berns packaged everything Morrison had recorded in those two days in March and released an album called *Blowin' Your Mind* without Morrison's consent or even knowledge. Morrison hated everything about it, including the cover and title which tried to make Morrison seem like a psychedelic rocker. He has since said when he saw the album's cover, "I almost threw up."

The release of *Blowin' Your Mind* was the beginning of the end between Morrison and Berns but because of the horrible contract he had signed, Morrison claims he has never seen a penny of royalties from "Brown Eyed Girl" or sales of the album. Perhaps this experience sours his opinion of the song since he has called it a "throwaway" and once said, "I've got about 300 other songs I think are better than that." While it's certainly his prerogative to think so, most fans would disagree. "Brown Eyed Girl" is easily Van Morrison's most pop-accessible song and it's nearly impossible to hear those "sha la la's" and not want to sing along. Certainly Morrison has written deeper, more powerful or introspective songs, but nothing in his canon comes close to being as danceable and as upbeat as "Brown Eyed Girl" (ok, maybe "Wild Nights" comes close). The song has been featured in many films and regularly appears on any list of greatest pop songs. It's probably a testament to Morrison's talent that even though he never wanted to be a pop singer, the one time he tried, he created an all-time classic.


**March 29th**


On this date in 1973, the O'Jays' enthusiastic call for international love and unity, "Love Train" was enjoying its one week stay at the top of the pop chart. The song basically interrupted Roberta Flack's chart dominance with "Killing Me Softly with His Song" as "Love Train" peaked on March 24th, ending a four week stay at #1 for Flack, but would bow out on March 30th, surrendering to Flack who would enjoy one last week at #1. Despite only staying at the top of the charts for one week, "Love Train" is a quintessential example of the Philadelphia soul genre that was quickly evolving into what became known as disco. But unlike so many of the songs of the disco era that concerned themselves with nothing more than getting down and boogieing, "Love Train" took on a much more important topic, nothing short of world peace.

Kenny Gamble and Leon Huff, the famed production team known as Gamble & Huff, were at the forefront of the Philadelphia sound (sometimes called Philadelphia soul or Philly soul). They worked with bands such as MFSB, Harold Melvin & the Blue Notes and the O'Jays, helping to create this unique style of music that brought elements of soul and funk together but wrapped them in a lush, orchestral sound, often using strings and a vibraphone to make their Philly soul stand out. Gamble & Huff, along with the production team of McFadden & Whitehead and a number of others, created this sound that helped usher in the disco movement that would come to dominate the seventies.

According to Eddie Levert of the O'Jays, when the band convened in the studio to work on "Love Train" Gamble & Huff had the tempo and rhythm worked out but no lyrics. Kenny Gamble, thinking of the world around him at the time, with the Vietnam War still raging on and so many other social issues on the front pages, came up with the lyrics for "Love Train" in mere minutes. As soon as the band saw the lyrics they knew the song could be big. "By the time we started laying down the vocals," Levert has said, "we knew we had a hit." He even feels the song was divinely delivered, adding, "'Love Train' felt like destiny. It had such perfect, timeless lyrics that it was almost as if they'd come from God, and we had to deliver them to the people."

And deliver they did. The O'Jays sang the song with such passion and urgency their vocals jump off the record. They also recorded a video for the song, something almost unheard of in 1973, mainly because there was no obvious platform for a music video to be shown. It's a simple clip that captures the theme of the song, as the band and a number of children hold hands and have some fun in a park (interspersed with shots of a train).

Years later the O'Jays and their signature song would become news once again. During the 2016 Republican National Convention, at which Donald Trump received his party's nomination, "Love Train" was not only played but a version called "Trump Train" with reworked lyrics calling for everyone to get join hands and, "Start a Trump Train" made an appearance. Levert and original O'Jay Walter Williams were very public about their displeasure with Williams saying, "Our music, and most especially, 'Love Train' is about bringing people together, not building walls," and Levert going even further saying, "I don't agree, whatsoever, with Trump's politics to the point where I think he just may be the anti-Christ." Some people were quick to point out that the O'Jays hadn't objected when their song "For the Love of Money" was licensed and used as the theme for Donald Trump's television show *The Apprentice* (which of course put money in their pockets unlike the public playing of "Love Train" at the convention.) Of course at the time Mr. Trump was simply a reality television host and not on his way to being the most powerful man in the world.

"Love Train" certainly is a call for unity. It's a plea for people all over the world to join hands and start a love train. And while the thought may be naïve, it's ambitious at the same time. Vietnam eventually ended but unfortunately the world has yet to come together to start that proverbial love train. There is still too much unrest both nationally and internationally which is a shame. When we hear the O'Jays' call to action to put aside our differences and ride their love train, you have to wonder why it couldn't just be that easy.

On this date in 1963, the Chiffons, a previously unheard of group, took over the #1 spot on the *Billboard* Hot 100 chart with "He's So Fine." The song had been composed by a young man who loved music and viewed his passion as a way to get his family out of poverty and though he accomplished that goal with "He's So Fine" the story has a somewhat tragic ending.

Ronald Augustus Mack (Ronnie Mack or Rocco to his friends) was born in the Harlem section of New York City during the summer of 1940. He taught himself to play piano as a child and performed in a doo-wop band called the Marquis as a teenager. The Marquis were a unique group for the time because they featured a female lead singer. It is perhaps here that Mack fell in love with the female voice and realized how commercially successful it could be. It may also be Mack's love for his own mother. His father had died when he was still a child and Mack's mother worked night and day just to keep a roof over the family's head and food on the table. Mack's sister Dottie has said: "I can remember me and my brother and sisters looking out the window waiting to see our mother come home from cleaning someone's house. Sometimes her knees would be bleeding and that would hurt my brother so bad, because with my father being dead, he knew he was now the man of the family."

Mack dreamed of making enough money that he could alleviate his mother's financial burden and he saw music as a means to that end. When the Marquis broke up he continued writing songs. Mack scored some success with a great upbeat doo-wop number called "Puppy Love" (not the Paul Anka song) with Little Jimmy Rivers and the Tops, which he wrote when he was still a teenager. Then one day he heard about a singing trio from James Monroe High School. He went to hear them sing and they auditioned for him in the school's cafeteria. He was blown away by the three teenage girls (Judy Craig, Patricia Bennett, and Barbara Lee) but thought they could use one more strong voice so he recruited Sylvia Peterson who had sung in Little Jimmy Rivers and the Tops. Mack became the quartet's manager and started writing songs for them, including one called "He's So Fine." He used his connections to get the group some recording time with the singing group the Tokens (who had just scored a hit with "The Lion Sleeps Tonight") producing the session. Jay Siegel of the Tokens agreed to work with the Chiffons based strictly on Ronnie Mack and his songs. Siegel would say later: "He came up with a composition notebook with all these amazing songs in it. They had the most incredible lyrics; not intellectual lyrics, but just the things that people speak of in everyday language."

At the recording session the singers were using "do lang do lang" as a background to provide the harmony, like any doo-wop band would do. It was an engineer working on the session who suggested they start the song with that vocal line, thus creating one of the most famous sounds of the early sixties. When the session was over everyone involved knew they had a hit. Now it was just a matter of finding a label to release it. They started with Capitol Records (for whom the Tokens were house producers) but they rejected the track saying it was "too trite...too simple." Unconcerned, they brought the song to another label. Then another. And another. In all ten labels turned down "He's So Fine" and Ronnie Mack started to lose hope. He also started feeling ill but refused to see a doctor right away. He had a record to sell and more songs to write and a family to save from the brink of poverty.

Finally, in late 1962 a small label named Laurie Records heard the song and expressed immediate interest. According to Siegel, during a meeting in their offices, "They locked the doors and said, 'You're not getting out of here. We want that record.' Of course, we'd already been turned down by ten companies. Give us eighty cents and we'd have given you the record." Laurie released "He's So Fine" and it shot up the charts in the winter of 1963, beginning a four week stay at #1 on this date.

Ronnie Mack was feeling worse and worse but he was also celebrating his success. One day he called his mother and his sisters into the living room and told them he had a surprise for them. When they walked in the room he opened a suitcase full of money and dumped it on all of their heads. Ronnie Mack's mother would no longer need to work till her knees bled just to feed the family. But the euphoria was short-lived. Ronnie Mack eventually checked into a hospital and was diagnosed with Hodgkin's lymphoma. Before the year was out, he was dead at 23 years old.

Jay Siegel of the Tokens would say, if Mack had lived, "he would have been one of the most successful songwriters of the sixties." In his short life he helped created the Girl Group sound that would dominate the pop chart throughout the decade with bands such as the Ronettes and the Supremes following in the Chiffons' footsteps. But his goals were more humble, to pull his family out of poverty and his one big hit accomplished just that. "He's So Fine" not only put the Chiffons on the map in 1963 but it provided enough of an income for Mack's mother to finally put her feet up and relax. His sister would say later, "He had a dream and he never gave up on it." Even through his illness he did everything he could to insure that dream came true.

## March 31st

On this date in 1958, Chuck Berry released his semi-autobiographical song, "Johnny B Goode." Though this was not his first contribution to the nascent rock and roll sound (that honor goes to 1955's "Maybellene") nor his most successful single (unfortunately that honor goes to the penis-joke of a song "My Ding-a-Ling" which is Berry's only career #1) it is his most iconic song and one of the greatest early examples of the power of the electric guitar and how it could drive the melody and create a hook that is impossible to ignore.

Charles Edward Anderson Berry was born to a middle class family in late 1926 on Goode Avenue in St. Louis, Missouri. He was exposed to music early on attending church with his parents and he soon discovered he had a passion for it. But he also ran into trouble as a teenager and found himself in jail for committing armed robbery. He formed a singing group while serving his time that was so impressive the authorities allowed them to perform outside of the facility. He was released on his 21st birthday and determined to follow his dream of making it in music (and avoid recidivism).

Within a few years he was playing in local clubs in St. Louis and displaying his showmanship on guitar. And though he was not above lifting riffs from other players, such as T-Bone Walker, he developed a unique style and sound that set him apart from all the others. His first big break came in 1953 when he was asked to join the extraordinary piano player Johnnie Johnson's band. Johnson, like so many bands of the era, played blues and R&B to satisfy their black audiences and country and rockabilly to please the white folks. From this musical stew boiled the early makings of rock and roll which Johnson and Berry were very much at the forefront of -- if not creating, then certainly propagating. A great example of this is Berry's first single, 1955's "Maybellene" which was inspired by (if not copied from) Bob Willis' country song "Ida Red." If you listen to both back to back you can almost hear one genre evolve into another. That evolution didn't take place overnight, it grew from songs being played over and over in smoky bars and clubs, tweaked here and changed there to please an audience and create reaction. That's how music develops and it's important to remember. Like the human thumb, it didn't just pop into existence one day, it evolved through natural selection (or in music's case, popular reaction). It slowly became what it is today. We know this about our fingers and we know it about music as well. And thankfully the fossils are right there on old records that still jump out of our speakers.

"Maybellene" sold over a million copies and soon enough Chuck Berry had gone from guitarist in a band to frontman. His next big single, 1956's "Roll Over Beethoven," was a bold and brash statement about the power of rock and roll. Berry was throwing out the old musical forms ("Roll Over Beethoven and tell Tchaikovsky the news") and ushering in the new one ("I got the rockin' pneumonia, I need a shot of rhythm and blues") and with the song reaching #29 on the pop chart it's fair to say the message was received. Loud and clear.

Berry then set out to record a song he'd written and had been playing live for a few years, going back to his time in Johnnie Johnson's band. Though he'd put the name "Johnny" in the title for his musical mentor, the song was mostly about Berry, starting with the word "Goode." It's not a misspelling as much as a nod to the street he grew up on. And though the protagonist doesn't come from St. Louis but rather from a log cabin way back in the woods of Louisiana, Berry could indeed play his guitar as easy as others rang a bell. When he sang the song live he included the lyric, "People passing by they would stop and say, oh my that little colored boy could play" but in the studio he changed it to "country boy" to avoid getting banned on radio.

For the song's opening riff, Berry borrowed again. It's ironic that so many future musicians would cite Berry as a source of inspiration and even claim to have stolen from him (when Keith Richards inducted Chuck Berry into the Rock and Roll Hall of Fame he famously said, "I lifted every lick he ever played") yet Berry was guilty of the same musical thievery. For "Johnny B. Goode" it was Carl Hogan's opening to "Ain't That Just Like a Woman" by Louis Jordan. Berry took the riff almost note for note but since "Johnny B. Goode" became the bigger hit, he'll always be credited for creating it.

It would be hard to oversell Chuck Berry's importance to rock and roll. Almost to a man, guitarists call him an inspiration. Perhaps John Lennon said it best when he said, "If you tried to give rock and roll another name, you might call it Chuck Berry." And in 1977, his signature song received the ultimate honor. When NASA launched the Voyager spaceships, whose missions are to explore the outer reaches of our solar system and beyond, they included something called the Voyager Golden Records which contain songs from earth. Should other intelligent beings ever find either of these ships, they can hear what we humans have been up to. Right there, alongside classical music from Bach, Mozart and Beethoven sits Chuck Berry's "Johnny B. Goode." So if aliens are out there, they too can sing along, "Go Johnny go go go" like so many of us have done all these years.

APRIL

# April 1st

On this date in 2002, after a nearly twenty year investigation by rock journalist Ima Phulin, it was revealed that Ringo Starr was not only the creative force behind most of the Beatles' hits but had also helped steer pop music over the course of the last four decades.

Phulin became interested in this topic as a young journalist in 1980 when she happened upon a meeting between Starr and Robert Pittman at which, it seemed to Phulin, Starr was giving Pittman instructions on how to start a channel devoted strictly to playing music videos. A year later when MTV launched, with, you guessed it, Pittman as the CEO, Phulin was intrigued. She reached out to Ringo Starr's people who refused to comment, other than offering his standard, "Peace and Love. Peace and Love." Phulin was undeterred and like Woodward and Bernstein a decade before, she began an extensive investigation that became known as Starrgate.

Phulin was able to get her hands on some secret tapes from Abbey Road studios that revealed the whole story line about John Lennon and Paul McCartney being such legendary songwriters was a myth. Starr is heard on those tapes instructing his bandmates on songs as far ranging as "Hey Jude" and "Revolution." On one tape, when George Harrison sings, "while my guitar gently sobs," Starr screams at him that he'd gotten the lyric wrong. "It's 'weeps,' you stupid git," Starr can be heard yelling followed by Harrison's plaintive "Yes, sir." Phulin also discovered in her investigation that Starr had created a pen name for himself, "Lennon - McCartney," to make it look like John and Paul had written all those songs and not him. When Starr finally came clean, on this date in 2002, his simple explanation was, "I wanted those wankers to get a little bit of credit for my prolific geniusness."

But if you thought Starr's influence was through after he orchestrated the Beatles' breakup (by introducing Lennon to Yoko Ono), you'd be wrong. Phulin was able to uncover example after example of Starr changing the direction of rock and pop since the early seventies. It's Starr who handed Led Zeppelin the opening line, "there's a lady who's sure . . ." telling them, "write a song long enough for fans to get to the bathroom and back." And it's Starr who talked Gene Simmons and Paul Stanley into wearing makeup, explaining to them, "Your music sucks, you better come up with a distraction." And when disco started gaining popularity it was Ringo Starr who called Robert Stigwood and said, "You should make a movie about this new dance music."

The list goes on and on. After single handedly creating MTV, Starr moved his attention to technology, discovering a way to digitize sound and creating the compact disc. It was Starr who told Steve Jobs that an MP3 player would sell in the millions and, after helping Sean Parker and Shawn Fanning create Napster, he then wrote the code for iTunes. Phulin also uncovered receipts of flannel shirts that Starr had bought for Nirvana, telling them, "Don't cheer up" as well as Starr's original notes with the dance instruction for the Macarena.

When Phulin finally presented all of her evidence to the music world, Starr finally came clean. Pressed as to why, he admits: "The drummer is often seen as the least talented member of any ensemble. I didn't want to ruin that paradigm. The world wasn't ready for it. So I worked behind the scenes and let everyone else take the credit." Did the "luckiest man in show business" thing bother him? He admits it did, saying "especially when Michael Bolton broke big. I mean that arsehole has zero talent so if people were lumping us together, I was pissed." As for his plans for the future, in 2002 Starr said he'd just created a singing competition he was calling American Idol that was set to air later that year. And he was working with a young rapper named Kanye West who was suffering from low self esteem. Starr was trying to pump him up and get him to believe in himself. It's an experiment that has gone tragically wrong.

Today we honor Ringo Starr for the creative mastermind he is, and we tip our cap to Ima Phulin for her unparalleled investigative skills.

# April 1st (the real one)

On this date in 1976, the Waverly Theatre in New York City played a midnight showing of *The Rocky Horror Picture Show*. The movie had premiered in Los Angeles in September of 1975 and opened in a few other test markets but after excoriating reviews and little fan interest the movie never got a nationwide release. But it would soon go from failure to cult following and is today one of the longest running films as theaters throughout the country still offer midnight showings that draw a large, eclectic and outspoken following.

Richard O'Brien wrote a musical called *The Rocky Horror Show* which first appeared in London's West End theater district in 1973. The plot follows a newly engaged couple who stumble upon the home of a transvestite who is channeling his inner Dr. Frankenstein and creating his own animated creature, albeit a perfectly sculptured man who can satisfy the doctor's every desire. O'Brien used the B movies that he loved so much as inspiration and created a campy and fun musical that won the *Evening Standard* Theatre Awards (the British version of the Tony's) for Best Musical. The musical also opened in Los Angeles and New York and began to build a buzz among theater goers. Music producer Lou Adler saw the show in London and immediately made an offer to purchase the film rights and placed it with 20th Century Fox. The movie filmed in England with a mostly British cast but Fox insisted on Barry Bostwick and Susan Sarandon playing the engaged couple (Brad and Janet). A pre-Bat-Out-of-Hell Meatloaf, who had already been on stage in *Hair*, as well as the Los Angeles production of *Rocky Horror*, landed the roll of Eddie. Tim Curry, who had similar stage experience as Meatloaf, landed the role of Dr. Frank N. Furter. Richard O'Brien performed the role of Riff Raff, assistant to the doctor.

O'Brien had not only written the book of *Rocky Horror* but all the music and lyrics as well. It's for this reason that he is revered among *Rocky Horror* fans and as the midnight showings became more and more interactive, with audiences participating by shouting out in the theaters, whenever Riff Raff appeared on screen it was to thunderous applause. It was this audience participation that helped make *The Rocky Horror Picture Show* such a cult classic. The movie is awful. It's poorly produced and the acting is cringe-worthy at times. But the music is very good, specifically Meatloaf's big number, "Hot Patootie – Bless My Soul," and the follow along dance song "The Time Warp," and the more the midnight crowds called out to the characters on the screen the more entertaining the movie became. Soon enough the theater crowds were bringing water guns to spray during the rainstorm scene and toast to throw when Frank calls for a toast. And of course when the cast is dancing to "The Time Warp" the theater aisles became filled with moviegoers bringing their knees in tight.

There is no explanation for what becomes a cult phenomena. Sometimes something catches on with a segment of the general public and becomes more popular than anyone could predict. And impossible to recreate. Indeed in 1981 O'Brien co-wrote a follow-up movie called *Shock Treatment* which was a critical and commercial disappointment and never found a following despite many a midnight showing. Meanwhile, *The Rocky Horror Picture Show* still runs in certain cities every Saturday night at midnight and plays to packed houses that yell and scream at the screen and dance in the aisles. It's a tradition that began on this date in 1976 and it's still going strong a generation later, at the late night, double-feature, picture show.

## April 2nd

On this date in 1989, the Bangles were sitting at #1 on the *Billboard* Hot 100 chart with their beautiful ballad "Eternal Flame." The song had arrived the day before, knocking "The Living Years" by Mike and the Mechanics from that spot. "Eternal Flame" had a one week run at #1 before bowing out to Roxette's "The Look." The song that was inspired by a rock and roll king's gravesite and modeled after an all-time great group would be the Bangles last chart-topper.

The Bangles were a four piece pop-rock band from Los Angeles that, from their earliest days, channeled Beatlesque melodies. Their first hit was the Prince-penned "Manic Monday." There are various rumors about why Prince would offer such a great song to the Bangles when he was writing and producing music for so many other bands at the time. The one about Prince loving their debut album sounds most likely. The one about him wanting to seduce Susanna Hoffs is more interesting (and Prince-like). However, when the song ended up in the band's hands it went all the way to #2 in 1986 and became a launching pad for the Bangles. They were the perfect MTV band, four beautiful women who could play and sing. "Manic Monday" and "Walk Like An Egyptian" (which went to #1) propelled their second album, *Different Light*, to #2 on the LP chart. They scored another hit in 1987 with a cover of Paul Simon's "A Hazy Shade of Winter" which appeared on the *Less Than Zero* soundtrack and climbed all the way to #2.

As the band began preparing material for their next album they decided to work with the songwriting team of Billy Steinberg and Tom Kelly. The duo were hitmakers throughout the eighties with Madonna's "Like a Virgin" , Whitney Houston's "So Emotional" and Cyndi Lauper's "True Colors" on their resume (just to name a few). As they sat with the two songwriters discussing material the band told a story of a private tour they'd just had of Graceland. As Hoffs explains: "The day we were there we were taken out to the Garden of Memories, and there was this little box which was supposed to have a lit flame in it, an eternal flame. Actually, that day it was raining so the flame was not on." Whether the flame was lit that day or not, a spark had been ignited. Steinberg instantly said, "Oh, eternal flame is a good title for a song." Hoffs helped the two songwriters complete the lyrics which is a beautiful ballad in which the singer hopes she's found her true love. There's no certainty to the song, with vocals that ask, "Do you feel the same?" and "Am I only dreaming, or is this burning an eternal flame?" It's that vulnerability that the song's producer, Davitt Sigerson, hoped to tap into when he suggested that Hoffs sing the song nude. When she questioned the strategy he told her Olivia Newton-John had done the same thing for one of her biggest songs. Convinced, Hoffs stripped and sang "Eternal Flame" with the rest of the band contributing, what Steinberg calls, "Beatles meets the Byrds" type harmonies. He would say later, "The bridge to the song, or the middle eight as the British would say, the part that starts, 'say my name, sun shines through the rain,' that part in particular is very Beatlesque."

The harmonies weren't the only thing Beatlesque about "Eternal Flame." Its march up the charts was Fab-Four-worthy as well. But it also proved to be their last shining moment. Susanna Hoffs' desire for a solo career led to the band's demise. Though they reunited some years later they've never been able to capture the magic of their late eighties run. Which perhaps answers the question if this burning is an eternal flame.

## April 3rd

On this date in 2003, 50 Cent was enjoying an incredible ride sitting at the top of the charts. "In da Club" had risen to #1 on March 8th, knocking Jennifer Lopez' "All I Have" from that position. It would stay at #1 for nine consecutive weeks, finally giving way to "Get Busy" by Sean Paul on May 10th. The song is not only 50 Cent's most successful single but, due to it's opening line, "Go shorty, it's your birthday," "In da Club" has become a modern day version of "Happy Birthday," making appearances at parties whenever someone is celebrating their annual trip around the sun.

Curtis James Jackson III was born in 1975 in Jamaica, Queens. His mother was a drug dealer and was murdered when he was just eight years old. Within a few years, a 12 year old Jackson was dealing drugs himself. When he was fifteen he was involved in a shooting incident, taking nine bullets to the legs, arms and face. Shortly after, he decided to leave the drug life behind and focus on a career in music. Like so many aspiring musicians, he made some low budget, do-it-yourself demos. Run-D.M.C's Jam Master Jay heard 50 Cent and was impressed. He took him under his wing and mentored the teenager, teaching him much about music and writing. Jay produced an album for 50 Cent but it was never released.

50 Cent produced another mixtape in 2002, this one called *Guess Who's Back?* This one found its way to Eminem and he was extremely impressed by what he heard. Eminem flew 50 Cent to Los Angeles to meet Dr. Dre. The two signed him to a reported one million dollar deal and set out to produce his debut. Over the course of five days they worked on seven tracks with 50 Cent. One of those turned out to be "In da Club."

The instrumental track for "In da Club" (which, unlike so much in hip hop is not sampled or interpolated from a previous work) had been produced by Dr. Dre and Mike Elizondo for Eminem's hip hop group D-12 with the goal that they'd write lyrics, rap to it and include it in the upcoming movie *8 Mile*. But D-12 couldn't make anything out of the track so it was shelved till Dre started working with 50 Cent. As Elizondo tells the story, 50 Cent listened to the track a few times then sat down and scribbled the lyrics that became "In da Club" in practically no time. 50 Cent had already worked on some of the tracks for his upcoming album and they had a darker vibe so he wanted this song to be more positive. He calls it "a celebration of life" adding, "every day it's relevant all over 'cause every day is someone's birthday." He mentions his shooting but even that has a positive twist ("Been hit wit a few shells but I don't walk wit a limp") and he celebrates his new contract with the line "I got a mill out the deal and I'm still on the grind."

With the backing of Eminem and Dr. Dre, 50 Cent was perhaps the most hyped rapper ever to release a major label debut. "In da Club" dropped on January 7th of 2003 and started a quick climb up the charts, hitting #1 in just two months. 50 Cent's album, *Get Rich or Die Tryin'* debuted at #1, selling almost 900,000 copies in its first week. By the end of 2003 it was the best selling album of the year having moved over 12 million units. And 50 Cent, who'd survived nine bullets as a teenager, was now one of the biggest names in hip hop and all of music.

### April 4th

On this date in 1932, Clive Jay Davis was born to a middle class family in Brooklyn, New York. When he was still a teenager both of his parents passed away and he moved in with his married sister to avoid being put into foster care. The story of how this young man would go from near orphan to one of the most important men in popular music, earning the nickname "The Man with the Golden Ear," is quite an extraordinary one.

Clive Davis was a smart young man. Despite the hardship of his parents' untimely deaths he was able to attend NYU because his grades earned him a full scholarship. He graduated *magna cum laude* then received a full scholarship to Harvard Law School. He began practicing law in the late fifties with a small firm that happened to have CBS as a client. He did some work for CBS and they were extremely impressed with this sharp young man with street smarts. Before too long CBS hired Davis to be a part of their legal department and he very quickly worked his way up the ranks. By 1967 he'd been named president of the label and he very quickly began focusing on the newest acts in rock and folk music. He made a fateful trip that June, attending the Monterey Pop Festival in California where he was blown away by Janis Joplin's performance. He signed the singer and her band Big Brother and the Holding Company and helped guide them to world-wide fame. Davis would do the same over the next few years with acts like Santana, Chicago, Bruce Springsteen and Billy Joel, just to name a few. In 1971 he saw an unsigned band from Boston named Aerosmith and promptly offered them a record deal, a moment the band celebrated in their song "No Surprize" with the lyric: "then old Clive Davis said I'm surely gonna make us a star just the way you are."

In 1973 Davis was unceremoniously fired from his position at Columbia. The label claimed he was misappropriating funds, including using corporate money to pay for his son's bar mitzvah. Davis has denied the allegations and claims the label just wanted to get rid of him. But either way, the man who was well on his way to earning the nickname "The Man with the Golden Ear" would not be out of work for long. He founded his own label this time, called Arista, where he helped launch Barry Manilow's career as well as signing already established acts like Aretha Franklin and the Kinks. One of the attractions for these artists was Davis' burgeoning reputation as a label chief who allowed for creative freedom but also had an innate feeling for what would sell. Franklin is a great example of this. Her final years with Atlantic Records had seen a steady decline in record sales to the point where many of her final releases did not even chart. Under Davis' guidance she was back in the Top 40 with 1982's "Jump to It" then climbed into the Top 10 with 1985's "Freeway of Love" and "Who's Zoomin' Who." Similarly, Davis would help revitalize the careers of Dione Warwick, Patti Smith and many others. He also established label imprints like Arista Nashville with artists like Brad Paisley and Brooks & Dunn, LeFace Records with Babyface and L.A. Reid and, even though he admitted to "not getting rap," Bad Boy Records with Sean Combs.

Perhaps Clive Davis' most famous discovery was Whitney Houston. Davis saw her perform one night and he immediately recognized her incredible talents. Davis signed her to Arista where her eponymous debut album sold 20 million units. And his most famous reclamation project, no doubt, was Carlos Santana. The fiery guitarist, who Davis had signed to CBS back in the day, had fallen out of music relevancy by the mid-eighties and eventually even stopped recording and touring altogether. Davis not only signed him to Arista but conceived of a project that would pair Santana up with contemporary singers like Dave Matthews, Cee-Loo Green and most famously, Rob Thomas. The resulting LP, *Supernatural*, sold 30 million units and produced two #1 singles.

How could a Jewish lawyer from Brooklyn become one of the most famous and successful people in the music industry? He has nurtured so many artists and bands through the years and his knack for knowing what will connect with the public is uncanny. He has an ear, a golden ear, that is right way more than it is wrong. He foresees changing tastes and responds by signing artists, whether they are unheard of or had previously been tossed aside by others labels. He often helps those artists select the right songs, matches them with producers and then handpicks which songs should be released as singles. A 2017 documentary called, *Clive Davis, The Soundtrack of Our Lives*, details many of these stories and more. It is well worth checking out to fully understand the story behind the Man with the Golden Ear.

On this date in 1994, Nirvana's frontman Kurt Cobain committed suicide. Many musicians before him (and some since) have overdosed on drugs and when that happens some people call it a form of suicide. Cobain ended things much more definitively. He left a suicide note, barricaded himself in the greenhouse above his garage, pressed the barrel of the 20-gauge shotgun to his head and pulled the trigger. Cobain was 27 years old and left behind a wife and daughter not even two years old.

Kurt Cobain has been called "a spokesman for a generation" as he and his band Nirvana helped create the sound we'd come to call grunge. He came to embody and personify the traits of Gen Xers: apathetic slackers who viewed the world cynically. It's a generalization, of course, and Cobain hated it. He was uncomfortable with it and the more famous he became the more he sought to escape his role. Heroin was his main source of checking out and numerous times in his short life he overdosed on the drug. Cobain also suffered from chronic bronchitis and often experienced intense pain due to an undiagnosed chronic stomach condition. He self-medicated with marijuana, oxycodone and heroin to alleviate the pain. Though he attempted rehab a few times he failed each one, returning to using quickly.

Cobain married Courtney Love in 1992. Love was a fellow heroin user and something of an enabler and Cobain's drug usage became worse after their marriage.

By the winter of 1994, Cobain, gaunt and strung out, appeared to those around him to be suicidal. Love called the Seattle police on March 18th to report that her husband had locked himself in a room with a gun. When the police arrived they found Cobain with several guns and multiple bottles of pills. Though he insisted he wasn't suicidal Love planned an intervention. A week later ten friends confronted Cobain about his drug use but he became belligerent and stormed out of the room. His friends wore him down though and he agreed to enter a detox center. He checked himself in on March 30th but after two days he hopped a fence and left the facility. He was seen in and around Seattle on April 3rd and 4th and those that spotted him said later he seemed distant and depressed. Love had lost track of his whereabouts so she hired a private investigator to find her husband.

At some point on April 5th Cobain entered the greenhouse above his garage. He propped a stool against the door, barricading himself inside. He wrote a one page suicide note that he addressed to his imaginary childhood friend Boddah. He placed his wallet on the floor, open to his driver's license and then took some drugs. Later, the medical examiner said it was most likely in the afternoon of April 5th that Cobain pulled the trigger. It was hard to be exact because Cobain's body wasn't discovered till April 8th.

In his suicide note Cobain lamented that he could not find joy in his fame and fortune. He wrote: "When we're backstage and the lights go out and the manic roar of the crowds begins, it doesn't affect me the way in which it did for Freddie

Mercury, who seemed to love, relish in the love and adoration from the crowd which is something I totally admire and envy. . . Since the age of seven, I've become hateful towards all humans in general." He ended his note: "I'm too much of an erratic, moody baby! I don't have the passion anymore, and so remember, it's better to burn out than to fade away." In the PS he addressed his wife and daughter directly, writing: "Frances and Courtney, I'll be at your altar. Please keep going Courtney, for Frances. For her life, which will be so much happier without me."

There are some who whisper that Cobain was murdered but it's absurd to think so. There's not a stitch of evidence that points to anyone but Cobain being in that room not to mention pulling the trigger.

It's tragic whenever anyone dies so young and even worse when they leave a young child behind. But things seemed destined to end ugly for Cobain from his earliest days of fame and his death was seen by many as a fait accompli. And by killing himself at 27 years of age, Cobain joins that mythical group of musicians who have passed away at the same age. Jones, Joplin, Morrison, Hendrix and now Cobain. It's a dark list of unrealized potential that will sadden and frustrate music fans forever.

### April 6th

On this date in 1974, the Swedish band ABBA won the Eurovision Song Contest. The band would quickly become worldwide superstars and they've gone on to be one of the most successful international bands in history. And then, just as it seemed their fame was about to diminish, a hit musical introduced them to a whole new generation.

ABBA came together as a singing group in 1972 in Stockholm, Sweden. They were made up of two couples: Björn Ulvaeus who was married to Agnetha Fältskog and Benny Andersson, who was engaged to Anni-Frid Lyngstad (they too would eventually wed after the band had broken internationally). By taking the first four letters of their first names they formed the word ABBA which they chose as their name, often writing it with the first B backwards. They released their first song, "People Need Love," soon after forming and had instant success in Sweden as well making a quick appearance on the U.S. charts. They were already demonstrating the traits that would catapult them to worldwide success: infectious melodies, awesome harmonies and upbeat lyrics. Their debut album, *Ring Ring*, was released in 1973 in Scandinavia as well as a few other countries like Germany, Australia and South Africa and it furthered their growing reputation.

In 1974, ABBA entered the Melodifestivale, which is Sweden's annual music competition to determine the group they'll send to the Eurovision Song Contest. The Eurovision Song Contest is an international talent competition that dates back to 1956. Every European nation submits an original song which is performed on a live television broadcast and then voted on. ABBA submitted

"Waterloo" and they won the 1974 Melodifestivale sending them on to that year's Eurovision Song Contest which was held on this date in Brighton, England. In the 18 year history of the competition a Swedish band had never won Eurovision, but ABBA broke that streak, beating a tough field of artists that included Olivia Newton-John who competed for England. Most Eurovision Song Contest winners enjoy a modest bump in popularity after the contest but for ABBA, whose star was already on the rise, the competition helped thrust them into the stratosphere. "Waterloo" was released in the U.S. and went to #6 on the pop chart. A year later they had back-to-back Top 20 hits with "I Do, I Do, I Do, I Do, I Do" and "SOS." Then in 1976, with disco music dominating the pop chart and dance floors of America, ABBA released "Dancing Queen." Once again it was the combination of Anni-Frid Lyngstad and Agnetha Fältskog's incredibly harmonious vocals, a contagious melody and fantastic lyrics written by Benny Andersson and Björn Ulvaeus (with their manager Stig Anderson's help) that made the song a hit. It went to #1 in April of 1977, three years after the band's big Eurovision win.

The next seven years would see ABBA consistently scoring pop hits in the U.S. and elsewhere. "Take a Chance on Me" went to #3, "The Winner Takes It All" peaked at #8 and "When All Is Said and Done" became their final Top 40, hitting #27 in 1982. But by the early eighties the band that had begun with two happy couples was fraught with internal struggles. Björn Ulvaeus and Agnetha Fältskog separated in 1978 and divorced in 1980. Ulvaeus promptly married music journalist Lena Källersjösix just months after the divorce was finalized. As for Benny Andersson and Anni-Frid Lyngstad, they were engaged for nine years before getting married in October of 1978. After two years they separated and ultimately divorced. Fame and fortune had taken its toll on the two couples and by the time they began recording new material in 1982 it was clear the end was nigh. It was only fitting that their final single was titled "Thank You for the Music." By the mid-eighties the band hadn't released anything new in a while and though they publicly denied breaking up, the music world figured they'd heard the last of ABBA. And that was true for more than a decade.

In 1999 a jukebox musical called *Mamma Mia!* opened in the West End theater district of London. Jukebox musicals use previously released songs (often by the same artist or from the same genre) as the musical score, fitting them into the plot (as opposed to traditional musicals where songs are written for the show). *Mamma Mia!* tells the story of a wedding that is about to take place on a beautiful Greek island. Every song in the production was an old ABBA number, from the hits like "Dancing Queen" and "Winner Takes It All" to the lesser known songs like "Money, Money, Money" and "Lay All Your Love on Me." The genius of the story line is how it sets up each song so it seems like it was written specifically for the scene. *Mamma Mia!* enjoyed incredibly long runs in London and on Broadway and was eventually made into a major motion picture starring Meryl Streep and Pierce Brosnan. The show reintroduced ABBA's wonderfully upbeat catalogue of songs to an entirely new generation of fans who fell in love with the Swedish band just as the world had in the seventies.

On this date in 1969, the Stooges were working on material at the Hit Factory in New York City which included their now iconic song "I Wanna Be Your Dog." Though the song was largely ignored by radio and the record buying public, it has gone on to be cited as an inspiration for, not one, but two, musical genres that emerged in the following decade.

James Newell Osterberg was born in 1947 in Muskegon, Michigan. He played drums in high school in a band called the Iguanas which is how he came up with one half of his stage name: Iggy Pop. He got out from behind the kit when he formed the Psychedelic Stooges with brothers Ron Asheton (on guitar) and Scott Asheton (on drums) and their friend Dave Alexander (who played bass). Pop was an outrageous frontman and the Psychedelic Stooges became known for their avant-garde live shows which often featured Pop using a vacuum cleaner or kitchen blender to create a wall of sound while Asheton pounded away on a set of oil drums with a hammer. Pop is credited for inventing stage diving as he would often hurl himself into the crowd and the one time he did this bare-chested he wound up landing on the floor and smashing a glass underneath him. When he returned to the stage he was bleeding and the crowd went wild. Pop began incorporating this into his shows as well, cutting himself with a piece of glass or a razor and finishing the show covered in blood, much to the crowd's delight.

The Psychedelic Stooges eventually shortened their name to the Stooges and fellow Detroit rockers, the MC5, took notice of the band and often had them as an opening act. In 1968 Elektra Records sent their publicist Danny Fields to Michigan to check out the MC5 in hopes of signing them. Fields caught a show where the Stooges were opening and he wound up offering both bands a contract. He would go on to manage the Stooges. Fields arranged for the band to come to New York to record their first album and, through his connections with the Velvet Underground, got John Cale to produce it.

"I Wanna Be Your Dog" is one of the earliest songs the band had written and it was a highlight in their live shows. They recorded it, along with seven other tracks during this week in 1969. "I Wanna Be Your Dog" is notable for a few reasons. First the song opens with a heavily distorted guitar sound. Many music historians would look at this years later as planting the seeds for heavy metal. "I Wanna Be Your Dog" also features a simple three chord riff and a continuously repeated single piano note (played by Cale). The simplicity of the music has led many of the same music historians to call this one of the first (if not the original) punk song. Indeed, though "I Wanna Be Your Dog" hardly sold, it is often mentioned by bands like the Ramones and the Clash as an inspiration for its straight ahead sound and raw energy.

The Stooges released three LPs between 1969 and 1973 before splintering apart. Pop went on to the most successful career of the four and ironically, the man known for stage diving and cutting himself just to please a crowd, has outlived the other three Stooges. Hindsight and history have been kinder to the band than record sales and radio play ever were and today they are revered as proto-punk gods who helped usher in a fierce new sound even as genres like soft rock and prog rock were dominating the scene. Wherever a couple of kids can get together, play three power chords and bang furiously on the drums, there lies the spirit of a band like the Stooges. There is nothing complex about "I Wanna Be Your Dog," not its lyrics or its instrumentation. But there is something magical in its simplicity as well as its desperation. It's the sound of youthful lust and rebellion and urgency and whether or not the world knew it at the time, it's a sound that would help create a genre that spit in the face of every musical institution that existed at the time. Well c'mon!

## April 8th

On this date in 1981, Blondie's "Rapture" was enjoying a two week stay at #1 on the *Billboard* Hot 100 chart. On March 28th it had knocked REO Speedwagon's "Keep On Loving You" from that perch and it would remain a few more days, till April 11th, when Hall & Oates' "Kiss On My List " took over. For Blondie, "Rapture" was their fourth and final chart-topper and it confirmed for everyone that the band was a true chameleon. They could be successful in just about any genre.

Blondie was a New York City band that became part of the Max's Kansas City and CBGB's punk scene even though they were never truly punk rockers. Their sound was far too polished and professional to be legit in that scene and as such, they truly foretold the new wave movement that would take punk's place. For many, Blondie was all about Debbie Harry. She was not only beautiful but she was a great singer and performer as well. And if the rest of the band, specifically guitarist Chris Stein and drummer Clem Burke, felt like they were simply her back-up band it certainly didn't slow down their momentum. Their third LP, 1978's *Parallel Lines* became their breakout moment, reaching #6 on the LP chart and producing two Top 40 hits: "One Way Or Another" which reached #27 and "Heart of Glass" which became the band's first #1. Already they were showing their diversity (or what some critics and cynics were calling "selling out"). They'd evolved from the straight ahead rock sound of their early years to include newer elements in their music. While "One Way Or Another" is certainly a rock song (and a clear precursor to new wave) "Heart of Glass" was nothing short of a disco song (in fact as a rock drummer, Burke refused to play the song live for a time). Were Blondie sell-outs or just so talented the band could master different genres? The question was bandied about among music fans as the eighties dawned but it didn't seem to deter them. Their next genre? Reggae. Blondie released a cover of an old Jamaican song called "The Tide Is High" in 1980 that also became another chart-topper for them. So it only made sense they'd dabble in yet another genre.

Debbie Harry had been hip to the hip hop scene from its earliest days. She used to visit some of the block parties that would take place in New York City where DJs would provide loops and MCs would rap over them. These were the beginning moments for the nascent musical style and Harry loved them. Music legend even has it that she was the one who brought her friend Niles Rodgers to a hip hop show one day and showed him how they were using his song "Good Times" to rap over. Harry had met Fab 5 Freddie at many of these events and fell in with his crowd. One day Freddie jokingly told Harry she should write a song about him and his crew. The rapper may have been joking but Harry took it seriously. She sat down with guitarist Chris Stein and they laid out a song that would include a section for her to rap over. The rap she came up with was very much like the early raps she'd heard in the streets of New York: ridiculous to the point of being comical. After name checking Fab 5 Freddy she goes off on a story about martians eating cars and you and then you eating cars and . . . it's all silly. Just like the Sugar Hill Gang's rap about going over a friend's house to eat. Rap was in its beginning stages and it would mature quickly but most of the earliest attempts were similar to Harry's rap - a chance for easy rhymes and fun patter. Blondie differed from the early rappers in that Harry and Stein created their own melody for their song instead of sampling existing records. Even today sampling is prevalent in the hip hop world which means rappers have to split song writing credit with the composers of the original. For Harry and Stein they are the only two listed as songwriters for "Rapture."

Blondie released "Rapture" in early 1981 and though MTV was still months away from launching there were already a few shows in the U.S. and England that were showing music videos and the industry was starting to see it as a strong promotional vehicle, especially when your band was fronted by someone as easy-on-the-eyes as Debbie Harry. Blondie produced a video that is as cheesy as Harry's rap and the song started climbing the charts. When it got to #1 it became the first song with rapping in it to top *Billboard*'s Hot 100 chart.

Blondie only lasted a few more years after "Rapture" became their last #1 and they never came close to the top of the charts again. The cynic will say they ran out of genres to ape. Fans would say they'd run their course and that during their years of influence they helped create new wave which would dominate the eighties. Either way, you can't argue with the band's success. Short-lived as it may have been, Blondie was by far the most successful band to emerge from that mid-seventies New York City scene. Their adaptability had to have something to do with that.

On this date in 1974, Blue Swede's version of "Hooked on a Feeling," which had already been covered a number of times and fundamentally changed from its original, was sitting at #1 on *Billboard*'s Hot 100 chart. It had risen to #1 on April 6th, knocking John Denver's "Sunshine On My Shoulders" from that spot and it would remain for one week, bowing out to Elton John's "Bennie and the Jets." But the song's one week stay at the top was only the beginning. It has enjoyed a long and rich history appearing in films and television shows and today, when most people hear it, they can conjure up a number of different images.

Songwriter Mark James composed "Hooked on a Feeling" which was originally recorded by B.J. Thomas in 1968. Thomas' version reached #5 on the pop chart. A few years later an English singer named Jonathan King recorded his own version of "Hooked on a Feeling" and gave it a slightly more uptempo feel. King also added the "Oogachaka" chant which was inspired by the 1959 Johnny Preston hit "Running Bear." King's "Hooked" went to #23 on the U.K. chart. It's this version that the Swedish band Blue Swede heard and liked. They added it to their set lists, often getting their audiences to chant along while they played the song. They had such success with it in concert that they decided to record their own version. They continued to use the "ooonga chackas," making them even more prominent than King had. Blue Swede made one other change from the original song to soften what some perceived as the obvious pro-drug reference. The original includes the lines:

> I got it bad for you girl.
> But I don't need a cure
> I'll just stay addicted
> And hope I can endure

Blue Swede removed the word addicted, changing the stanza to:

> Got a bug from you girl
> But I don't need no cure
> I'll just stay a victim
> If I can for sure

The Blue Swede version hit #1 in Sweden but was not initially released in the U.S. Somehow a copy of their version wound up in the hands of the owner of a record store in Connecticut. She began playing it for her customers who loved it and started calling local radio stations to request it. The song went viral (years before that was a thing) and soon enough EMI, whose Swedish arm, EMI Svenska, owned the rights, released it in the U.S. The song rose up the charts, out-selling Thomas' original and hitting #1 this week in 1974, making Blue Swede the first Swedish band to score a U.S. #1.

Blue Swede would have one more hit in the States ("Never My Love" which went to #7 in 1974) but for most American music fans they are far from the most famous Scandinavian band (ABBA probably has that distinction). Jonathan

King went on to a long and successful career in England, producing as well as broadcasting. He was probably best known as the man who discovered the band Genesis, that is until his 2001 conviction for indecency and buggery committed on young boys made him infamous for something other than music. B.J. Thomas enjoyed a long run of popularity throughout the sixties and seventies, topping the charts with "Raindrops Keep Fallin' On My Head" and "(Hey Won't You Play) Another Somebody Done Somebody Wrong Song" As for the songwriter Mark James, he has penned other classics like "Suspicious Minds", "Sunday Sunrise" and "Always on My Mind."

But of all parties involved, the song itself has probably had the most interesting ride. In 1992, Quentin Tarantino used it prominently in his movie *Reservoir Dogs*. A few years later on the television show *Ally McBeal* the writers came up with a concept where McBeal would dream of a "dancing baby" as she worried about her biological clock ticking away. The song the baby danced to? "Hooked on a Feeling" of course. In fact, some people refer to the dancing baby as the Oogachaka Baby. The song also made an appearance in the 2014 film *Guardians of the Galaxy* and it's been covered by various other artists including Carroll Baker whose 1978 version went to #1 on the country charts and David Hasselhoff whose 1997 version was accompanied by a video that is, well, unexplainable. Go ahead and pull it up on Youtube for the best laugh you'll have all day.

So whatever you associate the song with these days, whether it's a cult classic Tarantino movie or an animated dancing baby, no one can deny how catchy and memorable "Hooked on a Feeling" is. It's a joyous song of new found love that was made even more unforgettable with some chanting added to it. Give the song a listen today and see if you can stop from singing along to the chorus. It's doubtful you'll be able to.

### April 10th

On this date in 1976, Peter Frampton's double LP, *Frampton Comes Alive!* made its first appearance at #1 on the album chart. *Frampton Comes Alive!* would hit #1 numerous times throughout the year, ultimately spending a total of 10 weeks at the top and going on to be the highest selling album of the year. Today, it is the best-selling live LP of all-time. And yet, if it hadn't been for a record executive who wanted more songs, the whole thing may not have been such a smash hit.

Peter Frampton rose to fame in the music industry in England with a reputation as a fiery guitarist with matinee-idol looks. He was a founding member of the band Humble Pie and did some session work with artists like Harry Nilsson and George Harrison. It was during his work with Harrison that Frampton first used a talk-box, an instrument he would use famously a few years later. In 1972 he released his debut solo LP, *Wind of Change*. Despite the hype around him, the album underperformed. He toured extensively to support his debut and built a strong fan base so when he released his second solo effort, *Frampton's Camel*, expectations were again very high. The album failed to break big as did Frampton's next two LPs. Word was Frampton was a great concert act who was unable to capture his live magic in the studio. Which is why he and his label, A&M, decided to try a live album.

In the summer of 1975 Frampton recorded a number of his concerts in California and compiled them for a live album. When he presented the album to his label, Jerry Moss, the M in A&M, basically said "where's the rest?" Frampton responded by saying that's all they'd recorded and he didn't think the label would be up for a double LP. Moss, surprisingly said he wanted more and gave his blessing for a double album. This is fairly unprecedented in the music industry because double albums rarely sell as well as single LPs and so most double albums are released after an artist jumps through hoops to overcome their label's objections. But here Moss was asking for a double album and to make it all the more surprising he was asking an artist who had yet to live up to his potential.

With a release date set for early 1976 Frampton recorded a few more shows. These extra performances included live versions of "Show Me the Way" and "Baby, I Love Your Way," songs that hadn't been included in Frampton's first submission and would go on to be the album's big hits. "Show Me the Way" specifically was a song that Frampton had released a studio version single of in 1975 that hadn't even dented the charts. But when a live version was released on single, with its signature talk-box introduction, the song went to #6 and helped promote the album and propel it up the charts. *Frampton Comes Alive!* produced two more hit singles "Baby, I Love Your Way" and an edited version of "Do You Feel Like We Do" (the live single clocked in at 7:19 while the album version is over 14 minutes long and takes up most of side four). When Moss was asked later about expanding the album to two sides he was reluctant to take credit, saying simply: "I think every artist has their moment when they just hit a brilliance that's unexplainable. The audience and the sounds and the music sort of come together into a thrilling combination. And that album had that."

As quickly as Frampton's star had risen though, it came crashing down even faster. He released a studio album called *I'm in You* in 1977 that sold a million copies but fell far short of the bar that had been set by his live LP. Then, in 1978 he starred in the film *Sgt. Pepper's Lonely Hearts Club Band*. His performance probably would have been panned even more than it was were it not for critics focusing on how bad the whole movie was.

Frampton continued releasing solo LPs (that all underperformed) as well as touring with other artists. History will remember him as a talented musician who had one transcendent year when the stars aligned and a record executive gave his blessing for a double album. As Frampton has said, "When I kick the bucket, the first paragraph will be, 'The man responsible for *Frampton Comes Alive!* just dropped dead.'" Which makes Peter Frampton much more than a one hit wonder. He's a double album wonder, if there is such a thing.

On this date in 1981, riots took place in the impoverished Brixton section of London. The uprising, known as the Brixton Rising, was between the local African-Caribbean community and the police. When Margaret Thatcher was asked if funds could be directed to the area to help out she said, "money cannot buy either trust or racial harmony." Though the riots were eventually squelched, unemployment and poverty remained. All of this would inspire one of the most successful reggae songs of all time.

Eddy Grant was a musician born in British Guiana who moved with his family to London as a teenager. He was a socially conscious songwriter, penning "Police on My Back" as a teenager (which the Clash would cover years later). So when the Brixton Rising happened, Grant was moved to write about it. Grant was familiar with the neighborhood and knew the shopping district was called Electric Avenue because it was the first street in the area to get electric street lights. He wrote the opening line, "Now in the street there is violence," inspired by the riots. He then focused on the plight of the poor with lines like "Can't afford a thing on TV" and "Can't get food for the kid." Grant put his lyrics to an upbeat and powerful funk/reggae beat which is why many people who didn't study the lyrics simply thought the tune was a fun party song about rocking down to someplace called electric avenue. It's a classic case of lyrical dissonance.

"Electric Avenue" is also an early example of the hit-making power of MTV. The song was released in the U.S. in early 1983 when MTV still had an unwritten "no black artists" rule. It was Walter Yetnikoff, head of Epic, who famously threatened to pull all his artists from MTV if they didn't play the video for Michael Jackson's "Billie Jean" when it was released around the same time at "Electric Avenue." When MTV started showing "Billie Jean" (and their white viewer's heads didn't explode) the floodgates were opened. Other videos like "Electric Avenue" and Prince's "Little Red Corvette" followed in Jackson's footsteps and Grant was a prime beneficiary. His song hadn't started to climb the charts till MTV started showing his video but once they did it would rise to #2 during the summer of 1983.

Grant continued trying to make a difference with his music. In 1988 he released the anti-apartheid song "Gimme Hope Jo'anna" which was promptly banned in South Africa. He's also enjoyed success as a music industry entrepreneur. He owns a studio in Barbados called Blue Wave that is extremely popular and has been utilized by the likes of the Rolling Stones, Sting and Cliff Richard. And sure, poverty still exists (as Grant sings in "Electric Avenue," "There's lots of work to be done") and injustices happen everyday, but it's good to know there are artists out there like Grant who are socially conscious and looking to make a difference.

On this date in 1954, at a studio in New York City, Bill Haley & His Comets recorded a song called "Rock Around the Clock." Despite the fact that the song eventually helped launch the nascent rock and roll sound into the stratosphere of pop culture, it was recorded simply to fulfill a contractual agreement and fill the B-side of a single they were about to release. The song was out for over a year with nary a notice until it appeared in a film that changed everything. Here's how it all happened:

William John Clifton Haley was born in 1925 in Michigan and began his career in music as a yodeler. In fact, he was considered one of the top cowboy yodelers in America and for a while went by the name the Silver Yodeling Bill Haley. He moved on to country music and then, in 1952, formed a new band called the Comets. With his new band he began to focus on the emerging amalgamation of blues, rockabilly and country that was slowing taking shape. In April of 1953 Bill Haley & His Comets released "Crazy Man, Crazy" which peaked at #12 on the *Billboard* Juke Box chart (this is prior to the Hot 100 chart) and is considered the first rock and roll record to appear on a national American musical chart. The following year song publisher James Myers helped Haley leave his old record label and sign with Decca and part of their agreement was that one side of every single Haley released on Decca would include a song Myers owned the publishing rights for.

Haley's first single for Decca was a bizarre song called "Thirteen Women (and Only One Man in Town)" which is a post-apocalyptic tale where an atomic bomb kills everyone on earth but thirteen women and the singer of the song. Since Myers didn't own the publishing for "Thirteen Women" Haley looked through his catalogue and chose a number called "We're Gonna Rock Around the Clock Tonight!" which the country-western band Sonny Dae and His Knights had recorded the year before. Haley and his band recorded it (shortening the name to "Rock Around the Clock") on this date in 1954. They did three takes then decided the first was their best and that, with a little post production work, was the version that appeared on the B-side of "Thirteen Women (and Only One Man in Town)." They'd spent about a half an hour in the studio working on "Rock Around the Clock."

"Thirteen Women (and Only One Man in Town)" was released in May of 1954. It sold about 75,000 copies then slipped into obscurity. Haley's next release was his version of "Shake, Rattle and Roll" which climbed to #7 on the pop chart and further erased the memory of "Thirteen Women" and it's B-side.

Then, an amazing thing happened. Among the 75,000 copies of "Thirteen Women" that had been sold, one of them was owned by a ten year old boy named Peter Ford. He hated the A-side of the single but loved the B-side and he practically wore out the grooves playing the song on the record player in his bedroom. Peter Ford's father was an actor named Glen Ford who was currently shooting a film alongside a young Sidney Poitier called *Blackboard Jungle* about teachers in an inter-racial inner-city school. One day the older Ford mentioned his son's favorite song to the film's director, Richard Brooks, and Brooks decided to play "Rock Around the Clock" over the opening credits of the film.

*Blackboard Jungle* was released on March 19th, 1955 and to say the world would never be the same is actually understating the point. The movie caused riots in some theaters. Actually the movie didn't cause the riots as much as the music in the movie. Some theaters even began muting the movie till the opening credits (and song) were over but the song also appears at other times in the film so it did no good. Decca quickly re-released the single with "Rock Around the Clock" as the A-side and the song shot up to #1, becoming the first chart-topping rock and roll song. Marshall Lytle, the Comets' bassist, remembers the day the band realized what a big hit their song had become: "We were traveling on the New York Thruway from Buffalo to Boston to do a television show. I turned the radio on and 'Rock Around the Clock' was playing. This was a new Cadillac that Bill had just bought. It had one of those Selectrix dials where you just push the bar and it goes to the next station. I pushed the bar and it was playing again on another radio station. I pushed the bar again and it was playing again. At one given moment, it was playing five times on the dial. Within five minutes, I must've heard it a dozen times. I said: 'This is a monster hit.'"

It was indeed. And it would open the airwaves for Elvis Presley and Chuck Berry and Jerry Lee Lewis and so many others. That ten year old boy, Peter Ford, went on to a fairly successful career as a singer and actor but by far the largest impact he had on pop culture and music history was flipping that single over and playing the B-side, "Rock Around the Clock," so much his father took notice. The movie *Blackboard Jungle* helped ignite a fire that burns brightly even today. Rock and roll had taken off and once it did, no one was going to slow it down.

## April 13th

On this date in 2010, Train's huge comeback single "Hey, Soul Sister" had peaked at #3 on the pop chart. Though the song never made it to #1 in the U.S. it did top the charts in 16 other countries and went on to be one of the highest-selling songs of 2010 (and the best-selling song on iTunes that year). The song also helped the band's fifth studio album, *Save Me, San Francisco*, become a top-seller.

Pat Monahan started his music career in a Led Zeppelin cover band named Rogues Gallery in Erie, Pennsylvania. When they broke up in 1993 he moved west and started singing in coffee houses and local clubs in the Bay Area. He formed a band he called Train and when they couldn't get a record deal they released their self-titled debut independently. Eventually Columbia signed them and their second LP, *Drops of Jupiter* became a huge hit in 2001, peaking at #6 on the album chart. Their follow-up, 2003's *Private Nation*, did just as well and their fourth LP, *For Me, It's You*, wasn't as successful but it still got as high as #10.

Then, for some reason, the band took a hiatus. Pat Monahan released a solo album, *Last of Seven*, that only hit #82 on the LP chart and there was talk that maybe the band was finished. For a few years Train sat at the station and their fans waited. Then in 2009 they started working on new material. One song Monahan brought to the studio was something that was inspired by the Burning Man festival. Train had never played at the festival in the Nevada desert, nor had Monahan ever been to it, but he'd read about how they burn a wood sculpture of a man and how it sets off this spontaneous party with beautiful women, some naked, dancing around in the firelight. Monahan says the topic was on his mind one day when he hadn't gotten a lot of sleep and he claims to write better when he's sleep deprived so all of a sudden the lyrics for "Hey, Soul Sister" just came to him as if in a dream. He jotted them down with no melody, only knowing that he wanted the song to "bounce," because that's what the lyrics were about, a woman so hot the way she moves isn't even fair.

Monahan had chosen to do some work for the album with the Norwegian production duo Espionage (Espen Lind and Amund Bjørklund) and he brought the lyrics to them saying he wanted an "INXS-y type sound" for it. The two laid out a track for the lyrics with a catchy guitar opening, but Monahan wasn't happy with it. That's when Espen Lind picked up a ukulele and played the same opening riff on it. Monahan says he knew instantly that was the trick, saying: "It made the difference. It made my words dance. It made sense. These words were meant to dance with ukulele and not guitar." They completed the song and presented it to the band and everyone was happy except Train guitarist Jimmy Stafford. He'd never played the ukulele before and if the band was going to do the song live, he'd have to learn. Stafford explains: "At first, I tried to do it by using a guitar pick, and it didn't sound right. I had to go online and Google a ukulele lesson and noticed they're not using picks at all; it's more of a flamenco style. Once I got that down, then it sounded like the real deal."

"Hey, Soul Sister" was released in August of 2009 and perhaps because the band had been out of the spotlight for a while it didn't move right away. Their fifth album, *Save Me, San Francisco* was released in October of 2009. It debuted at #17 on the album chart but then started to descend and eventually even fell out of the *Billboard* Top 200. Then, as the band promoted "Hey, Soul Sister" everywhere, the song began to ascend in early 2010. Pop radio caught on and the song shot up even higher, eventually peaking at #3 this week in 2010. *Save Me, San Francisco* produced two other Top 40 songs, "If It's Love" and "Marry Me" and it announced to the music world that Train was rolling again.

On this date in 1983, David Bowie released his fifteenth studio album, *Let's Dance*. After a number of experimental albums in which he tested the limits of art rock and electronica (often called his Berlin trilogy because his three LPs, *Low* (1977), *Heroes* (1977) and *Lodger* (1979) were all made in that German city) Bowie wanted to return to the top of the pop chart and he tapped a down-on-his-luck disco producer to help him get there. The two created one of the most commercially successful albums of Bowie's career.

Niles Rodgers was a disco star and impresario, having produced hits for his own band, Chic, as well as others, most famously, Sister Sledge. He rode the disco wave as high as anyone which is why, when the eighties began and the phrase "Deader than Disco" became the law of the land, Rodgers found himself on the outside of the music industry looking in.

One day in 1982 Rodgers was hanging out with Billy Idol and the two walked into an after-hours club in New York City. Idol immediately spotted David Bowie and the three got to talking. Rodgers would reminisce later about the night, saying: "From the moment we started speaking, we never stopped talking to each other; he and I, it was as if we were in a bubble and no one else existed. It was probably the most significant few hours of both of our careers, especially if you talk in terms of what was to come: the numbers, the units sold, and the influence." Bowie must have been impressed with Rodgers and his deep musical knowledge because a little while later he asked him to produce his next album. The two then sat down for two weeks and listened to old records, trying to come up with a musical direction they wanted to take. Rodgers again describes that time: "This being way before the Internet, we actually went to the New York Public Library and to people's houses who had large record collections. We also went to record stores to go bin-diving." Finally they discovered their inspiration — a picture of Little Richard in a red cadillac. Bowie showed it to Rodgers and said, "I want my record to sound like this." Rodgers would say later: "He just had to show me a picture, and I completely understood. He wanted something that felt like the future but was rooted in rock and roll, something soulful, black, and R&B, but morphed and evergreen. And that's what *Let's Dance* is."

Rodgers' influence was felt immediately when the two started working together. One of the things Rodgers usually insisted on with his own songs was starting with the chorus or hook. As he's explained: "As a black artist, it was very difficult for me to get hits, because we had fewer radio stations to expose our music. So to get attention, a technique of mine was I always started my songs with the chorus: 'Ahhh, freak out!' and 'We are family!'" He suggested Bowie start "Let's Dance" similarly and it worked perfectly. Later when the song won some awards Bowie gave one to Rodgers with a note that said, "To my friend, Nile Rodgers: the only man who could make me start a song with a chorus."

Bowie also told Rodgers he wanted to record a version of the song "China Girl" which Bowie and Iggy Pop had cowritten years earlier and had appeared on Pop's 1977 album *The Idiot*. Rodgers came up with the guitar introduction for the song but thought it was so corny he almost scrapped it. When Bowie heard it he loved it, calling it genius.

*Let's Dance* was released on this date in 1983 (the title track had already been released as a single and was busy climbing the charts). The LP would go on to be a huge-seller. It peaked at #3 in June and produced three hits, the title track which went to #1, "China Girl" which went to #10 and "Modern Love" which peaked at #14. For Bowie it was a great moment in a career filled with them. For Rodgers, it was a career-saver. When reminiscing on the recording of *Let's Dance* and David Bowie himself, Rodgers would say: "This was a man who changed my life. When I made *Let's Dance*, Chic had broken up; I had had six failed records in a row... I was all by myself, and David and I formed a partnership. It was the two of us against the world. I never felt more loved; I never felt like a person trusted me more. I did *Let's Dance* in 17 days, start to finish – it was the fastest record in my entire life. And when I say 'finish,' I mean mixed, done, delivered. Which is why you've never heard alternate versions; there's only one version of those songs. And that's because we were on the same wavelength."

All from bumping into each other in after-hours nightclub. Pretty amazing!

## April 15th

On this date in 1972, "Roundabout" by Yes was sitting at its peak position of #13 on the pop chart. Though the band had one other higher charting song (1984's "Owner of a Lonely Heart" which hit #1) for most Yes fans, "Roundabout" is their signature work. It's got all the elements of a classic Yes track and indeed, it's the quintessential progressive rock song: long and winding with plenty of tempo changes, instrumentation that is superb to the point of almost classical, and lyrics that border on the mystical. It's amazing that something as mundane as driving through the countryside could produce such a timeless track.

Yes emerged from the late sixties rock scene in London and though they've undergone too many lineups changes to keep track of, the one constant has always been brilliant musicianship. Their compositions are sometimes more symphonies than rock songs and they were pioneers in the early days of the emerging progressive rock genre (often called "prog rock") along with bands like the Moody Blues and Procol Harum. Prog rock actually evolved from the psychedelic movement of the mid-sixties so some music historians trace its roots to the Beatles' *Sgt. Peppers* and the Beach Boys' *Pet Sounds*. What grew out of those trippy early offerings came a genre that delved into longer instrumentations that were often closer to free form jazz and even classical music than traditional rock or pop songs. One of the reasons prog rock bands have often stayed on the periphery of commercial success is the length of their songs. Traditional pop stations favor singles that clock in under four minutes. Many prog rock songs are just getting warmed up at the four minute mark. It wasn't till the advent of album oriented rock stations (AOR) that many of these bands even had an outlet for their music. But true prog rock bands could care less about pop success. They are much more interested in testing the boundaries of what can be recorded in the studio and played live and Yes certainly met those standards. By the time their third album had been released (1971's *The Yes Album*) they'd built a loyal following especially in the U.K. They toured relentlessly to support that LP which is how they found themselves in a van driving through Scotland.

The roads in this area are full of little traffic circles or roundabouts. When you're cruising along, a roundabout causes you to slow down, navigate the circle, then accelerate again. So whether you're at the wheel, in the passenger seat or, like so many traveling musicians, hanging in the back of the van with all the gear, a roundabout is obvious. It momentarily breaks the flow of the drive. Yes lead singer Jon Anderson and guitarist Steve Howe were in the back of the van one day, driving from Aberdeen to Glasgow when they started composing a song. Their tour was coming to an end and Anderson was eager to get home to London and see his wife again. Suddenly all these images and emotions started coming out in lyrical form. The landscape ("In and around the lake, mountains come out of the sky and they stand there,") Anderson's imminent arrival home ("Twenty four before my love you'll see I'll be there with you") and of course, the ever-present roundabouts. Some wordplays are harder to explain but when they are as hauntingly beautiful as, "Your silhouette will charge the view" who needs an explanation?

In the studio the song got all the usual Yes treatment, a beautifully composed introduction, including that unique sound that opens the song which is actually a piano strike played backwards, and incredible solos - most notably the keyboard work of Rick Wakeman.

*The Yes Album* had been a breakthrough success for the band and so as soon as their tour was over they got to work on their next LP. Where *The Yes Album* had been a big hit in the U.K., their fourth LP, *Fragile*, which would include "Roundabout" as well as "Long Distance Runaround" and "Heart of the Sunrise" would break the band worldwide. And much of that success had to do with an edited version of "Roundabout."

As the band readied *Fragile* for release their record company wanted "Roundabout" to get radio play. But the album version clocks in at eight and a half minutes and they knew this would be a deterrence. Sure the Beatles could get "Hey Jude" played but they were the Beatles after all. American pop radio wasn't going to make an exception for a band hardly anybody had even heard of. So Yes edited "Fragile" down to a radio-friendly three and a half minutes. Anderson would admit later to have mixed feelings about this, saying: "When we first heard the 'Roundabout' single, it was on the radio. We didn't know it was released. We were busy being a band on the road, and then we heard the edit and we thought, 'Wow, that must have been a big pair of scissors to edit that song.' I mean, it was just totally wrong musically. But it actually worked and all of a sudden we became famous, we had a hit record and more people came to see us, which was great, because then they would see the progression of music we'd been doing and they'd see us more as a band and not just wait for 'Roundabout.' Because we didn't do that 'Roundabout' in those days. We did the eight-minute version."

Eight minute version or even more. "Roundabout" is a crowd favorite and offers Yes an opportunity to showcase everyone in the band. Live, the song often goes on for about twice what it does on the LP, with guitar, keyboard and even drum solos. And of course, those lyrics. Those images of a drive through the Scottish countryside that somehow became beautiful poetry. It's a song that not only helped launch Yes but almost legitimized the whole prog rock movement in its nascent days.

## April 16th

On this date in 1969, MC5 was dropped by their record label despite the fact they'd finally placed a single on the *Billboard* Hot 100 chart. Their story is such a quintessential tale of rock and roll rebellion that the band has gone down in the annals of music history as pioneers despite their short-shelf life and virtual anonymity.

MC5 came together in Detroit in the mid-sixties, formed by high school friends Wayne Kramer and Fred Smith who shared a passion for music as diverse as R&B, jazz and good old American rock and roll. Joined by three others, lead singer Rob Tyner, bassist Michael Davis and drummer Dennis Thompson they named themselves MC5, short for Motor City 5. The band earned an early reputation for their high energy performances and soon came to the attention of poet and political activist John Sinclair. Sinclair had helped form the White Panther Party, a group of whites who stood in solidarity with the Black Panthers and whose ten point manifesto included: "Total assault on the culture by any means necessary, including rock and roll, dope, and fucking in the streets." Sinclair eventually became MC5's manager and their music took on an even more political leaning. At the 1968 Democratic National Convention in Chicago, the band played as part of the protests against the Vietnam War. There had been an entire day scheduled with various bands on the bill but most didn't show so MC5 wound up playing for an epic eight hours. The national attention this garnered them helped the band land their first record deal. Elektra signed them and since their live shows were such a huge part of their reputation, they decided to record one and release it as their debut album. That album, *Kick Out the Jams*, was released in February of 1969 along with the title track as the lead single.

Recording the band live also meant capturing some of their onstage banter with the audience and Sinclair and the band wanted much of that included, specifically their now famous introduction to "Kick Out the Jams," Rob Tyner's, "It's time to kick out the jams, motherfuckers!" After a few of their early, self-released singles had failed to chart, "Kick Out the Jams" actually cracked the *Billboard* Hot 100 chart in April 1969. Elektra had edited the introduction to the single, however, to: "It's time to kick out the jams, brothers and sisters" which infuriated the band and Sinclair. They became even more enraged when Hudson's, a department store chain in the Detroit area, made the decision not to stock their album.

Their response was simple and direct. They took out an ad in a local magazine that said simply:

"KICK OUT THE JAMS, MOTHERFUCKER! and kick in the door if the store won't sell you the album on Elektra. FUCK HUDSON'S!"

Though the label didn't have any knowledge of the ad until it ran, MC5 prominently included the Elektra logo. In response Hudson's decided to pull all Elektra albums from its shelves. The label responded by dropping MC5.

The band signed with Atlantic and John Sinclair was sent to jail for marijuana possession so they signed with a new manager, Jon Landau, to produce their next album, *Back in the USA* (years later Landau would come to fame working with Bruce Springsteen, producing his 1984 album, *Born in the USA*). *Back in the USA* and their third album *High Time* both lost money for Atlantic and the band was eventually dropped again.

So what is it that makes MC5 stand out in the history of rock and roll? Surely plenty of bands have had three albums and one mildly successful single on their resume. But MC5 was more than just a short-lived barely successful group. They were a force. Their live shows, especially in their early days were legendary for their energy and sense of chaos and anarchy. They played hard, fast and angry. Years later when the punk scene started growing in downtown New York and across the pond in London, many of the early bands cited MC5 and Iggy Pop's the Stooges as influences. MC5 has been called everything from "the most radical band on the planet" to "a complete and total disaster." They came from the hippie movement but then promptly kicked it in the teeth. They were signed by a major label then promptly dropped even as their single was on the charts. They were banned for vulgarity and eventually most of their members were arrested for drugs. They captured all the rage and energy and rebellion that we want in our rockstars and as Neil Young would sing years later, they even burned out, instead of fading away. If you have time today, crank up "Kick Out the Jams." Play it loud and defiantly the way it was meant to be played.

## April 17th

On this date in 1971, Three Dog Night's "Joy to the World" began an incredible six week run at #1 on the pop chart. Any time a song sits at #1 for over a month it's an incredible accomplishment. When it's a song that wasn't even initially released as a single, and dismissed as "childish" and "silly" by the band that recorded it, it's an even bigger achievement. Here's the story of how "Joy to the World" became such a huge hit and the answer to the mystery of those opening lines.

Hoyt Axton was a singer-songwriter from California who was commissioned to write a song for an animated TV special in the late sixties. He came up with the chorus for "Joy to the World" but then the special was cancelled. He thought the song had potential so he finished it up, using what songwriters often called lyrical placeholders for the opening verse. He fully intended to write a proper opening verse because "Jeremiah was a bull frog. Was a good friend of mine. I never understood a single word he said. But I helped him drink his wine" makes no literal sense nor did it have any secret meaning for Axton. There was no Jeremiah that Axton was thinking of and he didn't have any friends he couldn't understand. Still, he recorded a demo with the lyrical placeholders figuring if he never sold the song why bother writing the verses.

Axton happened to be opening for Three Dog Night around this time and one day they were shooting pool together prior to a show. Axton was playing a tape of some of his demos as background music and the band heard "Joy to the World" and asked if they could have it. Since Three Dog Night was a successful band (they'd reached the top of the charts that year with "Mama Told Me Not to Come") Axton was eager to give it to them. He replied, "Hell, you can put out a triple album of Hoyt Axton songs if you want." Three Dog Night was gathering material for their fourth studio album, *Naturally*, and they needed one more song so they decided this one would suffice. Before Axton could write a proper first verse though, they went into the studio and recorded "Joy to the World." They stuck it on the end of *Naturally* considering it nothing more than album-filler and then released "One Man Band" in November of 1970 as the lead single.

So how did "Joy to the World" become the band's most successful single? you ask. Good question. For that, we turn our attention to Larry Bergman, a radio DJ at Seattle's KISW-FM. KISW was an album oriented rock station (AOR) and so Bergman's job was to go through LPs the station had laying around and pull some tracks from them. He would tape the songs for on-air use and when he listened to *Naturally* he liked the album's last track so he stuck it on a tape. The song got played on air in early 1971 and the station instantly received phone calls asking about the song. KISW had a sister station, KJR-AM, which played a pop format and they too started getting requests for "Joy to the World." Bergman gave them a tape of the song as well and the song went into heavy rotation. With the buzz emanating from the great Northwest, Three Dog Night hurriedly released "Joy to the World" as a single in February of 1971. It went to #1 instantly in Seattle and within weeks it was a national hit as well. When the song went gold (selling a million copies) the band presented KISW with a gold record.

Then, as often happens, the lyrics fell under the microscope. Conjecture started with Jeremiah. Was he the biblical prophet? Or was he God? We humans often miss God's message so maybe that's what the third line meant. And of course the association with Jesus and wine is clear enough. Oh, and the fact that the song shares a title with a famous Christmas song didn't hurt. Before long Three Dog Night's "Joy to the World" was being analyzed in Sunday morning sermons. Axton, who wasn't a very religious man, found some humor in all this, insisting that he had no deeper meaning in the opening verse and sometimes wishes he'd had the chance to come up with proper lyrics. But he also came to embrace it. In 1979 he started his own record label and called it, you guessed it, Jeremiah.

"Joy to the World" was not only Three Dog Night's most successful song but it's gone on to have a rich history in pop culture, appearing in numerous movies, most notably the sixties throwback film *The Big Chill*. It's also been covered by artists as diverse as rock and roller Little Richard and punk rockers Ten Foot Pole. Because even if that first verse is enigmatic and nonsensical, there is nothing confusing about the message in the chorus, especially when it's sung with all the energy and enthusiasm that Three Dog Night gave it. Joy to the world. To all the boys and girls and even to the fishes in the deep blue sea. You can't get much more direct than that. No matter who Jeremiah is, "Joy to you and me" is a lyric we can all embrace. And most importantly, sing along to. Loud and proud.

## April 18th

On this date in 1984, "Footloose" by Kenny Loggins was finishing up its third and final week at #1 on the pop chart. It had climbed to the top on March 31st when it knocked Van Halen's "Jump" from that spot. On April 21st it would surrender the crown to "Against All Odds (Take A Look At Me Now)" by Phil Collins. *Footloose*, the movie, had a similar three week run as the box office king.

Dean Pitchford is an actor, novelist, screenplay writer and songwriter who, in 1979, read an article about a small town in Oklahoma that still had a "no dancing" law on the books from the 1800s. The article focused on that year's senior class, all 14 of them, who wanted a prom. They fought the town council and got the ordinance overturned. Pitchford was fascinated by the story so he traveled to the town to get more details and immerse himself in the area's culture and mindset. He had just contributed some songs to the movie *Fame* so he knew the potential a movie about teenagers and dancing could have. Pitchford sat down and wrote the entire screenplay with a working title of *Cheek to Cheek*. He loved the script but hated the title so he started playing around with different ideas. He wrote down "footloose and fancy free" during one brainstorming session then crossed out "and fancy free" and he had his title. He then wrote the lyrics to nine songs that would appear in the movie.

In 1982, Pitchford collaborated with Kenny Loggins and Steve Perry on a song called "Don't Fight It" which peaked at #17. Loggins already had a reputation for doing well with soundtracks, having gone to #7 with "I'm Alright" from 1980's *Caddyshack* so Pitchford reached out to the singer and got him to agree to write the music to Pitchford's lyrics for the title track as well as sing it. Pitchford collaborated with other musicians like Eric Carmen, Jim Steinman and Sammy Hagar on the rest of the songs for the movie. With a script, nine songs, and a star signed on to sing the title track, Pitchford was able to land a deal for *Footloose* and went into production in Payson, Utah, in 1983.

Tom Cruise was the first choice for the lead role of *Footloose* but he had signed on to do *All the Right Moves* so he was unable to fit it into his schedule. Rob Lowe was the next choice but he injured himself while dancing in the audition and was unable to take the part. Finally, 25 year old Kevin Bacon was cast, based mostly on his recent work in the film *Diner*. Bacon immersed himself in the role, even attending classes at Payson High School where he posed as a transfer student. With his skinny tie and new wave haircut he was treated pretty much the same as his character Ren would be in the movie, like a weirdo and an outcast.

The song "Footloose" was released in January of 1984, a month ahead of the film. Its music video was basically a four minute preview for the movie and it went into heavy rotation on MTV. By the time the movie was released the song was already in the Top 40 and *Footloose* opened up to three consecutive weeks of huge box offices. It would finish 1984 as the seventh highest-grossing film. The soundtrack was even more successful, spending over two months at #1 on the album chart and placing ninth on the list of top-selling albums for the year. "Footloose" was Kenny Loggins' only career #1 (he came oh so close in 1986 when another song from a movie, "Danger Zone" from *Top Gun*, made it to #2.) The song is not only Loggins' most successful but will forever be indelibly linked to Kevin Bacon. In fact, Bacon told Howard Stern once that he regularly tips DJs at weddings he attends NOT to be play the song. Apparently he doesn't always want to cut loose.

## April 19th

On this date in 1971, Cat Stevens' fourth studio LP *Tea for the Tillerman* was sitting at its peak position, #8, on the album chart. Though it is not Steven's highest-charting or best-selling album, it was his first Top 10 LP and it helped introduce him to a much wider audience who would quickly come to appreciate his unique combination of deft acoustic guitar playing and poignant lyrics. Before dropping out of the music industry altogether for nearly three decades, Stevens had made himself one of the most recognizable names in the new soft rock genre.

Steven Demetre Georgiou was born in post-war London in 1948. His family kept a baby grand piano in their home and he began playing it at a young age, teaching himself how to make music and play the right notes. As a teenager, inspired by the Beatles, he picked up the guitar and taught himself that instrument as well. He started playing in coffee houses and pubs and decided, if he was going to have a career in music he'd need to change his name. As he's explained, "I couldn't imagine anyone going to the record store and asking for 'that Steven Demetre Georgiou album.'"After a girlfriend told him he had "cat-like eyes" he decided upon his stage name. He signed his first record contract while still a teenager and though he didn't have any breakout hits early on, one of his earliest compositions, "The First Cut Is the Deepest" has gone on to be covered successfully by artists as diverse as P.P Arnold, Rod Stewart and Sheryl Crow.

Stevens contracted tuberculosis in 1969 which nearly killed him and wound up costing him a year of his life as he recuperated from the lung disease. But it's a year that would change his entire life as he questioned his own mortality, the meaning of life and religion and so many other issues that men in their young twenties are often too busy to contemplate. He began to meditate, took up yoga and became a vegetarian during this time. He also wrote as many as 40 songs that would make appearances on his next few albums.

Regaining his health, Stevens hoped to get his career going as well, He'd made a name for himself in London but was virtually unknown elsewhere. His fourth album, *Tea for the Tillerman*, and its lead single "Wild World" would change all that.

Stevens had written "Wild World" while dating actress Patti D'Arbanville but he denies it's about her. "It was not me writing about somebody specific," he has said, "although other people may have informed the song, but it was more about me. It's talking about losing touch with home and reality - home especially." Whatever his motivation, the song's lyrics are gentle and beautiful and when American radio got a hold of it, "Wild World" was destined to be a hit. Though it peaked just outside the Top 10, the song helped introduce Stevens to a new market and to promote *Tea for the Tillerman* which peaked at #8 this week in 1971. Soft rock was on the rise in popularity and Stevens' offerings fit in perfectly alongside artists like Elton John and James Taylor on the radio dial.

Stevens had an incredible run throughout the seventies, releasing successful singles and albums and becoming a dominant voice in this new genre of soft rock. And then, one day, he dropped out.

Stevens converted to Islam in 1977, changing his name to Yusuf Islam and walking away from the music industry and his successful singing and songwriting career. He remained quiet, at least musically, for the better part of two decades before easing his way back into the industry. In 2013 he was inducted into the Rock and Roll Hall of Fame, performing iconic songs like "Wild World" and "Peace Train." For anyone in attendance or watching at home, it felt like 1971 all over again.

On this date in 1970, Norman Greenbaum's "Spirit in the Sky" was sitting at its peak position, #3 on the pop chart, blocked from reaching #1 by the Beatles' "Let It Be" and Jackson 5's "ABC." The song has become an iconic example of rock meeting gospel and lifts most people up when they hear it, no matter what their religious upbringing may have been, or their current position on faith. Which makes sense since one of the most famous examples of Jesus being name checked in a rock song came from a good Jewish boy.

Norman Greenbaum was born in 1942 in Malden, Massachussets. He was raised in an Orthodox Jewish household and attended Hebrew school. Even into his adulthood he never changed his faith and identifies as Jewish. He loved folk music and the blues and by the time he was a student at Boston University he was playing in local coffee houses. He eventually moved to Los Angeles in the mid-sixties and formed something he categorized as a "psychedelic jug band" named Dr. West's Medicine Show and Junk Band. They actually charted in 1966 with a novelty song called "The Eggplant That Ate Chicago" but amazingly that was their only hit and soon enough they disbanded. Greenbaum found himself in San Francisco nurturing a solo career.

It was here that he happened to see a television show one day where two country stars, Dolly Parton and Porter Wagoner, were singing a religious song. Wagoner, specifically, made an impression on Greenbaum with his flashy suits and big pompadour and Greenbaum decided to challenge himself and write a religious rock song. The first thing he decided to do was include Jesus because he knew it would give the song a bigger audience. He has since said, "I decided there was a larger Jesus Gospel market out there than a Jehovah one." He then came up with the title of "Spirit in the Sky," channeling, of all things, the Westerns he used to watch as a kid. He explained years later: "If you ask me what I based 'Spirit in the Sky' on ... what did we grow up watching? Westerns! These mean and nasty varmints get shot and they wanted to die with their boots on ... It wasn't like a Christian song of praise it was just a simple song. I had to use Christianity because I had to use something. But more important it wasn't the Jesus part, it was the spirit in the sky. Funny enough ... I wanted to die with my boots on."

Like so many great songs, the lyrics came to Greenbaum quickly and easily. Almost, you might say, like they were divinely inspired. The music, however, took months. "I kept changing," Greenbaum has said. "I was never satisfied. ... It's based on an old standard blues riff. However, I changed it." Once he was happy with the melody and began working on the song in the studio two distinctive things took place. First, for the song's fuzz-tone opening riff, Greenbaum explains: "I knew this guy, and he knew electronics. So, rather than having a pedal and everything, he just put this little transmitter thing right into the guitar with an on-off switch. Somehow the sound has never been duplicated. Bands write me all the time, 'God, I've been trying to play that song for years and I can't even come close.' Interesting." The other unique feature of the song are the guitar fills which have an almost beep-like sound to them. Guitarist Russell DaShiell came up with that in the studio. DeShiell has said: "When the producer asked me to play some fills-in between the verses, as a joke I said how about something spacey like this and I did the pickup switch/string bending thing. I saw him stand up in the control booth and he said 'that's it! let's record that!' so we did." The Oakland-based Stovall Sisters were brought in to add backing vocals that, along with the hand claps, gave the song a decidedly gospel feel and "Spirit in the Sky" was ready to soar.

Of course with popularity comes scrutiny and sometimes Greenbaum gets some criticism for the third verse which begins "Never been a sinner. I never sinned," because some Christians, specifically Catholics, believe in something called original sin (which basically means everybody is born a sinner). Greenbaum has said: "I still get strange letters from heavy Christians that find it appalling ...I'm truthful in writing back. I say, 'You know, I flubbed that part.'"

But if you can look past that "flub," "Spirit in the Sky" is a transcendent song. When asked about its popularity Greenbaum has said, "it appeals to one's inner self and the need for redemption. Plus, heck, who wants to go to hell?" Nobody. We all want to go to heaven. And whether we believe that's for an eternity or just the sheer bliss of a soaring four minute song is a personal decision we all make. Greenbaum, a good Jewish boy singing about Jesus, gave us a path to the place that's the best. Crank it up and see if you can't get there.

## April 21st

On this date in 1983, Michael Jackson's "Billie Jean" was wrapping up its seventh and final week at #1 on the pop chart. The song had been released in the beginning of the year as the second single off Jackson's *Thriller* album. As "Billie Jean" climbed the charts so too did the album. *Thriller* hit #1 on the LP chart on February 26th and would remain there till the beginning of the summer, before returning sporadically a few more times in 1983. "Billie Jean" arrived at #1 on March 5th and would enjoy a seven week run. Then Jackson would vacate the top spot for just one week before returning with Thriller's third single, "Beat It." 1983 will forever be known as Michael Jackson's year and the popularity of "Billie Jean" is a huge reason for it.

There are two stories about Michael Jackson's inspiration for writing "Billie Jean." The most popular one he told during his lifetime was that there was no specific Billie Jean, the song represents a lot of women, namely groupies. Jackson and his brothers were constantly surrounded by female fans who were willing and ready to get intimate with any of them. Some of these women then claimed they had a child by one of the Jacksons. "There were a lot of Billie Jeans out there," Jackson once said, "every girl claimed that their son was related to one of my brothers." But Thriller's producer, Quincy Jones, said Jackson had a more specific woman in mind. Jackson had a stalker around this time. A woman who wrote Jackson numerous letters including one that claimed he was the father of her son though the singer claimed he had never met the woman. Jackson then received a package which include a gun and a letter giving Jackson a specific date and time that the woman would kill her child and herself and asked Jackson to kill himself at the exact same time so they could be together in the afterlife. The situation obviously freaked Jackson out and it's said he had nightmares for weeks. That's the woman Jones believes inspired "Billie Jean."

Whichever story is true, and there's a good chance they both are, Jackson wrote "Billie Jean" as he was working on material for *Thriller*, then recorded a demo and presented it to Jones. There have been rumors that Jones hated the song and didn't want it included on the album but he dismisses those as exaggeration. He admits to asking Jackson to make some changes. First, he thought the title should be changed to "My Lover" because people would think the song was about the tennis player Billie Jean King. Jackson stood his ground and the title remained. Jones also thought the 29 second introduction needed to be trimmed. When Jackson heard that he said: "But that's the jelly! That's what makes me want to dance," and as Jones would say later, "When Michael Jackson tells you, 'That's what makes me want to dance', well, the rest of us just have to shut up." The two butted heads so much over the song Jackson eventually insisted he be given co-producing credit for "Billie Jean."

Of course this being 1983, it was hard to have a hit without MTV's support. But Michael Jackson had one thing going against him in the beginning of 1983 - his skin color. MTV didn't have a "no black artist" rule but they may as well have. Years later MTV executives would claim that their initial intention was to launch a rock format channel, and it was only when they moved to a pop format that they started playing more black artists. Some see this is a convenient excuse. Whichever the case, what we do know is that CBS' president Walter Yetnikoff threatened MTV with going public about their anti-black stance as well as pulling every CBS artist off the channel if MTV didn't play the video for "Billie Jean." It was right around this time that MTV conveniently went to their pop format and found a place for "Billie Jean" as well as Prince's "Little Red Corvette." Many in the industry say "Billie Jean" helped promote MTV as much as MTV helped promote "Billie Jean." The song went on to sell ten million copies and MTV becoming more diverse in its playlist certainly expanded its popularity.

"Billie Jean" earned Grammy Awards for Best R&B Song and Best R&B Male Vocal Performance as well as the American Music Award for Favorite Pop/Rock Single. For an artist with as many hits as Michael Jackson it's impossible to call one of them a signature song, but there is no doubt that if you're old enough to remember 1983, and you hear that opening drum beat, the one Jackson called "the jelly," you can instantly picture his white shoes walking along that light-up sidewalk. Whatever his motivation or inspiration, he created a timeless classic to immortalize it.

On this date in 1978, Kansas was sitting at #6 on the *Billboard* Hot 100 chart with their song "Dust in the Wind." The ballad, a beautiful reminder about the fleeting nature of life, was a huge departure for the band but it would go on to become their most commercially successful single, even though the song's composer fought against it being recorded and released.

Kansas came together as a band in 1970 in Topeka, Kansas. They incorporated some complex symphonic arrangements and unique time signatures into some of their work, plus, besides your normal guitar and drums, Kansas featured a full-time violinist. Given all this, it would be fair to classify them as more than just a rock band, but pioneers in the emerging progressive rock genre as well. The band developed a following the old fashioned way, releasing albums and touring and slowly building a loyal and growing fanbase. Their fourth LP, *Leftoverture*, became their breakout, climbing to #5 on the LP chart and featuring the hard-rocking "Carry On Wayward Son" which peaked at #11 in the spring of 1977.

Around this time Kerry Livgren, Kansas' guitarist and primary songwriter, was reading a lot of Native American poetry and was struck by a particular line: "For all we are is dust in the wind" and it got him thinking. His band was doing well by this point and after years of toiling away in obscurity he was every bit a rock star. But what did it all mean? He'd eventually die and no amount of fame or fortune could prevent that. He picked up his guitar and started playing some beautiful, plaintive chords. His wife overheard him and said he should put lyrics to the melody. He responded by saying he didn't think it was a "Kansas-type" song but she encouraged him to try anyway. With thoughts of mortality and the ephemeral nature of life, he wrote "Dust in the Wind."

When Kansas gathered to record their next album, Livgren didn't immediately play the song for them. He still had his hesitations about it. They recorded "Point of Know Return" which would become the title track of their next LP, as well as a number of other songs in similar style. Near the end of the recording sessions it became obvious they needed one more song. Finally, Livgren presented "Dust in the Wind," even though he was sure his bandmates would reject it. But of course they didn't. In fact, they were floored by it. But even as they effused, Livgren regretted playing it for them and he asked his bandmates to forget about it. But they wouldn't let it go and finally they overruled him.

"Point of Know Return" was released in October of 1977 along with the album of the same name. Both did well, with the song peaking at #28 and the album selling solid numbers. Then, "Dust in the Wind" was released and became a huge hit, peaking at #6 in the spring of 1978. The LP would go all the way to #4 mostly driven by the success of the single. And then Kansas was in that precarious situation that some bands find themselves in. They'd won a whole new fan base with their mellow, acoustic, introspective hit, yet nothing else they played sounded like that. Kansas wasn't Simon and Garfunkel or America but they now had a whole lot of new fans that wanted them to be.

Despite the confusion among fans, Kansas continued on for many years as a successful rock band. They'd never achieve quite the level of success they did with "Dust in the Wind" but through the mid-eighties they were still hitting the Top 40 with songs like "People of the South Wind" , "Hold On" , "Play the Game Tonight" and "All I Wanted." Livgren has continued exploring questions about life and death and his conversion to evangelical Christianity in the early eighties eventually led to his departure from Kansas because the band wasn't looking to become a full-blown Christian rock band. In his solo work, he has delved deeper into the themes of life, death and religion. Nothing that he has written since "Dust in the Wind" though has struck the conscience of America quite as much as that simple song with its sobering life advice.

It does all slip away. And all your money won't another minute buy. And though the song doesn't offer counsel on what to do once you realize we are all just dust in the wind, it is this writer's humble suggestion that you enjoy the here and now as much as possible. All we do will eventually crumble to the ground but instead of dwelling on life's evanescence, we owe it to ourselves and our loved ones to make the most of the time we have. Love stronger. Live harder. Or as the Romans said, "carpe diem." Seize the day. Life is fleeting but we can squeeze the most out of it once we accept that fact and start making the most of every moment we have here on earth.


**April 23rd**

On this date in 1983, Dexys Midnight Runners made it to #1 on the *Billboard* Hot 100 chart with their song, "Come On Eileen." Here's how hard an accomplishment that was: 1983 was the year of Michael Jackson's *Thriller*. No one was a bigger star or hotter commercial success than Jackson that year. His song "Billie Jean" had a seven week run at #1 from early March through mid-April and then his follow-up, "Beat It" would go to #1 at the end of April where it enjoyed a three week stay. The only song that interrupted Jackson's nearly three month reign at the top of the charts was "Come On Eileen."

Dexys Midnight Runners came out of Birmingham, England in the late seventies melding rock and new wave with Celtic elements. Their band name was inspired by the popular amphetamine dexamfetamine which many musicians used to help power through their late night gigs. They used the nickname for the drug, Dexy, and added Midnight Runners because that's what the drug allowed them to do and, voila!, the unique band name was born. They were a big band going for a big sound even in their earliest days, incorporating a horn section and often fiddles to add that Irish flavor to their music. Their debut single, 1979's "Dance Stance" made it to #40 in the U.K. but since they didn't have a distribution deal in the States it was never released in America. The same can be said about their next few singles so while they were building a fan base in England they were practically unheard of across the pond. Even their single "Geno" which went to #1 on the British pop chart never got a U.S. release.

All that changed in 1983 and MTV had a lot to do with. MTV is often credited for leading what's called the Second British Invasion, because early on the channel played an inordinate number of British bands. Much of that had to do with the fact that England already had a number of shows that were playing music videos so most British bands in the early eighties were producing music videos and since MTV was desperate for content to fill 24 hours of programming, they often played whatever they could get their hands on. And when they got their hands on "Come On Eileen" the song went into heavy rotation. The video has a certain dirty, gritty quality. It's not slick or overly produced by any means. But there's a charm in that. And the video helped the song climb to #1.

So how did their biggest international hit come about? It started with a good rhythm. Dexys' lead singer Kevin Rowland has explained: "We wanted a good rhythm and we found one. Lots of records we liked had that rhythm: 'Concrete and Clay,' 'It's Not Unusual' by Tom Jones. Lots of records we liked had that 'Bomp ba bomp, bomp ba bomp.' We felt it was a good rhythm. We came up with the chord sequence ourselves and just started singing melodies over it. I remember thinking, 'We're really onto something here.'"

Once the catchy rhythm and melody was worked out it was time for lyrics and Roland tapped into a distant memory, specifically, his first love. Rowland was raised Catholic and he served as an altar boy as a kid. Like any boy hitting puberty, though, he became very interested in sex but since his religious beliefs treated premarital sex as a sin, it was a taboo subject. Nonetheless, he and his first girlfriend, yes, Eileen, did eventually break down and give in to the temptations of the flesh. Rowland tapped into that feeling of conflict he had as a kid. The lyric, "You in that dress, my thoughts I confess, verge on dirty," pretty much summarizes how most young men feel when dealing with the issues of sex and religion. Next came the chanting section. Again Rowland explains: "I came up with that, 'Too ra loo ra,' and I remember thinking, 'Wow, this is sounding really good.' You get a feeling when you're writing a song. Something happens. And in the end it kind of finished itself."

The final piece of the puzzle was the breakdown and tempo change towards the end which is followed by the upbeat fiddle section. The band repeated the "Come on Eileen taloo-rye-aye" while Rowland provided the counter melody with "now you're full grown, now you have shown, oh, Eileen." And if the fiddle section here sounds vaguely familiar, it was modeled after the Jewish traditional song "Hava Nagila."

Dexys Midnight Runners will always be considered the ultimate one-hit wonder. The nearest they came to #1 in the U.S. was their single "The Celtic Soul Brothers" which reached #86 on the *Billboard* Hot 100 chart. But that one hit lives on even today. Most everyone would recognize the song from just its opening fiddle and it's almost impossible-not-to-sing-along-to "taloo-rye-aye" parts. It's a slice of the early MTV era that anyone who lived through it could never, no never, forget.

On this date in 2015, "Uptown Funk" by Mark Ronson featuring Bruno Mars spent its 98th, and final day at the top of the pop chart. It had risen to #1 on January 17th when it ended Taylor Swift's seven week run with "Blank Space" and it would reside at the top for almost four months, 14 consecutive weeks in fact, before bowing out to "See You Again" by Wiz Khalifa featuring Charlie Puth. The song had taken over a year and a half to complete and driven one of its writers to near exhaustion from stress, but in the end it was all worth it. They completed a funk party that will surely stand the test of time.

Peter Gene Hernandez was born in 1985 on the island of Honolulu. He was born into a musical family, with parents who are musicians and an uncle who is an Elvis impersonator. By the age of three the young boy was already on stage, miming to Michael Jackson and, like his uncle, Elvis. In 1992, at just seven years of age he made his film debut, playing a little Elvis impersonator in *Honeymoon in Vegas*. He had already adopted a new nickname, using what his dad called him and going with Bruno Hernandez. When he moved to Los Angeles at 17 years old he changed his last name too because he didn't feel Hernandez had enough pizzazz. He explains, "The girls say I'm out of this world, so I was like, I guess I'm from Mars."

Bruno Mars was signed to a record deal when he was still a teenager but things didn't work out at his first label, Motown, and pretty soon Mars found himself struggling in Los Angeles. Things got so desperate he even resorted to DJing. "I told this person I could DJ," he once said, "because they said they could pay me $75 cash under the table. I didn't know how to DJ. I lost that job pretty quick." But pretty soon his music career got going, first as a producer and songwriter, and then eventually as a solo artist. His debut album, *Doo-Wops & Hooligans* was released in October of 2010, just days before Mars' 25th birthday. The album made Mars a household name with two chart-topping singles ("Just the Way You Are" and "Grenade") and "The Lazy Song" which reached #4. His follow-up, *Unorthodox Jukebox*, proved that Mars was going to avoid the sophomore slump. It topped the album chart in 2013 and gave Mars his third and fourth #1 singles ("Locked Out of Heaven" and "When I Was Your Man").

Mark Daniel Ronson was born in 1975 in the St John's Wood section of London, England. His family moved to New York City when Mark was just eight and he became childhood friends with Sean Lennon. He attended NYU and got into the downtown music scene, first as a DJ then as a producer. In 2003 he released his debut album, *Here Comes the Fuzz*, on which he does not sing or rap. He wrote (or co-wrote) and produced every track but brought in guest singers and rappers. Ronson continued producing tracks for other artists as well as releasing his own material (with guest singers) and eventually his path crossed with Mars. He produced three songs for the young singer's second album: "Locked Out of Heaven" , "Gorilla" and "Moonshine." The two vowed they would work together again.

When Mars was touring to support *Unorthodox Jukebox*, he and his band would often jam during their soundcheck. These spontaneous jams led to the funk groove that would evolve into "Uptown Funk." Ronson heard it one day and knew instantly they had to make that into a song. Ronson gives Mars all the credit, saying, "Bruno, I think, is probably one of the greatest hook writers of... certainly anyone I've ever worked with, if not this current generation of pop artists." But Mars was on tour and his schedule was as manic as could be. There was no time to fly him to a recording studio for a few days of non-stop work. Over the course of months, Ronson tailed Mars around the country. They'd work on the song in hotel rooms or backstages or studios they'd rent for a day on the road. The song was all but complete but Ronson still needed to add his guitar part. Suddenly, he started getting nervous thinking he wasn't up to the task. As he tells the story: "Bruno had done this great vocal, Jeff [Bhasker] had all these great synth parts. And while we were doing the guitars, I had done 50, 60 takes of it, and I couldn't get a part that I liked....We went out for lunch, and I sort of — I guess the pressure of this song and the guitar part — I fainted in the restaurant. And let's just say I redecorated the walls in the bathroom of this nice restaurant and had to be carried out."

Eventually, Ronson got his guitar part down and the song was added to the tracklist of his album *Uptown Special* which was slated for an early 2015 release. Ronson wisely selected "Uptown Funk" as the lead single and when that dropped on November 10th, 2014, it became an instant success. With its grinding bass, chicken-scratch guitar, incredible horn blasts and over-the-top, party lyrics, the song was destined for a long stay at #1.

"Uptown Funk" has been compared to the very best of James Brown and Prince's funk songs and indeed it stands up there with both of those iconic artists. Mark Ronson believes the reason for the song's success is that "it just sounds like a good time." Indeed it does. The song is a party from its opening through to the end and it forces the listener to react: hand clap, finger snap or full out dance. Don't believe me? Just watch.

## April 25th

On this date in 1992, "Jump," the debut single by a young hip hop duo named Kris Kross, bumped Vanessa Williams' "Saving the Best For Last" from the top of the *Billboard* Hot 100 chart. "Jump" would then stay at #1 for eight consecutive weeks, finally surrendering that spot to Mariah Carey's "I'll Be There." The young rappers not only ruled the charts that year but also influenced fashion and the lexicon. Believe dat.

Christopher Kelly and Christopher Smith became friends in first grade in Atlanta and soon began rapping together for fun. They eventually started performing at the local mall (Atlanta's Greenbriar Mall) where one day in 1991 a 19 year old named Jermaine Dupri spotted them. Though Dupri was still a young man himself he'd already formed one local rap group, the trio Silk Tymes Leather, and he thought Kelly and Smith (both 12 at the time) showed pure potential. He helped them get signed to Ruffhouse Records and began writing material for them.

As their debut album neared completion the clear standout song was "Jump." Dupri had written the rap but since he sampled six different songs to provide the music there are 14 songwriters listed for the track. He grabbed bits from "I Want You Back" by the Jackson 5, "Funky Worm" by Ohio Players, "Impeach the President" by the Honey Drippers, "Midnight Theme" by Manzel, "Escape-Ism" by James Brown and "Saturday Night" by Schoolly D.

The rap he wrote for Kelly and Smith or "Mac Daddy" and "Daddy Mac" as they were now going by, included two inside references. They'd begun calling the young boys' unique fashion style (which mainly meant wearing clothes backwards) "kross out" so in the beginning of the song when they rap, "As we stand there totally krossed out" they are name checking their own look. Also there was another group of young rappers from Atlanta at the time named Another Bad Creation and when the boys rap, "Don't try to compare us to another bad little fad" they are throwing shade on that group.

"Jump" was released on February 6th, 1992 but it wouldn't start selling for a number of weeks. When MTV started playing the video for the song it began to move and by March 31st, when their debut album, *Totally Krossed Out*, was released, the song made its first appearance on the pop chart, clocking in at #61. The following week it jumped all the way to #12 then it made it to #3 before taking over the top spot on this date. But it wasn't just the song that had permeated pop culture. People started copying the "krossed out" look and repeating some of the kid's terms like "believe dat." The song sold 2 million copies in 1992 and it helped their debut album top the LP chart as well. Michael Jackson asked the duo to open for him on the 1992 European leg of his Dangerous World Tour and also to appear in the video for his single "Jam." The future looked fly.

Kris Kross had some other successes over the next few years but nothing compared to "Jump." Their last single together (and with Dupri's help) was 1996's "Live and Die for Hip Hop" which only made it to #72 on the pop chart.

For Dupri, his career in music was only getting started. In 1995, he collaborated with Mariah Carey on her #1 hit, "Always Be My Baby." The following year he worked with Lil' Kim on the track "Not Tonight." He has since worked with Usher, Destiny's Child and Alicia Keys just to name a few. The decades weren't as kind to Kelly and Smith. They both continued making music as well as attempting to follow in Dupri's footsteps and manage and produce. Neither had anywhere near the success of their former mentor. Then in 2013, Chris Kelly overdosed on heroin and died. He was just 34. Jermaine Dupri called him "the son I never had" and Smith said "we were brothers." These days the surviving member of Kris Kross keeps himself busy with painting and sketching as well as working on his music and multimedia projects.

On this date in 1977, a brand new night club opened up on 54th Street in New York City. The site had formally housed an opera house and then a television studio but after a six week, $400,000 facelift it was now called Studio 54 and within no time would become the epicenter of the disco scene in New York and thus, world-wide. Like disco itself, the club's rise was meteoric and its fall precipitous. But in between, oh in between, the nights were fabulous and star-studded and cocaine fueled and bacchanalian.

Steve Rubell and Ian Schrager were both young men growing up in New York City looking to make a name for themselves. In 1975 they opened up a night club called the Enchanted Garden, in Douglaston, Queens and got a taste of how profitable and exciting life could be for club owners. But while Douglaston is about 16 miles from midtown Manhattan it can feel like a world away. The outer edges of Queens have more in common with any suburban area of the country than they do with all the late night excitement of the Big Apple and Rubell and Schrager yearned to be at the center of it all. Their opportunity arose in 1976 when CBS moved most of its broadcast operations out of its location on 54th street and put that spot up for sale. The nightclub scene was on the rise at the time and with disco crossing over from the dance chart to the pop chart it looked like there'd be no end to the public's insatiable desire for more, more, more. A number of parties made offers on the location on 54th street but Rubell and Schrager, with financial backing from Jack Dushey, landed the deal. They took control in the winter of 1977 and hurried the club for a grand opening. During the renovation they retained the theatrical rigs so they could have moving and changing scenery at the club. They also installed huge bass bins all over the club so the music would be felt as much as heard. Rubell and Schrager also took advantage of Carmen D'Alessio, a public-relations entrepreneur in the fashion industry, who knew everyone who was anyone. D'Alessio worked her Rolodex and made sure the opening night party was packed with celebrities. The next day, *The New York Post* ran a front page article about the opening with a picture of Cher in Studio 54. Rubell and Schrager had hoped to open the hottest nightclub in town. Before long, Studio 54 was the hottest nightclub in the world.

The list of celebrities who regularly showed up to party at 54 is legendary. Andy Warhol, Liza Minnelli, Elizabeth Taylor, Mick Jagger, Michael Jackson, Calvin Klein . . . And unless you were that famous, you had a tough time getting in. Rubell and Schrager installed a strict door policy that was enforced by their security and overseen by Rubell himself. He would stand on a stool overlooking the mob scene that showed up nightly and handpick the people who could get past his velvet rope. He called it "mixing a salad." He wanted just the right combination of black and white, straight and gay, male and female. And of course, everyone had to look fabulous and sexy and outrageous. Schrager used to joke, "If I didn't own the club I couldn't get in."

And once you were inside, the energy was off the charts. DJs spun the latest disco hits and the dance floor was always jammed. Drinks flowed and cocaine was snorted and couples made love up in the balcony or down in the dark recesses of the basement.

As the saying goes, pride goeth before the fall. For Steve Rubell it was both his pride and his big mouth that caused his fall. By 1978 he was bragging to anyone who would listen about how much cash he and Schrager were raking in. He told some people they made $7 million in their first year and in some newspapers he was quoted, bragging "only the Mafia made more money." Eventually the IRS decided to take a look and when they raided the club they discovered Rubell wasn't lying. The two were skimming millions in cash. Rubell and Schrager eventually plead guilty to tax evasion and spent 13 months in prison. But before they went away they hosted one more party at their famous club, calling it "The End of Modern-day Gomorrah." The club closed in February of 1980, not even three years after it had opened. In that short time it had become the most famous, the most glamorous, the most star-studded spot in the world.

Studio 54 re-opened about a year after it closed under new ownership but by that point everything had changed. Disco was dead and the new incarnation could never live up to the old one. Studio 54 closed its doors again a few years later and these days it has been converted back to a theater. You can go see musicals and plays there now and as long as you have a ticket you can always get in. No need to meet someone's standards just to get by the velvet rope.

If you go, and put your ear up against the walls you might just hear the echoes of the disco age. The bass still rumbles from somewhere deep in the past and the ghosts of Warhol and Taylor and Jackson still walk the aisles. Studio 54 had a brief reign as the hottest spot in all the world and if you look hard enough you can still see the glitter to this day.

### April 27th

On this date in 1932, Kemal Amin Kasem was born in Detroit, Michigan. He would go on to be one of the most recognizable voices in pop radio and his weekly countdown shows were must-listen-to programs for anyone who wanted to know what was riding the charts on any given week.

Kasem listened to radio programs as a child and dreamed of becoming a DJ one day. He got his first broadcasting experience in high school when he'd call the local sports on the radio. When he was drafted and sent to Korea he became a DJ on the Armed Forces Radio Korea Network and started sprinkling in facts about the songs he was playing. The trivia was well-received. It's something he continued to do after his stint in the army as he took various DJ jobs in Detroit, Cleveland, Oakland and then Los Angeles. It was in the City of Angels, on KRLA, that Kasem started becoming a national name. In 1964, Dick Clark hired him to host a teen-oriented music television show called *Shebang* and the exposure he gained from *Shebang* led to other jobs on television shows and small movie roles.

In 1969 *Scooby-Doo, Where Are You!* hit the air with Kasem voicing the role of Shaggy.

Then in 1970 Kasem launched the *American Top 40* program. It began as a three hour show that was carried by seven stations but it became an instant hit and was soon syndicated all around the country. By 1978 the show had expanded to four hours, mainly because of the increasing length of pop songs. The format was simple. Kasem took that week's *Billboard* Hot 100 chart, started at #40 and counted his way down to the #1 song of the week. Using the style he'd already perfected, Kasem provided some interesting facts or trivia about some of the songs or artists and these tidbits added to the overall quality of the show. He also started doing a "long distance dedication" and of course, his signature sign-off: "Keep your feet on the ground, and keep reaching for the stars."

Kasem was the voice of *American Top 40* for 18 years but a contract dispute in 1988 led to his departure. He then formed a competing show called *Casey's Top 40* which was picked up by the radio network Westwood One. Shadoe Stevens took over the reigns of *American Top 40* but the show clearly missed Kasem's banter and by 1995 it was cancelled. Eventually, Kasem gained the rights to his original show name and he was the DJ for *American Top 40* once again, from 1997 till he retired in 2004.

In 1992 Casey Kasem became the youngest inductee into the Radio Hall of Fame and five years later *Billboard* magazine honored Kasem with its first-ever Lifetime Achievement Award. He passed away in 2014 as one of the most recognizable and famous voices ever. He had, no doubt, kept reaching for the stars throughout his life and in doing so, became one of the most famous DJs ever.

### April 28th

On this date in 1973, Pink Floyd's eighth studio album, *Dark Side of the Moon*, rose to #1 on the *Billboard* Top 200 chart. They'd spent over a year developing the material for this LP, playing much of it live in concert to flesh it out, in hopes of having a breakthrough success that would expand their already rabid, yet cult-size fan base, especially in the U.S. where they'd so far failed to become a big name. Whatever expectations they'd had, *Dark Side of the Moon* far-exceeded them. Though it only remained at #1 on the album chart for one week, the LP went on to become one of the highest-selling and longest-charting albums in the history of rock and roll.

The earliest incarnations of Pink Floyd included Syd Barrett, who, for their first few years, was the visionary, lyricist and frontman for a band that was literally testing the outer limits of psychedelia in the mid-sixties. Barrett's artistry was enhanced by his copious LSD usage, and possible schizophrenia, and soon the previously outgoing and gregarious Barrett became socially withdrawn and prone to intense mood swings as well as periods of catatonia. In layman's terms, he'd gone mad.

Eventually Barrett was forced out of the group but this experience left an indelible mark on the remaining members of Pink Floyd. To a man, they became fascinated with what they saw as the razor thin line between genius and madness.

In 1971, when the band met to discuss their next project, bassist Roger Waters (who was already filling some of the creative gap left by Barrett's departure) proposed the idea for a "concept album" which dealt with things that "make people mad." All five members got to work on songs that would touch on the subject of lunacy and within weeks they were rehearsing material for what they were tentatively calling *Dark Side of the Moon: A Piece for Assorted Lunatics*. At one point the band discovered that another English group, Medicine Head, was releasing an album named *Dark Side of the Moon*, so they started calling their new work *Eclipse*, the same name as the song they intended as the final track for the album. When Medicine Head's album was a commercial failure they switched back to their original title but shortened it to just *Dark Side of the Moon*.

The early part of 1972 found the band performing much of this new material for audiences. They did over ninety shows throughout Europe, Japan and the U.S. and the album literally took shape based on how well it played live. At one point the band discovered that a bootleg of one of their performances was being sold in record stores and they were devastated, thinking this could ruin future album sales (they needn't have worried).

In between stints on the road the band convened at the famed Abbey Road Studios to begin recording sessions. They had come up with a concept of interspersing some dialogue throughout the album and so they took to recording people inside Abbey Road, asking them questions like "When was the last time you were violent?", "Do you ever fear you're going mad?" and "are you afraid of dying?" They recorded anyone and everyone they could find in the studio. One day Wings was working in a different room so they got Paul and Linda McCartney on tape but their responses were deemed too polished and playful. However, Wings guitarist, Henry McCullough, did contribute the excellent, "I don't know I was really drunk at the time." It was Floyd roadie Chris Adamson, who said "I've been mad for fucking years – absolutely years," which was given the honor of opening the album.

Though the finished result was similar to what Floyd had performed live, the biggest difference was the song, "The Great Gig in the Sky." During those 1972 preview shows that song (which was being called either "Religion" or "The Mortality Sequence" at the time) was a simple organ instrumental over which the band played spoken-word snippets from the Bible or speeches by Malcolm Muggeridge, a British writer known for his conservative religious views. When it came time to record this though they felt the song needed something different, perhaps because they were already using so many spoken word pieces in other parts of the album, so their engineer, Alan Parsons, suggested they try a young singer named Clare Torry, with whom he had just worked on another project. Torry was brought into the studio and asked to "improvise" as the track was played. At first she had no idea what was expected of her but she eventually got into it by pretending that she herself was an instrument. She belted out two takes, started a third, then stopped saying she felt she'd done her best work already. The band seemed unimpressed when she left the studio so she figured they wouldn't use anything she'd recorded. According to Torry she didn't know she'd made the album till she saw it in a record store and spotted her name in the credits. Torry's contribution to "The Great Gig in the Sky" makes that song one of the stand-outs on an album that is full of amazing songs.

Speaking of Parsons, he is given a lot of credit, and deservedly so, for the overall sound of the album. The band had lots of ideas (like Waters' suggestion of recording coins being dropped into a jar to make up the percussion track of his song "Money") but it took someone with studio-savvy to pull those ideas off. Parsons received a Grammy for his work on *Dark Side of the Moon* and it would help launch his own career. He attributes much of his success on the album to Monty Python. The band loved the English comedy troupe and whenever they were on television they would all take a break to watch. These segments alone in the studio gave Parsons extra time to cut tape and play with an effect to get it just right. When *Dark Side* became such a massive success, Pink Floyd used some of their new found riches to help fund the production of Monty Python's first movie, *Monty Python and the Holy Grail.*

And while we're on the subject of movie tie-ins, the urban legend that the band made *Dark Side* to sync up with the movie, *The Wizard of Oz* needs to be addressed. This rumor began at some point a decade or so after the release of the album and has only perpetuated with the advent of the internet (because rumors quickly become alternative facts online). The band scoffs at the notion that they did this intentionally and indeed if you attempt it, you'll spot only a few times when the two do seem "synched." Sure, Dorothy is balancing on the fence when the lyric "balanced on the biggest wave" is sung and the cacophonous moments of "The Great Gig in the Sky" do come just as the tornado hits, but there are far more examples where the music has nothing to do with what's happening on screen than the few coincidental moments when it does. Some have also pointed out that *The Wall* can be played during the movie *2001: A Space Odyssey* which just shows if you have enough free time, and marijuana, you can do amazing things.

Although *Dark Side of the Moon* only held the #1 spot on the *Billboard* Top 200 album chart for one week, it remained on that chart for a record breaking 741 weeks (over 14 years!)  Its worldwide sales figures are estimated to be about 45 million. It's an album that still sounds unique and original all these years later. The band set out to sing about madness and lunacy and in doing so they touched millions of music listeners, whether they struggled with their own sanity or not. If you have 42 minutes today, you should listen to *Dark Side of the Moon,* front to back in the track order as it was released. Crank it loud (preferably with headphones) so you can hear every little effect and spoken word piece. If you listen real close you may even hear the muzak version of the Beatles' "Ticket to Ride" being played in the background at the very end of the album. Having *The Wizard of Oz* playing simultaneously is optional of course (as is the marijuana) but surely either would enhance the experience.

## April 29th

On this date in 1979, the Police were stalled at #32 on the *Billboard* Hot 100 Chart with their debut U.S. single, "Roxanne." #32 isn't exactly a runaway success yet "Roxanne" helped break the band on both sides of the pond and has become one of the Police's signature songs.

The Police came together in early 1977 in London as the punk craze was at a fever pitch. None of the three members of the band were exactly punk rockers, though. First and foremost, they were a bit older than most on the scene. Bassist and singer Sting was 26, drummer Stewart Copeland was 25 and guitarist Andy Summers was already 35. Plus, their musicianship was far more advanced than the thrashing, three-chord-playing bands that were tearing up the scene. Sting was a lover of jazz and world music, Copeland had cut his teeth in a prog rock band and Summers had already played everything from R&B to psychedelia and was considered an excellent guitarist. Still, punk was in demand so the three started out playing songs simply and aggressively. If they were poseurs it was surely out of practicality. They wanted to land gigs and most bars and clubs were only hiring bands that could play it loud and straight and hard.

By the fall of 1977 they'd already developed a solid reputation on the club scene in London and were booked by the punk rock band the Damned to open for them in Paris. They arrived from London to find their accommodations less-than-desirable. The three were forced to share a room in a rundown hotel in a horrible section of Paris. The alleyway outside their hotel was filled with sex shops and crowded with prostitutes. Sting spent some time looking things over and he began to imagine what it'd be like to fall in love with such a woman. As he strolled the streets of Paris he saw a poster promoting the Edmond Rostand play *Cyrano de Bergerac* and it made him instantly think of the love interest's name, Roxanne (who is not a prostitute in the play but rather a beautiful and intellectual heiress). The lyrics came to him on the stroll. Sting would say later: "It was the first time I'd seen prostitution on the streets and those birds were actually beautiful. I had a tune going around in my head and I imagined being in love with one of those girls."

The next night the three musicians found out the trip to Paris had been worthless since the Damned had cancelled their show and they "pissed off back to England." But at the band's next rehearsal Sting sheepishly showed the others the song he'd written that night in Paris. Summers would say later,

"(Sting) was very shy at first bringing in his songs." But both of his bandmates liked what they heard and began working the song up. Sting had originally envisioned the song with a bossa nova beat but it was Copeland who suggested giving it a reggae feel. Summers explained: "We started playing around with it and came up with something where I was able to play four in the bar, Stewart put that slight reggae thing on, and Sting changed where he put the bass beats. We worked it up in one afternoon." When it came time to record the song Sting happened to bump into a standup piano that was in the studio just as the take was beginning which made him laugh out loud. Despite this obvious flub the band liked the take and decided to keep it in, which explains that random piano note and Sting's devilish laugh in the first few seconds of the song.

A&M initially released "Roxanne" in early 1978 in England only and the song was immediately banned by the BBC. The band couldn't believe it. As Sting has said: "There's was no talk about fucking in it. It wasn't a smutty song in any sense of the word. It was a real song with a real, felt lyric and they wouldn't play it on the grounds that is was about a prostitute." The Police tried to use this to their advantage, plastering posters around London promoting the song with "Banned By the BBC" emblazoned across them. Still, the single failed to gain any traction. It wasn't till the Police flew to the U.S. later in 1978 for a tour of the club circuit that "Roxanne" started to get some airplay in certain markets in America. A&M hadn't even released the song in the States but they'd do so quickly and then, based on the attention the song was getting in the U.S., they rereleased it in England. "Roxanne" peaked this week in 1979 at #32 and it got as high as #12 in England in its second run at the charts. And while these numbers weren't off the charts they paved the way for the Police who, within just a few years would become one of the biggest bands in the world. It's a good thing they hadn't been booked in a nicer hotel in Paris.


## April 30th

On this date in 1978, Cheap Trick recorded their second consecutive show at Tokyo's famous Nippon Budokan with an eye towards releasing a live album for their Japanese fans. The album would become one of the biggest imports in music history before their record label released the LP in the States and helped propel Cheap Trick from an underground (and under-appreciated) band to a household name. The album, released in the U.S. as *Cheap Trick at Budokan*, is one of the best-selling live albums in rock history.

Cheap Trick was formed in Rockford, Illinois in 1973. From their earliest days they played live as often as they could. They built a fan base in the Midwest by playing everywhere and anywhere they could find a crowd: bowling alleys, bars, warehouses. A gig was a gig and Cheap Trick rarely turned one down. They were signed by Epic Records and released their self-titled debut in February of 1977. The album fell under that common heading in rock history: critically acclaimed yet a commercial disappointment. Unfazed, the band kept playing live and seven months later they released their follow-up, *In Color*. Same deal. Critics loved it. Rock radio and the record buying public were less than enraptured.

Except in Japan. The band had never played there live but for some reason their records were selling well and the Japanese division at Columbia (which owned Epic) was eager to bring the band over. The Japanese division also had a standing agreement with Columbia that they could record and release live albums of any bands on their roster. The live albums would only be released in Japan so Columbia had no issue with it.

In April of 1978 the band made their first trip to Japan and they were blown away at the reception they received. Even at the airport. The band had flown across the Pacific on coach and yet they were greeted at the airport like the Beatles. They had to have guards posted at the hotels they were staying in. It was quite a shock for a band that walked the streets in their home country unnoticed.

Cheap Trick were booked to play Budokan on April 28th and April 30th, 1978. When they stepped on the stage for the first time they were blown away again. The wall of sound that greeted them was unlike anything they'd ever heard. 12,000 fans screamed at the top of their lungs throughout the band's entire ninety minute set. The same thing happened two nights later.

When the shows were over and recorded, the band was asked to mix the songs for release (again, just in Japan) and guitarist Rick Nielsen later admitted, "when we heard the tapes of the concert, we thought it sounded hideous." Hideous or not they finished the tapes, and then, since the project was slated as a single album and not a double, they had to select which tracks made the cut and which tracks didn't. When they were done, the Japanese division of Columbia had a Cheap Trick live album they titled *From Tokyo to You*.

Back in the states Cheap Trick were about to release their third LP, *Heaven Tonight*, which dropped a month after their epic shows in Japan. They set about promoting that album and started to work on new material giving little-to-no thought about the live album they'd left behind in Japan. Things at home returned to normal. They didn't need security to protect them and though their fans were enthusiastic it was nothing like what they'd experienced in Japan.

Then, a funny thing happened. Towards the end of 1978 some rock radio stations in the U.S. started playing tracks from the live album. Fans were ordering *From Tokyo to You* as an import, in some cases paying $40 or more for it to be shipped to the states. Epic approached the band about preparing a U.S. release but at first they demurred. They were close to finishing their fourth LP and they weren't exactly thrilled with the finished product of the live album to begin with. It is estimated that 30,000 copies of *From Tokyo to You* were imported to the U.S. before Cheap Trick finally acquiesced and signed off on an American release. *Cheap Trick at Budokan* was released in February of 1979 (for much cheaper than $40) and it became a huge hit. It has sold over 3 million copies and produced a Top 10 single in "I Want You to Want Me" (a song that hadn't even charted when a studio version was released in September of 1977).

Cheap Trick's next album *Dream Police*, performed much better than any of their previous studio albums but it was still considered a step backwards for the band. They were unable to capture the sheer energy and mania that they had in Japan (12,000 screaming fans is hard to fit in a studio). Since then the band has released numerous albums that are met with critical acclaim and inconsistent sales. In 1994 Cheap Trick released *Budokan II* which consisted of the rest of those live shows from 1978 that they couldn't fit on the single album. And a few years later they combined the two into one release titled, *At Budokan: The Complete Concert*. And because Cheap Trick, is, at its core, a live band, they continue to tour. They rock live shows. It is where they are clearly at their best and where they always will be. Sometimes they roll into towns unnoticed, sometimes they are met at airports by thousands of screaming fans. But when they hit the stage it's all the same. They're gonna leave you tired and sweaty and cheering for more.

MAY

On this date in 2014, "Happy" by Pharrell Williams was nearing the end of its eighth consecutive week at #1 on the *Billboard* Hot 100 chart. The song enjoyed an incredible ten week run at the top of the charts, from March 8th to May 16th, and with over 6 million copies sold or downloaded, it was easily the best-selling song of 2014.

Music lovers, especially those who enjoy hip hop and R&B, have known Pharrell Williams since the nineties. His name first appears as cowriter on the 1992 Wreckx-N-Effect hit "Rump Shaker." He then teamed up with his childhood friend Chad Hugo to form the production team called the Neptunes and they scored their first huge hit writing and producing Britney Spears' "I'm a Slave 4 U." In the years that followed the Neptunes would add hits like Nelly's "Hot in Herre" , Snoop Dogg's "Drop It Like It's Hot" and Gwen Stefani's "Hollaback Girl" (just to name a few) to their resume. In 2010, Williams was asked to contribute to the soundtrack for *Despicable Me* and four of his songs made the LP plus he composed most of the score.

So if, by 2013, you didn't know Pharrell Williams by name it just meant you didn't study things like who wrote which songs or who produced which artists. You certainly were familiar with his work.

But in 2013 Williams became a household name. In March of that year Robin Thicke released his dance number "Blurred Lines" which was not only produced and cowritten by Williams but featured him singing and appearing in the video. "Blurred Lines" spent a dozen weeks at #1 and was not only the Song of the Summer of 2013 but the highest-selling song of the year. Williams was also featured on Daft Punk's "Get Lucky" that summer which never quite made it to #1 (blocked by "Blurred Lines") but was a multi-million seller in 2013. Suddenly all the world had heard of Pharrell Williams.

Meanwhile, *Despicable Me 2* was being prepared and the producers asked Williams if he had anything to contribute. He offered them a few songs then remembered something he'd written a few years earlier and offered to Cee Lo Green. But when Green rejected it Williams had stuck the song away. The song was called "Happy." Green had gotten so far as recording the song but he was working on a holiday album at the time (called *Cee Lo's Magic Moment*) and his record label didn't see it fitting in. Williams has said that Green's version "smokes" his (which is hard to believe.)

So Williams recorded "Happy" himself for the *Despicable Me 2* soundtrack. Everything about the song is in line with the title. The lyrics are happy and carefree, Williams' infectiously high-pitched singing is radiant, and the fast, finger-snapping tempo is joyous as well. It's virtually impossible to hear "Happy" and not have your mood improved.

To give the song even more universal appeal, Williams put together two videos. The first is a traditional, song-length video that features Williams and others dancing and signing along with "Happy." The second video is the world's first (and probably still only) 24 hour long music video which resides at the website 24hoursofhappy. That video features the four minute song repeated 360 times and includes shots of various people dancing around Los Angeles and miming along with the song. Williams himself appears at the start of each hour. Minions (from the movie *Despicable Me*) appear in both the short video and the 24 hour version. These videos, featuring everyday people dancing and singing along to the song, spawned copycats and soon Youtube was inundated with homemade versions of the original, with everyone from cheerleader troops to senior citizen centers singing proudly that they were happy.

"Happy" spent 10 weeks at the top of the charts and sold over 13 million copies and downloads. The short video on Youtube has been viewed over 900 million times and the website 24hoursofhappy has had over 12 million visits (go ahead, I know you want to go there). But more important than its sales figures and internet clicks is the song's message. Williams wrote, produced and sang a song of optimism and empowerment. "Happy" is a reminder that we control our own moods, that you can tell bad news not to waste its time, you'll be just fine. That nothing can bring you down. It's not exactly rocket science and the lyrics aren't deep or introspective or groundbreaking, but sometimes everything works in a song and the message comes through loud and clear. That was certainly the case with "Happy." It literally has the power to cheer you up. Go ahead, give it a spin and see if you don't agree.

## May 2nd

On this date in 1969, the Who held a press conference at which they unveiled their latest album, *Tommy*, and helped introduce a new term into the musical lexicon. They were calling *Tommy* a "rock opera," a term most music fans, and even some critics, had never heard before. But after the popularity of *Tommy* the term would become commonplace and in many ways both genres, rock and opera, would be influenced. While many rock bands have taken their own stab at writing entire albums that contain a story arch, many opera companies, in an attempt to appeal to a broader fan base, have introduced rock or pop influences.

The Who emerged from London during those inchoate days of the early sixties when the bands that would spearhead the British Invasion were all forming in the bars and clubs in southern England. No doubt there were weekends when a young music lover could see the Rolling Stones on a Friday night, the Yardbirds open for the Kinks on a Saturday night, and then catch a set by the Who on Sunday. All of these bands were made up of post World War II babies who'd been influenced by American rock and roll in their adolescence and were now trying to follow in the Beatles' footsteps. The Who was no different except their chief lyricist and creative force, Pete Townshend, never seemed content to write standard rock songs. He wanted to tell stories and he saw music as his medium. As far back as 1966 he was working on a longer musical piece called *The Quads* which took place in an imagined future where parents could select the gender of their children. The Quads was about a family that wanted four daughters but somehow got a son, yet they raised him as a girl. The project was eventually abandoned but "I'm a Boy" was released as a single and became one of the Who's early hits in their homeland. A year later, Townshend composed the nine minute rock-suite, "A Quick One, While He's Away" which tells the story of a girl whose lover goes away so she takes up with another man (Ivor, the engine driver.) When her lover returns she confesses her infidelity and in the suite's finale, she is forgiven. By 1968, encouraged by the Who's co-manager Kit Lambert, Townshend began dreaming even bigger. Really big. He began to compose an entire album of songs that followed a theme. It would be an opera. A rock opera.

To be sure, Townshend didn't invent the concept. Music historians credit the psychedelic band Nirvana (not the grunge band from Seattle) and their debut album, 1967's *The Story of Simon Simopath* as the first rock opera. Then the following year the Pretty Things released their fourth LP, *S.F. Sorrow,* which was also a concept album or rock opera about a man named Sebastian F. Sorrow, and his journey through life. Townshend has denied being influenced by that album despite its obvious similarities to *Tommy.*

*Tommy* began as a story about a deaf, dumb and blind boy. While the project was still evolving, Townshend gave an interview to *Rolling Stone* magazine in which he talked about it, saying: "What it's really all about is the fact that ... he's seeing things basically as vibrations which we translate as music. That's really what we want to do: create this feeling that when you listen to the music you can actually become aware of the boy, and aware of what he is all about, because we are creating him as we play." As the concept developed Townshend had a conversation one day with the British rock journalist and writer Nik Cohn. Cohn told Townshend about a novel he was working on called *Arfur: Teenage Pinball Queen* and Townshend shared his ideas for *Tommy.* Cohn seemed unimpressed by the story line of *Tommy* and Townshend teased him, saying, "So you won't give it a good review?" When Cohn demurred Townshend replied, "What if Tommy was a pinball champion?" to which Cohn replied "in that case it would get five stars - and an extra ball." According to Townshend he wrote the song "Pinball Wizard" the next day and added the wrinkle to his story that Tommy, the deaf, dumb and blind boy, sure played a mean pinball. In his autobiography, Townshend admits, "I made a huge leap into the absurd when I decided the hero would play pinball while still deaf, dumb and blind. It was daft, flawed and muddled but also insolent, liberated and adventurous." Townshend was already following the Indian spiritual leader Meher Baba by this point and he was aware of Baba's saying that God was playing marbles with the universe. He loved the similarities between pinball and the visual of God playing marbles. With the element of pinball added, *Tommy* came to fruition and the band recorded the album in late 1968 and early 1969. As the project neared release they held a press conference on this date in 1969 to play their work for rock critics and journalists.

*Tommy* was almost universally praised and the band set out to tour in support of the album. While they were on the road that summer, the Who played their historic, middle-of-the-night set at Woodstock, which included the sun rising during the "See Me, Feel Me" section of *Tommy*'s finale. Townshend has called that single moment a career highlight, which, considering Townshend's career, is saying a lot. In 1975 a film adaptation of *Tommy* was released which starred Roger Daltrey as the title character. A Broadway musical of *Tommy* opened in 1991 and continues to tour from time to time. There have also been symphonic, ballet and bluegrass re-interpretations of the story through the years.

Of course, Pete Townshend wasn't done reinventing the medium of rock music. He'd channel even more of Baba's teachings for his *Lifehouse* project and though that was eventually abandoned, it begat the now classic song "Baba O'Reilly." And in 1973 he'd complete his second rock opera, *Quadrophenia*. Nik Cohn also wasn't done influencing music. It would be his 1976 *New York Magazine* article "Tribal Rites of the New Saturday Night" that inspired the movie *Saturday Night Fever*.

*Tommy*, like so many operas, is a challenge as far as listening to it and trying to follow a story line. Still, the album contains some signature Who songs like "Pinball Wizard", "Acid Queen" and "I'm Free." And then, of course, there's that finale. Many people call it "See Me, Feel Me" but that is really only part of the song called "We're Not Gonna Take It." If you have the time today (75 minutes to be exact) listen to the whole album. If not, give "We're Not Gonna Take It" a spin. It's a suitable synopsis of the story and contains some of Townshend's greatest lyrics (and considering Townshend's career, that's saying a lot.)


## May 3rd

On this date in 1984, Bruce Springsteen released "Dancing in the Dark" as the lead single for his upcoming *Born in the U.S.A.* album. He'd written the song out of anger and frustration from his manager's criticism of the album and insistence that it needed a hit song. Springsteen channeled those emotions and created exactly that, the most commercially successful single of his storied career.

By the mid-eighties Bruce Springsteen was a bonafide rock star. He had legions of fans who lined up to see him whenever he toured. And like so many rock acts that emerged from the seventies, he was more of an album artist than a singles artist. His LPs regularly sold huge numbers and often hit the top (or near the top) of the album chart. His work in the early eighties was a good example. His 1980 double LP *The River* hit #1 on the album chart while the lead single, "Hungry Heart," stalled at #5 on the pop chart. None of the other singles from that LP cracked the Top 10. In 1982, his sparse album, *Nebraska*, climbed to #3 yet neither of its singles even cracked the Hot 100. And Springsteen was fine with that. He'd much rather be viewed as a serious songwriter than a pop star anyway. And he certainly generated enough income in album sales to justify his healthy advances from Columbia.

But Jon Landau, Springsteen's manager and producer at the time, wanted to see his client stay as relevant as possible. Landau also correctly predicted that the music scene was changing and that rock was becoming less of the driving force it had been in the seventies. Pop music was taking its place and much of this was driven by MTV and the increasing importance of the visual aspect of music.

So as Springsteen was preparing material for his next album, Landau was in his ear to make it more accessible and radio-friendly. Springsteen did just that, keeping most of the material livelier than his previous few albums. Even the song that would become the title track evolved from a slower, acoustic version to the upbeat, drum-driven version we know today. Despite that song's themes of disillusionment in the promise of America, its sing-along chorus often makes people think it is a pro-U.S.A. anthem (most famously Ronald Reagan who used it during some campaign stops in 1984).

Springsteen eventually submitted the tapes for *Born in the U.S.A.*, feeling he'd met his manager's request and delivered an album that would sell well and keep the Springsteen name relevant. So he was very surprised when Landau said he felt the album needed one more song. And that song needed to be a hit.

Springsteen argued back and there are differing accounts of how intense that argument got. In his 2016 autobiography, *Born to Run*, Springsteen admitted, "We argued, gently, and I suggested that if he felt we needed something else, he write it." But, of course, it wasn't up to Landau to write a hit. That task fell to Bruce. And whether he was upset or just inspired, he channeled that emotion into a song which he wrote that night. In the lyrics, he admits to his frustration that he, "Ain't got nothing to say" and, perhaps, referencing MTV's influence, that he needs a makeover ("I want to change my clothes, my hair, my face.") He worked the song up with a very catchy melody and upbeat, 149 beats-per-minute tempo. And when Landau heard the song he knew it was the hit the album needed.

"Dancing in the Dark" song was released on this date in 1984 and it started climbing the charts instantly. It would get to #2 in late June where it sat behind Duran Duran's "The Reflex." The next week "The Reflex" slipped but instead of Springsteen claiming the top spot (which would have been a first in his career), Prince's "When Doves Cry" leaped-frogged from #3 to #1. Those two songs sat in that position for the next month, with "Doves" at #1 and "Dancing" at #2. Finally both began to slip in August, meaning Springsteen had been denied the top spot by Prince. To date, "Dancing in the Dark" is Springsteen's highest-charting song.

A video on MTV may have helped the song get to #1 but Springsteen was late in delivering that. He'd been initially opposed to even making any videos and when he decided he needed one the debate began about the concept. He hired Jeff Stein to direct, and Daniel Pearl as the cinematographer. Pearl had recently done work on the Police's "Every Breath You Take," and the original concept was similar, with Springsteen singing in a stark, dimly lit studio (and even dancing in the dark.)  But disagreements arose and the concept was scrapped. Brian DePalma was then hired to shoot a straight performance video. On June 29th, 1984, during Springsteen's concert at the St. Paul Civic Center in Minnesota, DePalma filmed the band's performance of "Dancing in the Dark." A young and virtually unknown actress named Courtney Cox (who would go on to fame in the 1990's sitcom *Friends*) was planted in the audience and Springsteen called her up to dance with him towards the end of the song. Though he felt he'd gotten all his shots, DePalma asked Springsteen to replay the song to ensure he had enough footage. The crowd in Minnesota was very understanding as Bruce and his band replayed "Dancing in the Dark" with DePalma and his film crew taking the stage to get some close-ups. The video arrived to MTV too late to help the song reach #1 but it did become Springsteen's first video to go into heavy rotation on the music channel and helped introduce him to a whole new generation of fans.

*Born in the U.S.A.* hit #1 on the album chart in the summer of 1984 and it would return in the winter of 1985. The album kept producing hits with "Cover Me" climbing to #7, the title track reaching #9, "I'm On Fire" peaking at #6, "Glory Days" stopping at #5 and "I'm Goin' Down" going up to #9. Landau had done his job as manager and producer: he'd given his artist direction and inspired him to write his most commercially successful collection of songs. As Bruce wrote in "Dancing in the Dark," "you can't start a fire without a spark" and Landau had provided that spark. Once fired up, Springsteen did his job as well. Frustrated at having to come up with one more song, he'd come up with one of his best, certainly in terms of commercial appeal.

### May 4th

On this date in 1970, members of the Ohio National Guard, which had been deployed to disperse an on-campus protest at Kent State, began firing into a crowd of unarmed students. Four young people were killed and nine were wounded. The incident, sometimes referred to as the Kent State Massacre, would not only inspire one of the great anti-war songs of all time, it would have a profound effect on the students at Kent State, some of whom would go on to become prominent musicians.

Kent State, like so many universities in the late sixties, was a hot bed for protests against the Vietnam War. Demonstrations were sparked after the April 30th, 1970 Cambodian Invasion and throughout the following weekend students at Kent State became more and more vocal and even violent, with rocks and bottles being thrown at policemen who had been called in to control the crowds. By Sunday, May 3rd, Ohio Governor Jim Rhodes was so frustrated he pounded his hands on his desk during a press conference and called the students "un-American." He promised to, "Eradicate the problem," and called on the National Guard to patrol the campus and quell any more protests. On Monday, May 4th, about 2,000 students arrived to continue voicing their discontent and very quickly tension between the protestors and the National Guard reached a boiling point. The guardsmen's first attempt at dispersing the crowd was tear gas but wind made that ineffective. This only seemed to embolden the protestors who chanted, "Pigs off campus," and hurled rocks towards the troops who slowly began to retreat. Then, without an order being heard, one guardsmen fired his pistol into the crowd. Another guardsmen followed and then more and within moments, 67 shots had been fired at the protestors who were now, literally, running for their lives. Nine students were injured and four were dead: Allison Krause and Jeffrey Miller who had been participating in the protest and William Knox Schroeder and Sandra Scheuer who had been strolling from one class to the next.

The photograph of a female student crying over the slain body of Jeffrey Miller became a lightning rod for the anti-war crowd.

Neil Young heard the news from Kent State and was moved by the senseless violence. He took a walk and composed lyrics for a song he'd call "Ohio" before he was back home. His lyrics directly reference the incident, mentioning "Tin soldiers and Nixon coming" and "Four dead in Ohio." He confronts the listener head-on by asking, "What if you knew her and found her dead on the ground?" Young then had his bandmates in Crosby, Stills, Nash & Young record the song and it was released just weeks after the incident. David Crosby would later say that putting Nixon's name in the lyrics was, "the bravest thing I ever heard." "Ohio" was banned on some radio stations but it still went on to be an iconic song among the anti-war, counter-culture groups.

"Ohio" is just one of the songs (albeit the most famous) that was written about the incident. Steve Miller wrote a song called "Jackson-Kent Blues" and the Beach Boys wrote and released "Student Demonstration Time" a year after the shootings. And a virtually unknown Bruce Springsteen also wrote a song called "Where Was Jesus in Ohio" which remains unreleased.

Meanwhile, the surviving students at Kent State were understandably moved. Many of them would eventually become musicians and look back at this day in 1970 as a turning point in their lives. Christine Ellen Hynde was one of those students and she'd eventually climb to international fame as Chrissie Hynde, lead singer of the Pretenders. Joe Walsh was another one. He would later say, "being at the shootings really affected me profoundly. I decided that maybe I don't need a degree that bad." Mark Mothersbaugh and Jerry Casale were also on campus that day. After the shootings, Mothersbaugh heard the song "Ohio" and it showed him how powerfully and instantly music can comment on social events. If someone had wanted to make a movie about the shootings, it would have taken a year or more to hit the theaters. But music was so much more immediate. CSNY had released their song within a month of the incident and that meant something to Mothersbaugh. He and Casale started thinking of the concept of "de-evolution," (meaning the human race was regressing and becoming dysfunctional) and they'd eventually form the post-punk band Devo.

Mothersbaugh said he rejected all of his hippie beliefs after the incident, saying, "I saw the depths of the horrors and lies and the evil," and he'd channeled those emotions into Devo's dark humor.

Neither the Kent State incident, nor any of the songs that came from it, ended America's involvement in the Vietnam War. That would take a number of years. In fact, it can be argued that no protest song has ever ended an armed confrontation. They may embolden the protestor, and give people something to sing at demonstrations, but it's doubtful any world leader ever pulled troops out of harm's way based on a song he heard on the radio. Still, there's a cathartic effect when an artist captures the zeitgeist of a movement in a song. Neil Young did that as well as any songwriter ever has just days after the Kent State shooting. To this day he considers it the best song he wrote for CSNY.


**May 5th**

On this date in 1970, "You Make Me Real," the only single released off the Doors' fifth studio album, *Morrison Hotel*, was sitting at its peak position just outside the Top 40. Somehow though, the single's B-side would go on to become one of the band's signature songs and one of the most popular, sing-along, bar songs of all time. And the whole song began from a casual comment made to Jim Morrison by another rock star and a typical jam session by the band. Here's the story:

1969 was a turbulent year for the Doors. It began in March when Morrison either did or did not flash the crowd in Miami and the fallout from the controversy caused cancelled concerts and bans from certain radio stations. Morrison spent much of the year fighting the legal issues that stemmed from the incident. The Doors released their fourth album, *The Soft Parade*, that summer and though it made it all the way to #6 on the album chart, the LP turned off some of their older fans as it strayed from their signature, blues-based sound. In September, Morrison was convicted and sentenced to six months in prison but an appeal meant he was free and the band decided to try to record another album. Then, just as recording got underway, Morrison was in more trouble, this time for harassing stewardesses on a flight. Morrison's drinking and drug use were out of control. He was clearly a ticking time bomb. The band's future was uncertain and, in many ways, it seemed the end was near.

This is the atmosphere surrounding the band as they gathered in late 1969 to record what would become *Morrison Hotel*. They were looking to return to basics and play some grittier rock and blues compared to their previous album. The blues specifically was something Morrison often enjoyed singing in the studio as the band warmed up and it was during one of these jam session that "Roadhouse Blues" began. While the band played the music, Morrison began riffing on a place called the Roadhouse. He'd never say if his lyrics were inspired by an actual location but many Doors' fans felt it was a place called Toping

Corral that was close to where Morrison was living at the time. To get there you had to take a road with many twists and turns which meant you definitely had to, "keep your eyes on the road and your hands upon the wheel." And the place did indeed have a few bungalows in the back where Morrison would often crash.

As the band was working on the song one day, Alice Cooper happened to be recording in another studio. According to Cooper he and Morrison were chatting between sessions and Cooper told the Doors' singer that he'd woken up that morning and had a beer. Cooper said he saw Morrison jot something down in one of his notebooks and then a little later he overheard Morrison deliver the now famous line, "Well, I woke up this morning, I got myself a beer." Cooper said to himself, "I just said that a second ago!"

For the sessions, the Doors asked the Lovin' Spoonful's John Sebastian to play the harmonica. He agreed but, in an attempt to distance himself from the controversy surrounding the band, he insisted he be listed in the credits as "G. Puglese." They also brought in the legendary bass player Lonnie Mack to play bass. But only bass. There have long been rumors that he played guitar on the track as well but those have been dispelled. Robbie Krieger did all the guitar work on the song which Morrison confirms going into the solo by yelling, "Do it, Robbie, do it!"

As *Morrison Hotel* took shape the band must have thought highly of "Roadhouse Blues" because they selected it as the first song on the album. But when it was time to release a single, for some reason they chose "You Make Me Real" and then picked "Roadhouse Blues" as the B-side (thus ensuring it wouldn't be released as a future single). Though the album didn't produce any hits it was very well received by both fans and critics. And somehow, over the years, "Roadhouse Blues" has become a jukebox favorite. It's also a staple in most bar band's repertoires. While no one but hardcore Doors' fans even remember "You Make Me Real," anyone who has listened to rock radio since the early seventies could probably sing every word to "Roadhouse Blues." And when Morrison sings that final, "Let it roll" it's impossible not to join in with the, "All night long" part even if you didn't wake up that morning and get yourself a beer.


**May 6th**


On this date in 1989, Madonna's "Like a Prayer" was in the middle of a three week run at #1 on the *Billboard* Hot 100 chart. The song and its accompanying video were shrouded in controversy but Madonna, as she's done so many times in her innovative career, used the bad press to her benefit.

1988 had been an odd year for Madonna. After marrying Sean Penn she'd chosen to focus on acting but her 1987 film *Who's That Girl* had been a commercial and critical failure. In 1988 she tried Broadway, starring in the David Mamet play *Speed-the-Plow* where her acting was some similarly criticized.

Other than the single "Spotlight" which was pulled from her remix compilation, *You Can Dance*, Madonna released no new music in 1988. She also underwent some personal milestones that year, turning 30 and seeing her marriage to Penn dissolve.

As she entered 1989 Madonna wanted to get back where she belonged, namely the top of the pop chart. But she'd matured since her early days (as artists are apt to do) and she wanted her work to reflect her new worldview. She also wished to channel some of the religious guilt she'd carried her whole life. Growing up Catholic, she was burdened by the sense of being sinful. As she would tell a reporter while promoting "Like a Prayer," "I have a great sense of guilt and sin from Catholicism that has definitely permeated my everyday life, whether I want it to or not... I'm always afraid that I'm going to be punished. And that's something you're raised to believe as a Catholic." Tying this into her latest work, she explained, "Both the song and album stemmed from this uneasiness; my direct prayers to God, it is beautiful and divine." She'd described "Like a Prayer" as the song of a passionate young girl, "so in love with God that it is almost as though He were the male figure in her life." Madonna worked with Patrick Leonard who co-wrote the song and also produced the session. They wanted a gospel feel for the track, befitting its religious themes, so they employed the Los Angeles Church of God Choir to sing background.

In early 1989 Madonna struck a deal with Pepsi. The soft drink was trying to win over the younger consumer and had recently signed deals with Michael Jackson and Whitney Houston. Madonna's deal called for a 2 minute commercial that would air before the song was released. Pepsi actually aired a commercial during that year's Grammy Award ceremony to promote the upcoming commercial which would feature the worldwide premier of a new Madonna song. On March 2nd, 1989, during *The Cosby Show*, Pepsi aired the clip, which featured Madonna watching an 8 year old version of herself (and vice versa) while "Like a Prayer" plays. It was a highly anticipated moment, and it is estimated that 250 million viewers saw the commercial worldwide. Pepsi had exactly what they wanted, a hot new song and a jubilant ad featuring one of biggest music stars of the day drinking their product.

Till the next day.

On March 3rd, Madonna released the song and its accompanying video. Pepsi had hoped the video would dovetail with its commercial so even if it didn't include the overly obvious Pepsi branding from the commercial, viewers would think of Pepsi whenever they saw the clip. But their deal with Madonna hadn't included artistic control over the video so they were as surprised as anyone when MTV premiered the video which features Madonna kissing a black saint, getting stigmata on her hands, and dancing in front of burning crosses. Religious groups freaked out and called for boycotts of Madonna's records and Pepsi products. Pepsi blinked, dropping Madonna quickly even though she got to keep her initial $5 million payment. And MTV benefited tremendously as everyone tuned in to see what the fuss was all about.

If the controversy cost Madonna any fans it was hard to notice. Her 1989 album (also called *Like a Prayer*) spent six weeks at #1 and sold over 4 million units. Besides the title track, the album also produced back-to-back #2 singles: "Express Yourself" and "Cherish." Madonna was back and the momentum from "Like a Prayer" would carry her into the nineties. If any pop star has ever figured out how to turn bad press into record and ticket sales it is certainly Madonna. "Like a Prayer" is just one of the examples throughout her storied career.

## May 7th

On this date in 1977, the Eagles' "Hotel California" went to #1, bumping Glen Campbell's "Southern Nights" from that spot. "Hotel California" would stay at #1 for one week before surrendering to "When I Need You" by Leo Sayer. Though it enjoyed just a one week stay at the top, the song is considered by most to be the Eagles' signature song and, in 1998, The Rock and Roll Hall of Fame named it one of the songs that, "shaped rock and roll." For decades people have analyzed the lyrics even though the song's writers claim their message is simple and direct.

The roots of the Eagles can be traced to 1971 when Linda Ronstadt asked two musicians, Glenn Frey and Don Henley, to join her band. The two became friends on the road and decided they wanted to start their own band. Throughout the years, the Eagles featured an ever-changing line-up of musicians but, until Frey's death in 2016, he and Henley were the two main constants.

In 1974, Don Felder was invited into the studio to add some slide guitar work on a song the Eagles were recording. The rest of the band loved what they heard and he was invited to join them. The next year Joe Walsh replaced Bernie Leadon, and the Eagles began drifting further away from the country rock sound of their early days. When he joined the band, Felder was told that if he ever had a musical idea, he should record it as a demo and then hand it over to Frey and Henley to write the lyrics. A year after joining the band he leased a house on the beach in Malibu, California and it's here that he clearly remembers coming up with the melody for what would become "Hotel California." He describes the setting vividly: "I remember sitting in the living room, with all the doors wide open on a spectacular July day. I had this acoustic 12-string and I started tinkling around with it, and those Hotel California chords just kind of oozed out. Every once in a while it seems like the cosmos part and something great just plops in your lap."

Felder did as he'd been told and brought the demo to Henley and Frey. They loved the slightly latin and reggae influences in what they heard. They began writing lyrics using a working title of "Mexican Reggae." As the song took shape, that title of course would change.

The opening verse of the song was inspired by the trip into the Los Angeles area. Felder has explained: "As you're driving in Los Angeles at night, you can see the glow of the energy and the lights of Hollywood and Los Angeles for 100 miles out in the desert." Henley added the often-analyzed line about the, "warm smell of colitas" to try to capture the scent of the drive. Many listeners thought it was a veiled drug reference (or even sexual innuendo) but according to the song's lyricists they had heard the desert plants that bloom with a strong pungent smell were called colitas so they used the word in the song. Felder again: "We try to write lyrics that touch multiple senses, things you can see, smell, taste, hear. 'I heard the mission bell,' you know, or 'the warm smell of colitis.'"

As the lyrics took shape Henley and Frey realized where they were headed: to a song about materialism and excess. They hadn't started out that way but, just like Felder's almost divine intervention with the melody, the lyrics sort of evolved in that direction without intent. Glenn Frey would say later that he and Henley wanted the song to be like an episode of *The Twilight Zone*, jumping from one scene to the next without much explanation. We begin on the highway, we find ourselves in the doorway and corridor and eventually we end up in the courtyard. Once the writers had grasped the fluid nature of the lyrics they were free to add their own imagery and even inside jokes, like the play on words, "She got the Mercedes bends." *The Stepford Wives* had been a cult favorite film in 1975 and it's perhaps where they came up with the night man saying, "We are programmed to receive." They also included a little shout out to Steely Dan, a band they enjoyed a friendship with. The year before Steely Dan had included the lyric: "Turn up the Eagles, the neighbors are listening" in their song "Everything You Did" and so the "steely knives" were the Eagles' nod back to Walter Becker and Donald Fagen.

The finishing touch for the song was the hotel imagery. Certainly any traveling band spends plenty of their days and nights in hotels so they are intimately connected with them. They chose the very popular Beverly Hills Hotel to serve as the metaphorical example of excess. As Henley would explain: "The Beverly Hills was still a mythical place to us. In that sense it became something of a symbol, and the 'Hotel' the locus of all that LA had come to mean for us."

The Eagles knew how important this song could be and they spent over a year shaping it. It was recorded three different times before the band deemed it acceptable. Even then the song took some work; there are over thirty edits on the master tape. The final, soaring guitar solo took three full days of practice and experimentation before Walsh and Felder recorded it together. The Eagles wanted to release the song as a single but their record company asked for an edited version (the song clocks in at over six minutes with that guitar solo). The band stood their ground and "Hotel California" was released as is. It went to #1 on this date in 1977 and it would go on to win that year's Grammy for Record of the Year.

So is it all really that simple? Are we not supposed to scrutinize every image and lyric? Does the "heaven or hell" line mean this is a song about the afterlife? After all when they sing, "We haven't had that spirit here since 1969?" that can't be a reference to the previous line's wine because wine is fermented while spirits are distilled. And what of that smell of colitas? How can that not be pot? Why is the champagne pink and why are we all prisoners and . . .

Don Henley insists he had no deeper meanings in mind. "The hotel itself," Henley has said, "could be taken as a metaphor not only for the myth-making of Southern California, but for the myth-making that is the American Dream, because it is a fine line between the American Dream, and the American nightmare." Glenn Frey would attempt to explain: "That record explores the underbelly of success, the darker side of paradise. Which was sort of what we were experiencing in Los Angeles at that time. So that just sort of became a metaphor for the whole world and for everything you know. And we just decided to make it Hotel California."

No doubt it's fun and interesting to study lyrics for hidden meanings, especially with a song as enigmatic as "Hotel California." Even when the songwriters claim there is no symbolism involved, we tend to analyze every word and image. It's part of the fun of loving music. As long as we don't lose sight of the fact that a song like "Hotel California" can be enjoyed on so many different levels. And one of those is on the surface. It's a great song to crank up and let it wash over you. If you do, without spending time or energy interpreting the thing, by the time that two minute guitar solo fades into the distance, you'll appreciate the song for what it is: a kick-ass rock tune no matter what it's about.

### May 8th

On this date in 1984, Island Records, in conjunction with the Jamaican label Tuff Gong released *Legend,* a greatest hits collection of Bob Marley and the Wailers. The album has become one of the highest selling LPs in history and has remained in the *Billboard* Top 200 album chart for years. Its success has helped make Bob Marley synonymous with reggae and the country of Jamaica.

Nesta Robert Marley was born in early 1945 in the Saint Ann Parish of Jamaica. Years later a Jamaican passport official would reverse his first and middle name because he said Nesta would sound too feminine in the U.S. By this point Marley was going by Bob anyway, or sometimes his nickname Tuff Gong. Marley showed a passion for music early on and by his teens he had moved to Kingston and was recording songs. In 1963 he formed the Wailing Wailers (later just the Wailers) and their single "Simmer Down" became a #1 hit in Jamaica in February of 1964. In 1964 he married Rita Marley who introduced him to Rastafarianism (he'd been raised Catholic). He also served a stint in jail in the late sixties (for marijuana possession) and his time there brought more social consciousness to his songwriting. Reggae music was in its infancy during this time and Marley was one of the pioneers in slowing the tempo of the island's music and emphasizing the bass drum on the third beat while all but eliminating the one beat (one of the distinguishing characteristics of reggae music which is popularly referred to as "one drop rhythm").

Marley met Johnny Nash in Jamaica while the U.S. singer was spending time on the island being influenced by the music there. Nash loved what he heard from Marley and recorded a few of his songs, took him on tour with him and brought him to London to record some of his own tracks. While in London, Marley met with Chris Blackwell who owned Island Records. Blackwell signed Marley immediately. He'd explain later: "I was dealing with rock music, which was really rebel music. I felt that would really be the way to break Jamaican music. But you needed someone who could be that image. When Bob walked in he really was that image." The first album Marley recorded for Island, *Catch a Fire*, is considered one of the greatest reggae albums ever released. In fact his output over the next few years, including iconic albums like *Natty Dread* and the pitch perfect *Exodus* helped bring Marley to international prominence as well as spread the reggae sound throughout the world. Marley became a bigger name in England but he was certainly not an unknown in the States.

As the story goes, Marley was diagnosed with cancer after a lesion was discovered on his toe. Doctors recommended amputation but he refused claiming it contradicted his Rastafarian beliefs. Eventually the cancer spread and claimed his life on May 11th, 1981. Bob Marley was just 36 years old.

*Legend* was released on this date in 1984, nearly three years to the date of Marley's passing. It would go on to sell incredibly over the next few decades and further the legend that was and always will be Bob Marley. If there's a downside to *Legend*, it's that most casual fans know Marley exclusively from the 14 tracks on the LP thus missing so many of his other classic tracks. Like any greatest hits compilation, *Legend* is a worthy synopsis of Marley's career but there is so much else to discover in the man's canon. One listen to *Catch a Fire* (of which only "Stir It Up" was included on *Legend*) and you begin to realize the depth of the man's genius. The same can be said for all of the albums he released throughout the seventies. Marley, similar to Dylan, was able to tap into a socially conscious message that spoke to an entire generation. Part mystic, part revolutionary and at all times humanitarian, Bob Marley was a musician with enough vision and talent to propel an entire genre of music from a small island in the Caribbean to world-wide significance. As he sang so famously in his song "Trench Town Rock," "One good thing about music, when it hits you, you feel no pain." Listen to Bob Marley today but go deeper than *Legend*. You'll feel no pain but he will surely hit you. Over and over and over.

On this date in 1970, the Guess Who arrived at the top of the pop chart with their often misunderstood rocker "American Woman." The song had come about completely spontaneously for the band and the only reason it was preserved for them to recreate later was a kid they discovered who was bootlegging their performance. Then, when they recorded the song and released it, many people mistook it for a pro-American anthem. Here's the intriguing story:

The Guess Who were a Canadian rock band, formed in Winnipeg in 1965. They achieved success in their homeland long before they broke in the States but by the late sixties they were regularly traveling back and forth across the border. According to the band's guitarist, Randy Bachman, they even got stopped at the border one time heading north and the guards, thinking they were draft dodgers, attempted to enlist them in the U.S. army. The band was very opposed to the Vietnam war, as were most of their fans in Canada, many of whom were, in fact, actual draft dodgers.

One day the band was playing a gig in Canada and Bachman broke a guitar string. His bandmates, knowing it would take their guitarist a few minutes to change his string and retune stepped off the stage. After Bachman had tightened the new string he discovered he didn't have a tuner so he went over to the electric piano and hit a note to give himself a reference. He then hit another note. He played the two notes back-to-back and everyone in the audience looked up at the stage. He realized he was playing a riff so he played the same two notes again and got an even better reaction from the crowd. He did it again and, as he would explain later: "Suddenly I realize I'm playing a riff I don't want to forget, and I have to keep playing it. So I stand up and I'm playing this riff. I'm alone on stage." Garry Peterson, the band's drummer, was the first one to join Bachman on stage and he started playing a beat to match the riff. Bassist Jim Kale was next and he provided the bottom to match Peterson's beat. Finally, lead singer Burton Cummings returned to the stage while the band was in full jam mode and Bachman screamed at him, "Sing something!" So Cummings did. He sang the first thing that popped into his mind: "American woman, stay away from me." Cummings would explain later: "What was on my mind was that girls in the States seemed to get older quicker than our girls and that made them, well, dangerous. When I said 'American woman, stay away from me,' I really meant 'Canadian woman, I prefer you.' It was all a happy accident." Cummings continued vamping, channeling his anti-war sentiments with lines like, "I don't want your war machines, I don't want your ghetto scenes."

When they finished the impromptu song they figured it'd be lost to memory. Bachman might be able to remember the riff and Cummings might recall some of his lyrics but the magic they'd created in the moment could probably never be recreated. That's when someone in the band spotted a kid in the audience with a portable cassette recorder. It was a fairly new technology at the time, and certainly not as ubiquitous as it would come to be in later years, but the band knew what it was immediately and what the kid must be up to. He was bootlegging their show. So they asked the young man for the tape and from it, they were able to transcribe the lyrics and rhythm. By the time they recorded the song, they only made slight adjustments to the words so what we know as "American Woman" was mostly a completely ad-libbed riff and lyric.

The Guess Who released "American Woman" in March of 1970 and it started a three week run at #1 on this date that same year. While many took the song for what it was, an anti-war and even anti-American rocker, some just heard the repeated "American woman" part and took it as a pro-U.S. anthem. One person who did get the song's true meaning was Pat Nixon. When the band blew up in the States (on the strength of their #5 hit "No Time" and their #1 hit "American Woman") they were asked to play the White House. Before the show, President Nixon's wife sent word to the band to ask them to leave "American Woman" out of their setlist. They respectfully obliged.

The Guess Who had been together for five years but at the height of their success things started to crumble. Bachman was on his way out and by 1971 he'd formed Bachman–Turner Overdrive which would go on to huge success throughout the seventies, releasing rock radio staples like "You Ain't Seen Nothing Yet", "Takin' Care of Business" and "Roll On Down the Highway." Bachman was replaced and the Guess Who continued on for a few more years but they'd never match the success they'd enjoyed with "American Woman." Maybe they just tried too hard, seeing how their most successful song was literally created spontaneously.

## May 10th

On this date in 1971, *Jesus Christ Superstar*, the album that would become the rock opera show and movie, had returned to the top of the *Billboard* Top 200 album chart. It had gone to #1 for a week in February, then surrendered that position to Janis Joplin's posthumously released LP, *Pearl*. But *Jesus Christ Superstar* wasn't done with its reign on the charts. It returned to the top on May 1st and would sit there for two more weeks before bowing out to Crosby, Stills, Nash & Young's live album *4 Way Street*. It was an amazing feat considering two things. First, the executives at MCA were afraid to even release the album for fear of backlash from religious groups (and they certainly didn't put their full promotional push behind it). And secondly, most rock aficionados look at 1971 as perhaps the greatest year ever, with classic albums coming from all corners; timeless works like: *Who's Next*, *Tapestry*, *Hunky Dory*, *Led Zeppelin IV*, *Imagine*, *Every Picture Tells a Story* and *Sticky Fingers* (just to name a few). For *Jesus Christ Superstar* to have found an audience (not to mention shelf space in a record store) was, quite frankly, miraculous.

Today, Andrew Lloyd Webber is considered an icon of musical theater. He has composed such classics as *Cats*, *The Phantom of the Opera* and *Evita*. But in the late sixties he was merely a composer looking to make it on the Great White

Way. He and lyricist Tim Rice had written *The Likes of Us* which they'd failed to find backing for. Then they'd brought *Joseph and the Amazing Technicolor Dreamcoat* to the stage in 1970 and suddenly they were known names. *Dreamcoat* is a retelling of the biblical story of Joseph so after successfully taking on the Old Testament they figured, Why not try the New Testament? Lyricist Tim Rice has said he was motivated by a line in the 1964 Bob Dylan song "With God on Our Side" in which Dylan sang:

> In a many dark hour
> I've been thinkin' about this
> That Jesus Christ
> Was betrayed by a kiss
> But I can't think for you
> You'll have to decide
> Whether Judas Iscariot
> Had God on his side.

It's a point of view rarely taken. The biblical portrayal of Judas is rather paper thin. There really isn't any time spent on why he would have betrayed Jesus. Luke and John both say that Satan entered him and Matthew mentions the famous thirty silver pieces, but other than that, no motivation is given for what is arguably the most notorious betrayal in history. So approaching the Jesus story from that angle, Webber and Rice wrote, recorded and released the album *Jesus Christ Superstar* before they even knew whether or not they could bring it to the stage. The album features Deep Purple lead singer Ian Gillan in the Jesus role, Murray Head (yeah, the "One Night in Bangkok" guy) singing Judas' parts, and Yvonne Elliman (whose "If I Can't Have You" would appear on the *Saturday Night Fever* soundtrack and reach #1 as a single) as Mary Magdalene. When the album became huge, it cleared the way for the 1971 Broadway production as well as the 1973 film.

The songs on the album focus on the final week of Jesus' life as told in the Gospel accounts, from his triumphant entrance into Jerusalem to that famous betrayal to his crucifixion. The subject matter is handled from a contemporary angle and the songs reside in that unique space where show tunes meet rock. The relationship between Jesus and Mary Magdalene is a major focus and while there is no physical aspect to it (like Martin Scorsese would flirt with in his 1988 movie *The Last Temptation of Christ*) the sexual undertones can get a little uncomfortable for some believers. And the Judas character, inspired by Dylan's song, is handled quite differently than usual. In fact some would argue that Judas, and not, despite the title of the piece, Jesus, is the real protagonist of *Jesus Christ Superstar*. He comes across as an almost tragic figure, a flawed man who makes a horrible mistake.

The final insult for some Christians came when Tim Rice told Time magazine: "It happens that we don't see Christ as God but simply the right man at the right time at the right place. We are basically trying to tell the story of Christ as a man. I think he increases in stature by looking at him as a man." Indeed, the fact that Webber and Rice didn't include a "resurrection" song or scene in their initial work (although some stage productions have inserted one) speaks to their beliefs of Jesus as a man versus Jesus as a God-figure.

All of this caused quite the stir with religious groups which, as it often does, gave the album free publicity. By the end of 1971, the double LP had become the highest selling album of the year and the show would run on Broadway and in London's West End for years. The 1973 movie was successful as well. Webber and Rice's unique take on Jesus Christ's final week, with its focus on Judas and Mary as two important supporting figures, had upset some but enthralled many. It's a classic album with a unique mix of rock grittiness and show tune panache and it not only found an audience in 1971, but somehow, perhaps through divine intervention, it became a huge-seller as well.

## May 11th

On this date in 1990, Sinead O'Connor was wrapping up her four week residence at #1 on the *Billboard* Hot 100 chart with her cover of "Nothing Compares 2 U." The song is by far her most successful single, in fact it's her only Top 40 hit and her career would quickly unravel after this. But before that, "Nothing Compares 2 U" introduced O'Connor to an international audience that fell in love with her voice before they became aghast at her social views.

Prince originally wrote the song "Nothing Compares 2 U" for one of his protégé bands, the Family. He had overheard a member of the band talking about a bad breakup and he penned the song, exploring the feelings of longing and despair for a lost lover. The song appeared on the Family's 1985 eponymous debut album but was never released as a single. After Sinead O'Connor's debut album *The Lion and the Cobra* became an underground hit she began collecting material for her follow-up. It was her manager, Fachtna O'Kelly, who recommended she cover "Nothing Compares 2 U" and when Prince gave his blessing O'Connor recorded it for her next LP, *I Do Not Want What I Haven't Got*. There is no doubt when you listen to O'Connor's version, especially compared to the original, that she tapped into the raw emotion of unrequited love that Prince had written about, specifically her delivery of the line, "I could put my arms around every boy I see, but they'd only remind me of you" and of course her soaring vocals in the chorus at the end. As O'Connor's second LP neared completion it was decided "Nothing Compares 2 U" would be released as a single and a video was shot which featured O'Connor singing the song in Paris. The original storyboard called for many scenes in and around Paris with a few close-ups of O'Connor singing but when the footage was examined later, everyone involved realized how dramatic the tight shot of her face was so they used that more than any of the B-roll. The video had a huge impact. O'Connor's near bald head was striking and the tears she sheds towards the end of the clip, which O'Connor has said was a sincere emotion and not something staged or planned, had a lasting effect.

"Nothing Compares 2 U" was released in January of 1990 and when the video went into heavy rotation on MTV that winter the song began a steady march up the charts. It hit #1 in the middle of April where it would sit for four consecutive weeks. *I Do Not Want What I Haven't Got* also climbed to #1 on the album chart that spring.

Sinead O'Connor received four Grammy nominations although in a bizarre move, and a precursor of things to come, she said she was rejecting the nominations (whatever that means) and she did not show up at the ceremony (where she won one Grammy, that for Best Alternative Performance). That spring O'Connor cancelled her appearance on *Saturday Night Live* in protest of guest host Andrew Dice Clay's misogynistic, homophobic jokes, saying, "It would be nonsensical of *Saturday Night Live* to expect a woman to perform songs about a woman's experience after a monologue by Andrew Dice Clay." While touring to support her album she also made some negative news when she played in a New Jersey venue that had a tradition of playing the Star-Spangled Banner before each show. O'Connor requested the venue not play the song, saying she had, "a policy of not having national anthems played before my concerts in any country, including my own, because they have nothing to do with music in general." The venue requested she reconsider and she threatened to cancel her show before they relented. When the story made national news Frank Sinatra said he'd like to kick her in the ass.

But all that was simply an appetizer to her main, career-ending moment, when she tore up a picture of the Pope in 1992 on *Saturday Night Live*. That combined with a series of releases that have been as far from main stream as seemingly possible have thrust O'Connor to the very edges of relevancy. These days when she says or does something odd, most people barely even notice. Still, it's worth remembering the winter and spring of 1990 when her face, that dramatic, striking face, was literally plastered all over MTV and broadcast into millions of homes. She struck a nerve with a song about loss and longing. She took painful lyrics written by Prince, poured even more anguish into them with her ethereal singing, and created a song that still touches the soul of anyone who's ever mourned a lover.

### May 12th

On this date in 1967, Procol Harum released their debut single, "A Whiter Shade of Pale." It would eventually peak in the U.S. at #5 (it made it to #1 in the U.K.) "A Whiter Shade of Pale" was not only Procol Harum's debut single it was the first song they ever wrote and recorded as a group and it would become an anthem throughout the legendary Summer of Love.

Procol Harum were formed after the English band the Paramounts broke up. Pianist and singer Gary Brooker formed a new band with organist Matthew Fisher, guitarist Ray Royer, bassist David Knights and oddly enough, Keith Reid who played no instruments nor sang. Reid was a poet who was interested in becoming a lyricist so Brooker included him in the band and encouraged his songwriting. When they got signed to Deram Records, a Decca Records subsidiary, they needed a name. Their manager knew someone with a cat named Procul Harun (Procul being the breeder's name) and so in the absence of anything better they adopted the name with slight variations to the spelling. The confusing name is often misheard or misspelled and many people think the second word is harem. It's also been given other explanations (like it's Latin for "beyond these things") but the name really did just come from a house cat.

As the band got started rehearsing Reid got started on what he was hired for: writing lyrics. He was at a party one day when he overheard someone saying to a woman, "You've turned a whiter shade of pale." He was intrigued by those words and remembered them clearly. He later sat down and wrote the song using interesting wordplay and intriguing imagery (who cares what a "light fandango" is when it can "turn cartwheels cross the floor?") He had a poet's background and the lyrics certainly read more like a poem than a pop song. Reid would say later: "I feel with songs that you're given a piece of the puzzle. The inspiration or whatever. In this case, I had that title, 'Whiter Shade of Pale,' and I thought, there's a song here." And when pressed on what, if anything, the song means, he attempts to explain: "It's sort of a film, really, trying to conjure up a mood and tell a story. It's about a relationship. There are characters and there's a location, and there's a journey. You get the sound of the room and the feel of the room and the smell of the room." This was 1967, after all, at the height of the psychedelic era, and words were less important literally than they were figuratively. There's a feeling you get listening to "A Whiter Shade of Pale" that goes far beyond what the words on paper may mean. And, of course, a lot of that feel has to do with the music itself.

When Reid gave his lyrics to Brooker, the pianist happened to be listening to a lot of classical music at the time so he started composing a melody inspired by that. "It does a bar or two of Bach's 'Air on a G String' before it veers off," Brooker said later. "That spark was all it took. I wasn't consciously combining rock with classical, it's just that Bach's music was in me at the time." It was in him and it came out masterfully. The tune matches the lyric's plaintive yearning perfectly.

"A Whiter Shade of Pale" was recorded in March of 1967 with the whole band present, including Matthew Fisher on the Hammond organ. Brooker and Reid presented the band with what they'd come up with and when they began to play, Fisher added the organ part that helped enhance the feel and emotion of the song. Though Reid had written four verses they only included two, although you can hear Brooker singing, "and so it was that later" as the song fades, leaving the listener with the impression that there was more. Sometimes when they played the song live they'd include an extra verse. You can find all the lyrics on the internet and it's understandable why the third verse never made it (about the mermaid) but the fourth verse includes a beautiful and intriguing couplet:

If music be the food of love
Then laughter is its queen
And likewise if behind is in front
Then dirt in truth is clean.

The song was released on this date in 1967 and quickly became a radio staple. The Summer of Love was about the start and there was a feeling that the counter-culture was taking over. Hippie ideals (as well as fashions) were everywhere and radios blared "San Francisco (Be Sure to Wear Flowers in Your Hair)" and "Light My Fire" and everything and anything from the Beatles' *Sgt. Peppers*. And "A Whiter Shade of Pale" was as much a part of the soundtrack of that summer as any song and sound.

Almost 40 years later, in 2005, Matthew Fisher filed a law suit claiming he deserved writing credit for improvising the organ solo. He won the suit with the judge confirming that Fisher's organ playing was part of the song's composition. The judgment has had a sweeping effect on the music industry, setting a precedent that someone who composes a "signature" part for an otherwise complete song should be credited as a cowriter.

Procol Harem never came close to matching the success of their debut song but with "A Whiter Shade of Pale" they'd given the Summer of Love and the whole psychedelic era one of its most poetic songs. So go ahead and "skip the light fandango" and give this classic (and classical) song a listen today. And be sure to watch the video too. One of the early, trippy attempts to match film to music.

### May 13th

On this date in 1978, Yvonne Elliman's "If I Can't Have You" went to #1 on the *Billboard* Hot 100 chart. The song rode the wave of disco's biggest commercial year and the movie that propelled it into the stratosphere, but it was a change of pace for Elliman who had built a reputation singing beautiful ballads. More proof that in the late seventies just about anything with a disco beat could climb the charts.

Yvonne Elliman was born in 1951 on the island of Honolulu, Hawaii. She showed a talent for music early on, playing ukulele by age four and piano just a few years later. By high school she was playing guitar and singing in a folk band and when she turned 18 she took a bold step, moving to London to pursue a career in music. In no time, she was singing regularly in bars and clubs and that's where she got her big break. One night Tim Rice and Andrew Lloyd Webber saw her perform and loved her voice. They were working on an album called *Jesus Christ Superstar* at the time and thought Elliman would be perfect for the Mary Magdalene songs. "I Don't Know How to Love Him," her ballad from *Jesus Christ Superstar*, went to #27 in 1971 and the LP was a huge-seller.

With the album's success Elliman was asked to join the stage show's traveling cast, which she did for the next four years. In 1973 she also appeared in the film version as Mary Magdalene. She also found work in the mid-seventies singing backup, most famously on Eric Clapton's version of the Bob Marley song "I Shot the Sheriff." The two would continue to work together for the next few years. She released some solo material during this time including a song called "Love Me" which climbed to #14 in 1976. "Love Me" is a song that had been written by Barry Gibb and Robin Gibb (two-thirds of the Bee Gees) and Elliman's version was produced by Freddie Perren. This brought her into the circle of these men so as they began to prepare music for an upcoming film about the dance scene in New York City, she was considered for a song.

Freddie Perren was already a legendary producer of classic disco songs, having produced "Love Machine" by the Miracles and cowritten and produced the Sylvers' "Boogie Fever." As the music started being compiled for the movie *Saturday Night Fever* he was brought in to oversee a recording session with Yvonne Elliman. At first it was suggested that Elliman sing the Bee Gees' penned "How Deep Is Your Love" which made the most sense as the song's slow feel was in the singer's wheelhouse. But RSO Records chairman and Bee Gees' manager Robert Stigwood, who was executive-producing the *Saturday Night Fever* soundtrack, insisted Elliman sing "If I Can't Have You" (which had also been written by the three Gibb brothers). He was adamant that the Bee Gees' record "How Deep Is Your Love." While "If I Can't Have You" was a departure for Elliman, she clearly pulled it off, showing that a talented singer can handle just about any genre.

When *Saturday Night Fever* started producing singles the first three went to #1: "How Deep Is Your Love" , "Stayin' Alive" and "Night Fever." But they were all sung by the Bee Gees so when "If I Can't Have You" was released, by a singer the public only knew for her ballads, no one was quite sure how it would be received. But this was 1978 and disco was white hot. One look at the charts from that year proves it: "Stayin' Alive" was #1 throughout the month of February. Andy Gibb (the Gibb brother not in the Bee Gees) took over for two weeks with his mid-tempo "Love Is (Thicker than Water)" which was bumped off by the Bee Gees' "Night Fever" which held the crown for eight straight weeks before surrendering it, on this day, to "If I Can't Have You."

Elliman has never matched the success she had with "If I Can't Have You" although it wouldn't be for lack of trying. In 1979 she tried her hand at disco once again, recording "Love Pains," which barely cracked the Top 40. She's had a few other minor hits since then but nothing nearly as close to her signature song, the beautiful and timeless, "If I Can't Have You."

On this date in 1969, Frank Sinatra's "My Way" was sitting at its peak position, #27, on the *Billboard* Hot 100 chart. Though Sinatra has had more successful offerings, "My Way" is easily his signature song. It's a song that was written specifically for him as a retirement song and going away message to the music industry. Of course, Sinatra didn't go anywhere. He'd continue recording and touring right up until his passing, which also happened on this date, in 1998.

Space does not allow for a full and proper synopsis of Frank Sinatra's career. Though he burst on the scene long before rock and roll, there is no doubt Sinatra was a "rock star." He had all the trappings: ridiculous levels of fame and fortune, the late night carousing, the marriages, the entourage. If anything, Sinatra created the template for what we expect in our musical legends. But Sinatra's career wasn't without its highs and lows. Indeed, it would be hard to imagine a more-than-sixty year career in entertainment that didn't have some ebbs and flows. There were times when Sinatra was on top of the entertainment world and as hot and happening as anyone. There were other times when he seemed out of step with the trends of the day. The late sixties were one of those times. Everyone from the Beatles to Simon & Garfunkel were dominating the airwaves and the charts and it seemed like there was no one left who appreciated a crooner with an orchestra.

Paul Anka, who, one could argue, was one of the early rock and rollers who helped marginalize Sinatra and his ilk, happened to idolize the man. He saw Sinatra as the pinnacle of cool and success so one evening when he found himself at a dinner with Sinatra and some others, he was shocked to hear his friend talking about retiring. Sinatra was tired of being secondhand news and getting outsold by all these greasy rockers. In no uncertain terms, Sinatra said, "I'm gettin' the hell out!" Anka was saddened but also motivated. He thought to himself, if a legend like Frank Sinatra is going to retire, he needs a proper song to send him off.

When Anka returned to New York he still had this on his mind. A few years earlier he'd purchased the rights to a French song called "Comme d'habitude" because he liked the melody and thought he could write English lyrics to it. His deal with the publishers allowed him to do just that but Claude François, the song's composer, was still entitled to future royalties for anything Anka came up with using the melody. He listened to the track a few times and then sat down to write Sinatra's grand farewell. He typed the words, "And now the end is near" and he was off and running. He tried to channel Sinatra and use words he could picture him singing. A line like, "I ate it up and spit it out" isn't something Anka would say but it was something he could picture Sinatra saying. He finished the song about 5am, New York time, and he was so excited he called Sinatra in Las Vegas and told him, "I've got something special for you." Sinatra recorded "My Way" on December 30th, 1968 and must have thought highly enough of it because he named his next album *My Way* as well. Years later, though, his daughter Tina would say her father hated the song and thought it was, "self-serving and self-indulgent."

"My Way" was released in early 1969 and though it didn't top the charts it became a big enough hit to upset Anka's record label. They couldn't believe he'd given away such a great song and they insisted he record his own version. Which he did. As did Elvis Presley. And Glen Campbell. And so many others. But really, there is only one, true version of "My Way" and it's sung by the man for whom it was written.

But instead of a going-away song, Sinatra just kept going. After a brief "retirement" he returned to recording and touring and had a very successful run late in his life with the *Duets* projects. In 1993 he released an album called *Duets* which featured contemporary artists singing with Frank Sinatra. The album went to #2 on the LP chart and helped introduce "Ol Blue Eyes" to a whole new audience. The follow-up, *Duets II*, would get to #9 on the charts a few years later.

Which brings us to this date in 1998 and Frank Sinatra's passing. He'd had ill health in his final years, suffering from heart and breathing problems, so when he was hospitalized from a heart attack it was clear that this time, the end was truly near. He was 82 and had achieved unprecedented levels of success throughout a career that spanned seven decades. He recorded more songs then anyone could even begin to count but there is little argument that what Paul Anka typed out for him, channeling Sinatra's vernacular and offering a send-off to the industry and the world, is his signature song. He did it all, Frank did, and yes indeed, he did it his way.


**May 15th**

On this date in 1982, the self-titled debut album by Asia, a prog rock fan's wet dream, went to #1 on the LP chart. The album would spend a total of nine weeks at #1 and sell over ten million units worldwide, and though the band was never able to match that success (and has undergone numerous line-up changes since), that debut album for many, is an all-time favorite slice of progressive rock merging with pop rock.

Asia was formed from the ashes of three historic bands: King Crimson, Yes and Emerson, Lake & Palmer. All three had been monumental in the creation of the genre that became known as progressive rock (prog rock for short). The genre is known for many things: long, winding songs, lots of time signature changes and accomplished musicianship. In 1981, four musicians from these bands came together to form a supergroup: bassist John Wetton (formerly of King Crimson), keyboardist Geoff Downes and guitarist Steve Howe (formerly of Yes) and drummer Carl Palmer (the Palmer in Emerson, Lake & Palmer). As the four began working on material for a debut album, their manager, Brian Lane, began to think up a name. He had two goals. First, he wanted a name that began with the letter "A" so the band's albums would be towards the front of a record store rather than at the back. Lane had managed Yes so he knew the drawbacks of a band being buried in alphabetical order. And he wanted something that sounded big and memorable. He thought, What could be bigger than the world's largest continent?

The artist Roger Dean was commissioned to create an album cover for the Asia's debut. Dean's exotic, fantasy-inspired landscapes have graced many an album cover, specifically Yes' masterwork, *Fragile*. Steve Howe would say, "There is a pretty tight bond between our sound and Roger's art." Indeed, the cover of Asia's debut album is as memorable to its fans as the songs themselves.

As Asia's debut neared completion, prog rock fans were literally salivating. Some, surely, expected an LP that contained maybe four songs, each 15 to 20 minute suites about space travel or middle earth. Those expectations, however, were dashed when *Asia* came out in March of 1982. The longest track on the album was 5:42 and every song, while maintaining a prog rock feel, had a pop music sensibility to it that made it radio-friendly. To make their commercial appeal even more pronounced, Asia didn't just release singles from the album, they produced music videos to go along with them. Music videos that quickly went into heavy rotation on the nascent MTV. "Only Time Will Tell" and "Heat of the Moment" both became Top 40 hits. "Sole Survivor" and "Wildest Dreams" also received a lot of air play in 1982 and have become rock radio staples ever since. Though the album wasn't treated well by critics (with Robert Christgau being the harshest calling the album "pompous" and "schlock in the grandest manner") and extreme prog rock fans were disappointed in the music's obvious commercial lean, rock fans ate it up. The LP went to #1 less than two months after its release and the band enjoyed unprecedented success in 1982. Asia embarked on a U.S. tour that began in theaters but quickly grew to stadiums to meet the demand for tickets.

Bands that are labeled as "supergroups" have traditionally disappointed fans in the long run. It's probably the burden of carrying such expectations that can wear a group down. Plus, any band that starts so well is bound to under-achieve with their next offering. And that can certainly be said for Asia. Their next LP, 1983's *Alpha*, sold a million copies and produced a Top 10 hit in "Don't Cry," but it is generally seen as a step backwards for the band. That trend continued with 1985's *Astra* (yes, the "A thing" continued with the album names, up until 2000's *Rare*). By then Wetton had been replaced by Greg Lake and Steve Howe left to form GTR.

Asia, in some form or another, has produced albums on a fairly regular basis ever since but they've never come close to capturing the heat of the moment that their debut did. Give it a spin today. If you're old enough to remember the summer of 1982 you'll be automatically transported back in time and relive some of your wildest dreams.

On this date in 1983, *Motown 25: Yesterday, Today, Forever* aired on NBC to incredible ratings. Over a third of the televisions turned on that night watched the show with some urban areas like New York, Philadelphia and Chicago scoring even higher ratings. What people saw was an incredible collection of stars from Motown's heyday performing their most iconic songs, including legends like Marvin Gaye and Diana Ross who were no longer with the label but felt obligated to return. But the most memorable moment of the evening, the song that everyone talked about the next day and the dance move that millions tried to copy after seeing it, was Michael Jackson's performance of "Billie Jean" which featured his first public exhibition of "Moonwalking."

It was Suzanne dePasse's idea to host an anniversary show for Motown in 1983. She'd worked for the label for years by this point and was one of founder Berry Gordy's most trusted advisors. Though Motown's star was fading by the early eighties, its past shone as brightly as ever and songs by the label's stars from the sixties and even seventies were still popular on radio, albeit oldies stations rather than pop stations. dePasse floated the idea by Gordy who liked the sound of it and deputized her to take the reigns and produce the show. The two of them began contacting past Motown stars to get them lined up. Some, like Ross and Gaye and Jackson, were now recording for different labels but after a generous helping of guilt and pressure, they all agreed to perform. The Pasadena Civic Auditorium was reserved and NBC signed on to tape the show for a future airing. On the night of March 25th, 1983, everyone came together and the show went off without a hitch. Looking back there were some curious decisions made as well as some controversial exclusions. Why Adam Ant was chosen to perform a duet with Diana Ross is anyone's guess. And the fact that the famous house band from Detroit, the legendary Funk Brothers, weren't even mentioned that night was just one more insult to the musicians who will never get their due credit (or compensation). Legend has it in fact that James Jamerson, the man who played bass on 30 of Motown's #1 hits, had to scalp a ticket just to get in.

The story behind Jackson's appearance varies depending on who tells it. Jackson had released *Thriller* in late 1982 and the album and its second single "Billie Jean" were flying off the shelves. Some say Jackson initially passed on taking the stage that night thinking he was already overexposed from his promotion of the album. In other stories he agreed to perform with his brothers as part of a Jackson 5 routine if and only if he also got a solo number. In the end, no matter whose story or memory you believe, that's what wound up happening. Jackson performed a medley of hits with his brothers ("I Want You Back", "The Love You Save", "Never Can Say Goodbye", and "I'll Be There") then they exited the stage and after a short introduction from Jackson, "Billie Jean" began playing through the house system. Jackson had decided he didn't trust the house band to recreate the song so he lip-synched to the track.

Jackson would say later he barely rehearsed his performance. He'd spent too much time focusing on rehearsing with his brothers for their medley so he just broke out some moves during the song and, since he had no back-up dancers to coordinate with, it's a plausible story. He'd say later: "I pretty much stood there and let the song tell me what to do. I kind of let the dance create itself."

But one move he had worked on was traditionally called "the backslide." The move had been around for decades or longer. Surely mimes have done a version of it forever (Marcel Marceau used to do a routine called "Walking in the Wind" that is basically the backslide) and James Brown had it in his arsenal of dance moves. But it was two young dancers, Casper Candidate and Cooley Jaxson, who taught Jackson the backslide. In 1979 Candidate and Jaxson had appeared on *Soul Train*, where they did an amazing dance to Jackson's "Workin' Day and Night." Jackson must have been watching that night because he contacted the dancers shortly after and asked them to teach him some of their steps. When they got together, the backslide was all Jackson wanted to learn. They taught him the move and he picked it up quickly. He claimed it didn't feel right and though Jaxson and Candidate tried to reassure him he had it down, he shelved it till he broke it out at *The Motown 25* special.

Jackson's entire "Billie Jean" performance that night was unforgettable. But when the bridge of the song came up and Jackson broke into what he would call The Moonwalk, everyone reacted; even the stage crew because Jackson hadn't shown the move in rehearsal. When his performance was over he was swarmed backstage by people telling him how great his performance had been. The next day he received a phone call from an 84 year old Fred Astaire who told him, "You're a hell of a mover. Man, you really put them on their asses last night." Jackson would say later, "It was the greatest compliment I had ever received in my life." But Astaire's call was just the beginning. Jackson was already a huge star but his performance on *Motown 25* had literally catapulted him into the stratosphere. While the television show helped revive a few careers, namely the Four Tops and the Temptations who toured together for years after their "Battle of the Bands" segment on the show, what it did for Michael Jackson is hard to overstate. He went into the show a huge name. After his electric performance and debut of his Moondance, life for Michael Jackson would never be the same. That night, he'd been crowned the King of Pop.

## May 17th

On this date in 1999, Ricky Martin's "Livin' La Vida Loca" had just begun its second week at #1 on the *Billboard* Hot 100 chart. The song would enjoy a five week run and catapult Martin to national fame in the U.S. as well as help usher in a whole new Latin dance sound right at the turn of the millennium. Martin's run of pop chart dominance may have been short-lived but the genre he helped introduce is still muy caliente.

Enrique Maciel Martín Morales was born in 1971 in San Juan, Puerto Rico. When he was seven years old he told his father he wanted to be a performing artist. Instead of squelching the little boy's dream his father simply asked, "How can I help?" Together, they found the boy an agent and within no time he was starring in television commercials. At twelve, he joined the famous Puerto Rican boy band Menudo and when he left them in his late teens he released a few solo albums (where he sang strictly in Spanish). He also did some acting in Mexico and, in 1994, appeared on the American TV soap opera *General Hospital*, playing a Puerto Rican singer. Then in 1996 he released a song in the U.S. called "Maria." The CD single (remember those?) sold fairly well, getting to #6 on the Hot Latin Songs Airplay chart and even cracking *Billboard*'s Hot 100 chart, peaking at #88. By the late nineties he felt he was ready to break in the States as a singer and he began to work on an album that would feature him singing in English and hopefully expose him to a market that he felt was primed for the taking.

As Martin began gathering material for that album he was presented a song that had been cowritten by the accomplished songwriter Desmond Child. Child had recently moved to Miami and was, in his words, "getting back in touch with my Latin heritage." He was going to Salsa clubs and listening to Latin artists and when he was presented the opportunity to work with Ricky Martin he jumped at it. He collaborated with Puerto Rican songwriter and producer Robi Rosa (who'd also begun his career in Menudo) with a goal to write, in Child's words, "the millennium party song from hell." The two wrote the song and then brought Martin in to record it using nothing but ProTools digital recording. Child would say later: "We were the first to record and mix a record all what they call 'in the box,' on ProTools. We were the first to go all the way to #1 with a song that was 100% non-analog." One of the advantages of the digital recording is its exceptional use of dynamic range compression, which, in layman's terms, means the song sounds louder than it actually is.

Ricky Martin's self-titled LP was set for a May, 1999 release. He planned to drop "Livin' La Vida Loca" in late March as the lead single. In an effort to promote both, Martin secured a spot performing at the 41st Annual Grammy Awards on February 24th, 1999. There are a number of award show performances that have stood out through the years and helped launch an artist's career from one level to the next. Madonna's incredibly sexy "Like a Virgin" at the 1984 MTV Video Music Awards stands out as a perfect example. Perhaps Martin's performance on the Grammys that night should be exhibit 1-A. Martin sang a spirited version of "Cup of Life," weaving seamlessly from Spanish lyrics to English. He received a spontaneous standing ovation and the next day, all anyone wanted to talk about was that new Latin singer. When "Livin' La Vida Loca" dropped a month later it flew off the shelves. Not only did the single go to #1 but Martin's album also hit the top of the charts and would eventually sell a staggering 15 million copies worldwide.

But the record buying public wasn't just interested in Ricky Martin. There suddenly seemed a huge demand for anything with a Latin beat. Artists like Marc Anthony and Jennifer Lopez and Enrique Iglesias and Shakira became huge sellers in the States and the Latin sound was all the rage as the world greeted the new millennium. And with Pitbull's ubiquitousness since his 2009 hit "I Know You Want Me (Calle Ocho)" the Latin beat looks like it's here to stay.

## May 18th

On this date in 1985, Simple Minds' "Don't You (Forget About Me)" climbed to #1 on the pop chart, knocking Madonna's "Crazy For You" from that spot. In just a week, it would surrender the top spot to the Wham! song "Everything She Wants." "Don't You (Forget About Me)" was a song written specifically for a movie and was turned down by numerous artists before Simple Minds agreed to record it. The song, and the movie, would become huge hits and even today they are joined at the hip, you can't think of one without thinking of the other -- and together they bring anyone who is old enough to remember it, back to the mid-eighties.

John Hughes made a name for himself in the early eighties. He wrote most of the script for *National Lampoon's Vacation* and then wrote and directed the coming-of-age comedy *Sixteen Candles*. Towards the end of filming *Sixteen Candles* he asked both Molly Ringwald and Anthony Michael Hall if they'd star in his next film as well. When they both agreed, he set out to write a script about a diverse group of high school students stuck in a library on a Saturday on detention. As production got underway, Keith Forsey, who was just coming off the success of composing "Flashdance... What a Feeling" for the movie *Flashdance*, was asked to write some songs for the movie. He spent some time on the set and was moved by some of the dialogue, specifically towards the end of the film when Hall's character asks the others if, when they return to school, they will all still be friends. Inspired by that scene he began to write lines like, "Will you recognize me? Call my name or walk on by?" and of course the urgent plea in the chorus not to be forgotten. Along with cowriter Steve Schiff, Forsey completed "Don't You (Forget About Me)," recorded a demo and presented it to Hughes. The director loved the song and he decided to use it in the opening of the movie.

Forsey then set out to get the song recorded but he was met with rejection after rejection. The list of bands who turned the song down outnumbers the students in detention in the movie. Everyone from the Fixx to Bryan Ferry to Chrissie Hynde were offered "Don't You (Forget About Me)" (which, keep in mind, was virtually guaranteed to make the soundtrack for a major motion picture) but turned it down. Hynde actually loved the song but had to pass on it because she was pregnant and didn't want to make a video. In fact, she loved it so much she told Jim Kerr, her husband and frontman for Simple Minds, about the song. But he didn't think much of it and Simple Minds generally didn't like recording songs the band didn't write, so initially they passed as well. It wasn't till Forsey flew to Scotland and sold Kerr and the band on the prospect that the song could help break them in the States that they agreed to record it. Simple Minds went into the studio and within three hours they'd completed "Don't You (Forget

About Me)," rearranging the song slightly, adding the "hey-hey-hey-hey" opening and the "la-la-las" at the end.

*The Breakfast Club* was released in early 1985 and though it wasn't one of the highest grossing movies of the year it earned over $50 million on a $1 million budget. It has since gone on to be one of the most memorable (and quotable) movies of the eighties. "Don't You (Forget About Me)" was released when the movie came out and benefited from massive MTV play as well as fitting into both rock and pop radio formats. The song hit #1 on this date in 1985. It would be the only chart-topper for Simple Minds. It's a song that nobody seemed to want to record but to this day, when anyone old enough to remember the mid-eighties hears those opening, thundering drums and those militant, "hey, hey, hey, hey's" they are instantly transported back to those five students serving Saturday detention at Shermer High School.

## May 19th

On this date in 1982, "Ebony and Ivory," a duet by Paul McCartney and Stevie Wonder, had just risen to #1. On May 15th it had bumped "Chariots of Fire" from that spot and it would enjoy an incredible seven week run, finally stepping down on July 3rd when the Human League's "Don't You Want Me" took its place at the top. The song has a simple message of racial harmony, using the keys on a piano as a metaphor for how we all could live together if we choose to. It would go on to become one of the most successful songs for both McCartney and Wonder and it was all inspired by a comedy routine.

Paul McCartney was watching television one day when the English comic Spike Milligan did a skit where he played a piano whose keys had been "segregated," separating the black keys from the white keys. It was a funny skit with a message. It ended with Milligan saying, "black notes, white notes, and you need to play the two to make harmony, folks!" A little while later McCartney got into an argument with his wife Linda and he found himself saying, "Why can't we get along like our piano keys?" The fact that the skit had stayed in his subconscious made an impression on McCartney and he sat down determined to write a song using the same theme. His composition is simple, one chorus that is repeated three times and one verse that is repeated twice. After pointing out how piano keys live in "perfect harmony" McCartney asks the simple question, "Why don't we?" When the song was completed, he knew right away he should sing it as a duet with an African American singer. He'd always loved and respected Stevie Wonder so he sent him a demo of the song with a note in braille. Wonder would tell Dick Clark: "I listened to the song, and I liked it very much. ... I felt it was positive for everybody. I won't say it demanded of people to reflect upon it, but it politely asks the people to reflect upon life in using the terms of music ... this melting pot of many different people."

McCartney and Wonder recorded the song together on the West Indies island of Montserrat in 1981. Perhaps because music videos were not all the rage just yet, nobody thought to make a video that day. So when it was decided "Ebony and Ivory" would be released as a single the two tried to coordinate their schedules again for a video shoot. Unfortunately they couldn't find a date that worked for both of them, so they cobbled a video together using separate shots of each singer and some fancy editing tricks to make them look like they are together on the same piano bench and playing in the same band. With today's technology, that sort of thing is easy to do, but back in the early eighties, it was a tough task. If you watch the video closely you'll pick up on it but it was done masterfully for the time.

"Ebony and Ivory" was released in late March of 1982 and it climbed the charts quickly, hitting #1 six weeks after its release. After its seven week run at the top it fell from the charts and then it became the subject of some ridicule. The song was mocked for being overly simplistic and sappy. *Blender* magazine named it the 10th Worst Song of All Time and in 2007, it was named the worst duet in history by BBC 6 Music listeners. *Saturday Night Live* also famously spoofed the song in a skit that may have aided in the public's change of opinion.

But whether or not the message in "Ebony and Ivory" is saccharine and overly simplified, there is no arguing its veracity. The world would certainly be a better place if everyone could see past skin color or nationality or faith and focus on our commonalities. If the keys on a piano can, oh Lord, why don't we?

### May 20th

On this date in 1979, KISS released their disco-infused single "I Was Made for Lovin' You." The song would become one of the band's highest-charting singles and in many ways opened up a whole new avenue for bands to get help with songwriting. Not bad for a song inspired by a late night visit to the most famous night club of the disco era and a challenge made by KISS' lead singer.

If you didn't live through the disco craze of the late seventies it's hard to imagine just how pervasive it was. Disco went beyond just music. It influenced fashions and advertising and pop culture. The dance beat was all-encompassing, which is one of the reasons the pushback against it was so fierce. It's not like you could change the radio station and ignore it. Disco was everywhere. And pretty soon artists and bands who were considered rockers were releasing songs with a four-on-the-floor disco beat. And not just releasing them but scoring hits as well. The Rolling Stones' "Miss You" was one of their most successful singles of the seventies. The same could be said for Rod Stewart's "Do Ya Think I'm Sexy." Rock fans were aghast. What did Jagger and Stewart have to do with disco?

Actually a lot. They both frequented the most popular nightclubs, disco palaces of the day, and heard that driving disco beat night after night. It's impossible for a musician to be exposed to a genre of music and not, eventually, want to take a crack at it. That's the exact origin of "I Was Made for Lovin' You." Well, half of the story anyway. Paul Stanley, lead singer and one of the chief songwriters for KISS was a frequenter of Studio 54. In his autobiography, *Face the Music: A Life Exposed*, Stanley wrote: "I loved going there to dance. I heard all these 126-beats per minute songs and listened to the lyrics and thought, "Gee I can do that." So like Jagger and Stewart before him, Stanley was influenced by dancing the night away to a driving disco beat and decided to try his hand at writing a disco song.

The other half of the story is this: In 1978 all four members of KISS decided to release solo albums. Each member worked with separate musicians and among the artists Stanley decided to work with were the singers for a band called Desmond Child & Rouge. Stanley and Child got along well and decided to try collaborating on some songs. They completed "The Fight" which appeared on a Desmond Child album and then, when Stanley got the idea to try to write a disco number, they collaborated on that as well. As Child explains: "Paul wanted to write a good disco song and I decided to help him with that. Paul started to write lyrics and chords then I played the song on the guitar and said 'OK, we'll do something to improve this and make it really a good song.'" The two completed the song and Stanley presented it to the band for inclusion on *Dynasty*, their first album following their solo LPs. By this point KISS was having some internal struggles which stemmed from Stanley and Gene Simmons losing patience with Peter Criss and Ace Frehley's heavy drinking and drug use. Things had gotten so bad that session drummer Anton Fig was brought in to do most of the percussion work on *Dynasty*. So even though Peter Criss is seen in the video for "I Was Made For Lovin' You," it's Fig who laid down that driving beat.

When "I Was Made For Lovin' You" became a hit, some wondered who this Desmond Child guy was. The song is credited to Desmond Child, Paul Stanley and Vini Poncia. Poncia is the song's producer and it's not uncommon for producers to get co-writing credit as they often add something in the studio that was missing, thus earning them future royalties. But Desmond Child wasn't a member of KISS nor was he listed as a producer. A few years later his name would appear again, this time on Bon Jovi's breakout album *Slippery When Wet* which featured a number of songs cowritten by the very same Desmond Child. Bon Jovi had actually been given Child's name by Stanley when the New Jersey rocker reached out to Stanley for songwriting help. Stanley was too busy to work with Bon Jovi personally so he recommended Child. This not only opened up an entire career for Child, who has gone on to write hits for artists as far ranging as Joan Jett, Aerosmith, Ricky Martin, Cher and Kelly Clarkson, but it also subtly gave bands permission to seek songwriting help from outside their own ranks. Throughout the seventies, most rock bands considered it anathema to go outside their own band for songs. It was one thing to do a straight cover of a preexisting song, like Hendrix doing "All Along the Watchtower" or Joe Cocker covering "With a Little Help from My Friends," but for some reason most bands never sought outside help when writing originals. When KISS scored a hit with a song cowritten with someone outside their own ranks, and then Child went on to help

Bon Jovi break through with "Livin' On A Prayer" and "You Give Love a Bad Name," it showed other bands there could be "gold in them thar hills."

If KISS were looking to cash in on disco's joy ride, they did it just in time. By the end of 1979 the backlash against the dance genre had reached a fever pitch and the terms "disco sucks" and "deader then disco" became ubiquitous on T-shirts and bumper stickers. To this day "I Was Made For Lovin' You" is a concert favorite whenever KISS tours but these days the arrangement they use de-emphasizes the disco feel of the original, giving it a harder rock sound that fits in with the rest of the band's setlist.

## May 21st

On this date in 1977, Stevie Wonder's "Sir Duke," a tribute to Duke Ellington and other musical greats, began a three week run at #1 on the *Billboard* Hot 100 chart. Wonder had been inspired by Ellington's death to write the song and it became a great tribute to not only past musicians but the overwhelming power of music itself.

Stevland Hardaway Morris was born six weeks premature in 1950 in Saginaw, Michigan. The combination of his early birth and the oxygen-rich atmosphere in the hospital incubator, resulted in his becoming blind in infancy. He displayed uncanny musical abilities as a young child, playing piano, harmonica and drums with an almost innate talent. By age 11 he'd written his first song, which he auditioned for Motown's chief Berry Gordy who signed the young boy immediately. A year later, at just 12 years old, and going now by the stage name, Little Stevie Wonder, he joined the Motortown Revue, touring the "chitlin' circuit" which was made up of theaters around the U.S. that accepted black artists. His performance in Chicago was recorded and released as the album *Recorded Live: The 12 Year Old Genius*. "Fingertips" was released as a single, coincidentally enough on this same date in 1963, and it went on to become Wonder's first big hit. His next few releases were commercial disappointments though and by 1965 it looked like the 15 year old might be dropped by Motown's Tamla label. "Uptight (Everything's Alright)," released towards the end of 1965, became a career-saver for Wonder. It hit #3 on the pop chart and convinced Gordy that Wonder wasn't quite washed up just yet.

In 1972 Wonder signed a new contract with Motown (his first one expired when he turned 21). He was not only given a higher royalty rate but more artistic control (something the micro-managing Gordy was loathe to surrender). Beginning in 1972, Wonder's work would take on a whole new direction. He became more adventurous musically and his lyrics began dealing with social and political issues as well as spiritual and mystical themes. His albums over the next few years: *Music of My Mind*, *Talking Book* and *Innervisions*, all paved the way for Wonder's career-defining double LP, *Songs in the Key of Life*. At fifteen he was at risk of being dropped by his label. A decade later he was universally acknowledged as one of the most important voices in music.

When Duke Ellington passed away in 1974 Stevie Wonder was already working on tracks for what would become *Songs in the Key of Life*. He was moved by the death of the jazz great. Ellington had been an influence on Wonder, both as a musician and as a bandleader. Wonder chose to commemorate the loss as only a songwriter can, by composing a tribute to the man. As Wonder explained later: "I knew the title from the beginning but wanted it to be about the musicians who did something for us. So soon they are forgotten. I wanted to show my appreciation." As the song took shape Wonder wasn't just showing appreciation to Ellington. He also gave shoutouts to other jazz and swing greats like Louis Armstrong, Ella Fitzgerald, Count Basie and Glenn Miller (or is that "Miller" a reference to Sodarisa Miller? Accounts differ depending on where you look). Wonder also rejoices in the power of music itself. Music had given this young blind man a career and led him to international stardom. When Wonder sings that music gives everyone, "an equal opportunity for all to sing, dance and clap their hands" he is, no doubt, thinking about his own upbringing. Music did not segregate against Stevie Wonder, despite his skin color and blindness, and so Wonder not only pays tribute to his heroes but to music itself for giving him that path. "You can feel it over," Wonder sings rejoicingly and indeed, one listen to "Sir Duke" and you can.

*Songs in the Key of Life* was released in late 1976. It debuted at #1 on the *Billboard* Top 200 chart and spent the next thirteen weeks at the top. It was the second best selling LP of 1977, behind only Fleetwood Mac's blockbuster *Rumours*. The album produced two #1 singles, "I Wish" and "Sir Duke" and is considered by most music fans as one of the most accomplished albums in music history. In "Sir Duke," Wonder sings, "Just because a record has a groove, don't make it in the groove." Wonder has produced plenty of albums that are "in the groove" throughout his career. None more so than *Songs in the Key of Life* and its classic tribute to the greats, as well as to music itself.

### May 22nd

On this date in 1989, Young MC released "Bust a Move." The song would eventually reach #7 on the pop chart, by far the highest position achieved by Young MC which makes him the quintessential One Hit Wonder (a title he even acknowledged in a future release). But that one hit was huge, not just for his own career but in helping hip hop crossover to the mainstream.

Marvin Young was born in London in 1967. His family moved to Queens, New York when he was still a child. He was a smart young man who attended Hunter High School in New York City then moved to Los Angeles, enrolling in the University of Southern California where he studied economics. He also loved rap from an early age and can remember calling WBLS, New York City's first and most famous dance music station, and asking for "Rapper's Delight." He credits rap pioneers like the Sugar Hill Gang and the Furious Five for his clean approach to rapping. As he began writing his own songs, they were PG rated, even in a time and age when Public Enemy and N.W.A. were releasing songs laced with profanities and sexual content. When he was criticized later for that approach, for playing it clean just to crossover, he takes the feedback with a grain of salt, saying he was cognizant of trying to appeal to as many people as possible and saying frankly, "I don't want to give a radio station a reason not to play (my song)."

While attending USC, Young met Michael Ross and Matt Dike who had just founded the record label Delicious Vinyl. They signed Young as an artist but before his first record could be completed they also asked him to write some lyrics for an artist they already had signed named Tone Lōc. Young obliged and wrote the #2 hit "Wild Thing" and co-wrote the #3 hit "Funky Cold Medina." But when those songs became massive hits, it was Tone Lōc who became the star. The videos played consistently on MTV but videos feature the performers not the writers, and Young found himself back in his dorm room still a virtual unknown (albeit with a much larger bank account).

As work finally got underway for Young's debut album, *Stone Cold Rhyming*, specific emphasis was paid on the album's standout track, "Bust a Move." The song is typical of Young's writing and rapping style: comical and innuendo-laced but free from vulgarity. The raciest line in the whole song is: "A chick walks by you wish you could sex her" and Young even tempers that by adding, "But you're standing on the wall like you was Poindexter." Young would say later that, besides playing it safe to sell records, a lot had to do with the life he was living at the time. "I was going back to a college dorm every night when I was making that record," he has said. "I wasn't even living in a neighborhood like I grew up in. I didn't really feel like I needed to live up to anything." Ross and Dike knew "Bust a Move" could be a big hit and they convinced Flea from the Red Hot Chili Peppers to play bass on the track. He was given a session fee (supposedly $200) which left a bitter taste in his mouth when the song became a hit. Flea would say later: "I feel as though I got ripped off. The bass line I wrote ended up being a major melody of the tune, and I felt I deserved songwriting credit and money because it was a #1 hit."

Though Flea is wrong about how high the song got, his frustration is understandable and probably shared by others because "Bust a Move" also features a sample of "Found a Child" by the group Ballin' Jack and the breakdown (following Young's "Break it down for me fellas") contains samples from two songs: "Scorpio" by Dennis Coffey and the Detroit Guitar Band as well as "Daytime Hustler" by Bette Midler. But these were the pre-Vanilla Ice days in rap, before crediting the writers of sampled material was mandatory, and so the only people who share writing credit for "Bust a Move" are Young, Ross and Dike.

Young would fail to have another huge hit in his career and some think it's the backlash he received for being too straight-laced and maybe playing it safe in an effort to sell well and find a large audience. Certainly as gangsta rap became huge, rappers like Young MC and MC Hammer were seen as "lacking cred." It's hard to compete with rappers rapping about bitches and hoes with a line like, "You say neat-o, check your libido." But Young has never seemed to mind the term One Hit Wonder. In fact in 1997 he titled his fourth album *Return of the 1 Hit Wonder*. That album, like most of his releases since *Stone Cold Rhyming*, failed to even make the charts.

## May 23rd

On this date in 1969, the Fifth Dimension's "Aquarius/Let the Sunshine In" spent its final day at #1 on the *Billboard* Hot 100 Chart. The song had enjoyed a six week stay at the top and it would go on to be the second highest selling single of the year. Pretty impressive for a song the band's producer was leery about even recording.

The 5th Dimension emerged from the LA music scene of the mid-sixties as a band with a unique sound, melding pop and R&B with infectious harmonies and focusing on uplifting lyrics. Their sound is sometimes referred to as "sunshine pop" or "psychedelic soul" and both descriptions are self-explanatory and perfectly accurate. They scored an early hit with 1966's "Go Where You Wanna Go" then cracked the Top 10 the following year with "Up, Up and Away." Their 1968 hit "Stoned Soul Picnic" made it all the way #3. As they were preparing material for their fourth album, they asked "Bones" Howe, who they'd done some work with on their previous albums, if he could secure the rights to "Aquarius" from the musical *Hair* for them to record. Howe was reluctant at first, explaining, "The thing that bothered me about it was that there'd been other releases of 'Aquarius' and none had done anything, so I was concerned about what we would do that would be any different." But instead of rejecting the idea altogether, he decided to go see the play firsthand. Howe was blown away by the finale, "The Flesh Failures (Let the Sunshine In)" which ends with an upbeat chanting of "Let the sunshine in!" He contacted the music publishers to see if he could make a medley of both songs, because as he would say later, "You don't mess with the music from a Broadway show." Once he was given permission he had to work out an arrangement because the songs are in a different key. The modulation between to the two sections of the song worked perfectly. It features a tempo change as well as a key change and takes the song from its dreamy opening fantasizing about the nirvana that will take place, "when the moon is in the Seventh House and Jupiter aligns with Mars" to the upbeat, gospel-like ending.

The 5th Dimension were touring at the time so Howe worked on the backing track in Los Angeles. He used the famous session musicians known as the

Wrecking Crew who have played on hits from artists as diverse as the Beach Boys, Sonny & Cher, the Byrds, the Mamas & the Papas and even Frank Sinatra. Once he was happy with the backing track he tracked down the band. They were opening for Frank Sinatra in Las Vegas at the time so he secured studio space in Sin City and they recorded their vocals. The band was so happy with the song they decided to name their next LP, *The Age of Aquarius* and they released "Aquarius/Let the Sunshine In" as the lead single in March of 1969. The song was perfect for the last year of the sixties. The decade was ending but some people still wanted to cling to some of the idealism of the time. Here was this infectious song on the airwaves singing about a time "When peace will guide the planets and love will steer the stars." The song became an instant hit and it climbed to #1 on April 12th. After six weeks it gave up the top spot to the Beatles' "Get Back" but the song remained popular throughout the rest of the year, especially that summer as Woodstock (billed as An Aquarian Exposition: 3 Days of Peace & Music) took place in upstate New York. The sixties may have been ending but the counter-culture ideas of peace, love and harmony were not going away quietly.

"Aquarius/Let the Sunshine In" not only spent six weeks at #1 it would go on to win Grammys for Record of the Year and Best Pop Vocal Performance by a Group. *The Age of Aquarius* would hit #2 on the album chart that year and produce a second #1, "Wedding Bell Blues." Though the 5th Dimension never quite reached this level of success again they continued to record for a number of years and following a hiatus, they tour to this day. Their unique sound will always be appreciated by anyone who loves harmonies and optimistic lyrics, or as they sing so passionately, "Just open your heart and let the sunshine in!"

### May 24th

On this date in 1997, Hanson's debut single "MMMBop" went to #1 on the pop chart, dislodging "Hypnotize" by The Notorious B.I.G from that spot. "MMMBop" would stay at the top of the charts for three weeks before giving way to Notorious B.I.G.'s tribute song, "I'll Be Missing You." The song that had helped the band of young brothers get signed to a major label deal had now made them international superstars.

Hanson consists of three brothers from Tulsa, Oklahoma: Isaac, Taylor and Zac. They first started performing as an a cappella group, making their debut public appearance in 1992 at the Mayfest Arts Festival in Tulsa. At the time Isaac was 12, Taylor was nine and Zac, all of seven. They called themselves the Hanson Brothers early on but eventually shortened it to just Hanson. They recorded and released two albums independently before being signed to Mercury Records. Their second independent release was titled *MMMBop* and included a song by the same name which the three brothers had written together. The song has a definite sixties, surf-rock feel to it which is no coincidence. The boys had grown up listening to plenty of fifties doo-wop and sixties rock. Zac would say later, "If anything, 'MMMBop' was inspired by the Beach Boys and vocal groups of that era - using your voice as almost a doo-wop kind of thing."

For a song with a nonsensical chorus ("Mmmbop, ba duba dop, ba du bop, ba duba dop . . .") there is actually meaning to it. "What that song talks about," Zac explains, "is you've got to hold on to the things that really matter." With a lyric like: "So hold on the ones who really care, in the end they'll be the only ones there," the boys were offering incredible advice at such a young age. Zac again: "Things are going to be gone, whether it's your age and your youth, or maybe the money you have, and all that's going to be left are the people you've nurtured and have really built to be your backbone and your support system." How a pre-teen can think of such things is a mystery but indeed the boys had come up with a song that was not only a classic "earworm" but would hold a lesson as well for their decidedly young fan base.

Mercury signed Hanson in 1996 and got them in the studio to work on material for a debut. They brought in the famed Dust Brothers to produce some of the tracks, hoping to add some credibility for the young boys. Plus longtime songwriters like Desmond Child and Barry Mann were asked to contribute material. But Mercury wisely decided to include the boys' best song from their independently released *MMMBop* and the label even released the track as their lead single. The song dropped on April 15th, 1997 and a little over a month later, on this date, the song made it to #1. Hanson performed the song everywhere, appearing on both David Letterman and Jay Leno's late night shows as well as a famous appearance on *Saturday Night Live* where they not only performed the song but then took place in a skit that found the band stuck in an elevator forced to listen to "MMMBop" over and over until they snap. Zac would say later, "You've got to take yourself lightly."

Hanson's major label debut album, *Middle of Nowhere*, was released in early May of 1997 and it would make it all the way to #2 on the LP chart.

Achieving such incredible success so early in a career can be difficult on any band, even more so for such young men. They were quickly the brunt of many jokes and their next few releases found an ever-decreasing fan base. Still, they record and tour to this day and not only have they all grown up but so have their fans who no doubt appreciate the message in "MMMBop" more today than they probably did when they were teenagers just like the band. Hold on to the ones who really care. It's excellent advice at any age.

On this date in 1971, the Rolling Stones' latest LP, *Sticky Fingers*, was sitting atop the album chart in both the U.S. and England, becoming the band's first chart-topper on both sides of the pond. Musically, the album is a landmark achievement for the band, as they were able to redirect public opinion away from the bad press of the last few years back on to what they did best: sing about sex, drugs and rock and roll. But all these years later, what people think about and talk about just as much as the music on *Sticky Fingers* is that historic cover. It appears at or near the top of almost every list of Greatest Albums Covers in history and the mystery surrounding it remains unsolved.

Sometime in 1969 Mick Jagger found himself at a party with Andy Warhol. Warhol, pop artist extraordinaire, had recently designed the album cover for the Velvet Underground's debut LP, *Velvet Underground & Nico*, with its simple painting of a banana. Warhol and Jagger got to talking at the party and the conversation turned to album covers. Warhol made a comment that stuck with Jagger. He said something about how cool it would be if an album cover featured an actual working zipper. Jagger was intrigued and as work developed on the next Stones album (with recording sessions taking place at Muscle Shoals Studio in Alabama as well as in London) he wrote a letter to Warhol and asked him to handle the design. In the letter Jagger writes, "In my short sweet experience, the more complicated the format of the album, e.g. more complex than just pages or fold-out, the more fucked-up the reproduction and agonizing the delays." Then Jagger added, "But, having said that, I leave it in your capable hands to do what ever you want." Warhol completely ignored Jagger's first point and ran with the second. He was going to do whatever he wanted, no matter how complicated it fucked things up.

Warhol set up a photo shoot and took a number of pictures of male models' crotches. Whether or not he had the guys "chub up" is open to conjecture but certainly in the picture that wound up being used there is a clear definition of a large penis beneath the jeans. Craig Braun, who was hired to take Warhol's design and make it a reality has no doubt. He says, "I used to kid Andy, 'I know you had that guy playing with his dick before you shot the picture!'" Because Warhol used a number of different models before selecting the final shot, he claimed to not even know whose crotch shot was ultimately used. What we do know though is that the rumors that circulated after the album was released, claiming it was Mick Jagger's crotch, were false. He wasn't at the photo shoot so there was no way the package was his (although Jagger was often slow to deny this, for obvious reasons).

The next step was to install a working zipper. This project fell to Braun who realized immediately that the raised part of the zipper would cause damage to the album when it was boxed for shipment. He fixed this problem by adding a second layer, a sub-cover, if you will. After all, if there's a working zipper, people will want to pull the zipper down. There should be something underneath for them to see, right? So his final design featured a working zipper that opened to reveal an image of cotton briefs. This solved the problem of the album in the sleeve being damaged. But it didn't solve the problem of the album that was sitting on top of the zipper being damaged. Braun hadn't thought about that. When the first shipments of *Sticky Fingers* went out, the third song of side two, "Sister Morphine," wound up being indented by the zipper from the album below it in the case. Braun's next work-around was ingenious. He later told the New York Times: "I got this idea that maybe, if the glue was dry enough, we could have the little old ladies at the end of the assembly line pull the zipper down far enough so that the round part would hit the center disc label. It worked, and it was even better to see the zipper pulled halfway down."

Imagine those "little old ladies" getting home from work and being asked what they did all day.

Warhol's cover, with its working zipper, was only part of the unique artwork of *Sticky Fingers*. The album also featured a logo for the band. This was another Mick Jagger idea and it was inspired by two things. First Jagger was always known for his prominent lips. Plus, he'd recently seen a painting of the Hindu goddess Kali, who is almost always shown with her tongue sticking out. Jagger wanted something similar to represent the band. He commissioned a designer named John Pasche to come up with something but since this was a last minute request by Jagger time was of the essence. Pasche sent a black and white version of the now famous tongue and lips logo to Braun who modified it slightly, painting it red, and included it on the inside of the album. This was the first use of the logo that would soon come to personify the Rolling Stones and is arguably the most famous band logo ever.

*Sticky Fingers* was released in early 1971. The Stones had been dealing with the fallout from the tragedy at Altamonte and the loss of their founding member Brian Jones. Jones had been replaced by Mick Taylor so *Sticky Fingers* is the first album to feature his incredible guitar work alongside Keith Richards. To say that the band successfully redirected the conversation is an understatement. Within no time the events of the past few years were all but forgotten and all music fans wanted to talk about was the new sound of the Stones. Where their previous release, *Let It Bleed*, had certain evil undertones, *Sticky Fingers*, from its bulging crotch cover to its bright red lips and tongue, was much more sexual. "Brown Sugar" not only dealt with sex but it seemed to focus on the taboo of interracial sex. And the album's incredible blues send-up, "Can't You Hear Me Knocking," which was essentially Mick Taylor's "welcome to the Stones" moment, features a stalker "begging" and "prowling" and "knocking down the dirty street." The album also featured plenty of drug references, from the whole languid "Sister Morphine" to the "cocaine eyes" in "Can't You Hear Me Knocking." But decades later, as much as the album is remembered for its music, it is also the artwork that so many people talk about. Rock critic Richard Harrington has said: "This album heralded an age of really imaginative and provocative packaging. It also introduced the greatest band logo of all time." Those two things are no small feat, along with some of the best Rolling Stones music of the seventies.

On this date in 1973, Edgar Winter's "Frankenstein" went to #1 on the *Billboard Hot 100 Chart*, bumping "You Are the Sunshine of My Life" by Stevie Wonder from the top. "Frankenstein" would hold the top spot for a week before giving way to Paul McCartney and Wings' beautiful ballad, "My Love." The song had started life as a B-side and would go on to become one of the most famous and successful instrumentals in the history of rock.

Edgar Winter and his brother Johnny grew up in the fifties in Texas, sharing a love of the blues as well as albinism. Edgar would say years later, "No one in school really gave me a hard time about being an albino... but then again I wasn't really popular." While Johnny focused on the guitar, Edgar picked up the keyboard. Both became prodigies at their chosen instruments. By the late sixties a young Edgar Winter was signed to Epic Records and released his self-titled debut album in 1970. Neither of his first two albums became big hits but they established an avid following. In 1972 he released a live album titled *Roadwork* which highlighted Winter's virtuoso keyboard work and impassioned vocals. *Roadwork* went to #23 on the LP chart and introduced Edgar Winter to a larger audience that loved his mixture of rock and blues.

Later that year, work began on Winter's third studio LP, which would be titled *They Only Come Out at Night*. He brought an early version of a synthesizer into the studio and started working on a hard rock jam that featured Rick Derringer (who was producing the session) on guitar, Dan Hartman on bass and Chuck Ruff on drums. As the four worked, the riff and melody Winter had written took on a life of its own. Each musician took a turn soloing, in fact Ruff did two drum solos so for a while the song had a working title of "The Double Drum Song." When they were done the track had to be edited in numerous places to make it fit on an album (and possibly the B-side of a single which is where Winter thought it would go). As Winter explained later: "Back in those days when you edited something, you physically had to cut the tape and splice it back together. It was all over the control room, draped over the backs of chairs and the couch. We were trying to figure out how to put it back together, saying 'Here's the main body; the leg bone's connected to the thigh bone.' Then Chuck Ruff, my drummer, says, 'Wow, man, it's like Frankenstein.' As soon as I heard that, I went, 'Wow, that's it!' The monster was born." Ruff's comment had given this epic, instrumental rock jam a fitting name.

As *They Only Come Out at Night* was prepared for release Winter decided "Hangin' Around" should be the lead single with "Frankenstein" as the B-side. But radio DJs started flipping the platter and playing the hard rocking instrumental so Epic quickly pulled the single and released "Frankenstein" as the A-side (with "Undercover Man" as the B-side). Within two months the song had reached #1 on the charts. "Free Ride" was released as the second single and it got as high as #14. "Free Ride" was written by Dan Hartman who would go on to a successful solo career himself, scoring a disco hit with "Instant Replay" and soft rock hit with "I Can Dream About You."

Though Winter would never match his 1973 success he has enjoyed a long and successful career as a multi-instrumentalist and a pioneer in using the synthesizer. His most successful song truly was a monster he'd created in the studio.

## May 27th

On this date in 1977, the Sex Pistols released their most controversial song to date, "God Save the Queen." The release was timed to coincide with Queen Elizabeth's Silver Jubilee, a celebration commemorating the 25th anniversary of her coronation and the publicity stunt worked to perfection. The song became the Pistols' biggest hit and the headlines it made thrust the band even further into the spotlight.

Malcolm McLaren was the undeniable brain trust behind the Sex Pistols. A Londoner, he'd spent time in New York City in the early seventies and was enthralled by the proto-punk movement that was fermenting in that city. He and his girlfriend Vivienne Westwood ran a boutique in London that they renamed SEX. Many young musicians hung out at the shop and McLaren began advising some of them on their careers, offering suggestions about some of the fashions and attitudes he'd witnessed in New York. Guitarist Steve Jones was one of those musicians and he eventually convinced McLaren (or did McLaren convince him? - it's open to debate) to manage his band. With Paul Cook on drums and Glen Matlock on bass all the band needed was a proper frontman. Rock legend has it that one day a young John Lydon was seen wearing a Pink Floyd shirt with the words "I hate" scrawled above the band's name. It was the exact attitude McLaren was looking for to be the frontman of his new band. Lydon was rude, crude and dirty, in fact his horrible body odor is what earned him the nickname Johnny Rotten. Lydon was convinced to tryout for the band even though he'd never sung before. When he did the others broke down in laughter at how bad he was. But McLaren convinced them that he was perfect. The band was going to be all about attitude and anger, two traits Lydon (Rotten) had in spades.

The foursome began rehearsing regularly in August of 1975 and the band was named the Sex Pistols because McLaren wanted them to be "sexy young assassins."

The Sex Pistols' first public performance was in November of 1975. McLaren encouraged their obnoxious attitudes and brash personas both on and off stage from the very start. He carefully cultivated their reputation in the local press as the angriest, rudest band in the land. How much of that was legitimate and how much of it was spurious will always remain a mystery. Certainly there was real angst among that generation in England. Rotten would say later: "Early seventies Britain was a very depressing place . . .It was completely run-down with trash on the streets, and total unemployment. Just about everybody was on strike. Everybody was brought up with an education system that told you point blank that if you came from the wrong side of the tracks...then you had no hope in hell and no career prospects at all." Then, in typical Rotten fashion, he concluded, "Out of that came pretentious moi and the Sex Pistols . . . and then a whole bunch of copycat wankers after us." So there is no doubt that the indignation displayed by bands like the Sex Pistols and the Clash and the Damned and Siouxsie and the Banshees was authentic. But there is also no doubt that McLaren packaged it perfectly and sold it to anyone and everyone he could.

McLaren encouraged his young charges to write their own songs early on. One of those songs started life with the title "No Future." Matlock had a hand in crafting the song as well as "Anarchy in the U.K." but as the band honed their sound and persona throughout 1976 he became the odd man out. There are various stories of how and why Matlock eventually left the Pistols and while the two most commons reasons ("he was too nice" and "he liked the Beatles too much") are probably not the whole truth, they fit nicely into the narrative of the Sex Pistols. With Matlock gone the final piece of the puzzle would be added in the winter of 1977. That's when John Beverly was asked to join the band as their new bassist. Beverly was the Pistols' biggest fan. He was at every show, thrashing away to their ferocious sound and he'd become good friends with Rotten so it was a natural fit. Except, Beverly didn't play the bass. But lack of musical prowess was far less important for a punk band than look and attitude (which Beverly had plenty of). He was given a new name, Sid Vicious, and told to learn the bass. McLaren would comment later: "When Sid joined he couldn't play guitar but his craziness fit into the structure of the band. He was the knight in shining armor with a giant fist."

Meanwhile the Pistols had already been dropped by one record label and were looking for a deal. EMI had signed the band in October of 1976 but after their famous cursing incident on British television the band had been dropped. McLaren then worked out a deal with A&M but on the day the band signed the contract they destroyed a bathroom in A&M's London office and were quickly dropped again. They signed with Virgin Records, their third record contract in six months, in May of 1977 just in time to release "No Future" which, by this point had evolved into "God Save the Queen." The song that had begun life as a rampage against England's economic system had been redirected to mock their royalty. And just in time for the big Silver Jubilee.

On June 7th, the day of the Jubilee, McLaren rented a boat with plans to have his band play their newest release, "God Save the Queen," from the River Thames, as close to Westminster Palace as they could get. Authorities shut the band down before they could even play the first note, which McLaren, of course, used as publicity to help the single move. And move it did. It reached #2 on the English pop chart and probably should have gone to #1 but it never made it. McLaren and the band will always believe that the chart was fixed to deny them a #1 because of the song's controversial nature.

The Sex Pistols flamed out quicker than any other punk band. After the release of their only LP, *Never Mind the Bollocks Here's the Sex Pistols*, in November of 1977, they embarked on a U.S. tour in early 1978 that was marred by fights and Vicious' ever increasing heroin use. At the last show of the tour, the band came out for an encore which Rotten introduced by saying, "You'll get one number and one number only 'cause I'm a lazy bastard." The band then launched into a cover of the Stooges' "No Fun" with Rotten repeating over and over, "This is no fun. No fun. This is no fun—at all. No fun."

The band broke up days later.

Whether they were singing about "no future" or "no fun," the Sex Pistols, in their few short years together, had helped change the musical landscape forever. Yes, they were calculating and, yes, they were packaged by McLaren, the brilliant promoter. But their emotions were real and their anger justified and they somehow made every other band seem like poseurs (or, in Rotten's words "wankers") if only for a brief time. Listen to "God Save the Queen" today but do it at maximum volume. Feel their energy and anger and attitude because if any band ever bottled that all together brilliantly, it was the Sex Pistols.

## May 28th

On this date in 1966, one of the most passionate love songs of all time, "When A Man Loves A Woman" by Percy Sledge, began a two week run at #1 on the *Billboard* Hot 100 Chart. It knocked the Mamas and the Papas' "Monday Monday" from that spot and it would stay at #1 till June 11th when "Paint It Black" by the Rolling Stones took its place. The song has been covered by numerous artists and appeared in both commercials and films and yet there remains to this day a burning question: who wrote it?

Percy Sledge was born in Alabama in 1940. As a young man he worked a number of different jobs while he attempted to make it as a singer. For a few years he would toil away Monday through Friday, then perform all weekend with a group called the Esquires Combo. Calvin Lewis and Andrew Wright were musicians in the band and they are listed as the only two writers on "When A Man Loves A Woman." According to them they wrote a song that was originally titled "Why Did You Leave Me?" They brought it to Sledge and had him sing it in their live shows. One day, Quin Ivy, who was an influential disc jockey and record producer in the area, heard the song and thought it had potential. He convinced Lewis and Wright to change the lyrics to be more optimistic, which they did, coming up with "When a Man Loves a Woman" entirely on their own.

Sledge told a completely different story. But part of the problem was Sledge told many different stories in his lifetime about how he came up with the song. In one, he used to sing the melody and some early form of the lyrics while working out in the fields in one of his day jobs. In another, he had just broken up with a girlfriend who was moving to California to pursue a modeling career and he showed up one day for rehearsal and told the band to play him a slow blues melody. With a broken heart, he improvised lyrics for "Why Did You Leave Me?" The band liked it and incorporated it into their set which is how Quin Ivy heard it, recommended the lyric change (when Sledge tells the story he came up with the lyric change) and had the song recorded. The obvious question for Sledge, then, was why he allowed Lewis and Wright to take credit for the song? His answer was always that he wanted to show his appreciation for them letting him into their band. Questions remained about who actually wrote the song up until Sledge's passing in 2015 and the mystery promises to remain unsolved. To this day though, only Lewis and Wright are listed as songwriters.

Quin Ivy's involvement with the song is undisputed. Everyone involved agrees that he heard the song in the band's set, recognized its potential and recommended the more optimistic lyric change. When he heard the result, he booked the band into the FAME Studios in Muscle Shoals, Alabama. Ivy then presented the song to Atlantic Records' Jerry Wexler who thought it had potential but mentioned that the horns were out of key. The band re-recorded the song, this time at Norala Studios in Sheffield, Alabama and Wexler loved this version. In fact legend has it Wexler called his superiors at the label and said he'd "just heard the song that will pay for our summer." However, somehow when Atlantic Records went to press the single, they used the original version of the song so those "out of key" horns have stayed with "When a Man Loves a Woman" all these years (though it's not something the untrained ear would pick up on).

For the average listener, the song has a simple melody but what makes it stand out is Sledge's singing. Though the chorus had been changed from "Why Did You Leave Me?" to "When a Man Loves a Woman" the song still teeters on the edge of despair. Sledge is exposing all the vulnerability that comes with opening one's heart to another. Lines like, "If she's bad he can't see it" and "She can bring him such misery" speak of a love that is near obsession. This is no carefree, whimsical love song. And whether Sledge wrote the lyrics or not, there is no doubt that his impassioned delivery is what makes the song an all-time classic. When Sledge pleads, "Baby please don't treat me bad" the listener understands how powerless he is in this relationship. If you've ever been that hopelessly and helplessly in love, there is no doubt Sledge has channeled all your fears in two minutes and fifty seconds of musical perfection.

On this date in 1983, Irene Cara's "Flashdance...What a Feeling" began a six week run at #1 on the *Billboard* Hot 100 chart. It bumped off David Bowie's "Let's Dance" and the song would stay at the top till July 9th when "Every Breath You Take" by the Police took its place. The song was Cara's only career #1 and is a great example of synergistic promotion. The song helped make the movie huge which also helped popularize the song. Not only would the movie *Flashdance* become a surprise box office hit, raking in over $200 million dollars and finishing 1983 as the 3rd highest grossing film (behind *Return of the Jedi* and *Terms of Endearment*), many people credit *Flashdance* for reviving the musical movie genre.

By the early eighties it had been a few years since a musical film had been a hit. Certainly 1978's *Grease* was huge at the box office, but since then musicals like *Sgt. Pepper's Lonely Hearts Club Band*, *The Wiz* and *Pennies from Heaven* had failed to live up to expectations, leaving Hollywood to wonder if musicals, or even movies that featured a lot of songs, were out. MTV factored into the equation. The thought was that people could see music and film intertwined at any time now so maybe they didn't need to go to a theater to see a musical. Which is why, when *Flashdance* went into production, it was given a fairly modest budget of $7 million.

*Flashdance*'s producers knew the movie would hinge on two things: the dance scenes and the soundtrack. For the dance scenes they chose to use multiple body doubles including Marine Jahan for most of the dancing scenes, gymnast Sharon Shapiro for the leap through the air in the audition scene and Crazy Legs for the breakdancing. The filmmakers tried to keep this hidden because they did not want to ruin the illusion that Jennifer Beals was not the one dancing. It's a secret though that eventually leaked out.

For the soundtrack, the producers recruited Phil Ramone to be the musical director and he asked disco legend Giorgio Moroder to compile some songs. Moroder and fellow producer Keith Forsey worked on a theme song for the movie. They wanted Irene Cara to sing the song because they loved her theme for the movie *Fame*. Cara was reluctant at first, afraid that working with Moroder would simply increase the number of people who compared her to Donna Summer, but she eventually agreed and helped complete the song and so Moroder, Forsey and Cara are all listed as cowriters. Though the word "flashdance" never appears in the lyrics, they titled it "Flashdance...What a Feeling" to tie in with the movie. Ramone asked Michael Sembello to contribute a song and his "Maniac" became the other huge hit from *Flashdance*. Sembello had already written "Maniac" but tweaked it to fit the movie (adding the line: "just a steel town girl on a Saturday night"). Ramone also recommended to the movie's producers that they incorporate break dancing into the film. He'd seen kids in New York City break dancing on the streets and thought it would be a cool and modern addition to the movie.

As *Flashdance* neared release expectations were low. When the movie opened in April of 1983 to mixed reviews it's safe to say everyone involved just hoped to make their money back and break even. But then, something amazing happened. People started talking glowingly about the movie and the positive word-of-mouth had an immediate effect. People started flocking to the theaters to see Jennifer Beals in all her sexy glory and radio stations started playing "Flashdance ...What a Feeling" in heavy rotation. The movie would eventually earn over $200 million dollars. The film's soundtrack sold over 20 million copies worldwide and both the title track and "Maniac" hit #1 in 1983. "Flashdance...What a Feeling" also won the Academy Award for Best Original Song.

Whether or not the movie was influenced by MTV, director Adrian Lyne has never said. But many people have pointed out the similarities between the quick editing used in many music videos and the dance scenes in Flashdance. And in the following years movies like *Footloose* and *Dirty Dancing* would not only successfully incorporate music and dancing, but they'd be edited with a similar feel. Moroder would continue writing for movies, scoring hits with "Danger Zone" and "Take My Breath Away" from *Top Gun.* Lyne would go on to produce other eighties' classics like *Fatal Attraction, 9½ Weeks* and *Indecent Proposal.* Jennifer Beals has enjoyed a long and rich history in acting but it's safe to say she's never been sexier than eating lobster in *Flashdance.* Or maybe getting the water dumped on her. As for Irene Cara, the biggest hits of her career have all been from movies. And while she's never climbed back on top of the charts she has enjoyed a fruitful career in films and music. And she's even re-recorded her lone #1 two more times, in 1995 for the *Full Monty* soundtrack and again in 2002, as a duet she recorded with Swiss artist DJ BoBo.

It's safe to say everyone involved in *Flashdance* took their passion and made it happen.

### May 30th

On this date in 1995, Hootie & the Blowfish, the band from South Carolina with the weird name and harmonious sound, were sitting on the top of the album chart with their debut LP, *Cracked Rear View.* The album would enjoy a four week run then return sporadically throughout the rest of 1995, eventually tabulating eight total weeks at #1. Hootie had enjoyed a long slow ride to the top and though they'd never match the success of their debut, no one old enough to remember 1995 will ever forget how ubiquitous Hootie & the Blowfish were that year.

The origins of Hootie & the Blowfish go back to the University of South Carolina in the mid-eighties. Mark Bryan, who loved to play guitar, was in the bathroom of his dormitory one day when he overheard an amazing voice. Turned out, it was a fellow freshman named Darius Rucker singing in the shower. Bryan convinced Rucker the two should play together and they started performing covers as a duo named the Wolf Brothers. As their popularity grew they decided to expand the band and start writing and playing original songs. They were in search of a name when one day Rucker saw two of his friends standing next to each other. One friend had a big head and wore rimmed glasses. His owl-like look had earned him the nickname Hootie. The other friend had big pronounced cheeks and was often called Blowfish. Rucker saw the two together and exclaimed, "Hey look, it's Hootie and the Blowfish." He liked how that sounded and brought it to the rest of the band and, for lack of anything better, they adopted it.

Hootie & the Blowfish played the bars and clubs in and around the Carolinas for years. When record labels ignored them they started making cassettes of their songs to sell at their gigs. In 1993 they went into a studio and recorded six originals. They called the resulting EP *Kootchypop* and self-released it on CD. They felt they were fighting a losing battle in the early nineties because the airwaves were filled with grunge rock and gangsta rap. Their sound was much more traditional and mellower, and featured some incredible harmonies. It's no doubt one of the reasons so many record labels passed on them. While the band sounded great and had some very good original songs already written and even recorded, they just didn't fit what was hot at the moment and for years they went unsigned.

Finally, in 1993, Atlantic Records offered Hootie & the Blowfish a contract. The band re-recorded some of the songs that had been on *Kootchypop* and added a few more to complete the eleven tracks on their debut. This being the mid-nineties, when "hidden tracks" were all the thing, the band also included a version of the Negro spiritual song "Sometimes I Feel Like a Motherless Child," the same song Richie Havens so famously played at Woodstock.

*Cracked Rear View* was released in July of 1994 along with the lead single "Hold My Hand." Neither became instant hits and so the band did what they'd always done, went back to playing live. Now, however, with the support of a record label, Hootie got some bigger gigs, including an opening spot on Big Head Todd & the Monsters' 1994 tour.

And then slowly their popularity began to grow. One day, Rucker and fellow bandmate Dean Felber were driving together when "Hold My Hand" came on the radio. As Rucker would explain: "It was the first time we had heard it on the radio. We were in Columbia, South Carolina. It came on the radio, and we were listening to it and about halfway through the song, he reached over and he turned it up, and we just started giggling. . . My heart raced. For me, it was a moment where I thought, 'Wow! This is radio... not just some college radio, we're on pop radio!' We had been playing for nine years! I thought this might really be starting to happen. . . That was a great day! You never forget the first time you hear your first song on the radio - that's hard to forget."

Rucker and Felber weren't the only ones to hear the song. Eventually everyone would. Radio stations started playing "Hold My Hand" and the album's second single "Let Her Cry" (which was released in December of 1994) in heavy rotation. It seemed the same reasons the band had gone unsigned all those years were the same things that made them so popular. The listening public needed a break from all that shouting and thrashing and anger and here was the perfect tonic. a band with a more traditional, soft rock sound with a debut single that, not unlike one of the Beatles' earliest hits, sang about something as sweet and innocent as hand holding. *Cracked Rear View* went on to sell 10 million albums in 1995 and is in the Top 20 of best-selling albums of all time. The LP produced four Top 20 hits.

Though Hootie & the Blowfish were unable to duplicate their initial success, Rucker has gone on to a successful career as a country singer. That same amazing voice that got him noticed in a dorm shower has served him well with hits like "Homegrown Honey", "True Believers" and his cover of "Wagon Wheel." And anyone who is old enough to have bought records in 1995 almost assuredly has a copy of the CD *Cracked Rear View* somewhere. It was one of those albums that virtually everyone owned and played out and, probably like Felber and Rucker did, cranked up every time you heard it.

### May 31st

On this date in 1986, Peter Gabriel's "Sledgehammer" had just broken the Top 40 on the *Billboard* Hot 100. The innovative video for the song was already in heavy rotation and it would help carry "Sledgehammer" all the way to #1 on the charts, becoming Gabriel's only career chart-topper. The song's popularity also helped Gabriel's 1986 LP *So* reach #2 on the LP chart. Gabriel gives credit where it's due, he believes the success of the song was all due to the video.

Peter Gabriel was a founding member of Genesis in the mid-sixties and served as the band's lead singer and eccentric frontman for almost a decade. His flamboyant stage presence helped get the band noticed and they soon became innovators in the progressive rock movement. When he left Genesis in 1975 many in the rock world were stunned. Gabriel then released four albums that he refused to title so they are listed using his name and whatever image was on the front cover (*Peter Gabriel/Car*, *Peter Gabriel/Scratch* etc). When his record company finally insisted he start titling his LPs he used two letter words. *So* became his 1986 release and "Sledgehammer" the lead single.

"Sledgehammer" is a euphemism for a man's penis. In fact, the song is filled with them: bumper cars, steam trains and big dippers. But it's not just male genitalia Gabriel was alluding to in the lyrics. When he sings "Open up your fruit cage. Where the fruit is as sweet as can be," he is referring to, well, you get it right? The whole song is a celebration of sex at its most raw and urgent. Gabriel explained later, "Sometimes sex can break through barriers when other forms of communication are not working too well."

This being the mid-eighties, no song had a chance for success without a great video. Gabriel enlisted director Stephen Johnson who had just done an innovative video for the Talking Heads' song "Road to Nowhere" in which he incorporated techniques like claymation and stop-motion animation. Johnson initially didn't love the song (his comment was, "I thought it was just another white boy trying to sound black,") but he agreed to direct the video nonetheless. Following the song's theme, the video opens with sperm cells swimming before we get some dangerously close up shots of Gabriel's face. Gabriel went all out to make the video a success. At one point he laid under a glass sheet for 16 hours and at another his face was painted blue with white clouds moving across it. The paint irritated his skin and left him with a rash. The video took five days to shoot and then Johnson, working with a team of seven animators, took another two days to edit it. The final product was mind-blowing for its time. No one had seen anything like it, on MTV or anywhere else.

When the video was submitted to MTV they loved it and immediately started playing it in heavy rotation. "Sledgehammer" was released on April 25th, 1986. It broke the Top 40 this week and eventually hit #1, ironically, knocking Genesis' "Invisible Touch" from that spot. Of the video Gabriel says, "I think it had a sense of both humor and fun, neither of which were particularly associated with me." At the 1987 MTV Video Music Awards, "Sledgehammer" was the runaway winner, taking home nine awards, the most ever for a single song. MTV has since said that "Sledgehammer" is the most played video in its history, and since the channel doesn't play videos anymore, that record seems safe.

# JUNE

# June 1st

On this date in 1969, in a hotel room in Montreal, John Lennon and his new wife Yoko Ono, along with a number of celebrities who were hanging out with the couple during their "Bed-In," recorded "Give Peace a Chance." Lennon had set out to write an anti-war anthem and months later, when he saw thousands of people singing the song at a rally in Washington, D.C., he knew he'd accomplished his goal.

Brian Epstein was the Beatles' manager since their earliest days and he is credited for packaging the band and helping to make them international superstars. No one would ever deny the talent in the band but Epstein's influence, especially early on, certainly helped. He cleaned up their rough edges from their hardscrabble days playing in Hamburg, Germany and presented the band as a wholesome alternative to some of the edgier rockers of the fifties. One of the things Epstein also urged the band to avoid was political commentary in their lyrics and during their interviews. He didn't see the point in turning off any of their fans (potential record buyers). His point couldn't have been made clearer when Lennon made the famous remark about the Beatles being, "more popular than Jesus" which caused the band a ton of bad press and helped make their last tour of the U.S. a nightmare. Epstein was not alone in this. Berry Gordy, head of Motown, had a similar edict with his artists: avoid politics!

But Epstein passed away in 1967 and by then his influence on the band had waned anyway. The boys were maturing and becoming more aware of worldly issues and they were no longer satisfied to just sing about holding hands and knowing secrets. John Lennon, especially, was interested in making statements with some of his songs. In the summer of 1967 he wrote "All You Need Is Love" which the band sang to the entire world during the first ever live television satellite show. The following year he wrote "Revolution" which had the potential to be a strong anti-war statement but Lennon couched it with some ambiguous lyrics ("Don't you know that you can count me out, in") and ended it with the overly optimistic finale that everything was going to be all right. It was like he was testing the waters before diving into the deep end.

On March 20th, 1969, John Lennon and Yoko Ono were married. Knowing how much publicity their wedding would generate they decided to use it to promote world peace. They went to Amsterdam for their honeymoon and announced to the press that they'd be spending an entire week in bed and that the press was welcome to come visit them. They called it a "Bed-In For Peace" a take on the popular "Sit-Ins" of the time, in which protesters remained seated in front of an establishment until they were arrested or their demands were met. The press, of course, showed up in droves and if they expected anything salacious they were certainly disappointed. Lennon and Ono were simply sitting up in bed, wearing pajamas and talking about peace. They'd also decorated their room with signs that promoted things like "Hair Peace" and "Bed Peace." It was your quintessential hippie moment.

Lennon and Ono were so happy with the press they received they decided to hold a second "Bed-In" a few months later in Montreal. They arrived on May 26th, 1969 and, once again, the press came out in large numbers. During one of his interviews, Lennon casually said to a reporter, "All we are saying is give peace a chance." The words must have stuck with Lennon because later that day he began to scribble lyrics for a new song. He had a simple goal: to write a song that could be sung at the rallies and demonstrations that were taking place to protest the Vietnam War. Later, he would tell *Rolling Stone:* "I wanted to write something that would take over 'We Shall Overcome.' I don't know why that's the one they always sang, and I thought, 'Why doesn't somebody write something for the people now?'" The verses were mostly nonsense, a list of things that "Everybody's talking about." But the chorus was anthemic, a simple and powerful message: "All we are saying is give peace a chance." In that regard the song is structured much like "All You Need Is Love." While the verses of that song are fairly forgettable, it's the chorus, the uplifting affirmation, "All you need is love," that makes the song a classic. The same can be said of "Give Peace a Chance." Lennon certainly could have spent some time in the verses expanding on his concept of peace and how it would affect the world (instead of just rattling off a list of rhymes like "Ministers, sinisters, banisters and canisters") but it's that chorus, the simple and easy to sing chorus, that makes what Lennon wrote in that hotel room in Montreal one of the all-time great anti-war anthems.

On Sunday, June 1st, John Lennon asked Derek Taylor, the Beatles' press officer who was traveling with him, to arrange to have video and recording equipment set up in the hotel room. Taylor found a local recording studio that was willing to help. The owner, André Perry, brought a four track recorder and some microphones. The room was filled with people, some celebrities (Tommy Smothers, Timothy Leary, Allen Ginsberg, Petula Clark and Murray the K) some journalists and some members of the Canadian branch of Radha Krishna Temple. Lennon presented his song idea to everyone and they ran through one rehearsal (which Perry recorded.) Lennon and Smothers played acoustic guitar and people in the room were encouraged to knock on the walls and floor to keep the beat. Happy with the run through Lennon counted off: "two, one, two, three, four," and everyone in the room participated in the performance of "Give Peace a Chance." After the first take Lennon declared it done.

The next day Perry brought a taped version of the song to Lennon and he was thrilled with it. Perry thought some of the vocals were distorted so they overdubbed them. As he would explain later, "We kept all the original stuff, we just kind of like improved it a bit by adding if you like, some voices." "Give Peace a Chance" was released as a Plastic Ono Band recording on July 7th, 1969. It peaked at #14 on the *Billboard* Hot 100 in September.

On November 15th, 1969 an anti-war demonstration took place in Washington, D.C. called the Moratorium to End the War in Vietnam. Over half a million people showed up. At one point Pete Seeger led the demonstrators in a ten minute version of "Give Peace a Chance" with Seeger ad libbing lines like, "Are you listening, Nixon?" and "Are you listening, Pentagon?" Lennon was watching on TV and called it, "one of the biggest moments of my life."

And indeed Nixon was watching too. When he was asked about the rally he said: "I understand that there has been, and continues to be, opposition to the war in Vietnam on the campuses and also in the nation. As far as this kind of activity is concerned, we expect it; however under no circumstances will I be affected whatever by it." And he wasn't. America's involvement in the war continued long past his presidency and since then wars have raged throughout the world. So it's fair to ask if Lennon or any other songwriter attempting to capture an anti-war message in a song has any efficacy. World leaders are above being swayed by a rally or a pop song. But it's also fair to ask what else should an artist do? Especially once they've achieved fame, which gives them the platform to get a message out to the masses. Someone like John Lennon was never going to be content writing simple love songs. His lyrics continued to evolve and attempt to affect change, most notably with "Imagine" which he wrote two years after "Give Peace a Chance." Lennon would tell an interviewer years later: "We think we have the right to have a say in the future. And we think the future is made in your mind." On this date in 1969, in a hotel room in Montreal, he attempted to plant a very simple message in everyone's mind. Give peace a chance.

## June 2nd

On this date in 1990, Digital Underground's "The Humpty Dance" reached its peak position on the pop chart, just outside the Top 10. The song was a last minute addition for the group's debut album *Sex Packets* and it only came about when everyone realized just how funny and commanding the fictional character Humpty Hump was. For an afterthought of a song, it's had a pretty rich history!

Gregory Jacobs was born in 1963 in Brooklyn, New York. He loved music as a child and taught himself to play piano and drums before discovering turntablism. He loved Parliament Funkadelic and his earliest compositions were P-Funk inspired jams with some rapping thrown in. Jacobs had moved to the Bay Area by the mid-eighties and he began using the rap name Shock-G. He dreamt of putting together a band similar to P-Funk that he would call Digital Underground.

One day while working at a music equipment store Jacobs met a man who was installing a home studio but didn't have the technical knowledge to complete the project. Jacobs offered to do the installation in exchange for some studio time and the resulting demos earned Jacobs a deal with Tommy Boy Records. Now Jacobs suddenly had a problem. Tommy Boy had signed Digital Underground based on Jacobs' description of this diverse group of musicians/characters but the concept was still just in his head. Jacobs would say later, "I always wanted Digital Underground to be this big super group, but we didn't have all the characters yet. Basically, most of the time if I had a vision of a kind of guy we needed, I'd just be that guy." But Jacobs rounded up some local musicians and created a song called "Doowutchalike" which was released in October of 1989 as Digital Underground's first single for Tommy Boy. In the song, Jacobs slips between rapping as Shock-G and also as another character he'd created called Humpty Hump. When it was time to shoot a video for "Doowutchalike" Jacobs took a trip to a party store and got a bunch of props. Jacobs explains: "The video was supposed to look like an insane party so we got all these accessories like the Groucho nose, shark noses, pig noses."

After the video was shot and "Doowutchalike" released, Jacobs started realizing Humpty Hump's potential. He began to create a history around the character to give him more life. As he's said: "Foolin' around with the Humpty voice was like doing hip hop ventriloquism . . . like a skit. I started the myth of Humpty during a college radio interview. I said that he was my brother from Tampa, an ex-lounge singer who got in a grease accident in the kitchen. He stood as a hero for all handicapped people around the world, because you can do anything. And people were buying that shit." Humpty Hump was even given a "real" name (Edward Ellington Humphrey III) and then it was time to give the character his own anthem. The problem was that the band's debut album was nearly ready for release so "The Humpty Dance" was written, recorded and added at the last minute. "Humpty was never part of a master plan," Jacobs says. "The album was almost done when we recorded the song. That's why there's no picture of Humpty on the album cover, because when the cover was shot we hadn't even written that shit yet!"

Jacobs came up with a bass line for the song and then used some samples to create the track. Showing his bias for Parliament he used two of their songs ("Let's Play House" and "Bop Gun") along with "Simple Song" by Sly and the Family Stone. For the lyrics, Jacobs channeled Humpty's braggadocios persona and created a rap that will live in eternity as one of the most memorable and hilarious ever performed. "The Humpty Dance" was released in the beginning of 1990 and its raucous video began getting regular spins on MTV. The song eventually peaked on this date in 1990 at #11, sitting two notches behind another 1990 hip hop party classic, "U Can't Touch This." So stop whatcha doin' and go watch the video of "The Humpty Dance." It is sure to amaze thee.

### June 3rd

On this date in 1964, the Rolling Stones were in New York City for the first time. Most music historians recognize this trip as the second wave of the British Invasion. They arrived less than 4 months after the Beatles and though they weren't already well known in the U.S. like the Beatles had been (the Stones' first album, *England's Newest Hit Makers* had only just been released in America two days earlier) they were still greeted by hundreds of fans at the airport and later that day caused a near riot when they showed up at the Astor Hotel in New

York City. You could say the Beatles had opened the door and the Rolling Stones came bashing through. Though the Stones were in America for only about three weeks, and their first U.S. tour consisted of all of a dozen shows, music history remembers this trip for a number of reasons.

One of the first things the band did was appear on Murray the K's *Swinging Soiree* radio show on New York's WINS. He was a big supporter of the band and had been hyping their trip to the States often on air. K interviewed them and then played their cover of Buddy Holly's "Not Fade Away." While that record was playing on air, he played the band a song called "It's All Over Now" by the Valentinos and suggested they cover it. A week later when the band was in Chicago at the famed Chess Studios they did just that. The Stones' version of "It's All Over Now" would go on to be their first #1 hit in the U.K.

From New York the Stones and their entourage flew to LA for an appearance on *The Dean Martin Show*. Martin was less than complimentary about the group (to say the least) saying, on air, "They're backstage picking fleas off one another" and then rolling his eyes after their performance. If you can find this on the internet it's definitely worth checking out. The legend has always been that the old guard of crooners didn't appreciate the new generation of rock and rollers and Frank Sinatra's quote about Elvis ("His kind of music is deplorable, a rancid smelling aphrodisiac. It fosters almost totally negative and destructive reactions in young people") and Martin's treatment of the Stones are two solid pieces of evidence to confirm that. Months later when Bob Dylan released *Another Side of Bob Dylan* he wrote in the liner notes, "Dean Martin should apologize to the Rolling Stones." That apology never came.

From Los Angeles the band started working their way back east, playing their first U.S. shows in San Bernardino, California and then San Antonio, Texas. Though they didn't have a show booked in Chicago they made sure to stop in the Windy City to visit the aforementioned Chess Records studio. They'd all grown up lovers of the blues and so much of that great music had come out of Chess. In his autobiography *Life*, Keith Richards would say, "2120 South Michigan Avenue was hallowed ground." But the boys weren't just tourists, they'd actually booked recording time at Chess and besides "It's All Over Now" they recorded a number of other tracks. This is also where, rock and roll legend has it, they witnessed Muddy Waters painting the ceiling and were infuriated by the sight of this legend doing odd jobs to make ends meet.

After a few more shows in places like Excelsior, Minnesota, Detroit, Michigan and Pittsburgh, Pennsylvania, the band arrived back in New York City for two shows at the famed Carnegie Hall. Instead of heading back to England as soon as the last show was over Mick Jagger and Keith Richards decided to stay in New York for one specific purpose. As Richards explained: "Mick and I hadn't come all the way to New York in '64 not to go the Apollo. James Brown had the whole week there at the Apollo. Go to the Apollo and see James Brown, damn fucking right. I mean, who would turn that down?" Many people believe Mick picked up some of his onstage moves from the Godfather of Soul, watching him at the Apollo and this is something Jagger does not deny. He has said: "I copied all his moves. . . I used to do James' slide across the stage. I couldn't do the splits, so I didn't even bother. Everyone did the microphone trick, where you pushed the microphone, then you put your foot on it and it comes back, and then you catch it. James probably did it best."

The Rolling Stones only played a dozen dates on this trip so you can't exactly call it a huge tour of the States. But as Charlie Watts has said, it was a beginning: "America was a joke when we arrived, but by the time we left we had an audience and by the time we came back we had made a hit record. It was all uphill, but the audience grew every time." Indeed it did. All these years later the Rolling Stones still sell out every time they tour the States and the short trip they made this week in 1964 helped lay the ground work for them becoming one of the biggest bands ever, on both sides of the pond.

## June 4th

On this date in 1968, the Rolling Stones began working at Olympic Studios in London on a song that Mick Jagger had recently penned as an homage to the devil. The song would take four days to complete, during which an assassination would lead to a critical lyric change. There's rarely been a better example of a band having their finger on the pulse of their generation's zeitgeist. Here's the story of "Sympathy For the Devil."

In 1967, Mick Jagger's girlfriend Marianne Faithfull gave him a Russian novel which had just been translated into English named *The Master and Margarita*. The devil is the main character in the book, and the story alternates between Satan visiting the Soviet Union and making sure Pontius Pilate puts Jesus to death. Jagger read the book and became very interested in the concept of the devil living amongst us and perhaps influencing modern events. He sat down and wrote lyrics for a song he initially called "The Devil Is My Name." The song's themes fit nicely with the Stones' image of being the bad boys of rock and roll. In its earliest incarnation it was a folk song. Jagger has said, "I wrote it as sort of like a Bob Dylan song." But then he brought it to his bandmates and the song took a whole new direction.

Jagger had hired filmmaker Jean-Luc Godard to capture the Stones working in the studio for a project they were initially calling *One Plus One*. With the cameras rolling Jagger presented his latest song to the band on this date in 1968. Keith Richards loved the concept but thought the song would be more powerful with a different rhythm. The band tried giving the song a Latin-jazz feel then switched to a straight samba beat. Once they stumbled on this they knew they had the right vibe and video footage shows the band working the song up to what we know of today. As they did, a few people who were hanging out in the control room started a spontaneous "woo woo" chant. The band loved that addition and added it to the final version. Of the beat, Jagger has said: "It has a very hypnotic groove . . .It doesn't speed up or slow down. It keeps this constant groove. Plus, the actual samba rhythm is a great one to sing on, but it has also got some other suggestions in it, an undercurrent of being primitive—because it is a primitive African, South American, Afro-whatever-you-call-that rhythm. So to white people, it has a very sinister thing about it." Richards has remarked about the song: "'Sympathy' is quite an uplifting song. It's just a matter of looking the Devil in the face. He's there all the time." Richards, in his sly way, then adds: "I've had very close contact with Lucifer. I've met him several times."

The band worked on the song throughout the day on June 4th and into the late morning on the 5th. When they left the studio they felt they had it complete but planned to return on June 8th to do some overdubbing. Then on June 6th, 1968, Bobby Kennedy was assassinated in Los Angeles. When the band returned to the studio to put some finishing touches on the song they realized one of the lines Jagger had written, "I shouted out who killed Kennedy" was now ambiguous. Jagger sang the line over, changing it to, "I shouted out who killed the Kennedys."

At one point while the band was working on the song a lamp that the film crew had brought into the studio started a fire. Some of the Stones' equipment was destroyed. Though the fire wasn't substantial it was the beginning of the "Curse of Sympathy" rumors. Conspiracy theorists also point to some controversy the song caused the band but really, the Stones were no strangers to bad press. In fact, some would argue they thrived on it and it only fed their burgeoning reputation. Some also claim that "Sympathy for the Devil" was the cause of all the troubles at Altamont but while it is one of the songs that was interrupted by fighting in the crowd, it was not the only one and it is not, despite popular belief, the song during which Meredith Hunter was killed. The truth is "Sympathy for the Devil" is most likely not cursed and has done the band far less harm than good. While it didn't sell as well as some previous Stones' singles it has become one of the band's signature songs and one of their favorites to play live.

## June 5th

On this date in 1967, the Doors had just put out their second single "Light My Fire." Earlier in the year they had released their debut self-titled album and first single ("Break On Through") but neither had much impact. But "Light My Fire" began a slow and steady climb up the charts, finally peaking at #1 in late July - right in the middle of what became known as the "Summer of Love." It also helped generate interest in their debut album which eventually hit #2 on the album chart, introducing America to a band it would soon come to revere.

"Light My Fire" was a true collaborative effort for the Doors. It was mostly written by guitarist Robby Krieger but Ray Manzarek came up with the organ introduction, Morrison helped with some of the lyrics ("the funeral pyre" is typical Morrison imagery) and drummer John Densmore, suggested the bossa nova beat. The album version clocks in at 7:06 so they had to trim the single to 2:52 to accommodate pop radio. Initially the band fought the idea of editing the song but it was actually Morrison who saw the advantage, saying, "Imagine a kid in Minneapolis hearing even the cut version over the radio, it's going to turn his head around." So they released the edited version and as it gained popularity on the radio, more and more people bought the album so they could hear the full-length version. 1967 was the Summer of Love and "Light My Fire" was as much a part of the soundtrack of that time as any song.

In September of 1967 the Doors appeared on *The Ed Sullivan Show* to sing "Light My Fire." Earlier that year the show's producers had been successful getting the Rolling Stones to change their lyric, "Let's spend the night together," to the more staid, "Let's spend some time together." They made a similar request to the Doors, asking them to change the line, "Girl, we couldn't get much higher," because of its obvious drug implications. In rehearsal Morrison sang, "Girl we couldn't get much better" and everybody seemed pleased. But when they performed the song later on live television he sang the original lyric. In the superb movie *The Doors*, Val Kilmer plays this moment much more defiantly, singing the word "higher" right into the camera. In reality Morrison delivered the line as he usually did: eyes closed and trance-like. The camera does however cut away to guitarist Robby Krieger who is clearly smiling at what they had just pulled off on live television. Sullivan and his producers, however, were not smiling, and they informed the band afterwards that they would never appear on the Ed Sullivan show again.

"Light My Fire" in many ways helped launch the Doors into national prominence. Their run as one of America's great rock bands was short but sweet. They released six studio albums in just over four years, and placed eight singles in the Top 40, but they left an indelible mark on the world of music and their back catalog still sells consistently to this day. The time to hesitate is through. Give "Light My Fire" (the full, album version) a spin today.

### June 6th

On this date in 1971, Jethro Tull's *Aqualung* was sitting at its peak position, #7 on the *Billboard* album chart. For Jethro Tull, who had already achieved major success in the U.K., Aqualung was their big break in the States. They would go on to enjoy an incredibly successful career with over 60 million albums sold and what *Rolling Stone* calls, "one of the most commercially successful and eccentric progressive rock bands."

The stories behind band name's etymologies range from the mundane to the fascinating and Jethro Tull's certainly falls near the latter. Ian Anderson, along with John Evan and Jeffrey Hammond had been in a number of lineups early on and they often found it hard to rebook a club gig so they started changing their name often, finding it was easier to convince a bar owner to take a shot at a new band rather than repeat a booking for a band they might not have loved the first time. Anderson has even said there were times he'd show up to a gig, look over the flyer for the evening and whatever band name he didn't recognize, that's the name he was using that night. As fate would have it, one night they were playing under the moniker Jethro Tull (a historical figure from the 18th century who was an agricultural pioneer) and the bar owner loved them and invited them back. So they were forced to keep the Jethro Tull name.

Though the band has undergone many personnel changes through its history, Ian Anderson has been the one constant. He has been the band's lead singer and chief lyricist and, because he didn't want to be a second-rate guitar player, his instrument of choice has become their signature sound. By the time the band started getting noticed Mick Abrahams had joined their ranks and he was far and away their best guitarist. This relegated Anderson to the role of rhythm guitarist but as he has explained: "I didn't want to be just another third-rate guitar player who sounded like a bunch of other third-rate guitar players. I wanted to do something that was a bit more idiosyncratic." That "something" turned out to be the flute. Anderson bought one and took a few week's worth of lessons before he started incorporating it into the band's sets. Though he mastered the instrument quickly he admits that early on, "Literally every night I walked onstage was a flute lesson."

Jethro Tull's debut album, 1968's *This Was*, reached #10 on the U.K. chart which was a testament to the following the band had already accumulated in England. Abrahams soon left the band, replaced by Martin Barre, and Jethro Tull's second LP *Stand Up* went to #1 in the U.K. That LP reached as high as #20 on the Billboard album chart and when its followup, 1970's *Benefit*, made it to #11 (and #3 in the U.K.), Jethro Tull seemed poised for a breakout.

As Anderson began thinking about their next LP his wife at the time, Jennie, showed him some photographs she'd taken of some homeless people in London. Anderson was moved with a sense of guilt that he was successful now and living a rock star life, yet here were some fellow human beings who literally didn't even have a pot to piss in. As all great writers do, Anderson took that seed of emotion and ran with it. He created a character, Aqualung, and wrote a song about him. Built around one of the most famous opening riffs in all of rock history, "Aqualung" opens the album of the same name with a grab-you-by-the-throat urgency. And then, because the character is mentioned in the album's next song, "Cross-Eyed Mary," people started calling *Aqualung* a concept album. It's a description Anderson has argued against and indeed there is no one theme that holds the album together. If anything there are two. Side one deals with the poorest among us, the sickly, the riff-raff and the people on the fringes of society while side two shifts its focus to God and how formal religions often obscure the true message of an all-loving deity.

Despite its incredible hook, "Aqualung" was not released as a single. The late sixties and early seventies had seen a rise in album oriented rock stations (AOR) which, unlike pop stations, were more interested in playing a band's entire repertoire, instead of just the radio-friendly hits, and Jethro Tull, along with bands like Led Zeppelin, was way more interested in album sales than singles' success. *Aqualung*'s sole single, "Hymn 43" barely cracked the Hot 100 chart while the LP peaked at #7 this week in 1971.

Disturbed by the concept that *Aqualung* was a concept album, Anderson decided Tull's next project would be a complete send-up of a concept album. He has called *Thick as a Brick*, "the mother of all concept albums" and with its one long track (split in half to cover the two sides of an album) he isn't far off. When that LP went to #1 in the U.S., it was obvious Tull could do just about anything, jokingly or not, and have it sell. The band had built a loyal following that loved its mix of hard rock and progressive rock (and that flute!) and those fans would carry the band to incredible success throughout the seventies.

## June 7th

On this date in 1969, a brand new band played their first live gig. It's something that has happened millions of times in the history of rock but what made this concert stand out is the new band was another one of the supergroups that were emerging from London in the second half of the sixties. And the concert was attended by over 100,000 people. The band would release one album during their time together and disband less than a year after forming. But in that time they left an indelible mark on rock history.

Most rock fans consider Cream to be the first supergroup. They came together in 1966 when guitarist and singer Eric Clapton, bassist and singer Jack Bruce and drummer Ginger Baker started jamming and playing a unique combination of blues and hard rock. Since the three musicians already had strong followings, the music press came up with the term "supergroup" to describe them. Cream lasted three years but if you ask Clapton it seemed like a lifetime. Bruce and Baker were always at odds and Clapton felt like he was always trying to keep the two focused and working together. Finally in 1968 he'd had enough and Cream produced their final album, appropriately titled *Goodbye*. They played their final concert in November of that year. Afterwards, Clapton busied himself with some side projects like playing guitar on the Beatles' "While My Guitar Gently Weeps" and participating in the Rolling Stones' *Rock and Roll Circus*.

Meanwhile, Steve Winwood was facing his own challenges in Traffic. That band had formed in 1967 and within a few years all four members were clashing over their direction. Winwood wanted to be more experimental while the others (and their record label) wanted them to be more commercial. Finally in early 1969 Winwood called it quits and left the band he'd helped to form.

Eric Clapton and Steve Winwood knew each other from the London music scene, in fact they had collaborated a few years earlier on a project Clapton had launched called Powerhouse. So with both of their bands defunct, Clapton called Winwood one day and asked him over to hang out and maybe jam. One visit turned into a regular thing and, as Clapton would write in his autobiography, "We'd drink and smoke and talk a lot, and play our guitars." The jam sessions were casual and loose with no formal direction until one fateful night. Clapton explains, "Steve and I were at the cottage smoking joints and jamming when we were surprised by a knock at the door. It was Ginger (Baker). Somehow he had gotten wind of what we were doing and had tracked us down." Winwood welcomed the drummer but Clapton had his trepidations, as he'd say, "Ginger's appearance frightened me because I felt that all of a sudden we were a band." That feeling only intensified when bassist Ric Grech joined the jam sessions. Before long the quartet were working on original songs and it became a fait accompli that a legitimate band was inevitable. Clapton, showing his hesitations, suggested the name Blind Faith. Winwood, who was more optimistic about the band, hated the name but went along with it because, as he'd say later, "If a band is successful, the name loses its meaning and just becomes a label." By March of 1969 Blind Faith were working on songs at Olympic Studios in London and the hype machine was in full force, with many dubbing the band "Super Cream."

Blind Faith debuted on this date in 1969 at an outdoor concert in London's Hyde Park. Over 100,000 fans showed up and feedback was universally positive. It seemed everyone loved the show except for one person: Eric Clapton. He thought the performance was sub-par and the adulation reminded him of his days in Cream when the band lived largely off its reputation. Nevertheless the band finished work on their debut, self-titled album and they got set to tour in support. *Blind Faith* was critically well received but the LP was controversial for its cover photo which featured a topless, seemingly underage, girl holding an airplane. In the U.S. the album was released with a picture of the band instead of the girl. Blind Faith toured to support their debut but Clapton was miserable again. He found himself playing mostly Cream songs since Blind Faith didn't have enough originals to fill a whole show. Other than the lack of friction between Bruce and Baker, Clapton felt like he was right back where he'd come from and he started hanging out with the tour's opening act Delaney & Bonnie instead of his bandmates. This eventually led to Blind Faith's demise after just one album. Clapton explained in his autobiography, "If Delaney and Bonnie had never played on the same bill as us it is possible that Blind Faith might have survived and regrouped at the end of the tour." But Clapton drifted further away from Blind Faith as the tour went on. By October of 1969 Blind Faith was all but dissolved and Clapton would begin working with several members from Delaney & Bonnie to form yet another supergroup, Derek and the Dominos.

On this date in 1968, Simon & Garfunkel's "Mrs. Robinson" began its second week at the top of the pop chart. The song had arrived on June 1st, replacing "Tighten Up" by Archie Bell & the Drells and it would have a three week run before giving way to "This Guy's in Love with You" by Herb Albert. For the duo from Queens, New York, it was their most successful single to date and they have a young, up-and-coming movie director to thank for helping them create the song.

Simon & Garfunkel had burst onto the folk rock scene when their debut single, "The Sound of Silence," climbed to the top of the charts in early 1966. Over the next few years they delivered consistent hits like "Homeward Bound" , "I Am a Rock" and their remake of the traditional English ballad "Scarborough Fair." Among Simon & Garfunkel's fan base was a young director named Mike Nichols. In 1966 Nichols made his directorial debut with *Who's Afraid of Virginia Woolf?* and he was quickly dubbed the "new Orson Welles." His next film was the coming-of-age comedy *The Graduate* which he began working on in early 1967. As editing got under way, Nichols used some of his favorite Simon & Garfunkel songs like "The Sound of Silence" and "April Comes She Will" as place holders for certain scenes before he could find the songs he'd actually use. But soon enough Nichols became, in his words, "obsessed by the band" and he thought their music would be perfect for his film. He met with Columbia Records chief Clive Davis in an effort to get the existing songs licensed. Davis loved the idea and thought it would help promote the duo even more. Paul Simon was apprehensive at first, viewing it as something of a "sell-out," but after meeting with Nichols and reading the script he agreed to allow the existing songs to be used. Nichols, figuring he had nothing to lose by asking, requested some new songs from the duo. Simon said he'd see what he could come up with.

When they met a few weeks later Paul Simon presented Nichols with a few new songs but the director didn't think they fit his film. Art Garfunkel then mentioned a song called "Mrs. Roosevelt" that Simon had been working on. The song was a lament to the passing of the "good old days" of America with a title character that may or may not have been Eleanor Roosevelt. When the duo played the song for Nichols he loved it and pointed out that the main female character in his movie was named Mrs. Robinson. Simon reworked that line to make it fit with the movie and Nichols used bits of the song throughout his film. It wasn't till a month after the movie was released that Simon completed the lyrics and he and Garfunkel recorded the full song. The single came out in April of 1968 and it hit #1 two months later, becoming the duo's second chart-topper.

Paul Simon's reference to Joe DiMaggio (asking where he'd gone) has been one of the most discussed lyrics of his prolific career. Simon is a huge Yankee fan who actually grew up more of a Mickey Mantle fan than a DiMaggio fan. Years after the song was a hit he found himself on *The Dick Cavett Show* and Cavett asked him why he hadn't used Mantle in the lyrics. Any songwriter could have predicted Simon's answer: "It's about syllables, Dick. It's about how many beats there are." Simon has also shared a story about meeting DiMaggio in a restaurant one evening. The Yankee great asked the songwriter what he meant by the lyric because he hadn't, in fact, gone anywhere. "I didn't mean the lines literally," Simon explains, "that I thought of him as an American hero and that genuine heroes were in short supply. He accepted the explanation and thanked me. We shook hands and said good night."

As it turned out, Clive Davis had been correct. *The Graduate* proved to be the perfect promotional vehicle for Simon & Garfunkel's music and they found an even bigger fan base with the movie's success. Since the beginning of his writing career, Simon had explored themes of alienation and disenfranchisement. Though Benjamin Braddock, Dustin Hoffman's lost and lonely character in *The Graduate*, wasn't written with Simon & Garfunkel as an inspiration, it turned out so many of their existing songs fit his struggle perfectly. But none more so than the new song the duo contributed to the movie. Simon had begun writing a song about lost innocence and the yearning for past heroes. He finished by creating a masterpiece for the film as well as one of the most successful songs of Simon & Garfunkel's illustrious career.

If you have time today, watch *The Graduate*. It's a funny and poignant time capsule of the late sixties and you'll never hear the word "plastics" the same again. But if you don't have the time to devote to a full movie, give "Mrs. Robinson" a spin. Rarely have a movie and a song been so perfect for each other.

## June 9th

On this date in 1990, M.C. Hammer's album *Please Hammer, Don't Hurt Em* started an amazing 21 week run at the top of the *Billboard* album chart. It went on to become the first hip hop album certified diamond by the Recording Industry Association of America (RIAA) for sales of over ten million. The lead single off the LP, "U Can't Touch This" was a huge reason for the album's success, even though it peaked at only #8 on the pop chart (it got to #1 on the R&B chart). The song benefited from some unique marketing and then was held back by a record company's gamble. Both paid off nicely.

Stanley Kirk Burrell was born in 1962 in Oakland, California. Before his teen years he was already hustling. He'd often hang around the parking lot of the Oakland Coliseum for A's games where he'd dance to music from a boom box for tips. A's owner Charlie Finley fell in love with the boy's energy and enthusiasm and he hired him as a bat boy, a job Burrell held from the time he was 11 till he was 18. It was the A's great Reggie Jackson who gave Burrell the nickname Hammer because he looked so much like Hank Aaron (who had the same nickname.) Burrell thought baseball was in his future but when he failed to be drafted out of high school he joined the Navy. After an honorable discharge Burrell turned his sights to music, forming a Christian rap band (called The

Holy Ghost Boys) before attempting a solo rap career, using the moniker M.C. Hammer. In 1986 he borrowed money from some A's players to start his own record label and self-released his debut album *Feel My Power*. His debut record, as well as his growing reputation for his high energy shows that featured scores of backup dancers, put him in play with the major labels. In 1988 Capitol Records signed M.C. Hammer for just under 2 million dollars.

Hammer's first album for Capitol, *Let's Get It Started*, topped the R&B chart and peaked at #30 on the *Billboard* album chart. In the late eighties, rap as a genre was growing exponentially in popularity and Capitol felt they had the right man in the right place at the right time. When Hammer submitted the tapes for his next LP, *Please Hammer, Don't Hurt 'Em*, his label instantly knew "U Can't Touch This" could be a huge hit. Capitol obviously wanted to get the video for "U Can't Touch This" on MTV (this was back when MTV still played videos) so they mailed 100,000 free cassette singles of the song to fans (this was back when cassette singles were a thing) along with a letter from Hammer asking them to call MTV and request the video (this was back when people still called other people). The ploy worked and MTV not only started playing it, the video went on to become the most-played of 1990 on the music channel.

Then, Capitol took an amazing gamble. In the spring of 1990 as "U Can't Touch This" was climbing the charts they slowed the production of the single. It became harder and harder to find a 7 inch version of the song and even the 12 inch singles were few and far between. Capitol's hope was that if music fans couldn't buy the individual song they'd shell out for the whole album. And it worked. "U Can't Touch This" surely would have topped the charts in 1990, most likely for multiple weeks. But instead, the song stalled at #8. Meanwhile the album went to #1 on this date where it would sit, with only a one week break, through November (*Step by Step* by New Kids on the Block was the album that interrupted Hammer's run of dominance for one brief week at the end of June).

"U Can't Touch This" uses one of the most famous samples of all time, Rick James' 1981 hit, "Super Freak." James, however, was notorious for not allowing rappers to use his work. According to the singer, his lawyers allowed Hammer to use the sample without his knowledge. He claims he didn't even know about it till a friend mentioned "U Can't Touch This" and then the song came on the radio they were listening to in the car. Even though Hammer had obtained the sample legally (and James was being compensated for it handsomely) James sued Hammer over not being listed as a songwriter. The suit was settled out of court when Hammer agreed to credit James, and "Super Freak" cowriter Alonzo Miller, as songwriters, thus increasing the amount of money they made from the song.

It is hard to overstate the influence Hammer had on pop culture in the early nineties. "You can't touch this" and "Stop! hammer time" became common catchphrases and his overly baggy pants started a short-lived fashion craze (c'mon, we all had 'em!) Plus like any dance video that got frequent spins on

MTV, many people started doing Hammer's moves (or attempting to, anyway). As with most things though that become über-popular there was, eventually, intense backlash, especially in the hip hop community where Hammer was seen as a sellout and poseur. He was mocked in multiple songs and videos by LL Cool J, Ice Cube and 3rd Bass just to name a few.

Hammer's next album, 1991's *Too Legit to Quit* – in which he dropped the M.C. from his name, wasn't as successful as *Please Hammer* but it still sold 3.5 million units. But his star was fading and by 1994 when he put out *The Funky Headhunter* it was clearly no longer Hammer Time. Still, for anyone old enough to remember 1990 (and own those baggy pants) we will never forget the impact MC Hammer had on music, fashion, dance floors and even the lexicon. So give it a spin today, and as Hammer would say, "If you can't move to this, then you probably are dead."

## June 10th

On this date in 1978, "You're the One That I Want" went to #1 on the pop chart, officially kicking off the "Summer of Grease." RSO Records (which was already riding high with the success of *Saturday Night Fever*) released the *Grease* soundtrack in April of 1978 and "You're the One That I Want" by John Travolta and Olivia Newton-John in May hoping to build anticipation for its film. The plan worked brilliantly with "You're the One That I Want" riding high as the movie opened on June 16th. *Grease* would be the highest-grossing film in 15 of the next 16 weeks and would finish 1978 as the top box office draw. It was the highest-grossing movie musical of all time until 2017 when Disney's *Beauty and the Beast* took its place.

*Grease* was a film adaptation of a Broadway musical but many of the most successful songs were written for the movie, including the title track (which was written by Barry Gibb and sung by Frankie Valli), the aforementioned "You're the One That I Want" and Olivia Newton-John's ballad, "Hopelessly Devoted to You." As casting got underway the lead role of Danny Zuko was offered to Henry Winkler but he turned it down. Winkler had already appeared as a leather-jacket-wearing tough guy in the 1974 film *Lords of Flatbush* and he was currently playing The Fonz on *Happy Days* so he wanted to avoid being typecast. The film's director Randal Kleiser then recommended John Travolta who he'd just worked with on the made-for-TV movie *The Boy in the Plastic Bubble*. Travolta literally came off the set of *Saturday Night Fever* and got to work on *Grease*. Few actors have ever starred in back-to-back iconic films like that.

Production took place during the summer of 1977, in fact, the day they filmed the "Look At Me, I'm Sandra Dee" scene in which Stockard Channing's Rizzo sings "Elvis, Elvis, let me be. Keep that pelvis far from me" was August 16, 1977. As every music fan knows, that's the day Elvis Presley died.

Travolta has admitted he missed most of the disco craze that *Saturday Night Fever* set off because he was busy every day on the set of *Grease*. He was in the middle of an unprecedented run in 1978. After early success on television in *Welcome Back, Kotter*, Travolta starred in 3 consecutive movies that were incredibly successful and centered around music (1977's *Saturday Night Fever*, 1978's *Grease*, and then 1980's *Urban Cowboy*). His career went into a tailspin in the early eighties and it wasn't until 1994's *Pulp Fiction* that he had a resurgence. Quentin Tarantino has said that once he cast Travolta in the role of Vincent Vega he wrote the twisting scene in the diner because, "You can't have Travolta in a movie and not have him dance."

RSO had a similar, in fact, more precipitous, decline in popularity. The same year that *Grease* was setting box office records they released the universally panned movie version of *Sgt. Pepper's Lonely Hearts Club Band*. The movie was a disappointing flop and, combined with the Bee Gees' 1980 lawsuit against the label for mismanagement, helped lead to the label and its production company's demise.

*Grease* has had many incarnations including a disastrous sequel in 1982, numerous returns to the stage and a live television version in 2016. None of these have ever captured the magic of the original film though, in which we were supposed to buy 34 year old Stockard Channing as a high schooler and with its overall message to women that if you want to land your man, you better dress sluttier and learn to smoke. If you have time today, watch the whole film. If not, give the "You're the One That I Want" a spin and relive the "Summer of Grease!"

**June 11th**

On this date in 1979, the Knack released their debut album *Get the Knack*. The album and its lead single "My Sharona" would go on to be huge hits which turned the band into overnight superstars. But as the saying goes, what goes up must come down. The backlash against the Knack was almost unprecedented and it undermined every effort the band made towards continuing its success. The Knack would never have another year like 1979. But oh, what a year it was.

Singer Doug Fieger had arrived in Los Angeles from Detroit in the early seventies looking to make it in the music business. His first LA band was the Sunset Bombers but when their lone album went unnoticed the band broke up. Fieger then started putting together another group of musicians, looking to form a rock band that would put a modern twist on classic, sixties rock. The punk scene wasn't as big in LA as it was in New York but there were still plenty of bands playing hard, unsophisticated and loud. But Fieger's goals were different. While he loved the energy of punk he believed in musical prowess and the power of great harmonies. He eventually put together a band he called the Knack and their first live appearance was in June of 1978.

The Knack took the LA club scene by storm. Within weeks they were playing in the hottest spots on the Sunset Strip and record companies were sending A&R men to check them out. Besides a huge fan base they also attracted some famous musicians who came to watch them play. Tom Petty was a regular and Ray Manzarek and Bruce Springsteen both showed up to check them out. In fact, one night Springsteen got up to jam with the Knack and as Fieger has said, "Bruce Springsteen gets up onstage with us on a Friday night, and on Monday, we have 14 record offers." The offer the band accepted was from Capitol which distributed the Beatles and so comparisons between the two bands began even before their debut was released. The Knack hit the studio in the spring of 1979 and *Get the Knack* was recorded in two weeks. Fieger has said: "I don't think we did two takes on any song, except for 'Maybe Tonight.' What we had to do was make the record quickly because to labor over it would have taken that spontaneity out of it."

As the album took shape it was Fieger's lusty ode to a young woman he was trying to date, Sharona Alperin, that was clearly the album's standout song. Fieger had met Alperin while she was still in high school, working at a clothing store. Though Fieger was in a long term relationship and Alperin had a boyfriend (and was just 17) Fieger was smitten and he invited Alperin to attend a Knack show. They became friends but very quickly he professed his love for her. She rejected him at first, citing the age difference and the fact that they were both in relationships, and Fieger, proving that unrequited love (or lust) can often be the greatest inspiration, sat down and wrote "My Sharona." Working with the band's guitarist Berton Averre, Fieger channeled all of his feelings towards the young Alperin into the song. "After I met Sharona," he would say later, "I knew the feeling I had for her would translate well with the rhythm of that song." Well, indeed. "My Sharona" has everything you could want in a rock song. It starts with a drum beat that is impossible to ignore, adds a guitar riff that is the definition of a "hook" and then moves on to Fieger's pleading, stuttering lyrics. And if that weren't enough, instead of the song ending two and half minutes in (like any good punk song would have) the listener is treated to Averre's soaring solo. After that, a dramatic caesura brings us right back to the simple driving beat and infectious hook, with Fieger repeating in desperate resignation, "ooooooo-ohhh, my Sharona."

*Get the Knack* is far from a one-hit album though. Its dozen tracks are all incredibly well produced and filled with unforgettable hooks. As "My Sharona" flew off record shelves and got virtually non-stop radio play, the LP became a big seller as well. "My Sharona" spent 6 weeks at #1 and the followup, "Good Girls Don't," went to #11. *Get the Knack* spent five weeks at the top of the album chart as well. 1979 was, in many ways, the Year of the Knack.

But then the backlash started. And it got loud. Some music fans felt the band was pre-packaged and the album formulaic. The Knack didn't help their own cause when they refused to do interviews which, instead of lending them "mystique" as they'd hoped, cast them as arrogant snobs. Soon enough "Knuke the Knack" was as common a phrase as "Disco Sucks." Their follow-up LP, 1980's ...*But the Little Girls Understand* reached #15 on the album chart but its two singles, "Baby Talks Dirty" and "Can't Put a Price on Love," showed the decreasing interest in the band. They hit #38 and #64 respectively on the pop chart.

Some bands are built to last and some just have one shining moment. The latter can certainly be said about the Knack. Some might even blame how popular they became during their one shining moment as perhaps there is such a thing as listener fatigue. The Knack wouldn't be the only band to suffer from it (we're looking at you Hootie & the Blowfish). But as seventies came to an end and a new decade was ready to dawn, there were many bands looking to alter the musical landscape for the eighties. The Knack, combining the brashness of punk with the musical sophistication of classic rock, was one of those bands. They may not have made it to the MTV generation, but they certainly helped create a look and a sound that would carry many an artist to fame on that channel.


## June 12th

On this date in 1970, James Taylor's "Fire and Rain" was still languishing outside the *Billboard* Hot 100 chart, four months after its release. The song would take another few months to finally crack the Top 100. It would eventually peak at #3 in late October of 1970. It was an incredibly slow ride for a song that today is considered such a forebearer for an entirely new genre of music as well as being Taylor's signature song.

James Vernon Taylor was born in 1948 in Massachusetts to a wealthy family. The Taylor's relocated to North Carolina when James was just three and he was raised there, learning to play cello and piano as a child. As a young man he was prone to bouts of depression and at 16 he was committed to a psychiatric hospital where he spent nine months. He wrote a number of songs during his time there and began to envision a career for himself as a musician. He was excused from the draft with a psychological rejection and then later he checked himself out of the hospital in early 1966. Shortly after, he moved to New York where he formed the Flying Machine and by the summer of 1966 he and his band were gaining in popularity. Taylor began using heroin around this time and eventually when the Flying Machine broke up he found himself penniless. A desperate call to his father rescued him and he entered rehab to get clean. Of his New York experience, Taylor would say later, "I learned a lot about music and too much about drugs."

After getting clean Taylor decided to relocate to London and try to make it as a solo artist. He was signed by Apple (the Beatles' new label) and recorded a self-titled debut album in 1968. When that LP failed to break, Taylor signed with

Warner and began working on a second album that would wind up being called *Sweet Baby James*. Side two of that LP opens with the now iconic "Fire and Rain." Taylor was only twenty years old when he wrote that song but it's a recap of the many things he'd experienced in his life up to that point. The "Susanne" mentioned in the opening verse was someone he'd come to know in the psychiatric hospital. Taylor would explain, "It concerned a girl called Susanne I knew who they put into an isolation cell and she couldn't take it and committed suicide." The second verse is about his own personal struggles at that point, dealing with depression and drug addiction and asking Jesus to see him, "through another day." And he even name checks his first band in the third verse with the line "sweet dreams and flying machines in pieces on the ground." But it's the simple and stunning chorus of "Fire and Rain" that makes the song so unforgettable. The words, "I've seen fire and I've seen rain. I've seen sunny days that I thought would never end" make Taylor sound like an old man looking back on a long life of incredible highs and lows. Though he was only twenty, he was able to channel his life experiences into such an amazing and poetic song. It's no wonder it was so powerful it eventually launched Taylor's career as well as an entire genre of music.

As the seventies dawned there was no such thing as soft rock and the concept of a singer-songwriter was applicable only in the margins of folk music (and certainly not on the pop chart). It's the main reason why "Fire and Rain" took so long to gain acceptance and climb the charts. The song was released in February of 1970 it wouldn't break the Hot 100 till September of that year. When it did it made a slow and steady climb, peaking at #3 the week of Halloween. That same week Elton John's "Your Song" was released and most musical historians look at these two songs as opening up the airwaves to a softer, more intimate sound. Artists like John Denver, Linda Ronstadt and Cat Stevens and bands like Bread and the Carpenters were soon filling the airwaves with a lighter, gentler sound that would soon be called soft rock or lite rock. And in many ways they owe a lot of their success to a twenty year old songwriter. So give "Fire and Rain" a spin today but pay close attention to the lyrics, specifically the coda. Taylor wrote about his pain but he also ended things optimistically with the, "There's just a few things coming my way this time around, now." line. It may seem like a throwaway but in hindsight, he could have been speaking of his career as well as the genre he was helping to popularize.

### June 13th

On this date in 1995, Alanis Morissette released *Jagged Little Pill*. Maverick Records had humble expectations for the album in the U.S. considering that Morissette was a virtual unknown so they had to be as surprised as anyone when the album's lead single "You Oughta Know" started getting solid radio play on some rock stations. There was something about the song's seething anger and Morissette's blatantly vulgar lyrics that set it apart from anything else. Her alternative rock, post-grunge sound was perfect for the time and within months of the album's release Morissette was a huge star and *Jagged Little Pill* was in everyone's CD cases.

Alanis Nadine Morissette was born in 1974 in Ottawa, Canada. By grade school she'd already mastered piano, was taking dance lessons and appearing on the Canadian children's show *You Can't Do That on Television*. She recorded a demo as a teenager and was soon signed to MCA Records Canada. Her debut album, *Alanis*, was released in 1991 and features a dance, pop sound that earned her the nickname "Canadian Debbie Gibson." She even landed the opening spot when Vanilla Ice performed in Canada. Her follow-up LP, 1992's *Now Is the Time*, was a less pop sounding, more ballad driven offering. It sold about half of what her debut did and MCA Canada dropped her. She was still a teenager in high school and at risk of having peaked as an artist.

After high school she moved to Toronto where she met record producer Glen Ballard who already had an impressive resume, having worked with artists like Michael Jackson, Paula Abdul and Wilson Phillips. Ballard was blown away by Morissette's talents, saying the two connected instantly. He told her if she moved to Los Angeles he'd work with her on an album. Morissette agreed and the two started recording demos, co-writing and performing all the instrumentation, just the two of them. Ballard told *Rolling Stone*: "I just connected with her as a person, and, almost parenthetically, it was like 'Wow, you're 19?' She was so intelligent and ready to take a chance on doing something that might have no commercial application." As the two got to work they set a goal of producing a song a day. In sessions that last sometimes sixteen hours they'd compose a song, record the track and Morissette would finish the vocals. The spontaneity on *Jagged Little Pill* is apparent to this day. It's a collection of songs that feel urgent and in-the-moment and do not suffer from overproduction.

Ballard found no takers when he shopped the demos until a 22 year old A&R man for Maverick Records named Guy Oseary heard them and offered Morissette a contract.

As Ballard and Morissette got to work completing the album, Morissette presented a new song called "You Oughta Know" which dealt with a recent break-up in which she'd been cheated on. But "You Oughta Know" wasn't your standard sappy break-up song. The lyrics were angry, finding Morissette asking: "Is she perverted like me? Would she go down on you in a theater?" and "Are you thinking of me when you fuck her?" After presenting the song to Ballard she thought better of it and decided against recording it but Ballard convinced her saying, "You have to do this." While Morissette says the song is autobiographical she has refused to reveal who it was written about. Much like Carly Simon's "You're So Vain" there are rumors about who "Mr. Duplicity" is, but Morissette has refused to confirm them. Actor Dave Coulier has admitted publicly that when he heard the song he knew instantly it was about him but he has also said he only admitted it to appease reporters who constantly ask him. We may never know whose philandering inspired the song but the music world should thank him. Because of his unfaithfulness the world has one of the greatest angry break-up songs it would ever hear.

*Jagged Little Pill* was released on this date in 1995 with Maverick offering a minimal promotional push. A month later "You Oughta Know" was released as a single and some modern rock stations started playing it in heavy rotation. The song promoted the album perfectly and both began climbing the charts. "Hand in My Pocket" was released as the second single and it too became a modern rock radio favorite. After years of hearing nothing but angry young men it was refreshing to hear a female rocker offering a take on alternative rock with a post-grunge attitude. "Ironic" was the next single (in which the lyrics are ironically not ironic) and it peaked at #1 in the spring of 1996. By this point *Jagged Little Pill* had sold over ten million units and earned Alanis Morissette and Glenn Ballard four Grammys including Album of the Year. Worldwide the album has sold over 30 million copies and Morissette's success is said to have opened the door for many female singers including Meredith Brooks, Pink, Michelle Branch, and fellow Canadian Avril Lavigne. Katy Perry calls *Jagged Little Pill,* "the most perfect female record ever made" and she's opted to work often with Glen Ballard as a result.

In 2005, in honor of *Jagged Little Pills'* tenth anniversary, Morissette released an acoustic version of her groundbreaking album called *Jagged Little Pill Acoustic.* The songs sound mellower but the writing is still crisp and Morissette's voice as clear and powerful, if a little less angry.

In one of the album's songs "You Learn" the twenty year old Morissette had offered advice, including, "I recommend biting off more than you can chew." Morissette was speaking from experience. She'd moved to Toronto right after high school and then to Los Angeles to make a record. She'd turned away from her teenybopper roots that had been successful to make an ambitious album that sounds as modern and fresh today as it did in 1995. She sang about real emotions that ranged from apathy to anger and she did it all without obvious commercial intent. She certainly bit off more than she could chew and in doing so, created an album that stands the test of time.

### June 14th

On this date in 1997, "I'll Be Missing You," a tribute to the recently deceased rapper The Notorious B.I.G., recorded by Puff Daddy, Faith Evans and 112 began an incredible 11 week run at #1 on the *Billboard* Hot 100 chart. In almost any other year "I'll Be Missing You" would have been the #1 song of the year but in 1997 it came in second, oddly enough, to another "tribute" song, Elton John's reworking of his classic "Candle in the Wind" to honor Princess Diana. And to this day "I'll Be Missing You" earns one particular musician about $2,000 per day while another, who feels he should be compensated, goes unrewarded. Here's the story:

In December of 1982 the Police were working on material for what would become their fifth and final studio album, *Synchronicity*. By this point Sting was the clear artistic leader of the band, being their main lyricist and singer and so things in the studio were often a bit awkward. Neither Andy Summers nor Stewart Copeland were being encouraged to contribute material as Sting's songs were far and away the band's most successful. So when Sting brought the makings of a song called "Every Breath You Take" into the studio the three got right to work as usual, fleshing out the song and turning a demo into something suitable for release. Sting had recently left his first wife to take up with Trudie Styler and he woke up one night with the words of this song pouring out of him. He sat down at the piano and had the melody and lyrics worked out in under an hour. But when he brought the song into the studio he didn't have a guitar part so Summers worked up the signature sound that would carry the song. Summers did not ask for, nor did Sting offer, a writing credit for his contribution, something Summers regretted when "Every Breath You Take" spent eight weeks at #1 and became the biggest-selling single of 1983. Sting is the lone songwriter listed on "Every Breath You Take."

Sean Combs grew up in the Harlem section of New York City in the seventies and eighties with an appreciation for a wide range of music. He has said that "Every Breath You Take" is one of his favorite songs. He started his career in music in 1990 as an intern at Uptown Records and by 1993 he'd launched his own label, Bad Boy Records. Rappers The Notorious B.I.G. and Craig Mack were early stars on the label and helped establish Combs as an industry mogul. Using the name Puff Daddy, Combs began releasing his own songs in 1997. "Can't Nobody Hold Me Down" spent six weeks at #1 in early 1997 and it seemed everything at Bad Boy Records was rolling. Till tragedy struck.

The Notorious B.I.G. was shot to death in Los Angeles on March 7th, 1997. Not long after, Bad Boy recording artist the Lox handed in a tribute song called "We'll Always Love Big Poppa" which started selling big numbers. This inspired Combs to record his own tribute to his fallen friend. He took a sample from the Police song he loved so much and, along with Faith Evans, who'd been married to The Notorious B.I.G., and the R&B group 112, he created "I'll Be Missing You." Combs would say later: "When I made the record, I was finally able to talk to (Notorious B.I.G.). That's all it was, a conversation."

In Combs' rush to release the song he failed to clear the sample with Sting. If he had, the two probably would have worked out the usual industry standard agreement where Sting would get songwriting credit as well as share in the publishing. But since Combs waited till after the song was released to get permission, Sting automatically got 100% of the publishing for "I'll Be Missing You." The song went to #1 for 11 straight weeks and sold over 3 million copies in 1997 alone. Even to this day the song sells and streams enough to earn Sting a reported $730,000 a year ($2000 a day).

Summers still gets performance royalties anytime "Every Breath You Take" is sold or played on the radio but he receives nothing for "I'll Be Missing You," a fact Summers calls, "the major rip-off of all time." As the guitarist points out, there's cruel irony in Sting receiving money for "I'll Be Missing You" while Summers and Copeland get nothing because Sting doesn't even appear on the recording while they do. The section of the original that Combs sampled contains no bass. So while you hear Copeland's drum beat, and Summers' signature guitar part, you hear nothing from the man who makes all the money from the song.

Once the financials were worked out, Sting actually appreciated his song being used as a tribute. He'd always had a love/hate relationship with "Every Breath You Take." The song had come to him during a confusing time in his life and he wrote it from the point of view of a possessive and obsessed lover, which is why he hated the fact that some people heard it as a love song and some of those even used it as their wedding song. Sting has said, "I think the song is very, very sinister and ugly and people have actually misinterpreted it as being a gentle little love song, when it's quite the opposite." So when Combs found a way to repurpose "Every Breath You Take" as a tribute, Sting was happy and even contributed, performing the song with Combs and his crew at the 1997 MTV Video Music Awards, where he sang the chorus. If Summers was home watching, he was surely seething.

## June 15th

On this date in 1968, Tommy James and the Shondells' "Mony Mony" reached its peak position, #3 on the *Billboard* Hot 100 chart. It was a party song that James had specifically set out to write as a "throwback" but then nearly gave up on the idea when he couldn't find the right female name to use in the chorus. Then James received what he felt was almost divine intervention and was able to complete the song, thus adding to the great playlist of party staples. Here's the story:

Thomas Gregory Jackson was born in Dayton, Ohio in 1947. He was a child model but once he started playing guitar he turned his attention to music. He formed his first band, the Tornadoes, when he was twelve. He soon started using the stage name Tommy James and changed the band name to the Shondells. Their first single, "Hanky Panky" went to #1 in 1966. James was still a teenager and he was already a rock star. The following year he reached #4 with "I Think We're Alone Now." During a time when most of the headlines in music had to do with the great bands coming over from England as part of the British Invasion, Tommy James was one of the few American rock stars making hits.

James decided he wanted to write and record a song that was a throwback to some of the party tunes of the previous years. He saw that the mood in music was changing with the psychedelic era and rock and roll was starting to become more serious, even calling itself simply rock. He cites 1957's "Bony Moronie" and 1964's "Hang on Sloopy" as inspirations so he and the band sat down to come up with something similar. Something fun and nonsensical that didn't necessarily need to change the world or blow anyone's mind.

The first thing they did was create the backing track. After giving it a go, they weren't happy with the drums but they did like one section, two bars to be exact so, according to Kenny Laguna, who played keyboards on the track, "before there were loops or anything else, we copied the two bars of drums 44 times and spliced them together, and that's the track of 'Mony Mony.'" James adds: "We pasted this thing together out of drums here, and a guitar riff here. It was called sound surgery." Once they were happy with the results of the "sound surgery" they sat down to add lyrics. Some of the lines came easy, like "Shoot 'em down, turn around, come home, honey" and "Don't stop cookin', it feels so good, yeah." But they knew they needed a two-syllable female name and they just couldn't find the right one. "We had most of the words to the song," James explains, "but we still had no title. And it's just driving us nuts, because we're looking for like a 'Sloopy' or some crazy name – it had to be a two-syllable girl's name that was memorable and silly and kind of stupid sounding."

James took the project home with him and along with Ritchie Cordell, who was producing the track they continued to brainstorm. According to James they were, "about ready to throw in the towel" when, "we go out on the terrace, we light up a cigarette, and we look up into the sky. And the first thing our eyes fall on is the Mutual of New York Insurance Company. M-O-N-Y. True story. With a dollar sign in the middle of the O, and it gave you the time and the temperature. I had looked at this thing for years, and it was sitting there looking me right in the face. We saw this at the same time, and we both just started laughing. We said, 'That's perfect! What could be more perfect than that?' Mony, M-O-N-Y, Mutual of New York. And so we must have laughed for about ten minutes, and that became the title of the song."

When it came time to record the vocals they wanted a party feel so they rounded up a bunch of people to join them in the studio. "We had our usual studio band," James says, "but we also dragged in people off the street, we had secretaries come downstairs. This was in the 1650 Broadway Building, the basement of 1650 was a big music industry building. All the writers and publishers were there, so we invited them all downstairs, and it was really a party that got captured on tape."

Then James made a curious decision for the time. He made a music video to go along with the song. There were very few outlets for playing a music video but James decided to make one and it's a wonderful documentary of the look and feel of the sixties captured in the moment. The effects may look cheesy today but for 1968 they were cutting edge and whoever got to see the video at the time was probably pretty blown away.

"Mony Mony" was released in March of 1968 and it peaked at #3 this week. For James it was a temporary foray into "party rock." He released the psychedelic classic "Crimson and Clover" later in 1968 and scored his second career #1 with it.

Of course, "Mony Mony" would have a second life when Billy Idol recorded it in 1981. His studio version went to #7, then a few years later he released a live version that hit #1 on the chart, coincidentally knocking Tiffany's cover of "I Think We're Alone Now" from the top spot. Billy Idol claims he recorded "Mony Mony" for the same reason James produced it: it's a great, fun, party song and he wanted to take a crack at it. So give it a listen today. It's sure to make you feel alright, I said yeah, yeah, yeah . . .

## June 16th

On this date in 1967, Aretha Franklin's "Respect" spent its final day at #1 on the pop chart. The song had arrived two weeks earlier when it interrupted the Young Rascals' run at #1 with "Groovin.'" It would be replaced by that same song. Two weeks at #1 does not make the song an all-time top-seller, but "Respect" has gone on to be, not only Franklin's signature song but, an anthem for both the women's lib movement and civil rights.

R&B singer Otis Redding wrote "Respect" after coming off a tour. As he was leaving his bandmates he complained about having been gone so long and one of them replied: "You're on the road all the time. All you can look for is a little respect when you come home." Like any great songwriter, Redding knew a great line when he heard it and he quickly wrote a song of lament in which the singer tells his woman she can do pretty much anything as long as she gives him respect when he gets home. She can do him wrong when he's not at home because she's sweeter than honey. Anything she wants or needs, she's got it. That's how desperately in love the singer is.

Redding released "Respect" in 1965 and it became his second consecutive Top 40 hit.

Aretha Franklin was born in 1942 to a mother who was a piano player and a father who was an extremely successful preacher. Her mother died before she was ten and Franklin began singing during her father's services soon after. He began managing her career and helped his daughter land her first record contract while still a teenager. Her first album, *Songs of Faith*, was released when Franklin was just 15 and she was well on her way to a career as a gospel singer. She toured often during this time with other gospel groups and she developed a crush on an older singer named Sam Cooke. Cooke told her he was leaving his group for a pop career and this seems to have planted the seed in Franklin to do the same. When she turned 18 she broke the news to her father that she wanted to be a secular singer. He was supportive and even helped her produce a demo that landed her a record contract with Columbia in 1960.

Franklin's years at Columbia were relatively unproductive and when her contract ended she moved to Atlantic Records. In January, 1967, she recorded her first song for Atlantic, "I Never Loved a Man (The Way I Love You)." The single reached the Top 10 and Atlantic rushed Franklin back into the studio to capitalize on her new-found-fame.

On February 14th, 1967, Franklin and her sisters, Carolynn and Erma met at the Atlantic Records Studio in New York City to record her next song. When engineer Tom Dowd asked what they'd be laying down, Franklin started to sing Otis Redding's "Respect." Dowd smiled, knowingly. He'd worked on the original with Redding just a few years earlier. But Franklin had a completely different message in mind for her version of "Respect" than Redding had for the original. With some subtle lyrical changes Franklin's version became an empowering song rather than a desperate lament. Where Redding opened up with, "What you want, honey, you got it," Franklin belted out confidently, "What you want, baby I got it." And instead of, "Do me wrong, honey, if you wanna," Franklin changed the line to, "I won't do you wrong while you're gone." By tweaking just a few words, Franklin had completely changed the tone of the song.

But Franklin wasn't done reinterpreting the original. She added a break in which she spelled out "R-E-S-P-E-C-T" and then added, "Find out what it means to me" and, "Take care, TCB" (an acronym for "taking care of business"). Her sisters, who were singing backup for the session, then go into a seemingly ad-libbed repetition of the line, "Sock it to me." The phrase would soon enter the vernacular and become a common punch line on the TV show *Laugh-In*.

Atlantic Records chief Jerry Wexler was in the studio that day to produce the session and he bears witness to the fact that Franklin owned the song. He has said, "The fervor in Aretha's voice demanded that respect" and indeed it did. From her pounding on the piano to her triumphant delivery, Franklin completely reworked the original. Where Redding sang "Respect" with a desperation in his voice, Franklin comes across as supremely confident. She knows she's got the goods and she is demanding respect! It's no wonder the song became an anthem for both the women's lib movement and civil rights. And when Franklin was asked about that fact later she would say: "I think it's quite natural that we all want respect. And we should get it."

"Respect" was released in late April of 1967 and within 5 weeks it had shot to #1. Franklin's debut album for Atlantic, *I Never Loved a Man the Way I Love You*, went to #2 on the LP chart. Almost overnight Aretha Franklin had gone from a struggling singer to the new Queen of Soul and it's a title she never relinquished. How's that for earning some respect?

On this date in 1971, Carole King's second album *Tapestry* began an incredible 15 week run at #1 on the *Billboard* album chart. Since 1968 King's life and career had undergone some seismic changes and now here she was, on top of the music world with an album that became anthemic for the women's lib movement.

Carol Joan Klein was born in New York City in 1942. Her mother was a piano player and even as a toddler young Carol had a curiosity about the instrument. When she was just four years old her mother began sitting her at the instrument, using phone books on the piano bench so she could reach the keys, and taught her to play. King would say later: "My mother never forced me to practice. She didn't have to. I wanted so much to master the popular songs that poured out of the radio." By the time she got to high school she'd changed her name to Carole King and formed a band called the Co-Sines. She attended Queens College where she met Gerry Goffin. The two were married in 1959 when King became pregnant and they both started writing songs together in the evenings while they made ends meet with day jobs. Within a year, they were able to quit their day jobs and focus full-time on music. One of their first compositions, "Will You Love Me Tomorrow," became a #1 hit for the Shirelles. The songwriting duo of Goffin and King were off and running. With King composing the music and Goffin writing the lyrics they produced hit after hit. "Chains", "The Loco-Motion", "Take Good Care of My Baby", "Up on the Roof", "One Fine Day", "(You Make Me Feel Like) A Natural Woman" . . . the list goes on and on. But by 1968 there was trouble in paradise as their relationship began to crumble. Goffin and King stopped writing together, divorced, and King moved to Los Angeles looking for a fresh start.

It was in California that King met James Taylor and Joni Mitchell. She released her first solo album, *Writer*, in 1970 filling the album mostly with songs she'd written with her ex-husband. The album did not make much of a splash but it did begin her collaboration with Taylor who played guitar on many of the tracks and, more importantly, encouraged King to write new songs and sing them herself. King has said, "James inspired me a lot. I write heavily under the influence of James Taylor."

The two musicians became so close they decided to record separate albums at the same time so they could utilize the same musicians. One day everyone would show up at A&M Recording Studios and work on King's material. The next day they'd head to Crystal Sound Studios and work on Taylor's. Both albums wound up being successful. Taylor's *Mud Slide Slim* proved that *Sweet Baby James* had been no fluke and he was a singer-songwriter who was here to stay. But Carole King's *Tapestry* was the true breakthrough. The album is bookended by songs of female empowerment and sexual liberation: "I Feel the Earth Move" and her version "(You Make Me Feel Like) A Natural Woman." The album was a bellwether moment for the feminists of the early seventies as the Women's Lib Movement took on more steam.

The lead single was a great promotional vehicle for the album. The sexually tinged "I Feel the Earth Move" was the A side but after a few weeks many radio DJs began flipping the single over and playing the B side, the mellow and lamenting, "It's Too Late." Eventually, *Billboard* declared the single a double A side and considers both songs to have reached #1.

*Tapestry* sold unprecedented numbers, especially for a female artist. King held the record for longest run at #1 on the album chart by a female artist for more than 20 years, till Whitney Houston's *Bodyguard* soundtrack spent 20 weeks at #1 in 1993. *Tapestry* has sold over 25 million copies worldwide. It received 4 Grammy Awards including Album of the Year and continues to this day to be an album on most people's Desert Island Disc list. King's life story has been retold for the theater in a show called *Beautiful: The Carole King Musical*. It's a story well worth the spotlight it's been given.

## June 18th

On this date in 1955, the song "Unchained Melody" hit the pop chart for the first of what would be many, many times. What started as a song for a prison film has become one of the great love songs in modern music.

In 1955 Alex North was contracted to compose the score for a prison film entitled "Unchained." In doing so North wrote the melody for what would become "Unchained Melody." He then asked Hy Zaret to work on lyrics fitting the movie's title and theme. Zaret thought the melody was too beautiful and he decided not to include the word "unchained" in his lyrics (as North had suggested), focusing instead on a more universal theme of someone pining for a lover he has not seen in a "long, lonely time." Despite that, the song was titled to fit the film and in 1955 alone, 4 versions of "Unchained Melody" charted, 3 of them getting to #1 on the *Billboard* pop chart.

A decade later the Righteous Brothers were working on their fourth album. Bobby Hatfield and Bill Medley (who are not, in fact, brothers) had agreed to do one solo song each per album. They both wanted to sing "Unchained Melody" so they decided to toss a coin and let fate decide. As luck would have it, Hatfield won the coin toss to take the lead vocal. Hatfield has a much higher singing voice than Medley so every time you hear that soaring finale, "I need your love," just know it was a 50/50 chance, the result of a coin toss, that we even have that moment on record.

The Righteous Brothers' version was originally released as a B-side (to "Hung On You"). It wasn't until radio DJs started flipping the single and playing "Unchained Melody" that the single started climbing the charts, eventually peaking at #4.

Today the song is listed as being co-produced by Phil Spector and Bill Medley although that fact is often contested. Medley claims Spector had nothing to do with it because Spector was only interested in producing singles and "Unchained Melody" was always intended as an album cut and B-side. Early copies of the single did not even credit a producer for "Unchained Melody" and only credited Spector as producing the A-side, "Hung On You." Later pressings of the single, after "Unchained" had become the hit, credited Spector as the sole producer. Medley, at his insistence, has been added as time has gone on.

The Righteous Brothers' version, after reaching #4 on the *Billboard* pop chart in 1965, would re-chart in 1990 when it was used in the movie *Ghost*. With the success of their original version, the Righteous Brothers rerecorded the song and both the original version and their reissue would chart, making the Righteous Brothers the first act ever to have two versions of the same song in the Top 20 at the same time.

"Unchained Melody" has been recorded more than 1,500 times by over 650 artists in multiple languages around the world. Its themes of pining for a lost love and how slowly time can go when someone is alone are universal. The lyrics, as Hy Zaret, insisted, do not include the word "Unchained" (or "Melody" for that matter) but the imagery of hunger and yearning speak to everyone. And in the hands of an amazing singer like Bobby Hatfield, the song became a masterpiece.

## June 19th

On this date in 2015, "See You Again" by Wiz Khalifa featuring Charlie Puth was back at #1 on the *Billboard* Hot 100 Chart. The song had had a six week run from April 25th to June 5th, then been interrupted for a week by Taylor Swift's "Bad Blood" before returning to the top for another six weeks. 12 total weeks at #1 for a song written to pay tribute to a fallen actor and would wind up being so powerful it helped a couple work out their acrimonious divorce - that's pretty impressive. Here's the story:

Charlie Puth was born in 1991 in Rumson, New Jersey. His mother is a music teacher who began teaching her son piano when he was just four. By his early teens he'd studied jazz, played at the local Count Basie Theater and recorded a Christmas CD that he sold door-to-door making $600. In 2009 he started his own YouTube channel where he'd post songs and comedy bits. His online following grew to the point where he came to Ellen DeGeneres' attention and she quickly signed him to a recording contract with her label eleveneleven. In 2015 he switched to Atlantic Records and his single "Marvin Gaye" went to #21, expanding Puth's fan base even further.

Cameron Jibril Thomaz was born in 1987 in North Dakota but he was a military brat so as a child he moved regularly. He lived in Germany, England and Japan before his family settled down in Pittsburgh. He started rapping at an early age and soon adopted the stage name Wiz Khalifa. He has given two different explanations for the Wiz part (1- it's short for wisdom, 2- because he's a wiz at everything he does). Khalifa is Arabic for "successor" and as the rapper says, "my granddad is Muslim, so he gave me that name." When Khalifa was just sixteen he contributed some songs to a mixtape of local Pittsburgh artists which brought him to the attention of major record labels. He was still a teenager when Warner Brothers signed him to a record deal but after delays in releasing his debut album he left them and signed with Atlantic which is how he became labelmates with Charlie Puth.

*The Fast and the Furious* was released in 2001 and after breaking the $200 million mark Universal Pictures realized it had struck gold. The combination of tough guys, action and plenty of car chases found a huge audience who ignored the bad reviews. When the sequel, *2 Fast 2 Furious*, also broke the $200 million mark, a franchise was born. Paul Walker, playing the role of Brian O'Conner, was an integral part of the franchise but halfway through filming *Furious 7* he was killed in a single-car collision. Production was delayed for script rewrites, and his brothers were used as stand-ins to complete some of his remaining scenes.

Atlantic Records was producing the soundtrack for the film and the movie makers decided they wanted to add a song that would pay tribute to Paul Walker so Atlantic put out a call to their artists for demos. Charlie Puth wrote a ballad called "See You Again" channeling his feelings for a friend who had passed away. He also envisioned Vin Diesel sending a final text message to Walker, writing, "I'll tell you all about it when I see you again." He submitted the demo and was pleasantly surprised when Atlantic chose it. They then commissioned Khalifa to write the rap verses for the song. Khalifa tapped into the sense of loss that he was going through at the time, having separated from his wife Amber Rose and being embroiled in a bitter custody battle over their son. Both writers tapped into very real emotions which helped "See You Again" become not only the perfect tribute to Paul Walker but a universally relatable song about not giving up hope even in the face of despair.

"See You Again" was released on March 10th, 2015. It didn't start climbing the charts till the movie was released a month later but when it did, it made a fast and furious race to #1.

Amber Rose has said that she was driving one day when she heard the song on the radio. When she heard her ex-husband rap:

> How could we not talk about family when family's all that we got?
> Everything I went through you were standing there by my side
> And now you gonna be with me for the last ride

it softened her heart. She called Khalifa in tears and the two worked out their differences and now have joint custody of their son. Puth has said their song, "brought the power ballad back" and Khalifa adds, "We brought the ballad rap back too." However you want to label their collaboration, the two young men created an incredibly powerful farewell song.

On this date in 1992, Mariah Carey's cover version of "I'll Be There" went to #1 on the *Billboard* Hot 100 Chart. The ballad ended Kris Kross' eight week run at the top and it would enjoy a two week reign before giving way to Sir-Mix-a-Lot's ode to big booty's "Baby Got Back." "I'll Be There" had been a last minute addition to Carey's unplugged setlist and her label had no plans to release the song as a single until MTV aired the show and demand became so great they'd have been fools not to.

The Jackson 5's Motown career got off to a pretty solid start. Their first three singles, "I Want You Back", "ABC" and "The Love You Save" all went to #1. Berry Gordy, Motown chief and architect of the band's early success, decided he wanted to expand their range. Instead of releasing a fourth "bubblegum soul" song, he wanted the Jackson 5 to take a stab at a tender ballad. He commissioned songwriters Hal Davis, Willie Hutch, and Bob West to come up with something. Using the New Testament passage, "For where two or three gathered in my name, there am I with them." (Matthew 18:20) as an inspiration they wrote "I'll Be There" which includes the beautiful line "Where there is love, I'll be there." The Jackson 5 released the song in August of 1970 and like their first three singles, "I'll Be There" reached #1 on the pop chart. Michael Jackson praised Gordy for the risk he took with the ballad and credited "I'll Be There" for expanding the band's fan base and showing the world they were capable of more than just sugary pop songs. The Jackson 5's fifth single, "Mama's Pearl," would break their streak. That song peaked at #2 on the chart.

Fast forward two decades. Mariah Carey, a young singer looking for a break, very famously slipped her demo tape to Columbia Records chief Tommy Mottola at an industry event. He listened to it on his way home, signed Carey to a record deal and began marketing her as Columbia's version of Whitney Houston. She released her self-titled debut album in 1990 and with a million dollars of promotional help from Columbia, Carey did the Jackson 5 one better. Her first five singles all hit #1 on the pop chart: "Vision of Love", "Love Takes Time", "Someday", "I Don't Wanna Cry" and "Emotions." She too would have her streak broken with a song that peaked at #2 ("Can't Let Go"). Needless to say, the early nineties belonged to Mariah Carey.

In the late eighties MTV had introduced a series they titled *Unplugged* in which an artist would appear in a very casual setting and play stripped-down reinterpretations of their hits using acoustic instruments. The first few artists to appear included Aerosmith, Elton John and Stevie Ray Vaughn. When Paul McCartney appeared in 1991, he released his performance on an album titled *Unplugged (The Official Bootleg)*. The album hit #14 on the LP chart and subsequently most artists who appeared on the MTV program coupled it by releasing a live album of their performance. In early 1992 MTV got Mariah Carey to agree to appear on *Unplugged*. Just days before the March 16th taping someone asked Carey what cover song she was going to do. When Carey looked at them inquisitively, they explained to her it had become a tradition for artists on *Unplugged* to do one cover song. She rehearsed "I'll Be There" as a duet with R&B singer Trey Lorenz and the song became a last minute addition to her setlist.

MTV aired Mariah Carey's *Unplugged* on May 20, 1992. Immediately, Columbia Records received requests for her version of "I'll Be There." They quickly made an edit, removing her on-stage dialogue and the song hit record stores on June 2nd. On this date in 1992, it climbed to #1. Her *Unplugged* album sold over 3 million copies and hit #3 on the LP chart. Carey went on to be the best-selling artist of the nineties. She's had 18 career chart-toppers and her 79 total weeks at the top of the *Billboard* Hot 100 are the greatest number for any artist.

## June 21st

On this date in 1966, a young and relatively unknown guitarist named Jimmy Page appeared on stage for the first time with the Yardbirds. Page, 22 at the time, had already enjoyed an incredibly successful career as a session musician in London, appearing (sometimes credited, sometimes not) on songs and albums by everyone from the Who and the Kinks to Joe Cocker and Petula Clark. When pressed about why he can't remember which recordings he played on, Page once explained: "I was doing three sessions a day, fifteen sessions a week. Sometimes I would be playing with a group, sometimes I could be doing film music, it could be a folk session ... I was able to fit all these different roles."

Two years earlier Page had been approached about replacing Eric Clapton in the Yardbirds but he'd declined because of his friendship with Clapton and because he was reluctant to give up his lucrative session work. So he'd recommended another friend, guitarist Jeff Beck. Then, in the spring of 1966, Page got to play with Beck, two members of the Who: drummer Keith Moon and bass player John Entwistle, and John Paul Jones, on a Beck side project (he was still in the Yardbirds). The session produced the song "Beck's Bolero." After the recording, the musicians were chatting about forming a super-group and Keith Moon made the now famous joke that it would go over like a "lead zeppelin." John Entwistle has insisted he was the one who made the joke but rock and roll legend favors Moon if, for no other reason than Keith Moon was a much funnier guy than John Entwistle. He'd even shown up to the session that day disguised in sunglasses and a Russian cossack hat. But either way, the joke was made, the name was floated out there and it would soon become reality.

Page has said the experience with Beck and the other musicians got him eager to join a band so when the Yardbirds lost yet another member, bassist Paul Samwell-Smith, Page finally joined the band. He played bass for a while before moving over to co-lead guitar with Jeff Beck. But the Yardbirds were beset with personnel problems. Beck eventually left the band along with Keith Reif and Jim McCarty. In 1968, Page reconfigured a new lineup just to fulfill some concert dates in Scandinavia. He recruited vocalist Robert Plant, drummer John

Bonham and bassist John Paul Jones. They completed the Scandinavian dates as the New Yardbirds but Page, remembering the joke Moon had made, decided to dub this new band Led Zeppelin (spelling it "Led" instead of "Lead" to avoid any mispronunciations). Atlantic Records signed the band, giving them an, at-the-time, record advance, over $200,000, and their eponymous debut album was released in early 1969.

Led Zeppelin would reshape rock music and help launch an entire sub-genre of rock called Heavy Metal. There have been few, if any, more influential bands in the history of rock and the seeds of their existence were sown on this date in 1966 when Jimmy Page stopped being a session player and got onstage with the Yardbirds.

## June 22nd

On this date in 1985, Bryan Adams' power ballad "Heaven" became his first #1 single, knocking the Tears for Fear song "Everybody Wants to Rule the World" out of the top spot on the *Billboard* chart. It would be replaced two weeks later by Phil Collins' "Sussudio." The song was written for a movie that turned out to be a complete flop, but it happened to include two songs that would go on to be huge hits. So, although the movie makers probably regretted producing the film, few on the soundtrack had any qualms about being involved in the project.

Bryan Guy Adams was born in Ontario, Canada in the final year of the fifties. By his teens he was playing in bands as well as working in local studios. In 1978 he met drummer and songwriter Jim Vallance and the two began a collaboration partnership that has lasted through the decades. Though Adams would go on to be a famous eighties rocker, one of the their first cowritten songs was the disco track "Let Me Take You Dancing." The early demos Adams and Vallance produced helped Adams land a deal with A&M Records for a reported one dollar. His self-titled debut was released just as the eighties had gotten started. Though it wasn't a blockbuster it certainly made A&M their dollar back and they green-lit a follow-up which helped establish Adams as an artist to watch. His third LP, 1983's *Cuts Like a Knife*, proved to be Adams' breakthrough, producing three Top 40 hits: the title track, "Straight from the Heart" and "This Time."

As his star was on the rise Adams was approached by the filmmakers of a movie called *A Night in Heaven* about a female teacher who falls in love with a male stripper. They were asked to contribute a ballad and they came up with the song "Heaven." Adams was opening for Journey on their Frontiers' tour and he and Vallance readily admit the song was inspired by, and even modeled after, Journey's "Faithfully." In fact, when they were recording the song and their session drummer had to leave the studio before it was completed, Adams was able to persuade Journey's drummer Steve Smith to help them finish "Heaven." When *A Night in Heaven* was released it was panned and became a flop, not even earning back its $6 million budget. Vallance has called the film "dreadful."

"Heaven" appeared on the movie's soundtrack in 1984 along with the original version of the song "Obsession" (performed by its cowriters, Holly Knight and Michael Des Barres). "Obsession" would be re-recorded and released as a single by the band Animotion and become a Top 10 hit.

Later that year Adams found himself working on his fourth studio album, *Reckless*, and he considered including "Heaven" but initially felt it didn't live up to the quality of the rest of the album, an opinion that was shared by his producer, Jimmy Iovine. But at the last minute Adams changed his mind and "Heaven" was added to *Reckless'* tracklist.

*Reckless* went on to sell twelve million copies worldwide, becoming the most successful album of Adams' career. After releasing "Run to You", "Kids Wanna Rock" and "Somebody" Adams decided the power ballad he didn't think lived up to the rest of the album, deserved to be released as a single. When it started climbing the charts the song proved to be a contender. It hit #1 on this date in 1985 becoming Adams' first career #1. For an artist known for upbeat rock, Adams has had four career chart-toppers, all mellower songs. While no one but the cast and crew remembers the movie *A Night in Heaven* (and even they would probably rather forget it), the ballad Adams and Vallance contributed has gone on to be a great example of power balladry in the eighties.

## June 23rd

On this date in 1962, Ray Charles' album *Modern Sounds in Country and Western Music* began an amazing 14 week run at #1 on *Billboard*'s album chart. The LP was a departure from Charles' previous work as it features covers of country, western and folk classics reinterpreted in different styles, including rhythm and blues, soul and jazz. Charles was already a well known figure in popular music but his 1962 offering would not only expand his fan base but bring more attention to the country music he'd tapped.

Ray Charles Robinson was born in 1930 in Georgia but his family moved to Florida when he was still an infant. Two defining and tragic moments took place in his childhood that would influence his entire life. When he was five he witnessed his younger brother drown in a laundry tub. Then soon after, he lost his sight. He'd already developed an interest in piano but now that interest became a full-blown passion. His father had left the family already and his impoverished mother was able to get Charles enrolled in a school for deaf and blind children where he was taught braille. When he was fourteen, his mother passed away and shortly after he was expelled from school. At fifteen, Ray Charles was a blind orphan. His prospects looked bleak. But his passion for music, and his extraordinary talent, would catapult him to worldwide fame.

But the going was tough at first. Charles moved from Jacksonsville to Orlando to Miami landing work in bands and hotel bars. His first big break came in 1950 when a record executive heard him playing in a Miami hotel. Before long he was signed to a record label and though that label went under, Atlantic Records picked up his contract and when his 1953 single "Mess Around" climbed to #3 on the R&B chart Charles' career was off and running.

As far back as 1959, Charles had expressed interest in experimenting with country music. In the liner notes for his 1959 LP, *What'd I Say*, Charles said he was influenced by the genre as a young man. "I used to play piano in a hillbilly band," he wrote, "and I believe I could do a good job with the right hillbilly song today." Shortly after his success with that album (and its title track which was not only a #1 R&B hit but climbed all the way to #6 on the pop chart) Charles' contract with Atlantic expired and he signed with ABC Records. His deal with ABC not only gave him a higher royalty rate but promised him more artistic control, something he exercised immediately with his 1960 cover of "Georgia on My Mind." Instead of recording an original work (as he did most often during his time at Atlantic) Charles' had sought to pursue his eclectic impulses as an interpreter and when "Georgia" became a #1 hit, he was emboldened to delve even deeper.

He decided he wanted to do an entire album of country songs, giving each one his own unique style. When the concept of the album was set, Charles' producer, Sid Feller, sent him over 250 songs to chose from. They weren't looking to copy the originals, but rather to add a "Ray Charles vibe" to them. Charles felt there were incredible similarities between country and blues, telling an interviewer: "The words to country songs are very earthy like the blues, see, very down. They're not as dressed up, and the people are very honest and say, 'Look, I miss you, darlin', so I went out and I got drunk in this bar.' With country songs and the blues, it is like it is."

*Modern Sounds in Country and Western Music* was released in 1962 and it quickly became a mainstream, crossover hit. Not only did it bring Charles even more fame (and fortune, specifically due to his higher royalty rate) but it helped bring national attention to country music which, before this, had enjoyed niche attention in certain areas but not the broad appeal it soon would. Today, the album is regarded by many critics as Charles' best studio work (both *Rolling Stone* and *Time* include it on their "Greatest Albums of All Time" lists) and it is often cited as a landmark album in American music because of its integration of soul and country music at the height of the African-American civil rights struggle. In the process of recording the album, Charles also became one of the first black musicians to exercise complete artistic control over his own recording career.

On this date in 1974, Lynyrd Skynyrd released what would go on to be their only career Top 10 hit, "Sweet Home Alabama." Though nobody in the band was from Alabama they'd all come to appreciate not just the Yellowhammer State but a specific studio that their song would help make famous. "Sweet Home Alabama" also started rumors of a feud between the band and another rocker, rumors that were unfounded and largely exaggerated. Here's the story:

Lynyrd Skynyrd rose to prominence with their 1973 self-titled, debut album that not only introduced the world to this new band from Florida but helped usher in a whole new sub-genre of music called southern rock. Along with the Allman Brothers and the Marshall Tucker Band, Skynyrd helped opened the airwaves to a brand of rock fused with blues, country and hard rock. These bands were not only proud of their unique sound but their heritage as well, often displaying confederate flags on their stages or album covers. So when Neil Young released "Southern Man" which decries the south for its racism and slavery, Skynyrd felt the need to reply in a song. That answer became "Sweet Home Alabama."

According to Lynyrd Skynyrd's guitarist Ed King, the opening riff and guitar solos came to him in a dream. Since the band was already working on their second album at the time he presented the basis for the song to his bandmates and guitarist Gary Rossington and singer Ronnie Van Zant helped him complete the track. They decided to pay homage to the south by way of Alabama, a state in which they'd spend a lot of time recording at Muscle Shoals Sound Studios (though they weren't in fact working there when the song was developed - they were at Studio One in Doraville, Georgia). They took Young's song on directly, including the lyrics:

> Well, I heard Mr. Young sing about her
> Well, I heard ol' Neil put her down
> Well, I hope Neil Young will remember
> A Southern man don't need him around anyhow

in the first verse. In the second verse they included a joke which not everyone got. They began that verse with the line, "In Birmingham they love the Gov'nor," but followed it with background singers singing "boo hoo hoo." George Wallace, who was the governor of Alabama at the time, is said to have loved the song which prompted Van Zant to say, "We're not into politics, we don't have no education, and Wallace don't know anything about rock and roll." In the third verse, Skynyrd wrote about Muscle Shoals in a line that is often misheard. The studio has a great backing band that has been nicknamed "the Swampers." The line that begins the third verse is, "Now Muscle Shoals has got the Swampers," a lyric that many people sing as, "Now Muscle Shoals has got the swamplands."

When the band got set to record the song King gave his signature count in and as he started playing his opening riff, Ronnie Van Zant asked the control room to turn up his headphones. When they listened back they all decided to keep the count in as well as the now famous, "Turn it up." When they got to the part about Neil Young, the band's producer Al Kooper shouted out "southern man." Another "mistake" they decided to keep in. This one is less obvious but if you listen close enough (in the left channel only) you'll hear Kooper's "southern man" right about the 55 second mark.

When the song was released it started to get immediate radio play. It would peak at #8 in October of 1974.

Then the stories began flying about the supposed feud between Lynyrd Skynyrd and Neil Young. While it made good fodder for magazine articles, there was no truth to it. Skynyrd had simply set out to answer Young's song. Van Zant is said to have loved Neil Young, in fact he often wore a Neil Young concert shirt on stage as he is on the cover of their *Street Survivors* LP. Nor was Young upset with the band. He wrote a number of songs for them to record, including "Powderfinger." Unfortunately they never got around to recording these before the tragic plane crash in 1977, which killed both Ronnie Van Zant and Steve Gaines. Some people even theorize that "Sweet Home Alabama" is less of a put-down to Neil Young then it is a back-handed compliment, that Skynyrd intended the whole song to be ironic (like the line about the governor) and that they don't think Alabama is "sweet" at all. That's probably too broad of an interpretation of the song but certainly, the band meant no insult to Neil Young.

So travel back to 1974 when southern rock was still incipient and give "Sweet Home Alabama" a listen today. Follow Van Zant's suggestion and "turn it up" and soak in one of the genre's emergent songs.

## June 25th

On this date in 1967, the first live, international, satellite television broadcast was held. The program, called *Our World*, was shown in 17 countries to an estimated 400 to 700 million people. Those who watched the two and a half hour event saw segments from each participating country that included songs or presentations from the likes of opera singer Maria Callas, painter Pablo Picasso and, most famously, the Beatles.

Representing the United Kingdom, the Beatles were asked to compose and perform a new song with a positive message. McCartney and Lennon both set out to write something (separately of course, they were no longer writing, "eyeball to eyeball" by this point). Days later, Lennon presented a demo for a song called "All You Need is Love." When he played it for the rest of the band, George Harrison was unimpressed, replying with typical English snarkiness, "Well, it certainly is repetitive." But since McCartney hadn't come up with anything, and the broadcast was approaching, the band decided to work Lennon's demo up to a complete song.

Using a technique he'd apply often, Lennon had written verses that were enigmatic, wrapped around a chorus that was simple and anthemic. This was the height of the protests against the Vietnam War and Lennon was starting to turn his attention to the peace movement. He admitted later he was fascinated by the power of slogans to unite people, saying: "I like slogans. I like advertising. I love the telly." When asked years later whether songs like "Give Peace a Chance" and "Power to the People" were propaganda songs, he answered: "Sure. So was 'All You Need Is Love.' I'm a revolutionary artist. My art is dedicated to change." Of the song and the broadcast Ringo Starr would say: "We were big enough to command an audience of that size, and it was for love. It was for love and bloody peace. It was a fabulous time. I even get excited now when I realize that's what it was for: peace and love, people putting flowers in guns." McCartney has opined: "The chorus, 'All you need is love,' is simple, but the verse is quite complex; in fact I never really understood it, the message is rather complex. It was a good song that we had handy that had an anthemic chorus."

For the broadcast, the Beatles invited many of their friends to create a festive atmosphere and to join in on the song's chorus. Mick Jagger, Keith Richards, Eric Clapton, Graham Nash, Keith Moon, Patti Boyd and Marianne Faithfull were among those who sang along. During the orchestral ending, snippets of both "Greensleeves" and Glenn Miller's "In the Mood" were played. McCartney also sang, "She loves you yeah, yeah, yeah" in the coda. The Beatles intended to release the recording from the broadcast as a single but Lennon was unhappy with his singing, so he re-recorded the solo verses and Ringo Starr also overdubbed his drums.

"All You Need Is Love" (backed with "Baby, You're a Rich Man") was released just a few weeks after the broadcast, midway through the Summer of Love. By mid-August it would get to #1, ending the Doors' three week run at the top of the chart with "Light My Fire." The Beatles were already the biggest band on the planet but certainly their international exposure on the *Our World* broadcast didn't hurt their fame. And if, as Harrison claimed, "All You Need is Love" is repetitive, it also promotes a simple message we all can embrace. Lyrics like "Nothing you can know that isn't known, nothing you can see that isn't shown," may be hard to interpret but that five word chorus is as simple and powerful as Lennon would ever get in his storied career. If only it were as easy to live those words each and every day as it is to sing them out loud.

### June 26th

On this date in 1909, Andreas Cornelis van Kuijk was born in the Netherlands. He would illegally immigrate to America at the age of twenty and go on to be one of the most successful managers in music history. Never heard of him? Sure you have. Read on.

As a child van Kuijk dreamed of going to America to be successful. He'd heard the legends of streets paved with gold and he just knew his fortune lay somewhere across the ocean. In his late teens there was a murder in his hometown which he may or not have been a suspect in. While history is unclear on the facts, what we do know is van Kuijk immigrated to the U.S. illegally. Shortly after arriving, he enlisted in the army, stealing the name of the officer who interviewed him to hide his illegal immigrant status. Using his new name, Tom Parker, he served two years (in Hawaii and Florida) before going AWOL. He was punished with solitary confinement and emerged with a psychosis that led to two months in a mental hospital. Eventually he was discharged from the army due to his mental condition. That's when he turned his attention to entertainment.

Parker had a penchant for promotion and huckstering. He worked in the carnival business for a while then moved to being a talent manager when he started promoting for singer Gene Austin. He later became Eddy Arnold's manager. In 1948, Parker received the rank of colonel in the Louisiana State Militia from Jimmie Davis, the governor of Louisiana and a former country singer, in return for work Parker did on Davis' election campaign. The rank was honorary since Louisiana didn't even have a militia, but Parker used the title the rest of his life, becoming known simply as "the Colonel" to many acquaintances.

Parker's big break came in early 1955, when he became aware of a young singer named Elvis Presley. Presley had a singing style different from the current trend, and Parker immediately sensed he could help make Presley huge. He soon became Presley's "special advisor" (Elvis already had a manager at the time) and was tasked with securing a new record contract with a bigger label. Sam Phillips, owner of Sun Records and the man who'd given Presley his start, set the price at $35,000 to buy Presley out from his Sun Records deal. It was a completely unheard-of sum at the time but Parker convinced RCA Records that Presley would be worth it and a deal was signed in November of 1955.

On March 26, 1956, after Elvis' current management contract expired, the singer signed with Parker. Presley's first RCA single, "Heartbreak Hotel" became his first #1, holding the top spot from April 21 to June 9th of that year. Parker arranged for Presley to appear on popular television shows such as *The Milton Berle Show* and *The Ed Sullivan Show*, securing fees that made him the highest-paid star on television. Elvis' career as the King of Rock and Roll was well underway and, no doubt, Parker was instrumental in guiding Presley to such unprecedented heights.

Parker was an innovative manager, coming up with many ways to make Elvis more money (and with Parker's 25% share, padding his own pocket as well) . Parker struck merchandising deals on everything from charm bracelets to record players, generating $22 million in sales in 1956 alone (back when $22 million was worth something). Parker even sold "I Hate Elvis" badges to make money off the non-fans. Presley was so happy with Parker's management that by the mid-sixties he re-signed with him, increasing Parker's cut to an unheard of 50%. Presley would say: "I don't think I'd have ever been very big if it wasn't for him. He's a very smart man."

Some people question some of the things Parker had Presley do throughout his career, the schlocky movies especially, but if a manager's job is to keep his client working and making money, no one can doubt Parker's efficacy. Presley survived the ebbs and flows of popularity that come with any twenty-year career in entertainment and in the end he was pulling in $150,000 a week in Vegas and playing sold-out shows wherever he appeared. The most legitimate criticism that can be levied at Parker is that Presley never toured abroad. In fact, he only played three shows in his entire career outside of the U.S. All three were in Canada in 1957 - none of which Parker attended. Some theorize that Parker's illegal immigrant status would have stopped him from getting a passport and exposed the fact that he wasn't a citizen. Though we'll never know the reason, there is no doubt that Presley missed lucrative opportunities to tour internationally and increase his popularity outside of the States. Parker has also been criticized for how he handled Presley's drug use. Some say he turned a blind eye, others say he even helped Presley find doctors who would fill the prescriptions he always needed filled. Either way, it was that drug use that led to Presley's death at just 42 years of age, in August of 1977.

Following Presley's passing, Parker was asked what he would do now. Parker responded, "Why, I'll just go right on managing him." And indeed he did, handling the estate's business affairs and promotion, until 1983 when the Presley family paid $2 million to buy out his contract. Ten years later, with the Presley estate more profitable then ever, Parker was quoted as saying, "I don't think I ever exploited Elvis as much as he's being exploited today."

Parker died in 1997 at the age of 87. Priscilla Presley gave a eulogy at his funeral and perhaps summed up Colonel Tom Parker perfectly, "Elvis and the Colonel made history together, and the world is richer, better and far more interesting because of their collaboration." She then concluded, "and now I need to locate my wallet, because I noticed there was no ticket booth on the way in here, but I'm sure that the Colonel must have arranged for some toll on the way out."

## June 27th

On this date in 1970, the band Smile played their last official gig. They had a small but ardent following in London but by far their biggest fan was Farrokh Bulsara who would soon join some of the musicians from Smile and form one of the biggest bands of the decade.

Guitarist Brian May formed the band Smile in 1968 with singer and bassist Tim Staffell and drummer Roger Taylor. Within a year the trio had signed with Mercury Records and although they did some studio work they would disband before they released anything on the label. Meanwhile, they played often in and around London and developed a following that included a young art student named Farrokh Bulsara. Bulsara's family was from Zanzibar and had moved to London to avoid unrest at home. Bulsara and Staffell were fellow students at

Ealing Art College so not only was Bulsara a fan of Smile he got to know the band personally. In an attempt to fit in culturally, Bulsara often introduced himself as Freddie.

In early June of 1970, Staffell broke the news to May and Taylor that he was leaving Smile to join a band named Humpy Bong. Smile had an upcoming gig on the books (on this date) and now they had no lead singer or bassist. So they recruited their biggest fan and satisfied the booking with Bulsara on vocals and a friend named Mike Grose on bass. In the following weeks Bulsara would change his stage name to Freddie Mercury and convince the band to change their name to Queen. They played their first gig as Queen less than a month later, on July 18th, 1970. They would go through a few bass players in the next few months before finding John Deacon. Drawing on his art school training, Mercury designed a logo for the new band. He called it the Queen Crest. It combines the zodiac signs of all four members: two lions for Leo (Deacon and Taylor), a crab for Cancer (May), and two fairies for Virgo (Mercury). The lions embrace the letter Q which wraps around a crown and the whole logo is over-shadowed by a phoenix - very similar to the royal coat of arms of England. The logo began as a simple line drawing but more intricate color versions have been used on later album covers.

Queen was signed to EMI Records and released their first album in July of 1973. Their self-titled debut received decent reviews but neither it, nor the only single off the album "Keep Yourself Alive" made a dent on the charts. But this was back when record companies actually allowed a band to find its sound and audience. EMI's patience began to pay off in 1974 with *Queen II* which went to #5 on the U.K. album chart (it only reached 49 in the States) and its only single, "Seven Seas of Rhye," got to #10 in U.K. Their next album *Sheer Heart Attack* was the real breakthrough and soon enough Queen was one of the biggest bands of the seventies. They sold over 150 million albums world-wide, landed 18 songs at the top of the U.S. pop chart and in 2001 were inducted into the Rock and Roll Hall of Fame.

Humpy Bong, by the way, released one single on Parlophone Records before disbanding.

### June 28th

On this date in 1975, the Eagles started a five-week run at # 1 on the album chart with their fourth studio LP *One of These Nights*. The Eagles had experienced growing popularity since their eponymous debut album in 1972, but *One of These Nights*, with three Top 10 singles ("Lyin' Eyes" which won a Grammy, "Take It to the Limit" and the title track) was the album that served as their breakthrough.

The origin of the Eagles is one of those rock and roll stories that hinges so much on coincidence it makes you wonder if there isn't a Rock and Roll God making things happen somewhere in the great beyond. In 1970, Glenn Frey (who had moved to LA from Michigan and formed his first band, Longbranch Pennywhistle) and Don Henley (who had moved to LA from Texas with his band Shiloh to record an album) happened to be at the famous Troubadour on the same night. They were two single guys just hanging out and for some reason they introduced themselves and got to talking. Neither recalled who initiated the conversation but clearly they were drawn to each and their commonalities became apparent as soon as they started speaking. It turned out they were both unhappy with their current band situations and yearned to do something more in the music industry. At one point in the conversation Frey said to Henley, "Do you want to go on the road with Linda Ronstadt and make 200 bucks a week?" Henley hadn't been on tour yet so he jumped at the opportunity.

The two joined Ronstadt's backing band and toured and also roomed together. On the road they began to discuss putting a band together. What had begun in the Troubadour as a casual conversation was now taking shape and the two became serious about the idea. One day they sheepishly broke the news to Ronstadt, thinking she might get upset and even throw them off the tour. Instead she was incredibly understanding and even helpful, suggesting they contact Bernie Leadon and Randy Meisner and even offering her house as a rehearsal space. Ronstadt has admitted to seeing great potential in the two musicians and was happy to be a part of the beginning of their journey. She even recalls coming home one day and being blown away by them. "They had rehearsed 'Witchy Woman'," she recalled, "and they had all the harmonies worked out, four-part harmonies. It was fantastic. I knew it was gonna be a hit. You could just tell."

The band started playing live and soon enough they were signed to David Geffen's brand new label Asylum Records. Leadon is often credited for coming up with the name the Eagles which was inspired by a peyote trip during which he started talking about the Hopi Indians revered eagles. Their first three albums built their reputation but it was their fourth LP, *One of These Nights*, which hit #1 on this date in 1975, that really helped the Eagles soar.

The Eagles went through a number of incarnations throughout their years, with some members leaving and some new ones joining, but Glenn Frey and Don Henley were always the backbone of the band. And even their relationship went through many stages. They started out as roommates on the road dreaming of forming a band and eventually became two of the biggest musicians in the world. They were contentious at times, conciliatory at other times. And though their relationship may not have been completely harmonious, whenever they sang together the harmonies were magical. When Frey passed away in January of 2016, Henley paid homage saying: "Glenn was the one who started it all. He was the spark plug, the man with the plan. He was funny, bullheaded, mercurial, generous, deeply talented and driven." Of those early days, Henley recalls, "we were two young men who made the pilgrimage to Los Angeles with the same dream: to make our mark in the music industry." With 150 million albums sold worldwide, you'd have to say they realized that dream and then some.

On this date in 1985, David Bowie and Mick Jagger recorded "Dancing in the Streets" for the upcoming Live Aid event which was just 2 weeks away. The song would go on to incredible success and earn millions for charity, yet to this day, the video is still the subject of ridicule. And rightfully so. It's one of the cheesiest examples of a mid-eighties music video . . . and that's saying a lot.

Bob Geldof, who had organized the Band Aid "Do They Know It's Christmas?" single to raise money for the Ethiopian famine victims, put together Live Aid to support the same cause. The event was promoted as a "global jukebox" with concerts scheduled in two different locations: Wembley Stadium in London and JFK Stadium in Philadelphia. One of Geldof's big ideas for the concert was that David Bowie and Mick Jagger would sing a song together, while one was in London and the other Philadelphia. Once everyone involved realized that the delay in the satellite feed would make that virtually impossible, the plan was altered. It was decided they'd record a song in advance, shoot a video, and have that shown at each concert.

"Dancing in the Streets" (like so many Motown songs) was written by committee. One of its three writers was a young Marvin Gaye (along with Ivy Hunter and William Stevenson, both of whom were songwriters for the Motown label). It was first recorded by Martha and the Vandellas and went to #2 in 1964. At the time, the song was seen to have two meanings. On its surface, "Dancing in the Streets" was simply a party song promising, "Swinging, swaying and records playing." But during the civil rights movement some felt the song was a call to march and demonstrate and it became something of an anthem during that time. The Rolling Stones actually helped propagate this perception when they borrowed the line, "Summer's here and the time is right," for their protest song, "Street Fighting Man." So it was decided "Dancing in the Streets" would be the song Bowie and Jagger would sing.

Bowie was working at Abbey Road studio on this day in 1985, recording the song "Absolute Beginners" for a movie with the same name. Jagger came down and they worked with Bowie's band on the song. They banged out "Dancing in the Streets" in just two takes then headed straight to the London docklands to film the song's video. Both singers were told to dance around and lip-sync to the song. Before long, it became obvious that they were each trying to one-up the other in terms showmanship. Bowie's drummer, Neil Conti places the blame on Jagger, saying, "It was a huge ego trip for Mick, he kept trying to upstage David." The result is semi-hilarious, as two of the biggest names in music prance, jump, skip and sashay through the three minute clip.

The video for "Dancing in the Streets" was first shown at the Live Aid concerts and then the single was released just weeks later. With plenty of promotion on MTV (for which no video was too cheesy) the song climbed the charts, peaking at #7 in the U.S. and going to #1 in the U.K. Like Band Aid and Live Aid, it helped raise millions for charity so it's hard to knock the effort of David Bowie or Mick

Jagger. But try and watch that video with a straight face and you'll see why so many place this clip at the top of any list of embarrassing music videos.

## June 30th

On this date in 1975, the Jackson 5 officially left Motown and signed with Epic Records. Though they'd reached unprecedented levels of success with Berry Gordy's label they were unhappy with the control he imposed over them and the minuscule royalty rate they had agreed to. Gordy had proven himself a ruthless and cunning business man but when the band found out they couldn't even continue recording under their own name, it was probably Gordy's most infamous moment.

Joseph and Katherine Jackson were a fertile couple. They had ten children during their marriage (one died as an infant) and as they all grew, they each showed a talent and an affinity towards music. Joe encouraged the boys and soon had them rehearsing songs and dance moves. Using the name the Jackson Five Singing Group (which they'd soon shorten to the Jackson Five) they started entering (and winning) talent shows in and around their hometown of Gary, Indiana. Inspired by these early successes Joe brought his sons to Chicago and then New York City where they continued winning talent contests performing mostly covers of Motown songs. In 1967 they made their first attempt at getting signed by Gordy but he initially passed. They continued honing their skills on the road, even playing in some strip clubs and eventually Gordy signed the band in 1969. He used his usual contract when signing the band and Joe has been criticized for not negotiating hard enough, signing away, among other things, ownership of the name the Jackson Five. While most bands on the label had been put together by Gordy and his team, so therefore it made sense he owned their name, the Jackson Five had come to him as a complete band. Yet he still now owned their name as well as had full control over their careers and was paying them a minuscule royalty rate of 2.8%.

But things didn't start out bad. They started out good. Very good in fact. The Jackson 5's debut single, "I Want You Back" was released in October of 1969 and by January of 1970 it had reached the #1 spot on the pop chart. In fact, the first four singles the band released all went to #1 and their streak was broken by only one chart position, with their fifth single, "Mama's Pearl," peaking at #2. By that point the nation had been swept up in Jacksonmania and the boys were ubiquitous, performing on television, appearing on magazine covers and even becoming stars in their very own Saturday morning cartoon. Gordy not only saw the marketability of the band but also the solo potential of the youngest boy, Michael. Soon enough, Michael Jackson was releasing solo singles for Motown even while continuing as a member of the Jackson 5.

Soon enough fortunes changed and by 1974 not everything the brothers released immediately went to the top of the charts. Joe and his boys were growing disgruntled by the control Gordy had over the band and the limits put on them to record their own material or even select which songs they recorded. And, of course, their royalty rate became a huge issue. They were still getting the same 2.8% they'd agreed to when they first signed with Motown and despite their track record Gordy refused to renegotiate. As their original five year deal was winding down Joe Jackson began approaching other labels, letting it be known that the band would soon be available. Epic stepped up with a 20% royalty rate and the band signed on. But as they made their exit from Motown, they found out that Gordy and his label would forever own the name the Jackson 5. So they signed with Epic as the Jacksons. That is, four of the five did. Jermaine Jackson did not follow his brothers. He'd begun dating Gordy's daughter Hazel (who he'd eventually marry) and Gordy promised him a solo career of his own. Randy replaced Jermaine thus making Michael no longer the youngest member.

The Jacksons' career on Epic was not nearly as successful as their time at Motown. They landed a few Top 10 hits during the disco era, 1976's "Enjoy Yourself" and 1977's "Shake Your Body (Down to the Ground)," but they were no longer the consistent hitmakers they'd been at the beginning of the decade. Much of that can be chalked up to Michael and his distractions. He was pursuing a film career that would soon see him star in the 1978 movie *The Wiz* as well keeping his solo options open. The success of his 1979 LP *Off the Wall* established Michael as a bonafide star and took him even further from the Jacksons. Though the band would go on (with and without him at times) it would fail to ever achieve the same level of success it had in its early years with Motown.

Which of course begs the question, did Gordy's control, which the band pushed back against, help them achieve such success? Was Gordy the visionary who knew how to get the most out of his talent? Or was he just a shrewd business man who signed the right acts and milked them for all he could? The truth, certainly, is somewhere between the two. But what's obvious is that on this date, in 1975, when the Jackson 5 left Motown, both the band and the label would be weaker without the other.

JULY

On this date in 1972, the Doobie Brothers released their second LP, *Toulouse Street*. The previous year their debut, self-titled album had underperformed so there was some pressure on the band to prove themselves. *Toulouse Street* did that and more. The album went to #21 on the LP chart and it produced two Top 40 singles, proving that the Doobie Brothers were a band to watch.

The Doobie Brothers came together in San Jose, California in the late sixties. Their original name was Pud which, thankfully, they decided to change. Like most musicians of the late sixties, heck, most young people of the time, they smoked a lot of marijuana. One day a friend suggested they change their name to the Doobie Brothers ("doobie" being a common street term for a joint) and after the band stopped laughing (they were probably high) they decided they liked the name. Early on the Doobie Brothers played a much harder sound than they'd become known for. They had an avid following of Hells Angels in Northern California and were obviously playing to their crowd. They landed a record contract with Warner Brothers and their eponymous debut was released in 1971. It failed to crack the *Billboard* Top 200 which was obviously a disappointment to everyone involved. But this was back when record labels gave their artists a chance to find their audience. Instant successes were nice but unexpected. Warner simply sent the band back into the studio and awaited a follow-up.

Lead singer and guitarist Tom Johnston clearly remembers coming up with a rhythm track on his acoustic guitar around this time that would ultimately change the fortunes of the band. He played it over and over one night and he said it made him think optimistically. "The chord structure made me think of something positive," he would say later, "so the lyrics that came out of that were based on this utopian idea that if the leaders of the world got together on some grassy hill somewhere and either smoked dope or just sat down and just listened to the music and forgot about all this other bullshit, the world would be a much better place." With these thoughts in mind, and this incredible melody, Johnston wrote "Listen to the Music" which the band would choose as its opening track for their second album.

*Toulouse Street* was released on this date in 1972 with "Listen to the Music" coming out as a single later that summer. Both performed much better than the Doobie's original offerings with "Music" peaking at #11 in November of that year and the LP making it to #21 a month later. *Toulouse Street* also produced "Jesus Is Just Alright" which made it to #35. Thus began a string of hits for the band that would dominate rock radio for the next decade. Even when Tom Johnston's health faltered from bleeding ulcers in the mid-seventies the band was able to persevere. They tabbed Michael McDonald to step in; at first temporarily for the ailing Johnston, then permanently once it was clear Johnston's condition was going to keep him from touring. The Doobie Brothers' first LP with McDonald was *Takin' it to the Streets* which included two Top 40 hits: the title tracks and "It Keeps You Runnin'." The Doobie Brothers hadn't missed a step.

It's heartening to think back to Tom Johnston coming up with "Listen to the Music" as the Doobie Brothers teetered on the edge of obscurity. If Warner Brothers had pressured the band for a hit he may not have felt as loose and easy going as you have to feel to create something so magical. You can credit that to doobies as well, of course. But whatever it was that put him in that state, it worked like magic. Sure, there's naïveté in thinking that if all the world's leaders got together and got high they'd cure all of our ills. But what's wrong with at least dreaming it? Especially if what comes from those thoughts is a song as joyous as "Listen to the Music." Johnston sings, "What the people need is a way to make them smile," and then he posits that listening to music and dancing our blues away is the answer. Naïve? Surely. Worth trying? I think we all should. Doobies, of course, are optional.


### July 2nd

On this date in 1966, Frank Sinatra's "Strangers in the Night" went to #1 on the *Billboard* Hot 100 chart, knocking the Beatles' "Paperback Writer" from the top spot. If you scan the list of #1 records in 1966, it's odd to see a crooner's name alongside such classic rock stalwarts as the Young Rascals, the Rolling Stones and the Lovin' Spoonful. But there Sinatra was, enjoying his first trip to the top of the charts since the mid-fifties. And despite the fact that the song was so successful for him, even taking home three Grammy Awards, Sinatra despised it throughout his lifetime.

It's hard to imagine the twentieth century in American music, or pop culture for that matter, without Francis Albert Sinatra. Yet truth be told, that was almost the case. He was born in December of 1915 and at thirteen and a half pounds the doctor needed forceps to remove him. This caused damage to his neck, cheek and ear drum and after the doctor cut the umbilical cord the infant was thought to have suffocated. It wasn't until the newborn's grandmother stuck him under cold water that he began to breathe.

Growing up, Sinatra fell in love with music and idolized Bing Crosby. He had a poster of the singer in his childhood bedroom and would sometimes boast that he was going to be "better than Bing." His parents ran a tavern in their hometown of Hoboken, New Jersey and young Sinatra would often hop up on the piano and belt out a song for tips. As a teenager he asked to join a local singing group called the Three Flashes. Legend has it that he was admitted mainly because he owned a car and the other three were sick of taking public transportation to their gigs. Whatever the reason, the Three Flashes became the Hoboken Four and before he was even twenty years old Frank Sinatra was on his way to fulfilling his dream. He quickly became the lead singer of the group, not just for his extraordinary singing but also for his matinée idol looks. He was the one who made the females swoon and before long he'd leave the Hoboken Four for worldwide fame and fortune.

In 1940 Sinatra made his first appearance with the Tommy Dorsey band and his star really started to rise. The bandleader was so enraptured by his new singer's voice there were times he'd almost miss his solo. Such was the effect young Frank Sinatra was having on everyone. And it wasn't just his voice that made him stand out. Sinatra had the innate ability to convey unbridled emotion in his delivery. And then there was his phrasing. The way he could fall slightly behind the beat without losing a song's rhythm. Tempo rubato is defined as disregarding the strict tempo of a song and if anyone was ever "Mister Rubato" it was Frank Sinatra. When Bono presented him with a Legacy Achievement Award at the 1994 Grammy Award ceremony he described Sinatra's rubato as, "not on the beat, over it. Playing with it, splitting it, like a jazzman."

In that same speech Bono said, "Frank never did like rock and roll," and there is no one who would argue with that. Sinatra was the original King of Pop, the greatest singer in the world and the most famous name in music for over a decade. From his colossal coming out party as a solo singer in 1942 till rock and roll burst on the scene in the mid-fifties, Sinatra was the man. Then, almost overnight, he seemed out-of-step with what was hot and cool and now. And Sinatra knew it. He criticized, both publicly and privately, everyone from Elvis to the Beatles and while his career from the mid-fifties to the mid-sixties can't exactly be described as "fading into oblivion," he had slipped much in popularity and record sales.

Which is why when he was presented with "Strangers in the Night" he recorded it, even though those close to him say he despised the song. He is said to have called it, "a piece of shit," and, "the worst fucking song that I have ever heard." But Sinatra also knew what would sell and he heard the commercial potential immediately in "Strangers in the Night."

Glen Campbell (who was then a session musician for hire) played rhythm guitar on the track. He was so in awe of being in the same studio as the Frank Sinatra that he couldn't stop staring at him. Campbell chuckles when he recalls, "Frank asked the producer, Jimmy Bowen, 'Who's the fag guitarist over there?'"

Perhaps the most memorable feature of "Strangers in the Night" is Sinatra's improvised scat during the coda. His "doo-be-doo-be-doo" left many fans lamenting that the song fades early and Sinatra's improvisation is cut off too soon. In fact, for his greatest hits compilation, *Nothing but the Best*, an extra ten seconds was added to the song, just a continuation of Sinatra's scatting. Cartoonists Joe Ruby and Ken Spears, who created the *Scooby-Doo* series have said they gave the title character his name as an homage to Frank Sinatra.

"Strangers in the Night" hit #1 on this date in 1966 and though it was only a one week stay at the top of the charts, for Ol' Blue Eyes it had to be a satisfying moment. In a career of ebbs and flows, to push past the Beatles and the Stones and every other rocker on the charts and make it to #1, proved that Sinatra was still the Chairman of the Board.

On this date in 1968, at a party at Joni Mitchell's house, David Crosby, Stephen Stills and Graham Nash played and sang together for the very first time, discovering the magic in their harmonies. Though their few short years together would prove turbulent, with the magic of those harmonies and some amazing songwriting, they managed to make some great music along the way.

David Crosby, Stephen Stills and Graham Nash all knew each other before this party at Joni Mitchell's house and they'd each had their share of success in the music industry prior to this happy accident. David Crosby had been a member of the Byrds until internal friction forced him out the year before. Stephen Stills was a member of Buffalo Springfield (along with Neil Young) who had just broken up. And Graham Nash, at the time, was in the Hollies. Stills and Crosby had been jamming together of late, thinking of collaborating, so when they found themselves at a party together at Mitchell's place, with her boyfriend Graham Nash in attendance, they decided to break out the guitars and sing for everyone. As Nash explains: "Halfway through the final joint we smoked that night, Crosby said, 'Hey Stephen play him that song we've been working on.' In the first two performances they did, I learned the words. I knew how Crosby was breathing, I knew how Stephen was starting and ending his sentences. When I put my harmony in there, we got about a minute into the song and had to stop and start laughing. We had never heard anything like that moment." The laughter may have come from the marijuana but there is no doubt that they also heard the euphony in their voices. There is something about these three men and their singing that makes the sum so much greater than the parts.

Nash was so excited he quit the the Hollies to work with Crosby and Stills.

The trio auditioned for the Beatles' label, Apple Records, but were somehow rejected. At the time the Beatles were experiencing a lot of internal strife and the story goes that the trio auditioned for George Harrison, who liked their sound, but when they asked if Paul McCartney would produce them he changed his mind and didn't recommend them to his bandmates. Whether that is accurate or not, Apple Records surely missed out. The three signed with Atlantic Records (Ahmet Ertegün had been a fan of Buffalo Springfield and was disappointed when they broke up) and got to work on recording their debut LP.

Besides working on music, the three musicians had to come up with a name. Based on their previous experiences in bands, they decided to use their surnames, thus insuring that they'd each maintain their individuality and that the band could not go on without any one of them. How they decided the order those names would appear in has been lost to history, but it is probably as simple as it sounds. Try those three names in any other order and they do not flow as easily off the tongue. And they even decided to use an ampersand to stand out. Crosby, Stills & Nash, it was.

Steven Stills stepped up in the studio and took over creative control of the band. He played most of the instruments on their debut and contributed what is arguably their greatest song, "Suite: Judy Blue Eyes." The titled is a play on the words "sweet Judy blue eyes" and the song was written by Stills as a lament about his breakup with his girlfriend, and fellow singer/songwriter, Judy Collins (who is, in fact, known for her beautiful blue eyes.) The song begins as a mid-tempo folk rocker then slows down in the middle section as Crosby, Stills and Nash show off their incredible harmonies. At the four and half minute mark the listener surely feels the song is winding down. And had it, "Suite: Judy Blue Eyes" would be a solid song of love lost and lament. But then the guitars seem to regain energy and the song builds back up. What's this? the listener may ask. Does this song have something more to say? We hear about canaries and sparrows singing, then the awesome alliteration, "Lacy lilting lyrics losing love lamenting." And then, the song takes off into a soaring, exuberant final minute of nothing but "do do dos" and, what is that, Spanish? The song finishes on one final "do do do" and the listener is left almost breathless. If ever a band had recorded the perfect opening track for their debut album, Crosby, Stills & Nash's "Suite: Judy Blue Eyes" is right up there among the best.

Less than a year after they'd discovered how harmonious their voices sounded together, Crosby, Stills & Nash released their eponymous debut album. Between the LP, which sold over 4 million copies, and their performance at Woodstock, Crosby, Stills & Nash let the world know that there was a new name, three to be exact, in rock music.

The rest, as they say, is rock and roll history.


## July 4th

On this date in 1976, Tom Petty and the Heartbreakers recorded "American Girl." Though the song wouldn't even make the *Billboard* Hot 100 chart, it has gone on to be one of Petty's signature songs as well as a favorite sing-along at bars and parties.

Tom Petty was born in 1950 in Gainesville, Florida. When he was just ten years old his uncle was working on an Elvis Presley film and he invited young Tom to the set. Petty would recall that meeting by saying, "Elvis glowed," and he would mark that moment as the beginning of his love for rock and roll. And, like so many his age, he also remembers seeing the Beatles on the Ed Sullivan Show and knowing instantly he wanted to make it as a rock star. "There was the way out," he would say later, "there was the way to do it . . . And it looked like so much fun." He began to take guitar lessons. One of his first teachers was Don Felder who would go on to fame and fortune as a member of the Eagles.

Petty's first band was called the Epics. They morphed into Mudcrutch and they were signed to a record deal and moved to Los Angeles. Mudcrutch released one single (which failed to chart) and then promptly broke up. From the ruins of his second failed band, Tom Petty decided to form Tom Petty and the Heartbreakers and began working on material for a debut album in the summer of 1976.

And so it came to be that on this date in 1976, while the rest of America celebrated its bicentennial, Tom Petty and his band recorded "American Girl." It's a song Petty remembers writing in his "little apartment in Encino" for which he credits the "waves crashin' on the beach" line. And it's also a song that Petty credits as starting a theme that would carry through much of his career: "writing about people who are longing for something else in life, something better than they have." That feeling of yearning with a sense of hope would indeed be a common thread throughout the next forty plus years of Petty's career.

What the song is not about though is a suicide. Rumors have long floated around that while Petty was still living in Florida, a female student at the University of Florida jumped to her death from the balcony of her dorm room. This incident is said to have left a mark on Petty's conscience which he channeled in "American Girl." Petty dismissed these claims as "an urban legend" and more succinctly "not at all true." In other words, just because the American girl in the song is on a balcony, doesn't mean she's going to jump.

"American Girl" wound up as the final track on Tom Petty and the Heartbreakers self-titled debut album which was released in November of 1976. Initially the album, and its lead single "Breakdown," sold much better in England than in the States. It would take over a year for the LP to peak at #55 on the *Billboard* album chart and while "Breakdown" did crack the Top 40, the next two singles off the album, "Anything That's Rock 'n' Roll" and "American Girl" failed to chart. Petty, of course, went on to an incredibly successful career, with over 80 million albums sold and a 2001 induction into the Rock and Roll Hall of Fame on his resume.

So how then did "American Girl" become one of his signature songs? Some of that can be attributed to the 1991 movie *Silence of the Lambs*. There is a scene in the movie where a female character is driving and listening to "American Girl." She is singing along passionately and keeping time by tapping on her steering wheel. Though the scene lasts only about 30 seconds it seemed to have reminded the audience about this great, long forgotten song. Movies can have that effect sometimes. Think of how *Top Gun* reintroduced "You've Lost That Lovin' Feelin'" or how "Old Time Rock and Roll" became even more popular once Tom Cruise sang along to it in his underwear in *Risky Business*. Since appearing in *Silence of the Lambs,* "American Girl" has shown up in other movies as well as TV shows. When Petty played the Super Bowl halftime show in 2008 he opened his set with the song. And on September 25th, 2017, Petty closed a concert at the Hollywood Bowl with "American Girl." It was his last show, and thus his last song, before he passed away of cardiac arrest just a week later.

On this date in 1976, the Ramones played one of the most significant club shows in the history of rock. And they weren't even the headliners.

The Ramones had been playing live for about two years by this point, becoming regulars at New York City clubs like Max's Kansas City and CBGB. There was a new movement beginning, a return to straight ahead rock and roll music, that was very much a reaction to what some saw as rock music becoming too big and bloated and self-important. The progressive rock sound, with its long, solo-filled songs, was something this new movement despised, as well as soft rock bands like America and Bread. The new sound emanating from New York City and London was the complete antithesis of all that. And the Ramones were very much at the forefront, playing fast and loud and masking their limitations as musicians with a ferocious energy and anger. Legs McNeil who cofounded *Punk* magazine (giving this movement its name) once described seeing the Ramones during this early phase: "They were all wearing these black leather jackets. And they counted off this song... and it was just this wall of noise... They looked so striking. These guys were not hippies. This was something completely new."

The Ramones signed with Sire Records and they recorded their debut album in the spring of 1976. They spent one week in the studio to lay down the album's fourteen tracks, which last less than thirty total minutes. The album cost $6,400 to record.

And nobody bought it. Hardly anyone even reviewed it. Sure, today, most music lovers own it and most critics have revisited it and recognize it as the pioneer of punk music. But at the time, the album was largely ignored. Except by a small group of young kids in England.

While the burgeoning punk scene was little more than a blip on the map in the States, it was creating quite the stir in London. Malcolm McLaren was a big reason for that. He had spent some time in New York and brought many of the punk rock elements back to the London music scene (McLaren would go on to manage the Sex Pistols). So when the Ramones actually put out a record, many of these young rockers were motivated to do the same. And when it was announced that the Ramones were coming over to play at the Roundhouse, tickets sold-out (even though they were just the opening act).

The Ramones made their international debut on July 4th, 1976, squeezing 14 songs into their set and playing for just over a half hour. The crowd called them out for an encore and they slammed through three more songs. They left the crowd drained and deafened and no one envied the headliners. That same night at a different club in London, the Sex Pistols played with a brand new band as their opening act. That band was the Clash.

Then on this date, July 5th, 1976, the Ramones played at the Roundhouse again and this time they were received like royalty. Members of the Sex Pistols, the Clash and the Damned were in attendance at this show and got to meet the Ramones. The night has taken on mythical importance in the history of rock and the stories sometimes seem extraordinary. There is one that has Johnny Rotten climbing up knotted bed sheets to get into the club and another has members of the Clash sneaking in a backstage door. There's also the great quote from Johnny Ramone, encouraging the Clash by telling them: "Look, we suck. We can't play. But don't worry about it, just do it." If any of these are not true, they ought to be.

The punk scene in London was set ablaze by the experience. In less than a year the Clash, the Sex Pistols and the Damned all released their debut recordings. Punk would prove to be a short-lived phenomenon but its elements went on to have huge effects on music, specifically the new wave scene of the eighties and the grunge movement a decade later. And while prog rock and soft rock continued on, punk rockers drew the line in the sand and said "enough!" Let's get back to basics and play something hard and fast.

## July 6th

On this date in 2002, Nelly's "Hot in Herre" was in the middle of a seven week run atop the pop chart. It not only served as Nelly's first #1 but also became the first chart-topping single for the song's producers, Pharrell Williams and Chad Hugo, who called themselves the Neptunes.

Cornell Iral Haynes Jr. was born in 1974 in Austin, Texas but he moved with his mother to St.Louis when he was still a young kid. And that's an important part of Nelly's history. He's from St Louis. He's proud of it. And he wants you to know that.

While he was still in high school, Nelly formed a hip hop group called St Lunatics (get it?) and though they had some local success they failed to land a major record label deal so Nelly started making solo demos and was signed by Universal Music Group. In the late nineties the hip hop world still centered around the East Coast - West Coast feud so Universal used Nelly's Midwest upbringing as his hook. Indeed Nelly's rap style is unique because of his twang and drawl, a fact he promoted by naming his debut album *Country Grammar*. That debut was released in June of 2002 and produced three Top 20 singles, the title track which climbed to #7, "E.I." which peaked at #16 and "Ride wit It" which made it all the way to #3. On the title track of *Country Grammar* Nelly rapped, "I'm from the Lou and I'm proud" and indeed the city embraced him as well.

Around the same time that Nelly was producing his debut LP, Pharrell Williams and Chad Hugo were gaining popularity as a production team called the Neptunes. They'd gained a reputation in the late nineties working with Kelis, Ol' Dirty Bastard and Jay-Z before scoring their biggest hit to date with Britney Spear's 2001 single "I'm a Slave 4 You." As Nelly started working on his follow-up album, he reached out to Williams and Hugo and they decided to work together on a track. The Neptunes have become known for their incredible beats and "Hot in Herre" is an early example of this. Nelly says, when they were recording the song, Busta Rhymes was in an adjacent studio and he came in asking: "What is that sound?!!?!? Oh my, God! Pharrell, where was that beat at? You were hiding that from me!"

"Hot in Herre" became the lead single for Nelly's second album, *Nellyville*, and it did exactly what a lead single should do. Dropped in April of 2002, two months before the album's release, "Hot in Herre" rose steadily up the charts and hit #1 the week *Nellyville* came out. "Hot in Herre" enjoyed a seven week stay at the top of the charts, eventually being replaced by *Nellyville*'s second single "Dilemma." That song, which featured vocals from Destiny's Child's Kelly Rowland, enjoyed an identical seven week stay at #1 on the *Billboard* Hot 100 chart. The summer of 2002 was the Summer of Nelly.

"Hot in Herre" begins with two quick samples (Neil Young's "There's a World" and Nancy Sinatra's "As Tears Go By") before settling into a groove sampled and looped from Chuck Brown's 1979 single "Bustin' Loose." Nelly also repeats the line, "I feel like bustin' loose," from that same song paying obvious respect to the original. "Hot in Herre" helped revive interest in Chuck Brown's work as the "Godfather of Go-Go Music," which is very popular in the D.C. area. The extra "r" in the title of "Hot in Herre" is yet another homage to St. Louis and the thick accent used "thurr." Chingy (who is also from St. Louis) did the same with his 2003 hit "Right Thurr" explaining, "That's just how we talk." Christina Aguilera (not from St. Louis) hopped on the extra "r" bandwagon with her song "Dirrty." After watching that video no one seemed to mind that she was carpetbagging. Nelly also mentions his producers in the lyrics, rapping, "Nelly took a trip from the Lunner to Neptune."

Though Nelly has never been able to match his 2002 success he has enjoyed a long and rich career both in music and in movies and television. His catch phrase has long been, "Don't forget where you came from" and based on his numerous philanthropic endeavors in and around St.Louis he clearly never has.

## July 7th

On this date in 1977, Styx released their seventh album, *Grand Illusion*. Yes, you read that correctly. Styx released their 7th LP on 7/7/77. And the numerology proved to be lucky for the band. *Grand Illusion* would be their breakthrough album after years of flirting with superstardom. And a song inspired by that very struggle would help propel them into the stratosphere. Here's the story:

The band that would become Styx began in Chicago in the early sixties when a 14 year old Dennis DeYoung started hanging out with two neighbors, Chuck and John Panozzo, who were twins. They formed a band called Tradewinds that would eventually morph into Styx. They signed a contract in the early seventies with an independent label from the Windy City called Wooden Nickel Records. They released five albums on Wooden Nickel to moderate success. The band was by no means failing but they hadn't exactly hit it big yet either. Their unique mix of hard rock with progressive rock elements was finding an audience, just not a huge one. Even with a Top 10 hit (1973's "Lady") Styx still found themselves as an opening act or playing in smaller clubs. The big time was within reach but they just hadn't gotten there yet. In 1975 they signed with A&M Records and their first release with them was more of the same; other than a loyal following in Chicago, they'd yet to really make it big.

All of this was on Dennis DeYoung's mind when he sat down to write a song for the band's seventh album. He was thinking of the struggle to make it. The determination to not give up. He channeled some sailing imagery as well as some religious themes and came up with a song called "Come Sail Away." The song starts simply and slowly with DeYoung on piano and singing about how he's got to be free. Slowly the band joins in and when DeYoung sings about missing out on the pot of gold you can almost hear his pain. But he promises to try, the best that he can, and that's when the song takes an upbeat turn. "Come Sail Away" not only takes flight musically but lyrically as well. There are gatherings of angels and a starship and then one of the trippiest breakdowns in recorded music. The song is six minutes of euphoric progressive rock and Styx suspected it was going to be the song to break them.

But they had a problem. A six minute problem. Sure there had been some longer songs by this point to get released as singles and be successful but those were few and far between and often by artists that had a hit-making track record. Styx needed a breakthrough song, and they didn't want a bunch of program directors to pass on their latest release because it didn't fit into their format. So they edited their song. They cut it down by half and released a three minute version to pop radio. Though this edit helped them it is anathema to any Styx or prog rock fan. "Come Sail Away" is six minutes of pure musical mastery. Its edited single climaxes too soon and eliminates the breakdown that literally takes the listener into orbit.

"Come Sail Away" became the hit the band needed. It helped propel *Grand Illusion* to #6 on the *Billboard* album chart and produced two Top 40 hits, "Come Sail Away" which made it all the way to #8 and "Fooling Yourself (Angry Young Man)" which peaked at #29. With momentum behind them, Styx would go on to incredible success over the next few years with Top 10 albums like *Pieces of Eight, Cornerstone, Paradise Theater* and *Kilroy Was Here* and their lone #1 hit, 1979's "Babe."

DeYoung had channeled his frustration for not making it big, and his hope that the band still could, with "Come Sail Away." And in doing so he created an all-time classic progressive rock song that helped Styx take flight. It's worth cranking this one up today but please, play the album version. Don't cheat yourself and climax too early.

On this date in 1967, the Beatles' *Sgt. Pepper's Lonely Hearts Club Band* began its second week at #1 on the *Billboard* album chart. The LP would spend a total of 15 weeks at #1 in the U.S. and an even more amazing 27 weeks at the top in the U.K. The album won four Grammy Awards, including Album of the Year, becoming the first rock LP to receive that honor. *Time* magazine declared *Sgt. Pepper's Lonely Hearts Club Band,* "a historic departure in the progress of music."

In 1966, the Beatles permanently retired from touring and become a full-time studio band. They began work on what would become *Sgt. Pepper's* in November of that year. They would spend four painstaking months trying to complete the album. Along the way, due to pressure from their record label, they released "Strawberry Fields Forever" and "Penny Lane" as a double A-side single in February of 1967. These songs, which had originally been planned for the album were pulled and replaced.

It was Paul McCartney, after recording the song "Sgt. Pepper's Lonely Hearts Club Band," who suggested that the band should craft the entire album as if it were recorded by the fictional Sgt. Pepper band. This alter ego, he theorized, would give them the freedom to experiment musically. McCartney felt the band, to a man, were burnt out and tired of their new-found fame and perhaps pretending they were someone else for a spell might spur their creative juices.

There is no doubt that the Beatles were also inspired by, and perhaps motivated to top, the Beach Boys' 1966 album *Pet Sounds* with its experimental, psychedelic sound. The Beatles' producer, George Martin, has said, "Without *Pet Sounds, Sgt. Pepper* never would have happened."

To appreciate *Peppers'* impact one must also know something about 1967 and specifically the Summer of Love. The counter-culture, flower-power movement was in full bloom. Hippies everywhere from San Francisco to Greenwich Village to London believed they were ushering in a new generation, a bohemian paradise with acid rock as the soundtrack and psychedelic drugs as the key to new levels of consciousness. The era's zeitgeist created fertile ground for the world's biggest band to release their most experimental project. *Sgt. Peppers* was the perfect album at the perfect time.

The last song on *Sgt. Peppers,* "A Day in the Life," is the masterful coda to the entire collection. As recently as a few years prior, Lennon and McCartney were writing songs, as Lennon once described "eyeball to eyeball." But things had changed by 1967 and "A Day in the Life" is a perfect example of how much. The song actually consists of two partial songs by each songwriter that the band and Martin wove together in the studio. Lennon, a voracious reader of newspapers, wrote the opening two verses (beginning with, "I read the news today, oh boy"), cobbling together bits and pieces of stories he'd recently seen. When he presented it in the studio as an unfinished song, McCartney offered a short piano piece he had been working on with lyrics about a commuter whose uneventful morning routine leads him to drift off into a dream. He also contributed the line that got the song banned from radio: "I'd love to turn you on."

Lennon then wrote the song's final verse inspired by another news story, this one about potholes. To complete the song a 41 piece orchestra was brought in and told to start playing the lowest note of their instruments and gradually play to the highest, thus creating the amazing 24 bar crescendo that ends with that famous, single, piano chord. That chord was produced by all four Beatles and George Martin banging on three pianos simultaneously. As the sound diminished, the engineer boosted the faders. The resulting note lasts 42 seconds. The studio air conditioners can be heard toward the end as the faders were pushed to the limit to record it. David Crosby was at Abbey Road studios when the Beatles were finalizing the song. He has since said: "I was, as near as I know, the first human being besides them and George Martin and the engineers to hear 'A Day in the Life.' I was high as a kite ... They sat me down; they had huge speakers like coffins with wheels on that they rolled up on either side of the stool. By the time it got to the end of that piano chord my brains were on the floor."

Most people, high as a kite or not, had a similar reaction the first time they heard *Sgt. Peppers* and that ending masterpiece, "A Day in the Life." And as awesome as the album is, music lovers will always wonder how much better it could have been if EMI hadn't insisted on a single in the winter of 1967 or if the Beatles had given them something other than "Strawberry Fields Forever" and "Penny Lane." It's hard to imagine improving *Sgt. Pepper's Lonely Hearts Club Band* but those two songs may have done it.


### July 9th

On this date in 1974, Frank Zappa's *Apostrophe (')* had begun sliding down the *Billboard* album chart after peaking at #10 the week before. Zappa had been releasing music for just eight years by this point yet this was already his eighteenth album. In a career that would span almost thirty years and feature over 60 albums this would be his highest-charting LP.

Frank Zappa was born in Baltimore, Maryland in late 1940. As a teenager, as rock and roll was exploding onto the scene, Zappa developed a keen interest in modern classical music. If that seems a little curious, it's a good introduction to Zappa's life and career. He never followed the norms and was wildly unpredictable as an artist and musician. And while those traits ensured Frank Zappa would remain on the margins of popular music, they also earned him an avid following of fans and critics who always looked forward to whatever mind-bending sounds Zappa had in store for his next release. And due to his incredible fecundity they never had to wait too long.

Frank Zappa had other musical interests to be sure. He loved R&B and some early rock and roll and when he dropped out of college after just one semester he decided to try to make a living in music by producing and composing. His first paid gigs were writing the scores for two low budget films which allowed him to tap into his love of classical music. But Zappa was never going to have a straight career in any specific genre and his passion for the absurd and avant-garde was apparent when he made his first television appearance, earning a slot on *The Steve Allen Show* where he appeared as a "musical bicyclist" and did indeed play the bike by plucking and running a bow over its spokes and blowing into its handlebars like a flute. It's a clip worth finding on Youtube for its humor as well as an early introduction to the artist that Zappa was well on his way to becoming. When he tells the band, "Try to refrain from musical tone" it tells you everything you need to know about Frank Zappa. He was more interested in experimentation or what the French call musique concrète. Keep in mind this is years before psychedelic rock would become an actual genre and Zappa was already stretching the boundaries of music and sound.

In 1965, Frank Zappa was asked to join a band called the Soul Giants. He did and quickly became their lead lyricist and singer. He encouraged them to change their name, which they did, to the Mothers. More than likely mothers was short for motherfuckers, a common term at the time for a talented musician. When the Mothers were signed to Verve by none other than producer Tom Wilson (he of Bob Dylan and Simon & Garfunkel fame) they were asked to change their name which is how they became the Mothers of Invention. Their debut album, *Freak Out*, was released in 1966 and it immediately established the band, and Frank Zappa specifically, as an important new leader in avant-garde music. And it wasn't just their recordings that were stretching the boundaries of sound. Their live shows, which featured improvised acts and audience participation in between the occasional song or two, were also becoming more performance art than actual concerts.

In late 1971, Zappa suffered two tragedies in the space of a week. On December 4th he was playing at the Casino de Montreux in Switzerland when a fan fired a flare gun in the arena that started a fire. The casino was burned down along with all of the band's equipment (a moment Deep Purple immortalized in their song "Smoke on the Water"). Then, just a week later, while playing with rented gear in London, a fan pushed Zappa off the stage. His bandmates looked down to see his body twisted and bleeding and they thought he was dead. Zappa, in fact, survived the fall but was wheel-chair bound for over a year and an injury to his larynx forced him to switch to a deeper, huskier vocal delivery.

In early 1974 Zappa released *Apostrophe (')* as a solo effort. The album follows a common theme in which Zappa dreamt he was an eskimo named Nanook. Its opening track "Don't Eat the Yellow Snow" became Zappa's first single to crack the *Billboard* Hot 100 and the LP peaked at #10 in the album chart.

Frank Zappa would continue producing and releasing music at a furious rate and though most of his albums and songs never gained much fame, they always attracted an avid audience that loved his sense of humor and adventure. In 1990 he was diagnosed with inoperable prostate cancer. He fought the disease for three years, ultimately passing away just shy of his 53rd birthday. His family announced his death by saying he'd, "left for his final tour." After all those years of experimenting and testing the boundaries of sound, as well satirizing anyone and everything, that was the perfect sendoff for Frank Zappa.

## July 10th

On this date in 1976, the Starland Vocal Band started a two week run at #1 on the pop chart with "Afternoon Delight." It would prove to be their only hit which means the Starland Vocal Band is often considered one of the original "one hit wonders" and by earning the Grammy for Best New Artist they were also early victims of that jinx. Still, their one big song is a timeless and well-loved classic of innocent innuendo.

The Starland Vocal Band (which included the married couple Bill and Taffy Danoff) were from Washington D.C. where they often frequented a restaurant named Clyde's of Georgetown. Clyde's had a happy hour appetizer menu called Afternoon Delight. The band fully admits they took (or is it stole?) the title of their song from that menu. In fact, in concert, Taffy would often introduce the song by mentioning the menu, adding, "Then Bill came home and we had our own afternoon delight." After the laugher from that line would subside she'd add, "we wrote the song instead of having a cigarette."

Clearly, the song's not-so-subtle double entendre is no accident. As Bill Danoff explains, "I didn't want to write an all-out sex song ... I just wanted to write something that was fun and hinted at sex." Their attempts at "hinting at sex" are comical (everything from, "Rubbin' sticks and stones together" to, "You've got some bait a waitin' and I think I might try a bite") as well as endearing. Indeed, if you compare "Afternoon Delight" to some of today's songs, where hinting has been replaced by blatant vulgarity at times, "Afternoon Delight" does have a timeless sense to it. It gives mid-day nookie a nice warm feeling as well as a great visual (those "sky rockets in flight").

"Afternoon Delight" was released as the first single for the Starland Vocal Band in April, 1976 and on this date it climbed to #1. The band's eponymous debut album made it to #20. The band parlayed their new-found fame into a television show, hosting a variety show on CBS throughout the summer of 1977. Among its staff of writers and performers was a thirty year old David Lettermen who had recently left his job as a weatherman in Indianapolis to move to Los Angeles to see if he could make it in show business.

None of the Starland Vocal Band's other albums would break the Top #100 and none of their other singles would break the Top #40. In fact, if you can even name another Starland Vocal Band song you should probably book yourself on *Jeopardy!* right now.

The term "one hit wonder" did not become popular until about a decade after the Starland Vocal Band's one big hit, and attempts to define the term have always been loose and casual. Some think it should mean any band that has just one Top 40 hit to its credit while others have a broader definition of the term. And while some use it derogatorily, there are certainly millions of bands who never even had one hit who would gladly accept the designation. Any list with the heading "One Hit Wonder" is sure to included the Starland Vocal Band.

Besides being an original one hit wonder, the Starland Vocal Band are also cited as one of the original bands to suffer from the "Grammy for Best New Artist Curse." They won the award (beating out Boston) and, as Bill Danoff says, "That was basically the kiss of death and I feel sorry for everyone who's gotten it since." There are plenty of exceptions to the curse (the Beatles won the award in 1965 and they did alright for themselves) but when you scan the list of past winners you can get a little overwhelmed by how many of them failed to live up to the promise that award inferred. Especially when you see who they beat out. A Taste of Honey winning over the Cars and Elvis Costello in 1979 is a great example.

"Afternoon Delight" has enjoyed a rich history in pop culture, quoted and featured in movies and TV shows including Will Ferrell (in his Ron Burgundy character) saying, "If you don't think this song is the greatest song ever, I will fight you" in the *Anchorman* DVD before the cast performs the song. Oh, and to this day, Clyde's of Georgetown has a gold record of the song hanging in their bar. One hit wonder or not, the Starland Vocal Band turned their Happy Hour menu into a timeless classic.

## July 11th

On this date in 1965, the Rolling Stones' "(I Can't Get No) Satisfaction" had just arrived at #1 on the *Billboard* Hot 100 chart where it would reside for the next month. Nothing would ever be the same again for the band from London. They were no longer riding on the Beatles' coattails; they were now bonafide hitmakers in their own right. And it all started with a dream.

The story behind the opening riff of "(I Can't Get No) Satisfaction" is rock and roll legend. On May 6th, 1965, the band played a show in Clearwater, Florida that was cut short when a number of young fans got into an altercation with the police on the scene. This type of thing was not unheard of for the Stones but the band was still upset by the situation and guitarist Keith Richards remembers going to sleep that night agitated at the events. Hours later, he woke up from a deep sleep with a riff, and the line, "I can't get no satisfaction" in his head. He used to sleep with his guitar and a recorder next to his bed for exactly these moments of inspiration so he immediately hit record and started playing the riff. According to Richards, he played it a few times and then fell back asleep. The next morning he listened back and heard about two minutes of guitar, "then me snoring for the next forty minutes." Unfortunately, that tape has been lost to history.

At first Richards thought the riff was too similar to "Dancing in the Streets" and he was afraid he'd nicked it from that song. But when he brought it to his bandmates they convinced him it was unique. Richards then thought the opening would sound better done with horns but when they ran his guitar through a fuzzbox (a fairly new invention at the time) he was happy with it. However, when Otis Redding released a cover of the song later in 1965 (using horns for the opening) Richards claimed he preferred that version. Despite his feelings about it, Richard's guitar opening for "Satisfaction" is, without question, one of the most famous and recognizable opening riffs in rock history.

Mick Jagger penned most of the lyrics for "(I Can't Get No) Satisfaction," channeling what he saw as over-commercialization in America. This was the band's third trip to the States in less than a year so Jagger was clearly seeing the difference between England and the U.S. Exactly a month after Richards dreamt the riff, the song was completed and released as a single. Despite the fact that Richards didn't think much of the song ("I thought it was album-filler," he has said) "Satisfaction" made a quick climb up the pop chart and hit #1 on July 10th, 1965.

Having a #1 single changed everything for the Stones. Jagger has said: "It was the song that really made the Rolling Stones, changed us from just another band into a huge, monster band... It has a very catchy title. It has a very catchy guitar riff. It has a great guitar sound, which was original at that time. And it captures a spirit of the times, which is very important in those kinds of songs... which was alienation."

"(I Can't Get No) Satisfaction" began an incredible run for the Rolling Stones and within a few years they were as a big a band as any on the planet. And since their closest rivals, the Beatles, had stopped touring, there was no one who could compare to the excitement the Stones generated every time they toured. Richards and Jagger eventually even found some satisfaction.

### July 12th

On this date in 1979, the Chicago White Sox held the second worst Major League Baseball promotional night ever (first place goes to the Cleveland Indians and their "10 Cent Beer Night." Google it.) The evening was promoted as the "Disco Demolition Night" by the White Sox in conjunction with 97.9 WLUP and their morning man, Steve Dahl. The "demolition" would consist of blowing up some disco records that fans brought to the stadium. It was supposed to take place during the break between games of a doubleheader. When all was said and done the second game couldn't be played and the White Sox lost by forfeit. By 1979 many in the country were sick of disco. In a few short years the musical genre had gone from underground, to popular to über-ubiquitous. Everywhere you turned or listened you saw and heard the disco fashions and beats. Even artists who had nothing to do with disco were hopping on the bandwagon and producing songs with a "four on the floor" beat and disco-type hook. Everyone, from Rod Stewart with "Do Ya Think I'm Sexy" to KISS with "I Was Made For Loving You," was making dance records. But the biggest slap in the face to rock fans was when the Rolling Stones released "Miss You" – not only as a 7" single but as a 12" dance record. Something had to be done.

That something started as a saying. The term "Disco Sucks" became pervasive. You saw it on tee-shirts and bumper stickers. And by the summer of 1979 the disco backlash was in full force. Which made the mood particularly ripe for Steve Dahl's big idea.

Dahl had been fired by a Chicago radio station, WDAI, in late 1978 when they switched from a rock format to a disco format. Though he quickly landed on his feet, taking over the morning shift at WLUP, his bitterness towards disco remained. He constantly mocked his old station on air and even recorded a parody of "Da Ya Think I'm Sexy?" which he called "Do You Think I'm Disco?" Then, he got his best (some would say worst) idea. And when he approached the White Sox with it, they were all ears. They were in the middle of bad season (they'd finish 14 games under .500 in 1979) and attendance was down. Too, their owner, Bill Veek, was known to try some unique promotional ideas to keep fans interested. He is quoted as saying, "You can draw more people with a losing team plus bread and circuses than with a losing team and a long, still silence."

Dahl pitched the promotion as a way to create an event to "end disco once and for all." The White Sox offered tickets for 98 cents (WLUP's location on the dial was 97.9) to anyone who brought a disco record with them to the ballpark. They expected to get a bump in the usual 15,000 or so fans they were drawing every night. Instead, close to 50,000 fans paid to get in and once the game was declared a sellout many more jumped the turnstiles. The Sox didn't even have enough man-power to collect all the records so many fans brought them to their seats. As game one played on, with the visiting Detroit Tigers ahead, it became obvious very few fans were there for baseball. Records soared through the air like frisbees (along with bottles and firecrackers) which became so dangerous Tigers' outfielder Rusty Staub urged his teammates to wear their battling helmets in the field. The smell of pot was so evident White Sox broadcaster Harry Caray mentioned it on air.

After the first game, a large box (rigged with explosives) was brought to centerfield. Steve Dahl, dressed in army fatigues and a helmet, emerged and started working the crowd into a frenzy with a "Disco Sucks!" chant. Then Dahl announced, "This is now officially the world's largest anti-disco rally," as he detonated the box of records. The explosion was so massive it burned a large hole in the outfield grass. It also ignited a riot. Fans stormed the field and began tearing up chunks of sod. Carey made announcements to get people back to their seats and the scoreboard flashed signs urging for calm. Even Dahl got on on the microphone and asked fans to vacate the field. But it was all to no avail. Chicago police in full riot gear arrived and 39 people were arrested for disorderly conduct. White Sox groundskeepers spent an hour clearing debris and trying to patch the grass but Tigers manager Sparky Anderson refused to allow his players to take the field given its condition. When they announced that game two would be postponed (it was later forfeited by the home team) hardly anyone in attendance seemed to mind.

Disco didn't die that night but it had taken a fatal blow especially in the pop culture arena. Dahl would say later: "Disco was probably on its way out. But I think Disco Demolition Night hastened its demise," which is probably the most accurate assessment of the evening. The genre that only a few years earlier was heard strictly in the nightclubs, retreated back to those very same clubs. It was renamed (because the word disco was verboten) to "club" or just simply "dance" and as technological advances like the drum machine and synthesizer became more prevalent the sound would morph into house and techno and electronica. None of these have ever reached the pop culture heights that disco did which is why they have avoided their own Demolition Night.

## July 13th

On this date in 1985, one of the most ambitious and successful benefit concerts in the history of rock took place on "both sides of the pond." Live Aid, which sought to raise money for famine relief in Ethiopia, was a dual-venue effort, with shows in London and Philadelphia. Over 170,000 people attended the two shows and almost 2 billion tuned in to watch the live broadcast. When it was all said and done, the show raised over $125 million in famine relief.

Live Aid was organized by Boomtown Rats lead singer Bob Geldof and Scottish singer Midge Ure who had previously organized the Band Aid project which produced the song "Do They Know Its Christmas?" As the story goes, Geldof was so moved one day when he saw footage of Ethiopians starving to death on BBC that he called his friend Ure and said, "We have to do something!" The two quickly wrote a song and then got their music industry friends involved to have it recorded. Geldof had seen the footage in October of 1984 and "Do They Know Its Christmas?" was out (and raising money) by that December.

At a Culture Club concert on December 22nd, 1984 at Wembley Stadium the band was joined on stage by a few other members of Band Aid (Culture Club's lead singer Boy George had sang on the song) for an encore of "Do They Know It's Christmas?" George was so moved by the experience he began talking about doing a benefit concert. Geldof and Ure once again went to work.

In January Geldof gave an interview to *Melody Maker* magazine that shows he was already dreaming big about the concert and planning the logistics. "The show should be as big as humanly possible," Geldof said. "There's no point in just 5,000 fans turning up at Wembley; we need to have Wembley linked with Madison Square Garden and the whole show to be televised worldwide. It would be great for Duran to play three or four numbers at Wembley and then flick to

Madison Square where Springsteen would be playing. While he's on, the Wembley stage could be made ready for the next British act like the Thompsons or whoever. In that way lots of acts could be featured and the television rights, tickets and so on could raise a phenomenal amount of money." He finished by saying, "It's not an impossible idea, and certainly one worth exploiting." Months later as plans took shape some of what Geldof predicted would come to fruition while some would not (most notably Springsteen's involvement). Live Aid did indeed take place on two stages, Wembley Stadium in the U.K. and JFK Stadium in Philadelphia. The show started at noon in England (7am EST) and went till 11pm in Philadelphia. The 16 hour concert featured more than 75 performances including a disappointing Led Zeppelin reunion and a transcendent set by Queen. The live crowd was 170,000 strong (70,000 at Wembley and 100,000 in Philadelphia) and over 40 countries broadcast the concert and held telethons to raise money. Despite all that, when Geldof heard how much was being raised during the day he became irritated and during an interview on the BBC he looked into the camera and said, "Give us your fucking money!"

Phil Collins decided he wanted to perform at both shows so he did an early set in England, hopped on the Concorde and flew across the Atlantic. Cher happened to be on his flight and when they got to talking she apparently knew nothing about the concert. Collins convinced her to show up in Philadelphia which she did and she took place in the finale. In Philadelphia, Collins did another solo set, played drums for Clapton and then was one of the drummers for the disastrous set by Led Zeppelin.

Led Zeppelin hadn't played together since John Bonham's passing in 1980. They decided to reunite for Live Aid using guest drummers and the resulting show (which featured just three songs, "Rock and Roll", "Whole Lotta Love" and "Stairway to Heaven") was universally panned. It started with technical problems and a hoarse Robert Plant hitting some sour notes. It went downhill from there. Jimmy Page blamed Collins, saying: "He didn't know anything. We played 'Whole Lotta Love', and he was just there bashing away cluelessly and grinning." Collins defended himself saying: "Robert wasn't match-fit with his voice and Jimmy was out of it, dribbling. It wasn't my fault it was crap. If I could have walked off, I would have. But then we'd all be talking about why Phil Collins walked off Live Aid." Plant doesn't lay blame but he did recap the experience by saying it was, "a fucking atrocity for us. ... It made us look like loonies." Led Zeppelin was so unhappy with their performance they refused to give permission to include it when the Live Aid DVD was put together (although you can find some clips on Youtube if you need to verify just how bad they were.)

On the positive side, most viewers and critics agree Queen's set (in which they squeezed 6 songs into just under 25 minutes) was the highlight of the concert. Lead singer Freddie Mercury, ever the showman, was everywhere, playing the piano for the opening of "Bohemian Rhapsody," prancing around with his sawed-off mic stand and generally owning the stage. When they ended their set, Elton John, who was yet to perform, said to them, "You bastards, you stole the show!"

There were fundraising concerts before Live Aid and there have been plenty since (including a Live Aid reboot in 2005 called Live 8) but no concert has ever brought together more talent across multiple continents for a single cause. And it all started with Bob Geldof being moved by a news report of starving people in Ethiopia.

## July 14th

On this date in 1977, New York City was waking up to a disaster. The night before, during a bad storm, lightning had struck an electrical substation on the Hudson River and the entire city was plunged into darkness. New York was already suffering through a horrible summer, with the economy in decline, rampant crime and the city gripped with fear by the Son of Sam murders. The Blackout of '77 caused widespread vandalism and looting, especially in the poorest sections of the city. On the morning of July 14th most of New York was still without electricity and as day broke the destruction became evident. You may ask yourself how this could be an excerpt in a book about music. Read on.

In the early seventies an urban movement was developing in the Bronx (one of New York City's five boroughs). DJs were setting up equipment at house parties or in outdoors parks. But they weren't just spinning records like in the clubs, they were manipulating the music by going back and forth between two songs, often two copies of the same record, focusing on the breaks in those songs; the sections where most of the melody and instrumentation drops out and the song is reduced to just a beat, often played by the drummer and bassist. Many of James Brown's records featured long, drawn out breaks and they were popular with these early DJs. DJ Kool Herc, a Jamaican born turntablist is often credited for creating this technique and it's helped earn him the title of "Father of Hip Hop." While the DJ spun what became known as "breakbeats" some people would dance in a very athletic and aggressive manner, often spinning on their heads or diving down on the ground and pushing themselves back up by one arm. This style soon became known as breakdancing. Also during these breaks, sometimes an MC would take the microphone and rhyme in a fast, rhythmic patter. Afrika Bambaattaa was another early and influential DJ in the Bronx. His goal, he said, was to get kids away from the violence of gangs by getting them involved in music. He called his followers the Universal Zulu Nation and announced the "Four Elements" of this new movement: DJing, breakdancing, graffiti and MCing. And early on, that was the order of importance. MCing, what would soon become known as rapping, was just one of the pillars of this culture, and nowhere near the main focus.

This movement spread, little by little, from the Bronx to other inner-city sections of New York in Brooklyn and Queens. But it was slow in developing mainly because not everyone could participate. Besides the talent involved, to produce a true street party you needed turntables, a mixer, a microphone and big speakers and amps; equipment that was not readily available especially in the impoverished sections of New York. It's been theorized that the looting following the blackout, during which plenty of professional sound equipment was stolen along with TVs and couches, broke this threshold and opened the doors for a lot of new talent. Grandmaster Caz, who was another early and influential artist from the Bronx, agrees with this theory. He has been quoted as saying: "During the looting, everybody stole turntables and stuff. Every electronics store imaginable got hit. Every record store. Before that blackout, you had maybe five legitimate crews of DJs. After the blackout, you had a DJ on every block. It made a big spark in the hip hop revolution." Whether it was the influx of new equipment or not, the timeline of rap's history seems to support this theory.

Prior to 1977 there were indeed just a few rappers in New York City and nobody was making records or attempting to sell their music. But things started gaining momentum in '77 and '78 as the MCs themselves started becoming bigger names than the DJs. Kurtis Blow was one of the first rappers to emerge and, with the help of Russell Simmons who became his manager, would become the first rapper to land a record deal when he signed with Mercury in 1979. Grandmaster Flash, who was one of the early and influential DJs on the scene, teamed with five rappers to form Grand Master and the Furious Five and they too signed a record contract in 1979 and were soon tabbed by the Clash to be their opening act. 1979 also saw the founding of Sugar Hill Records, a label started with the sole intention of recording and releasing rap artists. The new label's first release, the Sugarhill Gang's "Rapper's Delight," became the first hip hop hit, peaking at #36 on the *Billboard* Hot 100 chart in January of 1980. "Rapper's Delight" is also credited for giving rap its other name as many record buyers walked into stores asking for, "the new song that goes, 'hip hop.'"

In just a few short years, rap had grown from the streets and parks of New York City to a burgeoning new musical genre that was starting to get noticed. It would, of course, eventually dominate the world of music and pop culture. It probably would have happened anyway, but one of the darkest nights (pun intended) in New York City's history may have been the catalyst that set the wheels in motion. At least that's one theory that's been floated by one of the earliest rappers on the scene.

## July 15th

On this date in 1969, the zoning board of the town of Wallkill in upstate New York voted to ban the upcoming Woodstock Music & Art Fair. It was exactly a month till the beginning of the three day concert and for the third time, the organizers were forced to scramble and find a new location.

John Roberts, Joel Rosenman, Michael Lang and Artie Kornfeld had formed a partnership in January of 1969 titled "Woodstock Ventures" to produce a three day concert. Initially Kornfeld and Lang had wanted to open a recording studio in Woodstock, New York and approached Roberts and Rosenman to see if they'd be interested in investing. Roberts was heir to the Polident fortune and he and Rosenman were looking for investment ideas. They'd recently placed an advertisement in *The Wall Street Journal* identifying themselves as, "young men with unlimited capital." Part of Kornfeld and Lang's pitch about the studio included a music festival to help promote its launch. Lang had some experience organizing music festivals; he'd helped produce the Miami Pop Festival in 1968 which had 25,000 attendees. Roberts and Rosenman narrowed in on that idea and soon the studio was put aside and discussions centered on a weekend long concert. An agreement was struck with Roberts bankrolling Woodstock Ventures.

Initially Woodstock, New York was chosen for its hippie vibe. Bob Dylan had settled into the area and a steady stream of musicians (Jimi Hendrix, Eric Clapton and George Harrison to name a few) were spending time there. Local residents very quickly shut down the idea of a large concert taking place in their community though and the four organizers set about finding a suitable location. They thought they had that in nearby Suagerties but again the locals made a stink and the town shut down the plans. Throughout the spring of 1969, Woodstock Ventures was selling tickets for a three day concert in upstate New York that would take place from August 15th through the 17th, even though the organizers hadn't yet secured a location. Finally, they found a spot, leasing the Mills Industrial Park in Wallkill, for $10,000 and even adding the town's name to the posters they were distributing to market their concert. But yet again, local residents began to grumble and object. It was becoming increasingly obvious that the conservative towns north of New York City did not want to be overrun by hippies.

For over a month Lang, Roberts, Rosenman and Kornfeld moved forward securing bands (Creedence Clearwater Revival was the first major act to sign on) and even beginning construction of the staging at the site in Wallkill. But the people of the town continued to protest and finally an emergency meeting of the town's zoning board was called. They voted to block the concert on this date in 1969. Exactly one month before the show was to begin.

As devastating as this was for Woodstock Ventures and their upcoming festival, news reports of the ban proved to be good publicity. A number of different locations were offered and soon they selected Max Yasgur's farm in Bethel, New York. Despite even more opposition from the locals (including signs around town saying, "Buy No Milk. Stop Max's Hippy Music Festival"), Bethel approved the permits and finally a location was set for the upcoming, weekend-long concert. The organizers would have just a few weeks to get everything in place which is one of the reasons for the chaotic atmosphere that led up to the show. When everyone involved realized that there was no time to complete all the construction that had been planned, they decided to stop building the fences around the property and focus instead on building the stage. Three days before the show was scheduled to start, when thousands of attendees began arriving and simply walking through the open gaps in the fencing, the organizers decided to just make the festival free for everyone. Woodstock Ventures was nearly bankrupted from the festival and would not show a profit until the following year when a documentary film and soundtrack were released.

On this date in 1966, the Beach Boys' eleventh album, *Pet Sounds*, had already begun its descent down the *Billboard* LP chart. The album had peaked at #10, a modest showing for a band that was used to sending everything they released to, or near, the top. Yet rock historians often list *Pet Sounds* as one of the most groundbreaking and important records of all time. Here's the story behind a great American band and their seminal work.

Brian Wilson, the oldest of the three Wilson boys, grew up just south of Los Angeles in Hawthorne, California, fascinated by harmonies. As a teenager in the fifties he would listen to bands like the Four Freshmen and literally dissect what he was hearing. He'd then teach his family members (including his brothers and future bandmates Carl and Dennis) their own individual parts before recording them on the reel-to-reel recorder he got for his sixteenth birthday. Brian also met his cousin Mike Love at family functions and got him in on the singing.

The first band Wilson formed was called the Pendletones. The name was a play on the popular flannel shirt made by the Pendleton Woolen Mills that was a favorite among surfers at the time. They were already focusing on beach and surfing themes even though Dennis Wilson was the only avid surfer in the group. The first two songs Mike Love and Brian Wilson wrote together were "Surfin'" and "Surfin' Safari."

Brian's dad Murry Wilson was a songwriter and music producer and he arranged for the Pendletones to record both songs in October of 1961. Murry then brought the demo to Herb Newman, owner of Candix Records. Newman liked what he heard so he made an agreement to release both songs. Days later, when the first box of singles arrived the boys eagerly ripped it open, only to find the label had changed their name to the Beach Boys. When they questioned it they were told the label actually wanted to change their name to the Surfers but there was already a group with that name so they settled for the Beach Boys. Unfazed, "Surfin'" was released and sold well in the Southern California area, moving 40,000 units in just a few weeks. Soon enough Capitol signed the newly renamed Beach Boys and their first single for Capitol, "Surfin' Safari," went to #14 in the summer of 1962. Suddenly, the "California beach sound" or what would become known as "surf rock" was migrating east from its birthplace of Southern California.

For the first few years the Beach Boys seemed happy trading in this one genre and repeating surfing and beach themes. But as artists are wont to do, they matured. Specifically Brian Wilson, who not only aged but had his mind expanded when he started using psychedelic drugs. 1965's "California Girls" (which Wilson has said he wrote, "shortly after my first acid trip") was an early indication of the direction their sound was headed. They were still celebrating the Southern California vibe but in a much trippier way than ever before.

As Brian Wilson began working on what would become *Pet Sounds* a number of influences were at play. He had recently visited a Phil Spector recording session and became obsessed with Spector's signature "wall of sound." Also the Beatles had released *Rubber Soul* in December of 1965 and Wilson felt it was a great album with no filler songs. This was still a time in music when most artists aimed for successful singles, with albums often being a collection of songs that had been released as singles along with others deemed not good enough to make it on to a 45. Many musical historians point to *Rubber Soul* as one of the first albums that had a cohesive feel with no throwaway tracks. Certainly Brian Wilson did. He thought the Beatles had set a pretty high bar with *Rubber Soul* but he did not see it as insurmountable. He told his wife Marilyn, "I'm gonna make the greatest rock album ever made!" And finally there was Wilson's chance meeting with Tony Asher around the time. Asher was a young songwriter although his main successes to date had been jingles. But he and Wilson formed a fast friendship and when the Beach Boy told him he wanted to make an album that was "completely different" Asher agreed to collaborate.

Throughout late 1965 and the winter of 1966 Wilson and Asher wrote and recorded with little assistance from the rest of the band. They'd be called in from time to time to add their signature harmonies to some songs but while the list of guest musicians on *Pet Sounds* is a mile long there is nary any playing from the actual Beach Boys. It's for this reason that many consider *Pet Sounds* a solo Brian Wilson album. In fact, its lead single, "Caroline, No" was put out as a Brian Wilson, and not Beach Boys', song. This led to some inevitable in-fighting including the legendary moment when Mike Love blurted out in frustration, "Don't fuck with the formula." Love denies uttering the words, (he's called it "the most famous thing I ever said even though I never said it") but surely the feeling was there among Love and the band. And their record label as well. When Capitol heard the final tapes, with their experimental, psychedelia-infused sounds and weird effects they considered not releasing it.

While Love denies saying, "Don't fuck with the formula," another comment he made about the album not only hasn't been rebuked but gave the album its name. When Wilson played the tapes for Love he asked: "Who's gonna hear this shit? The dog's ears?" Wilson, who had already included a number of animal sounds in some of the songs, had his title.

While psychedelic rock predates *Pet Sounds*, it had remained on the margins of pop music throughout the early sixties. And though *Pet Sounds* sold disappointing numbers in the U.S., compared to previous Beach Boys' releases, it was by far the most popular album of the genre up to that point. The next few years would see an explosion of psychedelia in the rock world which many point to as the beginning of progressive rock as a genre. The Beatles readily admit that they were inspired by *Pet Sounds* when they sat down to work on *Sgt. Pepper's Lonely Hearts Club Band*, thus bringing the inspiration and competitiveness full circle between the two bands.

*Pet Sounds* became one of those albums that found appreciation in the years following its release. Sometimes that's how it is with great works of art. In 2003 when *Rolling Stone* polled a panel of artists, music journalists and producers to come up with their list of the "500 Greatest Albums of All Time," *Pet Sounds* wound up in second, right behind the Beatles' album it inspired. Perhaps its greatest influence is that *Pet Sounds* helped the rock world see albums as a more serious medium than singles. If the Beach Boys and the Beatles helped change that perception, within just a few years it was universally recognized in the rock world. The album opens with the Beach Boys signing in their timeless harmony, "Wouldn't it be nice if we were older." It's a simple song of innocence and yearning but perhaps Wilson was also thinking of rock and roll at the time. The genre itself was maturing and Wilson, who was at the forefront of some of that change, helped create one of its biggest catalysts with *Pet Sounds*. It's an album well worth revisiting today.

## July 17th

On this date in 1959, the short and tragic life of Billie Holiday came to an end. Despite having sold thousands of records and having performed to sold-out audiences, she was virtually broke. She was just 44 years old.

Eleanora Fagan was born in 1915 in Philadelphia. Her father, Clarence Holiday, left her mother, Sarah Fagan, shortly after her birth. Sarah was forced to take jobs on the road, leaving her young child in the care of friends or family members. When Eleanora was eleven, her mother returned home one day to find a neighbor attempting to rape her daughter. She was able to stop the attack. At twelve, Eleanora found work running errands in a brothel, which is where she heard her first jazz records, by the likes of Louis Armstrong and Bessie Smith.

Sarah and Eleanora moved from Philadelphia to Harlem where they both started working as prostitutes. Eleanora was only fourteen at the time. One day the brothel was raided and both mother and daughter wound up in jail.

Upon her release Eleanora began singing in clubs. She changed her name to Billie Holiday, Billie for Billie Dove, an actress she admired, and Holiday from her father's name. Her reputation grew quickly and she was able to get a lot of work in the late twenties and early thirties. At the time Harlem was a hotbed of jazz and there were clubs on just about every corner. Holiday made her recording debut at age 18 with Benny Goodman. Their record "Riffin' the Scotch" would become a minor hit, selling 5,000 copies and it gained her even more attention. She was becoming known for her unique style and phrasing as well as her ability to improvise, all traits that perfectly complimented the popular jazz sound of the day.

In 1935 Holiday signed her first record contract, with Brunswick Records. Her version of "What a Little Moonlight Can Do" sold well and furthered her reputation. In the next few years she had the opportunity to work with such jazz giants as Count Basie and Artie Shaw.

These larger bookings brought her out of the small jazz clubs of Harlem and into some of the larger ballrooms where, because of her skin color, she was often denied access to certain areas. "I was never allowed to visit the bar or the dining room as did other members of the band," she would lament. "I was made to leave and enter through the kitchen." When she toured the South, things were even worse and she was often the subject of racist taunts and heckling.

Her success continued well into the forties and she even landed a role in a major motion picture called *New Orleans* in which she starred with Louis Armstrong. But she was drinking heavily and even using heroin. In 1947 she was arrested for possession and spent almost a year in jail. After her release, because of her conviction, she was unable to get the necessary license to play in cabarets and clubs. She was arrested again in 1949 but this time earned an acquittal.

By the early fifties her health had deteriorated greatly from abuse. Her recordings from this time show the effects on her voice. It is rough and unable to project her former vibrancy. Still her career had some highlights, like the two concerts she played to a sold-out Carnegie Hall in 1956.

By 1959 Holiday had developed cirrhosis of the liver. On doctor's orders, she stopped drinking but soon relapsed. In late May she was hospitalized for treatment of liver and heart disease. The FBI had been investigating her for drug possession and they raided her hospital room, handcuffing her to her bed even though she lay there incapacitated. She was given last rites on July 15th and passed away two days later with less than a dollar to her name.

Any band member will tell you, there is nothing more collaborative than playing live. Each musician has their own responsibility, whether it's keeping the tempo or setting the rhythm. Even when they solo, they need to stay contextually within the confines of the original song and they need to bring their solo to an end by allowing their bandmates to re-enter the song on beat and in key. These rules go for the singer as well. They must be part of the overall fabric of the band and compliment the overall sound. Because no band is a collection of individual musicians. When it's done right, bands define the cliche that the whole is greater than the individual parts. And when a band plays in unison they can create a transcendent sound.

Imagine enjoying such a communal experience and then exiting the stage and being told you can't leave the theater with your white bandmates. You'll have to use the service exit. Oh and you know this beautiful hotel where you just got that standing ovation in the ballroom? It's for whites only so we've put you up at the motor lodge across town. No, these are not equal to the horrors of attempted rape and incarceration for prostitution, but injustices, no matter how big or small, gnaw at the soul. Holiday found two ways to deal with the pain and anguish of her life. First, she sang. And for the listener it's impossible not to hear the torment in her voice. And then she numbed herself with alcohol and drugs. There can be only two reactions to these. We must be sympathetic and understanding of the latter, and eternally grateful for the former. She may have died penniless but she left the musical world with a priceless collection of memories.

On this date in 2003, Beyoncé's "Crazy in Love" was ending its first week at #1 on the pop chart. The song would remain at the top for seven more weeks becoming the Song of the Summer of 2003 and one of the most successful singles of the year.

Beyoncé Giselle Knowles was born in 1981 in Houston, Texas. Her mother's maiden name was Beyoncé which is how her parents came up with her unique first name. She started dance classes at a young age and one day when her dance instructor was humming a song, Knowles began to hum along with her and hit a high note that was out of her teacher's range. Impressed with the young girl's skills, the teacher encouraged her singing. When Knowles was just seven years old she entered a talent contest at her school and beat out everyone, including students twice her age. A year later she went on an audition and met Kelly Rowland and LaTavia Roberson. The three became members of a group called Girl's Tyme which competed but lost on *Star Search* in 1992. Knowles' father, Matthew, sensed that his daughter had potential and he quit his job to manage Girl's Tyme. The group went through a number of lineup and name changes and eventually had been reduced to a quartet that featured Knowles, Rowland, Roberson and a schoolmate of Knowles named LaToya Luckett. They chose the name Destiny's Child after a passage in the Book of Isaiah and in 1996 Matthew landed them a record deal with Columbia. Their eponymous debut album was released in early 1998 which included the single "No, No, No" with Wyclef Jean that would make it all the way to #3 on the *Billboard* Hot 100 chart. In 1999 the group got to #1 for the first time with "Bills, Bills, Bills." A lineup change the following year would see Roberson and Luckett leave and be replaced by Michelle Williams. More chart-toppers followed including "Say My Name" and "Independent Woman Part 1" in 2000 and "Bootylicious" the following year. Also in 2001 Beyoncé (she was just going by her first name by this point) made her acting debut in the made-for-television movie *Carmen: A Hip Hopera*. In 2002 she starred alongside Mike Myers, playing Foxxy Cleopatra, in the comedy *Austin Powers in Goldmember*. The soundtrack for that movie included the first Beyoncé solo song, a funk number called "Work It Out." With Destiny's Child on a hiatus, it was obvious to anyone paying attention that Beyoncé was about to emerge as a superstar.

Around this time Jay-Z asked Beyoncé to appear on a record called "03 Bonnie and Clyde." There are differing reports about whether these two were already a couple at the time or whether working on the song together is what sparked the romance. But either way the song became a hit right around the time Beyoncé began working on her solo debut.

Beyoncé worked with a number of producers for her debut solo effort. She chose Rich Harrison to work with on "Crazy in Love." Before they began Harrison played an instrumental track for her that was based mainly on a sample from the 1970 Chi-lites' song, "Are You My Woman (Tell Me So)," that he was very excited about using. Beyoncé had reservations, saying it sounded too retro and that no one used horn riffs in the 21st century. At Harrison's insistence, Beyoncé acquiesced and the two set about writing lyrics. Beyoncé came up with the bridge. She looked at her self in the mirror and saw that her clothes were mismatched and her hair was messy and she started singing, "I'm looking so crazy right now." Harrison said, "That's the hook" and started to write lyrics using "crazy in love" as the theme. Beyoncé also started singing the "uh-oh, uh-oh, you know" part and Harrison incorporated that hook immediately.

Jay-Z came by the studio about three in the morning while Beyoncé and Harrison were still working. The idea for him to rap on the song was spontaneous. He sat down and wrote and recorded his part in ten minutes.

"Crazy in Love" was chosen to be the lead single off Beyoncé's debut solo album *Dangerously in Love*. It was released on May 18th, 2003, a full month before the album. The song's success would propel the album to open up at #1, selling 317,000 copies in its first week. It has sold over eleven million copies worldwide. "Crazy in Love" was the fourth highest-selling single of 2003 and it would take home Grammy Awards for Best R&B Song and Best Rap/Sung Collaboration. And as Rich Harrison predicted, many critics have praised the sampling of the Chi-lites horns as ingenious.

Beyoncé has gone on to worldwide success as one of the most popular singers and performers of the new millennium. She married Jay-Z in 2008 and as of this writing the couple has three children. She's sold hundreds of millions of records and starred in multiple movies. Pretty good for a runner-up on *Star Search*!

### July 19th

On this date in 1954, "That's All Right," by a 19 year old singer named Elvis Presley was released. The song had been recorded two weeks before and was already causing quite the stir in Memphis, Tennessee. And though the song failed to chart nationally, it's no stretch to say this release was the beginning of a seismic shift in popular music.

Elvis Aaron Presley was born in Tupelo, Mississippi, in 1935. His twin brother was delivered stillborn just a few minutes before him and so Elvis grew up an only child to Vernon and Gladys Presley. Vernon was never much of an earner and the three lived humbly, often relying on family members or government assistance. When Elvis was just three his father was sent to jail for forging checks and the boy and his mother had to move in with relatives. Elvis was always something of a "momma's boy" and his close bond with his mother was forged during these early years. For his tenth birthday Elvis asked for a bicycle but his parents couldn't afford it so they got him his second wish; a guitar.

Presley was thirteen when his family moved to Memphis, living in public housing and still struggling to make ends meet. One day in high school, a music teacher told him he couldn't sing. The next day he brought in his guitar and sang "Keep Them Cold Icy Fingers Off Me." The teacher was impressed enough to change her opinion saying she just didn't appreciate "his kind of singing." Presley was becoming more and more interested in music and his surroundings were helping. Living in public housing meant he was exposed to many different races and cultures and so, for Elvis, music had no color barrier. He was exposed to country, R&B, gospel and blues. One of his first jobs was at a local movie theater which was right next to Beale street, Memphis' most popular area for clubs. B.B. King remembered often seeing a young Presley checking out some of the musical acts.

In the summer of 1953 Presley, who was by now out of high school and working for a local electric company, walked into Sun Studio to make a record. This is a legendary moment in rock and roll history and it's been told so many different ways it's hard to know exactly what happened that day and why. What is for sure is that Sun's owner, Sam Phillips, was not in that day so his personal assistant, Marion Keisker, helped Presley in the studio. Keisker was impressed with the young man's voice and, knowing that her boss was always on the lookout for talent, especially, in Phillips' own words, "a white man who had the negro sound and the negro feel," she made an extra copy of the acetate to play later for her boss. She then asked Presley, "What kind of singer are you?" to which he replied, "I sing all kinds." When she pressed him further asking, "Who do you sound like?" Presley very famously replied, "I don't sound like nobody."

Phillips was indeed impressed by Presley's sound and he decided he wanted to work with the young singer. Presley returned to Sun Studio in June of 1954 and worked with Phillips on the ballad "Without You," but there was no initial magic in the studio. Phillips, to his credit, did not give up. He invited Presley back on July 5th, this time to work with local musicians "Scotty" Moore (on guitar) and Bill Black (on upright bass). Again Phillips didn't hear anything he felt was worth recording and he began to think he (and Keisker) had misjudged Presley's talent. Then, during a break in the session late on July 5th, Presley picked up a guitar and started playing and singing Arthur Crudup's 1949 blues number, "That's All Right Mama." He also started dancing around the studio as he played, probably out of frustration that the evening had been so fruitless. Moore and Black joined in, playing and also acting silly and foolish. Phillips (who was in the control room) interrupted and asked, "What are you doing?" When the musicians said they didn't know he told them to back up and try to find a place to start from. He also hit record. This was the sound he had been looking for.

Three nights later, on July 8th, 1954, Sam Phillips handed Memphis DJ Dewey Phillips a single of "That's All Right" (for some reason he'd dropped the word Mama from the title) with Elvis Presley listed as the artist (Scotty and Bill got second billing in a smaller font). Dewey played it on his Red, Hot, and Blue radio show and the phone lines lit up. He played "That's All Right" repeatedly during his show that night and also interviewed Presley on-air, specifically asking him what high school he attended in order to clarify his skin color for the many callers who assumed he was black.

Phillips readied the single for release and it came out on this date in 1954. The rest, as they say, is rock and roll history.

On this date in 1965, Bob Dylan released "Like a Rolling Stone." Very few songs have ever had the impact that this one had. It didn't just alter the musical landscape, it blew everything up.

Bob Dylan spent the early part of 1965 touring England. Though he'd already introduced some electric elements into his music on his fifth album, *Bringing It All Back Home*, which came out in March, his tour was still a traditional folk tour, nothing but acoustic guitars and Dylan singing his songs. But he was unhappy and feeling restricted as a folk singer. At some point on the tour he began writing a long-form poem that he has compared to "vomit" and "all about my steady hatred." The target of his anger is a fallen debutante who becomes a loner. When he returned from England he looked over the ten pages he'd written and wondered what to make of it. According to Dylan, "I had never thought of it as a song, until one day I was at the piano, and on the paper it was singing, 'How does it feel?'" And so he started crafting what he'd written into lyrics. He'd say later: "The first two lines, which rhymed 'kiddin' you' and 'didn't you,' just about knocked me out. And when I got to the jugglers and the chrome horse and the princess on the steeple, it all just about got to be too much." But he didn't quit. He eventually turned those ten pages into the lyrics for "Like a Rolling Stone." He then recorded a demo to bring to the studio along with a handwritten sheet of lyrics (in 2014 those handwritten lyrics sold for over $2 million).

On June 15th, 1965, Dylan arrived at Columbia's Studio A in New York City ready to get to work. Along with producer Tom Wilson were musicians Mike Bloomfield on guitar, Paul Griffin on piano, Bobby Gregg on drums and Joseph Macho on bass. Wilson had spent the earlier part of the day adding some electric instrumentation to the Simon & Garfunkel song "The Sound of Silence" which would turn that song into a hit and now here he was producing for Bob Dylan. They worked on some of Dylan's other songs, then, towards the end of the day, the folk legend broke out the demo for "Like a Rolling Stone." Dylan let the musicians hear the track and they went through a few rehearsals of it before the session ended for the day. The next day the band reconvened to record "Like a Rolling Stone." Tom Wilson had invited Al Kooper to come watch the sessions. As Kooper looked on, the musicians from the previous day launched into a rehearsal with Bobby Gregg starting things off with one loud drum beat before the band launched into the melody. With each take, Gregg's single shot would get louder and more shotgun like. With Paul Griffin at the piano, Kooper noticed nobody was at the organ and he was desperate to play on a Bob Dylan song so in between takes he walked into the studio and sat down at the Hammond. In his autobiography, Kooper described what happened next: "Imagine this, there is no music to read. The song is over five minutes long, the band is so loud I can't even hear the organ, and I'm not familiar with the instrument to begin with. But the tape is rolling, and that is Bob-fucking-Dylan over there singing, so this had better be me sitting here playing something. You can hear how I waited until the chord was played by the rest of the band before committing myself to play in the verses. I'm always an eighth note behind everyone else, making sure of the chord before touching the keys." After the first take Dylan gave his approval of Kooper's involvement so he stayed in the studio. They ran through eleven takes of the song that day and it's the fourth one that Dylan deemed the best so that's the version that got released.

With the song clocking in at over six minutes Columbia initially refused to release "Like a Rolling Stone" as a single. Radio was used to songs half that length so no one at the label even envisioned "Like a Rolling Stone" as anything more than an album track. Plus, truth be told, they didn't love this new direction Dylan was moving in. They'd signed him as a folk singer and in a few short years he'd forged quite the reputation in that genre. There were plenty of rockers fighting it out for shelf space and air time, Columbia would just as soon Dylan stay King of the Folkies. But then Shaun Considine, the coordinator of new releases for Columbia, slipped a studio acetate to a DJ at a prominent New York City nightclub. When the song played and the crowd went crazy, Considine knew he had a hit on his hands. As fortune would have it there were two radio DJs in the audience that night and they both called Columbia the next day asking for "the new Dylan song." Columbia was forced to release "Like a Rolling Stone" as a single. It hit record stores on this date in 1965, just days before Dylan infuriated the Newport Jazz Festival by going electric. The times certainly were a changin'.

Bob Dylan may have turned off some folkies but he'd turned on a whole new world of rock fans and inspired a whole generation of rockstars. The Doors' producer Paul Rothchild has said, "What I realized when I was sitting there is that one of us—one of the so-called Village hipsters—was making music that could compete with them—the Beatles, and the Stones, and the Dave Clark Five—without sacrificing any of the integrity of folk music or the power of rock and roll." Paul McCartney has said he was with John Lennon the first time they both heard the song and was amazed that it just kept going on and on. "It was just beautiful," McCartney has said. "He showed all of us that it was possible to go a little further." Elvis Costello commented, "what a shocking thing to live in a world where there was Manfred Mann and the Supremes and Engelbert Humperdinck and here comes 'Like a Rolling Stone.'" And when Bruce Springsteen inducted Bob Dylan in the Rock and Roll Hall of Fame he said, "That snare shot sounded like somebody'd kicked open the door to your mind. When I was 15 and I heard 'Like a Rolling Stone,' I heard a guy who had the guts to take on the whole world and who made me feel like I had to too." Springsteen added, "The way that Elvis freed your body, Dylan freed your mind."

Seek out "Like a Rolling Stone" today and give it a spin. Crank it loud so Bobby Gregg's snare shot startles you and then settle in and follow Dylan's angry trip and clever word play. Over half a century ago his snarling question "How does it feel?" woke up an entire generation. Let it challenge you as well.

On this date in 1987, Guns N' Roses released their debut album, *Appetite for Destruction*. It had a slow and steady climb to the top, first appearing on the *Billboard* album chart the week of August 29, 1987 and finally reaching #1 almost a year later, the week of August 6th, 1988. When all was said and done, *Appetite* stands today as the largest-selling debut album by any artist and the eleventh best selling album in U.S. history. And it could have been even greater.

Guns N' Roses started playing together as a band in 1985. Singer Axl Rose (who had been a member of the band L.A. Guns) and rhythm guitarist Izzy Stradlin (who had been a member of the band Hollywood Rose) got together and decided on the name as an ode to their previous bands. After replacing a few of the original members, the band's lineup was set with Slash (Stradlin's one-time Hollywood Rose bandmate) on guitar, Duff McKagan on bass and Steven Adler on drums. They started becoming regulars at Los Angeles' most famous clubs, namely the Troubadour and the Roxy, and they began to attract the attention of some record labels. In March of 1986, less than a year after forming, they were signed by Geffen Records. They released a four song EP in December of that year to keep their name visible while they withdrew from the clubs to concentrate on recording their debut.

The first big decision was finding a producer who could capture their raw energy. Hair metal bands were all the rage at the time but Geffen did not want an overly polished album. Guns N' Roses were awesome live and they sought to capture that energy on tape. They selected Mike Clink, a virtual unknown with no track record, to helm the recording sessions.

In early 1987 Guns N' Roses started work on their debut album. The members of the band had many original songs from their years of playing in other bands, as well as their short time together, so one of the hardest decisions was what to include and what to leave out. After choosing "Sweet Child O' Mine" as the album's ballad, they decided not to record "November Rain" or "Don't Cry," two incredible songs that would be shelved until 1991's *Use Your Illusion I*. One can only imagine how much stronger *Appetite for Destruction* would have been if at least one of these songs had been included.

The original cover art for the album, featuring a robot who looks to have just raped a woman and is about to be attacked by a flying metallic contraption, was so controversial that many record stores refused to display it or even carry it. Geffen finally convinced the band that their cover was killing their sales and the album was re-released with a new cover, an image that was originally designed as a tattoo, featuring a cross and five skulls (one for each band member).

Guns N' Roses toured extensively to support their debut. MTV was also very helpful, putting "Sweet Child O' Mine" in heavy rotation after its August, 1988 release. "Child" would become the band's first, and to date only, #1 single. Regarding Slash's unique guitar playing on this song, he says one day before the band began recording he was doing some warmups and started playing a circus-sounding melody. Stradlin asked Slash to keep playing the lick and then he came up with some chords to match. Rose, sitting in another room, heard the melody and was inspired to write lyrics about his current girlfriend, Erin Everly, daughter of Don Everly of the Everly brothers. When they recorded the song, Clink suggested they add a break near the end. Not knowing if the break would end or the band would come out of it, Rose started singing, "Where do we go?" The band loved it and they kept it in. To make the song more radio-friendly they edited Slash's guitar solo, a move that the band hated at the time but they couldn't argue with the results. "Child" helped push their debut to the top of the LP chart.

No one would claim that Guns N' Roses were a One Hit Wonder, yet it's also fair to say they failed to live up to the promise of their debut. *Appetite for Destruction* seemed to be ushering in a new sound, with a band as big and bold as they come. Yet within just a few years, grunge arrived and as "real" as Guns N' Roses looked compared to the high hair bands of the mid-eighties, Nirvana and Pearl Jam now made them look like poseurs. Then, internal squabbles began and Guns N' Roses was ripped apart almost as quickly as they'd come together. Still, it's hard to hear the manic tempo change at the end of "Paradise City" or Axl belting out, "I wanna watch you bleed" in "Welcome to the Jungle" and not be transported back to the late eighties when, for about a year or more, nobody was bigger or louder or badder than Guns N' Roses.

### July 22nd

On this date in 1985, ZZ Top's "Legs" peaked on the *Billboard* Hot 100 chart at #8. To date it is the band's highest-charting song although the trio from Texas is far more than a one hit wonder. Their signature beards and tongue-in-cheek humor have made them heroes to millions of fans who love their hard-core blues sound and incredible musicianship, all with a pinch of innuendo mixed in.

ZZ Top came together in Houston, Texas in the late sixties as three musicians who loved the blues. Their lineup was set early on: Billy Gibbons, guitarist, lyricist and the band's de facto leader, Dusty Hill, bassist and lead vocalist and Frank Beard on drums. Their first official show was in February, 1970 at a Knights of Columbus hall just outside of Houston. When the curtains opened the band was surprised to see one guy in the building. It's not often a show has more musicians on the stage than audience members watching, but the band played their entire set, even buying their lone fan a drink during their breaks.

Despite this inauspicious start ZZ Top began developing a strong following in Texas. They released their debut LP in 1971 and, tapping into the sense of humor that would be prevalent throughout their career, they titled it *ZZ Top's First Album*. It was another unpromising start for the band as the album, and its only single, failed to chart. But they kept at it, emboldened by the ever-growing crowds at their shows and their next few albums began to gain them notoriety outside of the Lone Star State. The band recorded and toured at a torrid pace for the next few years, releasing five albums between 1971 and 1976 and rarely taking any time off. They were either in the studio or playing live and soon fatigue had set in. They decided to take a hiatus after their 1976 Worldwide Texas Tour. It was a break that was originally supposed to be a few months but stretched out to almost two years. When they reconvened to start recording again, Gibbons and Hill had both grown long beards, leaving Beard the only one beardless.

Their first albums after the break were successful but as they started working on music for their next LP the music world had changed. MTV was now a formidable promotional vehicle; a fact that many rock-holdovers from the seventies found difficult to grasp. Whether they refused to release videos, or just cobbled together some live footage with little-to-no thought, many of these bands missed out on the opportunity that a video in heavy rotation on the music channel presented.

ZZ Top was not one of these bands. MTV was the perfect vehicle for the band. Not only did they create multiple videos for their 1983 LP, *Eliminator*, but since they were now incorporating synthesizers into their music, giving them a hard-rock-meets-new-wave sound, they fit right in alongside all the British bands that were invading MTV. *Eliminator* was named after a hot-rod that Gibbons had made for him and the car would not only appear on the album's cover but in the videos for the LP's singles: "Gimme All Your Loving", "Sharp Dressed Man" and "Legs." The first two songs, released in 1983, sold solid numbers and got plenty of exposure on MTV, introducing ZZ Top to a whole new audience. "Legs" was released in 1984 and peaked at #8 this week. *Eliminator* sold over ten million units, making it the band's most successful album.

Featuring the same three musicians since 1970, ZZ Top is the longest running American band with no lineup changes. Hill and Beard have deferred to Gibbons as their chief lyricist and bandleader which is one of the reasons they have avoided the clash-of-egos that can torpedo many bands Through the years, they've consistently delivered a unique mix of guitar or synthesized driven blues-based rock that is often sprinkled with double entendres. It's a sound that has helped them sell 25 millions albums and earned them a place in the Rock and Roll Hall of Fame.


**July 23rd**

On this date in 2011, Amy Winehouse died of alcohol poisoning. It was a tragic end for an incredibly talented singer who had once bragged about not going to rehab, but clearly needed to. And in dying at 27, she joined the mythical "27 Club," a group of famous musicians who have all passed away at that age. One can only hope she's the last member.

Amy Jade Winehouse was born in 1983 in London, England. Her uncles were all jazz musicians, her grandmother dated a jazz saxophonist and her father would often sing Frank Sinatra songs to her as lullabies. She grew up inundated with music. In fact, whenever she got in trouble in school, which was often, she would walk to the headmaster's office singing, "Fly Me to the Moon." Winehouse was a mischievous young child. But she was also precocious, demonstrating singing and dancing talents at an incredibly young age. She formed her first band, Sweet 'n' Sour, when she was just ten, then gained admittance to the prestigious Sylvia Young Theater School. There are differing stories about why she left that school, with her father and Young both claiming Winehouse simply transferred, but the one about her being expelled for not applying herself and for getting a nose ring match her future behavior and so that's the one most people go with.

By her late teens, Winehouse had decided that singing was her future and she put together a demo tape. A childhood friend of hers, soul singer Tyler James, passed that tape along and soon enough, Winehouse was signed to Simon Fuller's 19 Management company. Fuller did a superb job of whipping up excitement for the young singer and after something of a bidding war, she signed with Island and released her debut album, *Frank*, shortly after her 20th birthday. The LP received great critical response and sold well, especially in the U.K., and it seemed to anyone watching that a promising new career was just getting started.

But Winehouse was already demonstrating troubling behavior. She was partying way too hard and often appeared drunk on stage, sometimes unable to even finish her set. She also began dating Blake Fielder-Civil and their relationship was marked by bouts of violence as well as out-of-control drinking and drug use. Fielder-Civil would admit later that he introduced Winehouse to heroin and crack.

Before work could begin on a follow-up album, Winehouse's management company suggested she try rehab. She told them "no," then promptly fired them. Soon after this she was chatting with Mark Ronson who she'd tab to produce some tracks for her second album. As she recounted the story, she sang, "They tried to make me go to rehab and I said, 'no, no, no.'" They both laughed and Ronson asked her who wrote that song? When Winehouse told him, no one, that she'd just made it up on the spot, the producer encouraged her to flesh out the idea. Five minutes later she'd written the whole song. In the lines, "I'd rather be home with Ray," and, "There's nothing you can teach me that I can't learn from Mr. Hathaway," Winehouse tipped her cap to two of her obvious influences, Ray Charles and Donny Hathaway. In 2006, "Rehab" became Winehouse's breakthrough song, hitting the Top 10 in both the U.S. and England and helping to push her second LP, *Back in Black*, to #2 in the U.S. and #1 in England. Winehouse was being compared to some of the greatest singers of all time like Etta James and Sarah Vaughn. *Billboard* magazine effused that her voice was "Shirley Bassey-meets-Ella Fitzgerald."

But her erratic behavior continued. In August, 2007, during a pub crawl in London, Winehouse mixed heroin, cocaine, ecstasy, ketamine, whisky and vodka and wound up overdosing. She was schedule to begin a North American tour shortly after this but the plans were cancelled. A few months later she appeared on stage in Birmingham, England so intoxicated that the crowd booed her off. She canceled even more concert dates and then was denied a U.S. visa so the night in 2008 that she won five Grammy Awards she had to watch from home in England. She made repeated attempts to get clean over the next few years, all of which ended with Winehouse falling off the wagon, often right before a performance or public appearance. Then, on this day in 2011, Winehouse was found dead by her bodyguard after a night of drinking. The coroner's report would say she died of "alcohol toxicity" with a blood alcohol content five times the legal limit. Winehouse was two months shy of her 28th birthday.

The idea of a "27 Club" goes back decades but it gained serious consideration after Kurt Cobain killed himself in 1994. Some music journalists pointed out that 27 was the same age at which Brian Jones had died. And Jimi Hendrix. And Janis Joplin. And Jim Morrison. Even Robert Johnson, the famous blues guitarist who'd supposedly sold his soul to the devil in exchange for his incredible talent, had died at 27. And once it appeared in print it had to be so. Who cares that multiple studies have shown there is no statistical evidence showing musicians have a propensity to die at that age? So when Amy Winehouse died at 27 she was, of course, further proof of the club. Which is all simply coincidental. And tragic. The fact that anybody, famous artist or not, can leave us at such a tender young age is dreadful and we don't have to create mythical clubs to put them in. We just have to hope it stops. We have to hope people of any age stop abusing alcohol and drugs and losing their battles with depression. Because life is way too precious to take for granted.

The world will never know what future brilliance Amy Winehouse may have produced. We are simply left with yet another incredibly talent artist who left us too soon. If only she'd said, "yes, yes, yes."


## July 24th


On this date in 1981, Kim Carnes' "Bette Davis Eyes" ended its run at #1 on the pop chart. The song had spent nine of the past ten weeks at the top, interrupted once by the "Stars on 45 Medley." "Bette Davis Eyes" would wind up as the top-seller of 1981 and it would take home the Grammy Awards for both Record of the Year and Song of the Year.

Jackie DeShannon is a singer and songwriter from Kentucky who enjoyed a moderately successful career in the sixties and seventies. Her most successful song is "Put a Little Love in Your Heart" which went to #4 on the pop chart in 1969. In the early seventies she watched the 1942 film *Now, Voyager,* starring Bette Davis. DeShannon was inspired to write a song about the actress and, with fellow songwriter Donna Weiss, came up with "Bette Davis Eyes." DeShannon recorded the song and included it on her 1974 album, *New*

*Arrangement.*  In its original incarnation, "Bette Davis Eyes" has a honky tonk feel to it, featuring a prominent, upbeat piano. It sounds very much like a Leon Russell song.

Kim Carnes is a singer and songwriter from Los Angeles. In the early seventies she was a member of the bubblegum pop band Sugar Bear who released their records as part of a deal with the cereal Super Sugar Crisps. Instead of vinyl, Sugar Bear's songs were pressed on cardboard and could be cut out of the back of the cereal boxes. The Archies had a similar deal a few years earlier and it's sufficient to say they sold more cereal than Sugar Bear. After the band split up, Carnes and her husband, Dave Ellingson, began writing songs for David Cassidy. She also released solo recordings, including the Top 10 single, "More Love," in 1980.

As Carnes was preparing material for her 1981 LP, *Mistaken Identity*, it was Donna Weiss who suggested "Bette Davis Eyes" to the singer. Carnes credits her producer, Val Garay, and her keyboard player Bill Cuomo for coming up with the new arrangement. Indeed if you play the original and Carnes' version back-to-back, other than the lyrics, they are two completely different songs. Garay, for some reason, requested, "the cheapest sounding drum kit" for the song. Combined with an early synthesizer, the new arrangement has a smoldering, smoky, bar-room feel (which fits Carnes' voice perfectly). Besides the new arrangement, they made one minor lyrical change. The original song includes the line, "And she knows just what it takes to make a crow blush." That's a saying from decades earlier, meaning something that could cause unease or embarrassment. As Carnes worked on the song, no one in the studio knew the expression (and apparently nobody thought to Google it) so they changed the line to, "What it takes to make a pro blush." It's a lyric that's often misheard anyway; many people think she sings, "What it takes to make a girl blush."

Carnes' version of "Bette Davis Eyes" was released as the lead single to *Mistaken Identity* in March of 1981. There's some irony to that album title because as "Bette Davis Eyes" began getting steady radio play many people, hearing Carnes' raspy voice for probably the first time, thought that Rod Stewart had a new song out.

Though MTV hadn't gone on air just yet (that would happen on August 1st, 1981) Carnes worked with Australian film director, Russell Mulcahy, to put a video together for "Bette Davis Eyes." Mulcahy was a popular early director of music videos who was known for his quick edits and odd, visual non sequiturs. His work with Carnes is a typical Mulcahy production. Besides the performance shots of her singing while being just about blown away by a wind machine, the viewer is treated to an assortment of costumed characters who slap each other across the face and then pound on the floor in sync with the beat of the song. What characters like a sultan and a female pirate have to do with "Bette Davis Eyes" is anyone's guess. But once MTV went on air they played the clip often, helping to keep the song popular through the rest of the year.

In the song's wake, Bette Davis wrote letters to Kim Carnes and the songwriters to say she loved "Bette Davis Eyes" and to thank them for making her "a part of modern history." Turns out, the main reason Davis loved the song so much was that her granddaughter thought she was "cool" for having a hit song written about her.

It's worth trying to find both versions of "Bette Davis Eyes." It is fascinating how someone can hear the original and totally recreate it and turn it into the mega-hit it became. Especially when you consider that Val Garay received no writing credit for his contributions to the song's success. That's enough to make a crow blush.

## July 25th

On this date in 1965, Bob Dylan plugged an electric guitar in for his set at the Newport Folk Festival, sending shock waves (pun intended) through the audience and on through the rest of the music-loving public. This was a sea change in both Dylan's attitude and the world of folk and rock music.

By 1965, Bob Dylan already had a rich history at the Newport Folk Festival. He'd played there in 1963 just as he was becoming a big name in the folk world and his set, especially "Blowin' in the Wind" which he sang with Joan Baez, Peter Paul and Mary, and other festival performers, was very well received. In 1964, he was such a well-known name with the folkies in attendance, he was introduced with: "Take him, you know him, he's yours" (something that didn't sit well with Dylan). His set in 1964 was again well received although some people criticized him for being clearly stoned (which is an ironic criticism at a folk festival).

But by the following year Dylan was already planning the next phase of his career. In March of 1965 he released *Bringing It All Back Home* which featured his first use of electric instruments. The first single off that album, "Subterranean Homesick Blues," was Dylan's first to chart, just squeaking into the Top 40 the week of May 15th, 1965. Then in June he began working on his follow-up album, *Highway 61 Revisited*. He took a break in the recording sessions in July to write more material and to play the only live show he had scheduled that month, the Newport Folk Festival.

Dylan's performance at the 1965 Newport Folk Festival, and the crowd's reaction to it, has become the stuff of rock and roll legend. Here are the known facts: Dylan performed on Saturday, July 24th doing three acoustic numbers at a festival workshop (not on the main stage). The next night he took the main stage backed by a full band that included Mike Bloomfield on lead guitar and Al Kooper on organ. Both of these musicians were working with Dylan on his new material and played on "Like a Rolling Stone," the single Dylan had just released that week. Bob Dylan did three songs with the band on electric instruments: "Maggie's Farm," his brand new single and "It Takes a Lot to Laugh, It Takes a Train to Cry." During these three songs the crowd's reaction was mixed, including some "boos." He then left the stage but returned to play, acoustically, "It's All Over Now, Baby Blue" and "Mr Tamborine Man."

Here's the stuff that is legendary (meaning it may or may not be true but who cares, it makes for a great story). On the 24th, Dylan overheard festival director, Alan Lomax, make condescending remarks about the Paul Butterfield Blues Band who had played earlier that day. Mike Bloomfield, who was in the Paul Butterfield Blues Band as well as working with Dylan, was a friend so this really irritated Dylan. No one's quite sure if Dylan planned all along to do an electric set the next day or if Lomax's comments inspired a last minute change but according to Jonathan Taplin, a roadie at the festival, Dylan exclaimed, "Well, fuck them if they think they can keep electricity out of here, I'll do it." Dylan is said to have assembled the band that evening and rehearsed for the next day (which would lend credence to the "he did it on a whim" theory.)

As for the crowd's reaction, no one denies that he was met with cheers as well as some boos. But it's the reason for the negative reaction that is up for debate. Were they aghast that their folk hero was plugging in? Was it the poor sound system? Was it the length of the set? Pete Seeger, who was backstage at the time, blames the sound quality. He says he told the audio techs, "Get that distortion out of his voice ... It's terrible." Joe Boyd, who was responsible for sound mixing at the festival, not surprisingly, blames Dylan's use of electric equipment and a backing band. "I think there were a lot of people who were upset about the rock band, but I think it was pretty split," says Boyd. "I think that there was a segment of the audience, somewhere between a quarter and a half, that was dismayed or horrified or varying degrees of unhappy about what he was doing." Whatever the reason, and however passionately he was booed, one critic claimed Dylan, "electrified one half of his audience, and electrocuted the other."

Dylan was clearly affected by the reaction. At his next show, which took place in Queens, New York, in late August, he sat his band down before the concert and told them to expect anything from the audience. He planned that show to be acoustic for the first half and electric for the second half. The reaction that night is said to be similar to the Newport crowd, mixed, with a helping of boos once the second half began. Dylan did a world tour in 1966 with the same format and the electric set was often met with derision by the folkniks. There is footage from a show he performed in Manchester, England where, in between songs, an audience member clearly yells, "Judas!" (Dylan replies, "I don't believe you, you're a liar." Google it.)

Reaction in the music press was typically hyperbolic. Robert Polito, writing for the *New York Times*, claimed Dylan going electric was, "the cataclysmic finish of the folk movement." Apparently the Byrds didn't get that memo since they released their #1 single "Turn, Turn, Turn" a few months later. As for Dylan, he would wait 37 years before returning to the Newport Folk Festival. When he took the stage in 2002, he wore a wig and fake beard. He was met with nothing but cheers.

On this date in 1972, Bill Withers' "Lean On Me" was finishing its three week stay at the top of the charts. It was Withers' first and so far only #1 single and has become his signature song as well. And the whole song came about because of a new piano and a flat tire. Here's the story:

Bill Withers came to music later in life than most famous musicians. He was born in 1938 in a coal mining town in West Virginia and as a child he stuttered which caused him to be extremely shy. He enlisted in the Navy at 18 and served for nine years. He got over his stuttering during his time in the Navy and then became interested in music; both singing and songwriting. After his discharge Withers moved to Los Angeles and found work as an assembler for several different companies, including Douglas Aircraft Corporation. One night he was in a club to see Lou Rawls perform but the singer was late and Withers overheard the manager say, "I'm paying this guy $2,000 a week and he can't show up on time?" Withers was currently making $3 an hour so his ears perked up when he heard Rawls' pay and he became motivated to try to make it in the music industry. Using the money from his day job he recorded a number of demos and began shopping them around. He soon earned an audition for a brand new label called Sussex Records. They signed him and assigned Booker T. Jones (of Booker T. & the M.G.'s fame) to produce his debut album. Jones phoned in some favors and put together a rather impressive studio band for an unknown singer that included Stephen Stills on guitar. Withers was intimidated by the band and being in a recording studio and at first was too nervous to sing. But Graham Nash walked into the studio and as Withers recounts: "He sat down in front of me and said, 'You don't know how good you are.' I'll never forget it." Withers got over his fear just as he'd conquered stuttering and they were able to record a dozen songs in just a few sessions.

Bill Withers' debut, *Just As I Am*, which included "Ain't No Sunshine," was released in 1971. Even with a record contract and LP released, Withers was reluctant to quit his day job, believing the music industry was too fickle for a full-time career. In fact, the photo on the cover of *Just As I Am* shows Withers at his job at Weber Aircraft, holding his lunch pail, a clear sign that he was torn between careers. However, as the album and the single started selling, Withers had to chose between his nine to five and touring. Remembering how much Lou Rawls was pulling in, he went with music. Eventually his debut album would reach a very respectable spot (#35) on the LP chart and "Ain't No Sunshine" would peak at #3 on the *Billboard* Hot 100 in September of 1971.

Now a full-time musician, Withers treated himself to a Wurlitzer electric piano and began composing songs for a follow-up album. One day he was just running his fingers up and down the keys when the phrase "lean on me" came into his mind. He liked how that sounded and tried to build a song around it. So he asked himself how he had come up with those three words. What in his past, what in his psyche, had made that phrase come out. It was a very Freudian way of looking at songwriting and it worked. Suddenly Withers recalled a moment years earlier when he was driving through rural Alabama and he blew a tire. He pulled over and then realized he didn't have a spare. Withers, an African American alone in the South, became very nervous, even more so when a white man, who Withers has said, "looked like he was right out of the movie *Deliverance*," started to approach him. But the man offered help. He brought a tire from his house and they changed it together. Withers says that moment resurfaced when he started analyzing the words "lean on me" and he channeled it into this song. He has since said: "I think what we say is influenced by who we are, what's been our life experiences. I notice young guys writing about shooting each other in the city and stuff like that, well I would never have said anything like that because it was not my experience." His experience, especially that moment with a flat tire, had been a positive one of brotherhood so that is what he wrote about

As catchy as the entire song is, the most memorable parts are the two bridges (where Withers sings, "Just call on me brother"). The song takes on an almost gospel feel here. The coda is also quite powerful, as Withers repeats "Call me" fourteen times (although most radio stations faded early to fit the song under four minutes).

"Lean On Me" was released in April, 1972 and went to #1 on July 8th when it knocked Neil Diamond's "Song Sung Blue" from the top. It would spend three weeks at #1 before bowing out to "Alone Again (Naturally)" by Gilbert O'Sullivan. To date it's his only career #1 although his very next release, "Use Me," landed within one spot of the top in October of 1972. A decade later he collaborated with Grover Washington Jr., the incredible jazz saxophonist, to create "Just the Two of Us," another song that peaked at #2.

"Lean On Me" has been covered by many artists through the years, including a new jack swing version by Club Nouveau that also went to #1 in 1987. The original and the Club Nouveau version were both featured prominently in the 1989 Morgan Freeman movie of the same name. Artists as diverse as Garth Brooks, the Temptations, Mary J. Blige and Anne Murray have taken a stab at the song as well, attracted to its universal message of support and optimism. Bill Withers has been inducted into the Songwriters Hall of Fame and the Rock and Roll Hall of Fame. As for the man who gave him a spare tire, his name may have been lost to history but because of his generous actions (and Withers' new piano) the world has a song of hope that will live on forever. There *is* always tomorrow, as Withers sings, and when we feel down and out it is comforting to know we can call on others who will help us carry the load.

On this date in 1940, *Billboard* magazine published its first chart based on retail sales at music outlets. They called this the National List of Best Selling Retail Records. There were just ten spots and Tommy Dorsey's "I'll Never Smile Again" (with vocals by Frank Sinatra) will forever have bragging rights as the first #1 song on a *Billboard* chart based on sales figures.

*Billboard* magazine began publishing in 1894. Initially, it focused on the advertising industry and since, prior to radio and television, billboards and flyers were the primary form of marketing, the magazine adopted the name *Billboard Advertising*. It would shorten its name a few years later to simply *Billboard*. By the early 1900's the magazine had shifted its focus to outdoor entertainment like fairs and carnivals. There were sections that covered vaudeville and burlesque shows as well. One of its most popular regular items at the time was a "stage gossip" column covering the private lives of entertainers; a precursor to TMZ you could say. As motion pictures became popular, *Billboard* briefly began covering them as well but since *Variety* magazine already existed and had a corner on that market they decided to focus on music instead. In 1920, *Billboard* raised a lot of eyebrows when they hired an African-American journalist to write a weekly column about black performers. By the early twenties, capitalizing on the growing popularity of radio, *Billboard* published its first "chart," a listing of songs ranked by radio play.

The jukebox industry grew rapidly in the twenties and they began advertising regularly in *Billboard*. This led to a heavier focus on music and an interest in more charts. In 1936 *Billboard* added a Hit Parade chart which ranked songs based on sheet music sales. Then, in 1940, they started the National List of Best Selling Retail Records chart which was published for the first time on this date. Tommy Dorsey and Frank Sinatra not only have bragging rights of being the first #1 on the chart, they spent three months at the top before surrendering that position to Bing Crosby's "Only Forever." Early chart-toppers also include Glenn Miller, Sammy Kaye and Artie Shaw as the crooners and big bands dominated music throughout the forties.

In 1945 *Billboard* began charting album sales. At first the chart had only five positions and was published sporadically. It would take more than a decade for the album chart to be published weekly. Harry Belafonte's 1956 LP *Belafonte*, was the first #1 on a weekly *Billboard* album chart. This chart would be renamed and expanded multiple times in the next few years, and for a while Billboard differentiated between mono and stereo albums. It wasn't until 1963 that the chart was expanded to 200 albums and became known as the *Billboard* 200. Andy Williams' *Days Of Wine And Roses*, was the first album to be #1 on the *Billboard* 200 in August of 1963.

Meanwhile the singles chart was growing and evolving as well. By the early fifties *Billboard* published a number of charts. The National List of Best Selling Retail Records ran alongside charts like Most Played by Jockeys and Most Played in Jukeboxes. But as the rock and roll era dawned, *Billboard* consolidated all of these and in August of 1958 they published their first ever Hot 100 (which rolls off the tongue a little easier than the National List of Best Selling Retail Records). Ricky Nelson's "Poor Little Fool" will forever have bragging rights of being the first #1 on the *Billboard* Hot 100. In 1970, when Casey Kasem began his weekly *American Top 40* radio show, he used the *Billboard* Hot 100 as his guide each week, giving this chart even more importance. The thought of an artist scoring a #1 record became an even bigger milestone than ever before.

One could certainly argue that art should not be a competitive thing. That creativity should not be subjected to charts and tallies. That sales figures aren't a true measure of greatness in music or any of the arts. And that's certainly a legitimate argument. Still, we are a competitive society and so measuring anything and ranking it is satisfying to us. We like lists and charts and we refer to them both in the present and the past. Today's #1 record is meaningful, just as the #1 song the day one was born, ("You're My Soul and Inspiration" by the Righteous Brothers for yours truly) marks a significant moment in time. We use these lists to rank artists as well. The fact that the Beatles have 20 #1 songs, putting them ahead of Elvis with 18, is worth discussing. Although fans of The King can counter with the fact that Elvis had 79 cumulative weeks at #1 while the Fab Four had 59. Without charts we couldn't compare these, or point out that Rihanna stands a good chance of passing both the Beatles and Elvis before her career is through. So while a purist might question the importance of measuring music based on any criteria, for most people, ranking by sales figures is a pretty good way of going about it. And while there are scores of charts these days that compete for our attention, *Billboard*'s will always be the gold standard. And scoring a #1 hit will forever change an artist's fortunes.

## July 28th

On this date in 1992, Ice-T announced he was pulling the song "Cop Killer" from his album, *Body Count*. The decision was made after intense pressure from police groups and government officials across the country.

Tracey Lauren Marrow was born in Newark, New Jersey in 1958. He lost both of his parents before he was twelve and moved to Los Angeles to be raised by an aunt. In high school he was turned on to the author Iceberg Slim and used to memorize some of his passages and recite them for his friends. One day one of them said, "Yo, kick some more of that Ice, T," ("T" being short for Tracey) and Marrow's nickname was born.

Ice-T joined the Army out of high school and it was while he was stationed in Hawaii that he first heard the Sugar Hill Gang's "Rapper's Delight." He instantly became interested in hip hop and bought two turntables and some other audio equipment to learn how to DJ. After an honorable discharge, he was at a crossroads in his life. He'd been exposed to the gangster life in Los Angeles and started hustling when he returned to L.A. But he also had the talent and desire to make it in music. According to Ice-T, the decision to go straight came decisively one day: "I had a friend who I looked up to, 'cause he made more money than me. And he said, 'Yo, Ice, you got a chance. Do that rap thing.' And that word 'chance' messed up my mind. And I just gave up hustling completely." He released a number of singles in the mid-eighties on small labels before getting signed to Sire Records. He developed an early reputation for his hardcore lyrics that celebrated the gangster lifestyle. The term "gangsta rap" hadn't even come into vogue yet but Ice-T was helping to define the genre.

But Ice-T didn't just dabble in one genre. In 1991 he wrote and produced a song called "Body Count" that combined rap with heavy metal. He loved the song so much he formed a band called Body Count and set out to record an entire album combining the two genres. One day while they were working on material, Ice-T heard the Talking Heads' song "Psycho Killer" while driving to the studio. He walked in singing the song and someone said there ought to be a song called "Cop Killer." Ice-T went to work.

This was a particularly contentious time in Los Angeles as the Rodney King trial was taking place that winter and the video of King being beaten by the LAPD was ubiquitous on television. Ice-T has called "Cop Killer" a "protest record," saying that the song is, "sung in the first person as a character who is fed up with police brutality." As the album took shape, Ice-T wanted to title it *Cop Killer* but his record label, Warner Brothers, expressed concerns. However they didn't insist that he pull the song and allowed the album to be released.

And so it was. To very little fanfare.

*Body Count* debuted at #32 on the album chart (mostly on the strength of Ice-T's name) and then began to descend quickly from there. The only single off the album, "There Goes the Neighborhood" came and went without much notice. Then, in April of 1992, the four white police officers involved in the King case were acquitted, setting off massive riots in South Central L.A. Into this caldron, "Cop Killer" began to gain attention. CLEAT (Combined Law Enforcement Associations of Texas) was the first group to bring attention to the song. But they didn't just narrow in on the album, they called for a boycott of all Time-Warner products. In their press conference they sarcastically said, "Our quarrel is not with Ice-T but with the beautiful people who run Time Warner who like to present themselves as being in the business of family entertainment." They focused on the financial aspect as well, saying, "Our goal is to educate the average Time-Warner shareholder as to how low this corporation has sunk to earn a dollar."

CLEAT's announcement spread quickly in the media and with other law enforcement groups. The initial result? *Body Count* started flying off the shelves. The *Los Angeles Times* ran an article stating that sales of the album were up 60% in L.A. and 370% in Houston (where CLEAT's announcement had been made). Some retailers couldn't keep the album in stock. Even as objection to the song reached the highest levels of government, with sixty members of Congress sending a letter to Time Warner denouncing the song and Vice President Quayle calling "Cop Killer" obscene, Warner shipped half a million albums one week. At a Time Warner shareholders meeting in June, Charlton Heston read the lyrics to the songs "Cop Killer" and "KKK Bitch" (in which Ice-T raps graphically about banging a groupie whose father happens to be the Grand Wizard of the KKK) and urged the company to drop the album. Even President Bush made a statement criticizing Warner.

Ice-T defenders cited the first amendment, especially when some government officials started talking about bringing charges for indecency, sedition and even anarchy. Ice-T also initially defended himself and the song saying, "I ain't never killed no cop. I felt like it a lot of times. But I never did it." He then added, "If you believe that I'm a cop killer, you believe David Bowie is an astronaut," (an obvious reference to "Space Oddity").

Finally, Ice-T decided to pull the song. At a hastily called press conference on this date in 1992, he said the decision was mainly based on concerns for the well-being of the people who work at Warner. He said there had been death threats there and at the *Arsenio Hall Show* when he appeared on the program. According to Warner no one at the label had pressured Ice-T into making the decision, nor did they object when they heard the announcement. They requested retailers return all unsold copies (which did not happen in some cases) and a new version of the album was pressed without "Cop Killer."

Ice-T left Warner a year later and claimed censorship was an issue. "When you're in a business with somebody who might not wanna censor you," Ice-T explained, "economically people can put restraints on them and cause them to be afraid. I learned that lesson in there, that you're never really safe as long as you're connected to any big corporation's money." Warner chairman Mo Ostin, in a 1994 interview with the *Los Angeles Times*, said: "Warner got so thin-skinned after the incident at the shareholders' meeting. In the end, Ice-T decided to leave because he could not allow tampering with his work. And I can't blame him, considering the climate." Ostin also called Ice-T, "a terrific artist who spoke the truth."

Call it irony or things coming full circle, but in 2000, Ice-T landed a role on the NBC drama *Law & Order: Special Victims Unit*. He plays Fin Tutuola, a police detective.


### July 29th

On this date in 1974, Cass Elliot, otherwise known as Mama Cass, died in her sleep in the London apartment where she was staying while she played a string of shows at the London Palladium. She was two months shy of her 33rd birthday.

Ellen Naomi Cohen was born in 1941 in Baltimore, Maryland although she spent a significant part of her early life in Alexandria, Virginia where she attended George Washington High School and was a classmate of Jim Morrison. After high school, she changed her name to Cass Elliot and moved to New York to try her hand at acting. She later performed in a number of folk groups in the early sixties before joining a group called the New Journeymen. While they were rehearsing in the Virgin Islands, legend has it that Elliot was struck on the head with a copper pipe, and as a result her vocal range improved by three octaves. In a 1968 interview with *Rolling Stone,* Elliot confirmed the story saying: "Workmen dropped a thin metal plumbing pipe and it hit me on the head and knocked me to the ground. I had a concussion and went to the hospital. I had a bad headache for about two weeks and all of a sudden I was singing higher. It's true. Honest to God."

The New Journeymen consisted of husband and wife team of John and Michelle Phillips, Denny Doherty and Elliot. They changed their name to the Mamas and the Papas and also reconsidered their folk roots. Like Elliot, the others had emerged from the folk scene but were interested in expanding their musical horizons (and certainly potential incomes) with a more commercial, pop-oriented sound. John Phillips was the hardest to convince but eventually he agreed and the band, after just one audition, landed a deal with Dunhill Records. Their first single, "California Dreamin'" peaked at #4 in March of 1966. A string of hits would follow including their lone #1, "Monday, Monday." But by 1968 their chart performance had become erratic and they decided to disband.

Elliot then embarked on a solo career that got off to a disastrous start. In October of 1968 she was scheduled for a three week engagement in Las Vegas, playing two shows a night and earning $40,000 a week. She went on a strict diet and lost 100 pounds leading up to opening night. According to Elliot, the weight loss gave her ulcers and throat problems which limited her rehearsal time. On opening night, a star-studded audience packed the Circus Maximus theatre at Caesars Palace only to witness a nervous, weak and feeble Cass Elliot fumble her way through the show. The crowd was unsympathetic, with some booing and others walking out. After the show Elliot returned to the stage to apologize. Her second show later that night was even worse. Reviews were harsh with *Esquire* calling it a "disaster" and *Newsweek* hyperbolically comparing it to the Titanic: "Like some great ocean liner embarking on an ill-fated maiden voyage, Mama Cass slid down the ways and sank to the bottom." The show closed after only one night and rumors quickly spread of drug use.

Elliot landed on her feet though. She became a regular guest on talk shows and landed a few television variety shows of her own. She also returned to her original love of acting, appearing in a number of roles on television and in film. By 1973 she was even singing live again.

In the spring of 1974, following an appearance on *The Tonight Show* with Johnny Carson, Elliot collapsed. She played it off as exhaustion and she was soon off for a two week engagement in London where every show was a huge success. The night of the last show, July 28th, she called Michelle Phillips saying she had received standing ovations each night and she was elated. It seemed she was back on top of her game and her career prospects were indeed bright once again. She hung up the phone, retired for the evening and then died in her sleep.

When her body was found by police there was a half-eaten sandwich in the room. This fact was mentioned to the press prior to an autopsy being performed and very quickly the assumption became that Elliot had choked on her food and died. The autopsy, however, revealed that there was no food in her windpipe and that Elliot had, in fact, died of a heart attack. None of these facts have quelled the universal assumption that Mama Cass died from choking on her food. Frank Zappa mentions it in his 1985 song "We're Turning Again" with the lyric "We can visit Big Mama, we can whap her on the back, while she eats her sandwich!" And in the 1997 movie *Austin Powers, International Man of Mystery*, Mike Myers' character checks a list of people he once knew, mentioning Mama Cass, then crossing her name out, saying, "Deceased, ham sandwich." Sometimes an urban legend will just never die.

The apartment Cass Elliot died in was on loan to her from her friend, singer and songwriter Harry Nilsson. Four years later, Keith Moon, drummer for the Who, overdosed and died in that very same apartment. Nilsson, one can assume, hasn't been able to find any more musician friends who'd like to stay there.

### July 30th

On this date in 1988, Steve Winwood began a four week stay at the top of the pop chart with his song about overcoming obstacles in life, "Roll with It." Winwood had certainly overcome a few obstacles of his own by this point so maybe only fittingly, one of his biggest hits would also earn him a lawsuit and some black eyes in the music press for plagiarizing.

If there's ever been a piano prodigy, surely it was Stephen Lawrence Winwood. He was born in 1948 in Birmingham, England and was playing piano by the time he was four. In his pre-teens he was already playing in bands, supporting acts like Chuck Berry, B.B. King and Muddy Waters. Many of these U.S. artists in the fifties and early sixties would tour England with "pick-up" bands that were made up of local musicians and Winwood was already earning money playing his Hammond organ in such ensembles. When he was just fourteen he was a founding member of the Spencer Davis Group where he co-wrote their 1966, Top 10 hit "Gimme Some Lovin'." After his stint in the Spencer Davis Group he founded Traffic whose debut album, *Mr. Fantasy*, was released in 1967. Two years later Winwood left Traffic to join Eric Clapton in the supergroup, Blind Faith. Clapton only lasted for one album but Traffic was extremely successful, releasing gender-bending albums like 1970's *John Barleycorn Must Die* and 1971's *The Low Spark of High Heeled Boys*. Traffic trafficked at the intersection of prog rock and jazz fusion and they gained an avid following in the halcyon days of the early seventies rock scene.

By the mid-seventies Winwood burnt out. He was weary of the road and the grind of constantly coming up with new material so he dropped out of the music scene for a few years while he contemplated his future. In 1977 he returned with a self-titled debut album. Another few years went by before he released *Arc of the Diver* which featured the #7 hit "While You See a Chance." Solo success continued with 1986's *Back in the High Life* which peaked at #3 on the album chart and produced Top 40 hits like the title track, "The Finer Things" and Winwood's first solo #1, "Higher Love."

The following year Winwood began preparing material for his next album and one of the songs he wrote became the title track "Roll With It." The song offers some simple advice for getting through "hard times knocking on your door." You just "roll with it" and "then you'll see life will be so nice, it's just a step up to paradise." The song may not have any profound answers for overcoming hard times but its upbeat vibe and Winwood's enthusiastic delivery make it seem so simple. Just "roll with it, baby." "Roll With It" went to #1 on this date in 1988 where it stayed for four straight weeks.
Then the trouble began.

In 1990, the song publisher for the 1966 Jr. Walker & the All Stars' hit "(I'm a) Road Runner" filed a lawsuit claiming that Winwood (and his songwriting partner, Will Jennings), plagiarized their song. Some music fans also noted that "Come Out and Dance," a song from Winwood's recently released *Refugee of the Heart* album sounded eerily similar to Peter Gabriel's "Sledgehammer." Winwood defended himself in the press, saying in one interview: "There will always be someone who claims something is similar to something else. I don't steal songs off of people, I don't steal licks. I have influences, and my influences may be similar to Peter Gabriel's. Peter Gabriel himself has told me he was influenced by me. I don't take these (criticisms) seriously, because I'm not copying anybody."

As most of these cases do, Winwood settled for an undisclosed amount. Songwriters Holland-Dozier-Holland were credited with co-writing "Roll with It" and began receiving a portion of future royalties. Winwood was forced to just follow his own advice and roll with it, baby.

## July 31st

On this date in 1923, Ahmet Ertegun was born. He would go on to found the groundbreaking label Atlantic Records and along the way, help introduce white America to some of the most important African American artists of the fifties and sixties. He devoted his life to music and in a sad twist you could say it was music that cost him his life.

Ahmet Ertegun was born in Istanbul, Turkey to an affluent family. When he was just nine his older brother Nesuhi took him to see Duke Ellington and Cab Calloway and lit a passion for music in the young boy. The Erteguns moved to Washington, D.C. when he was twelve and Nesuhi continued to expose his younger brother to jazz greats like Billie Holiday and Louis Armstrong. Ertegun began to express interest early on in making records so his mother bought him a toy record-cutting machine. Ertegun would take instrumental songs, make up lyrics and sing over the original song, then cut a new record which he'd play for his friends.

In his early twenties Ertegun befriended Herb Abramson who was an A&R man for National Records. They quickly discovered they had a similar passion for jazz and R&B and they decided to start a record label. Ertegun borrowed $10,000 from his family's dentist and the two opened the Atlantic Recording Company in 1947 (years later that dentist would be bought out for over $2 million, a pretty good ROI). They both had a definite vision for their label early on. Ertegun explained it in his own words: "Here's the sort of record we need to make. There's a black man living in the outskirts of Opelousas, Louisiana. He works hard for his money; he has to be tight with a dollar. One morning he hears a song on the radio. It's urgent, bluesy, authentic and irresistible. He can't live without this record. He drops everything, jumps in his pickup and drives twenty-five miles to the first record store he finds. If we can make that kind of music, we can make it in the business."

In Atlantic's early days, that's the kind of records they made. Their first hit was Stick McGhee's "Drinkin' Wine, Spo-Dee-O-Dee" in 1949 and with the windfall that song brought in, they were able to sign artists like Ray Charles, R&B singer Ruth Brown and blues trumpeter Joe Morris. Atlantic not only signed the doo-wop band the Clovers but Ertegun decided to take a crack at writing songs for them as well. He penned "Don't You Know I Love You" and "Fool, Fool, Fool" using the pseudonym "A. Nugetre," (his last name spelled backward). Both songs went to #1 on the R&B chart. Ertegun also composed "Chains of Love" for Joe Turner which went to #2 on the R&B chart.

A huge part of being successful in the record business, especially over the long run, is foreseeing trends. As the fifties progressed, so did music, specifically the birth of rock and roll. In 1953 Ertegun made a wise move when he hired Jerry Wexler away from Billboard (Wexler had been an editor for the magazine where he coined the phrase "rhythm and blues") and the two would be quoted in an article the following year in Cashbox magazine, predicting the rise of rock and roll, describing music that would be, "up-to-date blues with a beat and infectious catch phrases and danceable rhythms.... It has to have a message for the sharp youngsters who dig it." Seeing the trend, Atlantic scored big with hits like Bobby Darin's "Splish Splash" and "Queen of the Hop." But they hadn't left their R&B roots behind and they continued to provide an incredible place for African American artists to thrive. Artists like the Drifters, Ben E. King, Otis Redding and Percy Sledge all flourished on the label. Ertegun has said, "Soul lyrics, soul music, came at about the same time as the civil rights movement, and it's very possible that one influenced the other." And when you talk of soul you have to mention the Queen of Soul, Aretha Franklin. She'd spent the beginning of her career signed to Columbia where she'd had some hits, but when she moved to Atlantic in 1966 her career really took off. And as rock and roll evolved into the rock sound of the sixties, Atlantic was there again, signing artists like Crosby Stills & Nash and Led Zeppelin. In 1970 when the Rolling Stones were shopping around for a new distribution deal for their own label, Ertegun met with Mick Jagger personally to close the deal. And when work got started on *Sticky Fingers*, the first album under the new contract, Ertegun was in the studio offering some advice to the band about their sound. During one session he suggested a change that their sound engineer tried and loved. When Ertegun left the studio the engineer asked the band, "Who the fuck was that guy?" and Keith Richards replied, "He's been making hit records since before you were born."

If there is one single reason for Ertegun's success it's that he loved music. From the day his brother brought him to that jazz show, Ertegun had a passion for the artistry of making music and records. And partying as well. He was famous for going drink for drink with his artists and staying out as late or later than any of them. Stephen Stills once said, "Ahmet had as much fun as any man alive" and Mick Jagger has said that Ertegun wasn't so much a father figure but "more like the wicked uncle with a wicked chuckle." If there was a show, no matter how big or small, Ertegun wanted to be there.

Which brings us to the sad end of this tale. In 2006, an 83 year old Ertegun attended a Rolling Stones' concert. He was backstage, meeting and greeting, when he fell. He slipped into a coma and six weeks later, he passed away.

But while Ertegun is gone, his legacy lives on. David Geffen has said, "Few people have had a bigger impact on the record industry than Ahmet," and Stephen Stills added, "He brought America's black and white cultures together through music." That was a goal of Ertegun's from early on and something he was proud of before his death, saying, "I did a little bit to raise the dignity and recognition of the greatness of African American music."

# AUGUST

On this date in 1981, MTV went on the air. One of their earliest tag lines was, "You'll never look at music the same way again" and throughout the next decade and more, that could not have been more true. To say MTV changed music as we know it is probably an understatement.

Music videos had been played on television prior to 1981. In the late seventies former Monkee, Michael Nesmith, had created a weekly television show called *PopClips* which showed music videos on Nickelodeon. There were similar shows in New Zealand (*Radio with Pictures*) and Australia (*Countdown*) but no one was doing a full-time broadcast devoted to showing music videos. However, with the advent of cable, there were a surfeit of channels and Warner Cable looked to fill that space by taking these weekly shows and expanding the concept to a 24 hour music channel.

Robert Pitman was selected by Warner to program MTV which was no easy task. At the time, very few songs came with accompanying videos, and those that did were often unwatchable. Nonetheless, the lineup was assembled and at 12:01am Eastern Time on this date in 1981, MTV went on the air with the words "Ladies and gentlemen, rock and roll." Film footage of the Apollo 11 launch and moon landing aired while they played an early theme song. MTV wanted to use Neil Armstrong's "One small step" quote but he refused to allow it. They would stick with the shuttle launch footage as a theme until the Challenger disaster in 1986.

After all the original VJs, Mark Goodman, Alan Hunter, Martha Quinn, JJ Jackson and Nina Blackwood, got to introduce themselves they played their very first music video, appropriately, "Video Killed the Radio Star" by the Buggles. Pat Benatar's "You Better Run" was the second video shown on the channel.

In the early years everything at MTV was low budget, from the cheesy sets to the fact that sometimes the screen would go black as technicians inserted a tape into the VCR or a video that was playing jammed. But that doesn't mean it didn't have an immediate impact. In the handful of markets that carried MTV early on, records sales began to rise on songs in rotation on the music channel. Artists like Men at Work and Human League were some of the first to "break" on MTV and show the record labels that the new format, like radio, had promotional power.

MTV took a lot of criticism early on for not showing many black artists. David Bowie even challenged Mark Goodman on air one day about it (Google it - it's a great clip). Walter Yetnikoff (president of CBS at the time) threatened MTV with pulling all of his artists (white or black) from their channel if they didn't start playing Michael Jackson's new "Billie Jean" video in 1983. MTV finally added it to its "medium rotation" playlist (two to three airings per day) but only after it reached #1 on the pop chart. This didn't exactly open the floodgates for black artists but soon Prince's "Little Red Corvette" and Donna Summer's "She Works Hard For the Money" were added to the rotation and eventually the channel became much more diverse.

By the mid-eighties MTV was a powerhouse and able to break records even better than radio. Budgets for videos increased as artists realized that if they had a unique video they could get a hit song. This is probably one reason for the abundance of one hit wonders in the eighties as bands without that much musical talent could get lucky with an eye-catching video and have a hit, only to never be seen or heard from again (we're looking at you, Dexys Midnight Runners).

In 1984 MTV produced its first awards show and Madonna's eye-popping performance of "Like a Virgin" set the bar for how to get noticed on these shows. Soon the channel's programming expanded to include special events like spring break and specialized shows like *120 Minutes, Headbangers Ball* and *Yo! MTV Raps*. Their *Unplugged* series produced incredibly intimate and memorable performances by Nirvana, Mariah Carey and 10,000 Maniacs just to name a few.

And as everyone knows, MTV is no longer a music station but more of a reality TV channel with shows like the *Real World, Jersey Shore* and *Teen Mom* taking the place of music videos and cheesy banter from V-Jays. The screen no longer goes black when a tech switches tapes either. Things have come a long way since its launch and it's hard to believe it now, but for about a decade or so there was no single entity as powerful as MTV for making hits and creating superstars. You can find that first broadcast on Youtube and it's worth looking up today, especially if you're old enough to remember the early eighties and ever sat around all day watching MTV hoping for your favorite video to be played. Those videos never did kill radio but they sure changed the musical industry.

## August 2nd

On this date in 1992, "Baby Got Back," Sir Mix-a-Lot's ode to women with large buttocks, was enjoying its five week run at #1 on the pop chart. The Seattle rapper's only #1 hit would go on to be the second largest seller of 1992, behind Whitney Houston's "I Will Always Love You." Years later, Mix-a-Lot finally revealed whose derrière inspired his song and it turned out to be a very famous butt.

Anthony Ray was born in 1963 in the Seattle suburb of Auburn, Washington which would put him in his late teens when rap was first spreading out of New York City. He heard the earliest rap songs on the radio and fell in love with the genre. But the problem for Ray was that nobody in the record business was scouring the great North West looking for the next hip hop star. So Ray did what so many musicians before and since have done; he bi-passed the record companies and set up his own label to release his music. He changed his name to Sir Mix-a-Lot and along with his DJ, Nasty Nes, established Nastymix. His first single, "I Just Love My Beat" (backed with "Square Dance Rap") was released in 1985. Rap was still a genre finding its footing at the time and Mix-a-Lot's sound was indicative of many of the earliest hip hop offerings, silly and fun with simple rhymes about everyday activities. Other releases followed before Mix-a-Lot gained some notice with 1988's "Posse on Broadway" which entered *Billboard*'s Hot 100 and peaked at #70. The Broadway in the title refers to a street in Seattle and not New York's famous theater row. In fact, "Posse on Broadway" name checks numerous spots in the Emerald City and is still a popular local tune.

Mix-a-Lot signed with Rick Rubin's Def American label and released the album *Mack Daddy* in early 1992. The second single off the LP is a song Mix-a-Lot has said came about while he was watching a Budweiser commercial during the Super Bowl. The models in the ad were too skinny for his taste and he thought of another woman he'd seen recently who was more up his alley. That was his inspiration behind "Baby Got Back" although it would take decades before he revealed who that other woman was. "Baby Got Back" was released in May of 1992 and, despite the fact that its video was initially banned on MTV, the song raced "like a turbo 'vette" up the charts. It hit #1 in the first chart week of July where it stayed for five straight weeks. MTV eventually saw its way to playing the video which only helped the song keep selling throughout the year.

Despite the obvious criticism that the song objectifies women, Sir Mix-a-Lot has stood by "Baby Got Back," saying it's not just about big butts but it's also a knock on women who, "damn near kill themselves to try to look like these beanpole models." He says women constantly thank him for the message that it's okay to have curves, or as Mix-a-Lot puts it, to be "thick and juicy."

So who was that other woman that Mix-a-Lot thought of when he got turned off by those skinny Budweiser models? In a 2014 interview with TMZ he said it was Jennifer Lopez who he'd seen dancing as a fly-girl on the TV show *In Living Color* which is funny because that he name checks Flo-Jo in the song (Olympic sprinter Florence Griffith Joyner) when he should have mentioned J-Lo. And it's even funnier that *In Living Color* parodied the song with "Baby Got Snacks," with Jamie Foxx playing the fictional rapper "Trail Mix-a-Lot." Little did they know that one of their own had inspired the song. "Baby Got Back" contains a few samples including one from the movie *Full Metal Jacket* of British actress Papillon Soo Soo saying, "Me so horny" (to complete the line "that butt you got makes . . . ") A few years earlier 2 Live Crew used that same sample in their controversial song "Me So Horny." The rhythm track also contains a sample of Channel One's song "Technicolor," specifically the whip-like snare drum. But this was right before the turning point in hip hop where composers of the original songs, used by either sample or interpolation, were credited and given a songwriting share. Which means Anthony Ray is the lone songwriter listed for "Baby Got Back" so he enjoys full credit whenever the song is used or covered. And those instances have been multiple through the years. "Baby Got Back" has appeared in movies, television shows and commercials. Plus it's been covered and reinterpreted by multiple artists. While the original is funny, if you want a great laugh, look up Joe Nichols' country version or Jonathan Coulton's breezy folk take on it. And then of course there's the Glee version which sounds exactly like you'd imagine.

In 2014, Sir Mix-a-Lot's most famous song had a resurgence of popularity as it was featured prominently in Nicki Minaj's hit song "Anaconda." Minaj, known for her own healthy derrière, could not have picked a better song to sample and celebrate. And if you want to see how much times have changed watch the two different videos back-to-back. Where Mix-a-Lot certainly used his share of scantily clad dancers (which made MTV ban it initially) his video would probably earn a PG-13 rating these days. Minaj's video is nothing short of soft-core porn. And after you're done, you may want to dial "1-900-mixalot and kick those nasty thoughts."

## August 3rd

On this date in 1985, Tears For Fears scored their first #1 hit with "Shout." The song would stay at the top of the charts for three weeks, assisted greatly by a video that was in heavy rotation on MTV.

Roland Orzabal and Curt Smith met as teenagers the late seventies in England working together as session musicians. They joined a band called Graduate that released one album in 1980 before Orzabal and Smith left to form Tears for Fears. Orzabal and Smith were both followers of American psychologist Arthur Janov and his trauma-based psychotherapy called primal therapy. Janov theorized that we repress negative memories from childhood that can be expressed (and often exorcised) in therapy by screaming or shouting. Janov received a lot of attention a decade earlier when John Lennon and Yoko Ono underwent primal therapy and produced the album *John Lennon/Plastic Ono Band*. Lennon's song "Mother," which features him screaming at his mother and questioning why she left him as a child, is basically a rock song masking as primal therapy. Orzabal and Smith were such believers in the therapy and Janov's writings that they named their band after a section in the Janov book *Prisoners of Pain* in which he referred to, "tears as a replacement for fears."

Orzabal and Smith both loved bands like Television and the Talking Heads so Tears for Fears' first album, *The Hurting*, had a definite synth pop sound to it. That album was huge in England, going to #1 on the album chart and including "Mad World" which made it to #3 on the singles chart. But neither made much of an impact in the States. Their first album continued their focus on psychology, with over half of the songs dealing with emotional distress or primal therapy.

When they began working on a followup LP, they moved to a slightly more mainstream, rock and pop sound. They'd name this offering *Songs from the Big Chair*, inspired by the movie *Sybil* in which a young girl with multiple personalities claims she only feels safe in the "big chair" in her therapist's office. The song that would launch the band to worldwide fame was the album's second single, "Shout."

Orzabal began the song by singing the chorus very repetitively, like a mantra. He then blended the verses into the chorus so they flow together more than most songs, layering the end of a verse, like, "You shouldn't have to shout for joy" with the chorus beginning on the "shout" in the verse. And with a chorus that urges the listener to "shout" and "let it all out" one can assume that Orzabal and Smith have returned to singing about primal therapy. But Orzabal disputes this assumption: "A lot of people think that 'Shout' is just another song about primal scream theory, continuing the themes of the first album. It is actually more concerned with political protest. It came out in 1984 when a lot of people were still worried about the aftermath of the Cold War and it was basically an encouragement to protest." Smith adds, "It concerns protest inasmuch as it encourages people not to do things without actually questioning them."

A huge reason for the song's success was a video that went into heavy rotation on MTV. Tears for Fears became just another English band to benefit from what become known as the second British Invasion. This was spurred on by MTV playing so many videos by bands from England. It wasn't that MTV preferred these bands, but early on they played what they could get their hands on, and since British television had provided a platform for videos to be played as far back as the late sixties, bands from England were more prone to make videos and, when they did, do more than just stick a camera in front of themselves while they played for an audience. It took a few years for American bands to catch up which is why the U.S. charts from the early to mid-eighties look a lot like the charts from the sixties when the Beatles and Stones were leading the first British Invasion.

Whether "Shout" is another nod to Arthur Janov or an encouragement to protest, there is no denying the song has a cathartic feel to it. The whole point of Janov's therapy is to bi-pass the cerebral cortex and get down to our primal selves; our inner beings. His patients achieved this through reenacting a painful moment in their lives and repeatedly screaming or crying. "Shout" may not make the listener recall any childhood trauma or pain, but it can feel good to sing along to, or better yet, to shout along to. It can be a great way to "let it all out."

### August 4th

On this date in 1978, *National Lampoon's Animal House* had just been released and was already receiving some glowing reviews. It would go on to be the third highest-grossing film of the year, earning $120 million. It not only launched John Belushi into superstardom but the movie had a huge impact on music as well.

*National Lampoon* first hit the newsstands in 1970 and within a few years had become an extremely popular magazine, known for its outrageous satire of all things Americana. As the magazine became more successful, it spawned radio shows, recordings, live theater and finally, in 1978, a major motion picture. When writers from the magazine decided to make a movie they pulled from their own backgrounds. They'd all gone to universities and many had been in fraternities so that became a natural setting. They chose to place the movie in 1962 because they saw that as America's last innocent year.

*Animal House* was filmed on a shoestring budget of just $3 million because no one foresaw its success. There was no track record for a film like this so how could they? When veteran actor Donald Sutherland landed a part he was offered either a flat fee or a percentage of the gross. Sutherland took the flat fee of $75,000, which ain't bad for three days of filming, but that decision ultimately cost him millions when the movie became a surprise hit. The rest of the cast were virtual unknowns, including Kevin Bacon who made his first film appearance and, most famously, John Belushi, who was already semi-famous from *Saturday Night Live* but would become the film's breakout star.

There are many party scenes in *Animal House*, frat parties and dances at the Dexter Lake Club, and so, musically, the movie could not have been set in a better time. Rock and roll in the early sixties was very much a continuation of the fifties sound, upbeat and fun with few serious themes. The movie is filled with these songs, some by the original artists, like "Twisting the Night Away" by Sam Cooke, "Tossin' and Turnin'" by Bobby Lewis and "Let's Dance" by Chris Montez, while others are covers. John Belushi gets the chance to sing "Money (That's What I Want)" and the garage rock classic "Louie, Louie" and a fictional band contributes "Shama Lama Ding Dong," an original song written for the movie and a remake of the Isley Brothers' classic party song, "Shout!"

The Isley Brothers wrote and released "Shout!" in 1959. The song had developed from their live performances where they would often cover Jackie Wilson's "Lonely Teardrops" which includes the repeated line, "Say you will." The Isley Brothers performed "Shout!" as a call and response to Wilson's song and when their audiences went nuts they knew they were on to something. Though their version didn't crack the Top 40 it has sold over a million copies and it became a popular song for bands to cover both live and in the studio. It is undeniably a great party song with its instructions on how to shout ("Kick my heels up," "Throw my head back") and multiple tempo changes including a caesura that begins with the line, "Now waaaaaaaaaaaait a minute." It only made sense for the producers of *Animal House* to include the song. And to do so, they created a fictional band called Otis Day and the Knights.

Lloyd Williams was chosen to sing both "Shama Lama Ding Dong" and "Shout!" and then actor DeWayne Jessie lip-synched the songs for the movie. When *Animal House* became a hit, Jessie changed his named to Otis Day and was very successful touring and performing songs from the movie. Propelled by the unforgettable scene from the movie, where members of the Delta house dance in togas, repeat back the "hey hey hey" parts and then, following Belushi's screamed "Gator," get down on the floor and gyrate, "Shout!" has remained a party classic all these years later. Bands cover the song frequently and DJs can chose between the original, the version from *Animal House* or any number of recorded covers.

Music serves many purposes in our lives. Some songs move us to tears. Some inspire us to take action. Some songs piss us off while others calm us down. "Shout!" has a purpose as well. From that opening, "well," that can be drawn out for over 5 seconds, depending on the version, through the final lines of: "Everybody shout, shout, shout" that fade slowly out, the song is a four minute celebration of movement and dance. It's a chance to escape and have fun. The song probably didn't need *Animal House* to secure its place as an all-time party classic but it sure didn't hurt either.

## August 5th

On this date in 1957, *American Bandstand* aired nationally for the first time. The show's host, Dick Clark was already a local celebrity in Philadelphia but he would soon go on to earn national prominence as arguably the most successful DJ of all time.

Richard Augustus Wagstaff Clark Jr. was born in 1929 just north of New York City. As a child he showed little interest in anything but the emerging new technology called radio. By ten he was telling anyone who'd listen he was going to be a DJ. That goal was made easier for the young man because his uncle owned WRUN, a station in Rome, New York that his father helped run. At sixteen he started working in the mail room at WRUN and, from time to time, would fill in on-air, using the name Dick Clay to avoid any confusion with his father. He attended Syracuse University, where he majored in advertising with a minor in radio.

Clark's first big broadcasting job came in 1952 when he became a DJ on WFIL in Philadelphia. WFIL had an affiliated television station and that same year they launched a show called *Bob Horn's Bandstand* which featured short musical films (precursors to music videos) and studio guests. From time to time Clark would fill in for Horn when he was on vacation. Then, in 1956, a 27 year old Dick Clark caught a very fortuitous break. Bob Horn was arrested for drunk driving and WFIL let him go. Clark was the obvious replacement and his timing couldn't have been more perfect. He took over as the show's host on July 9th, 1956 and a year later, on this date, WABC picked up the show, changed its name to *American Bandstand,* and began to air it nationally.

The show had an instant impact on music and pop culture. One of the first songs performed on *American Bandstand* was Paul Anka's "Diana." The song had been out for a month and was slowly creeping up the charts. After the nationwide exposure, the song shot to #1 on *Billboard*'s "Best Sellers in Stores" chart (the precursor to the Hot 100). Other songs had similar swift shifts in sales after appearing on the show and before long Clark became something of a musical kingmaker.

Rock and roll was exploding at the time and *American Bandstand* is often credited for bringing this new sound into the living rooms of America. For that role, there could be no one better suited than Dick Clark. Parents were fearful of this new, rebellious sound and the music industry, especially veteran singers and musicians who were being pushed aside in favor of these new young rockers, were leery of it. When Frank Sinatra was asked about Elvis Presley early on he replied: "his kind of music is deplorable, a rancid smelling aphrodisiac. It fosters almost totally negative and destructive reactions in young people." And Sinatra was not alone in his low opinion of rock and roll. But somehow Clark's affable personality and everyman good looks tempered that negativity and made rock and roll palatable, at least for some. Years later, Clark would look back on this and comment: "I was roundly criticized for being in and around rock and roll music at its inception. It was the devil's music, it would make your teeth fall out and your hair turn blue, whatever the hell. You get through that."

He did much more than just get through it. Clark's real genius was understanding the power of teenagers (or "the kids" as he often called them). He understood how quickly that generation follows trends and so, if his show was seen as introducing those trends as opposed to chasing after them, he'd be the one to watch. He once called himself "the fastest follower in the business" and that talent was crucial to *Bandstand*'s success. In that light, *American Bandstand* didn't just break music, it affected fashion and hair styles and dance moves. When Chubby Checker performed "The Twist" on *Bandstand* it not only launched his version of the song but it made the dance craze ubiquitous in the early sixties. So many other artists can point to *American Bandstand* as their debut or coming out party.

Clark's legacy should not just be limited to the music and fashions he helped introduce. He had an important impact on race relations as well. When he took over *Bandstand* the show had an unwritten "all-white" policy. He ended that very quickly, introducing African American artists early on followed by African American dancers. He told an interviewer years later: "I was aware that rock and roll and *Bandstand* owed their existences to black music and the black artists who sang it. By the time I had the show a year I knew it had to be integrated." By showing white and black kids dancing together, he was also showing that we are one people, especially when the power of music unites us.

Clark's success, of course, is not limited to *American Bandstand*. He was a true broadcasting genius, launching shows as diverse *as TV's Bloopers & Practical Jokes* and *Challenge of the Child Geniuses*. In 1972 he introduced *Dick Clark's New Year's Rockin' Eve* and for decades he was the last voice millions of Americans heard to end each year and the first to usher in a new one. And when ABC lost the rights to air the Grammy Awards he created the American Music Awards to take its place on the network.

But all those accomplishments pale in comparison to Clark and his impact on rock and roll in America. The cultural shift from the big bands and crooners of the forties and early fifties to the grittier sound and style of rock and roll is hard to comprehend for anyone who didn't live through it. But suffice to say that when big change takes place it is often met by a cultural bulwark. The old guard often fights hard not to lose any ground. In the case of rock and roll, it took someone as charming and disarming as Dick Clark to help clear the way. Even though he left us in 2012, for many, he'll forever be "America's Oldest Teenager."

## August 6th

On this date in 1990 Garth Brooks released the single "Friends in Low Places" three weeks ahead of his second album, *No Fences*. Brooks' debut LP had established him as a country artist on the rise. His sophomore release, and its lead single, which spent four weeks at #1 on *Billboard*'s Hot Country Songs chart, and won both the Academy of Country Music and Country Music Association awards for 1990 Single of the Year, would make him a superstar.

"Friends in Low Places" had an interesting path to the top of the charts. Earl Bud Lee, one of the song's writers, was out to lunch one day with some friends. When the bill arrived Lee realized he'd forgotten his wallet. In an attempt to make a joke he said to his lunchmates, "Don't worry, I have friends in low places. I know the cook." Lee's songwriting partner, Dewayne Blackwell, overheard the comment and the two saw the potential in that line right away. However, for some reason, they left the idea dormant until some months later when they were both attending a party to celebrate someone else's #1 hit. Perhaps they were encouraged or challenged by this because at that party they started talking about the "friends in low places" line and the song then came together quickly (which probably explains why the opening verse takes place at a party). With the song complete Lee and Blackwell sought to make a demo. Which is where Garth Brooks enters the story.

Troyal Garth Brooks was born in 1962 in Tulsa, Oklahoma. His mother was a country singer and his childhood home was filled with music. In fact his parents used to host talent nights at which all of their children were expected to perform. Brooks learned to play guitar and banjo at a young age yet, despite this, or perhaps because of it, he gravitated more towards sports than music as a teenager. In high school he participated in track and field and played football and baseball. He was good enough to earn a scholarship to Oklahoma State where he graduated in 1984. It wasn't until after college that he decided to pursue a musical career and so he headed off to Nashville.

Struggling musicians do all sorts of things to earn a living while they hustle to catch a break. For Brooks, that meant shoe sales. He landed a job selling shoes and boots which fortuitously allowed him to meet a lot of music industry folks. Ken Mellons, who was an unknown musician at the time and has gone on to his share of success, says he still has a business card Brooks handed him in an effort to network. Brooks also had the chance to sell Lee and Blackwell some shoes one day and when he mentioned his singing ability they hired him to cut some demos. Songwriters, especially those not blessed with a decent singing voice, will often write a song then create a demonstration version of it, or demo, to help shop the song to established artists and record labels. Lee and Blackwell had been happy with Brooks' prior demo work so after they completed "Friends in Low Places" they reached out to see if they could hire him yet again. But when they contacted Brooks he told them he'd signed a deal with Capitol Records and his first album was already complete and ready for release. Still, he agreed to help them with the demo.

When Brooks sang "Friends in Low Places" he loved it. He told the songwriters he wished he'd heard it a few weeks earlier so he could have included it on his debut album. Then he asked Lee and Blackwell if they would hold the song for him. Even though there was no guarantee the young singer would get a second album, and if he did it was at least a year away, they both appreciated his eagerness about the song so they agreed. Brooks has always been grateful that the two songwriters put that much faith in an unknown singer. "Friends" was the last demo Brooks would ever record.

Brooks' debut album had more than enough success that his label green-lit a follow-up. When he began to collect songs for what would become *No Fences*, "Friends in Low Places" was one of the first he recorded. Wanting to turn the song into a party he packed the studio with friends to sing the song's final chorus. At one point the microphone picked up the sound of a beer can opening and at another someone yells, "push Marie!" which was a reference to guitarist Jim Garver's wife who was in labor at the time (Garver, a wise man, was with his wife, not in the studio.) There is a third verse in the song that was left out of the studio version, possibly because it contains the word "ass." Brooks will often sing that verse in concert much to the delight of his rabid fans.

Garth Brooks has gone on to unprecedented fame and success as a singer. In terms of record sales he is the #1 solo artist in the U.S. Yes, you read that correctly, Garth Brooks has sold more records than Elvis Presley or Michael Jackson. And he is the only artist to have seven albums reach diamond status (10 million units sold). All this probably would have happened anyway but it's heartening to think back to the late eighties when Brooks was an unknown, handing out business cards at his day job trying to catch a break. And Lee and Blackwell creating a song from a spontaneous comment that went on to be a huge-seller. "Friends in Low Places" has brought joy to millions who have had the chance to hear Brooks play it live, as well as those who have sung it in a Karaoke bar or on a packed dance floor at a wedding. It's a song of bonding and friendship that tends to make people want to raise a glass (preferably of whiskey as the song suggests) and sing along. All because some songwriter forgot his wallet one day.

On this date in 1983 the coming of age film *Risky Business* had just been released. The movie not only became Tom Cruise's first big box office smash and helped establish him as a movie star but it revived Bob Seger's "Old Time Rock and Roll," ultimately making it one of his most recognizable songs. And he didn't even write it. Or did he?

Robert Clark Seger was born in Detroit, Michigan in 1945. His father played several instruments so he grew up in a home filled with music and by the time he was sixteen he had already formed his first band, the Decibels, and written and recorded his first original song, "The Lonely One." Like his father, Seger was a multi-instrumentalist, playing organ, piano and guitar for the Decibels. A few other bands followed before Seger signed his first contract, becoming a Capitol Records' artist in 1968. He released the single "Ramblin' Gamblin' Man" under the name Bob Seger System and when that began selling Capitol green-lit an entire album of the same name. Though that LP made it all the way to #62 on the *Billboard* album chart, two follow-up LPs didn't do nearly as well and by 1971 Seger had dropped the "System" and began recording solo. He'd continue to struggle to match his initial success until 1975's *Beautiful Loser* LP which included "Katmandu," a song that just missed the Top 40. The next year he released two albums under the name Bob Seger & the Silver Bullet band that would establish him as a rock mainstay: *Live Bullet* and *Night Moves*.

In 1978, Bob Seger did some recording for his next album, *Stranger in Town,* at the famous Muscle Shoals Sound Studios. His band had worked with him on some of the tracks but Seger also liked the sound of the Muscle Shoals Rhythm Section, also known as the Swampers, so he recorded with them as well. It was the Muscle Shoals Rhythm Section that suggested he give "Old Time Rock and Roll" a shot. He listened to a demo of the song that had been written by Thomas Jones and George Jackson and, according to Seger, he rewrote almost all of it. "All I kept from the original," Seger claims, "was the chorus: 'old time rock and roll, that kind of music just soothes my soul, I reminisce about the days of old with that old time rock and roll.'" Despite this, Seger never asked for a co-songwriting credit. "That was the dumbest thing I ever did," he would say later. His manager even told him he should ask to be added as a third writer but he declined, thinking the song was an album track and nobody would really like it anyway. Seger laments not being credited as much for financial reasons as for control. Because he's not a credited writer he has no say in where the song gets used. "It got into a Hardee's commercial because I couldn't control it," he laments. "Oh my God, it was awful!" Seger's account has been disputed by some of those who were familiar with the original demo of the song. They say Seger made little-to-no lyrical changes. Since Seger has never tried to get himself added as a cowriter, it's a moot point.

Despite Seger's low opinion of the song it was released in 1979 as the fourth single off *Stranger in Town*. As often happens with a fourth or fifth single from an album, "Old Time Rock and Roll" didn't make much of a splash. It peaked at #28 on the pop chart and after that, the song pretty much disappeared. By the early eighties Seger had even dropped it from his setlists at concerts because his fans did not consider it a must-hear song.

Then, *Risky Business* was released and Tom Cruise became a superstar almost overnight. And the scene featuring Cruise dancing in his underwear and lip syncing to "Old Time Rock and Roll" helped revive interest in the song. Capitol re-released the single and it just missed the Top 40 a second time. Before long "Old Time Rock and Roll" became a rock radio staple and Seger began featuring it prominently in his live shows. In 1989 the Amusement & Music Operators Association released a list called the Top 40 Jukebox Singles of All Time. "Old Time Rock and Roll" was ranked #9. Seven years later it had crept to #2. And in 2004 when Bob Seger was inducted into the Rock and Roll Hall of Fame he thrilled the crowd at New York City's Waldorf Astoria with a rousing version of the song. "Old Time Rock and Roll," with its easily sung chorus and danceable, rock-meets-disco beat, is not only a jukebox staple but a favorite at weddings and private parties as well. And no matter who actually wrote it, the sentiment that "Today's music ain't got the same soul" is pretty universal with all generations.

## August 8th

On this date in 1972, Alice Cooper's "School's Out" was sitting at its peak position, #7 on the *Billboard* Hot 100 chart. The song had arrived there on July 29th and would sit there for two weeks before it began to descend. As of today it is Cooper's highest-charting single (1989's "Poison" also peaked at #7 but spent only one week there) and is often considered his signature song as well as an annual favorite for kids wrapping up their school year.

Vincent Damon Furnier was born in 1948 in Detroit, Michigan. When he was ten his family relocated to Phoenix, Arizona where he attended and ran track for Cortez High School. When he was sixteen Furnier decided to participate in a local talent competition. He gathered a few fellow cross-country runners and they formed a band to do Beatles' songs with lyrics changed to be about their track accomplishments. The band won the competition and went on to some local fame as the Spiders. After they all graduated they were able to make frequent trips to Los Angeles and their fame continued growing. They changed their name to Nazz only to find out another band existed with that name so they were forced to find another one. Rock legend has it that Furnier sat down one day with a Ouija board and came up with "Alice Cooper," a name he adopted personally as well as for his band. He has since denied the rumor, telling the BBC, "It was like just pure urban legend. . . but it was a great story." The story matched the reputation Cooper was developing along with some crazy stage antics that included wearing makeup and having his head chopped off by a guillotine (fake, of course). He was on his way to creating an entire new sub-genre of music called "shock rock."

Before long Alice Cooper was recommended to Frank Zappa who was looking to sign some avant-garde acts to his label. As the story goes Zappa told the band to come to his house at 7 o'clock for an audition. Zappa of course meant 7pm (what musician would mean 7am?) so he was quite surprised to awoken by Cooper and his bandmates first thing in the morning. He signed the band immediately and their debut album, *Pretties for You*, was released in 1969. That same year the famous "Chicken Incident" took place which only furthered Cooper's wild-man image. At a concert in Toronto, Cooper tore open a feathered pillow (which was a regular part of his act) only to find a chicken inside (it had been planted there by his manager Shep Gordon). Cooper threw the chicken into the crowd (he claims he thought it could fly) and the audience proceeded to tear it up and throw the pieces back at Cooper. As shocking as that was (especially for the chicken) by the next day the story had evolved to Cooper biting the head off the chicken and drinking its blood. When he talked to Zappa about it and told him the truth, Zappa replied, "Whatever you do, don't tell anyone you didn't do it." Cooper would continue pushing the envelope in concert with pranks like staging his own execution by electric chair, beating up Santa Claus, stabbing baby dolls with a sword and draping a snake scarf-like around his neck.

In 1970 Cooper began working with producer Bob Ezrin and he scored his first legitimate hit with "I'm Eighteen." He soon went from underground, eclectic artist to a legitimate rock star which was clearly his status when he sat down to start preparing material for a 1972 album.

Cooper has cited two inspirations for writing "School's Out." He said he was once asked the question, "What's the greatest three minutes of your life?" His response was, "Christmas morning and the last three minutes of school." Cooper also said the old Bowery Boys movies inspired the title. The Bowery Boys were fictional New York City characters who were featured in nearly 50 films in the forties and fifties. They were heavily syndicated to television throughout the sixties and seventies so Cooper probably spent many an afternoon watching them. They would often use the expression "school's out," meaning "wise up." But being the inventor of "shock rock," Cooper had to take things a step further. Instead of school just being out for the summer, in Cooper's lyrics the school blows up and is out forever (which is pretty much every school kid's fantasy at some point).

Once again, Ezrin worked with Cooper on "School's Out" and it was his suggestion to have the chorus of children come in singing the childhood rhyme, "No more pencils, no more books, no more teachers' dirty looks." When the song was released some radio stations initially refused to play it, saying it promoted rebellion or violence in school. Teachers and school officials also spoke out against it which probably just helped the song gain exposure. The song was released in April of 1972, two months before Cooper's album of the same name. It entered the Top 40 in late June and then continued climbing throughout the summer of 1972, eventually peaking at #7. The song helped propel Cooper's album up the LP chart as well. *School's Out* peaked at #2 the same week its title track hit #7. Though Cooper only broke the Top 10 two other times in his career (1977's beautiful ballad "You and Me" went to #9 and, as mentioned, 1989's "Poison" hit #7) his albums became consistent sellers throughout the seventies as he established himself as the king of shock rock.

Not only has "School's Out" become an anthem for Cooper (and arguably his signature song) but it resurfaces annually as school years come to an end and children everywhere look forward to those "greatest three minutes."

## August 9th

On this date in 1995, Jerry Garcia passed away. He'd flirted with death before, most notably a decade earlier when he slipped into a five day diabetic coma, but this time around he was actually in rehab and trying to get healthy. Yet he succumbed to a heart attack, leaving millions of "Deadheads" in mourning.

Jerome John Garcia was born in San Francisco on August 1st, 1942. He was a rambunctious young man, smoking pot by age seventeen and stealing his mother's car when he was twenty. After a short stint in the army (punishment for the car theft), Garcia began hanging around the local music scene, meeting various future members of the Grateful Dead like Phil Lesh in 1962 and Bob Weir in 1964. He sang and performed mainly bluegrass and folk music in bands such as Mother McCree's Uptown Jug Champions and Sleepy Hollow Hog Stompers and the Warlocks. LSD was a popular drug at the time and Garcia began using it regularly, saying later that it changed everything for him.

Searching for a name for a new band he was forming, Garcia flipped through a Funk & Wagnall's encyclopedia one day and his finger fell on an entry for "grateful dead." The definition was, "a dead person, or his angel, showing gratitude to someone who, as an act of charity, arranged their burial." Garcia admitted later that he didn't really like the name, but, "just found it to be really powerful."

The Grateful Dead began performing regularly in the Bay Area and started developing a strong following. One of their first big performances was in 1967 at the Mantra-Rock Dance to benefit the Hare Krishna temple. The Dead shared the bill with poet Allen Ginsberg and bands like Moby Grape and Big Brother and the Holding Company with Janis Joplin. Their performance raised their local reputation even higher.

The Grateful Dead's eponymous debut album was released a few weeks later. In a sign of things to come, four of the album's nine tracks had to be shortened to fit on the LP. Their debut made little splash on the album chart (peaking at #73) and it wouldn't be certified gold (selling half a million copies) until 1971. Nonetheless the album was considered a big deal in San Francisco where they had become local celebrities. But Garcia would shepherd the band to much higher heights than just hometown heroes. Their music, which could never really be defined (was it rock, jazz, psychedelia, improvisation?) would pave the way for scores of "jam bands" to follow. They toured relentlessly, playing over 2,100 concerts in the 30 years between their formation and Garcia's death and released scores of studio albums. And if that weren't enough to keep a man busy, Garcia also played in side projects like the Jerry Garcia Band and various acoustic projects like Old and in the Way.

Garcia and the rest of the band were consistent drug users. Whether it was smoking pot, snorting cocaine or shooting heroin, the band experimented with just about everything. Combine that with Garcia's unhealthy weight, sleep apnea and cigarette smoking and it was no wonder his health deteriorated in his middle years. When he was 46 he succumbed to diabetes and fell into a coma for five days. When he awoke he was forced to learn how to play guitar all over again. They released a comeback album *In the Dark* in 1987, which became their bestselling studio LP and their concerts in the late eighties and early nineties are often considered among their best.

Garcia made attempts to get healthy, quitting smoking and becoming a vegetarian, but it was all too little too late (and the drug use never really did stop). He checked himself into rehab in the summer of 1995 (telling friends he was going to Hawaii for some time off) but just eight days after his 53rd birthday he was found dead.

Like every great musician, Garcia left a legacy of both recorded music and concert experiences that his ardent fans can relish forever. And surviving members of the band tour frequently enough that Deadheads can still enjoy their music live. Still, nothing is the same without Garcia at the center of the stage and surely every time Bob Weir plays "Brokedown Palace" or Phil Lesh performs "Box of Rain" (a song he wrote for his dying father) fans can look to the skies and know Garcia is smiling down behind his signature specs and full beard.

### August 10th

On this date in 2013, Robin Thicke's "Blurred Lines" began its eighth consecutive week at the top of the charts. It would stay there for a total of thirteen weeks, from June 22nd to September 8th, making it quite literally the song of the summer. "Blurred Lines" was not only the catchiest song of the year but it stirred the most controversy as well. And when all was said and done it was even the subject of a copyright lawsuit that sent shock waves through the music industry (and is still being appealed as of this writing).

Robin Thicke makes no secret of his love for Marvin Gaye's 1977 disco hit "Got to Give It Up," often calling it his favorite song of all time. So when he and Pharrell Williams got together in 2012 to work on a song, Thicke said, "We should make something like 'Got to Give It Up.' Something with that groove." The two started jamming and Pharrell immediately came up with his "hey hey hey" line. Within an hour they had laid down the basic track and written the lyrics (save for T.I's. rap which would be added later).

Before "Blurred Lines" was released, Thicke and his manager decided it needed a gimmick. Thicke had been an accomplished R&B artist till this point but had never had a crossover hit so they knew the song wouldn't sell just on his name alone (nor was Pharrell at that time, the household name he would become within the next year). The gimmick they came up with was naked models. They made a music video featuring Thicke, T.I., and Pharrell standing around casually singing while three models dance around them and pose (and one, for some reason, holds a lamb). In the unrated version the models wear nothing but skin-colored G-strings (Google it. Seriously, Google it, we'll wait). They also made an edited version where the models are (just barely) clothed. They released the unedited version on Youtube and within a week it was taken down with Youtube citing its anti-pornography stance.

The publicity this received was all the gimmick the song needed. In the spring of 2013 "Blurred Lines" started climbing the charts and the unedited video became one of the most shared links on the internet.

But very quickly controversy followed. Women's groups objected to the song, saying it promoted date rape, specifically the title and the lyric, "I know you want it" which encouraged the idea that, "'No' doesn't always mean 'No'." The video was also criticized for being misogynistic and objectifying women (not to mention lambs).

Negative publicity often helps an artist's popularity and such was the case with Robin Thicke and "Blurred Lines." The song has an undeniable hook and we'll never know how successful it would have been without the video and controversial press but with all that, "Blurred Lines" went to #1 where it stayed throughout the summer of 2013.

And that's when Marvin Gaye's family stood up and decided it was time to get their share. They accused the song's authors of copying the "feel" and "sound" of "Got to Give It Up." This was an historic claim. Previous lawsuits have attempted to show a writer copied a specific lyric or melody so much that a copyright was infringed upon. But since "Blurred Lines" doesn't take any specific series of notes from Gaye's song, "feel" and "sound" were their best arguments (and something Thicke had already admitted publicly to). And it proved to be a good one. On March 10th, 2015 a jury found Thicke and Williams (but not T.I.) liable for copyright infringement and awarded the Gaye family over $7 million and a share of future earnings. Most musicians and industry people have criticized the verdict saying it shows a complete lack of understanding of copyright laws and what has always been defined as "infringement." As of this writing, Thicke and Williams are appealing the ruling as they probably should. Artists have long been inspired by works that have come before them. So borrowing a song's "feel" and "sound" is often seen as a compliment or an homage. If the creator of the original is owed a copywriting credit, just how many songs will Chuck Berry have to be added to as a writer? Or Bo Diddley?

For Pharrell, "Blurred Lines" was just the beginning of a hot streak. 2013 also saw him performing with Daft Punk on their hit "Get Lucky" and in the winter of 2014 his own song "Happy" would rule the charts and airwaves. Thicke, however, has had a tough go of it since "Blurred Lines." His follow-up, "For the Rest of My Life" failed to chart as have a number of his subsequent releases. Clearly, the man needs a new gimmick.

## August 11th

On this date in 1978, the Rolling Stones' "Miss You" was finishing its one week stay at #1 on the pop chart. To date the Stones have not had another #1 ("Start Me Up" came oh so close, peaking at #2 in 1981) so the Stones' attempt at pilfering the disco sound, which infuriated much of their fan base and critics alike, can also be seen as their last climb to the top of the charts. Sometimes art, like politics, does indeed make strange bedfellows.

"Miss You" was the lead single off the Rolling Stones' 1978 album, *Some Girls* (as well as the opening track). Mick Jagger was the creative force behind much of the album (Keith Richards was dealing with a lot of legal issues resulting from a heroin bust the year before), specifically "Miss You," which was almost entirely written by Jagger. Speaking about his influences for the album, Jagger says: "Punk and disco were going on at the same time, so it was quite an interesting period. New York and London, too. Paris—there was punk there. Lots of dance music." Drummer Charlie Watts concurs: "A lot of those songs like 'Miss You' were heavily influenced by going to the discos. You can hear it in a lot of those four-on-the-floor rhythms and the Philadelphia-style drumming. Mick and I used to go to discos a lot... It was a great period." Watts adds: "I remember . . . coming back from a club with Mick singing one of the Village People songs - 'Y.M.C.A.' I think it was - and Keith went mad, but it sounded great on the dance floor."

The bass line, which drives the song as much as Watts drumming (an uncommon trait for a Stones' song and something that makes "Miss You" sound so much like a dance track) was created by Billy Preston who was working with the Stones at the time. Bassist Bill Wyman admits as much, saying: "I'd already gone home, and Billy picked up my old bass when they started running through that song. He started doing that bit because it seemed to be the style of his left hand. So when we finally came to do the tune, the boys said, why don't you work around Billy's idea? So I listened to it once and heard that basic run and took it from there. It took some changing and polishing, but the basic idea was Billy's." To make it seem even more like a disco track, "Miss You" became the first

Stones' song to be released as a 12 inch single (the preferred format for club DJs) as well as a traditional 7 inch. This extended version, called the "Special Disco Version," was released on pink vinyl and clocks in at eight and a half minutes. When you think of how pervasive disco was in the late seventies you just have to picture a Rolling Stones' song on pink vinyl called the "Special Disco Version."

While some hardcore Stones' fans hated the song because of its disco vibe, it became a hit. This was 1978, after all, and dance music was huge. One look at the charts that summer proves it. The Stones knocked Andy Gibbs' "Shadow Dancing" from the top spot and within weeks of "Miss You" vacating #1 "Boogie Oogie Oogie" by something called A Taste of Honey would start a three week run at the top. Donna Summer, Chic and, of course, the Bee Gees would all claim the top spot in disco's most dominant year.

Some credit (while others blame) the Rolling Stones for opening the door for other rock artists to experiment with the disco genre. Rod Stewart released "Do Ya Think I'm Sexy" and KISS produced "I Was Made For Loving You" all within a year of "Miss You." But who could blame these artists? Even Ethel Merman made a disco album.

In one of his last interviews, John Lennon also claimed some credit for "Miss You" citing his 1974 song "Bless You." "I think Mick Jagger took 'Bless You' and turned it into 'Miss You,'" Lennon said. "The engineer kept wanting me to speed that up - he said, 'this is a hit song if you'd just do it fast.' He was right. Because as 'Miss You' it turned into a hit." Lennon added: "I like Mick's record better. I have no ill feelings about it. I think it's a great Stones' track, and I really love it. But I do hear that lick in it." If you can track down "Bless You" you'll probably hear it too.

As if to prove that "Miss You" was no one-off foray into the world of dance music, the Stones' next album, *Emotional Rescue*, would include the title track that also sounded night-club ready. "Emotional Rescue" only made it to #3 in 1980, showing perhaps America's fatigue with disco, and by 1981 the Stones had returned to a much more traditional rock sound with *Tattoo You*. When that album was released and fans put the needle on the record to hear that unforgettable opening riff of "Start Me Up" you could almost hear the collective sigh from Rolling Stones' fans around the world. Their band was back from the clubs and ready to rock out once again.

## August 12th

On this date in 1973, "The Morning After," by a previously unknown singer named Maureen McGovern, was in the middle of a two week stay atop the charts. Months earlier the song had won a surprising Oscar and now here it was, sitting at #1 on the *Billboard* Hot 100 chart.

In March of 1972 songwriters Al Kasha and Joel Hirschhorn were summoned to 20th Century Fox for a meeting with movie producer Irwin Allen. Allen asked the two men if they'd be interested in composing the love theme for his upcoming film *The Poseidon Adventure*. Kasha and Hirschhorn were both eager for the project until they heard the deadline: tomorrow. The two spent the whole night at the piano and the next day presented a song called "Why Must There Be a Morning After?" Whether it was desperation or sincerity, Allen loved it. He suggested the title be changed to simply "The Morning After" (giving the song a slightly less ominous tone) and told Kasha and Hirschhorn to get it recorded.

The first version they produced was for the scene in the movie where the song would appear. For that, Renee Armand recorded vocals that actress Carol Linley would lip-sync. They then needed to find a singer for the version that would play over the movie's closing credits and appear on the soundtrack. Barbra Streisand was offered the song but she turned it down. Out of ideas, Kasha and Hirschhorn approached Russ Regan, head of 20th Century Records, to help them find a singer. Regan immediately thought of a demo tape he'd heard recently.

Maureen Therese McGovern was born in 1949 in Youngstown, Ohio. She was singing as early as three years old and by her young twenties she was working as a secretary by day and singing in a folk band by night. She recorded a demo tape which made its way to Regan and when he needed a singer for "The Morning After" he hired McGovern sight unseen.

*The Poseidon Adventure* was released during the 1972 holiday season and it quickly became a box office smash. It was the second highest-grossing movie of 1972 (behind only *The Godfather*) and with $127 million in tickets sold it became, at the time, the sixth highest-grossing film ever (nowadays $127 million is a disappointing opening weekend). The film received nine Oscar nominations, of which the award for Best Original Song seemed like a long shot because it was up against Michael Jackson's "Ben" from the rats-take-over-the-world movie of the same name.

But the 45th Academy Awards, held on March 27th, 1973 were nothing if not unpredictable. The evening is remembered for many things. Charlie Chaplin received the award for Best Score for *Limelight*, a movie that was twenty years old (it had been re-released in 1972, making it eligible) and Bob Fosse's *Cabaret* won eight Oscars on a night when *The Godfather* was predicted to clean up (the mafia movie did win three awards including Best Picture so it didn't exactly get shut out). And this is the night that Marlon Brando boycotted and sent Native American Sacheen Littlefeather up to reject his Oscar for Best Actor because of, "the treatment of American Indians today by the film industry," a speech that was met with a mixture of boos and applause. So when Cher tore open the envelope for the Best Original Song award and read, "The winners are Al Kasha and Joel Hirschhorn for 'The Morning After'" it was just one more surprise in a night full of them. Other than an award for Visual Effects, Best Song was the only Oscar *Poseidon* would take home.

At that point "The Morning After" had not been released as a single. But interest spiked after the award show and some radio stations started playing the song off the soundtrack. In May, 20th Century finally released the song as a single. It made its first appearance on the charts the week of June 23rd, cracking the Hot 100 at #99. From there it made a slow and steady climb . . . 86 . . . 42 . . . 29 . . . . It crept into the Top Ten on July 28th and then the next week, this song that had been written in a manic all-nighter and sung by a virtually unknown singer got to #1. Maureen McGovern, a secretary and coffee house folk singer just a year earlier, was at the top of the charts looking down on artists like Wings, Jim Croce and Diana Ross.

The equation of Al Kasha and Joel Hirschhorn plus Maureen McGovern and a disaster movie would equal Oscar success again two years later when "We May Never Love Like This Again" from *Towering Inferno* took home the Academy Award for Best Original Song. McGovern even got to appear in the film this time, playing a lounge singer. Kasha and Hirschhorn continued working together for many years, composing music for soundtracks, plays and even a game show theme song. When Joel Hirschhorn passed away in 2005 the *New York Times* noted in his obituary that his songs had sold more than 90 million records and appeared in twenty films. Maureen McGovern continued working in the film and television industry, singing "Can You Read My Mind," the love theme for the 1978 movie *Superman* and scoring another Top 40 hit the following year with "Different Worlds," the theme song for the television show *Angie*. McGovern has also appeared on screen (she's the singing nun in the 1980 disaster-spoof film *Airplane!*) as well as on stage, including Broadway shows like *The Pirates of Penzance*. and *Nine*. When she performs she often vocalizes the instrumental parts of her songs which has earned her the nickname "Stradivarius Voice." Her advice about music is to, "Listen with your heart," something you should do today with her first recording, "The Morning After." Though it was written for a disaster movie, there is a universal sense of optimism in the song. You don't have to be escaping from a capsized ship to appreciate a lyric like, "We have a chance to find the sunshine, let's keep on looking for the light," and hopefully we can all agree that "Only with love can we climb." It's a beautiful song composed in an all-night writing session and sung timelessly by a previously unknown singer and it still resonates today.

## August 13th

On this date in 1952, just one day after the song had been written, "Big Mama" Thornton recorded "Hound Dog." The composition is one of the earliest works by Jerry Leiber and Mike Stoller who would go on to unprecedented success as songwriters and producers. And even though Thornton's original version of "Hound Dog" became a huge hit on the R&B chart most people are more familiar with a different version of the song.

Willie Mae Thornton was born in Alabama in 1926. She was exposed to music at a young age from her parents; her father was a minister and her mother a singer at the local Baptist church. She moved to Atlanta, Georgia when she was just fifteen to join Sammy Green's Hot Harlem Revue, then in her young twenties she moved to Houston, Texas. Somewhere along the way she earned the nickname "Big Mama" which, at over 300 pounds, suited her perfectly. She signed her first contract in 1951 with Peacock Records but her first two singles were disappointments and Peacock began to wonder if she would ever reach her true potential. That's when they brought in two nineteen year old songwriters to work with her.

Jerry Leiber and Mike Stoller met in Los Angeles in 1950, becoming fast friends once they realized they both shared a love of blues and R&B. Their first collaboration, "Hard Times" which Charles Brown recorded, was a minor hit in 1952. They followed that up with "Kansas City" which was first recorded by Little Willie Littlefield and then taken to the top of the charts in 1959 by Wilbert Harrison. Based on their growing reputation for penning R&B songs they were invited to meet, and possibly write for, Willie Mae "Big Mama" Thornton. That meeting took place on August 12th, 1952. The two songwriters, both little Jewish guys just nineteen years old, were blown away by Thornton and her larger-than-life appearance. Leiber has admitted it was her appearance that impressed him the most: "She looked like the biggest, baddest, saltiest chick you would ever see. She must have been 350 pounds, and she had all these scars all over her face." Stoller would say, "She was a wonderful blues singer, with a great moaning style." After this initial meeting the two sat down to write a song for Thornton and decided on the theme of a woman who is sick of her man's philandering and decides to kick him out. Using a "hound dog" as a euphemism for a cheating man, the songwriters wanted to use the opportunity to allow Thornton to howl and wail. Once the theme was decided they wrote the song in no time, with Leiber scribbling the lyrics in pencil on ordinary paper and without musical notation (alas, that scrap of paper has been lost to history).

The two presented the song to Thornton the very next day and she was initially disappointed, wondering aloud, "Is this my big hit?" She then began crooning the song almost like Frank Sinatra would. When the songwriters attempted to correct her she got in their faces yelling, "White boy, don't you be tellin' me how to sing the blues." Unfazed, Leiber sang the song to demonstrate how they envisioned her performing it and that's when Thornton got it, hearing the underlying sexual humor in the line, "You can wag your tail, but I ain't gonna feed you no more." Thornton's next two versions were keepers and she added her own howls and ad-libbed lines like, "Aw, listen to that ole hound dog howl" and, "Aw, get it, get it, get it" during the guitar solo. She had clearly captured all the dirty grit and blues-based sexuality Leiber and Stoller had envisioned. One listen to Thornton's version and you have no doubt that she means everything she's singing (and more).

"Hound Dog" was released in early 1953. The song sold big numbers and spent seven weeks at #1 on the R&B chart. Despite that, Thornton, as well as Leiber and Stoller, saw mere pennies from Peacock. The incident inspired Leiber and Stoller to open their own label, Sparks Records, to avoid getting cheated again. As for Thornton, she would tell *Rolling Stone* years later: "Didn't get no money from them at all. Everybody livin' in a house but me. I'm just livin'."

Thornton's version was so popular it spawned its share of covers and answer records; songs written in response to a previous release. In the case of "Hound Dog" these included "Bear Cat (The Answer To Hound Dog)" by Rufus 'Hound Dog' Thomas and "Mr. Hound Dog's in Town" by Roy Brown, just to name a few. And there were also cover versions, including the most famous one, Elvis Presley's 1956 version.

There has been a lot of talk recently about cultural appropriation and if there's an initial example in music, Presley making a pop hit out of an R&B song that wasn't even written for his gender is probably it. Long before Vanilla Ice rapped and Justin Timberlake did his best Michael Jackson impression, Elvis was taking an R&B song and giving it a rock and roll feel as well as a comical sendup (just watch his appearance on Milton Berle when he sang "Hound Dog" and you'll agree). Initially, Leiber and Stoller were no fans of Elvis' version with Stoller saying: "I was disappointed. It just sounded terribly nervous, too fast, too white." Although he would admit, "after it sold seven or eight million records it started to sound better." Whether it's paying homage to, being influenced by or straight up stealing, it's hard to deny the difference between Elvis' version and the original, with all of Thornton's snarling and growling and grittiness. It's worth listening to both today just to see how differently two singers can interpret the same song.

**August 14th**

On this date in 1971, the Who released their 5th studio album *Who's Next*. Despite the fact that the album was the result of a failed project, *Who's Next* is the band's most critically acclaimed album and produced some of their most recognizable songs. But, as great as the album is, were it not for a curious decision of which songs to include, *Who's Next* could have been even greater.

In 1969 the Who released *Tommy,* an ambitious rock opera. The album and tour (and eventual film) are seen as high water marks for the collaboration of rock music with multi-media and storytelling. Inspired by *Tommy*'s success, Pete Townshend, the band's chief lyricist and composer, began thinking up his next big project. What he came up with was a futuristic rock opera called *Lifehouse*, which he envisioned being released as a double album and feature film. Townshend had two major influences during the time, he was reading the works of an Indian spiritual worker named Meher Baba and he was experimenting with a new musical instrument called a synthesizer. Ultimately the *Lifehouse* project would cause intense internal squabbling (singer Roger Daltrey has said the Who "were never nearer to breaking up") and it was eventually abandoned.

With *Lifehouse* dying on the vine, the band decided to hit the studio and start working on a more traditional album. In May of 1971 they did the bulk of the recording for what would become *Who's Next* at Olympic Studios in London with Glyn Johns producing. It was Johns who convinced the band to release their next work as a single album (*Tommy* had been a double LP) so when it came to selecting material, much of which had been written for the Lifehouse project, "Join Together" was left off the album. The song would eventually be released in 1972 as a non-album single and the fact that it peaked at #17 shows just how great a song it is. As strong as the track listing for *Who's Next* is, one can only imagine how much better it could have been with "Join Together" included.

The opening song on *Who's Next* is "Baba O'Riley" (sometimes erroneously called "Teenage Wasteland"). The title combines the names of Meher Baba and Terry Riley (an American composer Townshend respected). The song was originally part of the *Lifehouse* project and in one incarnation ran 30 minutes long. Townshend worked in his home studio creating the opening for the song, playing with an early synthesizer as well as cutting tape. He brought the final "demo" tape to Johns thinking the band could recreate it in the studio but Johns thought it was perfect and they used Townsend's homemade tape as an introduction to the song in the studio. To this day, when the Who perform live, the opening of "Baba O'Riley" is that same recording that Townshend made in his home studio. Since the guitar doesn't come in until almost two minutes into the song, Townshend often has some time to reflect on his work. He has said, "There is this moment of standing there just listening to this music and looking out to the audience and just thinking, 'I fucking did that. I wrote that.'" He did indeed. And it's arguably the most recognizable prelude to any song in the rock era.

The classic cover photo for *Who's Next* shows the band having apparently just peed on a concrete slab that protrudes from the ground. Drummer Keith Moon and bassist John Entwistle were inspired by Stanley Kubrick's 1969 film *2001: A Space Odyssey* (in which a similar monolith plays a prominent role) and decided to take the piss (pun intended) out of that and use it on the album's cover. According to photographer Ethan Russell, the band was unable to urinate in front of each other, so water was poured on the slab to achieve the desired effect.

Besides being recognized as one of the Who's best albums the sound quality of *Who's Next* is often critically acclaimed as well. In their early years the Who were considered one of those bands that were great live, but unable to duplicate the sound in the studio. With *Who's Next*, and much to Glyn John's credit, the band finally captured their powerful live sound on vinyl. And most of the songs on the album, the aforementioned "Baba O'Riley", "Won't Get Fooled Again", "Going Mobile", "Behind Blue Eyes" and even the hilarious "My Wife" (the only song written by Entwistle on the album) have become signature Who songs. If you have some time today, and want to experience an all-time great rock album, listen to *Who's Next* all the way through. For the full experience, include "Join Together."

On this date in 1965, Sonny and Cher's "I Got You Babe" had just begun a three week stay at #1 on the pop chart. While not an anti-war song per se, it was embraced by the counter-culture movement even though Sonny Bono wrote it to refute a song by one of their heroes.

Cherilyn Sarkisian was born in El Centro, California in 1946. Her earliest childhood ambition was to be famous and though she didn't know if that would be as an actress or singer, she was determined to make it happen. When she was sixteen she dropped out of high school and moved to Los Angeles to make it big. She started taking acting classes and supported herself by dancing in clubs on the Sunset Strip. And she hustled. Hard. She introduced herself to anyone and everyone she thought could help her catch a break. And it didn't take too long before she made the right connection.

Salvatore Phillip Bono was born in Detroit, Michigan in 1935. His family relocated to California when he was seven and he grew up aspiring to be a songwriter. After high school he worked a number of odd jobs to pay the rent while he pursued that dream. His first break came when he started working with the famed record producer Phil Spector. His next one came when he met a gorgeous sixteen year old in a coffee shop in Los Angeles. The two got to talking and before long they both realized they could help each other out. She was looking to become a singer and he was looking for talent.

Sarkisian had already decided to shorten her first name and just go by "Cher" and Bono had picked up the nickname "Sonny" somewhere along the way. Despite their age difference they became fast friends and Bono soon arranged for her to meet Phil Spector. The meeting went well and Cher began singing backup for Spector. She's on some of his best known recordings from the era, like "Be My Baby" by the Ronettes and the Righteous Brothers' "You've Lost That Lovin' Feelin'." Meanwhile, Bono and Cher began collaborating. Initially he wanted her to be a solo artist (with him writing and producing) but, due to her stage fright, she encouraged him to perform with her. Before long, they became a duo both onstage and in their personal lives. They experimented with a clever name for their act, "Cleopatra and Cleo," but when a few singles under that sobriquet failed they decided to simply go with "Sonny and Cher."

One day Bono heard Bob Dylan's caustic "It Ain't Me Babe" which features the folk singer rejecting a lover by telling her, "I will let you down" and, "It ain't me you're looking for." Bono sought to write a more optimistic song so while "I Got You Babe" might not be an "answer song" in the strict sense of the term, it was certainly inspired by Dylan's tune and tone. When Bono was finished with the composition he was so excited he woke Cher up in the middle of the night to demo it for her. She was unimpressed and went back to bed. Equally unimpressed was Ahmet Ertegun who ran Atlantic Records (Sonny and Cher were signed to their sub-label Atco Records). Ertegun wanted to release "I Got You Babe" as a B-side despite Bono's insistence that the song could be a hit. In an effort to convince his boss, Bono brought a copy of "I Got You Babe" to the

Los Angeles radio station KHJ, and made a deal with program director, Ron Jacobs. If the station would play the song once an hour, they could have it exclusively. Jacobs agreed, the song got a great response from KHJ listeners and Ertegun acquiesced.

"I Got You Babe" was released in early July of 1965 and it quickly became a radio favorite. It climbed the pop chart and hit #1 in mid-August where it would stay for three weeks before the Beatles' "Help!" bumped it from the top. There were two main reasons the song became a hippie favorite. First was the opening line, "They say we're young and we don't know," which spoke to the counter-culture's feelings that the older generation did not understand them. And when Cher sings to Bono, "Don't let them say your hair's too long," the lyrics again hit home for that generation who were constantly being told to cut their hair.

Sonny and Cher had a number of years of huge successes in the sixties but after Bono's repeated infidelities their marriage and working relationship eventually ended. Cher, having overcome her stage fright, went on to even greater success as a solo artist and actress. Bono, a hero to the counter-culture in his youth, became a conservative, Republican congressman (go figure). After years of estrangement, David Letterman brought them together on his *Late Night* show in 1987 and then pleaded with them to sing their most famous duet. It would take some egging on by Letterman and the studio audience but eventually the duo performed "I Got You Babe" one last time together, with not a little irony when Cher sang the long hair line.

## August 16th

On this date in 1962, the most famous and ignominious firing in all of rock and roll history took place when Pete Best was let go from the Beatles. And his bandmates didn't even have the guts to do it personally. They assigned the unhappy task to their manager who would break the news to him just months before the band was to become the biggest in the world. And to this day, he still doesn't know why.

By 1962, Pete Best had been the Beatles' drummer for two years, banging his way through all those marathon gigs in Hamburg, Germany, their Cavern Club residency and their short jaunts around the countryside of England, all crammed in the back of a van as they honed their skills, forged their reputation and built a loyal fan base. If John Lennon, Paul McCartney or George Harrison ever felt his drumming skills were lacking they never let him know. In January of 1962 the band signed Brian Epstein as their manager who promised to help them fulfill their dream of making it, "to the toppermost of the popper most." In June of that year, with Epstein working hard to find them a label (and being rejected repeatedly, most famously by Decca who told him, "guitar groups are on the way out, Mr. Epstein") the band signed with Paralophone Records.

Paralophone sent them to Abbey Roads studio to work with their producer, George Martin. In that very first recording session Martin expressed concerns about Best and even suggested the band use a session drummer for their recordings. The Beatles were friends with the fellow Liverpool band Rory Storm and the Hurricanes so of course they were familiar with the Hurricanes' drummer Ringo Starr. John Lennon, who was still the band's de facto leader at this point, asked Starr if he'd quit the Hurricanes and join the Beatles. When Starr accepted (on August 14th, 1962) the band gave Epstein the green light to sack Pete Best.

Two days later, Pete Best arrived at Epstein's office. The manager was very straightforward, saying simply: "I've got some bad news for you. The boys want you out and Ringo in." Best, shocked, could only mumble, "Why?" to which Epstein replied, "They don't think you're a good enough drummer, Pete. And George Martin doesn't think you're a good enough drummer." Then the final humiliation for Best came when he was told Starr was starting with the band that weekend. Best realized then and there that Starr had been invited to join the Beatles before he had even been let go. Lennon, in a moment of honesty, would say later: "We were cowards. We got Epstein to do the dirty work for us."

Starr took the stage as a Beatle for the first time two nights later.

Pete Best had a very strong following, especially with the band's female fans because he was often considered the best looking Beatle. At some of the Beatles' next performances a number of fans would chant "Pete forever! Ringo never!" in between songs and at one gig at the Cavern Club, George Harrison got into a shoving match with a Pete Best fan and wound up with a black eye. Brian Epstein had his car tires slashed and was forced to hire a bodyguard for fear of his own safety.

Best did his best to respond. He formed a band called Pete Best & the All Stars. They got a record deal with Decca (who were apparently already rethinking their guitar band stance) and released a single called "I'm Gonna Knock On Your Door." It failed to knock on the chart's doors. He was with a woman named Kathy who he'd met at a Beatles' show at the Cavern Club a few years earlier. Sometime after his firing he asked her if she still wanted to be with him. She said, "Pete, it's you I want. Not a Beatle." The two were married in 1963.

Best fought bouts of depression in the mid-sixties as Beatlemania swept the globe. He even attempted suicide one time. He sued Ringo Starr in 1968 over comments Starr made in a Playboy interview that insinuated drug use was the reason for Best's dismal (the case was settled out of court). He would move to the U.S. and try a few more times to make it in music, including an album he released titled *Best of the Beatles*, which was obviously a play on his name but also wound up fooling many record buyers. Eventually he gave up playing drums till he was coaxed back to the stage in 1988, appearing at a Beatles' convention in Liverpool. This led to Best forming the Pete Best Band, which toured regularly, playing sixties rock including some of his previous band's biggest songs. In 1995, the Beatles released their *Anthology* CDs which included a number of tracks from the band's Decca and Parlophone auditions with Best on drums. For the first time ever, Best received royalties from his work with the Beatles. It's estimated he made over a million dollars from *Anthology* although he's vague about exact figures. When asked if he's rich he replies, "in many ways."

Indeed he is. He and Kathy are still married. They have two daughters and five grandchildren. He's outlived the manager who fired him and two of the three Beatles who were too cowardly to do it themselves. When pressed about the past he has said: "What's the point in saying, 'I should have been this' or 'I could have been that?' That's yesterday. Forty years ago. What's important is what's happening today and tomorrow. When you realize that, you get on with it." It's truly been a long and winding road since that miserable day in 1962, but it's heartening to know Pete Best has indeed made the best of it.

## August 17th

On this date in 1969, the three day Woodstock Music & Art Fair was scheduled to end. Because of delays Jimi Hendrix actually closed the festival on the morning of Monday August 18th. Depending on how you look at it, Woodstock was either the high water mark for the counter-culture's peace and love movement of the sixties, a defining event, not just for the half a million attendees but also for an entire generation that impacted our world like few others, or it was a logistical and financial boondoggle of epic proportions that nearly bankrupted its organizers. What is irrefutable is that Woodstock is the single most famous concert of all time and despite repeated attempts by organizers the world over, it has never been duplicated.

Because of repeated delays with finding a location the organizers of the Woodstock Music & Art Fair were far behind schedule and two days before everything was set to start they were forced to decide between completing construction of the stage or building a fence around Max Yasgur's farm. They wisely choose the stage which in essence meant, at the last minute, Woodstock became a free event.

On Friday afternoon, August 15th, 1969, Richie Havens kicked off the concert. He was told to extend his set because other performers were delayed by traffic jams on the New York Thruway (mostly caused by the festival). Eventually he ran out of material and started playing a traditional Negro spiritual song called "Motherless Child" which dates back to the days of slavery when it was common practice to sell children of slaves away from their parents. Havens improvised new lyrics over the old song, repeating the word "freedom" like a mantra and getting the crowd, many of whom were still arriving, to clap their hands and chant along. "Freedom" is one of the most iconic performances of the entire weekend and the fact that it came about spontaneously is one of the most famous happy accidents in rock and roll history.

Delays would become one of the main stories of the weekend. Some were due to performers' travel woes (like Iron Butterfly missing their flight and thus the entire festival; John Sebastian, who was in attendance but not on the bill, was recruited at the last minute to take the band's place), others were caused by torrential rains that hit Friday evening and Sunday afternoon. Because of the delays some bands went on in the middle of the night, like Creedence Clearwater Revival whose lead singer John Fogerty has said: "There were a half million people asleep. It was sort of like a painting of a Dante scene, just bodies from hell, all intertwined and asleep, covered with mud." Fogerty said one guy on the hill was flicking his lighter and the band played their entire set directed at him. The Who took the stage at 5am Sunday morning and Pete Townshend has described them playing as dawn broke and half a million festival goers emerged from the darkness as a high point in his career. And because Hendrix didn't take the stage till Monday morning it is estimated that only about 40,000 people were left to hear his incredible rendition of "The Star Spangled Banner."

Much of what we know about Woodstock comes from the film and album that was released the following year (and finally helped the organizers of the concert actually make some money). Included were various stage announcements, some of which proved to be false. For example, the New York Thruway was never actually closed. And at one point the crowd was announced at "a million and a half people." While legendary, neither of these were factual. Whether or not the brown acid was bad and should be avoided is still open to debate.

Despite the delays and size of the crowd, Woodstock, as the organizers had hoped, was a peaceful gathering. There were no reported instances of violence. They had promoted the festival as "An Aquarian Exposition: 3 Days of Peace & Music" and indeed it was. For one shining weekend, we did indeed go back to the garden and prove that communal living in harmony with nature was possible. The cynic is free to say that those ideals had disappeared before the traffic on the Thruway dissipated. But champions of the counter-culture will say at least the moment happened. And it set, for all time, an example of what can happen when people come together in peace and harmony for a common goal. Whichever side of the coin you fall on, it's hard to listen to the Woodstock album or watch the movie and not know instantly that this was a defining moment as well as an appropriate coda, for the wild and crazy decade of the sixties.

On this date in 1983, the Police played to a sold-out crowd in New York City's Shea Stadium. Undoubtedly, this was a special night. For the Police, who admitted to a man they were huge Beatles' fans, playing at Shea was a thrill. In fact, Sting at one point announced, "We'd like to thank the Beatles for lending us their stadium." But unbeknownst to the more than 70,000 concert goers in attendance, this was a significant show for the three members of the Police for an entirely different reason. The night before, with the #1 song in the country, the #1 album on the *Billboard* LP chart and in the middle of one of the year's highest-grossing tours, they had decided to disband.

The Police had come together in 1977 in London while punk was all the rage. Their first show together as a power trio of Stewart Copeland on drums, Sting (Gordon Sumner) on bass and vocals and Andy Summers on lead guitar was, coincidentally enough on this same date, August 18th, in 1977. And while early on they certainly played with all the speed and energy that the times demanded, they weren't true punk rockers. They were a bit old for the scene (Copeland and Sting were in their mid-twenties, Summers, thirty-five) plus they actually had day jobs (Sting had been an English teacher, you can't get much uncooler than that). Oh, and their clothes weren't torn and tattered. No, instead, they saw punk as a way in the door and while you can hear some punk elements in their early work (notably "Next to You" and "It's Alright for You") Sting was already writing songs that had a myriad of influences including jazz and reggae.

A&M signed the Police to a record contract off the strength of a demo that Copeland's brother Miles helped them record (he would go on to manage the band) and in the spring of 1978 they released "Roxanne" in the U.K., a song Sting had written with a decidedly reggae beat about falling in love with a prostitute. It didn't trouble the charts.

In February of 1979, with their debut album *Outlandos d'Amour* now completed and in the stores, they released "Roxanne" in the States and it began to get some play (it would peak at #32). This led to a short U.S. tour of clubs (including punk's mecca, CBGB) and a rerelease of "Roxanne" back home where it finally caught some attention.

The Police's next album, *Regatta de Blanc,* continued their trend of moving away from the punk sound and scene (which by 1979 was already reinventing itself) and it spawned hits like "Message in a Bottle" and "Walking on the Moon" that would establish the Police as a band to be taken seriously as a new decade dawned. That new decade would give rise to a new genre of music called "new wave," where punk met technology (which is why it is also called "synth pop") and while the Police are often cited as one of the bands that helped popularize this sound they again continued to defy any specific genre.

By the early eighties Sting had clearly emerged as the leader of the band. He was the main songwriter and, as the band's frontman, there were certainly opportunities for his ego to get out of control. And, like almost all one-named singers, it did. Summers and Copeland mostly tolerated Sting's inflated opinion of self worth, and tried at times to knock him down a peg or two with some brotherly-love-type chiding (some of which was documented on MTV since *MTV News* ran constant pieces on the band), but by the release of 1983's *Synchronicity* there were clearly strains in the relationship. Add to that the fact that Sting was becoming frustrated by the limitations that a power trio placed on the type of music he could write and record and the environment had become toxic. Now, take all that drama, and shake it up with all the perks and attention that a #1 album and single provide, and it's a miracle the band even made it through 1983.

*Synchronicity* launched the Police from a popular band to another stratosphere. Released on June 17th, 1983 it shot to #1 within weeks and stayed there most of the summer. The album's lead single "Every Breath You Take" would also sit at #1 for most of the summer, while radio also picked up "King of Pain", "Wrapped Around Your Finger" and "Synchronicity II." With all this chart success, as well as internal squabbling, the band started a sold-out North American tour in Chicago on July 23rd. Halfway through it, the Police were scheduled to play Shea and with an off day before that show, the band had a meeting. Sting told Copeland and Summers that he felt they should disband after the tour. "This is as good as it gets guys," he said, "after this it'll be diminishing returns." The three members of the Police came to an agreement that night that they'd break up at the end of the tour.

The next day they took the stage in Shea's centerfield, at the top of the rock and roll world, yet knowing the end was now near.

Of the three, Sting's solo success is well documented. Summers released a few, mostly instrumental albums and also wrote and recorded for films. Copeland's post-Police career has been similar, composing for soundtracks and sitting in with other artists (that's him playing the hi-hat on Peter Gabriel's "Red Rain," for example). The three re-united for a 30th anniversary, world tour in 2007 (due to its success it stretched into 2008) during which everyone played nice. By the time the tour wrapped they'd sold nearly four million tickets and grossed over $350 million. Still, the band insisted it was a one-off experience and they were not reuniting nor recording any new material. If that turns out to be the case, the Police will have New York City to point to as the place they go to end things. Not only did they decide to disband the night before playing Shea but the final show of their reunion tour was at Madison Square Garden. They closed that last concert with "Next to You," the first track on their debut album. With Sting shouting, "Got this feeling, gonna lose my mind" and Copeland thrashing away on the drums, they had, if only for a moment, returned to their punk rock beginnings. The three left the stage arm in arm.

On this date in 1964, Dean Martin was sitting atop the *Billboard* Hot 100 chart with "Everybody Loves Somebody." In a year in which the charts would be dominated by rockers like the Beatles, the Animals and the Beach Boys, or soul acts like Mary Wells and the Supremes, somehow the "King of Cool" had returned to the top. It would be just another triumphant moment in an almost 60 year career that was full of them.

Dino Paul Crocetti was born in 1917 in Steubenville, Ohio to Italian-American parents. They spoke nothing but Italian at home and so young Dino didn't learn English until he began attending grammar school. He was often bullied for his accent and broken English. He dropped out of high school before graduation and became a boxer, using the name "Kid Crochet." It was a nice play on his last name but apparently a boxer named after a sewing technique doesn't strike fear in his opponents. Of his twelve fights, Martin would later say, "I won all but eleven." After hanging up his gloves he moved to New York City and began singing in local bands using the name Dino Martin, a close approximation to Opera singer Nino Martin. He sang with a number of bands in his early twenties. It was Sammy Watkins who recommended he change to Dean Martin, thus completing the Anglo-ization of his name. What Martin may have lacked in original singing style he more than made up for with his handsome looks and easy stage demeanor.

In the summer of 1945 Martin was performing at the Glass Hat Club in New York City. On the same bill was comedian Jerry Lewis. The two got to talking backstage and formed a fast friendship that would prove to be fortuitous to both of their careers. They put an act together, combining Martin's singing with Lewis' slapstick humor. The pair became very popular in the nightclubs of the mid-forties. Television appearances and a radio show soon followed before the ultimate prize came calling: Hollywood! From 1949 to 1956 Martin and Lewis made an incredible seventeen films. The exposure from these movies also helped launch Martin's singing career. He would score thirteen Top 40 hits during his years with Lewis, including "That's Amore" which made it to #2 in 1953 and "Memories Are Made of This" which became his first career #1 in 1955.

After splitting with Lewis, Martin made a conscious effort to become a "serious actor," a mission he accomplished with the 1958 World War II drama, *The Young Lions*. Starring alongside Marlon Brando and Montgomery Clift, Martin proved he was more than just a straight man for a slapstick comic and his solo career as an actor was off and running. But Martin's singing career struggled during this time. None of his late fifties' and early sixties' releases made the Top 40 and many of them even failed to crack the Top 100. Martin was not alone. Many of the crooners that had dominated pop music in the thirties and forties looked like yesterday's news once rock and roll broke onto the scene. But these singers didn't put their microphones away. They kept performing and recording and some of them formed what would become known as the Rat Pack. Dean Martin and Frank Sinatra were at the center of this group which performed to sold-out crowds in Las Vegas for years. The kids may have been into that new rock and roll stuff, but there were still plenty of grownups willing to pay to see their heroes perform.

Martin's son, Dean Paul Martin was 13 in 1964 and like most kids his age he loved the Beatles. This became a source of contention at home and one day Martin told his son, "I'm gonna' knock your pallies off the charts." The song that would fulfill this promise was an almost twenty year old composition, "Everybody Loves Somebody." Martin was working on material one day in the studio when his producer suggested the song. It's a typical standard, having been recorded multiple times by various singers. Martin had never recorded the song but he had sung it on Bob Hope's radio show in 1948. At his producer's suggestion, he sang it in the studio that day and everyone recognized its hit potential. The single dropped in June of 1964 and it made a steady climb up the charts. By early July it had cracked the Top 40 and a few weeks later it became Martin's first Top 10 since 1958's "Return to Me." But the Beatles were sitting at #1 with "A Hard Day's Night" and while Martin's song was impressive, no betting man would have placed money on a sugary ballad by an old time crooner knocking the kings of the British Invasion off the top. In the first chart week of August, "Everybody Loves Somebody" made it to #4 and then the following week it climbed to #2, directly behind young Dean's "pallies." Surely there was some good natured ribbing between father and son that week as anticipation rose over the August 15th chart. When it was published, the crooner had done it. He'd knocked the Beatles from the top!

"Everybody Loves Somebody" helped revitalize Martin's recording career and over the next few years many of his songs would be Top 40 hits. Alongside "That's Amore," "Everybody Loves Somebody" has gone on to become a signature song for Dean Martin and when he passed away in 1995, after an illustrious show business career that had seen him conquer music, television, stage and film, his family had the words "Everybody Loves Somebody" engraved on his tombstone. It's an apt epitaph for a man whose career was beloved by so many.


### August 20th

On this date in 1983, Stevie Nicks' "Stand Back" peaked on the *Billboard* Hot 100 chart at #5. The song had taken just a few months from inception to recording to releasing and now it was Nicks' most successful solo song to date (1986's "Talk to Me" would beat it by one spot, peaking at #4). And Nicks has Prince to thank for it all.

Stephanie Lynn Nicks was born in Phoenix, Arizona in 1948. Her grandfather was a frustrated country singer who taught his granddaughter to sing duets with him when she was just four. Her family moved often when she was growing up and Nicks remembers her youth as being lonely, except for her music. As a teenager she began writing songs and playing them on guitar and she joined her first band in high school. By her senior year she was living in California and one night she saw Lindsey Buckingham performing "California Dreamin.'" She was instantly attracted and got up to sing harmonies with him. Her grandfather's training came in handy as the two made sweet music right away. Nicks later joined Buckingham in a rock band called Fritz. They had the opportunity to open for Janis Joplin and Jimi Hendrix, two performers who influenced Nicks' singing style and intensity on stage. When Fritz disbanded, Buckingham and Nicks, who were now a romantic couple as well as collaborating musicians, formed a duo that they unimaginatively called Buckingham Nicks. The two released one, eponymous album before being asked to join Fleetwood Mac.

Actually Buckingham and Nicks were not asked to join Fleetwood Mac. Buckingham was. In late 1974 Bob Welch informed his bandmates in Fleetwood Mac that he was leaving to pursue a solo career. Mick Fleetwood, the band's drummer and co-founder, remembered hearing the Buckingham Nicks LP and being impressed by Buckingham's guitar playing. He got in touch and offered Buckingham Welch's old job. But Buckingham explained that he and Nicks were a package deal. Fleetwood accepted them both and the couple brought a smoother pop sensibility to Fleetwood Mac's previously harder, bluesier sound. The band went on to incredible levels of success throughout the rest of the seventies.

But a band like Fleetwood Mac, with multiple songwriters, limits an artist, especially one as prolific as Stevie Nicks. By the early eighties she'd amassed a number of songs that couldn't find their way onto Fleetwood Mac albums so she released her first solo LP, *Bella Donna*, in 1981. That album went to #1 and produced four Top 40 hits, inspiring *Rolling Stone* to dub Nicks the "Reigning Queen of Rock and Roll."

Around this time Nick's best friend, Robin Anderson died of leukemia. Nicks was devastated. She was determined to help Anderson's widower Kim take care of their baby so she said to him, "Well, we might as well get married." And so they did. On January 29th, 1983, Stevie Nicks married Kim Anderson and as Nicks would say later: "We didn't get married because we were in love. We got married because we were grieving." The marriage would last eight months. The evening of the wedding they were driving and they heard Prince's new song, "Little Red Corvette" on the radio. Nick's loved the sound of the song, especially the synthesizers. She started humming a melody inspired by what she'd just heard and got so excited she and Anderson pulled over and bought a tape recorder so she could capture it. She spent hours that night crafting the song (when you get married because you're grieving you apparently have nothing else to do on your wedding night) and eventually came up with "Stand Back."

Shortly thereafter, Nicks got to working on the song in the studio. On a whim, she called Prince and told him the story. He happened to be in Los Angeles where she was working and he popped over to the studio to play synthesizer on the track. Because Nicks and Prince were on two different labels they figured it would be better that his contribution went uncredited, although the two made a handshake agreement to split the publishing royalties 50/50. Prince, being the enigmatic artist he was, then just got up and left the studio. Nicks has described the whole experience as dream-like.

Nicks had high hopes for "Stand Back" so she procured a large budget for the video and hired Brian Grant (who'd directed successful videos like Peter Gabriel's "Shock the Monkey" and Olivia Newton-John's "Physical") to helm the project. They dreamed up an elaborate "Gone with the Wind" scenario with Nicks riding a horse up to an antebellum mansion. But when the video was done she hated it. She scrapped the whole thing and shot a simpler, performance-based video with Nicks singing directly to the camera and twirling around with her signature scarves. The video also features the obligatory choreographed dancers because what eighties video was complete without them?

To this day "Stand Back" is one of Nick's favorite songs to play live. She says it has an energy that, "comes from somewhere unknown," although it would seem to most that the energy, and sound, come from Prince's "Little Red Corvette" as well as his dream-like appearance in the studio.

## August 21st

On this date in 1961, Patsy Cline finished recording her vocals for "Crazy." The song would go on to be her biggest hit and help launch the career of an, at the time, unknown songwriter. And if it hadn't been for a coincidental meeting in a bar the whole thing may not have happened. Here's the story:

Virginia Patterson Hensley was born in Virginia in 1932. As a young teenager she was hospitalized with a terrible fever and a throat infection but upon her release her voice had changed. For the better. She'd say later, "When I recovered I had this booming voice like Kate Smith." She began to use that voice by entering (and winning) talent contests and soon she attracted the attention of country singer Jimmy Dean who often invited her to join him on his radio show. In 1953 she married Gerald Cline and though the marriage only lasted a few years she kept his last name after the divorce. Her second marriage was to Charles Allen Dick so you can understand why she kept Cline. It was her manager who suggested she use Patsy as a first name (from her middle name). In 1957, Cline scored her first big hit with "Walkin' After Midnight." The song went to #12 on the pop chart and #2 on the country chart and overnight a new country star was born. Though it would be a few years until her next big hit, Cline had made enough of a name for herself that she was a big star in Nashville throughout the late fifties and into the early sixties. In 1961 she scored big again with "I Fall to Pieces" which again went to #12 on the pop chart but this time became a #1 hit on the country chart. Unfortunately for Cline as "I Fall to Pieces" was climbing the charts she was involved in a very serious car accident that left her hospitalized for six weeks.

Willie Hugh Nelson was born in 1933 in Texas and he was always destined to be involved in the music industry. He wrote his first song at seven years old and was playing in bands by ten. In high school, he toured nationally with a polka band and in college he was a radio DJ as well as a singer at honky tonks. In 1960, hoping to make it in the music industry, he moved to the mecca of country music, Nashville. There, he sold some songs to other musicians and started hanging around Tootsie's Orchid Lounge, with two other struggling songwriters, Roger Miller and Kris Kristofferson. Tootsie's was a bar near the Grand Ole Opry that was a favorite watering hole for singers and songwriters and it's here that these two stories converge.

Patsy Cline's second husband, Charlie Dick, also frequented Tootsie's Orchid Lounge and one night, he and Willie Nelson got to talking. Legend has it that a song Nelson had written and sold came on the jukebox and when Dick seemed to like it, Nelson let him know it was his composition (which is one of those great stories that even if it isn't true, it ought to be). The young songwriter had a demo of a song he'd written called "Crazy." He'd offered it to singer Billy Walker who'd turned it down because, as Walker said, he thought it was a "girl's song." Dick was intrigued and since Cline was home recuperating from the accident he brought the demo tape home to play it for her. But she hated it. The melody was odd, blending jazz with country, and Nelson had recorded the guide vocals himself, speaking the lyrics of the verses slightly behind the beat. Cline initially said there was no way she could record it but when her husband played the demo for Cline's producer, Owen Bradley, Bradley heard potential in the song. He worked out an arrangement that was perfect for Cline and they made plans to record it on August 17th, 1961.

When the day arrived Cline limped into the studio on crutches. She took a few attempts at the song but each one ended in frustration. Her ribs were still bruised from the accident, making it impossible for her to hit the high notes. And perhaps her initial lack of enthusiasm for the song was coming into play. Whatever the reason, Cline, a singer who normally finished a song in one or two takes, was struggling. Nelson was in the studio watching her fumble with his song and he urged her to keep trying, knowing this could be his huge break. Much to his chagrin, after four hours of frustrating recording, Cline gave up and considered not finishing the song. But four days later, on this date in 1961, at the encouraging of her husband and her manager, who both sensed "Crazy" had hit potential, Cline took another shot at the song and this time she was able to hit all the notes and convey all the sadness in the lyrics.

"Crazy" was released on October 16th of 1961 as the follow-up to "I Fall to Pieces" and it was even more successful than its predecessor, reaching #9 on the pop chart. The song still stands up to this day as a painful ode to unrequited love and Cline's delivery is note-perfect. Sadly, "Crazy" turned out to be Patsy Cline's last big hit. Her next few releases would do well but not crossover as successfully and then in 1963, at just 30 years of age, Patsy Cline was killed in a plane crash.

For Willie Nelson, the success of "Crazy" helped him immensely. And not just financially. With a higher profile in Nashville as the song's writer he scored a record deal and his career as a performer, not just a songwriter, was underway. Nelson has become one of the most recognized names in country music and its sub-genre "outlaw country." Which just proves the power of networking. Or at least hanging out in the right bars.

## August 22nd

On this date in 1964, the Supremes began a two week run at #1 with their first hit song, "Where Did Our Love Go." Before this the Supremes were seen as a bit of a bust at their record label and if they had rejected this song like they attempted to, they may have stayed that way forever. Instead, their career soared and they became one of the most successful acts of the sixties.

To understand the inner workings at Motown Records one need only know about Berry Gordy's first job. Like his father before him, Gordy dreamed of being a songwriter but, living in Detroit, Michigan, and surrounded by job opportunities in the booming automobile industry of the fifties, as a teenager, Gordy worked at Ford. Car manufacturers long ago realized the efficacy of assembly lines. Instead of having one person build a car, assembly lines allow for multiple people to build many more cars by specializing. One person becomes a master at putting the lug nuts on the tires while another connects the gas line to the motor. And so on, down the line.

While working by day, Gordy wrote songs by night. And he was able to sell a few. Jackie Wilson had some success with a few of Gordy's compositions (or co-compositions), namely "Lonely Teardrops" and "Reet Petite" and Gordy, ever the entrepreneur, quit his day job and invested his profit from those songs into a new label. Tamla Records was founded in early 1959 and a year later Gordy changed the name to Motown (a blending, or portmanteau, of Detroit's nickname "motor town"). Gordy brought the same assembly line mentality to his label. Realizing that songwriting, musicianship and singing were all unique talents and it was easier to find individuals who excelled in each of these (rather than one person who could do all three) Gordy set up a system where a team of writers would compose a song, a house band would lay down the instrumental track and then singers would take their shot at singing the tune. It was a methodical approach to songwriting, which is often a haphazard endeavor, and it worked. Like a charm. Before long Motown's studio on West Grand Boulevard soon became known as "Hitsville U.S.A." And the hits rolled out of it as routinely as cars off the assembly line.

One of the legendary songwriting teams at Motown consisted of Lamont Dozier and brothers, Brian and Eddy Holland (usually referred to as Holland-Dozier-Holland or H-D-H). They wrote such legendary songs as "Locking Up My Heart" which the Marvelettes recorded in 1963, "Heatwave" which Martha and the

Vandellas took to the top of the R&B chart in 1963 and "How Sweet It Is (To Be Loved by You)" which Marvin Gaye scored a #6 pop hit with.

When they wrote "Where Did Our Love Go" in the spring of 1964 they intended it for the Marvelettes. At Motown the songwriters were not only responsible for writing songs but they would also assemble the house band (the famous Funk Brothers back then) and record the backing track, then find a singer or singing group to record the vocals. If no singer wanted the song, the writers had to pay for the recording session out of their own pockets (Gordy was a shrewd one!) So when the Marvelettes' lead singer, Gladys Horton, rejected "Where Did Our Love Go," saying, "It's the worst thing I ever heard," the writers began to search for someone, anyone, at the label to record the song so they could at least recoup their investment. Motown artist after Motown artist rejected "Where Did Our Love Go" until Lamont Dozier finally approached the Supremes. Diana Ross, Mary Wilson and Florence Ballard had been with Motown for two years by this point. They had released eight singles with one only one cracking the Top Forty ("When the Lovelight Starts Shining Through His Eyes" which peaked at #23). By Motown standards the band was just shy of being a failure. In fact, inside the walls of Motown, the Supremes were known behind their backs as the "No Hit Supremes." Yet even they rejected "Where Did Our Love Go." Diana Ross, the lead singer of the trio, felt the song was in too low of a key for her (because they'd recorded it in Gladys Horton's key). The trio considered having Wilson take the lead but finally the songwriters (who were far more established at Motown than the Supremes) persuaded them to record it with Ross reaching down to hit the low notes. When it came time to record their vocals no one was happy. Ross had a bad attitude throughout the session, which actually worked out for the theme of the song. You don't exactly wanna sing, "Where did our love go?" and admit to having a "burning, burning, yearning feelin' inside" that "hurts so bad" with a smile on your face and a chipper attitude. Wilson and Ballard were also unhappy during the session so instead of learning the proper backing vocals they just sang "baby, baby, baby" repeatedly. Then, towards the end of the session a disagreement arose and Gordy himself had to break it up. When it all was said and done and he asked to hear the song back, he shrugged and said it could be a Top 10, "but not a #1."

As it turned out, everyone was wrong about "Where Did Our Love Go." It sold incredibly well and landed at the top of both the pop and R&B chart two months after its release.

Now that their losing streak was over, the Supremes went on a tear, releasing #1 hit after #1 hit ("Baby Love", "Come See About Me", "Stop! In the Name of Love" and "Back in My Arms Again") all written by Holland-Dozier-Holland. They would eventually have twelve #1 songs, the most of any Motown group. The Marvelettes went in the opposite direction, they would never reach the top spot again in part because Holland-Dozier-Holland were now giving their best stuff to the Supremes. It would be fair to say they were the ones left wondering, where did our love go?

On this date in 1970, Lou Reed played his last gig with the Velvet Underground. The show was taped and released a few years later to satisfy a record contract and that album, *Live at Max's Kansas City*, would share a similar fate as every other Velvet Underground LP: critically acclaimed yet commercially disappointing. Though they sold very few records in their years together, the Velvet Underground has gained almost mythical status for their influence on so many artists and bands that followed them.

John Cale, a Welshman who moved to the States to study classical music, and Lou Reed, a Brooklyn kid who wanted to make it as a musician and songwriter, first started playing together in 1964. *The Velvet Underground* was a popular book at the time about deviant sexual behavior among consenting adults and Cale and Reed both liked the mysterious nature of the title. And since Reed had already written a song called "Venus in Furs" (with imagery of whips and shiny leather boots), they thought the name apt so they chose it for their new band. Cale told *Rolling Stone* once that his goal with Velvet Underground was to, "cross-pollinate rock with the avant-garde." A year later Andy Warhol became aware of the band and fell in love with their odd, down-tempo sound and underlying sexuality. He quickly became their manager and persuaded them to work with the German born singer, Nico. With Warhol's connections the band signed a contract and became a part of his multimedia roadshow, *Exploding Plastic Inevitable*, which combined Warhol's films with the band's music. Warhol also designed the cover art for their debut, *The Velvet Underground & Nico*. That LP was released in March of 1967 and though it sold poorly, peaking at 171 on the *Billboard* Top 200 album chart then quickly falling off it, it has taken on legendary status among music fans. *Rolling Stone* once called it, "the most prophetic rock album ever made" and famed producer Brian Eno has said, "Their debut album may have sold only 10,000 copies, but everyone who bought it started a band." Indeed, almost every punk band that ever rampaged through a set has cited the Velvet Underground as a source of inspiration. Why? Because what they lacked in musical prowess and artistry they made up for in attitude. Their sound was raw and droning and unrehearsed and they sang about prostitutes and drug dealers and transvestites and they were angry and nihilistic and quite frankly, they didn't give a fuck if you bought their records or not. And just to prove how their reputation has grown through the years, in 2013, when Lou Reed passed away, *The Velvet Underground & Nico,* with no specific promotion or marketing campaign, re-entered the chart and this time peaked at 121, 50 positions higher than when it was first released.

After their debut, the band severed ties with Warhol and Nico and hired Steve Sesnick to manage them. Under Sesnick's direction the band began playing harder. They recorded a second album, *White Light/White Heat*, in 1968 which peaked at an even more dismal 199 on the Top 200. Cale was trying to push the band in an even more experimental direction (he wanted to record a song with speakers underwater, for example) and finally Reed forced an ultimatum: him or me. Cale was tossed out of the band and replaced by Doug Yule. 1969 would see yet another album (*The Velvet Underground*) that made nary a dent on the charts.

By 1970 they were recording their fourth LP, *Loaded*, but by this point Reed was completely disillusioned with the band. When they edited out the bridge in his song "Sweet Jane" it was the final straw. Having signed a nine week deal to play at Max's Kansas City, Lou Reed stuck it out as long as he could. He quit the band with a handful of shows left in the run so his appearance on this night in 1970 was his last one with the Velvet Underground. *Loaded* would be released a few months later and it would fail to even crack the Top 200.

The Velvet Underground would release the live LP, *Live at Max's Kansas City,* which was from the show on this night in 1970, and then one more studio album (1973's *Squeeze*) before officially disbanding. Lou Reed would have slightly more commercial success in his solo career, most notably his 1972 single "Walk on the Wild Side" which became a #16 hit for him and his 1974 LP *Sally Can't Dance* which went to #10 on the *Billboard* 200 chart. Meanwhile, John Cale's post Underground work has been incredibly prolific as he continues to push the envelope of experimental art rock. But measuring any of them based on sales or radio play is unfair. The Velvet Underground gave voice to a segment of music lovers who wanted to dive into the deep end of the experimental pool. Part psychedelia, part down-tempo, part proto-punk, the Underground, especially on their debut album, challenged the listener to pay attention. There were no hooks, no finger-snapping moments, certainly no sing-along-able choruses. With Cales' droning playing and Reed's half spoken lyrics about drugs and sadomasochism, the Velvet Underground stayed safely away from any chart success. But their impact on music cannot be denied, if for no other reason than the number of musicians who followed them and cite the band as a source of inspiration. Brian Eno probably had it right. For every copy of their debut album, a new band was formed. And some of those bands or artists had names like Bowie and U2 and R.E.M and the Talking Heads and Morrissey and Nirvana and that's a pretty good legacy in anybody's book.

### August 24th

On this date in 1978, the Commodores' "Three Times a Lady" was in its second week at #1. It was the band's first chart-topper after ten years of playing together. A band's first #1 will often catapult them into a higher stratosphere of fame and strengthen their bond as bandmates. For the Commodores, "Three Times a Lady" had the opposite effect and would soon lead to the song's writer, Lionel Richie, leaving the band.

The Commodores came together in the late sixties at Tuskegee University. Founding member William King has said they flipped open a dictionary and randomly selected a name. "We lucked out," he has joked, "we almost became the Commodes." They signed with Motown in 1972 and consistently released funk and R&B songs that were met with varying degrees of success, most notably 1977's "Brick House." The funk celebration of a lady who is "stacked" was inspired by the idiom, "She's built like a brick shit house," but since the band wanted the song to get radio play they removed the curse word and left a single horn note in its place. The ploy worked, the song became a hit and it climbed to #5 on the pop chart. That same year the Lionel Richie written ballad, "Easy," peaked at #4. When the Commodores convened to record their next studio album, Richie presented his bandmates with yet another sugary ballad. This one was inspired by a speech his dad had made at his parent's anniversary party. His father thanked his mother profusely and said "I love you. I want you. I need you." Richie couldn't get these words out of his head and later when he sat down to write a song he began thinking about his own wife and how her support had helped his career. He wrote "Three Times a Lady" as an ode to both women, using his dad's "I love you. I want you. I need you" as the inspiration. The Commodores recorded the song and made it the lead single off their next LP, 1978's *Natural High.*

"Three Times a Lady" got to #1 on August 12th, 1978, ending the Rolling Stones' one week stay at the top with their disco infused hit, "Miss You." "Three Times a Lady" would enjoy a two week run at #1 before bowing out to Frankie Valli's theme song from the movie *Grease.* And when the band toured they clearly had to include it, and "Easy" in their setlist. The following year, inspired by his success writing slower, more intimate songs, Richie wrote two more ballads for the band, "Still" and the break-up song "Sail On." Both were Top 10 hits with "Still" reaching #1. In 1981, Richie wrote "Endless Love," but this time performed it as a duet with Diana Ross.

Commodores' concerts, which used to be non-stop funk-fests and dance parties, were becoming easy listening shows. While the band loved the success of the slower songs (and the money that comes with topping the charts and selling out bigger arenas), some members started to wonder if they were just becoming Richie's ballad-backing band. Fans were confused too. Some of their older followers came expecting to be on their feet all night but were forced to sit and listen to so many slower songs. Other fans came expecting to hear the songs they enjoyed on their easy listening stations only to be subjected to funky numbers like "Slippery When Wet", "I Feel Sanctified", "Lady, (You Bring Me Up)" and of course, "Brick House." When articles started appearing asking if Richie was too big for the Commodores, the band approached their main songwriter and asked him if he'd like to do a solo record. Richie said, "Yes," even though he admits it was like leaving his family.

Lionel Richie's eponymous debut album was a huge success, with three Top 10 singles including "Truly" which spent four weeks at #1. Based on the success of this first solo album, and Motown's desire for a follow-up, he had to break it to the Commodores that he was officially leaving.

The band would continue on without him to lesser degrees of success. "Night Shift," their tribute song to R&B singers Jackie Wilson and Marvin Gaye, was by far their biggest post-Richie single and although they have been able to return to a more straight forward funk sound, their concerts are still interrupted by a few Richie-written ballads. As for Lionel Richie, his solo work would make him one of the largest-selling and biggest names in music throughout the eighties. And while not everything he recorded was a ballad (especially the 1986 hit "Dancing on the Ceiling") Richie seems far more comfortable (and effective) singing an intimate slow song rather than getting down and dirty doing a funk number. Of course, with over a hundred million records sold in his career, it's safe to say his fans love what he releases no matter what tempo it is.

**August 25<sup>th</sup>**

On this date in 1975, Bruce Springsteen released his third, and contractually final, album for Columbia Records. The label that just a few years earlier had signed Springsteen with great hopes, had grown disillusioned with his lack of commercial success and were looking at this album as a make or break moment for the 26 year old singer. If this album performed like his first two, they were very likely to drop him. And Springsteen knew all of that which is why he took a grueling 14 months working on the album. The result, *Born to Run*, not only saved Springsteen from having to find a new label, it established him as one of the biggest names in music.

Bruce Springsteen was born in Freehold, New Jersey in 1949. Like so many singers his age, he became fascinated by music when he saw Elvis Presley perform on the Ed Sullivan Show in 1956. His mother, hoping to encourage her son, bought him an $18 guitar to practice on. When a teenaged Springsteen started landing some early gigs at Elks Lodges and trailer parks, she took out a loan and bought him an even nicer $60 Kent guitar. Springsteen kicked around the Jersey shore area as well as venturing into New York City with various bands in the late sixties and early seventies. He caught the attention of Columbia Record's producer John Hammond; the man who had signed Bob Dylan to the same label a decade earlier. Hammond facilitated the deal to get Springsteen signed, hyperbolically promising Clive Davis, the label's CEO, that the young Jerseyite was "the next Dylan."

Springsteen's debut album *Greetings from Asbury Park, N.J.*, was released in January 1973 to critical praise from the music press. But despite the rave reviews and Springsteen playing scores of shows to promote the album, sales were disappointing. Just nine months later Springsteen released his follow-up, *The Wild, the Innocent & the E Street Shuffle*, with virtually identical results.

In May of 1974, Bruce Springsteen and his E Street Band played some shows up in Boston. A rock critic by the name of Jon Landau was in attendance and his review of the shows included the quote: "I saw rock and roll's future, and its name is Bruce Springsteen. And on a night when I needed to feel young, he made me feel like I was hearing music for the very first time." At first

Springsteen cringed when he read the article. He knew the trappings that came with high expectations from his stature as "the next Dylan." Now here was a critic calling him the future of rock and roll. Still he was intrigued by the review and contacted its writer and was even more intrigued when Landau, who had also done some producing, started suggesting some recording techniques that could improve his next record. Springsteen decided this Landau guy might know what he was talking about and he asked him to co-produce this next, critically important, album. Landau agreed and one of the great rock and roll relationships had begun.

As work got underway, Springsteen was very well aware that this was the last album under his contract with Columbia and that things had changed significantly at his label. First, Clive Davis was gone, having been ousted amid allegations of misuse of funds and providing drugs to artists and disc jockeys (which most people would assume were in a record executive's job description). Plus the label had a new hot shot named Billy Joel whose debut album, 1973's *Piano Man*, had exceeded expectations. And by all accounts, Springsteen felt the pressure. He was agitated and moody in the recording studio. He would get exasperated that he heard things in his head he couldn't get his band to replicate. He recorded songs over and over looking for perfection. He spent months working on the title track alone, trying to find the perfect Phil-Spector-like Wall of Sound to go along with its lyrics of urgent passion and escapism. He focused obsessively over the song's introductions, believing the right hook could bring a listener in. He also sequenced the album specifically using a "four corners" approach so both Side A and Side B open with themes of optimism and escape ("Born to Run" and "Thunder Road") and close with feelings of loss and betrayal ("Backstreets" and "Jungleland.") He had a goal to make this record sound like "Roy Orbison singing Bob Dylan produced by Phil Specter" and that vision proved incredibly difficult to achieve. But after fourteen months of work, he did it.

Finally, on this date in 1975, Springsteen's masterwork was released. All the obsession had paid off. The Boss, as he was often called, was now a legitimate rock star of epic proportions. Two months later he would famously grace the cover of *Time* and *Newsweek* in the same week. His concerts became legendary rock and roll marathons. The album's title track, the one he labored over for six months, would become not just his signature song but the unofficial anthem of his home state. Oh, and Columbia renewed his contract too. And you can be sure he repaid his mother's $60 loan.

On this date in 1978, "Just What I Needed," the Cars' debut single, had just cracked the Top 40 on its way to #27. The song's original demo had helped the band get signed and now it was introducing the world, not only to a brand new band from Boston but a brand new sound as well.

Rick Ocasek and Benjamin Orr met in Cleveland, Ohio in the mid-sixties. They started playing in bands together, moving to Columbus, Ohio, then Ann Arbor, Michigan before landing in Boston. They formed a soft rock band called Milkwood and released a very Crosby Stills and Nash sounding LP in 1972. The album failed to chart and Milkwood disbanded. Their next attempt at making it in the music business was another short-lived band, this one called Richard and the Rabbits. Their band Cap'n Swing didn't work out either, nor did their coffee house acoustic duo simply called Ocasek and Orr (they'd apparently exhausted all the band names they could think of). By the end of 1976 Ocasek and Orr were both getting a little frustrated at playing live and forming bands and not finding that winning combination. But they gave it one more shot, this time recruiting David Robinson, who had previously drummed with the Modern Lovers, to join Greg Hawkes on keyboard and Elliot Easton on guitar. Orr would play bass and sing and Ocasek would play guitar and sing.

With this lineup (which Robinson suggested they call the Cars) they would take the stage for the first time on December 31st, 1976. That debut show was a hit and throughout the winter of 1977 the Cars began developing a strong following in the Boston area. The band recorded a demo tape of some of their songs and delivered one of them, "Just What I Needed," to some Boston rock radio stations. The band believed that song, which Ocasek had written and Orr sings lead on, had the best potential to break them. And they were right. Despite the fact that the band was unsigned and had no promotional push behind them, save for good old fashioned word of mouth, WCOZ and WBCN both started playing "Just What I Needed" regularly. Before long Elektra signed them to a record deal and, before the first anniversary of their first gig together, they were already recording their debut album.

That LP, *The Cars*, was released in June of 1978 and would peak at #18 on the *Billboard* Top 200 album chart. Even today the Cars' debut holds up as a riveting piece of work, combining good old rock and roll hooks with elements of electronica and even a bit of psychedelia and prog rock. It's an album worth listening to, front to back, in the original track order. The album opens with the infectious one-two punch of "Good Times Roll" and "My Best Friend's Girlfriend" and finishes with the trippy combination of "Moving in Stereo" and "All Mixed Up." Along the way the Cars rock hard but always with a polished and produced sound. Even the most punkish song on their debut, "Don't Cha Stop," has a futurist feel that seemed to be clearing a path for bands to evolve into the new decade. The Cars had much of the edginess of the punk bands of the day, but added an electronic feel to it, mostly through Hawkes' work on keyboard and synthesizer. This was before terms like "new wave" or "synth pop" had come in to vogue so there was really no template for this sound. But along with bands like Television and Blondie and the Talking Heads, the Cars were pioneers at smoothing out punk's rough edges and getting it ready for a new decade. It's no exaggeration to say that without the Cars, and a handful of other bands that became innovators with the new technology available to them, eighties bands like Duran Duran, Culture Club, Depeche Mode and Yaz would never have existed.

Over the next decade, the Cars went on to amazing commercial success but by 1988 they'd run their course and broken up. This time Rick Ocasek and Benjamin Orr didn't scramble to put together a new lineup. They'd had the success they'd hoped for and they separately pursued their own solo careers of recording and producing. When rumors circulated of a reunion, Ocasek adamantly denied them, saying at one point he'd rather have six months of diarrhea then tour for six months with his old band. In 2000, all possibilities of a reunion of the original lineup were put to rest when Benjamin Orr, just 53 years old, succumbed to pancreatic cancer. Eleven years later the four surviving members did indeed get together again. They recorded an album called *Move Like This*. Instead of replacing Orr on bass, Hawkes played the bass lines for most of the songs using a bass guitar Orr had owned. Ocasek and Orr usually split the singing duties but on *Move Like This* Ocasek sang lead on every track. He would admit later, "I was aware that on half of the new songs, Ben would have done better than I did. But we never wanted anybody from the outside." The band embarked on a short tour to support the album which ended with a performance at the House of Blues in Boston, about an hour's drive from where they played their very first gig in 1976. For a band called the Cars, they really had driven around the world and back.

**August 27th**

On this date in 2007, "Crank That (Soulja Boy)" had just cracked the Top 10. It would get to #1 on September 15th where it would reside for seven straight weeks. The song, that had been written by a then sixteen year old rapper named DeAndre Cortez Way, who goes by Soulja Boy, started a dance craze that some considered to be the biggest since the Macarena. Yet despite the song's popularity both on the charts and at private parties around the world, the lyrics have been analyzed and some say they are misogynist and indecent; allegations that Soulja Boy has denied.

One of the ways the internet has changed the world of music is that it has provided a path for artists to get their songs heard and noticed before they are signed to a major label. The list of stars who have "broken" on YouTube or SoundCloud grows every year and DeAndre Way is a prime example of this new path to success. DeAndre Cortez Way was born in 1990 in Chicago, Illinois. He moved with his family to Atlanta, Georgia when he was six which is where he fell in love with rap. At fourteen his father offered him some studio time to pursue his passion. A year later he posted his first songs on a website called SoundClick. After receiving positive reviews there he set up a MySpace page and YouTube account where he continued to offer his work for free.

In March of 2007, months before his seventeenth birthday, Way recorded "Crank That" in less than an hour using a digital audio computer called Fruity Loops. The ease of being able to create loops and musical beds to rap or sing over is one of the things that has opened the doors to so many new artists. Aspiring musicians no longer need studio time or even bandmates. They need a good computer and the right programs. As Way explains: "I can make a beat in my hotel room or I can make a beat in my dressing room, while getting ready for a show, and I can send it to Pro Tools, and bam, get it right back recorded on my laptop. Then I can post it for all my fans to hear." "Crank That" is a perfect example of this. But what shouldn't be overlooked in how quickly a song like this can come together, is that before any tune becomes a hit, it has to have a hook. Way, at 16 years old, created a catchy song by looping a steel drum beat then writing a rap that describes dance steps that are easily performed. That combination, catchy song and dance moves, has taken other songs to the top (most famously "Macarena" which spent fourteen weeks at #1 in 1996) and it would do the same for "Crank That."

Way then put together a low budget video in which he and two other young men demonstrate the dance that could be done to the song. By May, "Crank That" was getting radio play and his minute and a half long video was being viewed by millions. Way was quickly signed to Interscope Records and a new video (of the whole song) was shot and released. Way's original homemade, video has been viewed over 21 million times on Youtube, the professional one has received over a quarter of a billion clicks. "Crank That" got to #1 by mid-September where it spent seven weeks.

Then came the controversy. What exactly does Way mean when he raps, "Watch me crank that Soulja Boy, then Superman that hoe"? Internet speculation, backed up by the website Urban Dictionary, says (and if you're easily offended please skip the rest of this paragraph) that "cranking that" is slang for masturbation. And to "Superman" a woman is to ejaculate on her back, perhaps while she's sleeping, and then press a sheet on that spot so that the sheet will stick to her. When she gets up she'll have a cape (like Superman, only stickier). Certainly using the derogatory term "hoe" at the end of the line helped add fuel to the rumors. And with other lyrics like, "If we get the fightin' then I'm cockin' on your bitch ass," Way certainly can't deny the song is misogynistic.

Way replied to the rumors, telling BET, "Superman is just a dance," adding, "I heard about the e-mails going around and...basically, they trying to just stop my shine." When pressed further in the interview the young rapper was ready to move on and promote his next song, saying: "We're on to 'Soulja Girl.' We're on to the second single. 'Crank Dat' is slowly fading away. You tried, but it's too late." And while he hasn't followed up "Crank That" with any more chart-toppers, he did have some success in the years following it, with songs like "Kiss Me Thru the Phone" (#3) and "Turn My Swag On" (#19)

Whether or not the speculation is true, it certainly didn't hurt the song's popularity. Everyone from Mitzvah guests to athletes to daytime talk show hosts found themselves doing the dance. When "Crank That (Soulja Boy)" hit the top spot on the charts, Way became the youngest solo artist to write, perform and produce a *Billboard* #1 single. The song also became the first in internet history to be downloaded over 3 million times. Whatever "Supermaning a hoe" really means, it certainly didn't stop this young rapper from releasing one of the biggest songs of 2007.

## August 28th

On this date in 1982, Survivor's "Eye of the Tiger" began its sixth and final week at the top of the charts. The song was used during the "workout montage" in that year's hit movie *Rocky III*. It was the band's most successful single and yet they almost talked the movie producers out of using it. Good thing for them Sylvester Stallone couldn't get the publishing rights to the song he really wanted for that scene.

The original *Rocky* was a big success. It was the highest-grossing movie of 1976, earning over $200 million which, when compared to its $1 million budget, is sort of like the main character; an underdog that exceeds all expectations. The movie was also critically acclaimed. It received ten Oscar nominations and won three, including Best Film and Best Director. One of the nominations that didn't wind up winning was for Best Original Song, for Bill Conti's "Gonna Fly Now" (which lost to Barbra Streisand's "Evergreen" from *A Star is Born*.) "Gonna Fly Now" (often called the "Theme from *Rocky*") is used during the workout montage of the movie, most notably when Rocky is finally able to climb the steps to the Philadelphia Art Museum. If you are able to watch that scene, which ends with Stallone raising his arms triumphantly as the sun rises over the City of Brotherly Love, and not be motivated, you need to check your pulse. It's an inspirational moment for all ages and it helped "Gonna Fly Now" become part of pop culture lore. The song hit #1 on the *Billboard* Hot 100 chart and even today, anytime a "pump up" song is needed, Bill Conti's tune is first in line. In 1979, *Rocky II* was released and the filmmakers used an alternate version of "Gonna Fly Now" for the now obligatory workout segment.

When Stallone set out to produce a third installment in the *Rocky* series, he wanted to break away from Conti's sound and find something more modern and harder. He was given some tracks by the band Survivor and he liked their sound so he commissioned them to write a song for the movie, making it clear he wanted nothing like "Gonna Fly Now." The band was given a rough cut of the movie and the scene where their song would go had already been edited using Queen's "Another One Bites the Dust." Survivor's guitarist Frankie Sullivan and keyboardist Jim Peterik, who were set to write the song, were floored. The Queen song, with its thumping, disco-inspired, bass line and Freddie Mercury's impassioned delivery, was perfect. And they knew it. Sullivan and Peterik called Stallone and asked why he wasn't using it. They were basically talking themselves out of a job, which is commendable given the fact that at the time, Survivor wasn't exactly a household name. But Stallone told the two that he couldn't get the publishing rights from Queen. They didn't want their song used in the movie. So Sullivan and Peterik sat down with the goal of writing something even better than "Another One Bites the Dust," knowing that was going to be hard to beat.

As they worked on the song they were playing with the lyrics, trying to reference as much from the movie as possible. Lines like, "Went the distance" and, "Hangin' tough, staying hungry" are either lifted exactly from the script or approximated from it. The original demo was called "Survival" with the last line of the chorus going, "And the last known survivor stalks his prey in the night, and it all comes down to survival" because rival and survival are what's known as "perfect rhymes." But they finally realized that the visual of "eye of the tiger" (another line lifted from the movie) was more powerful and that "rival" and "tiger" are what songwriters call "near-rhymes" or "imperfect rhymes." When the band presented the song to Stallone he loved it. He made some suggestions to change the song slightly (which they did) but overall their original demo is what became the final product. Peterik has said they didn't mind getting suggestions from Stallone because: "He has a good ear for a hook. Just listen to his dialogues - he wrote those scripts. He came up with 'eye of the tiger' for that script and those hook phrases like 'I'm going to knock you into tomorrow.' All that stuff is Stallone, he's a genius with dialogue. Songs are nothing more than dialogue set to music as far as I'm concerned."

Rocky III became the fourth highest-grossing film of 1982 and "Eye of the Tiger" sold more copies than every other song that year but Olivia Newton-John's "Physical." And the song lives on today, showing up right alongside "Gonna Fly Now" whenever a motivational or "pump up" song is needed. Both convey the underlying message from the Rocky movies perfectly: that the only limits we have in life are ones we place on ourselves. If you want to climb the steps of the Philadelphia Art Museum or lose twenty pounds or run a marathon or whatever physical achievement you dream of, the first step, as the line in "Eye of the Tiger" goes, is "risin' up to the challenge." And if you're going to attempt to do something you've never done before, it wouldn't hurt to put a playlist together of songs that will motivate and inspire you. You can start with "Gonna Fly Now" and "Eye of the Tiger." Two songs that were perfect for the Rocky movies and two songs that are sure to get your blood pumping.

On this date in 1966, the Beatles ended a short and troubled U.S. tour with a show at San Francisco's chilly and foggy Candlestick Park. To a man, the band left the stadium that night thinking it would not just be the end of the tour but their last live show ever. And except for an impromptu appearance on the rooftop of Abbey Roads studio in 1969 they were correct. The Beatles never toured again.

The Beatles embarked on their third U.S. tour on August 12th, 1966. By modern standards the tour was very basic and abbreviated; eighteen shows scheduled in fourteen different cities over seventeen days (in a few locations they did two shows a day). As bad luck would have it, just as the tour began, the teen magazine *Datebook* reprinted a quote from John Lennon that had appeared in the *London Evening Standard* months before. Lennon had been asked about his interest in Christianity and he replied: "Christianity will go. It will vanish and shrink. I needn't argue about that; I'm right and I'll be proved right. We're more popular than Jesus now; I don't know which will go first – rock 'n' roll or Christianity. Jesus was all right but his disciples were thick and ordinary. It's them twisting it that ruins it for me."

The U.S. media grabbed a hold of the line, "We're more popular than Jesus," and ran with it, with headlines screaming blasphemy from sea to shining sea.

Brian Epstein, the Beatles' manager, considered cancelling the tour altogether but he decided to move forward. Before the first show, in Chicago, the band held a press conference where Lennon offered a feeble explanation and apology for his statement. Among his comments he said: "I'm not saying we're better or greater, or comparing us with Jesus Christ as a person, or God as a thing or whatever it is. I just said what I said and was wrong, or was taken wrong, and now it's all this." You can find the clip of this on YouTube and it's interesting to watch Lennon squirm through his answers while the other Beatles sit awkwardly beside him. Lennon clearly doesn't think he should have to apologize and it's obvious he had been talked into doing so. Compare this to their light-hearted press conferences of just a few years earlier and it's clear how quickly things had changed.

Still, the band was met with protests at almost every stop on the tour and local media focused more on Lennon's original statement and less on the music. Two shows in Memphis were almost cancelled when the city council publicly stated they'd rather their facilities not be used as a, "forum to ridicule anyone's religion." The local Ku Klux Klan nailed a Beatles' album to a wooden cross, vowing "vengeance." The band decided to go ahead with the shows but during the second concert someone threw a firecracker on stage. Everyone in the band and the production crew thought it was a gunshot and they turned to Lennon expecting to see him collapse on stage.

By the time the Beatles arrived in San Francisco their nerves were understandably frayed. Playing live was not something they enjoyed anyway.

Once they'd left the clubs and bars where they'd cut their teeth, they had always been frustrated playing stadiums and larger venues. The sound equipment of the day was certainly inferior and their rabid fans spent most of the concert screaming their heads off making it impossible for the band to even hear themselves. So without calling a band meeting and declaring they were done touring, they were pretty sure this would be their final show. Ringo Starr would say afterwards, "At that San Francisco gig it seemed that this could possibly be the last time, but I never felt 100% certain till we got back to London." He'd add: "John wanted to give up more than the others. He said that he'd had enough." Paul McCartney, feeling this could be the last show, asked their press officer Tony Barrow to record it on cassette (you can find that on the internet too if you search for it). Lennon brought a camera on stage and snapped a few pictures of the band with the crowd behind them; basically a "selfie" before that term actually existed. Again, Google it.

The Beatles would henceforth become a studio band. One can argue that their sound evolved to unprecedented levels because they devoted so much time to recording without the interruption of touring. They were also never bogged down with the question, "How are we going to play this live?" so when they thought to themselves, "Let's bring in a 40-piece orchestra to record this section," or, "Let's flip the tape and play these vocal backwards," they just went ahead and did it. By August of 1966 their records had already gotten experimental and their work in the studio non-traditional. Their first post-touring album, *Sgt. Pepper's Lonely Hearts Club Band,* would take all this experimentation to the next level. Music lovers and especially Beatles' aficionados can always wonder what the band would have looked like and sounded like if they'd continued touring but the fact is, when they boarded a plane to head home after that chilly show in Candlestick Park on this day in 1966, they'd never hit the road again as a band.

## August 30th

On this date in 1969, in the northern England town of Workington, a band called Black Sabbath played their very first gig. Until recently they were called Earth and an even earlier ensemble went by the name Polka Tulk Blues Band. But the combination of one member dabbling in black magic and a Boris Karloff film gave the foursome a new song, ultimately a new name and an entirely new direction. While they were at it, they'd pioneer a whole new genre of music.

The band that would eventually become Black Sabbath started forming in 1968 when Mythology broke up. Former members Tony Iommi (guitarist) and Bill Ward (drums), eager to form another band and keep working, saw an ad in a local music shop that said, "Ozzy Zig Needs Gig – has own PA." (PA being an abbreviation for public address system which is basically speakers and amplifiers.) Intrigued by the ad and needing sound equipment (what band doesn't?) they contacted this "Ozzy Zig" fella. This brought Ozzy Osbourne in as a vocalist and they subsequently recruited Terence Michael Joseph Butler (who went by "Geezer") to play bass. With some additional members they became the Polka Tulk Blues Band but eventually paired down to a foursome and chose the name Earth (which Osbourne hated).

Geezer was an avid reader of the occult. Books by Aleister Crowley and Dennis Wheatley were always with him and he even began to take part in black magic ceremonies. One night he awoke to what he believed was a figure from the dark side at the foot of his bed. He was so scared he immediately ceased dabbling in the dark arts. When he mentioned the experience to his bandmates they did what every musician thinks to do in these situations. They wrote a song about it. A theater across the street from where they were rehearsing was showing the Boris Karloff film *Black Sabbath* and they decided the name fit the song so they nicked it. The end result is a very dark and ominous song which includes the almost apocalyptic lyric: "Is it the end, my friend? Satan's coming 'round the bend." When they started playing the song live, it became a highlight of their shows. The band realized they had stumbled onto something unique and powerful. They decided to change their name to Black Sabbath and write more songs with similar themes and tones.

In the late sixties, with the hippie movement in full effect, Black Sabbath stood out like a sore thumb (more like an infected, rotting, decomposing thumb). While it seemed that every other band was doing psychedelic, flower-power themed music and singing about letting the sun shine in and getting together, here was this dark and brooding band playing harder than anyone else and singing about evil and Satan and death.

Black Sabbath quickly landed a record contract and their eponymous debut album, which they recorded in one day, was released on February 13th, 1970 (fittingly, a Friday the 13th). Although it sold fairly well (reaching #8 in the U.K. and #23 in the States) it was poorly reviewed, with *Rolling Stone* magazine calling it, "Just like Cream! But worse," and the Village Voice saying it was, "bullshit necromancy." Their follow-up, *Paranoid*, included some of their now iconic songs like "Iron Man", "War Pigs" and the title track. That LP went to #1 on the U.K. album chart and #12 in the U.S. Their third LP, 1971's *Master of Reality*, reached the Top 10 on both sides of the pond and solidified their reputation as the hardest and darkest band in the land.

The term "heavy metal" has been used forever in chemistry and metallurgy where elements are organized between light and heavy. But sometime in the late sixties the term found its way into music to describe a harder rock sound than was normally being played at the time. Though he wasn't the first to use it, famed critic Lester Bangs is credited for popularizing the term in essays about Led Zeppelin and Black Sabbath in the early seventies. As the seventies wore on and the genre mushroomed, the term became part of the everyday lexicon. We now use heavy metal to describe any hard, head-banging rock and it doesn't have to include themes like the dark arts and Satan, but they are often ubiquitous. Black Sabbath, which has gone on to sell over 70 million albums, is universally credited for being a pioneer in this genre. Along with bands like Deep Purple and Led Zeppelin, they are considered co-creators of heavy metal and in 2006 they were inducted into the Rock and Roll Hall of Fame. Good thing Ozzy Zig had his own PA!

## August 31st

On this date in 1974, Paul Anka's "(You're) Having My Baby" began its second week at the top of the charts. Anka's seemingly innocuous tribute to his wife Anne and their four daughters would become only his second #1 hit. It would also stir up controversy for being sexist and misogynist. And you thought we lived in overly-politically-correct times today!

Paul Albert Anka was born in 1941 in Ottawa, Canada. He sang at his local church when he was a child and talked of becoming a famous singer as if it were a predetermined fate. But he didn't just talk about it. He took action. When he was fifteen, he flew to Los Angeles to stay with an uncle and record an original song called "I Confess." The song was released on RPM Records and though it didn't sell well, it gave Anka a taste of what it could be like to be a professional singer and songwriter. Undeterred by the song's failure, he headed to New York City where he landed an audition with ABC Records. In that audition, he played piano and sang another original composition, this one about a girl at his church back home that he had a crush on named Diana. He was offered a contract immediately and since he was still a minor his father had to fly to New York to sign the deal for him. "Diana" was released while Anka was still fifteen and by the time it hit the top of the pop chart he had turned sixteen. Sixteen years old with a #1 hit in Canada, the U.S. and the U.K. That's an amazing start to a career!

"Diana" established Anka as a household name and in the years that followed he was a consistent presence on the pop chart with hits like "You Are My Destiny", "Puppy Love", "Put Your Head on My Shoulder" and "Lonely Boy." In the late fifties, with rock and roll dominating the charts, and scaring many parents, Anka was a safe alternative. His songs were sugary and sweet and his matinee idol looks helped his popularity. He also composed songs for other artists. In 1962 when Johnny Carson took over *The Tonight Show*, Anka composed a theme song for him. He also penned "She's a Lady" for Tom Jones and "My Way" for Frank Sinatra.

By the early seventies, Anka was performing regularly and at one residency, in Lake Tahoe, his wife Anne joined him with their four daughters. Even though she was not pregnant at the time (she would have their fifth child, another daughter, a few years later), Anka was moved at having his whole family together and he wrote "(You're) Having My Baby" as a loving tribute to his wife. He originally envisioned it as a solo song but when he tested it out with Odia

Coates, a female singer he often toured with, Anka decided to record the song as a duet. It was released as a single in June of 1974 and quickly rose up the charts. On August 24th it would dislodge Paper Lace's "The Night Chicago Died" from the top spot where it stayed for three straight weeks. Eric Clapton's cover of Bob Marley's "I Shot the Sheriff" was its successor at #1.

But instead of basking in the glow of a hit single, Anka was forced to defend himself from charges of chauvinism and, believe it or not, encouraging abortions. The feminist movement (or "women's lib" as it was often called), which had made amazing strides towards equality for women in the sixties and seventies honed in on Anka's song, specifically referring to the child in the lyrics as "my baby." Apparently, because Anka didn't sing "our baby" he was a sexist bigot. Add to that the line, "What a lovely way of saying you love me," and some women were foaming at the mouth. Their claim was that the song posited a woman's place in society as giving babies to their men and that bearing a child was the number one contribution they could make. The National Organization for Woman gave Anka their dubious "Keep Her in Her Place" award, and the magazine *Ms.* named him "Male Chauvinist Pig of the Year." As if that weren't enough, the Pro-Life movement also took issue with the song for its third verse where Anka sings, "Didn't have to keep it." Roe vs. Wade was only a year old at this point and many in the anti-abortion camp saw that line as giving permission, or even encouraging someone, to terminate a pregnancy.

Paul Anka insisted the song was simply an affectionate tribute to childbirth, and enough people agreed to make it a #1 hit, but he was upset enough at the backlash that, for a time, he dropped the song from his setlist. When he started singing "(You're) Having My Baby" live again he often sang "our baby" near the end of the song.

To date, "(You're) Having My Baby" is Paul Anka's final #1 song, though a year later he had a Top 10 hit with "Times of Your Life" which began as a jingle for a Kodak commercial before becoming a hit song. Anka has also had success acting in both films and television in a career that has spanned over six decades. And he doesn't intend on slowing down anytime soon. In a recent interview he said. "I've always believed that if you don't stay moving they will throw dirt on you."

# SEPTEMBER

On this date in 1988, "It Takes Two" by Rob Base & DJ E-Z Rock had just made its first appearance on the *Billboard* Hot 100 chart. The song would peak at #36 in mid-October which hardly makes it an all-time best seller. Still, some consider "It Takes Two" to be one of the greatest hip hop songs of all time (if not the greatest). Rank it however you like but there is no argument that "It Takes Two" is a classic party song that still packs dance floors more than three decades after its release.

Rap music grew from the inner-city streets of New York in the seventies so it's no surprise that most of the genre's pioneers were born and raised in the Bronx or Brooklyn or Harlem. Such is the case with Robert Ginyard and Rodney Bryce who were both in fifth grade in Harlem when they first started performing together in a group called the Sureshot Seven. After a few years, all but Ginyard and Bryce had left so the two began collaborating on hip hip songs. Ginyard, the duo's rapper, changed his name to Rob Base and Bryce, the duo's turntablist, became DJ E-Z Rock. Their first release was a song called "DJ Interview," and though it didn't sell well it helped Rob Base & DJ E-Z Rock earn a record contract. Their next single, "It Takes Two," would not only become their biggest hit but many would credit the song for helping propel hip hop into the mainstream.

From those early days of rap being mostly a street party genre, the musical beds for most hip hop songs were looped or sampled from existing songs. It's one of the reasons rap is so popular. Many times, rap songs have repurposed the melody or drum break of older songs in a way that the original artist could never have imagined. "It Takes Two" is a prime example of this. The song that Rock looped for Base to rap over is a 1972 funk number by Lyn Collins called "Think (About It.)" The song was written and produced by James Brown and it has all the components of a classic Brown track including a drum break that cried out to be rapped over. It's known today as the "Woo! Yeah!" break because as Brown's drummer played the beat, Brown did a call and response with his bandmate Bobby Byrd with Brown yelling "Woo!" and Byrd answering "Yeah!" As hip hop grew in popularity in the early eighties Street Beat Records released a multi-volume collection called *Ultimate Breaks and Beats* which contained songs from various genres that featured drum breaks ideal for looping and sampling (the set was often sold in pairs of identical records because if a DJ didn't have sampling technology he or she created a "loop" by going back and forth between records, repeating the same section over and over). Collin's "Think (About It)" was featured on one of these volumes although Rock and Base may already have been aware of the song before it appeared on a *UBB* release. Either way, the break lends "It Takes Two" an incredibly high energy rhythm track which is perfect for Base's aggressive rap style. He attacks the song with gusto and bravado, bragging that, "I'm the leader, the man superior" and, "Ladies love me, girls adore me" and most famously, "I'm not a sucker so I don't need a bodyguard." Rock and Base also created a dramatic prelude for the song. Using a sample of "Spacedust" by the Galactic Force Band, "It Takes Two" begins with a spoken word piece as the listener is warned:

> Right about now
> You are about to be possessed
> By the sounds of
> MC Rob Base and DJ E-Z Rock.

The transition between the opening and the first beat is an enthusiastic "Hit It!" It's a jolt that works perfectly, and the listener feels they've just entered a wild party. The song's energy and in-your-face attitude helped it break the Top 40 a few years before hip hop would start dominating the charts. This was around the same time that MTV, after ignoring hip hop since its inception, started airing *Yo! MTV Raps,* so if any year can be seen as rap's "coming of age" it is 1988. And Rob Base & DJ E-Z Rock's "It Takes Two" were one of the songs that helped push the genre forward.

With the success of the single, Base and Rock put together their debut album, also titled, *It Takes Two.* That LP would peak at #31 on the *Billboard* 200 chart and produce two more successful singles, "Get on the Dance Floor" which did not make an appearance on the Hot 100 chart but topped *Billboard*'s Dance Club Songs chart and "Joy and Pain" which peaked at #58 on the Hot 100. "Joy and Pain" samples the Maze song of the same name, another brilliant reuse of an original track.

In 1989, Rob Base released a solo LP, *The Incredible Base,* that would fail to match his debut's success, then five years later Rob Base & DJ E-Z Rock reunited and released *Break of Dawn.* The album and its lone single failed to chart. In 2014, Bryce, aka DJ E-Z Rock died at the tender age of 46 of complications from diabetes.

Anytime a list is made of top hip hop songs, "It Takes Two" is inevitably at or near the top. And rightfully so. For a genre that began at street parties in New York City, the song still sounds like a call to dance and celebrate. Near the end, Rock raps, "When I count to three, I want you to get busy, you ready now?" and then follows with, "One, two, three, get loose now!" Millions have "gotten loose" to this song since its release and there's no sign of its popularity waning. Give it a spin today but be forewarned, "you are about to be possessed . . ."

## September 2nd

On this date in 1975, KC and the Sunshine Band were making their first appearance at the top of the charts with their hit song "Get Down Tonight." 1975 was a significant year for this new "disco" sound as it continued to penetrate pop culture and Harry Wayne Casey (KC) and Richard Finch were at the forefront of the movement. They'd already written and produced another early disco hit, but this time around they kept the best stuff for their own band and the result was a breakthrough song that would establish them as disco kings for the rest of the decade.

Harry Wayne Casey and Richard Finch were both club goers from an early age in southern Florida, even sneaking into dance clubs before they were of legal age. They were both enamored by the early disco sound and sought to make their own records. In 1974 they secured studio time and were working on a song they'd written called "Rock Your Baby" while singer George McCrae happened to be in the same studio. They asked him to sing the song and they knew immediately his high falsetto was perfect for the record. To Casey and Finch's credit, they gave McCrae the song to release and when it became an international hit, selling over 11 million copies and helping to spread the word about this new dance sound that was emerging, it was his name and face that became associated with it. Actually the word "gave" is wrong since Casey and Finch benefitted financially from the record as well. Finch claims the first royalty check he received for co-writing and co-producing "Rock Your Baby" was $227,000 (and this is back when a quarter million was actually worth something). He promptly went out and bought his mom a Jaguar (even though she didn't have a driver's license). Besides the financial gain from the record, Casey and Finch also enjoyed a higher profile in the music industry.

Casey and Finch didn't give all their songs away though and in 1974 they also released KC and the Sunshine Band's debut album, *Do It Good*. While the LP failed to chart, its singles ("Blow Your Whistle", "Sound Your Funky Horn" and "Queen of Clubs") did make a dent on the R&B chart and get some play in the clubs. *Billboard* did not start a dance or club chart till October of 1974 (it was initially called the Disco Action chart) so their first singles couldn't be measured that way.

Casey and Finch got to working on a follow-up LP and one of the first songs they created was called "Get Down Tonight." Both songwriters openly admit they were inspired by Gilbert O'Sullivan's 1973 song "Get Down," even though they were never quite sure if O'Sullivan was singing to his dog or girlfriend (O'Sullivan has given different explanations himself so maybe he's not even quite sure either). "Get Down Tonight" has a unique introduction that is actually a guitar solo played at double time. Finch, an admitted "studio geek," had seen someone else playing with the speed of a tape to achieve a different effect so he tried it for the song's opening and loved how it sounded. The sped up guitar is prevalent throughout the song adding to its energy and urgency.

They say timing is everything in life and certainly for KC and the Sunshine Band 1975 was the perfect time to release "Get Down Tonight." Not only was disco breaking through to the mainstream but more and more radio stations were switching to a dance format and searching for records to fill the airwaves. And along came this catchy little chestnut that not only had a great beat but was urging the listener to do a little dance, make a little love, and get down tonight. The song enjoyed ridiculous airtime throughout the summer of 1975 and hit #1 at the end of August.

As "Get Down Tonight" was climbing the charts, KC and the Sunshine Band were wrapping up their next LP and that's when they went into the studio to record "That's the Way (I Like It)." Richard Finch would tell the SongFacts website, "We were all happy, and you could tell. We transferred the excitement of that hit feeling from 'Get Down Tonight,' and trust me, then we were all like, 'Oh, my God, this is amazing! We've done it! Let's put the magic on something else.'" One listen to "That's the Way (I Like It)" and you can hear exactly what Finch is referring to. Unlike the opening of "Get Down Tonight," which begins slowly with that ascending, sped up, guitar sound, "That's the Way (I Like It)" explodes out of the box. The band is playing hard and steady from the outset and the background singers are proudly belting out their "do do do's." All that is a grand introduction to KC's opening lyric "ahhh, that's the way I like it." Of course that line is interrupted by the back up singers agreement to his statement so when he sings, "That's the way" they come in with their, "Uh huh uh huh" before he can even finish the thought. What exactly do they like so much? The lyrics are vague on that fact. The only two verses refer to a woman who takes her man's hand and gives him all her loving. In the second verse she whispers in his ear. If that's enough to explain this joyous cacophony of sound then so be it, but it's hard not to get swept up in the wonderful exuberance of "That's the Way (I Like It)." By the end of the year the song would become the band's second #1. In total they had five chart-toppers and ten Top 40 hits by the end of the seventies.

As pioneers of the disco sound, KC and the Sunshine Band helped forge the way and show others how to make infectious, danceable songs that not only got club spins, but radio play as well. They released two of their best in 1975 and all these years later both songs are calls to action. To do a little dance. To get down tonight. And to enjoy it as best you can. Give them both a spin today and don't be surprised if you find yourself dancing around your room.


## September 3rd

On this date in 2002, a U.S. bankruptcy judge blocked the sale of Napster to the German media group Bertelsmann, in essence killing the deal that would have saved the peer-to-peer file sharing platform. Napster, which, at its peak at the turn of the millennium had 80 million registered users, had been offline since the summer of 2001. In just a few short years it had completely changed the face of music and the way consumers traded, acquired, and some would argue, stole songs. And now, it would stay offline and was ostensibly dead. Yet the changes it forced on the music industry reverberate even today.

Shawn Fanning was born in Massachusetts in 1980. He was a computer geek who, as a teenager, had earned the nickname "Napster" by someone who made fun of his hair. Still in his teens, he envisioned a program that would make peer-to-peer file sharing (specifically music files or MP3s) easier. Platforms like this already existed for advanced computer users (places like Usenet and Hotline) but Fanning wanted to create something much easier for the end user; something that combined a music search function with a file sharing system as well as instant messaging to make communication easier. Fanning was so sure that someone else was thinking similarly and was about to launch an identical website that he raced to finish his programming, staying awake at one point for 60 straight hours, writing code. He enlisted a friend and fellow computer geek, Sean Parker, who he'd met in hacker chat rooms, to help with the code, and his uncle, John Fanning, who was an early internet entrepreneur, having built the first internet chess server in the late eighties, to turn his program into an actual business entity. He gave his program his own nickname and Napster first went online in June of 1999 and within a month millions of users were trading files.

The company and its number of users grew quickly and exponentially. Fanning, a reserved and shy teenager, became the reluctant face of Napster and very quickly the spokesperson for the whole concept of file sharing. Some advocates saw the program as the epitome of what the internet promised: breaking down barriers and allowing for a free exchange of ideas and art. Others, specifically bands and record labels, saw it as nothing short of thievery. *Time*, in an October, 2000 article wrote: "As Fanning predicted, his program does everything a Web application is supposed to do: it builds community, it breaks down barriers, it is viral, it is scalable, it disintermediates--and, oh, yeah, it may be illegal."

To be sure, "file sharing" had been around for decades. The first time someone could purchase a piece of music on vinyl, she or he was now free to lend it or trade it with someone else. When the use of cassette recorders became widespread in the seventies the music industry launched their first anti-piracy campaign with the slogan "Home Taping is Killing Music." But while the making and trading of cassettes and mixed tapes may have put a dent in the industry, online file sharing was taking huge chunks out of it. And very quickly Napster found itself at the center of lawsuits.

Metallica was the first major band to fire back. In early 2000 it was brought to the band's attention that their entire catalogue of music was being shared on Napster. In fact, one of their unreleased songs, "I Disappear," began getting play on some college radio stations. The band filed a lawsuit on March 13th, 2000, less than a year since Napster had gone online. Rapper Dr. Dre filed suit a month later, after Napster refused his request to have his work removed from their service. Pretty soon, the Recording Industry Association of America (RIAA) sued Napster on behalf of five major record labels, claiming the website was facilitating the theft of intellectual property.

The RIAA's decision to take legal action, instead of trying to work out a deal with Napster, is often seen as a major misstep for the music industry. They were late to recognize how much the public loved the convenience of downloading songs (albeit for free) and it would take another computer geek, and music-industry outsider, Steve Jobs, to show them how to monetize this convenience. Meantime, the lawsuits and media attention that followed simply brought more awareness to Napster which attracted more users and the downloading continued to mushroom. Some colleges moved to block the site, not for any illegal issues, but because the downloading of music was clogging up their internet connections.

The RIAA sought a preliminary injunction to halt Napster's service which the company was able to get delayed throughout 2000. At the Webby awards in May of that year, Napster took home the prize for Best Music Site. That same month the House Small Business Committee met to discuss the popularity of online music services. Rapper Chuck D spoke at the meeting in support of Napster, calling it "a new kind of radio." Later, Chuck D would say, "I applauded what Shawn Fanning was doing. I thought he was the one-man Beatles. I thought what he had done with Napster was one of the most revolutionary things ever done in music, period." Others spoke of protecting an artist's work and about copyright infringement. The music industry was divided. Where some, like Chuck D, saw Napster as just another promotional vehicle, others saw outright theft of work that they'd created.

In June, Napster lost its first major lawsuit with the RIAA. They filed appeals so that they could stay online and, in an attempt to gin up some good will, they organized a free concert tour with Limp Bizkit as the headliner. Behind the scenes Napster was trying to negotiate deals with the labels. They struck out with every one of them save one, the German label Bertelsmann. Seeing the future in downloading and understanding the need to embrace this new technology and figure out a way to monetize it, Bertelsmann sought to partner with Napster and, in February of 2001 made an offer to the RIAA of $1 billion to drop their suit. The music labels balked and continued their fight.

Finally, in July of 2001, Napster was forced to shut down its site.

Instead of shutting off the spigot though, all closing Napster down did was give birth to scores of similar platforms like Kazaa and Limewire and Audiogalaxy. The music industry found itself in a game of legal wack-a-mole. Every time they sued and shut down one site, two more would pop up. It would take them years before they could work out deals with legal downloading sites and then as soon as they did, the streaming sites began. The music industry has failed to keep up, mostly because its an old behemoth and there will always be some 18 year old kid in his bedroom writing code for 60 straight hours in an attempt to find a new way to revolutionize technology and make things easier for the end user. Legal or not.

## September 4th

On this date in 1983, the Eurythmics were enjoying the view from the top of the *Billboard* Hot 100 chart with "Sweet Dreams (Are Made of This.)" The song had resulted from a fight between two bandmates and ex-lovers, and wound up being their only U.S. chart-topper.

Annie Lennox was born in 1954 in Aberdeen, Scotland. She studied at the Royal Academy of Music in London and kicked around in a number of bands including the Tourists where she first met and worked with Dave Stewart. Stewart is two years Lennox's senior and he too was a busy musician in London in the mid-seventies, bouncing from band to band trying to find that winning combination. When he and Lennox met as bandmates they also became a couple and when the Tourists broke up in 1980 they decided to form a duo. Their intent was to create pop music with electronics and a lean towards the avant-garde. They named themselves the Eurythmics after a musical class that Lennox had taken as a child. Just as they were getting started as a duo though, and getting signed to RCA Records, they were also breaking up as a couple. As amicable as any split may be, working together afterwards, especially in a creative and collaborative field, is fraught with difficulties. For Lennox and Stewart, the waters were often rocky.

They recorded their first album on a shoestring budget. They'd secured a small loan and bought some second hand gear and used it to create their debut LP, *In the Garden*. The recording process was so troublesome, Lennox had a nervous breakdown at one point and Stewart was hospitalized with a collapsed lung. *In the Garden* was released in 1981 and neither the album nor its two singles troubled the charts.

When they began work on their follow-up, Lennox and Stewart were still struggling to find harmony in their working relationship. One day they had an argument so bad Lennox was convinced they'd have to end the duo. But the next day she found Stewart at work, playing with a synthesizer riff he'd accidentally discovered by playing a bass track backwards. The two combined the riff with a plodding drum sequence and they realized they had a catchy backing track so they set out to write lyrics. Lennox wrote the line, "Sweet dreams are made of this" which she has since said is more of a mantra then a lyric. Still bitter from the previous day's argument, she also wrote, "Some of them want to use you," and, "Some of them want to abuse you" which motivated Stewart to say the song needed a counter-point to her acridity. Together they came up with the chord change that leads into the, "Hold your head up" section which gives the song a pleasant dichotomy of darkness and light, misery and hope.

Besides an infectious and brooding sound and lyrics that covered a full range of emotions, the Eurythmics had one more thing going for them that helped "Sweet Dreams" become a huge hit: a cool video. MTV was a kingmaker by 1983 and they started playing the video for the song, which features Lennox's androgynous/sexy look and shock of orange hair (an ode to David Bowie if not a blatant rip off), a masked Stewart playing a cello in an open field and, yes, a cow. Going back to their original goal of creating pop songs with a nod towards the avant-garde, the video had just enough surreal imagery to check all the boxes. Its heavy rotation on MTV might explain why the song didn't reach #1 in their homeland (it stalled at #2 in the U.K.) yet made it to the top spot in the U.S.

"Sweet Dreams (Are Made of This)" has been covered a few times, most notably in 1995 by Marilyn Manson. The band's hard, industrial rock version also benefitted from heavy video play and became Manson's first Top 40. And decades after its release, the song is still played in dance clubs, having been remixed often by the likes of Giorgio Moroder and Steve Angello. Though "Sweet Dreams (Are Made of This)" was their only #1, the Eurythmics released a steady stream of Top 40 hits throughout the eighties, most benefitting from equally eclectic and surreal videos. They broke up in 1990 and both Stewart and Lennox have gone on to solid success as solo artists. They have reunited a few times over the years, professionally if not romantically. Their collaborations are a perfect example of how friction can help create unforgettable art and in their lone #1 they offered perhaps their greatest advice: no matter how much people want to use and abuse you, hold your head up. Keep your head up.

### September 5th

On this date in 1970, Edwin Starr's "War" began its second week at the top of the pop chart. A week earlier it had dislodged Bread's "Make it with You" (have consecutive #1's ever been more complete opposites?) and it would enjoy one more week at the top before giving way to fellow labelmate Diana Ross and her version of "Ain't No Mountain High Enough." Before recording "War," Starr was considered a second tier talent at Motown but that fact would change with the success of "War."

By the late sixties the zeitgeist in the U.S. had changed and Berry Gordy, head of Motown Records, who had ridden high for a decade on R&B infused pop songs with little-to-no political message, was reluctantly recognizing that music can reach for a higher cause than just dancing in the streets. Still, he sought to protect his best-selling artists from alienating fans with "message songs" which is why, for example, he was encouraging Marvin Gaye to stop writing protest songs. Gaye kept submitting songs with a more serious tone and message and Gordy kept urging him to stick with what had made him famous. Gaye would famously say, "With the world exploding around me, how am I supposed to keep singing love songs?" (Gordy would finally acquiesce and allow Gaye to record his protest song "What's Going On?" in 1971.)

"War" was another song that Gordy was reluctant to release. Written by two of Motown's most successful in-house songwriters, Norman Whitfield and Barrett Strong, the song was originally recorded by the Temptations. Their version is slightly more upbeat than Starr's and though the lyrics are the same, it's sung with a bit more optimism and pop-radio friendliness; even though Gordy had no intention of allowing pop radio to get their hands on it. The Temptations' version was released on their album *Psychedelic Shack* in March of 1970. At the time the anti-war movement in the U.S. was at a fever pitch and many protestors heard the song and wanted it released as a single. But Gordy refused. While he knew many of the country's youth were against Vietnam he also knew there were some who were for the war. He did not want one of his most bankable groups to draw a line in the sand and risk splitting their fan base.

When Edwin Starr caught wind of this he stepped up and offered to record the song for a single release. Starr had come to Motown in 1968 when Berry Gordy purchased the rival Detroit label, Ric-Tic Records and absorbed all of their artists. Starr's first few Motown releases were unsuccessful although he did score a Top 10 hit with "Twenty-Five Miles." Gordy agreed to let Starr record and release "War," most likely figuring the singer was not that well known so who cared if he isolated some fans?

As it turned out, Starr's singing style suited the anti-war message of the song much better than the Temptations. Where they sang with their usual pop sensibilities, Starr brought a funkier, grittier attitude to the song. He practically spits out lines like, "It ain't nothing but a heartbreak." Whitfield and Strong also rerecorded the backing track to fit Starr's James Brown-esque delivery style and this too made the song more urgent and demanding.

Starr's version of "War" was released in June of 1970, a month after Kent State and at the literal height of the anti-war movement. It became a ubiquitous song on radio all summer and reached the top spot in just a few months. Even John Lennon, who had recently released "Give Peace a Chance" as *his* anti-war anthem had to give props and admit Starr's "War" was the strongest statement yet for pulling out of Vietnam. The song has been covered a few times through the years including an odd, new wave version by Frankie Goes to Hollywood in 1983 and a rocking live offering by Bruce Springsteen and the E Street Band which became a Top 10 hit in 1986. Wars between nations continue to this day and there will always be protests about them and songs sung in dissent. But it would be hard to match the power and contempt conveyed by Edwin Starr, answering the question, "What is it good for?" with his adamant disdain: "Absolutely nothing!"

### September 6<sup>th</sup>

On this date in 2014, Taylor Swift's "Shake It Off" became only the 22nd song ever to debut at #1 on the pop chart. It was downloaded over half a million times in its first week of availability. The song would spend two weeks at #1, then be interrupted by Meghan Trainor's eight week stay at the top of the charts wth "All About That Bass" only to return to the top for two more weeks in November. With "Shake It Off" and the album *1989*, Swift had completed her transition from cute young country singer to mega-watt pop star.

Taylor Alison Swift was born in 1989 in Reading, Pennsylvania. Before she was ten she was already performing with children's theater groups and her parents were sending her to New York for vocal and acting lessons. She'd soon shift her focus to country music, inspired by Shania Twain and Faith Hill and her family began traveling south to Nashville instead of east to New York. By 2003 they were making so many trips to country music's mecca that they simply relocated there. Even at a young age, Swift's talents and charisma made her superstardom seem inevitable. She quickly signed a recording contract and at sixteen was working in the studio on her debut. That self-titled album was released in 2006 and featured eleven songs, all either written or cowritten by Swift. The album went to #5 on the *Billboard* 200 chart and spent 24 weeks at #1 on *Billboard*'s Top Country Album chart. Her follow-up, 2008's *Fearless*, went to #1 on the *Billboard* 200 chart. Swift was not even out of her teens and she'd already secured her place as one of the top country-pop artists of all time.

Swift's next two LPs were equally successful and they continued her gradual shift from country artist with a pop sensibility to pop artist who vaguely had some country roots. As she began working on her fifth studio album, Swift was ready to make a full transformation and leave her country origins behind. She'd name that album *1989* as much for her birth year as the obvious eighties influence throughout the record. Instead of working with Nathan Chapman (who had produced or at least partially produced her first four albums) she brought in producers from the pop and dance world, specifically Max Martin who'd written and produced for Backstreet Boys, Britney Spears and NSYNC. And she left Nashville for the first time to do the bulk of her recording in more cosmopolitan locales such as Los Angeles and New York. Swift has said that during her work on the album she, "woke up every single day not wanting, but needing to make a new style of music than I'd ever made before."

Martin and Swift (along with fellow producer Shellback) co-wrote "Shake It Off." Swift saw it as an answer to her critics. As opposed to her 2011 song "Mean" though, which dealt with the same topic but resorted to calling her detractors mean and saying they make her walk with her head down, Swift now wanted a song of empowerment. Her message was, you can't control what people say about you but can control your reaction. "I want this song to go out into the world and not be about my critics," she explained. And her advice to anyone suffering from "haters" was to simply, "Shake it off."

The song has a fast tempo and features a bridge where the beat is carried by hand clapping and a cheerleading chant. All of this gives the song an infectious (or as Swift sings "sick") beat and hook. Though the lyrics are often seen as banal and repetitious (the phrase "shake it off" is sung 36 times and the word "shake" appears 70 times) there is no doubting the song's catchiness. Sometimes a pop song is best when it's simple and doesn't make the listener think too much. "Shake It Off" is a prime example of that. It's no wonder this was the lead single for *1989* and became such an instant hit. The album would be just as successful, selling well over a million copies in its first week and debuting at #1 as well.

But a song about haters was certain to attract a few more and sure enough Sean Hall and Nathan Butler, two songwriters who'd written 2001's "Playas Gon' Play" filed a copyright infringement suit against Taylor, Martin and Shellback. Their contention was that the chorus of "Shake it Off" (which goes: "Cause the players gonna play, play, play, play, play. And the haters gonna hate, hate, hate, hate, hate") too closely resembled their chorus ("Playas, they gonna play. And haters, they gonna hate"). The U.S. District judge who threw out the case wrote: "The allegedly infringed lyrics are short phrases that lack the modicum of originality and creativity required for copyright protection."

Whether Taylor Swift lacked a modicum of originality or creativity is in the ear of the beholder. What she has never lacked is success and with "Shake it Off" she not only kept her winning streak alive but she also accomplished her goal of going from a darling in the country world to a worldwide pop star. Still, haters gonna hate, hate, hate, hate, hate.

## September 7th

On this date in 1976, Paul and Linda McCartney were hosting a celebration in honor of Buddy Holly's 40th birthday. Eric Clapton was planning to attend with his girlfriend Pattie Boyd. But Boyd was taking forever to get ready, trying on different dresses and redoing her hair and make-up. Instead of getting frustrated about waiting and being late to the event, Clapton picked up his guitar and started playing and singing about what was going on. The result is one of the greatest love songs of all time.

Pattie Boyd and Eric Clapton had a very strange journey to their relationship. Boyd, a model, and George Harrison had met and fallen in love on the set of *A Hard Day's Night* in 1964. According to Boyd, when the Beatle first laid eyes on her, he asked her straight away if she'd marry him. When she declined, he asked, "Well, will you at least have dinner with me tonight." Two years later they were married. Though many of Harrison's more famous songs dealt with Eastern mysticism and spiritual enlightenment, he did pen his share of love songs and, to be sure, they were inspired by Pattie Boyd. He wrote, "I loved you from the moment I saw you," in "For You Blue" and, "You don't realize how much I need you," in "I Need You." And most famously, Harrison wrote "Something" while married to Boyd, a track Frank Sinatra called, "the greatest love song ever written."

In the late sixties Harrison and Eric Clapton started playing together and became fast friends. It was only natural that Clapton would meet and hangout with Boyd as well but soon complications developed. Clapton fell in love with his good friend's wife.

For years this love was unrequited and Clapton's only outlet was through songwriting (well, not his only outlet, Clapton actually dated Boyd's younger sister Paula for a while). His 1970 LP *Layla and Other Assorted Love Songs* was inspired by his growing obsession for his friend's wife. Songs like "Why Does Love Got to Be So Sad" (in which Clapton sings, "I've never been the same since I met you") and "Bell Bottom Blues" ("It's all wrong, but it's all right") and the title track ("Please don't say, we'll never find a way, and tell me all my love's in vain") were explicit pleas to Pattie Boyd veiled as rock songs. Finally, when Boyd and Harrison separated (as almost all rock and roll couples do), Clapton made his move and the two became a couple. By 1976 they were living together even though her divorce with Harrison was not yet finalized.

Which is how Eric Clapton found himself waiting for Pattie Boyd to get ready on this night in 1976. The McCartneys were hosting an event to kick off "Buddy Holly Week," a tradition that began that year and would continue for years to come. Boyd, perhaps nervous that she might bump into her ex that evening, was taking longer than usual to get ready. She would come downstairs from time to time and ask Clapton what he thought of her look. Each time he simply replied, "You look wonderful." Finally, Clapton started whiling away the time like he, and so many other musicians, are apt to do. He grabbed his guitar and started playing and singing whatever was on his mind. It was late in the evening. His girlfriend was wondering what clothes to wear. She put on her makeup and brushed her hair (which happened to be long and blond). She came downstairs and asked him if she looked alright. And he said, "Yes, you look wonderful tonight."

In the blink of an eye Clapton had the opening of a song. When Boyd finally came downstairs ready to go out she expected him to be angry but instead he excitedly shouted, "Listen to this!" He played her the opening verse and chorus and she loved it. Clapton would complete "Wonderful Tonight" later with verses about going to the party and having a bit too much to drink. It was released as a single in 1978, peaking at #16.

Boyd and Clapton would marry in 1979 and though their marriage only last a few years and would end, believe it or not, because of his cheating, their relationship produced some of Clapton's most impassioned writing and some of the most memorable songs of seventies. There is little argument that Pattie Boyd is the greatest muse in the history of rock, having inspired so many love songs by such legendary musicians.

The next time you're left waiting for someone, think of how Eric Clapton utilized his time on this night in 1976. Instead of clicking on the television or wasting time on Facebook, let your mind be free. You never know what timeless art you might create.

## September 8th

On this date in 1973, perhaps the greatest "baby-making" song ever, Marvin Gaye's "Let's Get It On" reached the top of the charts. Though it would spend only one week at #1, which certainly doesn't qualify it as an all-time great song commercially, it is often considered one of the most urgent cries for intimacy ever recorded. And to think, the song began as a call to get on with life after rehab. It's amazing what a woman can do!

Edward Benjamin Townsend was born in 1929 in Tennessee. After leaving the Marine Corps following a stint in Korea he decided to try to make it in the music industry. He had an early hit in 1958 with the ballad "For Your Love" then focused more on songwriting rather than recording. He wrote and sold songs to various artists throughout the sixties but as the seventies dawned he realized he had a drinking problem and he entered rehab to try and beat it. When he was released from rehab he wrote a song called "Let's Get It On" which had religious overtones and spoke of getting over troubles in your life. He presented the song to Marvin Gaye who, unbeknownst to Townsend, was also going through a ton of issues at the time.

Marvin Pentz Gay was born in 1939 in Washington, D.C. His father was a Pentecostal minister and by four, the young boy was singing at their services. He developed a passion for music early on and in his teen years played and sang in various bands and doo-wop groups. He eventually made his way to Detroit and in 1960 had the fortuitous opportunity of performing at a Christmas party at Berry Gordy's house. Gordy was impressed and he signed the young man to a contract with the Motown subsidiary label, Tamla. It was at the label that some people joked about his last name, asking, "Is Marvin Gay?" prompting him to add the "e." Going by Marvin Gaye now, he became a rare jack-of-all-trades at Motown. He sat in as a session musician, wrote songs for other artists and tried to make a name for himself as a singer. In the compartmentalized world of Motown this set Gaye apart and it probably helped him stick around when his first few releases failed to chart. Another thing that helped him stay in good graces with Gordy was that Gaye began a relationship with the owner's sister, Anna. The two married in 1963 and soon after Gaye's career as a performer took off.

By the early seventies though, Gaye had gone from a happy pop artist to a socially-conscious superstar. His 1971 album, *What's Going On* had been a breakthrough and it established Gaye as an artist speaking to a new generation. He was rewarded with a $1 million contract, making him the most profitable R&B artist of all time. Around this time Motown relocated from Detroit to Los Angeles. Gaye made the move with them even though his marriage to Anna was on the rocks. Gaye was also dealing with issues from his childhood at the time, realizing he was sexually repressed due to abuse he'd suffered by his father, you remember, the Pentecostal minister. This manifested itself with bouts of impotence and sadomasochist fantasies. In the midst of all this turmoil and uncertainty, Gaye met a seventeen year old named Janis Hunter and fell in love.

When Townsend presented his song about overcoming obstacles, Gaye asked if they could rework it. The songwriter, eager to work with Motown's highest profile artist had no objections. "Let's Get It On" evolved from redemption to sexual urgency, a theme that would carry through all of Gaye's 1973 album *Let's Get It On*. The title song is even reprised on the album with a song called "Keep Getting' It On." Gaye was clearly infatuated with Janis Hunter and the entire album can be viewed in the light of his sexual liberation.

Gaye and Hunter would have their first baby in September of 1974 and once his divorce from Anna was finalized the couple wed in 1977. As for Townsend he finally got his song of redemption recorded when he wrote "Finally Got Myself Together (I'm a Changed Man)" for the Impressions (that song would peak at #17 in 1974). Gaye fathered three children before his tragic death in 1984. He was shot and killed by his own father, once again, the Pentecostal minister! Townsend also had three children of his own before passing away in 2003. How many babies their most famous collaboration produced has yet to be calculated.

## September 9th

On this date in 1994, the Stone Temple Pilots released what most would consider their signature track, "Interstate Love Song." Like most of their work, this was a true collaboration, with bassist Robert DeLeo coming up with the melody and singer Scott Weiland writing lyrics that dealt with his incessant lying about his drug use. The song helped propel STP's second album to the top of the charts where it enjoyed a three week run. It also helped establish the band as a pioneer in the new grunge rock movement even as they showed they could venture into different genres. If only it had helped Weiland kick those drugs.

Rock legend has it that Scott Weiland and Robert DeLeo first met at a Black Flag concert in the mid-eighties. They began discussing various things when the conversation turned to their girlfriends. As they spoke they soon realized they were dating the same woman. Though Weiland told a different, and much more banal story of their meeting in his autobiography, legend has clung to the girlfriend story because it's just so rock and roll. However they met, the two put a band together called Mighty Joe Young that built a solid fan base in their hometown of San Diego. They signed a record contract and began working on their debut with producer Brendan O'Brien only to discover that a blues artist already had the name Mighty Joe Young. In need of a new name, the band brainstormed and discovered they all had fond memories of the STP Motor Oil stickers that were popular in their youths. They kicked around some ideas for a band name that would have the initials STP. After rejecting Shirley Temple's Pussy they settled on Stone Temple Pilots.

STP's debut album, *Core*, was released in 1992 and while some critics claimed they were "grunge imitators" the album sold extremely well and established the band as a loud and prominent new voice in the harder wave of rock that was sweeping out the hair metal bands of the eighties. While they toured to support *Core*, they were also writing songs for a follow-up LP and hoping to avoid a sophomore slump. The band traveled at the time in a Winnebago that pulled a trailer with all their gear. If someone in the band wanted some quiet time they would stretch out in the trailer with the equipment. They had walkie-talkies to communicate back and forth with their bandmates. One day, as they were traveling from city to city, DeLeo was back with the gear when he suddenly beeped into the Winnebago excited to share a riff he'd just come up with. He played them what he had through the intercom and the rest of the band was impressed.

Weiland was dealing with some guilt at the time. He was engaged to a woman named Janina Castaneda who was extremely concerned about his drug use. Before setting out on the road she'd made him promise he'd lay off the heroin and every day when they spoke on the phone he assured her he was clean. But he was lying. He was still using. Heavily.

So when Weiland heard the melody he channeled those guilty feelings and wrote lyrics from Castaneda's point of view. In the first verse he imagines her reading between the lines and hearing his lies. And then she leaves him on a "southern train." He concludes the second verse bluntly with "You lied. Goodbye."

The words "interstate love song" never appear in the lyrics but that's what he was writing, his love song to Castaneda while he rode along the interstates of America. The lyrics match the melody perfectly and they showed that STP were more than just hard rockers. If you didn't know "Interstate Love Song" was from a grunge band you'd maybe think it was from a southern rock band. The song sounds more country than alternative and the lyrics are far more personal than anything else the band ever produced.

Weiland and Castaneda were married just a week after "Interstate Love Song" was released (September 17th, 1994). They would divorce in 2000. Weiland would continue singing about drugs and lying to his loved ones throughout his career with STP as well as his solo work. His guilt was always bubbling just below the surface but the temptations of heroin and other drugs never did let up. On December 3rd, 2015, he was found dead on his tour bus. An autopsy would determine he died of an overdose of cocaine, ethanol, and the hallucinogenic methylenedioxyamphetamine. He was just 48 years old. Though the Stone Temple Pilots have continued on without Weiland they've never been able to match the success they achieved with his troubled voice in the band. He was truly one of those enigmatic artists that have come along from time to time in the annals of rock history. Mercurial, obsessive and brilliant. Scott Weiland, you lied. Goodbye.

### September 10th

On this date in 1960, Elvis Presley was riding high atop the pop chart once again. His song "It's Now or Never" began its fourth consecutive week at #1. It would stay there for one more week before giving way to Chubby Checker's "The Twist." Presley had come up with the idea for this song during his stint in the Army. He'd heard a Tony Martin song that was based on an old Neapolitan classic and he decided he wanted to record something in the same vein. The end result was the biggest international single of Presley's career.

Since there was a draft in America in the 1950s, when Elvis Presley turned 21 he, like every other young male in the U.S., became eligible. His manager, Colonel Tom Parker, approached the Pentagon to see what could be done about his celebrity client. They offered to have Elvis moved to the Special Services which would only require him to complete six weeks of basic training after which he'd be free to get on with his career, save for the occasional performance they'd ask him to do for the Armed Forces. The problem with those, in Parker's eyes, was that they'd be recorded and filmed with the U.S. Army profiting from any future showings. Parker was unwilling to allow this. He wanted complete and total control over everything Presley produced. So on March 24th, 1958 (a day called "Black Monday" by his fans) Elvis Presley entered the U.S. Army as a regular soldier.

Towards the end of his two year commitment, with Elvis stationed in Germany, he began planning his comeback for once he was released. He met a few times with his music publisher, Freddy Bienstock, so that songs could be ready for him to record as soon as he got back stateside. During one of these meetings, Presley mentioned a Tony Martin song he'd heard called "There's No Tomorrow." That song, unbeknownst to Presley, was actually based on the classic Italian song "'O Solo Mio." He told Bienstock he'd like to record something like that.

When Bienstock returned to his offices in New York City he found just two songwriters hanging around, Aaron Schroeder and Wally Gold. He explained what he needed and the two sat down and wrote the song in a half hour, which is perhaps how they came up with the theme of "now or never" - they might have realized that if they didn't finish fast enough and other songwriters showed up, they could lose their opportunity of writing one of Elvis Presley's comeback songs.

Upon Presley's release from the Army he was eager to get new music out. He was discharged in March of 1960 and he immediately spent two days in the RCA Studios in Nashville working with sound engineer Bill Porter. They recorded a dozen songs in those two days, of which "It's Now or Never" was the hardest to complete. The song is done mostly in a baritone (which was comfortable for Presley) but the big ending is in a tenor range and Presley was having a tough time hitting those notes. Finally, Porter told him to just do the ending, he could piece it together with what he already had. But Presley refused, saying, "Bill, I'm gonna do it all the way through, or I'm not gonna do it at all." And indeed he did. On the very next take, Presley nailed that big ending.

"Stuck on You" became the first single Presley released after his stint in the Army and his fans gobbled it up. The song, also from those marathon sessions with Porter, was released in late March, 1960 and it was #1 within weeks, where it stayed for four weeks. RCA held off releasing "It's Now or Never" till "Stuck on You" had run its course and when they did, it too shot up the charts. The song hit the top in mid August where it stayed for five weeks. It also hit #1 in the U.K., a rare occurrence for Presley who had all but ignored foreign markets in his career.

Whenever Presley performed "It's Now or Never" in concert, he would often interweave bits of "'O Solo Mio," paying homage to the roots of the song. And he never shied away from hitting the big notes, understanding the message in the song, to go for the moment, to reach for the here and now or, as they say in Latin, carpe diem, seize the day. It's now or never because, "Tomorrow will be too late."

## September 11<sup>th</sup>

On this date in 1814, two American statesmen were aboard a British warship that was sitting in the Baltimore Harbor. They were there to negotiate a prisoner exchange but when the British decided they were about to attack, they detained both men for a few days so they would not be able to alert their countrymen. By this point you may be thinking, what does this have to do with music? Read on and you'll find out.

Francis Scott Key was born during the American Revolutionary War. His father, a lawyer by trade, was an officer in the Continental Army. Key also studied law and by the early 1800's was married and had settled into his career. But then war broke out. There are a myriad of reasons why the War of 1812 was fought and since this is a book about music and not military engagements we'll skip over the issues and just say that 30 odd years after winning their independence from England, the still fledgling United States of America found itself at war once again against its former oppressor. Two years into the conflict, Key had become something of a statesman and one of his jobs was negotiating prisoner exchanges. That is how he wound up behind enemy lines aboard a British warship along with John Stuart Skinner, waiting for yet another bloody battle to break out. On September 13th, 1814, the British attacked Baltimore, bombarding Fort McHenry with their ships in the harbor and sending troops in by land. The American forces were successful in repelling the British and, on the morning of September 14th, Key awoke to see the American flag still proudly waving over the fort. Inspired, he sat down and wrote a poem to capture his emotions. He began, "O say, can you see, by the dawn's early light," and went on, describing the American flag with its, "Broad stripes and bright stars" and how, throughout the night, "The rocket's red glare," and, "Bombs bursting in the air" had shown him that the, "Flag was still there." All in all he wrote four stanzas, the first one ending with the question, "Does that star-spangled banner yet wave, o'er the land of the free and the home of the brave?" and the final three affirming that it most certainly did!

Key titled his poem, "Defence of Fort M'Henry," and had it published within a week after the battle was over. He then collaborated with a music publisher named Thomas Carr and they set his poem to, ironically enough, the tune of an English drinking song called "The Anacreontic Song." Carr decided to give the song a different title from the poem and he came up with "The Star Spangled

Banner." Though all four verses can be sung to the tune, most often it is just the first verse that is sung in public.

The U.S. did not have a national anthem at this point; most countries in fact didn't start adopting official songs as their "anthems" until the late eighteenth or early nineteenth centuries. So, for many years, "The Star Spangled Banner" was just another popular patriotic song in the U.S., right up there with "Hail, Columbia" which had been composed for George Washington's inauguration, and "My Country 'Tis of Thee" which uses the same melody as the United Kingdom's "God Save the Queen."

In 1916, with war once again raging, this time in Europe, President Woodrow Wilson decreed that "The Star Spangled Banner" be played at all appropriate military occasions. Two years later, during the 1918 World Series, "The Star Spangled Banner" was played during the seventh inning stretch of each game. If there was a competition for national anthem, "The Star Spangled Banner" was gaining momentum. Then, in 1930, the Veterans of Foreign Wars organization started a petition to make "The Star Spangled Banner" the U.S.'s official national anthem. The movement stalled because many people felt the song was too hard for the average person to sing. Indeed, if there's a criticism about the tune Key set his poem to, it is just that. One needs an extended vocal range to hit all the notes. The song was able to overcome those objections though, and in 1931 President Herbert Hoover officially signed a bill making "The Star Spangled Banner" the national anthem of the United States of America. It was soon being played before every baseball game, and then every major sporting event in America.

Through the years there have been many memorable, and sometimes controversial, renditions of "The Star Spangled Banner." Jose Feliciano was one of the first artists to reinterpret the song. His slow, bluesy rendition before game five of the 1968 World Series caused a national stir because it was different from the normal, traditional delivery. Some loved his take on the song, others saw it as disrespectful. Just a week after this, during the Olympic games in Mexico City, two African-American athletes, Tommie Smith and John Carlos, who had won gold and bronze in the 200 meter, made news when they gave a "Black Power" salute, raising black-gloved fists, during the national anthem. A year later, Jimi Hendrix played a soaring instrumental version of "The Star Spangled Banner" during his set at Woodstock. And perhaps the most famous version was performed by Whitney Houston in 1991 before Super Bowl XXV. She proved that day that while the tune is difficult for the average singer, in the hands of someone as talented as she, it can become a transcendent anthem of hope and patriotism. Over two hundred years ago, Key awoke to see the American flag still flying and he was moved to write the words that we still sing to this day. Our country has been through many more  "perilous fights" since and it is comforting to remember, today of all days, that we are still, "The land of the free and the home of the brave."

On this date in 1966, *The Monkees* made its debut on NBC. Though the television show only lasted two seasons, it would spawn scores of hit songs and albums and help launch a number of careers in the music industry.

In 1964, aspiring filmmakers Bob Rafelson and Bert Schneider saw the Beatles' film *A Hard Day's Night* and they had an idea. What if they created a television series about a rock band? They'd call this band the Monkees, so similar to the Beatles, it's a band named after a living creature but with a misspelling. But unlike the Beatles, the Monkees would be a struggling band and the show would focus around their wacky hijinks. Rafelson and Schneider sold the concept in April of 1965 and then it was time to put the fictional band together.

They ran ads in the *Hollywood Reporter* and *Variety* announcing auditions for the upcoming series: "MADNESS!! AUDITIONS. Folk & Roll Musicians, Singers for acting roles in new TV series. Running parts for 4 insane boys, age 17–21." Over 400 aspiring actors and musicians showed up who all read and played for the parts. Despite urban legend, Charles Manson was not one of the 400 to audition.

The four men who landed the roles and became the Monkees were: Micky Dolenz, who was hired to drum although he had no drumming experience (but he could sing), Davy Jones, a good looking English actor who could sing, Peter Tork, a folk singer and guitar player and Mike Nesmith, who'd already had some success in a few bands and as a songwriter.

Rafelson and Schneider wanted a very improvisational and avant-garde feel to their show. Episodes were loosely scripted and often contained little vignettes that didn't follow the story line and in retrospect seem more like modern day music videos. The actors were even encouraged to break the fourth wall occasionally and speak directly to the camera.

Don Kirshner was hired as the show's music supervisor. He'd already had success in the industry and was well on his way to earning his nickname, the Man with the Golden Ear. Kirshner was given the task of finding songs that could be hits for the fictional band. These songs would be played by studio musicians and then the Monkees would sing over those tracks. By the time the first episode aired he'd already delivered. The Monkees' debut single, "Last Train to Clarksville," was released in August of 1966, and was already climbing the charts by the show's debut. It would reach the top in November. Kirshner repeated this success with the band's second single, which was written by a then-unknown Neil Diamond, "I'm a Believer" and spent the first six weeks of 1967 lodged at #1 on the *Billboard* Hot 100 chart. The Monkees' eponymous debut album also hit the top of the charts. It was released in October of 1966 and went to #1 in November where it sat for thirteen weeks. It was knocked from the top by the Monkees' second album, *More of the Monkees*, which outdid its predecessor by spending eighteen weeks at #1. In 1967, the Monkees outsold the Beatles and the Rolling Stones. Combined.

This incredible success can be chalked up to the synergy between the show and the music. Viewers saw the band on TV and were inspired to buy their records. They listened to the records (or heard them on the radio) and were reminded to tune in to the show. It was ingenious and it worked. Until it didn't.

The Monkees' story certainly isn't unique in that success led to their demise. The rock and roll highway is littered with bands with similar stories. Where the Monkees stand out is that they weren't initially hired to play or create their own music. They were hired to act and, when called upon, sing. But when the show became a success everyone decided to capitalize and have the band tour. Touring and playing in front of thousands of adoring fans gave the band confidence that they could do more, specifically Mike Nesmith, who'd already had some success as a musician and who wanted to be more involved in writing the music. He didn't want to just play the part of a musician. He wanted to be one.

The band confronted Kirshner and things got heated between him and Nesmith. At one point Nesmith put his fist through a wall and told Kirshner, "That could have been your face." The producers of the show were forced to side with the Monkees and Kirshner was eventually let go. He'd seen the pros and cons behind a television show about musicians and his next venture would prove it. He helped put together *The Archies*, an animated show about a fictional band, because cartoons can't get too full of themselves.

The first post-Kirshner Monkees' album was *Headquarters* which only spent one week at #1. Its lone single, "Randy Scouse Git," which had been written by Micky Dolenz, failed to chart. And though there were some hits after Kirshner left, namely their final #1, "Daydream Believer," the band clearly missed Kirshner's golden ear.

By the end of the show's second season, Rafelson and Schneider had turned their attention to motion pictures and they allowed the show to be cancelled. The Monkees then starred in a motion picture called *Head* that was a complete flop. The next year Peter Tork quit the band. Without a TV show to promote their music, and someone like Kirshner to pick the right songs, they were failing to chart. When Nesmith left there was no point in the band going on.

*The Monkees* lived on for years in syndication and in the mid-eighties the band enjoyed some renewed popularity from the old shows playing on MTV. They reunited, sans Nesmith, and had a successful tour in 1986. Today, you can find some of the original episodes online and they are worth checking out. They are light and fun and quirky and something of a time capsule of the mid-sixties.

## September 13th

On this date in 1991, Nirvana displayed some of the most loutish behavior ever seen from rock stars. Forget trashing hotel rooms and showing up late to concerts. That stuff's for wannabes. Nirvana got so drunk and obnoxious they got thrown out of their own record release party.

Kurt Donald Cobain was born in Aberdeen, Washington in 1967. For his fourteenth birthday he was given a choice: a bicycle or a guitar. Cobain chose the guitar. In no time he was playing covers of classic rock songs as well as writing his own original music. After dropping out of high school, he formed a punk band called Fecal Matter. Though the band was short-lived they did produce a demo which Cobain gave to ex-classmate Krist Novoselic in hopes of starting a band together. Novoselic took over a year to listen to the tape. When he finally got around to it, he was impressed. He reached out to Cobain with enthusiasm and the two decided to start a band. Cobain gave this next outfit the name Nirvana. They went through a number of drummers before settling on Chad Channing who played on their debut album, *Bleach*, which was released in June of 1989 on the Seattle based record label Sub-Pop. Cobain and Novoselic were not happy with Channing though so when they were introduced to Dave Grohl, who was looking for a new band after Scream had broken up, they gave him an audition and they knew immediately that they'd found their drummer.

The trio then signed with David Geffen's brand new label DGC Records and began recording material for what would become their groundbreaking LP, *Nevermind*.

As the project came close to release, Geffen planned a party for the band on Friday, September 13th, 1991. Invitations to Seattle's Rebar went out that read, "Nevermind Triskaidekaphobia, it's Nirvana." Grohl, Cobain and Novoselic started drinking early in the day and they showed up shit-faced to their own party. Before long they started a food fight, throwing watermelon and slinging ranch dressing from the buffet tables. They also put some of their brand new CDs in the microwave (which causes a pretty cool effect, you should try it sometime). Finally, they were shown the door. For a while they stood in the alleyway of the club talking through a window with some their friends who were still inside but eventually they moved on to a friend's apartment where Cobain set off a fire extinguisher. They completed the evening at a club where Cobain saw a plaque commemorating a gold record for the band, Nelson. He ripped it down proclaiming it an "affront to humankind." No one in the club disagreed.

Their record release party was only the beginning of Nirvana's reign of terror in the music industry. Stories of backstage couches being lit on fire are some of their milder behavior. At MTV's Video Music Awards in 1992 Cobain got into it with Guns N' Roses' frontman Axl Rose and reportedly urinated on the piano he thought Rose was going to be playing in the show during "November Rain." Unfortunately for Elton John he wound up playing the piano Cobain had marked.

Of course, anger is a huge part of any punk band's DNA and make no mistake, while Nirvana is credited for launching a whole new genre of music, grunge is really just punk in flannel. Both genres share so much in common including the incredible impact they had on music given their short shelf life.

"Smells Like Teen Spirit," Nirvana's lead single off *Nevermind*, would race up the charts and hit #1 by January of 1992. The video was ubiquitous on MTV that entire winter and spring and though it doesn't feature any food fights or piano peeing, there is certainly a feeling of anarchy and chaos prevalent throughout the four and a half minute clip. This wasn't just a loud new song from a brash new band. This was a pronouncement that the eighties were officially over and it was time to make room for a new generation and their in-your-face sound. Hair spray and colorful clothes were out (heck, even the cheerleaders in the video of "Teen Spirit" are bland and colorless). Apathy and angst were in and you could either get the fuck out of the way or be shoved aside but either way you were making room for Generation X and their thrashing new soundtrack.

## September 14th

On this date in 1955, Little Richard was working in New Orleans trying to capture his raw and energetic live sound in a studio. He and producer Robert "Bumps" Blackwell grew frustrated at their lack of progress and headed out to a bar that happened to have a piano (not that this was a huge coincidence - every bar in New Orleans has a piano). Richard, in an attempt to blow off some steam from the fruitless recording session started banging on the piano and singing a song he had written and would often play live, but was so racy he hadn't tried to record it that day. Blackwell was immediately impressed and the two headed back to the studio to try to capture that sound. The song they produced that afternoon is one of the most groundbreaking recordings of all time.

Richard Wayne Penniman was born in 1932 in Macon, Georgia. His father was a deacon and the young boy was playing piano and singing in his dad's church at an early age. He was a diminutive child who earned the nickname "Lil' Richard." He loved gospel and when he was fourteen years old one of his favorite singers, Sister Rosetta Tharpe was performing in Macon so Richard made sure to be in attendance. But he did more than that. Before Tharpe hit the stage he climbed up there himself and started singing one of her songs. Before security could usher him off the crowd started cheering for him. Then Tharpe appeared side stage and encouraged him to keep going. Richard sang two songs before the show and Tharpe invited him back up to sing with her during her performance and she even paid him for being her "opening act." Richard has said he was hooked on becoming a singer from that moment on.

As he matured so did his musical tastes and eventually he started singing R&B (although he wouldn't tell his father right away because he called it "the devil's music"). Richard had some success but not enough to support himself so to make ends meet he found work as a dishwasher which is where he would write many of his songs in his head while mindlessly scrubbing dirty plates. He would also scream out of frustration sometimes as the dishes piled up, but instead of cursing he would yell, "Awap bop a lup bop a wop bam boom."

One of the songs he wrote over that sink was a raunchy rocker called "Tutti Frutti" which featured lyrics like, "Tutti fruity, good booty," and, "If it don't fit, don't force it. You can grease it, make it easy." That's the song he started playing in the Dew Drop Inn on this date in 1955, venting at his lack of progress as his studio time was slipping away. And that's the sound that Blackwell instantly realized they had to capture.

When the two returned to the studio they handed a local songwriter named Dorothy LaBostrie the song and asked her to clean it up. LaBostrie got right to work, replacing some of the song's racier lyrics with things like "aw rotty" (slang for alright) and leaving some lines open to interpretation like the one about the gal named Sue (who knows just what to do). When LaBostrie was finished rewriting the lyrics they had precious little studio time left and so the version that was released was just Little Richard's third (and final) attempt at the song. Blackwell also encouraged him to start and finish with his now signature, "Awap bop a lup bop a wop bam boom." They were so tight for time that Huey Smith, who had been playing piano during the entire session, didn't have time to learn the song so Little Richard played and sang. Earl Palmer, who was the in-studio drummer that day, says he just followed Richard's right hand on the piano to keep the beat. And Lee Allen only knew to come in with his sax solo when Richard let out his high pitched scream. The final product is an impassioned song that jumps out of the speakers with an urgency and spontaneity rarely heard before or since.

"Tutti Frutti" was released two months after it was recorded, towards the end of 1955, just as this nascent music called rock and roll was starting to edge its way onto the radio and into the record stores. Teenagers were rebelling against their parent's staid big band music and boring crooners and hearing the lustful screams of Little Richard sent shock waves through an entire generation of young music lovers. Even thousands of miles across the ocean, Richard's song was changing lives. David Bowie was nine years old when his father brought the record home for him to hear. "My heart nearly burst with excitement," Bowie would say later, "I had heard God."

Whether Richard's voice is that of God or just rebelling youth is certainly debatable. What we do know is that he was no longer washing dishes after "Tutti Frutti." Instead he, along with others like Presley and Berry and Haley and Holly, were about to permanently change the musical landscape. With "Tutti Frutti," Richard had created a template for so many others to follow. His opening "Awap bop a lup bop a wop bam boom" can be seen as a call for change, not just musically but culturally as well. The fact that it came from a slightly effeminate African American man made the song that much more mysterious and taboo, traits that scared the older generation but enthralled the younger one. The zeitgeist was changing, quickly, and in two and half minutes of rock and roll infused R&B, Richard was at the forefront, whooping and hollering and ushering in a new sound with outrageous energy.

## September 15th

On this date in 1984, Tina Turner's "What's Love Got to Do with It" began its third and final week at #1. On September 1st the song had knocked Ray Parker Jr's "Ghostbusters" from the top spot and in a week it would be replaced by John Waite's "Missing You." "What's Love Got to Do with It" and Tina Turner both share a similar story of being long forgotten and overlooked, only to emerge and take the pop world by storm.

Anna Mae Bullock was born in 1939 in Tennessee. As a young girl she sang in her church choir but it wasn't until she went to see Ike Turner as a teenager that she became interested in a career in music. She has said that his music put her, "into a trance" and she became a regular at his shows. One night during an intermission, one of Turner's bandmates invited her onstage and she belted out a song. Ike was impressed and he took the then seventeen year old Bullock under his wing. He gave her the name "Little Ann" and she released her first song in 1958. Ike would soon change her name again, this time to Tina because it rhymed with Sheena and Ike had a stage persona in mind for the young girl that would resemble the cartoon heroine Sheena of the Jungle. The first official release under this new name was 1960's "A Fool in Love" which became an instant success.

She was now officially part of the Ike and Tina Turner Revue, singing with Ike Turner and also becoming romantically involved with him. According to Tina, the two wed in 1962, although Ike has denied they ever legally married. Their relationship has been well documented and notable for Ike's repeated abuse. In a 1985 *Spin* article, Ike admitted as much, saying: "Sure, I've slapped Tina. There have been times when I punched her to the ground without thinking. But I have never beat her." The abuse was so bad Tina Turner attempted suicide at one point, swallowing 50 Valiums, after a fight with Ike.

As dysfunctional as their marriage was, musically, they found some success, releasing five Top 40 songs in their career including 1970's #4 hit, "Proud Mary." That cover of a Creedence Clearwater Revival song has become known as Tina's signature vocal as she completely reinvented the original and turned it into in a soul and funk masterpiece. But by the mid-seventies their relationships, both personally and professionally, had dissolved. Tina embarked on a solo career but for the next eight years she went largely ignored by radio and the record-buying public. After her 1979 LP, *Love Explosion*, failed to chart, her record company dropped her. For the next four years, Tina Turner was a singer with no label.

In 1983, Capitol Records A&R man, John Carter, despite some objections from his label, signed Tina Turner. He also agreed to help produce what he envisioned as her comeback album, *Private Dancer*. As the two began collecting material for that album they listened to a demo called "What's Love Got to Do with It." The song had been written some time earlier by Terry Britten and Graham Lyle and offered to Donna Summer who had sat on it for years without recording it. When Turner heard the demo she disliked the song but her manager convinced her to record it and so she did, with Terry Britten producing the session.

Capitol released Tina Turner's cover of the Al Green classic, "Let's Stay Together" well ahead of the album's release and it did surprisingly well, peaking at #26 on the charts. They then released her version of the Beatles' "Help!" but that single failed to chart. As May of 1984 approached Capitol had little hope for the album or its third single "What's Love Got to Do with It" so when the song began moving up the charts that summer everyone was surprised, save for John Carter who had predicted this all along. The single's success also spurred on album sales and though *Private Dancer* never hit #1 (1984 was the year of Prince's *Purple Rain* and Bruce Springsteen's *Born in the USA* and those two LPs effectively blocked the top of the album chart from July of 1984 to February of 1985) it sold over 25 million copies worldwide. And though she hadn't written the lyrics, no one who hears Tina Turner sing, "Who needs a heart when a heart can be broken?" whether they know her history or not, could deny that she sings that line with more passion than anyone else ever could.

"What's Love Got to Do with It" took home the Grammy Awards for Record of the Year and Song of the Year. It also provided the career changing momentum Turner had been looking for. She went on to great success both as a singer and actor. It's one of the great comeback stories in rock and roll history, enabled by a song that itself had been long overlooked and even forgotten.


### September 16th

On this date in 1969 Neil Diamond released a song he'd written and recorded a year earlier inspired by a photo he'd seen some time before that. It would go on to be one of Diamond's most successful songs commercially and by far his most universally loved recording. And to think, he wrote it in less than an hour and simply as a way to get his money's worth out of a recording session. Some throwaways turn out to be, well, diamonds.

Neil Leslie Diamond was born in Brooklyn in 1941. He became interested in music at an early age and was in a high school choir with Barbara Streisand. At a summer camp in his teens he had the chance to see folk singer Pete Seeger perform and according to Diamond that was a monumental moment in his musical maturation. He began to try his hand at songwriting immediately after the Seeger show.

Though his parents encouraged his musical ability they also wanted him to have a reliable career to fall back on so Diamond attended New York University as a Pre-Med student. But he often found himself bored in class and when his mind wandered it always went to writing poetry or song lyrics. He even cut classes from time to time to take a train uptown to Tin Pan Alley, the area in Manhattan where so many music publishers and songwriters had their offices. There, he'd network and try to sell some of his songs. In his senior year, he was offered a job at Sunbeam Music Publishing. He dropped out of school, ten credits shy of graduation to accept the position. Diamond would say later: "I never really chose songwriting. It just absorbed me and became more and more important in my life." He had some success early on selling songs (most notably "I'm A Believer" to the Monkees) as well as performing his own originals (like "Cherry, Cherry" which reached #6 in 1966). However, by the late sixties, after almost a decade in the music business, he hadn't had that breakthrough moment that would make him a superstar.

In 1968 he found himself in Nashville with a recording session scheduled the next day. Looking over his songs he realized he only had two that he wanted to record but he probably had time in the session to record three originals. Not wanting to waste time or money, he sat down to write one more song to record the next day.

He let his mind wander trying to think of a topic to write about. What popped into his head was a *Life* magazine article he'd read years before about the Kennedy family which featured a cover shot of their daughter Caroline riding a horse while her parents look on. He'd always thought it seemed very sweet and he started playing with that concept and the words "sweet Caroline." He built a song around that and according to Diamond the entire thing, from conception to melody and lyrics, was done in an hour.

The next day he recorded all three songs and it was "Sweet Caroline," that last minute addition to the playlist, that became a hit. The song peaked at #4 and sold over a million copies. Some 50 years later, it is still a cherished classic. "Sweet Caroline" is sung heartily at baseball games, karaoke bars and weddings. The lyrics are simple and easy and the melody infectious (or as people usually call back during the song, "So good, so good, so good!")

Diamond wouldn't reveal which "Caroline" inspired the song until almost 40 years later when he mentioned it in an interview, then sang the song to Caroline Kennedy at her 50th birthday. Since then he's changed his story some, saying sometimes that he wrote the song about his then wife Marcia (but since he needed a three-syllable name he didn't sing "sweet Marcia"). Most people have stuck with Diamond's original admission though because what could be cuter than a world famous song being inspired by a few innocent photos of a kid riding a horse?

Neil Diamond has gone on to an amazing career. He's sold over 100 million records and had ten #1s and almost 40 Top 40 hits, earning the nickname the "Jewish Elvis." Given Diamond's talents, all of this success probably would have happened anyway. Still, it's intriguing to think about that career-changing moment when Diamond sat alone in a hotel room the night before a recording session and let his mind wander to come up with one more song. The opening lyric pretty much says it all, "Where it began, I can't begin to knowing . . ."

On this date in 1984, Billy Squier's song "Rock Me Tonight" was beginning its descent down the pop chart after peaking at #15. Though the song was Squier's highest-charting single, it would also prove to play a large role in his career demise, based largely on a cringe-worthy video. MTV is credited for helping boost a lot of careers but in Squier's case, it may just get the blame for undermining one.

William Haislip Squier was born in 1950 in Massachussets. He took piano lessons as a child and when he was ready to quit, his grandfather bribed him to continue. He soon began enjoying them (thanks, Grandpa!) and then bought a used guitar from a neighbor and taught himself to play. He saw Eric Clapton perform in Boston in the late sixties and has said that that was the moment he decided to pursue music as a career. He spent the seventies cutting his teeth with various bands that never quite made it before signing a contract as a solo performer in 1980 with Capitol Records. His debut album, *Tale of the Tape*, peaked at just #169 on the *Billboard* 200 chart. Though it contained no hits, one song, "The Big Beat" has been sampled over 200 times by hip hop artists who love the song's, well, big beat.

It was Squier's second album, *Don't Say No* that burst him onto the scene. The 1981 LP established him as a rocker who could produce catchy opening riffs, hard beats and power cords. Songs like "In the Dark", "Lonely Is the Night", "My Kinda Lover" and "The Stroke" became rock radio staples in the early eighties. *Don't Say No* peaked at #5 and spent almost two years on the album chart. His follow-up, *Emotions in Motion*, was not as successful but it contained the Top 40 rocker, "Everybody Wants You." As the musical landscape was changing in the early eighties, with pop overtaking rock in popularity, Squier was one of the few true rock stalwarts showing that an electric guitar was still the most powerful instrument, especially in the hands of a true axman.

Squier was on vacation in Greece with his girlfriend when he came up with the idea for the song "Rock Me Tonight." He actually created the song while he was swimming, came out of the water and said to his girlfriend, "I've got a hit for the next record." And indeed, as Squier's next album, *Signs of Life*, took shape it was obvious "Rock Me Tonight" would and should be the lead single. And since MTV was the number one promotional vehicle at the time, he had to have an accompanying video.

Squier chose to work with director and choreographer Kenny Ortega for this particular project. At the time, the highlight of Ortega's resume was working with Gene Kelly on the film *Xanadu*, so it was certainly a peculiar choice to say the least. Somehow the two dreamed up a scenario in which Squier would wake up naked on a bed of satin sheets, dress himself in a dancer's outfit, then preen and prance around the bedroom, singing his new song. At one point, Squier crawls across the floor towards the camera and at another he tears away the shirt he's wearing. It's a shot Ortega must have loved because he shows it twice then freezes on the image of Squier's shirtless torso. Squier then puts a new shirt on, this one, apparently keeping with the video's theme, a pink tank top. Squier finally picks up his guitar three minutes into the song (the most masculine thing he'll do in the clip) and he's suddenly joined by his band as they play the rest of the song together.

When Squier saw the final product he said, "What the fuck is this?" But he allowed the video to be released so he has no one to blame but himself. He'd say later he wasn't aware he could have scrapped the whole project and only realized it when Bruce Springsteen did that with the first video shot for "Dancing in the Dark." Regarding the clip, he'd elaborate later: "The video misrepresents who I am as an artist. I was a good-looking, sexy guy. That certainly didn't hurt in promoting my music. But in this video I'm kind of a pretty boy. And I'm preening around a room. People said 'he's gay' or, 'he's on drugs.' It was traumatizing to me." Squier has also called the video, "an MBA course in how a video can go totally wrong." Of his own culpability, Ortega says: "If anything, I tried to toughen the image he was projecting. If it has damaged his career, he has no one to blame but himself."

MTV started playing the video as soon as they got their hands on it in June of 1984 and the song began its ascent up the charts. It would peak at #15 in early September and on this date in 1984 it had already slipped a spot and would continue to tumble off the charts. The video continued on MTV and became a viewer favorite, in much the way traffic slows down while passing an accident. It was one thing to have artists like Prince or even David Bowie showing their effeminate side, but the world was not ready for a rocker like Billy Squier to get so outrageously flamboyant. In a poll of over 400 music industry insiders, Squier's video was voted the worst ever made by a major artist and record label. Mike Kelber, who ran the Capitol Records division, called it, "a whopping steaming turd," and Van Halen's manager, Pete Angelus, stating the obvious, has said Squier, "shouldn't have put on a fucking pink T-shirt and danced around like that."

Kenny Ortega would bounce back, choreographing *Dirty Dancing* and directing the musical movie *Newsies* as well as the *High School Musical* movies, projects that might seem more fitting for a choreographer. Squier, though his career didn't end instantly, would never reach his earlier heights again. Can it all be blamed on the video for "Rock Me Tonight?" Seek it out today on the internet and you decide.

## September 18th

On this date in 1970, Jimi Hendrix, the most legendary and incendiary guitarist of his generation, died in an apartment he was renting in the Notting Hill section of London. The coroner would rule he died of asphyxiation caused by vomiting while intoxicated with barbiturates. The woman he was staying with, Monika

Dannemann, said later that Hendrix took nine of her sleeping tablets, eighteen times the recommended dosage. Hendrix was just 27 years old.

Johnny Allen Hendrix was born in Seattle, Washington in 1942. In grade school he would carry a broom with him and mimic playing a guitar. A social worker sent a letter home to his father saying if the child wasn't given a guitar it could result in psychological damages. His father refused. Sometime later the young Hendrix was helping his dad clean a neighbor's house and he found a ukulele with one string. The woman whose house they were cleaning told the boy he could keep it and he began teaching himself to play with that one string. He saved money from other odd jobs and bought his first real guitar at age fifteen. He never put it down.

After serving a year in the Army, Hendrix moved to Tennessee and started playing in bars and clubs. He backed up artists like the Isley Brothers and Little Richard. He was becoming known, not just for his extraordinary playing ability, but his showmanship on stage. One of his early tricks was to play the guitar with his teeth.

Hendrix moved to London where he hoped to step out front and make a name for himself. He formed the Jimi Hendrix Experience with bassist and guitarist Noel Redding and drummer Mitch Mitchell. The trio began playing regular gigs and very quickly became the buzz all about Swinging London. One of their early live performances was a night where the star-studded audience included Eric Clapton, John Lennon, Paul McCartney, Jeff Beck, Pete Townshend, Brian Jones, and Mick Jagger. Rock legend has it that every musician in attendance was in awe and half-afraid that the music scene was about to change dramatically based on this one man's ridiculous talent. Clapton especially, who was considered a guitar great by this point, was both impressed and a little bit scared.

In October of 1966, the Who's managers, Kit Lambert and Chris Stamp, signed the Experience to their newly formed label, Track Records, and released their debut single "Hey Joe." The band's second single "Purple Haze," earned them even more attention in England as it reached #6 on the U.K. pop chart. In May of 1967 their debut LP, *Are You Experienced*, was released and sold well in England.

While the band had gained a lot of attention overseas, they'd failed to garner nearly as much in the U.S. That all changed in June of 1967 at the Monterey Pop Festival. It was Paul McCartney who recommended the Experience to the festival's organizers and Brian Jones who introduced them, calling Hendrix the most exciting performer he'd ever seen. They played an incredible set that ended with Hendrix destroying his guitar and then lighting it on fire. The picture of the Hendrix kneeling in front of the fire as if conjuring the flames to burn higher is one of the most iconic photographs in rock and roll lore.

Jimi Hendrix was as much a part of the soundtrack of 1967's "Summer of Love," as the Beatles and the Doors and as engrained in the fabric of the sixties' counter-culture movement as any pop or political figure. His version of "The Star

Spangled Banner" at Woodstock, much like his burning guitar at Monterey, is a seminal moment in the hippie saga. And just like so many of his generation, be it Rock God or your average, everyday beatnik, he struggled with drugs and alcohol. There's a fine line between what Timothy Leary promoted with his famous, "Turn on, tune in, drop out" catchphrase and straight up substance abuse. Hendrix attempted to walk that fine line like a tight rope without a net. One night of over-indulgence cost him his life. Though his flame had been doused, in his short time on earth, he left the world with more than enough transcendent recordings and images to last us for decades to come. And by joining that mythological group of artists who die at the age of 27, known as the 27 Club, he assures that the mystery surrounding what could have been for this incredible guitar hero will always be greater than the reality. In one of his songs, Hendrix asked the listener, "Are you experienced?" Spend some time today listening to him wail on guitar and you can answer with a definitive yes!

## September 19th

On this date in 1970, Neil Young released *After the Gold Rush*. Though he was only 24 at the time, he had already accomplished so much as a musician and artist. And his career was really just getting started. All these decades later Young is considered one of the most important voices in rock history and a musician who has always followed his instincts and creativity.

Neil Percival Young was born in 1945 in Toronto, Canada. In the mid-fifties he fell in love with the new rock and roll sounds that were blaring from his transistor. He idolized Elvis Presley and loved everyone from Fats Domino to Chuck Berry. The first instrument he picked up was a plastic ukulele and after reaching the limitations of that toy he was given his first real guitar. Throughout his teens he formed or was a member in many different bands, including one of the odder combinations of musicians you'll ever see, the Mynah Birds which featured Neil Young and Rick James (yeah, that Rick James). The Mynah Birds were actually signed to a deal with Motown but then James got arrested and the band broke up. Young's next venture was with Buffalo Springfield where he first worked with Stephen Stills. Their 1967 hit "For What It's Worth" not only put the band on the map but many musicologists say it helped popularize folk rock. After Buffalo Springfield broke up, Young released two solo LPs (one with a new backing band he'd assembled called Crazy Horse) before joining Crosby, Stills & Nash to form Crosby, Stills, Nash & Young. CSN originally offered Young a sideman position but he said he would join them only if they made him a full band member. Understanding how important he could be to their lineup, they did just that and the newly formed CSN&Y released their groundbreaking album *Déjà Vu* in early 1970. Later that year, days after the Kent State Massacre, Neil Young penned "Ohio," one of the most urgent protest, anti-war songs of the era. The song was released less than a month after the shooting.

The four musicians in CSN&Y decided they'd each release a solo project after the success of *Déjà Vu* before working together again. Young got right to work and had *After the Gold Rush* ready for release by the end of the summer of 1970. Among the musicians Young chose to work with was a 19 year old Nils Lofgren who would go on to fame as both a solo artist and a longtime member of Bruce Springsteen's E Street Band. Young released two singles from *Gold Rush*, "Only Love Can Break Your Heart" and "When You Dance I Really Love You." While both are well respected tracks in Young's canon, two other songs from the album are far more memorable.

First is "Southern Man," Neil Young's scathing attack on racism in America. With images of burning crosses and bullwhips cracking, Young confronts the "Southern man" with the simple question, "When will you pay them back?" and urges him, "Don't forget what your good book said." Young had taken on the Vietnam War with "Ohio" and now he was confronting endemic racism. He was proving there was no topic too big or controversial for him.

The topic of the other memorable song from *After the Gold Rush,* the title track, isn't so clear. Sure there are references to Mother Nature and how she is on the run in the 1970s, a line Young updates when he plays live, today changing it to, "Look at Mother Nature on the run in the twenty-first century." But the rest of the song is dreamlike and enigmatic with knights in armor and silver space ships and, in all three verses, the sun. The song is delivered beautifully, with a simple piano to set the melody and a french horn that plays the solo. Young's voice is tender and vulnerable and all this adds up to a sound the listener gets lost in, forgetting about the meaning of the song and just diving deeper into the ethereal sound. Indeed, even Young has admitted to not understanding "After the Gold Rush." When Dolly Parton covered the song years later she asked Young what it meant and he told her: "Hell, I don't know. I just wrote it. It just depends on what I was taking at the time. I guess every verse has something different I'd taken."

Neil Young's next album, 1972's *Harvest* would cement his status as a bonafide rock star and a man whose talents for songwriting and musicianship had few peers. He has gone on to an incredible career and continues to be a voice for causes he believes in. And though it's sad that racism and unnecessary wars still exist, and that Mother Nature is still on the run, it's heartening to know artists like Neil Young will always be there to point out society's shortcomings and challenge us to be better.

### September 20th

On this date in 1975, David Bowie made his first appearance at #1 on the *Billboard* Hot 100 Chart with his caustic look at celebrity, "Fame." The song was a true collaborative effort between Bowie, a new guitarist he'd just started working with and one of Bowie's musical heroes who he'd invited to the studio one day. Throw in Bowie's seething rage at being screwed over by his current management and voila! You had the makings of a chart-topper.

David Robert Jones was born in 1947 in the Brixton section of London. The pivotal moment of his young life came when he was nine years old and his father brought home a box of singles of American rock and roll pioneers like Elvis Presley and Fats Domino and Little Richard. When the young boy played "Tutti Frutti" he would later say he'd, "heard God." He was fifteen when he formed his first band and began using the stage name Davy Jones. But in 1966 when *The Monkees* went on the air he was forced to change it or be confused with their Davy Jones. He took another piece of Americana as inspiration, using the last name of the legendary pioneer James Bowie and the knife he made famous. His first release was 1967's "The Laughing Gnome" and within just a few years David Bowie had established himself as one of the most important and unique voices in rock music. His 1972 LP, *The Rise and Fall of Ziggy Stardust and the Spiders from Mars*, in which Bowie adopted the persona of an androgynous rock star from outer space named Ziggy Stardust established Bowie as an innovator with few peers.

While David Bowie toured the U.S. extensively throughout 1974 with his Diamond Dogs Tour, he became infatuated with the burgeoning soul/Philly sound that was growing more popular in the States (and would eventually evolve into disco). He even renamed his tour the Soul Tour in its last legs. During a break in August of 1974, Bowie took up residency at Philadelphia's Sigma Sound Studio where he brought together a number of African-American musicians and singers (including a then-unknown Luther Vandross) to create what he would later call "plastic soul." Most of the tracks that would make up his next album, *Young Americans*, where recorded in Philadelphia in August of 1974.

One of the musicians who Bowie worked with in Philadelphia was a guitarist by the name of Carlos Alomar. Bowie loved his work so much he invited him to play on the last leg of his tour. Alomar introduced Bowie to a 1961 Flares' song called "Foot Stompin" which they worked into their setlist at the end of the tour and also played on the *Dick Cavett* show after the tour wrapped up. If you can find that clip on Youtube you'll see what inspired "Fame." Alomar had rewritten a guitar riff for "Foot Stompin'" and after hearing it night after night on tour Bowie decided he had to make a song out of it.

Bowie spent the winter of 1975 in New York City hoping to finish the work he'd started in Philadelphia. He was, by his own words, "obsessed" with soul music at this time so he invited Carlos Alomar to New York to help complete the album. He'd also met his idol, John Lennon, the year before and the two had become fast friends. One day he invited Lennon to hang out at the Electric Ladyland Studios where Bowie was recording. Lennon was advising Bowie at the time about his management situation. Bowie had just been hit with a bill for expenses from his recent tour and recording sessions and he basically realized he was broke. Lennon was encouraging Bowie to fire his manager, Tony DeFries, which he'd eventually do, and take more control of his own career.

That was the mood Bowie was in that day when Lennon arrived at the studio. Alomar began riffing on the jam he'd come up with for "Foot Stompin'" and Lennon, not wanting to be left out, picked up a guitar and started playing along. As Alomar explains, "In funk music, what you want to do is put down a lot of holes, leaving space for people to dance." As the trio jammed, Lennon filled one of those holes very simply by singing the word "fame." It was perfect and it was all Bowie needed. He wrote the rest of the song in no time, channeling his anger at his current situation and his disillusionment with celebrity. He would say later: "I think fame itself is not a rewarding thing. The most you can say is that it gets you a seat in restaurants." Even though Lennon had contributed just the one word, Bowie included him as a songwriter, acknowledging that his musical hero had taken a jam session and given it direction and purpose with that one word.

Bowie completed the album in New York City that winter and *Young Americans* was released on March 7th, 1975. The lead single was the title track and it did well in the U.S., peaking at #28. Then, in July, "Fame" was released as the second single and it began a decisive march up the charts, eventually knocking Glenn Cambell's "Rhinestone Cowboy" from the top on this date in 1975. The song's caustic view of fame and celebrity would somehow, ironically, only give David Bowie more of it.

### September 21st

On this date in 2004, Green Day released their seventh studio album, *American Idiot*. The album would go on to be a huge comeback for the punk rock trio from California, selling fifteen million copies worldwide, spawning five successful singles, winning a Grammy for Best Rock Album and eventually being turned into a Broadway musical. Not bad for an album that was recorded just because some tapes of a completely different album were stolen.

Green Day had burst on to the musical scene in 1994 with their major label debut, *Dookie,* which contained the hit songs "Basket Case" and "When I Come Around." Their straight ahead, three-chords-with-a-vengeance style was a throwback to the seventies' punk rock sound and they rode the wave of the grunge movement with their youthful energy and angst. Like so many punk bands though, they found success took its toll (it's hard to stay angry when the world is now at your feet) and their next few albums saw them slipping in commercial sales as well as pop culture relevance. Following 2000's *Warning,* which saw the band completely moving away from its punk rock roots (and sales continue to fall) the band took a break. When they reconvened three years later, Billie Joe Armstrong, Mike Dirnt and Tre Cool, decided to return to their earlier style and sound. Throughout that summer they worked on an album of songs they decided to call *Cigarettes and Valentines.* But just as the record was being finished, the master tapes were stolen. Though older versions of the songs as demos were still around and even, in some cases, backup tapes existed, the band took this as a sign. They decided to start a whole new album from scratch.

To begin with, the trio got competitive. They decided to each write a thirty second song, trying to outdo each other. The short snippets they came up with were woven together in a musical suite that became the album's penultimate song, "Homecoming." The band liked the rambling, wide-open sound of that song so much they recorded another medley, this one titled, "Jesus of Suburbia" which also helped them start seeing a vision for this new project. Armstrong would then write the title track, addressing some of the socio-political issues of the day, and suddenly these new songs had a theme. Before long the band started referring to their current project as a "punk rock opera" which would make it the first of its kind. Armstrong took a break from working with the band for a while and traveled to New York City where he wrote "Boulevard of Broken Dreams" and "Are We the Waiting." He also began to shape the album's storyline while in the Big Apple. He saw the piece as telling the story of people, "going away and getting the hell out, while at the same time fighting their own inner demons." When he returned to California, the band got to work and over the course of five months, spending over $650,000, they completed *American Idiot.*

One of the last songs to be written for the album ultimately became the title track. Though the entire LP isn't politically charged, "American Idiot" certainly is. One day, while driving to the studio, Armstrong heard a Lynyrd Skynyrd song on the radio and, as he'd say later: "It was like, 'I'm proud to be a redneck' and I was like 'oh my God why would you be proud of something like that? This is exactly what I'm *against.*" He wrote the song and then played it for Dirnt and Cool and asked them if they were ok with it. The lyrics are controversial to be sure, especially with America at war with Iraq and Afghanistan at the time and George W. Bush seeking re-election. Armstrong sings about being controlled by the media (brilliantly calling it, "the subliminal mind fuck") and how he is, "not part of a redneck agenda." The chorus also includes the fantastically enigmatic line, "Television dreams of tomorrow." That's one of those lyrics that is so open to interpretation you could write a thesis on it. Of course, following it up with: "We're not the ones who're meant to follow," lets everyone know how Armstrong and the band felt about the "propaganda."

Though the band was unsuccessful with their ultimate goal of making sure George W Bush wasn't reelected, or as Cool said, making, "the world a little more sane," they were at least successful in questioning the war in Iraq and taking shots at the "television media." Sometimes a band attempts to affect change and while it might not be successful on the broader scope, it can alter the attitudes and opinions of those listening. This was certainly the case with Green Day. In a decade they'd gone from whining about, "nothing and everything all at once," to decrying, "a redneck agenda" that they felt had dragged us into unwanted wars. Those who love *American Idiot* have to be grateful to whoever stole those *Cigarettes and Valentines* tapes and to the band for realizing it was a sign that they could do something much bigger and better and more important. In the decade that is called "the oughts," *American Idiot* is as significant as any record released. Play it today if you have the time but play it loud. Angry and defiant is meant to be cranked.

On this date in 1981, the Rolling Stones' 18th studio album, *Tattoo You*, had just climbed to #1 where it would reside for the next nine weeks. *Tattoo You* was critically praised as a return to form for one of the world's greatest rock bands and, to date, it is their last album to top the charts. Not bad for a collection of songs cobbled together from previously rejected and unfinished tracks.

The seventies were an odd decade for the Stones. Optimistically, their fans could point to the fact that the band, unlike so many of their peers from the sixties, made it through the decade together and were still commercially relevant. Critics complained that they had strayed too far from the raw and gritty early sound that had established them. But then, the Stones had always adapted and followed trends, hadn't they? They released *Their Satanic Majesties Request* during the psychedelic era and they answered the Beatles' *Let It Be* with their own *Let It Bleed*. When they missed out on Woodstock they planned Altamont. So if the seventies had seen them dabble in soft rock with "Angie" and "Wild Horses" and disco with "Miss You" and "Emotional Rescue" and even a little punk with "Shattered," these were just a few more genres the band proved they could mimic and even master.

So as the eighties began, the Stones were in a unique spot and promoters were begging for a world tour. But why tour when you haven't got a new album to promote? And how do you record new work when your chief songwriting duo is barely speaking to each other?

That last question was answered by the album's associate producer, Chris Kimsey, who had worked with the band throughout the seventies. He sifted through hours and hours of tapes from the recording sessions that had produced their last handful of albums. When he was done he presented the band with enough of their own rejected material to make up a new LP. Some were bits of songs that needed completion; some were instrumental tracks that needed lyrics. All of them were worth completing and including on a new Rolling Stones' release.

The quintessential reclamation project of *Tattoo You* was the album's opening track and its lead single, "Start Me Up." The first incarnation of the song was recorded during the 1977 sessions for *Some Girls*. At that point the song was called "Never Stop" and it had a reggae vibe to it. As the Stones often did when they were trying to work a song out in the studio they had played it over and over during a six hour recording session, often jamming for fifteen to twenty minutes like jazz musicians, straying from the melody but never too far to return and seeing if anything magical might arise. Eventually they deemed the song unsuitable and Keith Richards even said to Kimsey, who was producing that particular session, that he didn't like the song and he thought maybe he'd heard the melody somewhere else anyway (something Richards is always leery of). Then he told Kimsey to erase the tape. Fortunately, the producer ignored that order.

During that fruitless six hour session the band had stuck with their original reggae vibe for the song except for two takes which found Richards and drummer Charlie Watts giving it a more straightforward rock sound. Kimsey, in his search for material for the new album, had gone back and listened to all six hours of the session. It was the rock arrangement, which included one of Richard's signature opening riffs, that he felt was worth exploring. To the band's credit they agreed and after a few lyrical changes and overdubs, they produced a song that stands shoulder-to-shoulder with anything they'd ever recorded.

Other songs on *Tattoo You* have similar histories of being rejected in previous sessions only to be dusted off and finished for the album. The oldest of these was "Waiting on a Friend" whose backing track had been done in 1972 in the sessions that produced *Goats Head Soup*. The Stones neglected to credit Mick Taylor for his work on this song (he was with the band at the time before departing in 1974) and when *Tattoo You* became such a huge success, Taylor asked for, and received, his share of royalties.

*Tattoo You* and the almost yearlong world tour to promote it, helped remind the world that the Rolling Stones were truly the greatest rock band still standing. While the Who, the other last great sixties' band, were on their way to breaking up, the Stones were actually finding a whole new generation of fans. And while the eighties were not without some solo projects and even a few missteps (there is simply no explanation for "Too Much Blood" - the song or its *Nightmare on Elm Street* inspired video), the band would even make it through their third decade intact, no doubt spurred on by the tour-de-force that *Tattoo You* proved to be. One can only imagine what else is buried in their old, rejected studio tapes and jam sessions.

### September 23rd

On this date in 1939, Glenn Miller's "In the Mood" had just been released and was already gaining popularity. This era predates the most popular charts so it is hard to say just how successful "In the Mood" became but all these decades later it is still one of the most recognizable rhythms and a staple in just about every orchestra's repertoire. And though the origins of that famous rhythm may never be known, we do know the man who made it internationally recognizable. Here's the story of the song of the tragic tale of Miller's life.

Glenn Miller was born in Iowa in 1904. He loved music from an early age and saved up money from milking cows to buy his first trombone when he was just eleven. He'd mastered it, as well as the mandolin and clarinet, before he graduated from high school. "Dance band music" was just coming into vogue at the time, as the Roaring Twenties were starting to roar, and Miller determined early on that music was his calling and he would someday lead a famous big band. Throughout the twenties and early thirties Miller perfected his craft, playing in numerous bands alongside accomplished musicians like Tommy

Dorsey, Gene Krupa and Benny Goodman. He formed his first band in 1937 but they failed to distinguish themselves with a unique sound and after less than a year Miller broke the band up, realizing he needed something distinctive to set himself and his next orchestra apart.

He discovered that something in New York City when he auditioned saxophonist Wilbur Schwartz. Schwartz had a unique sound to his playing and Miller had him play lead clarinet, surrounding him with four other saxophonists. He'd say later, "The fifth sax, playing clarinet most of the time, lets you know whose band you're listening to." With this new and exceptional sound, the Glenn Miller orchestra started releasing hit after hit. Charts still counted sheet music sales more than record sales so it is hard to say just how dominant Miller was in the late thirties and early forties but it's been estimated he scored 23 #1 hits in just four years, which would give him more than Elvis Presley's 18 and the Beatles' 20.

One of Glenn Miller's earliest releases was "In the Mood" which came out in September of 1939. The melody of "In the Mood" is so simple and catchy it seems to the first time-listener that it's something familiar. And in fact it may be. There were many records that had already been released that have a similar melody. One listen to Wingy Manone's 1930 song, "Tar Paper Stomp" and you can hear the origins of "In the Mood." Fletcher Henderson's 1931 "Hot and Anxious" also includes a similar riff as does the Mills Blue Rhythm Band's 1935 song "There's Rhythm in Harlem," albeit at a much faster tempo. But this is before the day when every song got published with copywriter protection so credit often went to whoever made the song famous. In the case of "In the Mood" that would be Glenn Miller, who isn't listed as a composer on the track but for all intents and purposes has become synonymous with the song. He made it his own, incorporating the "tenor fight" during the first break of the song, and including that incredible ending where the tune rises triumphantly to the unforgettable climax. Miller's recording brought joy to thousands of dance floors in its day and it continues to do so today.

Glenn Miller was soon the most famous band leader in the world. His shows were huge-sellers, his records flew off the shelves and he even made appearances in motion pictures. But then war broke out and Miller, despite being in his late thirties, decided to join the effort. The Navy rejected him based on his age. Then he approached the Army so he could, in his own words, "be placed in charge of a modernized Army band." The Army accepted him and before long he'd formed a 50 piece Army Air Force band that performed hundreds of shows for U.S. troops stationed in England. His music was not only being used to boost morale among the troops but was being broadcast into Germany and used as anti-fascist propaganda. One of the messages Miller recorded was, "America means freedom and there's no expression of freedom quite so sincere as music." On December 15th, 1944, Miller flew from England to France to make arrangements to bring his band there. The small plane he was in went down at sea, killing Miller and two other occupants. Their bodies were never recovered.

Though Glenn Miller died at just 40, his legacy and music lives on. When most people hear the words "big band" they think first of Glenn Miller and the sound they hear is that infectious opening of "In the Mood." Though it had been released in 1939, before the U.S. was dragged into World War II, it was still a popular number by the time the war ended. One listen to it, and you can almost hear the feeling of joy and celebration that the millions of soldiers returning home from the war must have felt. The U.S. and its allies had been victorious, defeating fascism and saving the world from totalitarianism. There are scores of other songs from the era that capture the same emotion but none better than "In the Mood." Give it a listen today and see if you can't be transported back to that critical time in history when the world was literally saved from destruction.

## September 24th

On this date in 1991, the Red Hot Chili Peppers released their fifth studio album, *Blood Sugar Sex Magik*. After years of living in the margins of pop success this is the album that would propel them into the stratosphere. And it was a song where they stepped away from the driving funk and rap that had defined them as a band up to that point which would help them get there. That song, "Under the Bridge," began as a very personal and private poem and would go on to become the band's most successful single ever.

The Red Hot Chili Peppers started playing together in 1983 in Los Angeles. Anthony Kiedis, guitarist Hillel Slovak, bassist Flea and drummer Jack Irons were all high school classmates who loved punk rock, funk and rap and decided to try to meld these genres together. Their raucous live shows quickly gained them a large following and they were signed to EMI, releasing their eponymous debut album in 1984. Though the LP failed to chart the Chili Peppers became favorites on college radio stations and their underground fame grew outside of southern California. Hoping to dive deeper into their funk roots, they tapped George Clinton to produce their sophomore release, *Freaky Styley*. Much like their debut, this album didn't sell well but it continued to help them find a fan base in colleges and clubs. 1987 would see them release *The Uplift Mofo Party Plan* which found the Peppers introducing some heavy metal elements into their sound. That album sold better and peaked at #148 on the album chart. From the outside looking in, the band seemed poised for a breakout.

But trouble was brewing. As their reputation grew, so too did Kiedis and Slovak's drug use, specifically heroin. In June of 1988, tragedy struck. Hillel Slovak, 26, died of an overdose. The band was devastated and at a crossroads. Jack Irons left and went into years of depression. Flea and Kiedis decided to keep the band going with Kiedis promising to seek help. It was around this time that Kiedis channeled his sadness for his friend's death, his own frustration at struggling with drugs, and his love for his hometown of Los Angeles into a poem he called "Under the Bridge." Kiedis admits that there are times he feels his, "Only friend is the City of Angels" and references a, "bridge downtown" where he, "drew some blood" and gave his life away. The bridge is a real place where he used to buy heroin and shoot up. He wrote the poem as a deep and personal reflection and then put it away, never thinking it could become a song.

In 1989 the Peppers released their fourth LP, *Mother's Milk*, which made it to #52 on the *Billboard* 200 chart. For their next album they asked famed producer, Rick Rubin to work with them. Rubin's resume was already star-studded, having founded Def Jam Records in the early eighties in his New York University dorm room, then going on to produce such epic artists as Run-DMC, the Beastie Boys and the Black Crowes. The Peppers had actually asked Rubin to work with them a few years earlier but he'd turned them down because of Kiedis and Slovak's drug problems. This time, though, he agreed and then made a unique suggestion that the band move into his ten bedroom mansion during the recording process. The mansion is supposedly haunted, and urban legend says Harry Houdini once lived there, all of which lent an aura of mysteriousness during the recording process and gave the album its name.

As the band worked on new material, Kiedis showed Rubin his notebook where he kept his lyrical ideas and poetry. Rubin read "Under the Bridge" and suggested the band turn the poem into a song. Kiedis doubted it would work, thinking the poem far too intimate and not exactly in the Peppers' raucous style. But Rubin pushed back because, as he'd say later, "My thinking was that the Chili Peppers were not limited to being a funk band with rapping." Eventually Kiedis acquiesced and his bandmates loved it. They each wrote their own musical parts and "Under the Bridge" was completed and included on *Blood Sugar Sex Magik* which was released on this date in 1991.

"Give it Away" was released as the first single off *Blood Sugar Sex Magik* and it became the Peppers' first single to chart, peaking at #73. The band and their record company then needed to select a second single. A few record executives went to a Peppers' show at which Kiedis missed his vocal cue to "Under the Bridge" only to have the audience pick him up and sing, in virtual unison, the first verse. After the show, Kiedis apologized to the executives for "fucking up" the song only to have one say, "Are you kidding me? When every single kid at the show sings a song, that's our next single."

"Under the Bridge" was released in March of 1992 and it peaked at #2 in June (to date the Peppers have never had a #1). It would take Kiedis another few years to finally kick drugs completely (he claims to be clean since 2000) and it's hard to argue that anything good comes from a young musician dying, but "Under the Bridge" has served for so many as a message of hope and salvation. For anyone who doesn't want to feel like they did in their darkest days, Kiedis provided inspiration to stop hanging under the bridge, but use it instead to cross to a better side.

On this date in 1965, Barry McGuire's "Eve of Destruction" went to #1 on the *Billboard* Hot 100 chart when it ended the Beatles' three week stay at the top with "Help!" McGuire would enjoy a one week stay at #1 before being bumped off by the McCoys' "Hang on Sloopy." Thus was the state of the music and the culture in 1965, as bubblegum pop and more serious rock fought it out on the charts and radio stations. "Eve of Destruction," with all its pessimistic, apocalyptic imagery, was a big part of that musical transition and it all came from the sleepless night of a nineteen year old songwriter.

P. F. Sloan was that nineteen year old songwriter. By 1964 he'd already achieved some success both as a performer (at fourteen he'd recorded and released his debut song, "A Little Girl in the Cabin") and as a songwriter, having contributed songs to Jan and Dean and others. But he was very much affected by the troubling news of the day. Many cite Kennedy's assassination in November of 1963 as the "End of the Fifties" and soon after, as the Baby Boomer generation matured, they became aware and involved in other issues such as civil rights and the anti-war movement. Sloan started listening to folk artists like Woody Guthrie and Bob Dylan around this time as well which helped shift the focus of his songwriting from the California beach sound fluff to more serious topics.

It was around this time that Sloan had a bout of insomnia. As most songwriters are inclined to do, instead of staring at the ceiling or counting sheep, he scribbled some lyrics and wrote a song. Then another. And another. Sloan has said he penned five songs that sleepless night, each reflecting his worried mind. During one of those songs, he claims he heard an inner voice that he has since identified as God. He scribbled the opening line: "The eastern world is explodin'. Violence flarin' bullets loadin'" and he was off. He pulled many issues from recent headlines, like the "War of Water" in Israel which is referenced in the lyric, "And even the Jordan River has bodies floatin'." And he asked that inner voice if he believed we were on the eve of destruction? He says the inner voice even helped him, namely correcting the line, "Think of all the hate there is in Red Russian" to "Red China." Sloan would say later he felt the whole song was a "love song" as well as "a prayer."

When he presented his new songs to the publishing company he was working for he was told "Eve of Destruction" was "unpublishable" and was even asked not to write anymore songs like it. It was an opinion that was only confirmed when the Byrds considered the song but then rejected it. However the Turtles did record a version of "Eve of Destruction" and included it as an album track on their debut LP, "It Ain't Me Babe."

This is where Barry McGuire enters our story. McGuire was a member of the folk group the New Christy Minstrels in the early sixties where he co-wrote and sang lead on their most successful single, "Green, Green." He left the Minstrels in 1965 and decided to try a solo career. As he was searching for material, he was told of this young, quirky songwriter named P. F. Sloan and was invited to check out his songs. McGuire liked what he saw and a recording session was scheduled that included Sloan on guitar. McGuire was able to lay down two songs but as the clock was winding down on the three hour session he figured he was done. Someone suggested he take a crack at "Eve of Destruction" but McGuire's voice was fried and he hadn't really studied the song yet so it was decided he'd lay down a guide vocal that he could replace at a later date. McGuire did just that, literally reading the vocals off a sheet of paper as he sang. When he began the line, "I can't twist the truth, it knows no regulation" with an "ahhhh" it was because he'd lost his place on the sheet of paper and needed a second to find it. McGuire also didn't bother hitting the high note in the final chorus, figuring he'd go for it when he re-recorded his vocals. That recording session wrapped up on a Thursday and on the following Monday McGuire got a call from someone telling him to turn on his radio. KFWB, a leading rock station in Los Angeles at the time, had gotten a leaked copy of McGuire's rough cut version of "Eve of Destruction" over the weekend and was already spinning it. McGuire never would have a chance to go back and smooth out his lyrics and correct that "ahhhh" which is one of those happy accidents that occur in music history. As it turned out, McGuire's gravely-voiced delivery is painfully perfect for the record's bleak lyrics and dire warnings. McGuire would say later that, "Sometimes raw and naked is the way it's supposed to be," and this has never been more true than with "Eve of Destruction."

1965 was indeed a turning point in American culture. From the "Bloody Sunday" incident in Selma, Alabama, where civil rights demonstrators were beaten and tear-gassed by State Troopers, to the first U.S. troops arriving in Vietnam, it certainly felt for many like the eve of destruction. And the pop chart bore witness to this. The Rolling Stones were telling everyone they couldn't "get no satisfaction" and the Beatles were crying "Help!" and amidst all this came a song from an unknown singer and an equally unknown songwriter reminding everyone, "If the button is pushed there's no running away." And as a nation's youth wondered why they were old enough to be drafted but not to vote, they had this new song asking the same question. "Eve of Destruction" spent just one week at #1 on the charts but its impact was felt throughout the rest of the decade and beyond. Sloan had helped show songwriters and artists that a "statement song" didn't have to be relegated to the margins of commercial success. Especially with the largest generation America had ever seen maturing and becoming more aware of political and social issues, songs that spoke to the very heart of the zeitgeist would soon become pop hits and protest anthems. "Eve of Destruction" isn't the first song to do this, but it's one of the first to achieve chart success, helping to open the airwaves for so many others to follow.

On this date in 1964, Roy Orbinson's "Oh, Pretty Woman" reached #1 on the *Billboard* Hot 100 chart where it would enjoy a three week stay. It knocked the Animals' "House of the Rising Sun" from the top perch and on October 17th "Do Wah Diddy Diddy" by Manfred Mann would take its place. Incredibly, for such a legendary singer as Orbison, this was only his second #1 single and it would prove to be his last. Not bad though for a song written in the time it takes your wife to go shopping.

Roy Kelton Orbison was born in Vernon, Texas in 1936. He had poor eyesight as a child and was forced to wear thick, corrective eyeglasses (which would transform years later to his distinctive dark sunglasses). When he was six he was given a guitar and he would say later, "I was finished, you know, with anything else." Music would be his primary focus for the rest of his life. Growing up in the south, especially in the pre-rock and roll era, he was exposed mainly to country music. He formed his first band in high school and when they were offered $400 to play a dance, Orbison became convinced that music could be his career. This theory was solidified a year later when Orbison saw Elvis Presley perform. Presley was already a rising star and only one year older than Orbison so he decided to go where Presley had come from. In 1956, Roy Orbison traveled to Memphis, Tennessee and he and his band the Teen Kings auditioned for Sam Phillips. Phillips loved their sound and immediately recorded and released "Ooby Dooby." The Teen Kings soon disbanded but Orbison stayed in Memphis and became part of the early Sun Studio stable of rock and roll pioneers. But Orbison didn't just sing upbeat numbers. His rich and emotion-filled voice was perfect for ballads and breakup songs which was exemplified with 1960's "Only the Lonely (Know the Way I Feel.)" Orbison seemed to find his groove with "Only the Lonely" and other songs followed in the same vein, like 1961's "Running Scared" (his first career #1) and "Crying." In just a few short years he'd carved out a unique career for himself as a successful artist who could not be pigeonholed. Part rockabilly, part country, part balladeer, Roy Orbison was as unique a voice in the early sixties as any artist.

The legendary story of how "Oh, Pretty Woman" was created begins in the Orbison household in Nashville, Tennessee in the early summer of 1964. Orbison is working with his songwriting partner, Bill Dees, trying to come up with some new material. Orbison's wife, Claudette, walks in to say she's heading out to do some shopping. Orbison asks if she needs any money and Dees replies, "Pretty woman never needs money." Claudette probably smiles and maybe even thanks him for the compliment, then heads into town. Songwriters know a good line when they hear it and Orbison and Dees realize they may have stumbled onto something worth pursuing. Then Dees starts banging his hand on the table, trying to imitate the pace a person would walk as Orbison sings, "Pretty woman walking down the street." They make eye-contact and now they know they've got something good. The song pours out of them effortlessly. Dees, who would often say "mercy" when something impressed him, contributes the line that only Orbison could sing with his perfectly salacious growl. They both admit later they probably got the "yeah yeah yeah" part from the Beatles' "She Loves You" which was all over the airwaves at the time. Before Claudette returns home, the song is completed.

Orbison would have "Oh, Pretty Woman" recorded and released within weeks of its creation. The song became an instant hit, reaching the top of the charts only a month after its release.

Not only would Orbison's career begin to cool off after "Pretty Woman" but his life was met with great tragedy as well. Just two years after she inspired the song, Claudette was killed in a motorcycle accident. She would die in her husband's arms. Two years later, in 1968, while Orbison was touring Europe his home burned to the ground, killing two of his three sons. The man who could famously pack so much emotion and passion into his rich voice, suddenly had too much emotion to deal with. It would take almost two decades for his career to bounce back and just as it was, as he was enjoying a second life with the Traveling Wilbury's, he died of a heart attack in 1988. He was just 52 years old. Roy Orbison, the man with the dark sunglasses and voice from the Gods was gone long before his time.

### September 27th

On this date in 1994, the Dave Matthews Band released their first major-label album, *Under the Table and Dreaming*. The band had been together for almost three years at this point and they'd built a solid fan base the old fashioned, grass roots way, by playing gig after gig to impassioned crowds. With an album release and additional promotion, they were soon one of the biggest bands in the world.

David John Matthews was born in Johannesburg, South Africa, in early 1967. While he was growing up, his family moved often between South Africa and the U.S. which has given him a unique worldview. When he was nine he started playing guitar. Just a year later he lost his father which, some say, informs his "carpe-diem" inspired outlook and subsequent lyrics. Back in South Africa, now in his teens, he faced conscription into their military and, since he is a pacifist, he fled his homeland to avoid being drafted. He settled with his mother in Charlottesville, Virginia, where he became a popular face on the local music scene. He often went to see Tim Reynolds, another local musician, who would occasionally invite Matthews to the stage and encouraged him to pursue his own songwriting. In early 1991, Dave Matthews did just that, forming a band and giving it his own name.

Frustrated that they couldn't land a record contract, in 1993 the Dave Matthews Band created their own label, Bama Riggs, and released an album called *Remember Two Things*. The album had been recorded live in August of 1993 and it debuted on the college charts as the highest independent entry; an impressive accomplishment and a testament to the reputation the band had already forged.

Doing things independently, and out of the norm, became the norm for the Dave Matthews Band. Early on, taking a page from the Grateful Dead, they encouraged fans to bootleg their shows, even providing a direct patch from the soundboard so fans could get the best possible sound. Matthews felt their live shows were worth spreading around and certainly the propagation of these tapes helped build their reputation. They encouraged fans to trade tapes of live shows (instead of selling them for profit), an unwritten policy that continues even to this day.

Major record labels finally caught on to their burgeoning success and RCA signed the Dave Matthews Band in 1994. They released their debut, major-label album, *Under the Table and Dreaming* on this date in 1994 and made their first national television appearance in February of 1995, playing "What Would You Say?" on *Late Night with David Letterman*. Subsequent appearances on Jay Leno and *Saturday Night Live* would help expose DMB to a wider audience. *Under the Table and Dreaming* had a slow build, growing on word-of-mouth and consistent radio play on alternative rock and college radio. It eventually peaked at #11 on the album chart in June of 1995 and has gone on to sell 6 million copies. Their follow-up LP, 1996's *Crash*, debuted at #2 on the album chart which speaks highly to the anticipation the music world had for more material from the band. Their albums have been consistent sellers ever since.

But the Dave Matthews Band is more than just the sum of their albums and singles. For most DMB fans, the real attraction, like the band surmised early on, is their live shows. Dave Matthews' concerts are known for their rock-jazz-jam fusion and their tight sound. The band was wise to allow their fans to record their shows because that is truly where the magic in the Dave Matthews Band lies. Matthews has also developed what his fans call Davespeak, his interesting, non-sequiturs between songs which are often random and have nothing to do with the next song. But they make their shows all the more fascinating because, besides, "What will they play next?" their fans often wonder, "What will he say next?" As for Tim Reynolds, though he never officially became a band member, he will often join them live and he and Matthews still do acoustic shows from time to time. The two have also released three live albums together. And for Dave Matthews' fans that is a big part of the attraction: his unpredictability. When they play live, even on an extended tour, they rely less on a setlist and more on a spontaneous, play-what-we-want-when-we-want attitude. It's why many DMB fans will follow the band and see a dozen or so shows consecutively, because each night is a different concert. The Dave Matthews Band connected with an entire generation in the mid-nineties and many of those fans will be lifelong followers of the band. Because they never know where they'll wind up.

On this date in 1968, the Beatles' "Hey Jude" reached the top of the charts where it would remain for nine straight weeks. The song was the first single released on the band's new label, Apple, and it was the first #1 single in the history of *Billboard*'s Hot 100 chart that clocked in over seven minutes long. In fact, many musicologists believe the song's success opened up the airwaves for songs that were longer than the previously desired three and a half minutes as, within just a few years, Eric Clapton's "Layla" and Don McLean's "American Pie" were huge hits. But as big and record-setting as "Hey Jude" eventually became, it's important to remember it's a song about a little boy struggling with his parent's divorce. And maybe that's why it was so successful. Unlike so many Beatles' songs of the era, it didn't aspire to change the world or start a revolution. Its goal was simply to cheer a kid up.

By 1968 the Beatles were all grown up. They'd seen and experienced a lifetime in just four short years since exploding on to the international stage. But as famous as they'd become, they had some of the same struggles that any of us do. One of those was the bitter separation and eventual divorce between John Lennon and his first wife Cynthia. Their marriage had produced a son, Julian, who was five when his dad left his mum. Paul McCartney loved the boy. At that point McCartney had no children of his own and he was the doting uncle, visiting Julian and Cynthia constantly and bringing gifts for the young boy. As an adult Julian would look back on his childhood and say he was closer with McCartney than his own father.

On one of those trips to see Julian, after Lennon had left to be with Yoko Ono, McCartney became very sad, envisioning what the boy must be experiencing and what was in store for him. He came up with a ballad he called "Hey Jules," offering advice for the young boy and words of encouragement like taking a sad song and making it better.

He presented the song to his bandmates (after changing "Jules" to "Jude" because, according to McCartney, "It sounded better") with the assurance that there was one line he needed to fix. When Lennon heard the line, "The movement you need is on your shoulder," he told McCartney to leave it. Lennon thought it was the best line in the song. Speaking of Lennon's opinion of "Hey Jude," when he first heard it he thought McCartney had written it as a message to him (specifically the line, "You have found her, now go and get her" which he understandably took as a message about Yoko Ono).

On July 31st, 1968, the Beatles began recording the song. They'd rehearsed it a number of times in their usual Abbey Road studios but on this night they headed to Trident Studios to take advantage of their eight track recorder. McCartney started the recording while drummer Ringo Starr was out of the room which wasn't a problem since the drums don't kick in till just about a minute into the song. McCartney remembers seeing Starr tiptoe by him, take his seat at his drum kit and start perfectly on beat. Happy with the first take, the band wrapped the session then reconvened the next night with a 36 piece orchestra to play the transcendent final four minutes of the song. After the orchestra played their parts the Beatles asked them if they'd clap and sing along the "na na na" parts for double their fee. All but one musician agreed. The Beatles also gathered anyone else they could find to help out and McCartney lead this make-shift chorus in four of the most magical minutes of music that have ever been laid down on tape. As everyone else supported the melodies with those ascending "na na na's" and emphasized the beat with hand-clapping and foot-stomping, McCartney repeated, "Hey Jude" over and over like a man possessed.

Since the Beatles were not touring anymore they came up with a unique way of promoting their new song. They filmed a promotional video in which they lip-synched and mimed playing their instruments along with the track they'd already recorded. For the ending, over 100 people were brought onto the set to sing and clap along. The video was first shown on television in England then offered to other television programs throughout the world and it helped the song become such a monster hit.

If Paul McCartney's goal was to cheer Julian Lennon up, you could argue whether he accomplished it or not. After all, Julian claims he didn't even know the song was about him till a decade or so later. But no one can listen to that incredible coda and not be uplifted and moved to sing and clap along. It's some of the most joyous and uplifting sounds you'll ever hear. If you search the internet, you'll probably find the video the Beatles produced for "Hey Jude" and it's well worth watching today.

### September 29th

On this date in 1986, Run-DMC.'s version of "Walk This Way" was sitting at its peak position, #4 on the *Billboard* Hot 100 chart. The song not only helped catapult hip hop into the mainstream but it also revived the career of a great American rock band that would go on to enjoy an even better second act than their first. That's a pretty big accomplishment for a song the band didn't even want to cover or release as a single.

New York City in the mid to late seventies was the breeding ground for rap music. The genre began in the streets and parks of the city's poorest sections of the Bronx, Brooklyn and Queens. DJs would set up their gear and provide a musical bed by looping break beats that MCs would then rap over. As the genre started gaining popularity some early promoters and producers emerged on the scene, looking to take these artists from the streets to stages and studios.

One of these was Russell Simmons who was born and raised in the Hollis section of Queens. Russell encouraged his younger brother Joseph to get involved and he started out as Kurtis Blow's DJ before taking the microphone himself and beginning to rap. The younger Simmons got his friend Darryl McDaniels rapping as well and the two started showing up at Two-Fifths Park in Hollis that DJs often frequented. One of the most popular DJs at the park was

Jason Mizell and the three quickly became friends. Russell had already given his brother the nickname Run and now he suggested DMC for McDaniels, and Run-D.M.C. for the group. McDaniels would say later, "When we heard that shit we was like, 'We're gonna be ruined!'" But they went with Russell's suggestion because he was already achieving success in the business and promised to help them get a record deal. With Mizell changing his name to Jam Master Jay the names were all set and soon enough Run D.M.C. signed with Profile Records and released their debut single "It's Like That" in 1983. The song did very well, reaching #15 on *Billboard*'s R&B chart, and Profile green-lit an entire album. *Run D.M.C.* was released in March of 1984 and it stands today as a groundbreaking LP in the history of rap music. Not only did the album put Run D.M.C. on the map but it helped introduce new elements of hard rock into rap music. Soon the term "rap rock" was being used for this fusion that Run D.M.C. very much helped spearhead. Their second album, *King of Rock*, continued to not only make Run D.M.C. one of the biggest names in hip hop but also pushed rap rock further into the forefront of pop music.

As Run D.M.C. began preparing material for their third album they decided to work with Rick Rubin. Rubin had founded Def Jam Records along with Russell Simmons and he brought a wealth of music knowledge to the studio. One day Rubin played the Aerosmith album *Toys in the Attic* in the studio and the three members of Run D.M.C. immediately recognized the beginning of "Walk This Way" because it was a common drumbeat for DJs to loop back in the day. But none of them had heard the whole song nor did they know a thing about Aerosmith. They had no clue that the band had been dominant in the rock world for much of the seventies but had struggled of late while various members went through rehab. When Rubin suggested they remake "Walk This Way" McDaniels and Simmons hated the idea. But Mizell seemed open to it so Rubin put him in touch with Aerosmith's guitarist and the song's cowriter Joe Perry to find out if he and Steven Tyler would play on their cover version. Aerosmith's most recent album, *Done with Mirrors*, had underperformed so Perry and Tyler agreed and with their participation lined up, Simmons and McDaniels acquiesced. Although even after the recording was done, the two saw the song as album-filler and not single-worthy. Again it came down to Rubin's persuasion to convince Run D.M.C. that their version of "Walk This Way" could be a big hit. A video was made that pitted Tyler and Perry in a studio right next to Run D.M.C. as the two bands compete for who can be loudest. Eventually Tyler busts through the walls with his mic stand just in time to sing the chorus and soon they're all on a stage together playing for a cheering crowd.

The Run D.M.C. version of "Walk This Way" was released on July 4th, 1986 and started to get frequent plays on both pop radio and rock radio stations. The video became the first rap video to get heavy rotation spins on MTV. "Walk This Way" became the first rap song to break the Top 5 on the *Billboard* Hot 100 chart and Run D.M.C.'s third album, *Raising Hell*, went to #1 on *Billboard*'s R&B album chart (it hit #6 on the *Billboard* 200 chart). Besides the sales success, "Walk This Way" and *Raising Hell* helped put hip hop into the mainstream.

Where many had dismissed it as a passing fad, music journalists now more than ever began writing and talking about rap as a legitimate new genre of music that would have a cultural impact for years to come. And were they ever right! Hip hop soon became a dominant force not only in popular music but in setting tones in fashion and behavior as well. And as if that weren't enough influence for one song, Aerosmith enjoyed an incredible resurgence in popularity after Run-D.M.C. covered "Walk This Way."

In hindsight, turning Aerosmith's original version of "Walk This Way" into a rap song seems like a no-brainer. The song opens with an incredible drum-beat hook that was already a popular choice for those early DJs to loop and for MCs to rap over. Plus, Tyler's delivery in the verses is more like fast patter than singing. There's no huge difference between Tyler's verses in the original and McDaniels and Simmons' rapping in the cover version. Still, it took a ballsy young producer to convince the rappers that it could work, and a rock band down on its luck to agree to participate. Put those elements together with RUN-D.M.C.'s incredible skills and you not only had a huge hit but a song that would propel an entire genre forward.

### September 30th

On this date in 1960, Chubby Checker's version of "The Twist" was finishing its first week atop the *Billboard* Hot 100 chart. It would fall from that spot but then return again in January of 1962 at the height of the "Twist Craze" that it had ignited and that swept across the nation, spawning scores of follow-up songs about the dance. Checker's version was a cover, or as the original songwriter and singer would call it, "a clone." But it was Checker's version that became famous while almost no one even knew there was an original with equal or even greater qualities. And all that can be attributed to Dick Clark. Here's the story:

Songs mentioning twisting have been around for a long time. As far back as the mid-1800s there was a song called "Grapevine Twist." And in the thirties, the famous ragtime musician, Jelly Roll Morton, included the line "Mama, mama, look at sis, she's out on the levee doing the double twist" in his song "Winin' Boy Blues" (although Morton was probably singing about sex and not dancing). But it wasn't till 1959 that someone wrote a song devoted entirely to actually doing the dance. That came from Hank Ballard. He was offstage one day, watching his band the Midnighters warm up and saw them doing a dance that he described, "as if they were trying to put out a cigarette." It looked fun and easy to do, so he figured he'd compose a song about it. Was he, like Jelly Roll Morton, using "the twist" as a euphemism for sex? Given his reputation, probably. When he promises, "We're gonna twisty twisty twisty, till we tear the house down" it can certainly be interpreted either way. Although once he starts bragging about how good his sis is at twisting, the double entendre starts getting a little creepy. Ballard believed "The Twist" could be huge and even start a dance sensation, but his record company didn't share his enthusiasm and they stuck "The Twist" on the B-side of his song "Teardrops On Your Letter." Still, when Hank Ballard and the Midnighters performed live, "The Twist" was a highlight and the whole audience followed the band and did the dance. Word quickly got to Dick Clark, who was always looking for the next big dance craze for his nationally televised show *American Bandstand.*

There are two versions of what happened next. Some say Clark attempted to book Ballard and his band but they were unavailable. It's hard to believe, given how popular *Bandstand* was, that any band wouldn't have reworked their schedule to make an appearance. The other story is that Clark was leery of having Ballard perform on his show because the Midnighters were known for some raunchy songs like "Work with Me Annie" in which Ballard is basically begging for sex and "Sexy Ways" featuring explicit lines like, "Wiggle till your hips get tired and weak."

Whatever the reason, what we do know is that Dick Clark commissioned a new version of "The Twist," one that he could play on his show, oh and if he could throw a bone to a friend with a recording studio, that would be a bonus too (because of recently passed payola laws Clark couldn't personally have a financial stake in the recording). Clark chose a local Philadelphia singer named Ernest Evans because of his ability to imitate many popular singers of the day and he connected Evans with Cameo-Parkway Records with whom Clark had a great relationship. Evans recorded the song doing his best Hank Ballard imitation. Before its release, Dick Clark asked Evans if he wanted to use a stage name. It was Clark's wife who suggested Chubby Checker using Fats Domino as the inspiration (Fats becoming Chubby and Domino turning into Checker). So pretty much everything about Chubby Checker to this point was a facsimile.

When Ballard heard Checker's version he actually thought it was his own. When he realized it wasn't he said, "They cloned it." And he wasn't far off. Listen to both versions, especially the vocals, and you can tell why Ballard was confused and not a little miffed. And though he and his band missed out on the performance rights, and all the fame that comes with performing a hit song on television and on tour, at least, as the song's writer, Ballard enjoyed the publishing money that poured in after the song became a huge hit. After a while, he didn't mind that he'd been cloned.

Chubby Checker performed "The Twist" on American Bandstand multiple times, helping to promote the song and then to feed the fire of this new trend in dancing. Checker would keep the Twist-money flowing in, releasing "Let's Twist Again" which peaked at #8 in 1961 and "Slow Twisting'" which went to #3 in 1962. That same year his version of "The Twist" returned to #1 for two more weeks. Other performers hopped on board releasing scores of songs about twisting like "The Alvin Twist" by the Chipmunks and "The Peppermint Twist" by Joey Dee and the Starlighters (which replaced "The Twist" at #1 in its second stay at the top of the charts). Even Frank Sinatra got involved with his 1962 song "Ev'rybody's Twisting'" (not a career highlight for Ol' Blues Eyes.) Ballard himself took a shot at capitalizing on the craze but his 1962 song "Do You Know

How to Twist" peaked at just #87 on the Hot 100. Apparently everyone knew how to twist by this point and no one was interested in hearing from the guy who'd gotten the whole thing started.

Like all huge sensations in music (and any art), twisting eventually burnt out. But it has also seen periods of revitalization and renewed interest. And every time that happens it is Chubby Checker who is there, re-releasing a new version of "The Twist" like his 1988 rap version with the Fat Boys or just re-recording the original (which he's done plenty of times). Ballard, up until his death in 2003, seemed more content to bask in his reputation as an early rock and roll pioneer. He was voted into the Rock and Roll Hall of Fame in 1990, an honor that hasn't been bestowed upon Chubby Checker despite his rather vocal campaigning to get in. Maybe if there were a Hall of Cloning . . .

# OCTOBER

On this date in 2005, "Gold Digger" by Kanye West and Jamie Foxx was in the middle of a ten week run at the top of the *Billboard* Hot 100 chart. The song had reached #1 in mid-September when it ended Mariah Carey's ten week run of dominance with her smash hit "We Belong Together" and it would remain there till Thanksgiving when Chris Brown's "Run It!" took its place. "Gold Digger" would help launch Kanye West's career as one of the most successful rappers of all time.

Eric Marlon Bishop was born in 1967 in Terrell, Texas. He grew up excelling at two things: music and telling jokes. In college he tried to make it as a standup comic and when he noticed that comedy clubs tended to call up female comics first, he changed his name to Jamie Foxx to fool the clubs (and to honor his comic hero Redd Foxx). His big break came in 1992 when he joined the cast of *Living Color* and then in 1996 when he landed his own sitcom, *The Jamie Foxx Show*. He also appeared in films such as 1992's *Toys* and *On Any Given Sunday* in 1999. In 2003 he sang the chorus on Twista's #1 hit, "Slow Jamz," which was produced by Kanye West.

Kanye Omari West was born ten years after Foxx in Atlanta, Georgia. His parents divorced when he was three and he moved with his mother, a college professor with an English doctorate, to Chicago, Illinois. West showed a propensity for poetry from an early age and by third grade he was writing his own rap songs. He was given a digital sampler soon after and began experimenting with producing techniques like sampling existing songs and looping them to create musical beds to rap over. Much to his mother's chagrin he dropped out of college to pursue a career in music, an event he would immortalize a few years later when he named his debut album *College Dropout*.

West first broke into music as a producer, working with artists Foxy Brown and Nas before landing the opportunity to work with Jay-Z. West produced four tracks on Jay Z's 2001 album *The Blueprint* including the LP's most successful single, "Izzo (H.O.V.A.)" which went to #8 and brought a ton of attention to Kanye West who would soon step out from the producer's console and into the studio to be the main attraction.

West released his debut album in early 2004. It was a commercial as well as a critical success and West quickly began work on a follow-up. One of the songs for that album had actually been rejected by the rapper Shawnna for whom West had written a song called "Gold Digger" using a sample of the Ray Charles' song "I Got a Woman." When Shawnna turned down the song, whose chorus went, "I'm not saying I'm a gold digger but I don't miss with no broke niggas," West rewrote the song from a male's perspective. While West was working on the song, the movie *Ray* was released with Jamie Foxx's Oscar award winning portrayal of Ray Charles. Inspired by the performance, West reached out to Foxx and asked him if he'd sing on the track. Foxx interpolates Charles' original lyrics with one vital change. Where Charles sang of a woman who, "gives me money when I'm in need. Yeah, she's a kind of friend indeed" Foxx sings of a woman who, "takes my money when I'm in need. Yeah, she's a trifling friend indeed." Built around that chorus, West then raps about a woman who has a "baby by Busta" and "used to fuck with Usher" but who he loves anyway. In the second chorus she has another baby, which just means eighteen years of child support, even though, instead of buying toys, "She went to the doctor got lypo with ya money." The entire song is comical and infectious and, with a radio edit that eliminated the "N" word, it is no surprise it shot up the charts and spent ten weeks at #1.

*College Dropout* had announced to the world that there was a new rapper to pay attention to. With the success of "Gold Digger," and West's second album, *Late Registration*, Kanye West was now one of the biggest names in music. And he knew it. If West is criticized for one thing, it's his over-exaggerated feeling of self-worth. He has said: "I am the number one human being in music. That means any person that's living or breathing is number two," and, "When you're the absolute best, you get hated on the most," and, "I am Warhol. . . I am Shakespeare in the flesh." Although he's not above poking fun at that ego either. He once said, "My greatest pain in life is that I will never be able to see myself perform live," and in 2016's "I Love Kanye" he rapped, "I love you like Kanye loves Kanye."

Perhaps the most Kanye-West moment of all time came when he interrupted Taylor Swift's acceptance speech for Best Video at MTV's *VMAs* in 2009, saying, "Yo, Taylor, I'm really happy for you, I'ma let you finish, but Beyoncé had one of the best videos of all time!" Or maybe it's when he went off script during the Hurricane Katrina telethon and said, "George Bush doesn't care about black people," while a stunned Mike Myers could just stare at the cameras. Both are pop culture moments that are often replayed and rehashed and they exemplify West and his outspoken and brash personality. He's forged an incredibly successful career as a rapper, producer, fashion designer and entrepreneur and he and his wife Kim Kardashian are one of the most famous couples in the world (especially if paparazzi exposure counts as criteria for fame). It's worth digging up "Gold Digger" today and enjoying one of West's most recognizable and commercially accessible songs.

## October 2nd

On this date in 1971, Rod Stewart's "Maggie May" began an incredible five week run at #1 on the *Billboard* Hot 100 chart. The song also helped Stewart's LP, *Every Picture Tells a Story*, make it to the top of the album chart and both would ultimately help launch Stewart's worldwide stardom. Not bad for a song that the record company didn't even want included on the album and only released initially as a B-side.

Roderick David Stewart was born in London in 1945. He loved music as a child and began busking (singing on the streets for tips) as a teenager. He also loved attending live music shows and, when he was just sixteen, he snuck into the Beaulieu Jazz Festival where he not only enjoyed the music, but also had his first sexual experience. In his autobiography he described the episode: "On a secluded patch of grass, I lost my not-remotely-prized virginity with an older (and larger) woman who'd come on to me very strongly in the beer tent. How much older, I can't tell you - but old enough to be highly disappointed by the brevity of the experience."

Stewart's big break came just a few years later. He'd gone to see Long John Baldry perform and on the way home he was waiting for a train when he started playing his harmonica to pass the time. Unbeknownst to Stewart, Baldry was waiting at the same station. When he overheard Stewart's playing he immediately asked him to sit in with his band. When Baldry discovered that Stewart could not only sing, but that he had very unique, raspy voice, he made him an official band member. Rod Stewart was still a teenager but he was able to quit his day job as a gravedigger and focus entirely on music. He had success early on in the music industry both in groups like the Jeff Beck Group and Faces and as a solo artist. By the late sixties he found himself contributing songs for Faces and trying to come up with material for himself so he was admittedly tapped for topics.

At some point he thought back to that experience at the jazz festival and decided to write a song about it. The lyrics are semi-graphic, describing their sex as wrecking the bed and the woman as wearing him out and though she's stolen his heart, Stewart vows to go back home "one of these days." Whether he didn't want to use the woman's real name or he didn't remember it is unclear but he chose Maggie May which is an obvious play on the old traditional English folk song about a prostitute called Maggie Mae.

Working on the song in the studio, guitarist Martin Quittenton came up with the chords and was added as the song's cowriter. Mandolin player Ray Jackson, who was in the studio to help on a different song they were working on ("Mandolin Wind") also contributed to the song but was not added as a songwriter. To add insult to injury he's not even mentioned on the album. The liner notes read: "The mandolin was played by the mandolin player in Lindisfarne. The name slips my mind."

When Stewart submitted his third solo album *Every Picture Tells a Story*, Mercury, his record company didn't like "Maggie May." Stewart insisted he had nothing else and that the song would have to be included. They acquiesced, then released it as the B-side to the album's lead single "Reason to Believe" in July of 1971. The single did not perform well but then some radio DJs started flipping the disc over and playing "Maggie May" and getting requests for it. Mercury re-released the single with Stewart's story of lost virginity as the A-side. Suddenly the song began climbing the charts and on this date it became Stewart's first U.S. #1. *Every Picture Tells a Story* also hit #1 on the the U.K. and U.S. album chart. Rod Stewart, who was already well known in England but virtually unknown in the States, was now a huge name on both sides of the pond. He was a consistent presence on the charts and on radio throughout the seventies and even into the eighties, often touching on similar themes as "Maggie May" and playing off his image as a Lothario. He has scored sixteen Top 10 singles and four #1s and sold over 100 million records worldwide in an over-fifty-year career. The real Maggie May may have been disappointed by the brevity of their sexual encounter, but Stewart has proved he can last long enough when it comes to remaining a star.

## October 3rd

On this date in 1992, one of the clearest examples of "career suicide" took place when Sinead O'Connor tore up a picture of the pope on *Saturday Night Live*. O'Connor had been riding high for the last few years with commercial and critical success, yet in one instant, she destroyed her career and would never come close to the popularity she was enjoying at the time. Yet years later, as case after case came out against Catholic priests in Ireland and around the world who had abused children, O'Connor can at least claim to have had a point. Little solace though for her derailed career.

Sinead O'Connor's first LP, *The Lion and The Cobra*, was released in 1987 and it established her as an artist to watch. Her voice is both powerful and ethereal which comes across well on the album's lone single "Mandinka" which received a lot of play on college radio stations as well as spins on MTV. Her follow-up album, 1990's *I Do Not Want What I Haven't Got* turned her from an underground sensation to an international star. The album's lead single, the Prince-penned "Nothing Compares 2 U" spent six weeks at #1 in the spring of 1990 and the album had a similar run on the *Billboard* 200. She also received great reviews for her work during Roger Water's The Wall - Live in Berlin concert (at which she sings a haunting version of "Mother") and for her contribution to the Elton John/Bernie Taupin tribute album *Two Rooms* (her version of "Sacrifice" is a highlight of that compilation.) By 1992, the music world was excited to see what O'Connor would do next.

But no one was prepared for her appearance on *Saturday Night Live*.

The first song O'Connor performed that night was "Success Has Made a Failure of Our Home," a track from her recently released third album, *Am I Not Your Girl?* She returned later in the show and performed a powerful a cappella rendition of Bob Marley's "War" staring intensely at the camera. She changed some lyrics in the song to include a reference to child abuse. In rehearsal she ended the song by holding up a picture of a refugee child but live, she ended by singing the lyric "Victory of good over evil" and as she sang "evil" she held up a picture of the very popular current pope, John Paul II. As the word "evil" ended she tore the photo three times while saying, "Fight the real enemy." She then tossed the pieces at the camera, never breaking her steely stare.

*Saturday Night Live*'s producer Lorne Michaels made the immediate decision not to flash on the applause signs and so the audience, stunned as it was, remained silent. The show cut to a lower angle shot of O'Connor who begins to remove her ear pieces before the final cutaway to commercial. Four seconds of dead silence may not seem like much but on television it can seem like an hour. NBC did not edit the performance out of the West coast tape-delayed broadcast that night, but future reruns have used the footage from the rehearsal.

NBC received thousands of protesting phone calls in the following days. The following week, *SNL*'s guest host, Joe Pesci, began the show by holding up the picture of the pope taped back together, which received thunderous applause. Madonna, who spoofed the incident in her next *SNL* appearance by holding up a picture of Joey Buttafuoco, saying, "Fight the real enemy," before tearing it up, would come out publicly against O'Connor. She told one interviewer, "I think there is a better way to present her ideas rather than ripping up an image that means a lot to other people." It was surprising to many that Madonna, who has often been the provocateur in her career, wouldn't support someone else's outrageousness.

Two weeks after the show, O'Connor was scheduled to perform "I Believe in You" at the Bob Dylan 30th Anniversary tribute concert at New York's Madison Square Garden. When she walked out on stage she was met with a very vocal, yet mixed, reaction. The cheers and boos would not subside. Kris Kristofferson who was part of the band that night leaned over and said, "Don't let the bastards get you down," to which O'Connor replied, "I'm not down." When the crowd refused to let up, O'Connor signaled for the band to stop playing and she launched into an improvised, and shouted, version of "War." She then left the stage and Kristofferson followed her and hugged her while she cried.

*Am I Not Your Girl?* was a curious follow-up to *I Do Not Want What I Haven't Got.* It's a collection of cover versions of old jazz standards and show tunes. It sold over a million copies (which often happens to the follow-up of a hugely successful album) but failed to produce any hits or attract radio play. Her next album, *Universal Mother*, continued this downward trend and O'Connor's career, commercially at least, has never come close to where it was before her *Saturday Night Live* appearance. Yet, in the decades that followed, as her popularity waned, the instances of abuse in the Catholic Church, both in Ireland and in the United States, began to emerge. In 2009, the Ireland Child Abuse Commission released a lengthy report detailing thousands of cases of emotional, physical and sexual abuse at the hands of clergy as well as church leaders. None of these allegations have ever included Pope John Paul II so one could argue that Sinead O'Connor's protest was poorly aimed, but if she meant to bring attention to this atrocity, even at the cost of her own career, she accomplished that goal.

On this date in 1969, Creedence Clearwater Revival began a four week run at #1 on the *Billboard* 200 chart with their third LP, *Green River*. Creedence has never had a #1 song, a frustrating five of their singles have peaked at #2 on the pop chart, yet *Green River* and their 1970 album *Cosmo's Factory* both topped the album chart. 1969 was a breakthrough year for CCR with two successful albums and an appearance at Woodstock.

The band that would eventually become Creedence Clearwater Revival began as a trio featuring John Fogerty, Doug Clifford and Stu Cook, who all attended the same junior high school in El Cerrito, California. They performed under the name the Blue Jackets for awhile till they were signed to a record contract at a small label called Fantasy Records where they changed their name to the Golliwogs. John's brother Tom joined the band around this time, rounding out the lineup. In 1967 Fantasy Records was bought by Saul Zaentz who loved the band but understandably hated their name. After much debate they came up with a new name by combining three things. First, Tom Fogerty had a friend named Credence so the band started there, adding an "e" to the first name so it would resemble the word "creed." There was also a popular television commercial at the time for Olympia Beer that promoted its "clear water" so they borrowed that. And they capped it all off with the word "revival" to show their commitment to the band. Fantasy released their eponymous debut album in July of 1968. It was their cover of the decades-old rockabilly song, "Suzie Q" that first got CCR national attention, with the single peaking at #11 in November of 1968. In January of 1969 the band released their second album, *Bayou Country*, which earned them even more fame. "Proud Mary," the lone single from *Bayou Country* made it all the way to #2 in March of 1969. The band was poised for a breakout.

Their third album, *Green River*, was released in August of 1969, two weeks before their appearance at Woodstock. "Bad Moon Rising," the lead single off the album, had already peaked at this point (again, at #2) and the title track was already beginning its ascent up the pop chart (it too would peak at #2).

"Bad Moon Rising" went on to become one of CCR's signature songs. John Fogerty, who wrote the song, says he was inspired by the movie *The Devil and Daniel Webster*, specifically a scene where a hurricane wipes out a town. He penned the words, "I feel the hurricane blowing. I hope you're quite prepared to die" and he was off and running. Despite the song's apocalyptic message he gave it an upbeat tempo. "Bad Moon Rising" also contains one of the most famous misheard lyrics in all of rock music. When Fogerty sings, "There's a bad moon on the rise," many listeners hear, and often sing back, "There's a bathroom on the right." Fogerty even has fun with this in concert sometimes, pointing to the restrooms as he sings the line.

Creedence would release four more albums in the next three years, and get two more singles ("Travelin' Band" and "Looking Out My Back Door") all the way to, you guessed it, #2. Internal strife and friction would eventually lead to the band's demise with John Fogerty going on to a very successful solo career. There have been some partial reunions through the years and one chance for the four original members to play together (at Tom's wedding) but mostly lawsuits and squabbling have kept them apart. When Tom Fogerty died in 1990 he buried any chance that the original four would come together for a tour. Three years later when CCR was inducted into the Rock and Roll Hall of Fame things were so contentious that John refused to be on the same stage with Cook and Clifford. Tom Fogerty's widow arrived with an urn of her husband's ashes which she thought she'd bring to the stage when the band was introduced, only to be left at her seat. Fogerty, being the famous one, was able to keep the pair (and the urn) from appearing that night as John gave the acceptance speech and then performed with an All Star band. Rarely have the lyrics to a band's biggest song been more prescient: "I see trouble on the way."

## October 5th

On this date in 1961, Bobby Vee's "Take Good Care of My Baby" was ending its three week stay at the top of the *Billboard* Hot 100 chart. Vee had gotten his start in music a few years earlier on one of the darkest days in the industry, and now here he was at #1. The story is one for the ages, with triumph literally rising from the ashes of tragedy.

Bobby Vee was born Robert Velline in April of 1943. He fell in love with rock and roll the moment he heard it coming through his transistor radio while growing up in Fargo, North Dakota. He loved everything he heard but especially Buddy Holly. He loved Holly's sound so much that in high school he even formed a group to play some of Holly's music (as well as some other early rock and roll songs). So it was understandable that he and his friends were excited beyond belief when it was announced that the "Winter Dance Party" tour, which featured Holly along with Dion, the Big Bopper and Ritchie Valens, would be making a stop in Fargo. Velline and his friends all bought tickets and anxiously awaited that day, February 3rd, 1959, to arrive.

It was with shock and grief that Fargo (and the rest of the world) woke up that morning to the news of a plane crash. Along with the pilot, Roger Peterson, three musicians were all killed: Holly, Valens and the Big Bopper. The rock and roll world was devastated but someone made the decision that the show must go on. A Fargo radio station put out a call for local musicians to perform that night along with Dion, who hadn't been on the ill-fated flight, because, according to rock and roll legend, he was too cheap to kick in for it.

The fifteen year old Velline and his band volunteered. They didn't even have a name yet so they made up the name the Shadows (which is pretty dark considering the circumstances). They went from practicing Buddy Holly songs in hopes of landing some school dances to literally taking his place at a show the day he died. It was as unfortunate yet fortuitous beginning of a career as anyone could imagine.

After the show, inspired by his ability to mimic Holly's style, he wrote and recorded a song called "Suzie Baby" which sounds like a slowed down version of Holly's "Peggy Sue."

Vee would spend the next few years on the road. At one point his band included a musician who was going by the name Elston Gunnn. Gunnn had been born Robert Allen Zimmerman. He'd leave Vee's band before long and change his name yet again, this time to Bob Dylan, before embarking on a solo career (you may have heard of him).

"Take Good Care of My Baby" was written by the legendary songwriting team of Carole King and Gerry Goffin before they became so legendary. They'd just recently had their first big hit when the Shirelles' version of "Will You Still Love Me Tomorrow" went to #1. They originally offered "Take Good Care of My Baby" to Dion. He gave it a listen but passed on it, choosing instead to record a song he'd just written called "Runaround Sue" (which hit #1 just two weeks after "Take Good Care" vacated the spot). After Dion passed, the song made its way to Bobby Vee who, with a young Don Kirshner producing, recorded and released the song immediately. Ten days after King and Goffin had signed over the song to Bobby Vee, they heard it on the radio.

Though he never made it back to the top of the charts, Bobby Vee enjoyed a long and successful career, releasing music throughout the sixties and repackaging his old hits for compilations into the seventies. He toured regularly in the following decades, usually as part of an oldies tour which featured other rock and roll legends, sometimes, no doubt, even Dion. No matter how many thousands of shows he performed though, he never could or would forget that first one. For the rest of the world it was the "Day the Music Died" yet for Robert Velline it was the beginning of a career on stage.

### October 6th

On this date in 1982, a previously unknown singer and dancer using just the one name Madonna, released her first single, "Everybody." While the song failed to crack *Billboard*'s Hot 100 chart, it did do well on the dance chart, peaking at #3 on *Billboard*'s Hot Dance/Club Play Chart. One of the greatest careers in pop music had officially begun.

Madonna Louise Ciccone was born in 1958 in Bay City Michigan. When she was just five years old she lost her mother to breast cancer. She became terrified that her father would be taken from her too and she often couldn't sleep unless he was nearby. When she was eight her father remarried and Madonna admits to resenting him for this for decades and for developing a rebellious attitude thereafter. Rebellious or not, Madonna was a straight A student and a cheerleader. She received a dance scholarship after high school and considered a career as a dancer. But one year into college she dropped out and moved to New York City determined to make it in music. It was the first time she'd ever been on a plane or in a taxi. She was nineteen years old and had $35 to her name.

Madonna found work as a backup dancer fairly soon, landing a spot on "Born to Be Alive" singer Patrick Hernandez's 1979 world tour. On that tour she met and started dating musician Dan Gilroy. When the tour ended they formed a band called Breakfast Club together. She left Breakfast Club to form Emmy, a band with another boyfriend, Stephen Bray. Unhappy with band work, Madonna started writing her own music with an eye towards a solo career. She recorded three of her own songs, "Everybody" , "Ain't No Big Deal" and "Burning Up" and started approaching club DJs to see if they'd play her music. The first DJ to play a Madonna song in public was Mark Kamins at New York's Danceteria. He played "Everybody" and when the song got a great reaction on his dance floor he told Madonna he'd get her a record deal if she allowed him to produce her. Kamins approached Chris Blackwell who owned Island Records but he passed. Then he talked to Sire Records A&R man Michael Rosenblatt who not only loved Madonna's sound but her attitude as well. Rosenblatt would say later that Madonna, "will do anything to be a star, and that's exactly what I look for in an artist: total cooperation."

Sire offered Madonna a $5,000 advance and she signed a contract to release two singles (not exactly a long term commitment on Sire's part). By the time they went into the studio to record "Everybody," Madonna and Mark Kamins were romantically involved. Sire initially thought about marketing Madonna mysteriously, perhaps in hopes that some would think she was a black artist. To this end the cover for "Everybody" did not feature a picture of her (a rarity for a new artist) but rather a collage of a New York city street scene. This plan went out the window quickly though when Madonna insisted on a video for "Everybody." She understood the power of MTV (which had only been on air about a year by this point) and saw videos as taking the place of touring. She was able to procure a $1500 budget from Sire, about a tenth of what most artists were spending at the time, and shot a performance video featuring her and some back-up dancers. They sent the video to clubs around the country that were using videos and there was no doubt that this visual exposure helped the song in the nightclubs.

Though "Everybody" and it's follow-up single "Burning Up" were not commercially successful, they did impress Sire enough that they extended her first record deal to include a full album. Madonna went into the studio to record more material for her debut and chose to work with yet another current boyfriend, John "Jellybean" Benitez. It was Benitez who recommended a song called "Holiday" for Madonna to record and it was "Holiday" (Madonna's third single) that broke her nationally. That song would make it to #16 on the pop chart and suddenly everybody knew this young dancer/singer from the Midwest.

Madonna has gone on to unprecedented levels of success in the music industry, having sold over 300 million records and well over a billion dollars in concerts tickets throughout her career. It's an amazing thing to think back to her flight to New York City with $35 in her pocket and a head full of dreams. Could she have envisioned that much success? Knowing Madonna's ambition, probably.

## October 7ᵗʰ

On this date in 2006, Justin Timberlake's "Sexyback" began its fifth consecutive week atop the *Billboard* Hot 100 chart. It would last two more weeks at #1, giving Timberlake's new LP, *FutureSex/LoveSounds*, the type of promotion any artist hopes for when they release a lead single. *FutureSex/LoveSounds* would spend two weeks at the top of the album chart, establishing Timberlake as one of the premier pop artists of the time.

Justin Randall Timberlake was born in 1981 in Memphis, Tennessee. He was a natural performer as a child, singing country and gospel before the age of ten. When he was eleven he appeared on *Star Search* and then a year later landed a spot on *The Mickey Mouse Club* where his castmates included Ryan Gosling, Brittany Spears, Christina Aguilera and future bandmate JC Chasez. After his stint with Disney he was recruited by boy band impresario Lou Pearlman who was looking to duplicate the success he'd had putting the Backstreet Boys together and eventually formed NSYNC in 1995. NSYNC's eponymous debut album sold eleven million copies in the halcyon pop craze of the late nineties and their next albums established them as one of the most successful boy bands of the era.

In 2002 NSYNC took a hiatus and Timberlake released his debut solo album, *Justified*. The LP went to #2 on the album chart and though it failed to produce a #1 single, with three Top Twenty hits ("Like I Love You" , "Cry Me a River" and "Rock Your Body") it established Timberlake as an artist to watch.

Timberlake would take his time with a follow-up but he certainly didn't sit around doing nothing. He proved to the world he is a multi-talented artist by acting in movies and making comedic appearances on *Saturday Night Live* and *The Tonight Show Starring Jimmy Fallon*. By 2005 he was ready to work on a second solo record.

"Sexyback" began as a song called "Be Gone with It." Timberlake knew the song needed something catchier and as he worked on the lyrics he came up with the "sexy back" concept and added it to the song. The rest of the lyrics are vague and leave some things open to interpretation. He mentions shackles and slavery so many took the song as a call for S&M. While the video is certainly sexual there are no *50 Shades of Grey* type imagery.

As for the inspiration for the music, Timberlake has said he envisioned David Bowie singing a James Brown song. This probably explains the Brown-esque shout-outs like, "Take it to the bridge," and, "Take it to the chorus." Timberlake said he listened to Bowie's "Rebel Rebel" about fifteen times before writing the song. He and producers Timbaland and Nate Hills used a lot of unique concepts in the recording of "Sexyback," over-modulating Timberlake's vocals and using synthesizer sounds that were more common in Electronic Dance Music, which at the time was still an underground musical genre. In fact, some would argue that "Sexyback" helped popularize EDM and bring it into the mainstream. The drum track also has a very disco sounding, four-on-the-floor, feel to it. Timberlake has called the whole song, "an experiment gone right."

Right, indeed. While his record company wanted to release "My Love" as a lead single, Timberlake had a hunch that "Sexyback" was the better call. That's a disagreement that a newer artist will often lose but with Timberlake's reputation he won and proved to be prescient (although in his label's defense, "My Love" also hit #1, albeit for just three weeks). Besides the chart success, "Sexyback" would help Timberlake earn a Grammy and a People's Choice Award and MTV named him Male Artist of the Year for 2006. Whatever exactly he's singing about, the world loved it.

**October 8th**

On this date in 1985, Dire Straits' "Money for Nothing" was nearing the end of its 3 week stay at #1. The song would go on to become the band's most successful single and indeed their only chart-topper to date. Not bad for a song inspired by an overheard conversation.

Dire Straits was formed in London, England in the late seventies. They released their first album in 1978 and very quickly found an avid rock audience with songs like "Sultans of Swing" and "Romeo and Juliet."

Mark Knopfler was the main lyricist, lead guitarist and singer for the band so it fell on him to come up with material every time the band recorded. At some point in the mid-eighties, Knopfler found himself in a hardware store in New York City. He was standing in front of a wall of televisions that were tuned to the latest craze: MTV. He overheard a guy who worked in the store commenting on some of the videos, putting down the music and the musicians in some very non-politically-correct terms. Knopfler got a kick out of what he was hearing and didn't want to forget anything so he borrowed a pen from someone else at the store and jotted down some notes, leaning on a kitchen counter display. He wrote down things he'd overheard like, "What are those, Hawaiian noises?" and, "That ain't working." Knopfler then created a few of his own lines in the same vein and before he left the store he had most of "Money for Nothing" written.

Knopfler had recently reached out to MTV asking how his band could get on their channel. He was told, "Create a hit song and make a great video." Simple enough. With his hardware store scribblings he felt he had the makings of a great song so he sought the help of two people he knew in the industry who'd already had MTV success. First he talked to Billy Gibbons of ZZ Top and asked him for advice on getting his signature fuzz tone on his guitar. Gibbons would comment later, "He didn't do a half-bad job, considering that I didn't tell him a thing." Then he reached out to Sting and asked him to add something to the song. The ex-Police lead singer sang the a cappella opening, "I want my MTV," to the tune of his Police hit "Don't Stand So Close to Me." For his troubles, Sting was given a co-writing credit.

Once Knopfler felt he had a hit song, he set out to make a great video. He decided to use some cutting edge (for the time) computer animation using an early program called PaintBox. The characters in the video were initially supposed to have more details but when the budget for the video ran out they went with what they had. Looking at it today the graphics are incredibly rudimentary and any kid with the right app could make something more realistic on their phone or tablet, but for the time, the "Money For Nothing" video was considered very advanced and it helped Knopfler accomplish his goal of getting played on MTV.

Mark Knopfler has had to answer for some of the language he used in "Money for Nothing." His explanation that he was singing in the first person of this hardware store worker and using language he either directly overheard or could picture that guy saying hasn't always been enough to assuage every critic. Sometimes when he sings the song live he'll change the word "faggot" to "queenie" simply to avoid more controversy. But controversy or not, "Money for Nothing" went on to be Dire Straits' most commercially successful song. It also earned the band a Grammy and an MTV Video award plus it helped catapult their 1985 LP, *Brothers in Arms,* to one of the world's bestselling albums, having moved over 30 million copies. Not bad for a little eavesdropping.

### October 9th

On this date in 1965, the Beatles started a four week run at the top of the pop chart with their somber ballad, "Yesterday." The melody had come to Paul McCartney a year earlier in a dream but he was so afraid he'd heard it elsewhere he sat on it for months before even writing lyrics to it. And the song was such a departure from the Fab Four's early sound that the band refused to have the single released in England fearing it would derail their fame. Yet half a century later, "Yesterday" is one of the most covered songs of all time.

Sometime in 1964, Paul McCartney awoke from a dream at his girlfriend Jane Asher's apartment in London with a plaintive melody in his head. He sat down at the piano and played it a few times so he wouldn't forget it. But the tune was so recognizable to him he thought sure he must have heard it somewhere else. For weeks he'd hum it to anyone who would listen and ask them if they recognized it. When no one could identify it, he finally decided it was an original and started filling in lyrics to match the melody.

Since their earliest days of songwriting, McCartney and John Lennon would often use lyrical "place holders" in a song just to determine the number of syllables and the cadence that a specific line would need. They'd then go back and fill in better words. McCartney's first place holder lyrics for his work-in-progress went: "Scrambled eggs, oh my baby how I love your legs. But not as much as I love scrambled eggs." McCartney then started taking every opportunity he could find to work up the song. He'd sit at a piano any chance he got and sing it and work on the lyrics. He (or Lennon, there are differing accounts) came up with the idea of starting lines with one, three syllable word. "Yesterday" and "suddenly" became catalysts into the lyrics and McCartney admits that the rhyming of day with stay and away was simplistic. The song finally came together and none-too-soon as his bandmates had grown tired of hearing it incessantly. Then, because the ballad didn't really fit the rock and roll image the Beatles had forged for themselves, McCartney offered the song to fellow London singer Chris Farlowe who turned it down for the same reason: it was too soft.

Finally on June 14th, 1965, just a few days before his 23rd birthday, Paul McCartney recorded "Yesterday." The band had just wrapped up "I'm Down" at Abbey Road Studios and while the other three headed out for a post-recording-session pint, McCartney stayed around with producer George Martin to record the song. It was the first time a Beatles' song had ever been recorded by just one member of the band.

McCartney recorded two takes, playing acoustic guitar and singing with a microphone pointed at the guitar and another for his vocals. In the first take he sang two lines out of order and can then be heard suppressing a laugh about it. He nailed his second shot at the song. Three days later McCartney added some additional vocal work and a string quartet was brought in to enhance the melody. Years later when the Beatles' *Love* project got underway, in which they remixed some of their hits, this rudimentary recording method became an issue because there exists no clean track of just McCartney's vocals or just his guitar. It's another indication that the band, including McCartney himself, didn't exactly see "Yesterday" as an important song or they would have recorded it properly.

This became even more evident when the song was suggested as a single. The Beatles objected, fearing the song, which had an Adult-Contemporary feel to it, would turn off their younger fans. There was even discussion of releasing the song as a Paul McCartney solo, but Brian Epstein, the band's manager, squashed that idea. It's a sign of how powerful the band was in England (and not yet in the States) because they were able to convince Parlophone (their U.K. label) not to release it yet Capitol, which distributed them in the U.S., went right ahead.

Backed with "Act Naturally," "Yesterday" was released on September 13th, 1965 and quickly moved up the charts. On this date in 1965 the song became the Beatles' fifth consecutive #1 single. It spent four weeks at #1 and sold a million copies in its first five weeks.

It is sometimes claimed that "Yesterday" is the most covered song in the history of recorded music. Indeed there are over 3,000 commercially released versions of the songs (including an insufferable number of Muzak versions). Other songs have made similar claims though, most notably George Gershwin's "Summertime" which has ten times that number of versions. Be that as it may, it sometimes seems the only artist who hasn't taken a crack at releasing a version of "Yesterday" is Chris Farlowe. He must still think the song is too soft.

## October 10th

On this date in 1969, the Archies' "Sugar, Sugar" was enjoying a four week run at #1 on the *Billboard* Hot 100 chart. The song, which had knocked the Rolling Stones' "Honky Tonk Women" from the top of the charts on September 20th and would go on to become the best-selling single of the year, had been rejected by one made-up TV show band only to be turned into a hit by another made-up TV show band.

Don Kirshner, co-founder and co-owner of the music publishing company Aldon Music since 1958, had been hired in 1965 by the producers of the new television show *The Monkees* to find songs with commercial potential for their on-screen band to sing. He met his goal with incredible success. The first two songs he found for the band, "Last Train to Clarksville" and "I'm a Believer" both topped the charts. The first two albums he helped them with, *The Monkees* and *More of the Monkees*, also reached #1 on the *Billboard* album chart. The formula was perfect: Kirshner would find a song with hit potential, a studio band would produce the backing track for the actors on the show to sing over, the song would debut on the show, then the single would climb the charts. It seemed like a can't-miss equation for years to the come. Till the train was derailed.

Problems arose when the members of the band insisted on having a say in the music that was being released under their name. At first the show's producers compromised by letting the actors (who also had musical backgrounds) perform the songs. This appeased the Monkees for a bit but then they wanted to also use songs they'd written. The conflict came to a head one day with an argument between the band members and Kirshner and his lawyer over whether the band should record a song Kirshner presented called "Sugar, Sugar." At one point Monkee Michael Nesmith punched a hole in the wall and screamed, "That could have been your face!" Eventually the show's producers sided with the band and Kirshner was shown the door.

Undeterred, but obviously educated on the synergistic powerhouse a television show with hit music can be, Kirshner got involved with the upcoming cartoon series *The Archies*. He assembled the band that would record the music for the show and chose the songs they'd record. As his nickname the "Man with the Golden Ear" would imply, he was once again successful. After two moderate hits,

"Bang-Shang-A-Lang" and "Feelin' So Good (S.K.O.O.B.Y-D.O.O.) he had them record the song the Monkees had fought so hard not to: "Sugar, Sugar."

Just like his hits for the Monkees, "Sugar, Sugar" created a promotional loop in which all parties benefited. The song was played on the television show which encouraged viewers to go buy the single. The song was played on the radio which reminded listeners to tune in to the Saturday morning cartoon. The promotion took one more successful step when Post struck a deal to place the single on the back of their Super Sugar Crisp cereal boxes.

Besides being the most successful song of 1969, beating out other chart-toppers like the Beatles' "Get Back", "Aquarius/Let the Sunshine In" by the 5th Dimension and Zager and Evans' "In the Year 2525," "Sugar, Sugar" is often seen as the signature song of what became a sub-genre of pop called "bubblegum music." The genre was given that name because of its similarities to bubblegum: both are popular with teens and pre-teens, they are sweet and easy to chew but offer little substance. Other bubblegum pop songs include the Ohio Express' "Yummy Yummy Yummy" and "Simon Says" by the 1910 Fruitgum Company.

It's an interesting dichotomy that as music got more and more serious, this offshoot of light and fluffy songs became more prevalent on air and on the charts. Perhaps it's even a survivalist thing for music lovers who want to avoid everything they hear being heavy and thought-provoking. Sometimes a little pop inaneness isn't so bad. For every song aimed at changing the world, maybe it's important to have a ditty that's about nothing. The same year the Beatles were asking everyone to come together and Simon and Garfunkel were singing about the whores on seventh avenue, a song with no deeper message than how sweet it is to kiss a girl ruled the charts for a month. Interpret that however you wish but it's doubtful you can listen to the opening line of "Sugar, Sugar" and not smile. At least a little. And at the end of the day, isn't that what music is all about?

### October 11th

On this date in 1975, a brand new sketch comedy show called *NBC's Saturday Night* aired on WNBC. Despite tepid ratings early on, and a deluge of complaint letters and phone calls from viewers who were offended (and apparently didn't know they could just change the channel) NBC stuck with the program. All these decades later, and after a name change to *Saturday Night Live*, it is a decision that has paid off handsomely for the Peacock Network as well as the show's creator Lorne Michaels. And since this is a book about music and not television shows it should be mentioned that *SNL* has provided the musical world with countless unforgettable moments.

Weekend programming has always been an after-thought for television networks. There are fewer adult viewers on the weekends so Saturday and Sunday nights are often filled with re-runs, second class shows or old movies.

For years that's how NBC approached their Saturday nights. For about a decade, from 1965 on, the network simply replayed old *Tonight Show* episodes. But in 1975 Johnny Carson requested they stop this. He wanted to start taking some more nights off and use his own re-runs to fill the nights he wasn't live. The network approached the creators of *National Lampoon,* a highly successful humor magazine, about producing a show to fill their late Saturday night time slot. When they passed, the network approached comedy writer Lorne Michaels who jumped at the opportunity. Michaels then raided *National Lampoon*'s staff, poaching some of their writers as well as John Belushi, Chevy Chase, Gilda Radner and Bill Murray who had been a part of their off-Broadway shows *Lemmings* and *The National Lampoon Show.* At the time, ABC had a show called *Saturday Night Live* with Howard Cosell so Michaels called his new offering *NBC's Saturday Night.* From day one Michaels' vision was simple: a variety comedy show that would combine live sketches with pre-taped bits and musical performances but with a edginess not seen before in television comedy shows.

The very first show, which aired on this date in 1975, featured George Carlin as guest host and Billy Preston and Janis Ian as musical guests. In just their second week, *SNL* was already making news in the music world. With Paul Simon as the host and Art Garfunkel as one of the musical guests, a reunion was inevitable. And sure enough after a little good natured ribbing from Simon, who said to his one-time partner, "So you've come crawling back," the two performed "The Boxer" and "Scarborough Fair." Paul Simon, who is a close friend of Lorne Michaels, has been at the center of many a magical musical moment on the show, perhaps most famously his delivery of "Still Crazy After All These Years" while wearing a turkey suit (it was their Thanksgiving episode, after all). Though he only got a few bars into the song before stopping, it's an early moment in the show's history that would help define their ethos: nothing was too over the top or outrageous. Certainly not for that time slot.

Those first few years were not easy for the show. NBC was getting overwhelmed with complaints from offended viewers and ratings were poor. More than once the network came *this close* to taking the show off the air but with nothing worthwhile to take its place, they hung in there. And by 1977, the ratings were not only improving but the reputation around the show was as well. Pretty soon *SNL* became the "cool kids club," a show you had to watch or else miss out on what everyone would be talking about Monday morning. Catchphrases like, "You look MAH-velous," and, "Isn't that special?" and, "Schwing!" entered the lexicon and recurring characters like Mr. Bill and Father Guido Sarducci made it worth waiting up on Saturday nights.

And of course, there were always the musical guests, many of whom saved their most outrageous moments for *SNL.* Google "Saturday Night Live Music" and you'll find scores of lists from experts who opine about the most memorable musical moments from the show's history. And if you've watched over the years you probably have your own favorites. If you go back far enough, maybe your list includes Elvis Costello, who in 1977 started "Less Than Zero," the song he'd told the show he would perform, only to stop it moments in before saying, "Sorry ladies and gentlemen, there's no reason to do this song here," before launching into "Radio Radio" a song that castigates corporate broadcasting. It's a move that prompted Lorne Michaels to give him the finger from side stage and then ban Costello from his show. Or maybe you remember when Mick Jagger licked Ron Wood's lip during the Stones' 1978 performance on the show. Or in 1981 when a 22 year old Prince danced around the stage in a trench coat and bikini bottoms while playing a wild rendition of "Partyup." Or maybe your memories are more recent and include Mariah Carey, who in 1990 was just bursting on the scene, performing an amazing version of "Visions of Love." Or a year later when Nirvana tore up that same stage with "Smells Like Teen Spirit." There have been awkward moments as well (like when the tape stopped during an Ashlee Simpson performance and showed the world she was lip syncing) and controversial ones too (no more so than Sinead O'Connor tearing up the picture of the pope) but mostly there have been amazing and unforgettable performances from everyone from Queen to Kanye West.

*SNL*, a comedy show first and foremost, has given the musical world more than its share of highlights and Lorne Michaels knows the reason why. He told *Spin* magazine: "*The Tonight Show* would have Crosby, Stills and Nash in 1987. They would wait until there was no danger at all, whereas we were more in touch with music, I think, because we were just putting on the music we were listening to. We were fans." And as fans they have provided a platform for some unforgettable moments.

## October 12th

On this date in 1978, Nancy Spungen, Sid Vicious' girlfriend, was found dead by a single stab wound to her abdomen in the room she was sharing with the ex-Sex Pistol in New York City's famed Chelsea Hotel. In her short twenty years she'd led a very troubled and tragic life and now she was dead, most likely at the hands of her boyfriend, although we'll never know for sure since Vicious did not live long enough to face charges in her death. The Nancy and Sid story is truly one of the most tragic in the annals of rock and roll history.

The Sex Pistols rose to fame during punk rock's incendiary genesis. Formed by manager Malcolm McLaren they sought to be the nastiest, loudest, rudest, most anti-establishment bunch of punks ever brought together. In fact, early on they fired bassist Glen Matlock for liking the Beatles too much. Matlock's place was taken by lead singer Johnny Rotten's friend and self-appointed "ultimate Sex Pistols' fan," Sid Vicious (despite the fact that Vicious couldn't play bass at the time). McLaren would later say, "If Johnny Rotten is the voice of punk, then Vicious is the attitude." That "attitude" came along with a very serious heroin problem.

Nancy Spungen was born in 1958 in Philadelphia and had a very troubled childhood. She was diagnosed with schizophrenia at 15 which helped explain her constant temper tantrums and violent fits. Her mother once said, "I know it's normal for babies to scream, but Nancy did nothing but scream." She was also an exceptionally smart child and after skipping a grade in high school she was accepted into the University of Colorado at just 16 years of age. Just months into her freshman year though, she was caught with marijuana and expelled. She would move to New York City at 17 where she worked as a stripper and prostitute. She also became a groupie on the scene. hanging with bands like Aerosmith, the New York Dolls and the Ramones. A year later, she moved to London to meet the Sex Pistols. When Johnny Rotten showed no interest in her, she began a tumultuous relationship with Sid Vicious.

Sid and Nancy's nineteen month love affair was punctuated by constant fighting, physical abuse from Vicious and copious amounts of drugs. When the Pistols broke up, the couple moved to New York City and checked into the Chelsea Hotel. The Chelsea already had a long and storied history at this point, home to many musicians and artists. Everyone from Bob Dylan to Iggy Pop has taken up long term residence at the Chelsea. In 1953 writer Dylan Thomas died while staying there and in the late sixties Arthur C. Clarke wrote his science fiction masterpiece *2001: Space Odyssey* while residing at the Chelsea. So when Sid and Nancy moved in, it seemed like just another eccentric couple staying at the hallowed hotel.

That is, until the morning of October 12th, 1978. According to Vicious he woke up that morning in a drug induced stupor with no memory of the night before. He then discovered Spungen sprawled out on the bathroom floor. She was dead. When police arrived and began investigating, they quickly discovered Vicious had recently bought the knife that was used to kill her. Vicious gave conflicting reports, saying at times he had no memory, then one time telling police, "I stabbed her but I didn't mean to kill her."

Amazingly, his lawyers were able to get him out on bail. While awaiting trial he attempted suicide using a broken light bulb to slit his wrist. This incident led to a stay at Bellevue Hospital, where he attempted suicide again, this time by jumping from a window shouting, "I want to be with my Nancy." Released again, in December of 1978, he assaulted a man in a nightclub and was sent away to Rikers Island for enforced detoxification.

On February 1st, 1979, Sid Vicious was released from Rikers having completed almost two months in a methadone detoxification program. His family and friends threw him a party to celebrate. Somehow he got his hands on heroin at the party and he overdosed. His family and friends tried to revive him, walking him around the party until they thought it was safe. But Sid Vicious died in his sleep that night, only to be found the next morning by his own mother. He was 21 years old, a year older than Nancy Spungen was when he mostly likely took her life.

Sid and Nancy had made a death pact to be buried next to each other but the cemetery where Spungen was buried refused to be associated with Sid Vicious and wanted to avoid any publicity. His mother, who had found her son dead, was now left to scatter his ashes on his late girlfriend's grave. It's an appropriate ending for what is truly the most harrowing and heartbreaking story of wasted youth in all of rock and roll history.

## October 13th

On this date in 1987, Sting released a double LP called *Nothing Like the Sun*. The album is considered his masterwork, combining a myriad of musical genres and influences into what Anthony DeCurtis, for *Rolling Stone*, called, "a powerful and often hypnotic album." Sting had disbanded the Police a few years earlier, in part because he was frustrated at the restrictions a power trio placed on the type of music he could produce. With this, his second solo studio album, combining everything from jazz to funk to acoustic to rock to world beats, it is within reason to say *Nothing Like the Sun* was the album Sting was born to make.

When the Police broke up in early 1984, at the very height of their fame and commercial success, most music fans anxiously awaited Sting's solo work. He was, after all, the creative driving force and main songwriter for the Police so it's no wonder that his first solo release, 1985's *Dream of the Blue Turtle*, went to #2 on the album chart. In this first solo album, Sting showed why he'd wanted to stretch his wings past what the Police could play, introducing elements of jazz fusion into his already deep repertoire of rock, new wave and reggae. He used a variety of musicians on this album but, showing his jazz leanings, he featured two prominently: pianist Kenny Kirkland and saxophonist Branford Marsalis. The next year, 1986, Sting released a double live album, *Bring On the Night*, which was recorded during his 1985 solo tour and which again featured both Kirkland and Marsalis prominently.

It was during 1986 that two significant events happened that would not only change Sting's life but dramatically influence the direction and mood of his next work. The first was the death of his mother. Sting had had a complicated relationship with his mother which he wrote about in his 2005 memoir *Broken Music*. She'd had an affair while he was growing up which caused obvious tension in his childhood household. He describes a rather cold and loveless upbringing where he turned to music as consolation. "Without the piano as an outlet," he wrote, "I may well have become a delinquent." While he wasn't estranged from his mother when she died he didn't go to her funeral. The second significant event was Sting's participation in A Conspiracy of Hope, a short tour on behalf of Amnesty International aimed at raising awareness of human rights. These shows heightened Sting's awareness of global issues which certainly informed his writing.

Amid all this emotional turmoil Sting began work on his second solo studio album in March of 1987 at a recording studio on the Caribbean island of Montserrat. Besides the aforementioned Kirkland and Marsalis, who were now playing an even bigger role in Sting's band, there were a number of guest guitarists like Eric Clapton, Mark Knopfler and even ex-Police bandmate Andy Summers, who made the trip to Montserrat to contribute to *Nothing Like the Sun.*

There is certainly a somber tone to the album, most notably in songs like "Fragile," which Sting mentions in the liner notes was a tribute to Ben Linder, an American civil engineer who was killed by the Contras in Nicaragua in 1987, and "They Dance Alone," which Sting wrote after witnessing women in Chile dancing by themselves with a picture of their lost loved ones pinned to their dresses as a silent form of protest against their dictator Augusto Pinochet. And though a mother figure is mentioned only a few times on the album, most notably in the opening track "Lazarus Heart," in which a man has a flower growing from a stab wound in his heart and when he shows his mother it is she who is holding the sword (Sting said he dreamed it) one can feel the sense of loss throughout. Sure, there are a fewer lighter moments, like the lead single "We'll Be Together" and the hysterical Noah's ark send-up "Rock Steady," but overall *Nothing Like the Sun* is serious and solemn and at times down-right gloomy.

But it is magical as well. For amidst all this loss there is a shimmer of hope. After the rains of "Rock Steady" they do indeed find dry land. After reminding us how important it is to learn from the past in "History Will Teach Us Nothing" we are urged optimistically to, "Be what you come here for." And even the stab wound in the heart in the opening track grows a flower. "Every day another miracle" Sting reminds us. And to most anyone who has heard *Nothing Like the Sun* start to finish (the way we used to listen to albums) we are forced to agree. This is the album Sting was born to make.

### October 14<sup>th</sup>

On this date in 1983, Cyndi Lauper released her debut album *She's So Unusual.* The lead single, "Girls Just Wanna Have Fun" had been out about a month and was already getting solid radio and MTV play. "Girls" would eventually peak at #2 and help drive Lauper's debut LP to #4 on the album chart. In just a few short years she'd gone from being told she'd never sing again, then to declaring bankruptcy, to now being one of most recognizable names, faces and voices of the new MTV generation.

Cynthia Ann Stephanie Lauper was born in 1953 in Queens, New York. She grew up an eccentric child, always coloring her hair and wearing odd outfits. She even changed the spelling of her first name to Cyndi just to be different. And she also loved music; everything from the Beatles to Billie Holiday. By twelve years old she was composing her own songs on an acoustic guitar. Lauper got a GED after being expelled from high school (like any good eccentric) and by the early seventies she was playing in bands, doing covers of Jefferson Airplane and Led Zeppelin songs. In 1977 she damaged her vocal cords and a doctor told her she'd never sing again. She took a year off then worked with a vocal specialist and regained her voice.

In 1978, Lauper met a saxophonist named John Turi and the two formed a band called Blue Angels. The Blue Angels landed a recording contract and released their self-titled debut in 1980. The album went nowhere and when the band fired their manager he fired back with a lawsuit. Lauper was forced to file bankruptcy and yet again she lost her voice. She worked in retail stores in New York and as a waitress for a while, till she regained her voice and started singing in small bars in New York City. She was eventually discovered and signed to Portrait Records, a subsidiary of Epic.

Lauper recorded her solo album at the Record Plant in New York City during the summer of 1983. She co-wrote a few of the songs, did some originals that others had written and included a cover version of Prince's "When You Were Mine." "Girls Just Wanna Have Fun" was written by Robert Hazard who recorded a demo version of it in 1979 and then failed for years to find anyone to sing it. Hazard's version was written and sung from a man's perspective, relishing in a world where girls, well, just wanted to have fun. Lauper liked the song and reworked the lyrics to change the point of view to her own. As the album shaped up it was clear to everyone involved that "Girls" could be a huge hit so there was no doubt it should be the lead single. MTV was already a kingmaker by this point so Lauper and her management knew they needed a strong video to go along with the song. But they had a very limited budget to work with. The solution? Volunteers! They phoned in as many favors as they could, even getting the video equipment loaned to them for no cost. Wrestling manager Lou Albano played Lauper's father in the video which led to many appearances by the two together at wresting events. Lauper's real mother played her on-screen mother.

"Girls Just Wanna Have Fun" was released on September 6th, 1983 and the music video was added to MTV's rotation immediately, playing virtually non-stop throughout that fall and winter. The song eventually peaked at #2 in March of 1984, parked behind Van Halen's "Jump" for two consecutive weeks. After "Girls" peaked, an incredible five more singles would be released off *She's So Unusual*, including the beautiful ballad "Time After Time" which went to #1, the "is she singing about female masturbation?" number "She Bop" and even the Prince cover. By the time it was all said and done *She's So Unusual* had sold 16 million copies worldwide and would introduce the world to Cyndi Lauper. The girl from Queens has gone on to sell 50 million albums and 20 million singles in her career. It's safe to say she wouldn't have to wait tables anymore.

### October 15th

On this date in 1955, Elvis Presley performed at the "Big D Jamboree" at the Cotton Club in Lubbock, Texas. Presley was performing pretty regularly by this point all over the country as rock and roll was emerging as a popular musical genre with the growing baby boomer generation and he was quickly becoming a chief pioneer of the new sound, so this show wasn't unlike so many in those early years, except for the opening act, Buddy and Bob. The duo of Buddy Holley and Bob Montgomery, were local musicians who'd landed the opening spot based on their talents and local celebrity. But after that night, life, for one of them, would never be the same.

Charles Hardin Holley was born in Lubbock in 1936 to a musical family. He was the fourth and last child and earned the nickname "Buddy" early on. His siblings taught him banjo and guitar at a young age and he played with them in talent contests. In high school he became friends with Bob Montgomery with whom he shared a love of bluegrass. They started performing as Buddy and Bob at school dances and parties. They grew so popular in Lubbock that the local radio station, KDAV, gave them a weekly radio show. Elvis Presley came through Lubbock earlier in 1955 and the two were in attendance. Afterwards, impressed by the energy of this new sound, they started incorporating rock and roll and rockabilly into their shows and their popularity grew even more. They started opening for many of the national rock and roll acts that came through town including Bill Haley and the Comets and, on this date in 1955, Elvis Presley. Singer Marty Robbins was part of this jamboree and his manager, Eddie Crandall, was so impressed by Buddy Holley that he connected the dots and got him signed by Decca Records. It was Decca that misspelled Holley's last name on their initial contract and instead of fighting it, the young singer just changed his name and became Buddy Holly.

During his short time at Decca, Holly wrote a song called "That'll Be the Day" after seeing the movie *The Searchers* in which John Wayne's character uses those words as a common catch phrase. Holly recorded a slower version of the song that went nowhere, much like everything he released during his short time at Decca. He soon left that label and signed with Brunswick. Decca attempted to block Holly from leaving so he released his more rock and roll sounding version of "That'll Be the Day" on Brunswick under the band name the Crickets. The song became Holly's breakthrough and reached #1 on *Billboard*'s brand new Best Sellers in Stores chart, selling over a million copies.

Holly became an early and influential figure in rock and roll. In his few short years of releasing records and touring the States as well as the U.K., he would influence an untold number of young musicians. When you consider how many bands covered his songs like "Rave On" and "That'll Be the Day" you begin to realize the impact he had on that next generation of rock and rollers, both in the U.S. and abroad, where the seeds of the British Invasion were already being planted. Holly also wrote or co-wrote many of his own songs which was also groundbreaking for the time. Other than folk artists, there weren't many "singer-songwriters" just yet and Holly showed the world it was possible to do both. And with his song "Everyday" (which was the B-side of Holly's second big hit, "Peggy Sue" and got a fair amount of radio play as such) he also showed these early rockers it was acceptable to have a soft and tender side.

There's more than a little irony in the fact that the song that introduced Holly to the world includes the line, "That'll be the day that I die," since less than two years after its release, Holly did indeed perish in the infamous plane crash that has become popularly known as the Day the Music Died. We all know music didn't, in fact, die that day, but certainly scores of future potential great songs by the Big Bopper, Ritchie Valens and, of course, Buddy Holly did go down with that plane. What direction those artists would have taken us we'll never know but for Holly, his few years as a major artist had a lasting and profound effect on the future of rock and roll.

## October 16th

On this date in 1981, "Endless Love," a duet by Lionel Richie and Diana Ross, spent its final day at the top of the pop chart, ending an incredible nine week stay at #1. Making the success of the song even more unbelievable are two facts. The movie for which the song was commissioned was a disappointment at the box office. And the recording session was riddled with last minute changes. How this song became one of the most successful singles of all time for Motown Records is nothing short of a miracle.

Diana Ernestine Ross was born in 1944 in Detroit, Michigan. She began singing professionally as a teenager as a member of the girl group the Primettes which included future Supremes, Mary Wilson and Florence Ballard. Within a year the band came to the attention of Motown Records' owner Berry Gordy who, when he first heard them sing, claims Ross' voice, "stopped me in my tracks." But when he found out their ages he advised them to come back after they finished high school. In January of 1962 Gordy made good on his promise, signing the band after insisting on a name change and the Supremes soon became an integral part of Motown's success throughout the sixties. But Diana Ross was the clear star of the group and after Ballard was let go, Gordy changed their name to Diana Ross and the Supremes. The fact that Ross and Gordy were romantically involved by this point didn't hurt Ross' chances at becoming a superstar. By 1970 she was releasing solo material and throughout the seventies her career flourished as both a singer and an actress, specifically in her debut role as Billie Holiday in 1972's Lady Sings the Blues which earned Ross an Oscar nomination and a Golden Globe award. In 1981, Diana Ross' contract with Motown was up and she was courted by many different labels, eventually signing with RCA, landing a seven year contract for $20 million dollars. At the time it was the most lucrative record contract ever awarded. Her last recording for Motown was a duet with another Motown artist who would soon be leaving a band to venture out as a solo performer.

Lionel Brockman Richie Jr. was born in 1949 in Tuskegee, Alabama. He attended Tuskegee University where he became a founding member of the Commodores. The band signed with Atlantic Records in 1968 before moving to Motown where they enjoyed success throughout the seventies as a funk/R&B

outfit most notably with their #5 hit, "Brick House." But Richie was more than just a dance artist. He showed his more soulful side with 1977's "Easy" and 1978's "Three Times a Lady" which became the Commodores' first #1.

By the late seventies it was obvious Richie was not long for the Commodores and a solo career was inevitable. He wrote "Lady" for Kenny Rodgers which became a #1 hit in 1980 and brought Richie to the attention of Franco Zeffirelli who was directing a film adaptation of Scott Spencer's novel *Endless Love* and looking for someone to pen a theme song for the movie. Richie accepted the job and wrote the song thinking he'd sing it by himself. It wasn't till Zeffirelli approved the song that he told Richie he wanted it sung as a duet. Richie had never written a duet before so this was virgin territory for him. He reworked the lines and created melody parts, then met with Diana Ross to record the song. But when Ross looked things over she insisted on even more changes. Basically, she wanted all his lines. Richie reworked the song yet again to accommodate Ross' requests and the two sang the song in one, hurried session that Richie would later called a "disaster."

Out of that disaster of a recording session emerged one of the greatest duets of all time. Though the movie the song was commissioned for underperformed, "Endless Love" spent nine weeks at #1 and became the second highest-selling single of 1981 (behind "Bette Davis Eyes.") The song also represents a turning point for both singers' careers. Ross left Motown even as "Endless Love" was ruling the charts and for Richie, the duet was the first song he'd performed outside the Commodores. With its success, Motown became insistent on a solo album from him. He recorded his self-titled debut a year later and when it too became a huge-seller he finally decided it was time to leave the band.

"Endless Love" still stands as both Lionel Richie and Diana Ross' most successful single (as solo performers as well as with their groups). In 1994, Mariah Carey and Luther Vandross recorded a version which became Vandross' biggest hit, peaking at #2. Both versions of the duet have been used by thousands of couples as their "first dance" and still receive solid play on adult contemporary radio.

### October 17th

On this date in 2009, Jay-Z's "Empire State of Mind" debuted on the *Billboard* Hot 100 chart at #10. The song, which also featured fellow native New Yorker Alicia Keys, would soon become Jay-Z's first, and to date only #1 hit and it takes its place alongside scores of great songs that celebrate the Big Apple.

Shawn Corey Carter was born in 1969 in Brooklyn, New York where he was raised in the hardscrabble Marcy housing project. As a child he would often wake his family with late night jam sessions that found Carter banging out drum beats on the kitchen table and rapping at the top of his lungs. To encourage his interest in music his mother bought him a boom box and soon enough Carter was creating makeshift songs. He became known among friends as "Jazzy," a nickname that soon transformed into "Jay-Z." His first big break in music came when Big Daddy Kane hired him as his hype-man and in 1994 he released his first solo single, "In My Lifetime." When he couldn't find a label to sign him he set up his own imprint, Roc-A-Fella Records, and released his first LP, *Reasonable Doubt*, in 1996. That album climbed to #23 on *Billboard*'s 200 chart and let the music world know there was a unique new voice emerging in the hip hop world. Jay-Z wasn't the first rapper to talk about his tough upbringing or admit to drug dealing and violence in his songs, but he did it with a unique lyrical artistry and rugged yet nimble flow. His albums soon became chart-toppers and within just a few years he was one of the most successful artists and businessmen in music (or as Jay-Z would famously rap, "I'm not a businessman, I'm a business, man"). In 2009 he was presented with a song that celebrated New York City and even mentioned the housing project he grew up in and he decided to record it. But the song had an anthemic chorus with a definitive beat played on piano so Jay-Z knew exactly who he wanted to accompany him on the track.

Alicia Augello Cook was born in 1981 in the Hell's Kitchen section of New York City. As a child she loved playing piano and her mother encouraged this, sending her for music and dance lessons as early as seven years old. She graduated from the Professional Performing Arts School as valedictorian at the age of sixteen and was accepted into Columbia University at the same time she was being courted by Columbia Records. Eventually Cook had to decide between the two Columbias and she chose the music industry. She also decided she needed a stage name. Her first idea was Alicia Wild but her mother told her it sounded like a stripper's name and then she suggested Alicia Keys to her daughter because of the obvious relationship to the piano.

Before long Keys became frustrated at Columbia Records as her career was delayed by management's indecision on how to market her. The fact that Keys' music doesn't fit neatly into a specific genre threw off the powers-that-be at Columbia and eventually she left the label before an album could be released. She found a home at J Records where her sound, a mix of soul, R&B and jazz, was encouraged rather than compartmentalized.

Keys burst onto the musical scene in 2001 when her debut single, "Fallin'" and her first album, *Songs in A Minor*, both topped their respective charts. She very quickly became one of the hottest new artists of the new millennium, known as much for her soaring voice as her incredible piano playing skills.

Songwriters, and native New Yorkers, Angela Hunt and Jane't Sewell-Ulepic were both traveling abroad in early 2009 when they found themselves missing their hometown. They wrote a song called "Empire State of Mind" and decided to send it to Jay-Z's Roc Nation to see if he'd be interested in recording it. He loved the track, re-wrote the verses in rap form and then considered who he could find to play the chorus. He originally thought of Mary J. Blige before realizing that

Alicia Keys would be perfect. Both singers were New Yorkers but Keys brought the added benefit of her piano wizardry.

"Empire State of Mind" was released this week in 2009 and it debuted at #10 on *Billboard*'s Hot 100 chart. Jay-Z's timing could not have been better since the New York Yankees were in the postseason and would eventually go on to win their 27th world championship that fall. "Empire" continued to climb after the Series and on November 28th it became Jay-Z's first career #1 as the main performer (he'd been the featured artist on previous chart-toppers).

New York has probably had more tunes written about it than any other city so it is hard to say which one is the signature song for the Big Apple. But in terms of capturing everything the city has to offer in four and half minutes, it would be hard to top "Empire State of Mind." From Jay-Z's bold and brash rapping ("I'm the new Sinatra, and, since I made it here I can make it anywhere") to Key's anthemic chorus calling New York a, "concrete jungle where dreams are made of," "Empire" has it all. Jay-Z becomes a practical tour guide, leading the listener around the city from his humble beginnings in Brooklyn to his current residence in Tribeca ("right next to DeNiro.") Along the way we meet "Dominicano's right there up on Broadway," get a glimpse of the Statue of Liberty and a shout out to the Twin Towers that fell on 9-11 ("Long live the World Trade.") And as each verse ends Keys returns with that soaring chorus. The song is loud and manic and in-your-face which makes it the perfect ode to New York City.

## October 18th

On this date in 1988, the supergroup Traveling Wilburys, released their debut album, *Traveling Wilburys Vol 1*. Though the thought of such a band had long been on George Harrison's mind, it was his need for a last minute song that got the project rolling. The result was, in *Rolling Stone*'s words, "the ultimate supergroup." Here's the story:

In early 1987 George Harrison put an end to his self-imposed, five year hiatus from recording and began working on material for a new album. He asked Jeff Lynne, he of ELO fame, to co-produce the project. As work progressed, Harrison mentioned to Lynne how much he'd like to form a supergroup. Lynne loved the idea and basically said, "Count me in." The project Harrison and Lynne worked on throughout 1987 became a huge success. *Cloud Nine* sold solid numbers, eventually peaking at #10 on the LP chart and the album's first single, a cover of Rudy Clark's "Got My Mind Set on You" became Harrison's third, and final, #1 hit. The second single off the album, Harrison's nostalgic ode to his former band, "When We Was Fab," also became a Top 40 hit and suddenly the ex-Beatle was red hot.

George Harrison found himself at Bob Dylan's home in Malibu, California, in April, 1988 needing a song for the B-side of his next single, "This Is Love." Also hanging out were Lynn, Roy Orbison and Tom Petty. Harrison saw an old box in Dylan's garage with a label that read "Handle with Care." He wrote the opening line, "Been beat up and battered around," and the other four musicians began contributing. Since Dylan's place had a home studio, they laid down the track right there and then and Harrison submitted it to his record company. But when Warner Bros, who distributed Harrison's Dark Horse label, heard the song and found out who was playing on it, they refused to release it as a B-side. They wanted more from this new collection of rock greats. And based on how easily their first composition had come about, Harrison was eager to work with the others again.

They decided early on, perhaps as a way to fight the "supergroup stigma" to adopt new names and personas for the project. Harrison and Lynne had had a running joke going while they recorded *Cloud Nine*. Whenever a slight mistake was made in the studio Harrison would say, "We'll bury it in the mix." They said it often enough that "we'll bury" became a nickname for any error and "we'll bury" soon morphed into "Wilbury." So the quintet dubbed themselves the Wilbury brothers, with each musician taking on a different name (Roy Orbison became Lefty Wilbury, Harrison chose Nelson, Lynn picked Otis, Dylan selected Lucky and Tom Petty took the name Charlie T Jr), and they called the band the Traveling Wilburys. Even the drummer they worked with, Jim Keltner took a pseudonym: Buster Sidebury. Though the five famous musician's pictures prominently grace the cover of their first album, their real names never appear. From songwriting credits to the liner notes, Dylan, Harrison and Orbison, some of the most famous names in rock history, are all absent.

But of course the public knew. When "Handle with Care" and *Traveling Wilburys Vol 1* were released, on this date in 1988, nobody fell for the fake names. Just as two decades earlier nobody wondered who Sgt. Pepper's Lonely Hearts Club Band really was, the public saw through the Wilburys' disguise and bought the band's music eagerly. The album would peak at #3 on the *Billboard* LP chart.

But then, tragedy struck. In December of 1988, Roy Orbison died at just 52 years old of a heart attack. The band released the second single "End of the Line" with a beautiful tribute to "Lefty." In the video for the song, the four surviving Wilburys play around a rocking chair that holds Orbison's guitar.

A tour would have been a hard thing to pull off anyway, what with five successful musicians, each with their own demanding schedules, but Orbison's death seemed to take any enthusiasm away from the project. At least for a while. The four remaining Wilburys reunited in 1990 and released a second LP, intentionally misnumbered, *Traveling Wilburys Vol 3*, which they dedicated to "Lefty." There were discussions of a tour but again it never came to fruition, something Petty thought was for the best. "Then you're obligated to be responsible," Petty said of the prospects of a Wilburys' tour, "and it's not in the character of that group. It would make it very formal." Indeed, if the band can best be described as anything it was informal. From the day a chance meeting in Bob Dylan's backyard turned into a song that was deemed too good to bury as a B-side, the Wilburys weren't in it for a buck or stardom. Each had already achieved that and more in their own right. Harrison had a simple criteria for anyone in the band, they had to be someone he could "hang with." And if you listen to their music, especially that first album, that spirit comes through. You'll hear five friends, five incredibly talented and successful friends, just hanging out and creating some cool music. There's spontaneity and humor and even some good life advice and it's all mixed in with jaunty, catchy tunes. In "End of the Line," they sang together, "It's alright, if you live the life you please," and as musicians and artists you'd have to say that each of them did just that.

**October 19th**

On this date in 1987, despite intense objections from their record label, including the offer of a bonus to go back and record a completely different album, Australia's INXS released their sixth LP, *Kick*. The album produced four Top 10 singles (including the band's one and only chart-topper) and sold over ten million copies. Safe to say the label's instincts were wrong on this one.

INXS began as the Farriss Brothers in 1977 in Sydney, Australia (brothers Andrew, Tim and Jon Farriss were early founders of the band). They changed their name early on, inspired by the English band XTC and a local Australian jam named IXL. Their first single was released in 1980 and over the course of the next five years they slowly built a fan base in Australia, England and the U.S. In 1986 they broke the U.S. Top 10 for the first time with their song "What You Need." *Listen Like Thieves*, their fifth studio album peaked at #11. The band seemed poised for a breakthrough.

As they convened to record material for their next album, they chose to focus on what worked with "What You Need," a unique blend of rock and funk with what Andrew Farriss called a "balls-to-the-wall chorus." Following this formula, the band created song after song: "New Sensation", "Need You Tonight", "Devil Inside" and "Mystify." When they were done they excitedly presented the tapes to their label, Atlantic Records. When the response was bewilderment and disappointment the band was shocked. Atlantic executives said there was no way they could get the music on rock radio and the only way they could promote it was on black radio but since the band had no reputation in the R&B world that would be like starting all over. Atlantic asked INXS to rework the album but the band felt it was their best work and they stood their ground. Finally the president of the label offered the band $1 million to go back to Australia and make an entirely new album.

But the band refused. They insisted they'd gotten it right the first time and they wouldn't change a single note. Finally the label acquiesced and released "Need You Tonight" as the lead single a month ahead of the album's release. The song's video prominently features Michael Hutchence, INXS' lead singer and sex symbol, singing directly into the camera. Hutchence, with shirt open to his navel, long hair and black leather pants, was a smoldering rock star cut from the Jim Morrison mold. MTV started showing "Need You Tonight" in heavy rotation and when *Kick* was released on this date in 1987 the album started climbing the charts immediately.

By early 1988 "Need You Tonight" went to #1 and *Kick* peaked at #3 on the album chart. "Devil Inside" was the album's second single and it peaked at #2 in April of 1988. "New Sensation" then peaked at #3 and *Kick*'s fourth single, "Never Tear Us Apart" also broke the Top 10, peaking at #7. 1988 was by far the most successful year for INXS as single after single climbed the charts and *Kick* sold millions of copies. The band embarked on a sixteen month worldwide tour and they took home five awards at that year's MTV Video Music Awards.

INXS's subsequent album's would not match *Kick*'s success and then in 1997 their charismatic lead singer, Michael Hutchence, was found dead in his hotel room. The band has shouldered on, replacing Hutchence with a variety of singers, including one they found via a reality TV show called *Rock Star: INXS*. They've sold 55 million albums through the years making them the third most successful Australian band behind AC/DC and the Bee Gees. It's a feat made all the more amazing when you consider their most successful album, the one that accounts for nearly half of those 55 millions albums sold, was rejected by their record company who urged them to rework it. To the band's credit they refused and it's that album that *Kick*-ed their career into overdrive.

### October 20th

On this date in 1977, a plane carrying Lynyrd Skynyrd and their road crew crashed in a heavily wooded area in Mississippi. Two members of the band, a backup singer and three others were killed on impact. The band that had helped create southern rock would never be the same again.

In the mid-sixties, a few teenage friends from Jacksonville, Florida came together to form a band. They were students at Robert E. Lee High School where a physical education teacher named Leonard Skinner was a strict disciplinarian and constantly hounded the boys about their long hair. They started using his name for their band as a mocking tribute and soon came up with the odd spelling for it. By 1970 they were a popular band in and around Jacksonville, often opening for national acts when they came through town. Al Kooper (of Blood, Sweat and Tears fame) got to see them perform and promptly signed them to his Sounds of the South label and promised to produce their first album.

Their debut album came out in 1973 with the phonetically helpful title *(Pronounced Leh-nerd Skin-nerd)*. The album sold a million copies and included their opus, "Free Bird." Their follow-up, *Second Helping*, included the song "Sweet Home Alabama" which hit #8 on the pop chart. The band was quickly becoming known for their incredible live performances and they toured relentlessly in the U.S. and abroad.

On October 17th, 1977 they released their fifth studio album, *Street Survivors,* which had been recorded during two breaks in their touring schedule earlier in the year. The album featured a cover shot of the band with flames shooting up behind them. It was just three days later, following a concert at the Greenville Memorial Auditorium in Greenville, South Carolina, that the band and some of their crew boarded a flight to their next stop, Baton Rouge, Louisiana. Rock and roll legend has it that Aerosmith had considered using the same plane and crew earlier in the year, but passed on it due to concerns over both the safety of the plane and the readiness of its crew. Towards the end of the flight from Greenville to Baton Rouge the plane ran low on gas, perhaps due to an engine problem, and the pilot attempted an emergency landing at a small air strip near Gillsburg, Mississippi. The plane clipped some trees and crashed. Singer Ronnie Van Zant, 29, and guitarist Steve Gaines, 28, were both killed instantly. Along with the band members, vocalist Cassie Gaines, assistant road manager Dean Kilpatrick, pilot Walter McCreary and co-pilot William Gray all perished. The rest of the band and crew suffered a myriad of injuries. Artimus Pyle, the band's drummer, along with two crew members crawled from the wreckage through swampy woods until they found a local farmer. The farmer was startled to see the bloodied men in such a remote area and he initially drew his gun for safety before they were able to convince him to call for help.

Soon after the tragedy, Theresa Gaines, Steve's widow, asked the record company if they'd change their most recent album cover out of respect for the deceased. *Street Survivors* was withdrawn from the record stores and given a new cover sans flames.

Lynyrd Skynyrd disbanded and for the next decade various members performed together under band names such as Rossington-Collins Band, Vision, and the Allen Collins Band. In 1987, Lynyrd Skynyrd reunited with Ronnie Van Zant's younger brother Johnny as their new lead singer. But tragedy continued to plague the band. Guitarist Allen Collins was paralyzed after a drunk driving accident in 1986 that killed his girlfriend. He died in 1990 at just 37 years old. Bassist Leon Wilkeson died in 2001 of chronic liver and lung disease. He was 49 years old. Keyboardist Billy Powell died at 56 in 2009 of a heart attack. A year later, Leonard Skinner, the disciplinarian who despised long hair and loud music, and who had unwittingly given the band its name, died at age 77.

Gary Rossington, at 64 years of age, is the only original member left. Of course, this hasn't stopped Lynyrd Skynyrd from touring as heavily as ever. They helped create the genre of southern rock and as long as there's an audience of fans who want to hear such classics as "Gimme Three Steps", "What's Your Name" and their signature song, "Free Bird," they'll continue to tour, through hell and high water.

On this date in 1977, after years of frustrations and rejections, including one famous record executive who literally threw them out of his office, Meatloaf and Jim Steinman saw their masterwork, *Bat Out of Hell*, finally get released. The album that nobody in the music industry wanted would soon go on to be one of the bestselling LPs of all time.

Marvin Lee Aday was born in Dallas, Texas in 1947. He somehow earned the nickname "Meatloaf" (he has given so many versions of the etymology of his moniker that no one really knows the truth behind it) and was singing and acting by high school. He moved to Los Angeles to make it in the entertainment industry, still straddling the line between theater and music. In the early seventies he toured as an actor and singer in a musical called *More Than You Deserve* that had been had cowritten by Jim Steinman. Steinman recognized traits in Meatloaf's voice and delivery that were perfect for his writing style. Steinman envisioned music, even rock songs, as over-dramatized, mini-plays and Meatloaf's ability to act as well as sing passionately fit with the writer's methodology perfectly. When Steinman began working on his next project, a modern-day re-imagining of the *Peter Pan* story called *Dream Engine*, he included Meatloaf in the project. As the work took shape they both felt that three of the songs were exceptional: "Bat Out of Hell", "Heaven Can Wait" and "The Formation of the Pack" (which was retitled "All Revved Up with No Place to Go.") Soon the *Dream Engine* project was put aside and Steinman started directing his energies towards a more traditional rock album. As other songs took shape Steinman and Meatloaf began performing them live, in and around New York City, with Steinman on piano and Meatloaf singing. Sometimes Ellen Foley, who Meatloaf had met when he performed in *Hair*, would join them for the song "Paradise by the Dashboard Lights."

Crowd response was always tremendous and Steinman and Meatloaf began shopping around looking for a record deal. Instead of recording a traditional demo though, they would perform their songs live in the conference rooms of the record companies they were courting. Rejections started piling up. Dave Sonenberg, who was Steinman's manager, has said it felt like they were creating record companies just so they could be rejected. The final insult came during their audition for CBS. The iconic Clive Davis actually interrupted them mid-song and started berating Steinman, asking, "Do you know how to write a song? Do you know anything about writing? Have you ever heard any rock-and-roll music?" After they exited the CBS offices Steinman stood on the streets screaming, "Fuck you Clive!" The two were about ready to give up.

Till Todd Rundgren came along.

Rundgren heard them play one night and he approached them wanting to produce their album. In fact, Meatloaf quotes him as saying, "I've got to do this album." He got it. He heard how over-the-top it was, passionate yet a pastiche at the same time. Horny and hilarious. He felt it was a parody of Bruce Springsteen and all his themes about cars and young love. Steinman and

Meatloaf told Rundgren they had a deal with RCA Records (though they did not) and in late 1975 recording got underway. Halfway through the sessions Rundgren discovered that there was no deal so he started trying to find someone to pay for the studio time (he'd self-financed things till that point) and release the album. Finally Cleveland International Records, a subsidiary of Epic Records, heard some of the work and accepted the album.

Most of the recording took place in Woodstock, New York, with a band Rundgren had assembled with himself playing guitar, Roy Bittan and Max Weinberg (both from Springsteen's E Street Band) on piano and drums respectively, and Edgar Winter playing saxophone. Members of Rundgren's band Utopia also contributed to the album. When it came time to record the baseball play-by-play (which is a euphemism for the make out session during "Paradise") they recruited Yankee's announcer Phil Rizzuto. When the record was released, Rizzuto, an Italian Catholic, claimed he had no idea that his contribution was a metaphor for teenage, backseat groping. Meatloaf denies this, saying Rizzuto only claimed ignorance to combat criticism from his parish priest.

Cleveland Records released *Bat Out of Hell* on this date in 1977, despite the fact that everyone at Epic hated the record. Promotion for the album was minimal and sales out of the box were slow. The album first started to move in England after the BBC showed a clip of the title track being performed. Response was so good they requested another clip and were sent "Paradise by the Dashboard Lights." With little record company support, Steinman and Meatloaf put together the Neverland Express band and hit the road, initially opening for Cheap Trick. As the tour progressed and the record started selling, they became the headliners.

*Bat Out of Hell* has gone on to sell over 40 million copies worldwide. It's an amazing accomplishment for any album, all the more extraordinary for a collection of songs that no one in the industry wanted. But you can't really blame record executives. They have a formula and are looking for something to plug in. To fit a mold. *Bat Out of Hell* with its over-the-top, hard-rock-meets-show-tunes feel and intense, wall-of-sound production, didn't sound like anything that had come before it. It's worth re-visiting today and listening start to finish.

### October 22nd

On this date in 1976, Bob Seger released his ninth studio album (but his first credited to Bob Seger & the Silver Bullet Band), *Night Moves.* Though he'd been recording and releasing music since the late sixties this is the album, and the title track, the song, that put Seger firmly on the map as a rock and roll star speaking to a new generation. Good thing he took some extra time to complete this seminal work.

Bob Seger released his first studio album, *Ramblin' Gamblin' Man*, in 1969 under the name the Bob Seger System. The album got as high as #62 on the *Billboard*

200 Chart. The title track was released as a single and went to #17. After that his next few albums and singles did not chart nearly as well and Seger was at the risk of becoming a niche singer with just a strong following in and around his hometown of Detroit. Which is why, after his 1975 album, *Beautiful Loser*, he wanted some extra time to prepare his next work. With his record company pressuring him for his next release he put out a live album, *Live Bullet*, mainly to appease them and buy himself some more time.

The title track for *Night Moves* was one of the songs Seger labored over. He'd had the idea for it as far back as 1973 when he'd gone to see the movie *American Graffiti*. He left the theater with a nagging thought: I have a story to tell too. His story was about growing up in rural America (he was born in Lincoln Park, Michigan, what's known as "downriver" from Detroit) and specifically about losing his virginity as a young man in the backseat of a car. It's a universal story that so many can relate to and isn't that the most important trait in any art?

So he began to write a song about his first sexual experience. As a skilled lyricist he was able to allude to things poetically without being graphic, namely the brilliant line: "working on mysteries without any clues," which anyone who has fumbled through their first sexual experience can relate to. As the song took shape Seger realized his imagery of summer was also an analogy for youth and so he wanted to end the song with a reference to autumn which would show how he'd aged. His problem was that the last verse he'd written (beginning with: "I woke last night to the sound of thunder...") was a completely different tempo than the rest of the song. Bruce Springsteen's *Born to Run* album had just been released while Seger was mulling this over and he thought about the tempo changes in the song "Jungleland." He decided to just connect the two sections similarly and it worked perfectly. After taking years to write, "Night Moves" was completed quickly in the studio in just a few takes and Seger knew it would be a monster song for him. He has said: "When people ask 'Do you know when you've written a hit?' the usual answer is no. This song was an exception."

In terms of themes and topics, "Night Moves" certainly doesn't tread on virgin territory (pun intended). Songwriters and composers have forever reminisced about the "good old days" and looked back at their youth through a lens of nostalgia. And they probably always will. But something about Seger's writing, his everyman delivery and even the simple guitar strumming that opens the song, struck a chord (again, pun intended). "Night Moves" was released as a single in December of 1976 and it moved steadily up the pop chart, peaking at #4 in March of 1977. It would soon become a rock radio staple and one of Seger's signature songs. The album of the same name helped establish Bob Seger as a rock and roll giant and it began an incredible streak of success for him. 1978's *Stranger in Town* went to #4. . . 1980's *Against the Wind* went to #1. . . 1982's *The Distance* went to #5.

Bob Seger has accomplished the goal he set for himself leaving the theater that day. He felt he had a story to tell. And he's found millions of fans and record buyers who have wanted to hear it.

On this date in 1999, Carlos Santana's huge comeback song, "Smooth," began an incredible twelve week run at the top of the charts. "Smooth" and Santana's *Supernatural* album were the brainchild of Arista head Clive Davis who looked at Santana as an older artist in need of relevance. The result is one of the great comeback stories in rock history.

Carlos Santana was born in 1947 in Mexico. His father was a mariachi musician who taught his son to play the guitar and violin at an early age. His family relocated to San Francisco where a teenaged Santana started hanging around the local music scene, rubbing elbows with the Grateful Dead and others. It was a happy accident one day that brought attention to his incredible guitar skills. Paul Butterfield was scheduled to perform at the famed Fillmore West but he was too intoxicated to go on. Fillmore's owner, Bill Graham, threw together a bunch of local musicians to fill the time slot. Santana wound up being a part of the impromptu group and standing out from all the others. Columbia Records was currently looking to sign some rock artists after years of ignoring the genre and under the label's stewardship of their new CEO, a young Clive Davis, they signed Carlos Santana. He very quickly made a name for himself with his incendiary guitar work and fusion of latin sounds with rock music. Santana played at Woodstock and in the early seventies had back-to-back #1 albums with *Abraxas* and *Santana III*.

But by the late eighties Santana, like so many of his peers from the classic rock era, had fallen out of favor. By the mid-nineties he even found himself without a label.

That's when Clive Davis reached out to him yet again. Davis was at Arista now and he had an idea that he hoped would propel a comeback for the guitar legend. He wanted Santana to do an album with a number of contemporary artists. Santana agreed and the two began gathering material and commissioning songs to be written. One of the songwriters they approached was a relatively unknown named Itaal Shur. Shur listened to some of the songs that had already been done for the album and he didn't hear a cha cha. Knowing Santana had had great success with songs done in that time signature, with previous hits like "Black Magic Woman" and "Oye Como Va," Shur sat down to write a song with a cha cha rhythm. When he submitted his first demo, which included a guitar solo that he figured Santana would improve upon, the label liked the melody but not the lyrics. They teamed Shur up with Rob Thomas (of Matchbox 20 fame). Thomas was brought in initially just as a songwriter but after he and Shur reworked the lyrics the two submitted a new demo with Thomas singing the redone lyrics and Davis was impressed enough to ask the Matchbox 20 singer if he'd perform it with Santana. Thomas jumped at the chance. To Shur's delight Santana played the guitar solo almost note for note as he'd done on the two demos.

*Supernatural* and "Smooth" were both released in June of 1999 and with the song getting ubiquitous radio play they both ascended their respective charts.

By October "Smooth" and *Supernatural* had each gone to #1. They'd both spend a total of 12 weeks at the top. When "Smooth" hit #1 it gave Santana the dubious honor of having the longest time between his first charting single (1969's "Jingo") and his first #1 song. *Supernatural* would produce one more chart-topper ("Maria Maria" which was a collaboration with Wyclef Jean) and it was so successful Davis and Santana worked on a follow-up a few years later, bringing in other artists to collaborate with the guitar great. That album, *Shaman*, debuted at #1. The formula was so effective there's now a term for it in the music industry. When an older artist teams up with a younger one and achieves chart success they call it the "Santana Effect."

Clive Davis has had a storied career as a record executive so it's hard to say which of his many accomplishments is his greatest. But certainly his reclamation of Santana's career has to rank right up there. He rightly predicted that teaming the rock legend up with younger artists would introduce him to a whole new audience. 30 million copies later, *Supernatural* did exactly that. If you've got enough time today, give the whole album a listen. If not, just crank up "Smooth." Either way, appreciate both Santana's talents and Davis' vision. Combined, they created one of the most popular albums of all time.

## October 24th

On this date in 1962, James Brown recorded his performance at the famed Apollo Theater in Harlem, New York, financing the project himself because his record company had shown no interest in releasing a live album. He was even prepared to self-finance the release of the LP but finally his label agreed to put it out. The result, *Live at the Apollo*, became a huge-seller and the record that crossed Brown over from strictly an R&B artist to a true international superstar.

James Joseph Brown was born in Barnwell, South Carolina in 1933. He grew up in abject poverty and began performing at a young age as a way to make some money. He would sing or dance for anyone who would spare a dime. Brown did other things for money as well, and at sixteen he was convicted of robbery and sent to juvenile detention. It was there that Brown formed his first band, a gospel group, and upon his release he was determined to make it as an entertainer rather than a criminal.

He put together an R&B group that quickly became know for their outrageous live performances. Little Richard caught their act and loved them. He recommended them to his manager who signed them and helped them land a record contract. James Brown and the Famous Flames released their first single in 1956. That song, "Please, Please, Please," did extremely well on the R&B chart (peaking at #5) yet only made a dent on the pop chart (#105). Their next song, "Try Me," did slightly better but the disparity continued (#1 on the R&B chart - #48 on the pop chart). Meanwhile, Brown was furthering his reputation with his live performances. His singing was fervent, his dance moves electric and his band was as tight as a snare drum (they better be since Brown was known to fine them, mid-performance, for missing a cue or hitting a bad note).

Brown yearned to cross over to more widespread popularity and he believed that releasing an album from one of his concert appearances was the key. The problem was his label, King Records, disagreed. A live album, they believed, especially one that didn't contain any new material, had little commercial potential. To that point, only a handful of jazz artists had successfully put out live recordings, and none of them had gone on to be big sellers (they were jazz artists, after all). Failing to convince anyone at the label that the project was worth it, Brown made plans to perform at the Apollo Theater, where he knew from experience the crowd would be raucous and responsive to the "call and response" technique he often used at his shows. He then arranged to have the show recorded.

Afterwards, Brown's record company listened to the tapes and decided they'd release the LP, if for no other reason than to keep one of their highest profile artists happy. *Live At the Apollo* was put out in the spring of 1963 and it quickly moved up the charts. It would spend over a year on the *Billboard* Top 200 album chart, peaking at #2. Because there was no dead air between the songs on the album, some radio DJs would just play the album all the way through, pausing for chatter or commercials only when they flipped the platter.

Brown finally had his crossover hit. While he continued to have more success on the R&B chart than the pop chart he could now point to some of his singles as legitimate hits. 1964's "Papa's Got a Brand New Bag" went to #8 on the pop chart. 1965's "I Got You (I Feel Good)" got as high as #3. And while his legacy will probably always be his live shows rather than his records, at least with *Live at the Apollo* (and the subsequent live albums he released) he was able to capture some of that incendiary magic on vinyl for those who never had a chance to see him in person.

### October 25th

On this date in 1986, Bon Jovi's *Slippery When Wet* hit #1 on the *Billboard* 200 Chart. The album would spend only one week at the top, but then return in January of 1987 for a seven week stay. The album was a true breakthrough for the band from New Jersey. Pretty much exactly as it was designed to be.

John Francis Bongiovi was born in New Jersey in 1962. He began playing piano and guitar at the age of thirteen and by sixteen he was playing in bands and performing at local bars and clubs. At some point he reworked his name to the more stage-friendly Jon Bon Jovi. After high school, he took a job at the Power Station, a Manhattan studio where his cousin, Tony Bongiovi, was co-owner. There, Bon Jovi made several demos, including one produced by Billy Squier, and sent them to record companies with no luck. He also recorded a song called "Runaway" with studio musicians. He had a contact at the New York radio station WAPP (103.5FM "The Apple") who wanted Bon Jovi to let WAPP include the song on the station's compilation of local homegrown talent. He agreed and the song started to get airplay in the New York area in the winter of 1983. He put a band together, gave it his reworked last name, and started playing showcases and opening for other local talent. Bon Jovi quickly caught the attention of Mercury Records who signed the band and released their debut eponymous album in January of 1984. It included "Runaway" which became a Top 40 hit.

After two albums that were moderately successful (their debut which peaked at #43 in 1984 and *7800° Fahrenheit* which went to #37 a year later) Bon Jovi were eager to take a quantum leap forward and become true superstars. Surely, they had all the makings for success. With the growing influence of MTV they were a band made to be seen, specifically their lead singer Jon Bon Jovi who had matinee idol looks and some of the highest hair of the decade. Plus their sound was hot; an awesome mix of glam rock, heavy metal and pop rock that was radio friendly and filled with hooks. All they needed was an album that would launch them into the stratosphere.

So they and their record label, Mercury, decided to make some changes to achieve that result. First, they decided to bring in a songwriter to collaborate with Bon Jovi and guitarist Richie Sambora. Bon Jovi reached out to Paul Stanley of KISS but Stanley told him he was too busy to help. Then Stanley made a suggestion that would prove to be extremely helpful: Desmond Child. Child had cowritten one of KISS' biggest hits "I Was Made For Loving You," and Stanley felt he could help the guys from Jersey. Child met with them a few times in the basement of Sambora's mother's house and their collaboration would produce four songs that made it on the album: "You Give Love a Bad Name", "Livin' on a Prayer", "Without Love" and "I'd Die For You." The band and their label also specifically softened Bon Jovi's sound just a bit, going for a more mainstream approach rather than the harder sound of their first two LPs.

As work progressed they had over 30 songs for the album which they then auditioned for groups of teens in the Tri-State area. Which songs made the album, and which would be released as singles, were all determined by feedback from these listening sessions. Mercury even nixed the band's first album cover (which featured a rather hot woman in a torn tee-shirt. The woman is wet and we can only assume, slippery). They didn't want anything to get in the way of this album being a huge hit and the thought that some retailers might not stock it because of the cover was unacceptable. The second cover the band submitted (and which Mercury approved) was simply a black garbage bag that someone sprayed a hose on and wrote the album's name in.

"You Give Love a Bad Name" was released on July 23rd, 1986, a month ahead of the album. It quickly grabbed the public's attention and became ubiquitous on the radio and MTV. That's all a band can hope for from a lead single, get noticed and build anticipation for the album. The song follows one of Jon Bon Jovi's credos about songwriting: "Don't bore us, get to the chorus." Bon Jovi is well aware that the chorus of most songs is the most recognizable part and getting there quickly can help a song become a hit. "Bad Name" literally opens with the chorus shouted at the listener before the music even starts and if that doesn't draw you in, nothing will.

When *Slippery When Wet* dropped, a month after "Bad Name" had been released, it began to fly off the shelves. Then, even before the lead single had peaked, Mercury released "Livin' On a Prayer" as the second single. This is rare because usually a record company wants a song to have run its course before releasing the next single off an album, but in this case the strategy worked. "You Give Love a Bad Name" would continue climbing and hit the top spot on November 29th. "Livin'" would follow it to #1 in early 1987.

The band had what they wanted. A mega hit. *Slippery When Wet* would go on to be highest-selling album of 1987 and it would certify Bon Jovi as true international superstars. When their next album, 1988's *New Jersey* hit #1 just two weeks after its release there was no doubt that Bon Jovi had laid claim to being one of the most successful and iconic bands of the eighties. Just like they'd planned.

## October 26th

On this date in 1970, "Take Me to the Pilot," a single by a relatively unknown English singer and pianist named Elton John, was released in the U.S. The B side of the single was "Your Song" which had already been out for months on John's eponymous second album. Within weeks, radio DJs began flipping the single and playing "Your Song" and soon the record was re-released with the A and B side reversed. "Your Song" would peak at #8 in January of 1971, introducing America to this new, young talent and, some say, helping open the radio airwaves to a whole new genre of music. Not bad for a song that was written in minutes and is described by its lyricist as "childish and naïve."

In 1967, Ray Williams, an A&R man for Liberty Records, placed an ad in the British music paper *New Musical Express* looking for talent. A seventeen year old Bernie Taupin responded hoping to land some songwriting assignments. So did a twenty year old pub pianist named Reginald Kenneth Dwight. They both failed the audition. However, instead of sending them both on their merry way, Williams thought the two might be able to collaborate. He gave Dwight a few of the lyrics Taupin had submitted and encouraged the piano player to write music for them. Thus began one of the most successful lyricist/musician collaborations in the history of music. Around this time Dwight changed his name to Elton John, an homage to saxophonist Elton Dean and blues singer, Long John Baldry.

One of their earliest collaborations was "Your Song." Taupin was at John's parents' house having breakfast on their rooftop terrace (hence the "I sat on the roof and kicked off the moss" line) and the lyrics came to him right there at the table. He scribbled them down on a piece of paper. The coffee ring stain on that paper gives testament to how and where it was written. Looking back Taupin sees the song for what it is; a teenager's innocent feelings about love. While he calls it "childish and naïve" and sometimes even cringes at what he calls his, "extraordinarily virginal sentiments," he also understands why it became so successful: "Because it was real at the time. That was exactly what I was feeling. I was seventeen years old and it was coming from someone whose outlook on love or experience with love was totally new and naïve." Taupin, by the way, has never revealed who the song was written about and John says he even gets a little defensive when asked.

As quickly as the lyrics were written so too did Elton put them to music. He claims it was less than twenty minutes from the time Taupin handed him that coffee stained piece of paper till he had the arrangement all worked out.

While John's first few singles went mostly unnoticed ("Border Song" got to #92 in early 1970) "Your Song" put him on the map. From then on, John's singles and albums sold well in the U.S. and in England. Some musicologists also point to "Your Song" and James Taylor's "Fire and Rain" (which went to #1 in late 1970) as the two songs that opened the airwaves for a new, soft rock, easy-listening genre. Make no mistake, there have been singer-songwriters playing laid back songs forever, but they certainly did break through to the mainstream in the early seventies with artists like Elton John and James Taylor opening the doors for everyone from Billy Joel and Seals and Croft to America. Even bands like Fleetwood Mac, who were known as harder rockers, found their best commercial success by mellowing their sound to fit this genre.

That's a pretty good legacy for a song written in just a few minutes over breakfast.


### October 27th

On this date in 1973, "Midnight Train to Georgia" by Gladys Knight and the Pips began a two week stay at the top of the *Billboard* Hot 100 Chart. In the history of pop music it is certainly not uncommon for a song to be inspired by a conversation with a songwriter or even a comment that the lyricist might have overheard. So in that regard, "Midnight Train" is in good company. What sets it apart is how famous the person was who made the unwitting remark to the writer that prompted the song.

Jim Weatherly played quarterback at the University of Mississippi in the early sixties. When he went undrafted he decided football wasn't in his future so he decided to pursue his other passion, songwriting. He moved to Los Angeles and began trying to sell songs. He also joined a flag football league where he met, and became friends with, an actor named Lee Majors. One day he called his friend at home and Major's new girlfriend, Farrah Fawcett, answered the phone. She told Weatherly that Lee wasn't home, then she mentioned that she was packing for a trip home to see some family. She told the songwriter she had to catch a midnight plane to Houston.

After hanging up the phone Weatherly couldn't get "midnight plane to Houston" out of his head. There was something romantic and lyrical there. He started to imagine that Fawcett was leaving LA for good and that Majors might follow her, giving up his dream of making it in show business to be with his new love. When he came up with the line, "I'd rather live in her world than live without her in mine," he knew he was on to something. About 45 minutes after hanging up the phone with Farrah Fawcett he had written a song called "Midnight Plane to Houston."

In 1971, Weatherly signed with a manager who convinced him to record some of his own compositions to improve his chances that big name artists might hear them and want to record the songs themselves. He put "Midnight Plane to Houston" on his debut album as well as another song he'd written, the caustic breakup tale, "Neither One of Us." His manager's strategy worked. Gladys Knight recorded "Neither One of Us" and Cissy Houston expressed interest in "Midnight Plane to Houston." She loved the imagery in the song about someone choosing between their love and their dreams, but she thought the title needed to be changed. As she's explained, "My people are originally from Georgia and they didn't take planes to Houston or anywhere else. They took trains." She also had a concern that the Houston in the title would be confused with her last name. After Weatherly gave permission for the title and lyric to be changed to "Midnight Train to Georgia," Houston recorded it and released the song as a single in 1972. Meanwhile, "Neither One Us" was becoming Knight's most successful song to date (it peaked at #2 in the spring of 1973) and she became interested in recording more songs penned by Weatherly. When she heard Houston's "Midnight Train to Georgia" she wanted to make her own version. Released in August of 1973, Gladys Knight and the Pips' "Midnight Train to Georgia" went to #1 on this date, becoming the one and only chart-topper of Knight's career.

Neither Farrah Fawcett nor Lee Majors had to give up their dreams and return home. They both achieved incredible success in Hollywood. They married the same year the song she'd inspired went to #1. Their marriage lasted almost a decade, or what they call in Hollywood, a lifetime. At some point Weatherly did leave LA to return to Mississippi where he'd grown up. But it wasn't out of failure or to give up on his dreams. He continued to write and record and though he'd never match the success of his earliest years, he has enjoyed a fruitful career as a songwriter.

On this date in 1978, NBC aired the made-for-TV movie *KISS Meets the Phantom of the Park*. KISS was at the height of its popularity at the time but within the next few years they'd be torn apart by internal struggles and their fame would begin to slip. Some point to their acting debut as one of the reasons for this decline. Others simply to the fact that they'd been a novelty act for millions of adolescent fans who were growing up and requiring more from their favorite bands than fireworks and make-up. But whatever the reason, there is no doubt that *KISS Meets the Phantom of the Park* is one of the worst movies ever filmed and the fact that it aired almost exactly a year after The Fonz jumped over a shark on *Happy Days* (thus creating the term "jumped the shark") is somehow appropriate because KISS as a band had just done the same thing.

1977 had been a big year for KISS. Their sixth studio album, *Love Gun*, had gone all the way to #4 on the album chart and then their second live offering, *Alive II*, went to #7. Their concerts were sellouts and their merchandise was flying off the shelves. KISS' manager, Bill Aucoin, felt this was the perfect time to capitalize on the band's popularity and take them to an even higher level. He came up with a two-tiered approach to do just that.

Phase one was the "Solo Albums" project. Instead of working on an immediate follow-up to *Love Gun*, each individual member of the band produced their own solo album in 1978. The albums were all released on the same date, September 18th, 1978, marking the first time a band has ever had all its members release a solo project on the same day. Though they were solo LPs, they were all marketed as KISS albums and tied together with similar album covers, all featuring a headshot of the artist in full KISS makeup painted by Eraldo Carugati. Each album sold about a million copies making the project fairly successful.

Phase two was a movie. Inspired by their successful appearance on *The Paul Lynde Halloween Special*, Aucoin believed his band was ready for the big screen and so he sought a movie deal in which the members of KISS would play superhero versions of themselves (something that had actually begun the year before with the release of the KISS comic book). The project was pitched to the band as *A Hard Days Night* meets *Star Wars*, and really, who wouldn't sign up for that? Aucoin was unable to entice a major motion picture studio to get involved (which is why the project ultimately wound up on television) but he did sign a production deal with Hanna-Barbera and they enticed the famed horror director, Gordon Hessler, who had classics like *The Oblong Box* and *Cry of the Banshee* to his name, to helm the project. Screenwriters were hired and told to follow the band around for a while to pick up their mannerisms and get a sense of their rapport. Every time the writers were present, guitarist Ace Freely (who was known for his eccentric behavior and was opposed to the idea of the movie) wouldn't say anything but "ack." When the first draft of the script was submitted that's the only line Frehley was given. He objected and the writers hastily gave him some more dialogue.

Shooting took place in May of 1978 at Magic Mountain, an amusement park just outside of Los Angeles. None of the four members of KISS had any acting experience and they'd been given minimal training. To make matters worse, Frehley and drummer Peter Criss were battling substance abuse issues at the time. They'd often show up on the set clearly inebriated or even miss whole scenes (like the one where Frehley's stunt double, who was African American, had to stand in for him). On the day shooting wrapped, Criss and KISS' tour manager Fritz Postlethwaite were involved in a serious car accident. Criss then missed the post-production sessions where his dialogue would have been looped over what was shot, forcing the movie makers to use a stand-in to voice over all of Criss' dialogue. The only time his actual voice is heard in the movie is the scene where he sings "Beth." Speaking of the music in the movie, in an obvious attempt at cross promotion, most of it came from the solo albums, while some of the songs used came from KISS' catalogue.

Calling the resulting film a train wreck is actually an insult to train wrecks. Between the horrible acting, the comically low-budget special effects and the disjointed dialogue, *KISS Meets the Phantom of the Park* is so tragically awful it's almost hard to turn away from it. During the fight scenes it's so obvious that stunt doubles are being used you wonder why they even bothered putting make-up on them. The band disliked the movie so much for making them look like buffoons that for years no one in their crew was permitted to even mention the film in their presence. Yet much like other dreadful movies, *KISS Meets the Phantom of the Park* has actually taken on cult status (we're looking at you *Rocky Horror Picture Show*). And in recent years even some of the members of KISS have changed their opinion about it. Frehley has said, "I couldn't stop laughing from the beginning of the movie to the end," and Gene Simmons now compares the film to the infamous B-movie classic, *Plan 9 from Outer Space*.

The year after the film aired, KISS released *Dynasty,* which peaked at #9 on the album chart and contained one of their most successful songs, "I Was Made For Loving You." So tying their commercial decline to their film debut may be a bit of a stretch. But as the eighties dawned there was no arguing the fact that KISS' popularity was waning. They spent most of the next fifteen years shuffling their lineup and releasing fairly forgettable albums. Somehow, the band that was as much about their visual appeal as their musical quality, missed out on the whole MTV craze.

In 1996 KISS reunited after a number of years of inactivity. Their resulting tour lasted over a year and grossed over $43 million. Since then, they've become steady earners on the road and were inducted into the Rock and Roll Hall of Fame in 2013. So who knows, maybe it's not too late for The Fonz to make a comeback.

On this date in 1971, Duane Allman went out for a ride on his Harley Davidson. As he approached an intersection, a large flatbed truck came to an abrupt stop in front of him. Allman was traveling way too fast to stop in time. He struck the back of the truck and was thrown from his bike. He began to skid across the road and then his Harley landed on top of him. Many of his internal organs were crushed. Allman was clinging to life as he was brought to the hospital but desperate attempts to save the guitar phenom went for naught. He died hours later. He was 24 years old.

Duane Allman had two passions growing up: playing guitar and riding motorcycles. Early on, in fact, it was his younger brother Gregg who excelled at guitar and Duane took it up as sort of a sibling rivalry. One day the brothers went to see B.B. King in concert and Duane said to Gregg, "We got to get into this." They both doubled their efforts, perfecting their craft and then they started playing publicly. In 1961, they formed a band called the Escorts and they opened for the Beach Boys one day. Their next outfit had the adorable name the Allman Joys which eventually became the Hour Glass. They released two albums as the Hour Glass in the late sixties but were frustrated that their record label was trying to turn them into a pop band when all they really wanted to do was play the blues.

Hour Glass broke up in 1968 but the work Duane had done for the band caught the attention of Rick Hall, owner of FAME studios in Muscle Shoals, Alabama. Hall hired Duane as a studio musician. It was around this time that a happy accident led to Duane learning to play the slide guitar. He was recovering from an injury from falling off a horse when one day his brother Gregg stopped by with a bottle of pain killers and the debut album by Taj Mahal. About two hours later Gregg received a frantic phone call from his brother saying he had to see him immediately. When Gregg arrived Duane was excited to show him how he'd taught himself to play slide guitar. After listening to "Statesboro Blues" on the Taj Mahal album, and hearing the slide guitar, he'd emptied the bottle of pills and used it to get the same effect. "Duane had never played slide before," the younger Allman would say, "he just picked it up and started burning. He was a natural." "Statesboro Blues" would become a regular song for the Allman Brothers and Duane's slide guitar would become a staple sound for the whole "Southern Rock" movement.

Duane only worked as a full-time session player for a few months but in that time he got to play with many greats, from Aretha Franklin to Percy Sledge and from Boz Skaggs to Wilson Pickett. It was Allman's guitar work on Pickett's cover of "Hey Jude" that caught the attention of another guitar great. When Eric Clapton heard the guitar solo in that song he had to know who that was, as Clapton has said, "immediately!"

The Allman Brothers Band was formed in early 1969 and released their self-titled debut album in November of that year. The following year, while the band was finishing up recording their second LP, *Idlewild South*, Clapton had the opportunity to finally meet the guy who'd played on that Wilson Pickett track. He had just begun working in Miami on songs for what would become *Layla and Other Assorted Love Songs*, when he found out the Allman Brothers were playing a show in town. He went to check them out. According to rock and roll legend, when Clapton arrived Duane Allman was playing a guitar solo and when he spotted Clapton in the crowd he just froze and stopped playing. Dickey Betts, the band's other guitarist, picked up the solo but then he too spotted Clapton and had to turn away for fear of freezing up as well. After the show, Clapton was hanging out with the band backstage and he mentioned he was in town to record an album. Duane asked if he could come by the studio and watch them record and Clapton responded by saying, "And bring your guitar, you gotta play." Allman took him up on the offer and his playing on the title track as well as other songs on the LP led producer Tom Dowd to say, "The song and the whole album is definitely equal parts Eric and Duane." (Guitar World has a site on the internet where they've isolated parts of "Layla" that is fascinating - Google it). After his death, Clapton would call Duane Allman, "the musical brother I'd never had but wished I did."

In the summer of 1971, the Allman Brothers released their third album. This one was a live offering called *At Fillmore East*. Meanwhile, Duane continued doing some session work, sometimes even spontaneously dropping in at a recording studio and contributing to whatever was being worked on. He'd receive cash payments for these but no official credit which makes it virtually impossible to compile a complete discography of his work.

The Allman Brothers Band were very much at the forefront of the burgeoning southern rock sound which is a combination of rock, blues and country. Duane's slide guitar work became emulated by many others and it became a signature part of genre. Shortly after Duane's death, Lynyrd Skynyrd began dedicating "Free Bird" to him whenever they played it live (leading some to think it was written for him, but in fact it was written before Allman's death).

Gregg Allman joined his brother in rock and roll heaven in 2017 when he succumbed to liver cancer. The brothers did as much to put southern rock on the map as any two people and now they can play together once again. And who knows, if heaven has motorcycles, they're probably riding together too.

### October 30th

On this date in 1987, George Michael released his first solo LP, *Faith*. Michael had previously been one half of the duo Wham! (common trivia question: "Who was the other guy in Wham!?") but he wanted to change his teenybopper pop star image to a more serious singer and songwriter. Not only would he accomplish that with *Faith* but he would also create an album that would dominate the charts (twelve weeks at #1) and produce six Top 5 singles. And then a few years later, he sought to blow it all up again.

George Michael and Andrew Ridgeley (there's your answer by the way) came together as Wham! in the early eighties. Their early work dealt with some serious issues but in an effort to have more commercial success they chose to focus on lighter fare. Which is the only way to explain "Wake Me Up Before You Go-Go." The song not only became their first U.S. #1 single but also their signature song. With lyrics like. "Don't leave me hanging like a yo-yo" (you're limited when you try to rhyme with "go go") and an overall message of, "Let's not fight, let's go dancing," "Wake Me Up Before You Go-Go" (the song and its accompanying video) was typical eighties pop: upbeat and fun with nary a serious message to be found (although Michael and Ridgeley do wear shirts in the video that say "Choose Life" — perhaps in an effort to distract the viewer from some of the worst lip-syncing ever filmed). It's a no wonder that Michael wanted to break away from that image.

George Michael always saw himself as more than just a teen-idol and he aspired to be seen as a serious writer. His next career move made major strides towards that goal.

His first foray into solo recording was the single "Careless Whisper." The song was released in 1984 while he was still with Wham! and it appears on their final album *Make It Big* (plus it was cowritten by Ridgeley) which is why the song is sometimes credited to the duo and not as a solo piece. The lyrics of "Careless Whisper" hint at where Michael wanted to go with his writing. At first listen the song is about a man who has "cheated a friend" and though he wants to reconcile he understands they probably won't (and, "maybe it's better this way.") In the line, "Guilty feet have got no rhythm," Michael shows exactly how far he's come as a writer. Counter that with the banal logic of, "Let's not fight, let's go dancing" and you see a maturity not just in writing but in worldview. Michael had things to say.

Michael spent most of 1987 shuttling between studios. He did some work for his debut album in Denmark (at Puk Studios) and the rest in London (at Sarm West Studios). Michael not only wrote the entire album he also insisted on so much creative control that Columbia let him produce it himself. The resulting work is a masterpiece. There are some down and dirty funk numbers like the lead single, "I Want Your Sex" and "Monkey." The title track, which is a straight ahead rockabilly song. A jazz infused ballad called "Kissing a Fool." And some smoldering R&B like "Father Figure" and "One More Try." Michael brings together elements and influences as far ranging as Bo Diddley, Marvin Gaye and Prince and it all worked. His singing throughout the album is passionate and clear.

*Faith* received critical praise upon its release and it quickly began to climb the charts. It would hit #1 three separate times, propelled there each time by another successful single. "I Want Your Sex" peaked at #2. Then the song "Faith" shot to #1. "Father Figure" matched that success as did "One More Try." The album's fifth single, "Monkey" also hit the top spot before its sixth release, "Kissing a Fool" stalled at #5. Another contributing factor to the album's success was Michael's world tour. He played 137 shows in five months in 1988, visiting North America, Europe, Asia and Australia. And of course, Michael had MTV on his side as well. His videos, especially for the song "Faith," ran so frequently one might assume the M now stood for Michael. If you lived through the eighties, surely you can conjure up the image of Michael in his torn jeans and leather jacket leaning against the jukebox, without much effort. By the end of 1988 Michael had the highest-selling album and the highest-selling single of the year (the title track), which hadn't been accomplished by an artist since 1970 when Simon & Garfunkel did it with *Bridge Over Troubled Water* (the album and single of the same name).

And then, just to show George Michael's restlessness, he sought to blow it all up yet again. He found himself loathing the image of himself in the video for "Faith" and in the video for his song "Freedom! '90" he blows up the jukebox and burns his leather jacket.

George Michael passed away on Christmas day, 2016. He was just 53 years old. Throughout his career he followed his muse and trusted his instincts and while he never matched his success with *Faith* he certainly was one of the most successful artists of the MTV era. Give *Faith* a spin today, the whole album if you have the time, or the title track if you don't. If you're old enough to remember the late eighties you'll probably be transported instantly back to that era. Enjoy the ride.

## October 31st

On this date in 1975, Queen, despite passionate objections from their record label, released "Bohemian Rhapsody" as a single. If you are too young to remember rock music prior to 1975 it's hard to appreciate the impact "Bohemian Rhapsody" had because you've always lived in a world where it exists. But prior to this song, no one had ever had the creativity, or the audacity, to record and release something like "Bohemian Rhapsody." Once it was out there, and once rock radio started playing it and music fans started buying it, music would never be the same again. Suddenly, anything was possible, musically and creatively. Queen had broken some of the last barriers that existed.

Queen began working on their fourth studio album, *A Night at the Opera*, in the summer of 1975. One day, lead singer Freddie Mercury came into the studio with a song almost completely written and worked out in his head. As soon as the band started working on the track, it became clear this was no ordinary song. Mercury got his three other bandmates to record the backing track in no time, leaving big gaps of space for what he told them would be "the opera stuff." As work progressed the band and their producer Roy Thomas Baker, began referring to the song as "Freddie's Thing." Though the backing track took no time it was the vocals that took forever. Queen was actually working in a fairly advanced studio for the time so they had access to a 24 track recording system.

Still, Mercury envisioned more vocal layering and so they started "bouncing down" the tape, meaning they'd record multiple layers of vocals, then record them all onto one track, which would free up the other 23, so they could then layer even more vocals. There are sections of "Bohemian Rhapsody" where the vocals are layered some 180 times - all on a 24 track tape machine. Brian May, the band's guitarist, remembers taking a piece of the tape and holding it up to a light and he could see through it. That's how often it had been run through the recorder.

In the end it took three weeks to record the vocals, with the four members of Queen sometimes singing up to ten hours a day. There are sections of "Bohemian Rhapsody" where it sounds like an entire chorus is singing but it's not. There are no other voices on the record but those of Mercury, May, bassist John Deacon and drummer Roger Taylor.

Speculation remains about what exactly (if anything) the song is about. Some theorize Mercury is talking about his experience of being forced to leave his native Zanzibar as a child. Others see it as Mercury's "coming out" song. Mercury would only admit that the song was about "relationships" and he also once said it was nothing but "random, rhyming nonsense." Regarding the overall meaning of the lyrics, May once said: "Freddie was a very complex person: flippant and funny on the surface, but he concealed insecurities and problems in squaring up his life with his childhood. He never explained the lyrics, but I think he put a lot of himself into that song."

Whether there is a deeper meaning to the lyrics or whether it is just "random rhyming nonsense" will probably be an unanswered question as it seems Mercury took any further clues to the grave with him. What he left behind though was a song that broke almost every barrier left to be broken. Who in their right mind would think that a song that combines balladry and hard rock with opera was even worth recording, not to mention releasing as a single? Those were the challenges Queen's record label faced, not to mention the song's length, and the band's insistence that they wouldn't edit it for radio. And if Queen had been a newer band without their previous track record of delivering hits, the record company may well have won the argument. But as *A Night at the Opera* was readied for release it was "Bohemian Rhapsody" that Queen insisted be the lead single. The band even made a video (years before such a thing was mandatory) to be played on Britain's *Top of the Pops* show and even that proved to be innovative for the time.

"Bohemian Rhapsody" peaked at #9 in the U.S. on its initial release (it went to #1 in the U.K.) The song enjoyed a resurgence in 1991 when it was featured in the movie *Wayne's World*. It was rereleased and this time got all the way to #2. But really, with a song as groundbreaking and unique as "Bohemian Rhapsody" a resurgence was never needed. The song had never left the playlist of any rock radio station and there are very few music lovers who can hear the opening a cappella question, "Is this the real life?" and not reach for the volume knob and turn it up. Way up. And we didn't need Garth and Wayne to tell us to freak out at the guitar solo either. We'd been doing that all our lives.

Audacious or genius (in reality, probably both) "Bohemian Rhapsody" broke so many barriers in the mid-seventies there were hardly anymore to be broken after that. Crank it up today.

NOVEMBER

On this date in 1963, the Rolling Stones released their second U.K. single "I Wanna Be Your Man." The song had been written by John Lennon and Paul McCartney and given to the Stones after a chance meeting. It was an early hit for the group, getting to #12 on the British pop chart but its significance goes far beyond its sales figures. "I Wanna Be Your Man" showed the Rolling Stones, Mick Jagger and Keith Richards specifically, how easy it could be to write original songs. Once challenged, the two came up with some of the greatest rock and roll songs the world has ever known.

The Beatles were a pioneering band for many reasons but the fact that they wrote their own songs is a huge one. Before the Beatles, most artists, outside of the folk world took songs that professional songwriters had written and composed and then recorded them.  To be sure, there were others before the Beatles, Buddy Holly most notably, but the examples of artists who were also composers were few and far between.  But Lennon and McCartney saw the advantages of breaking this mold. The first was financial. When a song sells there are two parties who benefit: the songwriter(s) and the performance artist(s). Instead of splitting the pie, if they recorded their own songs they'd get both halves. So, for example, on their debut album, *Please Please Me*, they made more money from "I Saw Her Standing There" (an original Lennon-McCartney composition) than they did from "Twist and Shout" (which is a cover). And then of course there's the creative aspect. Most artists would rather sing songs they've written themselves, expressing feelings and emotions and sharing experiences that are unique to themselves. So for Lennon and McCartney it was never even a question. If they were going to be recording artists, they were going to follow in Buddy Holly's footsteps and write their own songs.

Andrew Oldham, the Rolling Stones' manager, understood all this as well. Though he wanted the Stones to be the "anti-Beatles" in so many ways, one of the few things he wanted his young charges to take from the Beatles was songwriting.

The two young bands knew each other by 1963 with the Beatles already on their way to superstardom and the Stones hoping to follow in their wake. So one day when McCartney and Lennon happened to run into Oldham and he told them the Stones were rehearsing and he'd love for John and Paul to come check them out, the two Beatles agreed. It was this chance meeting and the subsequent rehearsal which led to the Stones recording "I Wanna Be Your Man." It was a song Lennon and McCartney were already working on but hadn't yet finished and so at the rehearsal when Oldham chided his young band once again about writing their own songs (in front of their two guests) John and Paul sat down, finished "I Wanna Be Your Man" and offered it to the group. The Stones completed the song and released it as their second single in their homeland.  It rose to #12 on the U.K. Singles Chart and helped bring even more attention to the band.

Jagger and Richards were so impressed they became determined to write their own material. Rock and roll legend has it that shortly after this experience, Oldham locked the two in a room, telling them, "Don't come out till you've written a song." The result was "As Time Goes By" which they thought was, "a terrible piece of tripe" (Richard's description) but their manager thought was a hit. He suggested they change "time" to "tears" and since the song was a ballad (and they were more of a rock and roll band) they sold the song to seventeen year old Marianne Faithfull (the Stones would record their own version in 1965). When her version went to #9, and Jagger and Richards received the windfall as songwriters, they needed no more convincing. By February of 1965 their first original song, "The Last Time" went to #1 in the U.K. and then that summer, they wrote, recorded and released "(I Can't Get No) Satisfaction" which broke the band internationally.

In just two short years they'd gone from watching two young men scribble lyrics down on a piece of paper and complete a song, to writing their own hits. It's amazing what a little motivation and rivalry can do.

## November 2nd

On this date in 1996, the Bayside Boys' remix of "Macarena" (a song by the Spanish duo of Los Del Rio) began its fourteenth and, thankfully, final week at the top of the pop chart. The song, and its associated dance, had become a pop culture phenomenon earlier in the year and by the time it reached the top spot in early August you couldn't throw a rock and not hit someone doing the dance that went along with "Macarena." By the time it slipped from the top, Macarena-push-back was already well underway and like most flash-in-the-cultural-pan moments, pretty soon "Macarena" was considered unplayable in most clubs and at most parties. Decades later the song has yet to achieve "throwback" status which means the world has still not recovered from 1996 and the ubiquitous over-playing of "Macarena."

Antonio Romero Monge and Rafael Ruíz Perdigones started playing together as Los Del Rio (English translation: those from the river) as far as back as the early sixties in their hometown of Dos Hermanas, Spain (which is indeed by a river). The first three decades of their career were uneventful until one fateful day when they were booked to entertain at a party for one of Venezuela's richest men, Gustaco Cisneros. It was at that party, while Los Del Rio were performing, that a beautiful flamenco dancer got up to perform. Monge was so taken by her beauty that he improvised the lyric: "Dale a tu cuerpo alegría, Magdalena, que tu cuerpo e' pa' darle alegría y cosa buena." (Translation: "give your body some joy, Magdalene, 'cause your body is for giving joy and good things too.") In Spain, calling a woman Magdalena is to associate her with Mary Magdalene which implies she is sexy and sensuous. The two liked what Monge had improvised and created a song using that as the opening lines. They recorded a few different versions of "Macarena," one of which became fairly popular in Puerto Rico when then-governor Pedro Rosselló used the song as his unofficial campaign anthem when he was seeking reelection (it worked; he won.) Since Puerto Rico is a popular spot for cruise ships, many vacationers heard the song and began asking for it when they returned home.

Which is how it appeared on the radar of Miami radio and club DJ "Jammin' Johnny" Caride. Caride was getting asked for the song regularly by club-goers so he sought it out (this is back before you could just download a track onto your phone) and he heard potential in the song. He brought it to his partners at Bayside Records and the trio added English lyrics and gave the song a more traditional American dance beat.

All that explains the song which is only half the story. The rest, of course, is the dance. As the music video was being prepared for the Bayside Boys' version of "Macarena" somebody had the ingenious idea that if there were a line dance to go along with the song, it might give it a hook. Mia Frye, a dancer and choreographer was recruited to come up with something simple and repetitive. Something, as she has said, "a child with no sense of rhythm could dance." She created the sixteen movement dance and taught the other nine dancers who appear in the video. Once the video was unleashed on the public, all hell broke loose. The dance indeed was so easy everyone could do it. And before long everyone was. Throughout 1996 no place was safe, there were no "Macarena-Free Zones." Bars, clubs, weddings and Mitzvahs were all subjected to the song and its dance. In August, the New York Yankees set the world record for Most People Doing the Macarena when more than 50,000 fans performed the dance at their Macarena Night (one of the few records Yankee fans don't brag about).

"Macarena" went on to sell over 11 million copies. It was the most successful song of 1996 by a long shot. But even by the end of that year "Macarena" fatigue had already set in. When Los Del Rio released a holiday version of the song entitled "Macarena Christmas" (which was really just a mash-up of their original song with some popular Christmas carols) the song only peaked at #57. Nothing they've done since has even charted. "Jammin Johnny" Caride and his Bayside Boys have never come near matching their "Macarena" success either. Mia Frye has been relegated to Reality TV in France. But if the past few decades have not been kind to all the guilty parties involved, they can always look to 1996 when they combined their talents to literally take over the world. They created a song and a dance that left its mark (or scar depending on how you look at it) on anyone who lived through that year. Whether you loved it or hated it, there was no denying its impact. 1996 will always be remembered as the Year of the "Macarena."

## November 3rd

On this date in 1990, Vanilla Ice's "Ice Ice Baby" got to #1 on the *Billboard* Hot 100 chart, making it an historic record. "Ice Ice Baby" became the first song by a rapper to top the pop chart (it wasn't the first song with rap in it to get to #1 though, that honor belongs to Blondie's "Rapture.") You'd have to think that most artists who are considered One Hit Wonders look back with appreciation on the lone song that they're known for. But for Vanilla Ice, after all he went through with his only chart-topper, you have to wonder if part of him doesn't regret he ever wrote the damn thing.

Robert Van Winkle was born in 1967 in Dallas, Texas. As a child, his family moved often between Dallas and south Florida so he called both home. He fell in love with rap and the hip hop culture just as he was becoming a teenager and it was emerging as a viable musical genre. At thirteen he learned to break dance and since he was the only white kid in his neighborhood doing it, the black kids started to call him Vanilla. He also started entering rap battles around this time so his nickname evolved to MC Vanilla. At some point he created a break dance move he called "The Ice" and that's how his nickname ended up Vanilla Ice.

According to Ice he wrote "Ice Ice Baby" as far back as the mid-eighties and it was part of his live show long before he landed a record contract. When he did, with a small independent label called Ichiban, he released "Ice Ice Baby" as the B-side to his rap reworking of the song "Play That Funky Music." Though that single went largely ignored some DJs flipped the record over and started playing the B-side. When "Ice Ice Baby" started gaining attention, a video was quickly thrown together (shot on a rooftop in Dallas for around $8,000) and the song was given its own release, this time by SBK Records. "Ice Ice Baby" became a huge hit but it only spent one week at #1 because of a calculated risk that SBK took. They limited the number of singles they shipped in hopes of creating demand for Ice's album, *To the Extreme*. The strategy worked brilliantly and the album spent sixteen weeks at #1 in 1990 and early 1991.

And that's when the Ice hit the fan.

One night Brian May, guitarist for Queen, was in a nightclub in Germany when "Ice Ice Baby" came on. He recognized the hook right away. It was from a song that he had cowritten along with his bandmates and David Bowie called "Under Pressure." He approached the club DJ to inquire about the song and he was told it was already a hit in the U.S. Queen and Bowie sought credit and compensation but Ice initially denied he'd sampled their song, something anyone with two good ears knew he had done. Eventually there was a financial settlement made by Ice and SBK and all five "Under Pressure" songwriters were added as composers to all future pressings of "Ice Ice Baby." This was the early days of rap and Ice's high profile experience dealing with the sampling issue is actually pointed to as the moment rappers realized they couldn't just sample someone else's work without giving proper credit and compensation. It soon became common practice for original songwriters to be listed as composers and received their portion of any royalties when sampled. There are some composers, like Billy Squier for example, who have made more money from their songs being repurposed in rap records than they ever made on the original recordings.

Once Ice had ironed things out with Queen and David Bowie you would think his struggles were over and he could just enjoy his new found fame and fortune. You would be wrong. Suge Knight, who had just started his hip hop label, Death Row Records, wanted his piece of the action. He approached Ice about signing over some publishing points to him and, though Ice claims no one at Death Row had anything to do with the creation of "Ice Ice Baby," he did just that, surrendering millions in future royalties. Legend has it that Knight hung Ice by his ankles over a balcony to "persuade" him to sign over those points. Knight, of course, denies that story and while Ice is vague on the details, he does admit to being very scared on that balcony and the fact that he signed over even more of his royalties speaks to how frightening it must have been.

With "Ice Ice Baby" ruling the airwaves, Ice's version of "Play That Funky Music" was reissued and once again he found himself in hot water. He hadn't credited Robert Parissi, the song's original writer, so Ice found himself in yet another copyright dispute. Parissi was given half a million dollars and added as a composer to all future pressings.

And then, as quickly as Vanilla Ice had burst onto the scene, he was viewed as a novelty act or worse, a poseur. He was criticized for rapping about the streets when he grew up in middle class, white neighborhoods. His appearance in the 1991 movie *Teenage Mutant Ninja Turtles II: The Secret of the Ooze* and the song he contributed for the soundtrack, "Ninja Rap," didn't help. His follow-up album, *Extremely Live*, was a concert album that included some new material. The album hit #30, mostly on the strength of his name because it was generally panned by critics and its lone single "Rollin' in My 5.0" did not chart (although Ice had finally learned his lesson by this point, giving Steve Miller, whose "Fly Like an Eagle" he sampled in the song, writing credit).

"Ice Ice Baby" is one of those songs that was so popular it was overplayed at the time and people soon grew tired of hearing it. But after years of being on the shelf, many now appreciate it for what it is, a goofy rap song with an infectious hook that brings people back to the early nineties when hip hop, especially the songs that crossed-over to mainstream success, was mostly just fun and made you want to dance. There are very few among us, who lived through that time, that can hear someone say "stop" without thinking "collaborate and listen." That's the sign of a successful song that becomes part of an era's pop zeitgeist. "Ice Ice Baby," for all the trouble it caused Vanilla Ice, is still a time machine that can transport the listener back to those innocent early days as rap rose to prominence. Give it a spin today.

On this date in 1958, Tommy Edwards' second version of "It's All in the Game" was riding high atop *Billboard*'s brand new Hot 100 chart. The song had arrived a month earlier and would remain for another two weeks, making it one of the highest-sellers of the year. It had been about fifty years since the melody was first composed and almost a decade since someone sat down to write lyrics for it, and now here it was, a quintessential example of a doo-wop ballad for all time.

In 1911, a man by the name of Charles Dawes composed a classical piece. He called it "Melody in A Major" although it is often referred to as "The Dawes Melody." It is such a beautiful piece of music it is often taught to classical musicians in training which is where Carl Sigman first learned it. Sigman had taken training to play classical music before embarking on a career as a pop song writer. By the early fifties he already had a number of hits under his belt, most notably "Pennsylvania 6-5000," "Enjoy Yourself (It's Later Than You Think)" and "What Now, My Love?" "The Dawes Melody" had always stayed with Sigman and he often considered penning lyrics for it. One day, he thought of the term "it's all in the game," which was common vernacular at the time, similar to today's "it is what it is," and once he inserted that into the melody the rest of the song virtually wrote itself. "It's All in the Game" was recorded in 1951 by a number of artists including Dinah Shore, Sammy Kaye and Tommy Edwards. Edwards had the most success with the song, with his version reaching #18 on the Best Sellers in Stores chart (the precursor to the Hot 100).

Seven years later Edwards was nearing the end of his contract with his record label and based on his poor recent performances he was sure to be dropped. For his last release he decided to re-record one of the only songs he'd had success with, "It's All in the Game." This time around though he gave the song a doo-wop arrangement since that genre was huge at the time. It was this version that shot to #1 for six straight weeks.

When the song reached #1 it had historical significance for *Billboard*. Since Charles Dawes, having composed the melody, is a cowriter, and since Dawes went on to be Vice President of the United States (under Calvin Coolidge) and for his work on the Dawes Plan after World War I he was presented with the Nobel Peace Prize, "It's All in the Game" has the honor of being the only song to ever hit #1 that was composed by a U.S. Vice President and also the only song to ever hit #1 that was composed by a Nobel Prize winner. (If you're wondering if Bob Dylan receiving the Nobel Prize for Literature in 2016 affects that record the answer is "no." Dylan has two #2 singles but has never had a chart-topper.) All this may have meant something to Dawes had he not passed away in 1951 at 85 years old, the same year the original versions of "It's All in the Game" were being released.

For Edwards, his second shot at "It's All in the Game" salvaged his career for a while. He spent the next few years producing Top 40 hits like "Love Is All We Need" and "I Really Don't Want to Know." By the mid-sixties he had once again fallen out of commercial favor and his last handful of singles failed to chart. He passed away in 1969 of cirrhosis of the liver. He was just 47 years old. The lyricist who came up with words for "The Dawes Melody", Carl Sigman, continued a successful songwriting career. After "It's All in the Game" he wrote "Ebb Tide" (another example of Sigman taking an existing instrumental piece and adding words) and the theme to the "Robin Hood" television show. He would live to the ripe old age of 91, passing away in 2000. He'd written a simple and beautiful song to match a timeless melody and his words will forever remind us that many a tear will fall, but it's all in the game.

## November 5th

On this date in 1956, *The Nat King Cole Show* debuted on NBC television making Nat King Cole the first African American entertainer to host his own weekly show. Though this should have been a significant step forward in racial equality, NBC's failure to land any national sponsors for the show, which led to its demise after just 13 months, demonstrated how far we had to go as a nation.

Nataniel Adam Coles was born in Alabama in 1919. His mother was the local church organist and she taught her son to play at an early age. By his mid-teens he'd developed a love of jazz and he made his first recordings in 1936. Around the same time he dropped the "s" at the end of his last name and started going by Nat Cole. He'd add the "King" a few years later for how closely his name then sounded to the children's nursery rhyme character Old King Cole. In his early years he focused on his skills as a jazz pianist playing nothing but instrumentals. Then one fateful night, a drunk patron demanded he sing a song and so Cole belted out the only one he knew the words to, "Sweet Lorraine." The patron tipped him 15 cents but more than that he'd opened up Cole's future by showing him how unique his soft baritone voice could be.

The King Cole Trio signed with the brand new Capitol Records and became the fledgling label's first real stars. In fact, their signature circular building, which has been their home since the fifties, was often referred to as "The House that Nat Built" because of how important his success was to the label. So many of his signature singles like "The Christmas Song", "(Get Your Kicks On) Route 66", "Unforgettable" and "Mona Lisa" were recorded during his first decade of incredible success at Capitol as Cole became one of the biggest stars in the nation.

Which is why it was only logical that he was offered a television show. Cole originally signed a contract with CBS in early 1956 but when a show never materialized there he began talks with NBC. His first broadcast, a fifteen minute show, aired on this night in 1956. With no national sponsor. And that trend continued week after week, despite solid ratings and an incredible lineup of guest stars like Tony Bennett, Ella Fitzgerald and Sammy Davis Jr (many of whom appeared for scale - the minimum their union would allow - in hopes of helping the show be profitable). Advertising agencies were able to sell spots in certain local markets, in New York Rheinghold beer was a sponsor, in Los Angeles Gallo wine and Colgate became advertisers, but all the big companies were afraid of becoming national sponsors for fear that some white people would boycott their products. An executive at Max Factor cosmetics admitted as much when he actually went on record saying, "A Negro can't sell lipstick for us." Cole was flabbergasted and replied, "What do they think we use? Chalk? Congo paint?" He then added, "And what about a corporation like the telephone company? If a man sees a Negro on a television show, what's he going to do, call up the telephone company and tell them to take out the phone?"

NBC continued airing *The Nat King Cole Show* till December of 1957, losing money each week despite solid ratings. When the show was cancelled Cole praised the network saying: "They supported this show from the beginning . . . they tried to sell it to agencies. They could have dropped it after the first thirteen weeks." He placed the blame squarely on the advertising industry saying, "Madison Avenue is afraid of the dark." When asked about being a trailblazer Cole would say he was the "Jackie Robinson of television."

Despite his show's cancellation, Cole's success as a recording artist continued throughout the fifties and even into the sixties as the musical tastes of the nation were certainly changing and many of his jazz-playing and crooner-singing peers were in commercial decline. He recorded an LP entitled, *L-O-V-E*, in December of 1964 right around the time he started experiencing unexplainable back pain. When friends convinced him to see a doctor, an X-ray revealed a malignant tumor on his lung. He was forced to miss a performance that same month and Frank Sinatra filled in for him. By early 1965 he was bedridden. On Valentines' Day he and his wife took a drive along the Pacific Ocean. He died the next day at 45 years of age. At his funeral Robert F. Kennedy, Count Basie, Frank Sinatra, Sammy Davis Jr., Johnny Mathis, George Burns, Danny Thomas and Jimmy Durante all served as pallbearers. Jack Benny, in his eulogy, said: "Nat Cole was a man who gave so much and still had so much to give. He gave it in song, in friendship to his fellow man, devotion to his family. He was a star, a tremendous success as an entertainer, an institution. But he was an even greater success as a man, as a husband, as a father, as a friend."

That final album he recorded, *L-O-V-E*, was released the same month Cole passed away. It would get to #4 on the album charts. Later in 1965 Bill Cosby became the first African American actor in a lead role of a television show when he landed the part of Alexander Scott in *I Spy*. Five years later, NBC aired *The Flip Wilson Show* which was a huge ratings success and sponsors lined up to advertise.

On this date in 1970, at Nipmuc Regional High School (which is now Miscoe Hill School) in a small Massachusetts town called Mendon, five young men, all in their early twenties played their first live gig together. Tickets were about a buck and one person in attendance said afterwards he was, "blown away by their sound." Despite that high praise, it's doubtful anyone in attendance that night, or any of the band members for that matter, could have predicted that this group would go on to become what some consider "America's Greatest Rock Band."

Earlier in 1970, two bands happened to play together at the same gig, Chain Reaction and Joe Perry's Jam Band. The drummer and backup singer for Chain Reaction, Steven Tyler, loved what he heard from the other band and he approached them about joining forces with the caveat that he no longer wanted to be stuck behind the kit. He envisioned himself as a frontman and lead singer and felt that Perry's incredible guitar playing and his own talents could be a great combination. Perry agreed and a new band was born, with Tyler and Perry joined by bassist Tom Hamilton, drummer Joey Kramer (from Perry's band) and Roy Tabano on rhythm guitar. They began rehearsing and smoking copious amounts of marijuana. One day they sat down to think of a name and Kramer mentioned that he'd been doodling the word Aerosmith ever since hearing Harry Nilson's album *Aerial Ballet*. The rest of the band thought Kramer was referring to the Sinclair Lewis novel, *Arrowsmith*, but when he showed them the unique spelling, the band liked it and chose that over their second choice, the Hookers.

It was Perry's mom who helped Aerosmith land their first gig. She taught in the area and knew someone at Nipmuc Regional High School who helped them secure the gymnasium. In a sign of things to come, the band caused some trouble that first night. Tyler broke into a locker and took a school shirt which he then wore on stage. And there were signs that the band snuck booze in and were drinking on stage. They must have played well enough though as one guy in attendance said, "It seemed obvious they were going to go someplace."

Someplace indeed. After replacing Tabano with Brad Whitford, Aerosmith began garnering quite the reputation for their ferocious live shows. One night their manager invited Columbia head, Clive Davis, to come see them at the New York City club Max's Kansas City. Davis agreed to come check them out but the only problem was, Aerosmith wasn't scheduled to play that night. The band paid Max's to secure a place on the bill that evening and Davis was blown away. He offered them a recording contract and their self-titled debut was released in January of 1973, a little more than two years after their first gig together.

Aerosmith achieved incredible success over the next few years, carving out a place for themselves in hard rock's pantheon. Their albums sold well and their live shows were an attraction for any fan of blues-based rock. But the drug use that had begun with marijuana had grown along with the band's success. Tyler and Perry became known as the Toxic Twins for their dangerous combination of heroin, cocaine and other narcotics. Tyler has since said that he spent approximately $6 million dollars on drugs during the time he was using. Some around him claim that's a conservative estimate. And as you'd imagine, with rampant drug use comes unpredictable behavior. In 1979 tensions in the band exploded and Perry left the group. Whitford soon followed. Aerosmith continued on without them, though their popularity waned in the early eighties. Then, on a fateful night in 1984, Aerosmith played a show in Boston that Perry and Whitford attended. Backstage, everyone got along and within no time the two were back in the fold. The reunited Aerosmith began a tour called Back in the Saddle. Their resurrection was complete just a few years later when Run-D.M.C. covered "Walk This Way," helping to launch hip hop into music's mainstream and reminding the music world about this great band.

There is a strong argument to be made for Aerosmith being the best American rock band. Of course that is a subjective title but what's not up for debate is their chart success. The band has sold over 150 million albums and scored 21 Top 40 hits. They were inducted into the Rock and Roll Hall of Fame in 2001, their first year of eligibility and Perry and Tyler have also been inducted into the Songwriters Hall of Fame. It all began with a humble show in a high school gymnasium on this date in 1970. And despite all the set-backs along the way, Aerosmith has achieved unprecedented levels of success. Celebrate them today by cranking up some of their best known songs.

## November 7th

On this date in 1943, Roberta Joan Anderson was born in Alberta, Canada. She would survive a childhood illness and then, using the stage name, Joni Mitchell, she would go on to become one of the most influential singer-songwriters of the twentieth century.

As a child Anderson leaned more towards athletics but when she contracted polio at the age of nine she started focusing more on her creative side. She yearned to play guitar but since her mother saw it as a "hillbilly thing" she initially settled for learning the ukulele. Eventually she taught herself guitar by studying the Pete Seeger songbook. Since the polio had affected her fingers she had to improvise many tuning techniques and she later looked at this as a blessing in disguise as it allowed her to, "break free of standard approaches to harmony and structure." Throughout her career it would be the combination of her unique open tuning with her wide-ranging contralto voice and incredibly poetic lyrics that would set her apart as a performer.

She also had a passion for art and attended the Alberta College of Art and Design in Calgary for one year to study painting. She sang in coffeehouses and busked throughout this time to help make ends meet. She was twenty when she told her boyfriend that she was pregnant. He promptly left her. Abortion was illegal in Canada then so she gave her baby girl up for adoption, an experience she kept private most of her life but hinted at in her songwriting (most notably in her 1982 song "Chinese Cafe" which includes the lyric: "Your kids are coming up straight. My child's a stranger. I bore her but I could not raise her.")

She met musician Chuck Mitchell in Toronto in 1965 and they married 36 hours after meeting. She started using the name Joni Mitchell and the couple moved to Michigan where they both started playing together in coffeehouses and restaurants. She was composing her own music more and more now and after her relationship with Chuck dissolved she moved to New York City in 1967 to try to sell some songs and maybe land a recording contract.

Mitchell accomplished both of those goals very quickly. She was able to sell some of her compositions to established recording artists, most notably "Both Sides Now" which Judy Collins had a Top 10 hit with in 1968. She also found herself playing a club in Florida one day when David Crosby walked in. He was immediately struck by her sound and invited her to join him in Los Angeles where he introduced her to all his industry contacts. Mitchell was soon signed to Reprise Records and her debut album, *Song of a Seagull*, was released in 1968. She painted the cover of her debut album as well as her 1969 follow-up, *Clouds*, which earned her a Grammy Award for Best Folk Performance.

That same year Mitchell was invited to perform at Woodstock but her manager said she'd get more exposure appearing on *The Dick Cavett Show*. She sat in her hotel room in New York City that weekend, watching the news from upstate New York. She composed a song combining beautiful imagery of the festival with an anti-war message and some religious themes. "Woodstock" has not only become one of her signature songs but it embodies most of the hippie generation ethos in one beautiful track. It's amazing that the definitive song about the festival was composed by someone who watched it on TV.

And then, she released *Blue*. The album is her masterwork, a singer-songwriter at the top of her game, tapping into her insecurities and infatuations and pouring her heart out in song. The album was a critical and commercial success and has been cited as an influence by artists as diverse as Sarah McLachlan, Prince and Bjork.

Mitchell continued writing and recording music and her songs have continued to touch the hearts of those who hear them. She has the unique ability of covering a wide range of topics in her music, everything from the most personal and intimate emotions to a diverse number of causes that she believes in, including the environment and social equality. Still, she considers herself an artist first and foremost, saying at times she's a, "painter derailed by circumstance." Whatever those circumstances may be, music lovers the world over are glad she got derailed. Her songs have added to the soundtrack of so many lives.

On this date in 1982, Michael Jackson and producer Quincy Jones finally stopped mixing their new album and handed the tapes over to their record label, Epic. The release date for Jackson's sixth studio album was just weeks away but the two had continued tweaking and working on every last detail of the album up to the last minute because Jackson so badly wanted a mega-hit record, something to outdo Jackson's 1979 LP, *Off the Wall*. Not only would they accomplish that goal but the album they labored over so obsessively would go on to become the highest-seller in U.S. history.

Michael Jackson made his professional debut as a singer in 1964 at the age of six when he started performing with his four older brothers as the Jackson Brothers (they'd change their name to the Jackson 5 a year later). The band toured the Mid-West and South, opening for such legendary acts as Gladys Knight, Sam and Dave and the O'Jays. Even early on it was clear that young Michael was the star of the group. He stood out, not just as the youngest and cutest member, but as the one with the most charisma and stage appeal. In 1969 the Jackson 5 signed with Motown and they went from an opening act to "Jacksonmania!" almost overnight. Their first four singles were all #1's: "I Want You Back", "ABC", "The Love You Save" and the ballad "I'll Be There." Motown saw the potential of a solo career for Michael early on, releasing his first solo single, "Got to Be There," in 1971. For a number of years Michael maintained both aspects of his career, performing with his brothers as well as by himself. When the band left Motown for Epic Records he moved his solo career to that label as well. In 1978 Jackson appeared in *The Wiz* where he got to work with Quincy Jones. The two developed a friendship and decided to do an album together

The result was a huge success. *Off the Wall*, with its four Top 10 singles, established Michael Jackson as a true superstar. But despite the commercial and critical success of the album, Jackson was disappointed, mainly about receiving just one Grammy (Best Male R&B Vocal Performance for "Don't Stop 'Til You Get Enough"). He felt the song should have taken home Record of the Year (which went to the Doobie Brothers for "What a Fool Believes") and his LP should have won Album of the Year (which Billy Joel took home for *52nd Street*). Jackson was determined not to let it happen again.

Michael Jackson and Quincy Jones began work for what would become *Thriller* in April of 1982. In the next few months they'd record 30 songs and pull from a myriad of genres. Disco was done by this point so the dance tracks on the LP have a more modern feel to them. Plus they incorporated some rock sounds, specifically in "Beat It" which features a soaring guitar solo by Eddie Van Halen. They went with a funkier, bass driven groove in "Billie Jean" and "Wanna Be Startin' Something" and a hard hitting drum track in "P.Y.T. (Pretty Young Thing)." The album also included some slower R&B ballads where Jackson got to show off his more sensitive side. The duo worked on the album for months, racking up production costs of $750,000.

And when the album was finally set for release, they almost blew the whole thing by picking the wrong song to release as the lead single. "The Girl Is Mine," Jackson's duet with Paul McCartney, is the cheesiest song on the whole album and misled the public as to what the rest of *Thriller* consisted of. Though the single sold well (based on the two artists singing it, how could it not?), it did not promote the album properly and *Thriller* got out of the box slowly. Then in January of 1983 "Billie Jean" was released as the second single and now the world turned its interest to the entire LP. *Thriller* went to #1 on the album chart in late February of 1983 where it would sit for seventeen straight weeks. After getting bumped from the top spot by the soundtrack to *Flashdance* it would return again and again to #1, spending a total of 26 weeks at the top of the album chart. Seven of the nine songs on the LP were released as singles with "P.Y.T." performing the poorest, peaking at #10. And indeed when the 26th annual Grammy Award ceremony took place on February 28th, 1984, Michael Jackson was announced to the podium a record eight times. That night he was truly crowned the King of Pop.

### November 9th

On this date in 1967, a brand new publication called *Rolling Stone* released its very first issue. It was printed in newspaper style, with no staples and all in black and white. In the very first "Letter from the Editor," Jann Wenner explained he chose the title from three inspirations: the Muddy Waters' song "Rollin' Stone" , the band the Rolling Stones and Bob Dylan's "first rock and roll record" which was titled "Like a Rolling Stone." He then went on to write that the new publication, "is not just about music but also about the things and attitudes the music embraces." And in typical sixties' lexicon he added, "We've been working quite hard on it and we hope you can dig it." All these years later, music fans continue to dig it.

Initially *Rolling Stone* avoided delving into politics or social issues. The first few years the magazine focused on music and pop culture and since they were originally founded in San Francisco there was certainly an emphasis on the hippie culture and its epicenter of Haight-Asbury. By the early seventies though, the magazine started adding some political coverage especially with the addition of Hunter S.Thompson who became a contributing editor and made *Rolling Stone* the magazine to read. *Rolling Stone* had an amazing stable of writers and contributors during the seventies. Besides Thompson they featured Jon Landau, Lester Bangs, P.J. O'Rourke, Cameron Crowe and Patti Smith.

Bands saw appearing on the cover of the publication as such a coveted spot that Dr Hook & the Medicine Show even wrote a song about it. As a result *Rolling Stone* did indeed put them on the cover, however they used a cartoon drawing instead of a photograph and ran the headline, "What's Their Names Make the Cover."

By 1973 *Rolling Stone* was being printed more like a traditional magazine with four colors and stapled in the center. In 1980 they switched to the larger ten inch by twelve inch format. They'd switch back to a more traditional size magazine in 2008.

But it's not just the print format that has evolved through the years. The editorial focus has shifted numerous times as well. After being the vanguard for the counter-culture movement throughout the seventies they saw the changing zeitgeist as a new decade unfolded and throughout the eighties they became more of an entertainment focused magazine. This, of course, led to criticism that they were shirking their responsibility at guiding the political debate and in recent years, specifically with the writing of Michael Hastings and Matt Taibbi, they've focused once again on relevant issues of the day (albeit from a decidedly liberal point of view).

Music lovers' main criticism of the magazine is that it over-idolizes the days of classic rock and is often slow to embrace new musical trends. But it will often go back and rewrite its own history once a genre or band has proven itself. Led Zeppelin is a perfect example. The magazine largely ignored them early on, yet nowadays, whenever they write about the band they do so in the most glowing of terms. Heavy metal and hip hop are two genres the magazine seemingly has no use for.  And then, of course, there was the 2014 story "A Rape on Campus" which told the harrowing story of a gang rape on the University of Virginia campus which proved to be untrue. *Rolling Stone* was lambasted for their lack of fact-checking in what seemed in hindsight a race to sensationalism. The resulting defamation suit cost the magazine millions.

Still*, Rolling Stone* continues to be a powerbroker in the music industry. Scoring a cover article is considered a coup for any band or pop culture figure. And while its main readership may be online these days, it's still a place so many music lovers go to catch up on what's new in their beloved industry. So yeah, Mr. Wenner. I think you can be confident, we dig it.

### November 10th

On this date in 1976, Blue Öyster Cult was sitting at #12 on the *Billboard* Hot 100 Chart with "(Don't Fear) the Reaper." It would prove to be their highest-charting single ever and, because of a late night television comedy sketch, the song would take on legendary status. Still, the song's writer laments that people misunderstood his message and thinks his band (which aptly has the word "cult" in its title) would have been better off without this lone Top 20 hit.

Blue Öyster Cult came together as a band on Long Island, New York, under the name Soft White Underbelly. They recorded one album for Elektra in 1968 under that moniker before changing lead singers and their name. They came up with Blue Öyster Cult from a poem their manager, the famed record producer Sandy Pearlman, had written in which a group of aliens (with the name Blue Oyster

Cult) come to earth and secretly begin changing history (think Scientology, only believable). To make their new name all the more mysterious, two dots were added over the "O." Today we call this a "metal umlaut" because other hard rock or heavy metal bands such as Motörhead, Mötley Crüe and Queensrÿche have adopted similar markings (as did the satirical band Spınal Tap). In addition to a new name, the band created their hook and cross logo which has appeared (sometimes prominently and other times hidden) on every one of their album covers. Pearlman envisioned Blue Öyster Cult as an American answer to Black Sabbath and he encouraged the band's hard rock sound and their themes of cosmic mythology and mediaeval wizardry. If there was ever the perfect soundtrack to play Dungeons and Dragons to, BÖC provided it.

Which is why, when lead guitarist Donald Roeser (who used the stage name Buck Dharma) had a psychological breakthrough one day as he contemplated his own mortality and wondered whether he'd be reunited with past loved ones after his death, it fit the band's themes when he wrote the lyrics and accompanying music to "(Don't Fear) the Reaper." Dharma wrote the song to inspire people not to fear death, that it is inevitable so there is no use worrying about it anyway, and, oh, by the way, you'll be reunited and, "together in eternity," with your loved ones so you have that to look forward to. Dharma, thinking of young lovers, included Romeo and Juliet in his lyrics and he simply guessed that 40,000 people die everyday (this was before the age of Google so it was actually harder to get a fact like that at a moments' notice. I'll pause here while you Google "How Many People Die Everyday?" 151,000. Pretty depressing). Of his most famous song, Dharma himself says: "I was thinking about my own mortality. I wrote the guitar riff, the first two lines of lyric sprung into my head, then the rest of it came as I formed a story about a love affair that transcends death. I was thinking about my wife, and that maybe we'd get together after I was gone."

When the band sat down to record the song, they gave it a much more accessible sound than many of their previous offerings, layering vocals harmonically in what many consider an imitation of the Byrds' sound and softening the drums and including a cowbell as a percussion instrument. They also included a dramatic caesura in the middle of the song where the instruments drop out, the guitar comes back in gently and the song rebuilds for its finale. They've never explained the caesura but perhaps the symbolism is death. The beginning of the song, our life on earth, then everything comes to an end but sure enough, there is an afterlife. Or, maybe they just felt like including a false ending.

"(Don't Fear) the Reaper" spent twenty weeks on the pop chart, peaking this week in 1976. But instead of enjoying their new found exposure, Dharma found himself defending his song. His inclusion of Romeo and Juliet led some listeners to think the song was promoting suicide. He would say later: "Romeo and Juliet, I used as an example of a couple who had faith to take their love elsewhere when they weren't permitted the freedom to love here and now. What I meant was, they're in eternity cause they had the faith to believe in the possibility. It frankly never occurred to me that the suicide aspect of their story would be plugged in to people's take on 'Reaper,' making it an advertisement for suicide. . . It would bother me to know the song gave someone an excuse to commit suicide." Dharma also felt that, with a charting hit, the band lost their direction for a while. As he has said: "it was good for business, but bad for art. Ever since 'The Reaper' was a hit we've been under pressure to duplicate that success. The body of our work failed. . . everyone tried to write a hit single and that's a bad mistake. The Cult is never destined to be successful at a format. To be a singles' band you have to win the casual buyer."

If the band was consciously trying to write hits, they failed miserably. Their only other Top 40 song, "Burnin' For You" peaked at #40 in October of 1981. Since then BÖC has remained as they always were, a band with a small yet loyal following.

And then, 24 years after the song's initial success, came "more cowbell." In the spring of 2000 Christoper Walken was the guest host on *Saturday Night Live*. As is custom on *SNL*, all the cast members submit proposals for sketches early in the week, most incorporating the talents of the guest host. Will Ferrell submitted a sketch in which Walken would play a music producer working with Blue Öyster Cult while recording "(Don't Fear) the Reaper" in the studio. During the recording session, Walken keeps pleading for "more cowbell" thus encouraging Ferrell (who plays the fictional Gene Freckle) to play his cowbell more and more enthusiastically, knocking into the other bandmates and cracking up some of the other players as well. When Walken exclaims: "Guess what? I got a fever, and the only prescription is more cowbell!" a new saying had entered the lexicon.

While the *SNL* skit brought new attention to Blue Öyster Cult's most famous song, its message has been with us forever. As Dharma wrote, the seasons don't fear death, "Nor do the wind, the sun or the rain." So why should we? Whether you believe in an afterlife or not, there is no denying that death is inevitable. So if we stop worrying about it and live our lives every day to the fullest, we'll be better off. And if maximizing every day also means having a good laugh, you can always watch the "More Cowbell" sketch. Hopefully it cracks you up like it did Jimmy Fallon.

### November 11th

On this date in 1972, Mott the Hoople was at their highest-chart position ever, with "All the Young Dudes" sitting at #37 on *Billboard*'s Hot 100 chart. The song was given to them by one of their most famous fans in an effort to save the band from breaking up. The plan worked. Though "All the Young Dudes" was only a modest hit it earned the band many more fans and instead of disbanding, they'd remain active throughout the seventies. Here's the story:

Mott the Hoople's self-titled debut album, released in 1969, was one of those LPs that didn't sell extraordinarily well but did create a small, cult like following. But at least that album cracked the *Billboard* Top 200 album chart (at #185). Their next three LPs failed to do so and their record label was close to giving up on the band. That's when Mott's bass player, Pete Overend Watts, called David Bowie asking for work. Bowie was a big fan of Mott the Hoople so he was devastated when he found out that they were going to disband. He felt he had to do something. He offered to produce an album for the band if they stayed together plus he got them some time in a recording studio (their record label was unwilling to shell out any more funds for recording). Then, Bowie offered them a song he'd already written and wanted to include on his upcoming *The Rise and Fall of Ziggy Stardust and the Spiders from Mars* album. The band gave a listen to the song but turned it down. That song, "Suffragette City" would go on to be one of Bowie's signature songs. Still wanting to offer a song for the band in hopes of saving them, Bowie sat down and wrote one for them. Rock and roll legend says he sat cross-legged in lead singer Ian Hunter's apartment and penned it in no time. This song, "All the Young Dudes," Mott the Hoople loved. In fact, drummer Dale Griffin remembers thinking, "He wants to give us that? He must be crazy!" Mott the Hoople took Bowie up on his offer to produce their next LP which, of course, included "All the Young Dudes."

The ending of the song was completely ad-libbed when they were working in the studio. During the coda, where the chorus is repeated over and over in "Hey Jude" style, Hunter recalled a recent gig where he was being heckled and just started speaking the, "Hey, you down there, you with the glasses," part. The band and Bowie loved it so they kept it in.

"All the Young Dudes" not only became Mott the Hoople's biggest hit but also an anthem for the Glam Rock era where sexual lines were being confused if not blatantly crossed. The line, "Lucy looks sweet 'cause he dresses like a queen," not only makes the song a glam rock anthem but also a gay anthem as well. None other than David Bowie was giving permission to dress and act as you wish. The song is also a kiss off to the previous decade's Rock Gods with the line: "My brother's back at home with his Beatles and his Stones. We never got it off on that revolution stuff," and by name checking T-Rex, Bowie was practically creating a playlist for glam rockers.

There is nothing sonically unique about glam rock; it's simply rock music. The "glam" comes from the outlandish attire and make-up worn by the performers and also adopted by many of their fans as well as some of the themes in their songs. Mott the Hoople never exactly went full-glam like Bowie or Marc Bolan, so though they sang one of the era's defining songs, you're hard pressed to find pictures of them with glitter eye shadow and lipstick (like you can of Bowie and Bolan). Still, by recording a song that David Bowie penned for them, the band not only salvaged their own recording career but they provided a track that will forever capture the zeitgeist of that era, when dressing like a queen was more important than all that revolution stuff (what a drag.) Give "All the Young Dudes" a loud and proud spin today and see if you can't feel the vibe as one era came to an end and another was just beginning.

On this date in 1991, Naughty By Nature was sitting at #6 on the *Billboard* Hot 100 chart with its single "O.P.P." To date, it's the highest the East Orange, New Jersey based hip hop trio has ever been on the charts. Besides having a hit song and entering a new phrase into the lexicon of the early nineties (for a while, you couldn't be into anything - you had to be "down wit it," that's how much "O.P.P." permeated the culture), Naughty By Nature also gave us one of the great, early examples of how powerful sampling could be in rap music.

Naughty By Nature was made up of rappers, Treach and Vin Rock and DJ Kay Gee. They released an album in 1989 using the name New Style then fellow New Jersey rapper Queen Latifah took them under her wing. She got them signed to her record label, Tommy Boy Records, and encouraged them to change their name and find a more commercial sound.

One day Kay Gee was scratching the Jackson 5 hit song, "ABC" and Treach heard it and wanted to build a song around it. The issue of sampling was huge at the time as Vanilla Ice was going through his well-publicized problems regarding his song "Ice Ice Baby" and whether he should be sharing writing credits with Queen and David Bowie (who had written "Under Pressure"). The band approached Motown to get clearance for the sample and Motown demanded 75% of the publishing for the new song. Despite that exorbitant demand, they moved forward, as Kay Gee explained to *Rolling Stone* magazine: "One hundred percent of nothing is nothing, and 25 percent of 2 million sold is a lot. We knew that it was gonna be huge, so we didn't care."

Treach remembered a drug dealer in his neighborhood who used to say he was, "down wit O.P.M.," meaning other people's money. Treach started playing with that idea, changing the last letter to a "P" and having it mean different things for a man or for a woman and not saying what it meant but explaining it. This way they could get the song played on radio. As Treach has said: "The record probably would have been banned if radio had known what we was talkin' about. It took them a year or two to figure out what it meant. If you weren't listening or weren't really into hip hop, it wasn't easy." The song also features a classic "call and response" which helped launch its popularity. Few among us could ever hear the question, "you down wit O.P.P?" without yelling back, "yeah you know me!"

The final piece of the puzzle for Naughty By Nature was the video for the song. MTV was still playing music videos in the early nineties and, where just a few years prior the only hip hop videos that ever got played were relegated to their *Yo! MTV Raps* show, by 1991 their airwaves were flooded with MC Hammer, Vanilla Ice and Salt-N-Pepa. "O.P.P." went into heavy rotation on MTV and it changed everything for Naughty By Nature. Where before they could go wherever they pleased, once the video came out they were as recognizable as any stars. Treach has said: "We went into malls and security was like, 'Yo, don't ever come in here again without tellin' us' because it was a mob. We had to run out the back door to get away."

Naughty By Nature came close to matching their early success with 1993's "Hip Hop Hooray," which also uses a "call and response" to elicit listener reaction. That song peaked at #8. Internal squabbles between the three men have caused them to stop recording together although from time to time they have performed as the original trio, delighting fans and taking them back to the early nineties when the simple question, "You down wit O.P.P?" could get everyone answering in unison, "Yeah you know me!"

**November 13<sup>th</sup>**

On this date in 1992, Boyz II Men's "End of the Road" reached its own end of the road at #1, wrapping up a record breaking thirteen straight weeks perched at the top of the *Billboard* Hot 100 chart. The band that nobody had heard of just two years ago now had the most successful single of all time.

The roots of Boyz II Men can be traced to 1988 when four young men, Nathan Morris, Marc Nelson , Wanya Morris and Shawn Stockman, who were attending the Philadelphia High School for Creative and Performing Arts were practicing their harmonies in a men's room one day. In walked Michael McCary, with his incredibly deep and smooth voice, and he spontaneously joined in. The quintet knew instantly how great they sounded together and started practicing regularly (school bathrooms were their favorite place to rehearse because of the excellent acoustics). The young men were inspired by the band New Edition and decided to name themselves Boyz II Men, a take on the song "Boys to Men" from New Edition's 1988 LP *Heart Break*. They lost Marc Nelson along the way leaving them with the quartet that would go on to international fame.

The first step towards that fame came when the band snuck backstage after a New Edition show to meet their idols. They sang New Edition's "Can You Stand the Rain" for Michael Bivins, who along with fellow bandmates Ricky Bell and Ronnie DeVoe had just announced they were forming a New Edition spin-off called Bell Biv DeVoe. Bivins was blown away and offered to manage the group and produce their first LP. The combination of new jack swing beats with classic a cappella harmonies gave Boys II Men a unique sound that would be dubbed "hip hop/doo-wop." The band, with Bivins at the controls, recorded their debut album, *Cooleyhighharmony*, in the fall of 1990 and released their first single, "Motownphilly," in January of 1991. That song peaked at #3 in September of that year, introducing the world to this new group and their incredible harmonies.

Meanwhile, work was being done on an Eddie Murphy comedy called *Boomerang* and Antonio "L. A." Reid and Kenneth "Babyface" Edmonds were commissioned to come up with songs for the soundtrack. Babyface had recently gone through a divorce and when he sat down to write a song with Daryl Simmons, Simmons divulged that he was currently going through a similar breakup. With sadness and loss on their mind the two came up with the lyrics and melody for "End of the Road." When they presented it to Reid, he recognized the song's hit potential immediately, saying, "That's a smash!" Babyface offered to sing the song but Reid thought it would be perfect for Boyz II Men. The band was opening for MC Hammer so on an off day in the touring schedule they flew to Philadelphia to record their vocals. The four young men tapped into the emotion of the song so perfectly that they were literally moved to tears in between takes. Stockman told *Rolling Stone:* "Each time we played it and sang it, we got more and more into it. Guys were, like, crying and everything in the studio." Morris felt the song was a gift from above, saying, "It had to be the Lord that brought us that song and said, 'Here you go, Boyz II Men, here's something to help you blow up.'"

Blow up indeed. While "Motownphilly" and its follow-up "It's So Hard to Say Goodbye" had given notice that Boyz II Men was a band to keep your eye on, "End of the Road" made them superstars. The previous record for the longest consecutive stay at #1 had been held by Elvis Presley, whose double-sided single, "Don't Be Cruel" and "Hound Dog" had spent eleven weeks at #1 in 1956. The quartet smashed that record by two weeks. "End of the Road" also won the Grammy for Best R&B Performance by a Group with Vocal and Best R&B Song. And they weren't nearly finished; they'd beat their own record just a few years later when "I'll Make Love to You" spent fourteen weeks at #1. The band that had come together singing in a school bathroom and had to sneak back stage to get their big break, had conquered the world of music in just a few short years. They'd not only gone from boys to men they'd transformed from unknowns to international superstars.

## November 14th

On this date in 1994, Sheryl Crow was sitting at #2 on the *Billboard* Hot 100 chart for a frustrating sixth straight week, lodged firmly behind Boyz II Men's "I'll Make Love to You." Though Crow's song never would make it to #1 (in fact, to date, Crow has never been to the very top of the pop chart), "All I Wanna Do" did help introduce the musical world to this fresh new voice, although, as it turned out, we'd probably all heard her before.

Sheryl Suzanne Crow was born in Missouri in 1962 to a musical family; her mother was a piano teacher and her father, a trumpet playing lawyer. After college, she followed in her mother's footsteps, teaching music at a local elementary school while she sang with a number of bands and made some money doing jingles. Her voice was heard nationwide singing: "It's a good time for the great taste of McDonalds." Eventually Crow moved to Los Angeles to see if she could make it in music and before long she was singing backup for artists like Stevie Wonder, Rod Stewart and the Eagles. One day while singing for a Johnny Mathis record she overheard some other singers talking about auditioning for an upcoming Michael Jackson tour. She made note of where and when it would be and showed up uninvited. She landed the job and wound up singing backup on Jackson's Bad World Tour, performing in front of over four million people. After coming off the road with Jackson she landed other high profile backup jobs, recording, performing and even writing songs for Tina Turner, Phil Collins, Celine Dion and others. One day, while singing for Don Henley, the Eagle great pulled her aside and told her to stop supporting other artists. She was too talented to be a backup singer and her songs were too good to let others sing. With Henley's encouragement she began shopping for a record deal. She signed with A&M and in 1992 began work on a debut album. But as the album neared release, she and her label both thought it was subpar. The material was deemed "too slick" and "overly-produced" and at the last minute the album was shelved.

At a crossroads in her career, Crow started dating a musician named Kevin Gilbert who would get together weekly with a bunch of other musicians for a loose and informal jam session they dubbed the Tuesday Night Music Club. Crow started attending and before long she and the other musicians were working on original material that she would eventually turn into her debut album.

"All I Wanna Do" is an example of this collaboration. Crow read a poem one day called "Fun" and she connected with its characters who sit around and drink all day. She contacted the poet, Wyn Cooper, and asked him if she could take his poetry and set it music. Cooper was thrilled and Crow, along with other members of the Tuesday Night Music Club, set the poem to a mid-tempo, jangling beat. She added a spoken intro, which began with, "This ain't no disco," an obvious ode to the Talking Heads' "Life During Wartime," and delivered the verses in a half-spoken, almost conversational, singing style that reminded many of the Stealers Wheels' "Stuck in the Middle with You."

As work neared completion on the album, Crow didn't feel "All I Wanna Do" was worthy of inclusion but her brother talked her into it, telling her the song was a hit and she'd be crazy to leave it off. Crow included "All I Wanna Do," gave her debut album the name *Tuesday Night Music Club* and this time she and A&M had no hesitations. The album was released in the summer of 1993 along with the slow and melodic "Run Baby Run" as a lead single. Neither were very successful and then Henley gave Crow her second big boost when he asked her to open for the Eagles on their Hell Freezes Over reunion tour. In just a few short years she'd gone from singing backup for Henley to opening for him. And exposure from that tour helped her start gaining some recognition. When her next two singles, "All I Wanna Do" and "Leaving Las Vegas" started selling so too did her album. "Leaving Las Vegas" was another song inspired by literature as the title was borrowed from the book of the same name by John O'Brien.

A year after the album had been released it was suddenly everywhere. And "All I Wanna Do" is a big reason. It captured much of the ethos of the early nineties. The same sense of apathy that enraged the grunge bands was evident, but instead of pissing Crow off, she simply raised a drink and got a, "Good beer buzz early in the mornin'." The song was the perfect tonic for that rage which is probably a big reason for its success. And it not only helped promote *Tuesday*

*Night Music Club,* which has sold over 8 million units, but it helped launch Crow's career. She hasn't had to sing jingles or backup since then, becoming a huge star just as Don Henley had predicted.


## November 15th

On this date in 1990, German record producer Frank Farian called a press conference to tell the pop world what it pretty much already knew: that the Grammy Award winning duo Milli Vanilli was a lip syncing fraud (not his words). The band that had burst onto the scene just a year before and rose to popularity with their combination of catchy songs, exotically good looks and choreographed dance moves, was now exposed as a hoax. And none of their lives would ever be the same again.

The Milli Vanilli story can be traced to a Maryland-based band called Numarx. They released a dance track in 1987 called "Girl You Know It's True" which got little notice in the States but was a club hit in Germany. Frank Farian, a German record producer and talent manager, who had had some success with a disco group called Boney M, heard the song and thought he could make it an international hit. Farian was also very aware of the changing priorities in pop music, driven by the power of MTV, that an act's look was as important (if not more so) than its sound. He assembled a group of studio musicians to reproduce "Girl You Know It's True." He then found three American soldiers, singers John Davis and Brad Howell and rapper Charles Shaw, who were stationed in Germany, to sing and rap on the track. Farian then went on a talent search to find the frontmen who could lip-sync the song for a video. He knew what he wanted: good looking young men with rhythm who could be the face of the song. When dancers Rob Pilatus and Fabrice Morvan walked into his office one day looking for work, he knew he'd found his frontmen.

Farian released the first Milli Vanilli album in Europe called *All or Nothing* using a picture of "Rob and Fab" as the cover. No credit was given in the liner notes to anyone who played or sang on the album which was not uncommon in Europe. In fact, Farian had done this before with impunity. He often sang the songs for his disco band Boney M, who would lip-sync to them in concert. When Arista signed the band for U.S. distribution, Farian handed in a reworked album titled *Girl You Know It's True* and credited the singing to Rob Pilatus and Fabrice Morvan. A video was put together for the lead single (the title track) and it immediately went into heavy rotation on MTV. The video checked off all the boxes to be a hit: catchy song, good looking singers with great dance moves, a little bit of rap. This type of sound was huge in the late eighties, this combination of Euro-dance with a touch of rap and Milli Vanilli was in the right place at the right time. And in their skin tight biker shorts doing the running man dance, they had quite the visual appeal to set them apart. "Girl You Know It's True" was ubiquitous on radio and MTV throughout the summer of 1989 and Milli Vanilli would reach the top of the charts with each of their first four singles

("Girl" as well as, "Baby Don't Forget My Number", "Blame It On the Rain" and "Girl I'm Gonna Miss You").

But cracks started to show early on. According to people at MTV, the first time Rob and Fab were interviewed and everyone heard their thick German accents and rough English skills, rumors started spreading that maybe the duo weren't the ones singing on the record. Then, at a show in Connecticut in the summer of 1989, as they were performing "Girl You Know It's True," the tape that they were lip-syncing to got jammed. It just kept repeating, "Girl you know it's Girl you know it's Girl you know it's . . ." Rob and Fab ran off the stage but according to Downtown Julie Brown, who was MCing the show, no one in the audience seemed to care. In December of 1989 Charles Shaw (the actual rapper on the song) came forward with the truth, claiming he'd been paid just $6,000 for his work with no percentage of record sales. Farian quickly cut him a $150,000 check and suddenly Shaw wasn't talking anymore.

All of this suspicion did not slow down record sales, video plays or even awards. At the Grammy Awards in February of 1990, Milli Vanilli beat out Tone Lōc, Neneh Cherry, the Indigo Girls and Soul II Soul for Best New Artist.

The band was on a roll and Farian began preparing material for a follow-up album. As work progressed through the summer of 1990 Pilatus and Morvan began insisting that they be allowed to sing and even write some songs for this next album. But Farian refused. He wanted to duplicate their previous success, with him producing all of the songs with studio musicians and singers and Rob and Fab playing the performer role. Things came to a head just as the album was being finalized with Rob and Fab threatening to come forward with the truth. So Farian decided to beat them to it, calling a press conference on this date in 1990 to pull back the curtain on his great ruse.

The new album was quickly reworked and released only in Europe. It was given the title *The Moment of Truth* and credited to the Real Milli Vanilli. The front and back cover art work was changed at the last minute but they forgot to change the text on the spine so that still read the original album title: *Keep On Running*. In the U.S., RCA looked to distance themselves as much as possible from the controversy so the album was released under the band name Try 'N' B. The Recording Academy decided to take back their Grammy so if you look at the list of Best New Artists by year, 1990's is listed as "vacated."

Pilatus and Morvan moved to Los Angeles where they released an album under the name Rob & Fab. It sold about 2,000 copies. Despite this, a few years later, Farian started to work on a Milli Vanilli comeback record called *Back and in Attack*. This time he included Rob and Fab along with some of the original musicians and singers. But as the album was finishing up Rob Pilatus was arrested for drug possession and theft. Farian bailed him out of jail and paid for a stint in rehab but just as a promotional tour was about to get underway, Pilatus was found dead in his Frankfurt hotel room of an alcohol and drug overdose. He was 32 years old. Morvan has stayed active in the music industry although he's never come near to duplicating the success of his Milli Vanilli days. Farian has fared slightly better. He produced the Euro-dance band Le Bouche in the nineties and helped them score a hit with "Sweet Dreams (Ola Ola E)." *Back and in Attack* remains unreleased.

## November 16th

On this date in 1981, a band named Tommy Tutone released a song that would drive women named Jenny, and people with a specific phone number, crazy. The song became a monster hit, largely because of the song's video, leaving Tommy Tutone as the quintessential One Hit Wonder.

In the late seventies, musicians Tommy Heath and Jim Keller came together to form a band in California. They originally called themselves Tommy and the Tu-Tones but shortened that to Tommy Tutone. Their eponymous debut was released in early 1980, climbing to #68 on the album chart with its only single, "Angel Say No," just cracking the Top 40.

Alex Call was a friend of Jim Keller's and when his own band, Clover, broke up in the late seventies he took a stab at going solo and also selling songs to other bands. One day he was sitting in his backyard, thinking about writing a song that would, in his words, "fuckin' rock out." He channeled the Kinks and early Rolling Stones, aiming to create what he described as: "A timeless rocker akin to the archetypal rock-n-roll instrumentals that I dug when I was a kid. I wasn't looking to copy those songs, but I wanted something that had that primordial rock vibe." He came up with the opening riff, the melody and the chorus with the name "Jenny" and the phone number 867-5309 which he pulled from thin air but loved how it fit perfectly with the rhythm. From there he went inside to his little home studio and laid down the track with the limited lyrics he had. By chance, Jim Keller, stopped over that same day. Call played Keller what he had and told him he was stuck for any more ideas and then Keller just blurted out, "Al, it's a girl's number on a bathroom wall." They both laughed at that because it was so obvious to them, yet Call had missed it. Within twenty minutes the two had written the verses and completed the song. Because Keller was in a band with a record deal and Call was not, Keller took the song and presented it to the rest of his bandmates. Someone suggested they change the phone number to a phony 555 exchange (like what happens in the movies when they say a phone number) but they all agreed that ruined the song so they kept it as it was. "867-5309/Jenny" was recorded and released as the lead single to their second album, *Tommy Tutone 2*. A low budget video was made which shows the protagonist of the song so obsessed with this woman he winds up in therapy, outside her window peeping in and ultimately arrested for his crimes. In 1981 MTV was brand new and desperate for videos so "867-5309/Jenny" got plenty of plays and helped promote the song.

As "Jenny" started climbing the charts some people's phones started ringing off the hook. Anyone in any area code with the number 867-5309 started getting prank calls at all hours of the day, with most simply asking for Jenny before hanging up. The band started getting approached at gigs by angry people with that number but were forced to change it. Even just women with the name Jenny were bothered by the song. Call says, "I've met a few Jennies who've said, 'Oh, you're the guy who ruined my high school years.'"

When Call or Keller was interviewed about the song, they often made up stories, sometimes saying the song was inspired by a Jenny who worked at a recording studio or that one of them had actually seen the phone number written on a bathroom stall. The truth, that Call had come up with the name while sitting in his backyard and the number just sounded great when sung with the tempo of the track, was just too boring.

"867-5309/Jenny" was released on this day in 1981. The song peaked at #4 in May of 1982 and would end up being Tommy Tutone's only hit song. The band took a hiatus after their third album flopped but today they still tour, usually as part of an eighties' package tour. Call continued to write songs, and though artists such as Pat Benatar and Huey Lewis have recorded his compositions he's never matched the success he had with Jenny and that phone number, which still lives on even today. A few years ago a New Yorker who had the number 212-867-5309 tried to sell it on E-bay. The bidding got to $80,000, mostly from businesses who thought it would be good promotion to have such a recognizable number. But then the auction was shut down because phone numbers are not technically owned by their users. The name and number are also often used as a brush-off by women. Many a guy has been given a cocktail napkin by a woman after asking for her number, only to find out it says, "Jenny - 867-5309." And if you Google "most famous phone number," well, you can imagine what comes up. Phone calls may no longer be "the price of a dime" but when anyone thinks "famous phone number," it's likely they'll blurt out 867-5309.

## November 17th

On this date in 1971, the band Faces released their third album, with the clever title *A Nod's As Good As a Wink... to a Blind Horse*. The annals of rock and roll are littered with bands who were unable to capture their ferocious live sound in the studio but there is probably no better example of this than Faces. They are considered by many to be a great live band, with their concerts often erupting into spontaneous parties and they were indeed one of the highest-grossing touring acts in the first half of the seventies. But their albums never quite captured the raucous madness that was a live Faces show. *A Nod's As Good As a Wink* did come closest and it went on to be their most successful release.

Faces formed from the ashes of the Small Faces. When Steve Marriott left that band (to form Humble Pie) the remaining members (keyboardist Ian McLagan, Ronnie Lane on bass and drummer Kenney Jones) recruited Ronnie Wood to take Marriott's place on guitar and Rod Stewart to take over vocals. Their record company urged them to keep the name Small Faces since they already had a strong following, especially in their native England, but they wanted a new identity so they shortened the name to simply Faces.

Faces toured and recorded at a furious rate. They released their debut LP in March of 1970, their follow-up in February of 1971 and their third album on this date in 1971. In the meantime they played to packed houses regularly and, if that weren't enough, Stewart began focusing on a solo career. In fact his third solo album, *Every Picture Tells a Story*, which had been released a few months prior to *A Nod*, was the beginning of the end for Faces. Stewart's solo success, with "Maggie May" hitting #1 in October of 1971, was forcing him further and further away from the band and by the time they started working on their fourth LP, *Ohh La La*, he was practically nonexistent in the studio. By 1975 they were all but finished, so when Ronnie Wood was offered Mick Taylor's old job by the Rolling Stones it was a no-brainer. Wood's departure was the final nail in the Faces' coffin although the band has reformed from time to time for one-off appearances.

*A Nod's As Good As a Wink... to a Blind Horse* made it all the way to #6 on the *Billboard* album chart and "Stay with Me" (Stewart and Wood's hilarious account of sleeping with a groupie named Rita) hit #17 on the pop chart. But Faces are one of those bands that none of their recordings could ever do them justice. Anyone who ever saw them live will tell you there was magic in their performances. In his autobiography, Stewart claimed Faces was the first band to kick soccer balls into the audience. And the first band to have a full bar on stage ("It saved the time and energy wasted hopping off into the wings for refreshments," he wrote). They were imperfect musicians who never started a show with a set-list (between each song they'd huddle up to discuss what they should play next). Stewart felt this was a key to their success as he wrote in that same autobiography: "Our sloppiness and looseness turned out to be the thing that made us vulnerable and appealing and, in the end, entertaining. You want an entertainer to give the impression of being capable of a fuck-up." Fuck-ups aside, Faces knew how to throw a party and if you were lucky enough to see them back in their torrid touring days of the early seventies, you'll probably never forget it. Whether you did or not, give *A Nod's As Good As a Wink... to a Blind Horse* a spin today. Or if you don't have the time, at least crank up "Stay With Me," and try to appreciate one of rock's most underrated bands. They were far from perfect, but there was genius in their "fuck-ups" nonetheless.

**November 18th**

On this date in 1976, Richard Hell performed at CBGB in lower Manhattan with his brand new band Richard Hell and the Voidoids. This was by no means the first time Hell had played on that famous stage, in fact rock and roll legend has it that he actually had a hand in building the thing, but this was the first time he played there with the band and the lineup that would finally get his punk anthem "Blank Generation" recorded and released. Hell is as much of a punk-pioneer as any Ramone or Sex Pistol, and if you've never heard of him it's because, in the true punk spirit, he grew bored and frustrated with the music scene early on and moved on to other artistic endeavors.

Hell was born Richard Lester Meyers in Kentucky in 1949. He met Tom Verlaine while still in school and the two became fast friends, causing trouble wherever they went. They found themselves in Alabama at some point and were arrested for arson and vandalism. Hell eventually dropped out of high school and moved to New York City to be a poet but by 1972 he'd turned his attention to music and he and Verlaine would form the proto-punk band the Neon Boys in 1972. Their manager, Terry Ork, approached Hilly Kristal, CBGB's owner, in an effort to get his and other rock bands to play in his club. CBGB (which stands for Country, Blue Grass and Blues) had opened in 1973 with an emphasis, as the name implies, on more sedate forms of entertainment like country music and even poetry readings. Kristal, perhaps as a stall tactic, told Ork he couldn't host any rock bands because he didn't have a proper stage for them. As the story goes, Hell, Verlaine and some others rolled up their sleeves and got to work and built a stage. Soon enough, CBGB was transforming into a rock club with an emphasis on bands that played loud and hard and fast. The term "punk" was just starting to be used by this point to describe these young, brash bands.

The Neon Boys would evolve into Television, and by 1975 they had gathered quite a following in the music scene in downtown New York City. Hell was an energetic and charismatic frontman and the song he'd written called "Blank Generation" had already become an early punk rock anthem. The song captures all the ethos of the genre in one fast and furious three minute rampage: anger, anarchism, desperation. It's all right there in Hell's greatest contribution to the movement. Hell also became a fashion plate for the scene. He was one of the first to spike his hair and take the stage in ripped clothing, often held together by safety pins. It's a look and attitude that many copied, in fact Malcolm McLaren, who was right there at the genesis of the punk scene in New York City, took many of these elements back home with him to London and implemented them when he created the Sex Pistols.

By 1975 Hell and Verlaine had fallen out and soon after, Hell formed the band that bore his name and would take the stage at CBGB for the first time on this night in 1976. Richard Hell and the Voidoids would go on to release two albums, neither of which troubled the charts. But today the first one, 1977's *Blank Generation*, is revered as an innovative record for the whole punk movement.

Punk got commercialized pretty early on. The authenticity of the scene was gone within a few short years. When you could buy jeans that were already frayed and torn and held together with safety pins (for more money than non-ripped jeans) the whole punk spirit was essentially gone. Hell kicked around the music scene for a little while longer but eventually returned to his original love of writing. He's released books and poems and in 2013 he published an autobiography called *I Dreamed I Was a Very Clean Tramp* in which he writes: "Half of the beauty of rock and roll, is that anyone can do it." Certainly he and his contemporaries proved that in the mid-seventies you didn't need any special musical talent. Rock and roll wasn't just for the prodigies or virtuosos. If you had authentic emotion and an ability to express it (and were able to help build a stage) you could scream your message into a microphone and make a connection with an audience. Or maybe an entire generation. Hell belonged to that generation. The blank generation. Still does. But as he adds in that timeless punk anthem, he could also, "take it or leave it." That was the overall attitude of punk rockers from day one: anger mixed with apathy. Fury with indifference. Attitude with lassitude. Before 5th Avenue got hold of it, that was the maddening enigma of punk rock and no one embodied it better than Richard Hell.

## November 19th

On this date in 1981, Journey' s "Don't Stop Believin'" was making a slow and steady climb up the charts. It had been released on October 6th and entered the Top 40 a month later. The song would peak at #9 in mid-December and though it is not Journey's most commercially successful song (that honor belongs to "Open Arms" which went to #2 in 1982) no one who has ever attended a wedding or sang at a karaoke bar or seen an eighties' cover band would ever argue that it's not Journey's most recognizable song. And it all began with a lead singer's inability to fall asleep on the road.

Journey was formed in San Francisco in 1973 as members of two former bands (Santana's and a band called Frumious Bandersnatch) came together and started playing jazz fusion. After three albums that weren't exactly big sellers, the band must have come to the realization that nobody buys jazz fusion albums and they decided to take their band in a different direction. At the urging of their record label they decided to hire a frontman and start playing a more accessible form of rock (you know, with words and a melody). They hired singer Steve Perry and when their first album with him (1978's *Infinity*) went to #21 they knew they were on to something. Subsequent albums did slightly better (1979's *Evolution* went to #20 and then 1980's *Departure* peaked at #8) and the band started tasting real success. They were poised for a breakout. While touring, they started to prepare material for what they hoped would be the catalyst to worldwide fame.

It was on tour one night that Steve Perry found himself unable to sleep. He was in a hotel in Detroit and after tossing and turning for some time he decided to look out the window. He was caught by how the street lights cast a glow directly underneath them but nowhere else. He'd see people passing under a streetlight and then they'd seemingly disappear. This idea of disappearing sat on his mind as did the words "streetlights people." Perry began working on lyrics, inspired by his sleepless night in Detroit, and including mysterious imagery like strangers waiting up the boulevard and rolling dice just one more time. He included the line, "Born and raised in South Detroit," even though any Detroiter will tell you there is no such place or neighborhood in their fine city.

Perry brought the lyrics of the song to a band rehearsal one day and "Don't Stop Believin'" evolved as a true collaborative effort.

The structure of the song is unique in that the big pay-off, the part you most want to sing along to ("Don't stop believin', hold on to that feeling...") only comes at the end. The chorus ("Strangers waiting up and down the boulevard") is a good section but the real power in the song are the words of the title and Perry only sings them at the very end. Perhaps that's one of the charms of the song. There's a built-in anticipation that forces the listener to be patient and wait through the slow and powerful build up till everything climaxes in that high energy finale. Or maybe the charm is that the lyrics talk of winners and losers and smoky rooms and cheap perfume - imagery that is timeless and universally relatable and poetically romantic. Or maybe it's the combination of Jonathan Cain's keyboard opening, Neal Schon's soaring guitar work and Perry's raspy voice. Whatever it is, "Don't Stop Believin'" is one of those songs that forces people to sing along, nay, scream along. It's a song that grabs the listener and pull them in and doesn't let up till the end.

Journey's 1981 album *Escape* would indeed become the band's breakthrough moment. The LP produced four Top 20 hits and has sold over 12 million units. And while their chart dominance only lasted a few years, Journey continues to tour to this day, getting crowds everywhere to scream along to their signature song. Even though it's not Steve Perry fronting the band anymore, the song he began on a sleepless night in Detroit will forever be a staple at parties and in bars. Everywhere, in fact, but in South Detroit.

### November 20th

On this date in 1991, Prince was sitting atop the *Billboard* Hot 100 Chart with his song "Cream." He had taken over the #1 spot two weeks earlier, bumping Karyn White's "Romantic" from the top. "Cream" would enjoy a two week run at #1 before being knocked off the top by, brace yourself, Michael Bolton's unnecessary cover of "When a Man Loves a Woman." As if that atrocity isn't enough, "Cream" was Prince's last #1 so you could say his days as a chart-topping artist were ended by Michael Bolton. There is no explaining taste.

Prince Rodgers Nelson was born in 1958 in Minneapolis, Minnesota. He signed his first record contract when he was just seventeen and 1984's *Purple Rain*, the album and movie, catapulted him into superstardom. Throughout his career, Prince had a very fickle relationship with commercial success. It seemed that every time he attained it, he pushed back against it. Every time his bandwagon got full he veered off the road and tossed those new-found fans aside. Instead of following up *Purple Rain* with a *Purple Rain Two* type of album he released the much less commercially accessible *Around the World in a Day*. When his *Batman* soundtrack returned him to the top of the charts he subjected his fan base to the movie *Graffiti Bridge*. And when that movie under-performed (and rightfully so) he released *Diamonds and Pearls*, his most successful work of the nineties.

As *Diamonds and Pearls* was nearing completion Prince's label wanted him to release "Cream" as the lead single. They heard its potential and suspected it would be a hit and perhaps help the album move numbers closer to his eighties' LPs. Prince, however, wanted the funk orgy "Gett Off" to be the lead single and since Warner was done arguing with their pestilent pop star they let him have his way. "Gett Off" peaked at #21 so no one would say it was a flop but it didn't promote *Diamonds and Pearls* the way "Cream" eventually would. When it was released (in September of 1991) the song and the LP began their ascent. They'd both peak in November, the song at #1 and the album at #3.

Prince was rarely forthcoming about the origins of his songs and at first listen "Cream" is a simple ode to a beautiful woman (actually she's "filthy cute" and she knows it) who Prince is urging to "get on top." The word "cream," other than its obvious sexual connotations, isn't really explained in the lyrics nor does it have any meaning besides being repeated over and over. It's not exactly one of Prince's deeper songs. But when he released his *Hits/B Sides* compilation he mentioned in the liner notes that "Cream" was written, "while standing in front of a mirror." This is a claim Prince would often make in concert before launching into the song. Whether it's true or not, that explanation gives a different meaning to lines like: "You're so good. Baby there ain't nobody better," and, "Make the rules. Then break them all 'cause you are the best." Prince may have lacked the obedience to deliver a commercially viable product each and every time, but he never did lack for confidence.

After *Diamonds and Pearls*, Prince began a slow and steady decline in his commercial appeal. After a decade or more of being a pioneer in pop and dance music, he, for the first time in his career, began following trends, namely hip hop. His attempts to incorporate rap into his nineties music would make him feel like a poseur, something he'd never been, and this, in many fans' eyes and ears, was the main reason his sales began to sink. Plus he was confusing the public with stunts like writing "slave" on his face and changing his name to an unpronounceable symbol. When he left Warner and began releasing his own music through separate distribution deals, he no longer had the full promotional strength of a major record label behind him and he slipped even further into pop culture irrelevance. His career had a slight resurgence in 2004 when he was elected into the Rock and Roll Hall of Fame. He embarked on a world tour and released an album, *Musicology*, that got all the way to #3, though even that success is a bit inflated since Prince very cleverly boosted album sales by including a CD with every concert ticket he sold on that tour (a loophole that *Billboard* closed after Prince's tour).

As enigmatic and incredibly talented as Prince was, his success is hard to measure in commercial terms. Sure he sold tons of records and had chart success but with just five #1 singles in his career and six #1 albums, his numbers don't measure up to some of the greats in music history. Michael Jackson, for example, who Prince is so often compared to, had more than twice as many #1 songs. But Prince's influence on music goes so much deeper than chart success and sales numbers. He was an innovator throughout the eighties, a decade where substance was often outweighed by style and flash. Prince, incredible musician, singer, wordsmith and dancer, uniquely combined substance with style, art with flash. And while he'd never get back to #1 on the charts after this date in 1991 (and others like Michael Bolton would) no one would question his legitimacy as a musical icon. He did indeed make the rules. Then break 'em all 'cause he was the best.

## November 21st

On this date in 1970, the Carpenters' "We've Only Just Begun" began its fourth and final week lodged at #2 on the *Billboard* Hot 100 chart. The song would never reach the top, blocked by a combination of "I'll Be There" by the Jackson 5 and the Partridge Family's "I Think I Love You." In the history of pop music there are plenty of stories of successful songs being bogarted for ad campaigns. "We've Only Just Begun" may be the only example of the exact opposite taking place.

Paul Williams is a jack-of-all-trades in the entertainment industry. He's done everything from acting in films and on television, to writing scores for movies to singing and performing his own music. And he's written plenty of hits for other artists as well.

In 1969 he and fellow songwriter Roger Nichols were approached by Crocker National Bank to write a song for an ad campaign they were working on. When Williams innocently asked the ad agency, "What rhymes with Crocker?" they said that they weren't looking for a jingle. The concept they had was to appeal to young people who were just getting started in life. They wanted to shoot images from a wedding while a sweet sounding ballad played that fit the tone of a couple beginning their life together. They wanted to end the commercial with the message: "You've got a long way to go. We'd like to help you get there."

Williams and Nichols sat down and came up with a short ditty with the chorus, "We've only just begun," and the commercial first aired in the winter of 1970.

Soon after Richard Carpenter, one half of the singing sibling duo the Carpenters, saw the commercial and thought he recognized Williams' voice. Since they were both under contract to A&M Records it was easy enough for Carpenter to confirm his suspicion and he asked Williams if there was a complete song because he'd like to record it. Here's where there are differing stories. Williams claims he and Nichols had already written the verses and a bridge, believing the song had potential. In other places, it's been reported that Williams simply told Carpenter that the rest of the song existed, then he and Nichols huddled up to finish it. Either way, as Williams has said: "Roger Nichols and I expanded it as a complete song and never in our wildest dreams imagined it would be a hit. And then an angel sang it. When Karen Carpenter sings your songs, you are blessed."

Blessed indeed, for artist and composer. With "We've Only Just Begun" the Carpenters had scored back to back hits to start their recording career. "(They Long to Be) Close to You" had gone to #1 in the summer of 1970 and with two hits under their belt they'd go on to win the Grammy that year for Best New Artist. Williams would go on to write or cowrite plenty more Adult Contemporary hits including "Rainy Days and Mondays" for the Carpenters, "Evergreen" for Barbra Streisand and "The Rainbow Connection" which Jim Henson sang as Kermit the Frog in the 1979 film *The Muppet Movie*. He attributes his success to his authenticity, saying he writes about real events and with real emotions. Regarding his success with "We've Only Just Begun" he laughs when he says, it had, "all the romantic beginnings of a bank commercial. . . I think it was a hit because of, obviously, Karen's amazing vocal, but I think that any time we write authentically and honestly about what's going on in the center of our chest, because people are so much alike, there's a big a chance that it's going on in the center of your chest, too." As for the Carpenters, they enjoyed incredible success throughout the seventies, selling some 90 million records and playing to adoring fans throughout the decade. But in 1983 Karen Carpenter, at just 32, died of heart failure due to complications from an eating disorder.

We'll never know how many mortgages the commercial sold for Crocker Bank but the Carpenter's song has brought joy to millions and, with its imagery of "white lace and promises," was a very popular wedding song back in the day as well. You can probably find the original commercial on Youtube but to appreciate the voice of an angel, seek out the Carpenter's version and give it a listen today.

## November 22nd

On this date in 1986, Boston's *Third Stage* began its fourth and final week at the top of the *Billboard* 200 album chart. The LP that had been delayed for eight years due to internal band strife, squabbling with management and even a lawsuit with their record company, was now the biggest of the band's career. And much of it had to do with a leaked demo and the public's demand for more music from Boston.

Tom Scholz is the creative force behind Boston. He started writing music in the late sixties while attending the Massachusetts Institute of Technology. When he graduated MIT with a masters he started working at Polaroid, using his salary to build a state-of-the-art home studio that was the rival of most professional studios. He wrote and recorded many demos in that basement studio that would go on to become Boston classics; songs like "Peace of Mind", "Rock and Roll Band" and "More Than a Feeling." The demos attracted the attention of Epic Records who signed Boston and set up studio time for the band. Scholz, however, insisted that their record be recorded in his home studio and that he co-produce, so that he'd have as much creative control over the project as possible. He felt his standards were higher than anyone else's and if his name was going to be attached to a project he wanted it done right. The fact that Boston's self-titled debut went on to be one of the most successful debut albums of all time, selling 17 million copies and spending 132 weeks on *Billboard*'s Top 200 chart, seems to back up Scholz's demand for creative control. And also for not being rushed. When Epic wanted a follow-up and pressured him to complete it, despite taking two years to write and record *Don't Look Back*, Scholz was quick to blame the fact that the album didn't live up to its predecessor on having to rush through the record. *Don't Look Back* has sold seven million copies so it shouldn't be seen as an abject failure, although many of those sales came in the mid-eighties when the band returned again to popularity and their back catalog became some of the best-selling of any artist.

When Scholz began working on a third LP things became very dicey between him and Boston's management. He also became even more deliberate in the studio. He's an admitted "studio geek" and he was becoming obsessed with every new technological advancement in sound. Eventually, he advised the rest of the band that it was going to be awhile, if ever, that a new record would be complete and they were free to pursue other endeavors. Epic wanted a new album so badly they actually filed a lawsuit against Scholz to compel him to complete one (because nothing stirs the creative juices like a legal gun to the head). As the lawsuit continued, CBS (Epic's parent company) decided to withhold royalties from the band until the suit was settled. Scholz half-heartedly worked on material while he fought the legal battle. He also formed Scholz Research and Development Inc which designed and manufactured sound gear including a line of amplifiers called Rockman that are highly regarded in the industry.

Then, in 1984, six years after anyone had heard from Boston and with no news of a new album or material being anywhere near completion, a few radio stations started playing a song called "Amanda" and calling it, "a new song from the band Boston." Someone, presumably at Epic, had leaked the song. After a few weeks of airplay, CBS caught wind of the song being played and their president and CEO, Walter Yetnikoff, sent a cease and desist letter to the stations. But the attention the song had garnered in this short time inspired Scholz to get back to work on finishing the band's third album. He won his lawsuit, with CBS paying back millions in royalties and releasing the band from their contract. He then finished work on *Third Stage* and released it on MCA.

In September of 1986 the power ballad "Amanda" was officially released as the lead single and *Third Stage* also hit the record stores on vinyl as well as on the emerging new technology, compact disc. The song and the LP both hit the top of their respective charts in November of 1986 and *Third Stage* became the first CD-formatted album to be certified gold (500,000 copies) by the Recording Industry Association of America.

The band has failed to produce anywhere near those numbers with their subsequent releases (all spaced out way further than any record company would prefer) and while Scholz's high standards and methodical recording techniques can be credited for Boston's amazing sound, it must also be blamed for their lack of output. Although you can be sure an MIT grad has figured that out.

## November 23rd

On this date in 1949, Marcia Griffiths was born in Kingston, Jamaica. She's gone on to an incredible career in music, earning the nickname the Empress of Reggae and whether or not you've heard of her before, it is almost guaranteed you know some of the songs she's sung on and, unless you've spent the last 30 years in a cave, you've probably line-danced to her most famous song.

When Griffiths was just 13 years old she was singing along with a young neighbor who was playing guitar and a passerby (who happened to be the Jamaican singer, Phillips James) overheard her and was blown away. James encouraged the young girl to try out for an upcoming show and she won a spot to perform with the legendary ska band Byron Lee and the Dragonaires. The crowd loved her so much they called her out for an encore but since she'd only rehearsed one song she was unable to return to the stage. One song, it turned out, was enough, because the very next day she received two record contract offers. She selected the offer from Studio One and under the tutelage of the early reggae producer Clement Dodd (often called Sir Coxsone) she recorded her first song, "Feel Like Jumping," at age fourteen. This led to duets with singers such as Bob Andy, Tony Gregory and the legendary Bob Marley. Getting to work with Marley early on (with whom she recorded "Oh My Darling" in 1964) was a great opportunity and it encouraged the teenager to pursue a career in music.

A number of years later Griffiths was performing in Kingston and Marley's wife Rita Marley and another singer named Judy Mowatt happened to be in attendance. After the show Griffiths asked the two women if they'd like to try harmonizing and as soon as they sang together they knew it was magic. The next night Griffiths invited them on stage and, with nary a rehearsal, the three singers blew the audience away. They formed a group called the I-Threes and began performing regularly. Bob Marley came to see them often and loved their sound so much that when he lost Peter Tosh and Bunny Wailer in his band he decided to hire the I-Threes as his backup vocalists. This was 1974 and Marley's star was on the rise. Eric Clapton's cover of his "I Shot the Sherriff" had brought worldwide attention to reggae and soon enough he was touring the world. Marcia Griffiths was right there with the band during those meteoric years. She sang on some of his most recognizable recordings like "Waiting in Vain" , "Is This Love" and "One Love/People Get Ready."

But Griffiths' career was not relegated to being a backup singer. She released plenty of her own work, fifteen albums total. In 1982, she released a cover of

"Electric Boogie," a song written and originally recorded by Bunny Wailer in 1976 (Griffiths sang backup on the original). She had great success with it in her native Jamaica, reaching the top of the charts. Choreographer Ric Silver was hired to create a dance to go along with the song for the opening of a New York City nightclub. As his line dance, that he called the Electric Slide, took off, Griffiths rereleased "Electric Boogie" to capitalize on the craze. In January of 1990 her cover of "Electric Boogie" reached #51 on the pop chart, making it the most successful song in the U.S. recorded by a female reggae singer. The Electric Slide not only helped make Griffiths a household name but it made line dancing a trend at clubs and private parties.

There's a communal feeling dancers get when they are stepping in unison and it is something that is highly requested by some partiers. The repetitive nature of a line dance is what makes it popular, it has to be simple and easy to learn (and easy to execute after a few cocktails). It's this redundancy, along with the frequent playing of the associated song, that drives some people crazy. Line dancing is one of those things most people have strong opinions about, either for or against. Some people can't wait to take four steps to the right and four to the left, etc etc, while some people will only do it at gunpoint.

The Electric Slide swept across the U.S. in the early nineties and it was still popular when The Macarena came along and took over dance floors with a fury. Then towards the end of the millennium, an artist named DJ Casper took the Electric Slide and added some extra steps, rebranding it as the "Cha Cha Slide." Artists were seeing the immediate connection between creating a popular dance and record sales. In 2007 "Cupid Shuffle" with its corresponding line dance, was another big hit. The following year V.I.C. released a song called "Wobble" and to show how connected at the hip the dance is to the song's success, that single was out for three years before it entered the charts. When it did, it's because the Wobble dance had finally become popular at parties and in clubs (which thus, helped sell records - or in the case of "Wobble," downloads). "Crank That (Soulja Boy)" and "Watch Me (Whip/Nae Nae)" are two more recent examples of songs that benefitted from having an associated dance. All of these songs and dances can trace their roots to Marcia Griffiths' "Electric Boogie" and Ric Silver's simple and repetitive Electric Slide.

So now you know whom to credit. Or blame, depending on your opinion of line dancing.

### November 24th

On this date in 1982, Stevie Ray Vaughn and his band Double Trouble recorded the song "Pride and Joy" which would appear on his debut album *Texas Flood*. It was an original composition by the brilliant blues guitarist and it would not only make him a household name in rock music but would inspire an entire resurgence in interest in the blues in America. Vaughn has been compared favorably to axmen such as Muddy Waters, Otis Rush (whose classic 1958 blues song "Double Trouble" inspired Vaughn's band's name) and even Jimi Hendrix. And tragically, (much like Hendrix himself) his career was short yet influential and he left a legacy of incredible performances behind for generations to rock out to.

Vaughn was born in Dallas, Texas in 1954 and his older brother Jimmie, 3 years his senior, probably had the most influence on him as a child. Jimmie played guitar and so young Stevie wanted to learn as well. When he turned seven he got a guitar as a birthday gift and taught himself to play by ear. Since the records that were laying around the house were mostly blues albums, that's what he taught himself to play. By the time he was eleven he was playing in a band and by sixteen he was in a recording studio for the first time, laying down tracks with his band Cast of Thousands. He soon dropped out of high school and moved to Austin for its much richer musical history and opportunities.

The band Double Trouble came together in 1978 in Austin under Vaughn's leadership and guidance and they were soon creating quite the buzz throughout Texas. The band underwent some lineup changes but the one constant was Vaughn's incredible guitar work and blues singing. Their big break outside of the Lone Star State came in the summer of 1982 when they were invited to play at the Montreux Jazz Festival in Switzerland. Their set was well received with one reviewer writing: "He had no album, no record contract, no name, but he reduced the stage to a pile of smoking cinders and, afterward, everyone wanted to know who he was." One person who wanted to know who he was happened to be David Bowie, who caught the band's set and was so impressed he asked Vaughn to play on his upcoming album. That's Stevie Ray Vaughn's guitar work on "China Girl" and "Let's Dance" in case you thought the blues was the only thing he could play. Another chance encounter in Switzerland was with Jackson Browne who caught the band's set in the lounge of the Montreux Casino, and wound up joining them on stage and jamming with them all night. He was as impressed as Bowie and he offered the band free use of his personal recording studio in downtown Los Angeles which is where they convened on this day in 1982 to record "Pride and Joy" (a song Vaughn had written about a girl he was dating).

As "Let's Dance" began to sell big numbers Bowie made plans for a world tour. Realizing how essential his guitar work had been on the album, he invited Vaughn to be a part of the band but Epic had just signed Vaughn and Double Trouble and so the young guitarist had a decision to make: guaranteed money and the glory of a worldwide tour backing up a rock icon, or focus on the chance of making a name for himself and his band. He began rehearsing with Bowie for the Serious Moonlight Tour but then decided he wanted to focus on his own music. He actually gained notoriety in the industry for the decision he made and it helped build anticipation for his debut LP.

*Texas Flood* was released in June of 1983 and Vaughn and Double Trouble spent the rest of the year touring. In 1984 the National Blues Association named

Vaughn their Entertainer of the Year, marking the first time a white man had ever won the award.

The next few years would be marked by periods of recording and touring interspersed with stints in rehab while Vaughn fought his alcohol and drug addictions. His father had been a heavy drinker and Vaughn had suffered abuse at his drunken hands and this gene had clearly been passed down. According to Vaughn, at the height of his substance abuse he was consuming a quart of whiskey and snorting a quarter ounce of cocaine each day. But as the eighties came to an end it looked like Vaughn had conquered his demons and he was performing again and sounding better than ever.

On August 26th, 1990, he performed a show in Wisconsin alongside other guitar greats like Buddy Guy, Robert Cray and Eric Clapton. Even his brother Jimmie Vaughn was on the bill and the two got to play side-by-side that night. After the show, most of the musicians boarded four helicopters that were to take them to Chicago. Vaughn got on the third helicopter along with some of Clapton's people (including his agent and bodyguard.) The other three helicopters made it through the fog that night but Vaughn's did not. Just after midnight it struck the hill of a ski resort and everyone on board was killed. Jimmie Vaughn was given the sad task of identifying his brother's body. A few days later everyone from Buddy Guy to David Bowie to ZZ Top were in attendance at his funeral. Niles Rogers offered the eulogy and Stevie Wonder, Jackson Browne, and Bonnie Raitt sang "Amazing Grace." Here was yet another guitar great and rock and roll legend struck down in his prime.

They say if heaven has a band it must be pretty kick-ass and some even argue that's why God calls so many of these great musicians home before their time. While all that is clearly conjecture, what we do know is Stevie Ray Vaughn played guitar and sang the blues like a man possessed.

## November 25th

On this date in 1976, The Band performed their farewell concert, at San Francisco's Winterland Ballroom. The show was filmed by director Martin Scorsese and released in 1978 as *The Last Waltz*, perhaps the most critically acclaimed concert film and "rock-umentary" of all time.

Ronnie Hawkins is a Canadian rockabilly artist of American descent who rose to fame in the late fifties and is credited today with advancing rock music north of the border. His backing band was called the Hawks and it was filled with talent, mostly because of a shrewd strategy that Hawkins employed. Whenever a band started becoming popular anywhere near Toronto, where he had a stranglehold on the music scene, Hawkins would hire their best musicians for his own band. Using this poaching method, the Hawks built up a roster that was the envy of any band. At their height, the Hawks included Levon Helms, Richard Manuel,

Rick Danko, Garth Hudson and Robbie Robertson. Eventually though, the strategy backfired as the Hawks became so good, they were no longer content to be Hawkins' backing band. In 1963 they left him and, on their own, they performed under various names like the Canadian Squires and Levon and the Hawks. A few years later they heard Bob Dylan was looking for a backing band for his first U.S. "electric" tour and they landed that gig, appearing with Dylan under the name Bob Dylan and The Band. In between tours, Dylan invited the band to join him in Woodstock, New York and they agreed, renting a large pink house to crash in. They collaborated with Dylan during this time but also worked on original material of their own. When it came time to release their own music, they still hadn't settled on a name. Since everyone always knew them as someone else's band, and they were often just called "the band," they decided to adopt that as their name. When it came time to come up with a title for their debut album they made a similar decision. Since most of the work had been done at that large pink house, the LP was simply titled *Music from Big Pink*. That album, which not only features a few tracks written or cowritten by Bob Dylan but a cover that was painted by the folk legend, was met with great expectation in the rock community. And though it did not sell record numbers, it is respected today as a highly influential album and helped establish The Band as an important new voice in the folk rock and roots rock genres.

Over the next few years The Band furthered that reputation with landmark albums like their eponymous second LP and 1970's *Stage Fright*. Songs like "The Weight", "Up on Cripple Creek", "Rag Mama Rag" and "The Night They Drove Old Dixie Down" have become rock radio staples. But by 1976 they were weary of the road, specifically Robbie Robertson who urged his bandmates to retire from touring. When he got their agreement, he began planning a farewell concert. He envisioned something grandiose and memorable and then he reached out to his friend Martin Scorsese to find out if the filmmaker would be interested in taping the show and making it into a documentary. Scorsese signed on and plans got even more elaborate.

Thanksgiving happened to fall on this date in 1976 so as concert attendees filed into the Winterland Ballroom they were greeted with turkey dinners. Once the show got underway, it was clear this was going to be a star-studded evening. The Band had many admirers among rock's glitterati and many of them came out to perform alongside them at their farewell show. Most importantly to The Band, the two men who had helped them get their start, Ronnie Hawkins and Bob Dylan, each made appearances that night. Others included Muddy Waters, Van Morrison, Eric Clapton, Joni Mitchell and Ringo Starr. Neil Young, who sang "Helpless" with The Band, hit the stage with a noticeable bit of cocaine still in his nostril from a backstage bump. Post-production special effects were able to erase the drug but they couldn't do anything about Young's obvious coked-up demeanor.

Scorsese and a crew of seven cameramen filmed the show along with backstage interviews with the performers. Because of other film commitments it would take the director a year before he could even begin editing. *The Last Waltz* was not released until April of 1978. When it was, along with a triple album from the concert, both were met with critical acclaim. Today most film critics and musicologists list *The Last Waltz* as the greatest concert film ever. It's worth finding today on the internet or some streaming service.

## November 26th

On this date in 1979, "No More Tears (Enough Is Enough)," a disco duet featuring Donna Summer and Barbra Streisand was enjoying the view from the top of the pop chart. It had arrived there two days earlier, knocking the Commodores' ballad "Still" from the #1 spot and the song would enjoy a two week stay before giving way to another one-word-titled ballad, "Babe" by Styx. Coincidently, the song was the fourth #1 for both Summer and Streisand but it was Streisand's first trip to the top with a dance song. And it all began when she proved she could sing to a driving disco beat on her own. Once she'd managed that, the duet with the two divas seemed inevitable.

LaDonna Adrian Gaines was born in 1948 in Boston, Massachussets. Using the stage name Donna Summer she earned her title as Queen of Disco by releasing hit after hit with a "four on the floor" dance beat throughout the seventies. Her work with producer Giorgio Moroder would not only make her an international superstar but it would provide a road map for so many other dance artists who followed in their wake. After scoring tons of chart-toppers on *Billboard*'s dance chart, but always falling short on the pop chart, she finally broke through in 1978 scoring a #1 hit with "MacArthur Park." The following year she rang up back-to-back #1 songs with "Hot Stuff" and "Bad Girls." In the pop and dance world, there was no one bigger than Donna Summer in the late seventies.

For Barbra Streisand, her path to "No More Tears" was a bit less obvious. Born Barbara Joan Streisand in Brooklyn, New York in 1942, she became known early on as a singer who could hit soaring notes and deliver passionate ballads. In 1964 she became a household name when her song "People" from the Broadway play *Funny Girl* went all the way to #5. Her first trip to the top of the charts came a decade later with the heartbreaking ballad "The Way We Were." She'd reach #1 again in 1977 with "Evergreen (Love Theme from A Star Is Born)" and a year later she was back on top with a duet with Neil Diamond called "You Don't Bring Me Flowers." Besides singing, Streisand had a highly successful acting career and in 1978 she was cast to appear alongside Ryan O'Neal in the romantic comedy *The Main Event*. With disco all the rage at the time the movie producers thought they'd capitalize on the craze by having Streisand sing a dance song for the soundtrack. She was amenable so Paul Jabara, who'd just written "Last Dance" for Donna Summer for the *Thank God It's Friday* movie, was brought in and asked to pen a song. The result was "The Main Event/Fight" which got all the way to #3 and erased, for most fans, the bitter taste of how awful the movie was.

Streisand's record company, Columbia, was interested in having her take a stab at another dance track and they approached Casablanca, Summer's label, to see if a duet could be worked out. The record companies struck a deal where the single would be released on both labels and sales would be added and split in half when calculating royalties. Plus, Streisand and Summer would be free to include the song on each of their upcoming LPs. Jabara was brought in again and Moroder asked to produce the session. By everyone's account there was no Clash of the Divas in the studio, however during the long drawn out note Summer attempted to keep up with Streisand and wound up falling off her stool when she ran out of breath. But Jabara, who was in the studio that day, reports: "There was Streisand, hands flaring, and Donna, throwing her head back - and they're both belting, sparking each other. It was a songwriter's dream. Seeing them on their stools opposite each other was so mind boggling, my head nearly turned 360 degrees, like Linda Blair's did in *The Exorcist.*"

Though the song went on to top the charts, Streisand and Summer never had the opportunity to sing it together like they had that day in the studio. Summer would often perform the song live with one of her back-up singers taking Streisand's parts but Streisand, who barely tours or even performs live, only had the chance to sing this in front of an audience after Summer's untimely passing in 2012. During her Back to Brooklyn Tour in late 2012 she would sing part of this and lament the fact that Donna Summer was no longer around to sing it with her. The next year Summer was posthumously inducted into the Rock and Roll Hall of Fame. "No More Tears (Enough Is Enough)" had been her last career #1. For both singers, their duet of female empowerment will always be one of their most successful songs.

### November 27th

On this date in 1970, just months after the Beatles had announced their breakup and released their final album, *Let It Be,* George Harrison released *All Things Must Pass.* For many, the album is just another reminder at how deep the talent was in the Fab Four. Besides the pop genius of Paul McCartney and the caustic vision of John Lennon, here was Harrison at the height of his artistic craft. And to prove the point, many of the gems on the album were actually songs rejected by the rest of the Beatles for their final albums. And yet, *All Things Must Pass* is often considered by critics and music fans, the best solo album of any ex-Beatle.

George Harrison was the youngest Beatle and by the time he'd been introduced to John Lennon by Paul McCartney the two older bandmates were already collaborating and writing songs, as Lennon so famously described, "eyeball to eyeball." In Harrison's first few years with the Beatles he seemed happy and content to play lead guitar and harmonize to either old rock and roll songs that the band covered or whatever new tune Lennon and McCartney had come up with. But soon enough he expressed interest in taking a stab at composing songs and there's some debate about how this was received by John and Paul. Some say they encouraged Harrison and the fact that some of his earlier contributions are cowritten by one or the other would lend credence to that. But an album represents a very limited space for songs, a single album may include a dozen or so, and therefore the Beatles, like so many bands with multiple songwriters, would often clash over which songs should make the cut. Lennon and McCartney, due to their prior experience and expertise, scored the vast majority of those slots, leaving precious little real estate for the other two Beatles. While Ringo Starr rarely showed up with a song he thought worthy of making a Beatles' LP, increasingly, Harrison did. And in retrospect, when his Beatles' compositions are held up against those of Lennon and McCartney's, his songwriting was as advanced and informed and worthy of inclusion.

This struggle inevitably led to frustration and by the end of the sixties Harrison had resorted to releasing solo albums. In 1968 his soundtrack to the movie *Wonderwall* became the first solo album by a Beatle even though the band was still (technically) together. He followed that up in 1969 with an experimental album called *Electronic Sound*. Meanwhile, he was trying to get his songs recorded by the band and included on their albums. A task he accomplished, most famously with songs like "Here Comes the Sun" and "While My Guitar Gently Weeps" but failed to do with compositions such as "All Things Must Pass." As early as 1969 Harrison was voicing his frustration and thinking of releasing a solo album of his songs (and not just the instrumental and experimental stuff he'd included on his first two solo releases). When, in April of 1970, it was officially announced that the Beatles were broken up, he got right to work.

Harrison had worked with Phil Spector on the Beatles' final album and he asked the producer to helm the recording sessions for his first solo effort. Spector marveled at how much material Harrison had already written and it was clear early on that this had to be a double LP. Harrison then brought an incredible array of musicians together, including his good friend and fellow guitar genius Eric Clapton, to play on the LP. After years of focusing on the sitar, Harrison returned to playing mostly guitar, introducing the slide guitar sound that would mark much of his future work.

Thematically, Harrison continued his exploration into religions (Eastern and otherwise). Songs like "My Sweet Lord", "Awaiting On You All" and "Hear Me Lord" find Harrison struggling with guilt and how it affects his relationship with his Lord. He also offers uplifting life advice in "Beware of Darkness and "Art of Dying" as well as a beautiful love letter to the fans who were always hanging outside Apple Studios with "Apple Scruffs." If you listen to the album as a whole there is a definite underlying sadness and sense of loss. This could be due to his marriage with Patti Boyd (although the two wouldn't separate for another few years, there was already trouble in paradise) or the breakup of the band.

Certainly the album's cover, in which Harrison looks expressionlessly at the camera, sitting on a stool surrounded by four garden gnomes that have been toppled over, and the title of the album, have been interpreted as Harrison's statement of how he felt about being free from the constraints of being a Beatle. And when looked upon in this light, lyrics like, "Tell me, who am I without you, by my side," from "What Is Life" and "Isn't it a shame how we break each other's hearts and cause each other pain," from "Isn't It a Pity" take on a whole new meaning.

When it was all said and done the album consisted of four sides of traditional songs and two sides (a third LP) of jam sessions (called the Apple Jams).

When *All Things Must Pass* was released it was met with immediate critical acclaim, with most commentators focusing on the who-knew-this-guy-had-so-much-talent angle. The *New York Times* said: "If anyone had any doubts that George Harrison was a major talent, they can relax ... This is a release that shouldn't be missed." And this was only just the beginning for Harrison. Through the next two decades he'd continue to release albums that were met with critical acclaim, as well as commercial success. In the late eighties he was also a member of the supergroup the Traveling Wilburys and in the mid-nineties he had a huge hand in the creation of the Beatles' *Anthology*. But a few years later, he was diagnosed with throat cancer, something he blamed on his decades of smoking. He died in November of 2001 and three years later he was posthumously inducted into the Rock and Roll Hall of Fame as a solo artist. As he had told us all in the title track of his seminal work, which was released on this date all those years ago: "All things must pass. All things must pass away."

## November 28th

On this date in 1964, the Kinks' "You Really Got Me" peaked at #7 on the *Billboard* Hot 100 chart, introducing them to America and making them part of the early wave of the British Invasion. The song was written and recorded by the band while they were in limbo with their record label, having under-performed with their first two releases. And if the original version had been released they may have stayed that way. But a razor blade to a speaker cone saved all that. It helped make popular a sound that thousands of guitarists would copy and it launched the Kinks' career. Here's the story:

The Kinks came together in London at the time when so many bands were playing skiffle and early American rock and roll covers. Brothers Ray Davies (singer and guitarist) and Dave Davies (lead guitarist) were joined by Pete Quaife (bass guitar, backup vocals), and Mick Avory (drums and percussion) and the band was managed early on by Shel Talmy. They were signed to Pye Records in the U.K. and their first two singles, a cover of Little Richard's "Long Tall Sally" and a Ray Davies' original called "You Still Want Me," both failed to gain traction either in England or the States. Pye threatened to cancel the band's contract if they didn't score a hit with their next release. This was the spring of 1964 after all and Beatlemania was already spreading like wildfire and bands like the Stones and the Who were gaining legions of fans.

Around this time Ray Davies went to a club and was watching some women dance. He was mesmerized. He'd tell *Rolling Stone* years later: "I just remembered this one girl dancing. Sometimes you're so overwhelmed by the presence of another person and you can't put two words together." He may not have been able to put two words together in the club but when he got back home he put his thoughts down in lyrical form. There's nothing deep or complex in Davies' words but he does convey that feeling of being struck by someone else's beauty: you don't know what you're doing and you can't sleep at night. He composed the song on piano with a mid-temp, jazz and blues feel featuring a saxophone to carry the melody. When he played the song for his brother, Dave thought a meatier opening riff played on guitar and a faster, rock and roll style beat, might help convey the song's message of urgency.

This disagreement caused confusion in the recording studio. With Talmy producing, the Kinks initially recorded a much slower, laid-back version of "You Really Got Me." Later, when the band heard it played back they knew they could do better. Their opinion was confirmed when Dave Davies' girlfriend said the song wouldn't make her, "drop her knickers." That being the ultimate goal of any rock and roll song, they knew they had to re-record it.

But then Pye cut them off. Their label was unwilling to give the band anymore studio time, assuming they'd drop them after this third song and then not be able to recoup any past expenditures. Eventually Talmy broke the stalemate and agreed to fund another recording session. It was at this second session that Dave Davies, looking for that tougher sound for the song's opening riff, took a razor and slashed the speaker cones of his guitar amp. The resulting "fuzz tone" was exactly what the band wanted and it was this version of "You Really Got Me" that became the band's first big hit. When they followed it up with an eerily similar "All Day and All of the Night" (which also peaked at #7 in the U.S.) they were securely back in the good graces of their record company.

There's always been some debate (to put it kindly) between the Davies brothers about whose idea it was to slash the speaker cone. Dave takes full credit for it and even calls Ray a liar when he implies he had a hand in it. To be sure, the Kinks were not the first band to use this type of effect, blues players have utilized the unique sound a torn speaker cone provides for years and by 1964 there was already an early version of a fuzz tone pedal available to musicians (so they could achieve the same effect without ruining a speaker cone). But the success of "You Really Got Me" helped popularize this sound and by a year later, when the Stones hit #1 with "(I Can't Get No) Satisfaction," featuring that now famous opening riff with a similar fuzz tone, every guitarist was adding a fuzz tone pedal to their arsenal.

Disagreements aside, the Kinks went on to a long and successful recording career that stretched well into the nineties before they disbanded to focus on solo projects. In 2010 Pete Quaife died of kidney failure. A few years later, the record label that didn't want to finance that one last recording session was officially liquidated. Ray and Dave continue to squabble at times although they have also reunited from time to time as well. Because no matter who gets the credit, they are both responsible for creating some unforgettable early rock and roll numbers.

**November 29<sup>th</sup>**

On this date in 1980, Kenny Rogers' smash hit "Lady" began its third consecutive week at the top of the *Billboard* Hot 100 chart. It was only halfway through its stay at #1 as "Lady" would go on to be the biggest pop song of Rogers' career. Incredible considering the man who wrote the song for him almost decided to record it himself.

Kenny Rogers' career goes as far back as the late fifties when he recorded country songs as a young man under the name Kenneth Rogers. He was also a member of the First Edition (later Kenny Rogers and the First Edition) which dabbled in country as well as soft rock and even psychedelic rock. When they broke up in 1976 Rogers embarked on a solo career and by 1977 he was becoming a household name in pop and country music. "Lucille" went to #5 on the pop chart and #1 on the country chart and the following year "The Gambler" reached #16 on the pop chart and again, #1 on the country chart. His desire to continue crossing over and achieving pop success as well as country fame is what led him to reach out to Lionel Richie one day and ask him for a song.

By 1980, Lionel Richie had forged a reputation as a songwriter who could compose beautiful ballads. He'd scored mellower hits for his band, the Commodores, with songs such as "Easy", "Still" and "Three Times a Lady." So it wasn't that odd of a request when a country star of Rogers' magnitude reached out with a song request. Richie sat down and wrote the opening verse and chorus of a song he was calling simply "Lady," and then, realizing how good this particular piece could be, started second guessing whether he should give it away or not. Richie spoke to his lawyer for advice, explaining that if he sang the song himself it could be a "smash." His lawyer agreed but added, "If you give it to Kenny, it will be bigger than you ever thought."

Richie saw the wisdom in his lawyer's advice so he brought the half-finished song to Rogers for his opinion. Rogers liked what he heard but asked for the second verse. Richie said it was coming and a recording session was set up. The day of the recording, Richie still hadn't written a second verse so Rogers wondered out loud where it was and as he explained to *Us Weekly*: "They said, 'Lionel's in the toilet writing it right now.' I go, 'What?' And they said, 'Yeah, he can't write unless he has the pressure to write.'"

What Lionel completed in the toilet and what Rogers recorded that day turned into a monster hit for both of them. "Lady" became the first song of the eighties to top all four of *Billboard* magazine's singles charts: country, Hot 100, adult contemporary and Top Black Singles. As Richie explained, the fringe benefit for him personally was that it opened him up to a whole new audience. As he's said: "I picked up all of Kenny's following too. And that happened to be the rest of the world."

Richie would capitalize on this new found exposure in just a few years as he embarked on his own solo career. He also claims that "Lady" is the most financially rewarding song of his career, or as he joked to *Entertainment Weekly*, "I have an estate that 'Lady' bought." For Rogers, "Lady" would be the only time as a solo artist he'd hit #1 on the pop chart, although he did return in 1983 with "Islands in the Stream," a duet with Dolly Parton. He has continued to be a presence on the country charts ever since. The collaboration between Rogers and Richie was so successful it led to Richie producing Rogers' 1981 album, *Share Your Love* for which Richie penned a few more songs (no word on whether he finished those in the loo as well). The two have also maintained a friendship that has lasted, well, through the years.

## November 30<sup>th</sup>

On this date in 1977, *Bing Crosby's Merrie Olde Christmas* aired on CBS TV in the U.S. The special would air on Christmas Eve in the U.K. It was Crosby's final Christmas special after decades on both television and radio and, despite some drama, it would produce quite possibly the most famous holiday duet of all-time.

For an entire generation, Bing Crosby is synonymous with Christmas. In 1942 he recorded the song "White Christmas" which is not only the best-selling Christmas song but, with over 100 million copies sold, it's the highest-selling single of all time. Crosby also started doing Christmas show specials back in 1936. At first they were radio broadcasts, then in the fifties he moved his annual show to TV. In 1977, it was decided he'd record his show abroad, calling it *Bing Crosby's Merrie Old Christmas*. The premise was that Crosby and his family were spending the holidays at the estate of a distant relative in England. The show's producers sought to bring in some local talent to give the special a U.K. feel. The Trinity Boys Choir, Stanley Baxter and Twiggy all made appearances. And somehow, they got David Bowie to agree to join Crosby for a duet.

On September 11th, 1977, David Bowie walked in to Elstree Studios in London for the taping of the special. It's unclear whether Crosby knew who Bowie was that day but neither Crosby nor the show's producers liked what they saw from the young singer. Bowie was sporting lipstick and an earring and looking very much like the post-glam rock star he was. In truth, Bowie was only there because his mother was a big fan of Bing Crosby and he'd been enticed with a promise that the show would also air the video to his newest song, "Heroes." And his attitude showed it. When the show's producers asked Bowie if he'd remove his earring and wipe off the lipstick he told them he'd consider it. Then, when they told him what they had in mind, that he and Crosby would sing "Little Drummer Boy" together, Bowie balked, saying, "I hate that song."

Suddenly they seemed poised to lose the opportunity of having both legends sing together on the show. The producers scrambled. The show's musical director, Ian Fraser, along with the episode's writers Buz Kohan and Larry Grossman sat down at a piano and wrote original lyrics for Bowie to sing as a counter melody to "Little Drummer Boy." The new lyrics begin with: "Peace on earth, can it be? Years from now, perhaps we'll see?" which Bowie would sing while Crosby continued the lyrics to "Little Drummer Boy." Then Crosby would join in with Bowie, singing "Every child must be made aware. Every child must be made to care. Care enough for his fellow man. To give all the love that he can."

After this Crosby would return to "Little Drummer Boy" while Bowie continued with original lyrics like, "I pray my wish will come true" before ending with both singers harmonizing a very optimistic, "Can it be?"

In little over an hour the trio had completed the new lyrics and melody. Bowie was pleased with what they had come up with and after taking out his earring and wiping off his lipstick they were set to record. And what a magical taping it turned out to be. After the two exchanged some light banter about their holiday traditions Bowie started playing some notes on the piano. Then they both sang the opening lines to "Little Drummer Boy." If Bowie truly hated the song, he did a good job of hiding that emotion before starting to sing the counter-melody of the new lyrics. The final product is extraordinary. Whether Bowie and Crosby are singing separate lyrics or harmonizing the same lines, their voices work in perfect unison.

Days after the taping, Crosby would say Bowie was a "clean-cut kid and a real fine asset to the show." Crosby stayed in England throughout September and played a concert in Brighton on October 10th. A few days later he flew to Spain to play golf and hunt partridge. On October 14th, after completing a round of golf he suffered a massive heart attack and died at the entrance to the clubhouse. His final Christmas special, featuring the now historic duet with David Bowie, aired a few weeks later, becoming CBS's second posthumous music special of 1977 (they'd aired *Elvis in Concert* just months after Presley's death).

After the show aired nobody heard much about "Peace on Earth/Little Drummer Boy" for a few years. Then in the early eighties bootleg copies of the song began to circulate. Finally in 1982, RCA Records released the song as a single just in time for the holiday season. The song just barely missed the Top 40 in the U.S. but it climbed all the way to #3 in the U.K. Since then the duet makes frequent appearances on holiday compilations and the video, which is well worth checking out especially now that both singers have left us, is often shown and shared around Christmastime. It's amazing that something created so spontaneously and out of desperation for fear that Bowie might just decide to forgo the taping, has become such a holiday staple for so many. Can it be?

On this date in 1972, Johnny Nash's "I Can See Clearly Now" spent its last day at #1 on the *Billboard* Hot 100 chart after an incredible four week run. The song was not only Nash's most successful single but it helped introduce reggae to an American audience that would embrace this new sound. Within no time, other artists were incorporating reggae's one drop drum beat and emphasis on the bass rhythm and Jamaica's ruling Reggae King would finally break in the States. All because Nash's girlfriend knew some people in Jamaica.

Johnny Nash was born in Texas in 1940. By his late teens he was already signed to a record deal and releasing easy listening songs with a voice that sounded almost identical to Johnny Mathis. In 1965 he cofounded JAD Records in New York City. One of his first signings was the Cowsills, the group of sibling singers that would inspire *The Partridge Family*. A few years later he was dating a woman who had some contacts in Jamaican television and radio and so he made the trip with her to the island. His 1965 R&B song "Let's Move and Groove Together" had been a major hit in Jamaica so he was not unknown there and he very quickly fell in with the music scene. Reggae was fairly new at this time, having evolved from the island's traditional ska and rocksteady "riddim" so Nash arrived at the genesis of the genre. He was introduced to a struggling artist named Bob Marley and his band the Wailers and he signed them to a deal on JAD. Though none of their JAD releases were successful, their work with Nash while he was on the island would prove timely for helping their sound migrate off the island. Nash also recorded some songs himself while there and you can instantly hear the reggae influence in songs like "Hold Me Tight" (which went to #5 in the U.S. in 1968) and his cover of the Sam Cooke classic "Cupid" (which hit #39 in 1969).

When Nash returned from Jamaica his love of reggae came back with him. He began working on his next album and would include four songs written or cowritten by Bob Marley, including "Stir It Up" which would go on to become a signature song for Marley. Having helped introduce reggae in the U.S., he then helped it become even more popular with the title track of that next album, "I Can See Clearly Now."

Nash aimed to write a song of hope and redemption, using the analogy of rain to represent the bad times we all go through and the "bright, bright, sun-shiny day" to represent the good times. His message was one of encouragement as he tells the listener in the bridge (using a dramatic key change to drive home the point of optimism), "Look all around, there's nothin' but blue skies." Using the same reggae vibe that had influenced his recent work, the song has an infectious and cheerful feel. Nash recorded "I Can See Clearly Now" in London using members of the Average White Band who were two years away from breaking with their own song of hope called "Pick Up the Pieces."

Musicians are often trend followers and once reggae was introduced it began permeating a lot of pop songs. Paul Simon's 1972 song "Mother and Child Reunion" has an obvious reggae feel and Eric Clapton would soon score a #1 hit covering Bob Marley's "I Shot the Sheriff." And when Nash toured to support his new album he brought Bob Marley along with him which further helped introduce the Reggae King to the world outside of Jamaica.

Nash released his version of Marley's "Stir It Up" as the lead single for his upcoming album in March of 1972 and it peaked at #12 on the pop chart a month later. Then in June he released "I Can See Clearly Now" and the song began a slow and steady climb up the charts. It would hit #1 in early November, knocking Chuck Berry's ode to his penis, "My Ding-A-Ling," from that slot. "I Can See Clearly Now" finally surrendered the top spot on December 2nd, 1972 to "Papa Was a Rolling Stone" by the Temptations. But the song has never left the hearts and minds of anyone who needs a quick pick-me-up, a shot in the arm of optimism and a reminder that bad feelings slip away and tomorrow can be a "bright, bright, sun-shiny day."

## December 2nd

On this date in 1987, the *Dirty Dancing* soundtrack was into its third week at #1 on the *Billboard* 200 album chart. It would hold the top spot through the end on the year, for nine straight weeks, then get bumped by a combination of George Michael's *Faith* and Tiffany's self-titled debut, only to return to the top of the chart in March for another nine week stay. With 32 million units sold the *Dirty Dancing* soundtrack is one of the most successful releases of all time and the film it came from was a box office smash as well. Not bad for a movie that was shot on a shoe-string budget because no big Hollywood studio wanted it.

*Dirty Dancing* is based on a semi-autobiographical script by Eleanor Bergstein who wrote the screenplay and then shopped it around in vain to just about every studio in Hollywood before Vestron Pictures, a fledgling new studio, bought the rights and set a $5 million budget. Emile Ardolino, who had won the 1983 Academy Award for the documentary, *He Makes Me Feel Like Dancing*, was brought in to direct not based on his experience (he'd never helmed a major motion picture before) but for his passion for dancing. The filmmakers wanted to use real dancers in the movie and not body-doubles as had been done so famously just a few years earlier with *Flashdance*. Jennifer Grey, daughter of the Oscar-winning actor and dancer Joel Grey (of *Cabaret* fame), was given the female lead and Patrick Swayze, a Joffrey Ballet trained dancer, was offered the male lead. Swayze's agent encouraged him to turn down the role, thinking it might affect the bad boy image he'd developed in movies like *The Outsiders* and *Red Dawn*, but Swayze loved the script so he took the part against his agent's advice.

Jimmy Ienner was given the task of producing the soundtrack which would be a mix of songs from the early sixties and a few new ones composed just for the movie. He contacted Frank Previte, who Ienner had worked with previously and asked him to write a song for the movie. Previte, whose New Jersey based band

Franke and the Knockouts had recently broken up, was busy searching for a new record contract so he told Ienner he didn't have the time. Ienner told him, "This could change your life" and Previte agreed to give it a shot. He penned "(I've Had) The Time of My Life" as well as "Hungry Eyes."

Meanwhile, delays in shooting caused some outdoor scenes to be shot in mid-autumn. By the time they filmed the scene where Swayze and Grey practice their big jump in the lake they had to spray paint the leaves green to make it look like summer. The water temperature was as low as 40 degrees and there are no close-ups in that scene because both actors' lips were blue.

Both the film and its soundtrack were released in August of 1987. The film opened to mostly positive reviews and as it grew in popularity that fall it is said to have boosted attendance at dance classes. The soundtrack and its lead single, "(I've Had) The Time of My Life," both started climbing their respective charts and would peak at #1 in November. "Hungry Eyes" would get as high as #3 as would Patrick Swayze's contribution to the soundtrack, "She's Like the Wind."

As for Franke Previte, you would have to say Jimmy Ienner was pretty accurate in his assessment of how important writing songs for *Dirty Dancing* could be to his life. Not only did he make a ton of money off the initial record sales but in 2010 when the Black Eyed Peas released "The Time (Dirty Bit)" he was given songwriting credit for their use of lyrics from "(I've Had) the Time of My Life" which brought him another windfall. And all these years later, "(I've Had) the Time of My Life," which Bill Medley and Jennifer Warnes so passionately sing, is still a great closer at parties. It's a pretty amazing accomplishment for a movie no one wanted and a soundtrack its producer had to convince people to participate in.

### December 3rd

On this date in 1976, Londoners were confused and a bit frightened as a huge pink pig was spotted flying over their city. Flights at Heathrow were cancelled and some farmers phoned the police complaining that their animals were scared of the flying swine. And to this day, it's unclear if it was a genuine mistake or an ingenious publicity stunt.

Pink Floyd had emerged from the psychedelic era of the sixties and quickly made a name for itself as one of the most unique and experimental bands of the era. Their early albums were not big sellers but they built an avid fan base which grew exponentially when Floyd released their seminal work, *Dark Side of the Moon,* in 1973. That LP would spend the next fifteen years on the *Billboard* 200 chart. Their followup, 1975's *Wish You Were Here*, wasn't as successful but it nonetheless hit #1 on both sides of the pond. So as the band recorded their next LP and prepared for its release they were understandably anxious about having another big seller. But Pink Floyd wasn't the type of band to write hits. Their music hadn't changed much since those early, experimental days. It had become a little more accessible but the band still leaned towards long, compelling solos and introductions to songs that lasted minutes instead of the industry-standard seconds. As their latest album took shape, loosely based on George Orwell's *Animal Farm*, with a ten minute song called "Sheep," an eleven minute song called "Pigs (Three Different Ones)" and a seventeen minute song called "Dogs," the theme became obvious. The band chose the simple name of *Animals* for this album and then set about deciding on an appropriate cover. This is back when album covers were still important and with a twelve inch by twelve inch space to fill, bands often gave a lot of thought to the image that would help them promote their latest work (and with good reason, since many music fans spent hours analyzing each cover).

The band went back to the well, hiring artist Aubrey Powell who had actually gotten his start by designing Floyd's second album cover *Saucerful of Secrets*. After this, Powell and Storm Thorgerson had formed Hipgnosis, an art design studio focusing on album covers. Through the years they'd helped create some of the most iconic albums covers in rock history, including the Electric Light Orchestra's debut, Styx's *Pieces of Eight* and, of course, *Dark Side of the Moon*'s simple yet unforgettable 'prism/pyramid' design. So when they sat down and explained their latest album to Powell, with its themes of anti-capitalism and criticism of the military-industrial complex, it was up to him to come up with a concept. He suggested a few designs that the band rejected, then lead singer Roger Waters mentioned the Battersea Power Station, which he regularly drove by. Waters explained later to *Rolling Stone*: "I'd always loved Battersea Power Station, just as a piece of architecture. And I thought it had some good symbolic connections with Pink Floyd as it was at that point. One, I thought it was a power station, that's pretty obvious. And two, that it had four legs. If you inverted it, it was like a table. And there were four bits to it, representing the four members of the band." The band thought the building was perfect and so Powell commissioned a German zeppelin manufacturer named Ballon Fabrik to build a 40 foot long balloon shaped like a pig.

On December 2nd the balloon was filled with helium and brought to the Battersea Power Station where Powell hoped to get a picture of it flying above the building. The balloon was tethered to the building's long smoke stacks and a sharp shooter was on stand-by in case the moorings broke. Unfortunately inclement weather that day caused the photo shoot to be postponed to the following day. But nobody informed the guy with the gun that he needed to return. December 3rd, 1976 was a better day for the shoot, clear and cold but with a steady wind. As Powell began to set up the shot a wind gust ripped the pig free from its restraints and it began to fly off into the distance. Londoners making their Friday evening commute looked up to see this huge flying pig and had to think it'd been a rough week at work. Some farmers called in to the police to complain that their animals were running and scared and as the swine approached Heathrow, flights were grounded. The Royal Air Force was brought in to chase the pig which eventually landed miles away in Kent.

Aubrey Powell was arrested and the band still didn't have their cover shot. They finally decided to just cut and paste a flying pig into an existing shot that had been taken of the building (remember this is years before Photoshop), which is probably what they should have done all along. But then they wouldn't have gotten all the headlines about their album cover disaster which certainly didn't hurt sales of *Animals*. The album hit #2 in the U.K. and #3 in the U.S. and has sold over four million copies. The Battersea Power Station is decommissioned but the abandoned building still stands in southwest London. Locals report that it is often frequented and photographed by Pink Floyd fans. As for the pig, after its uncharted flight over London, Roger Waters named it Algie and the band started breaking it out during their concerts. It became as related to the band as the tongue is to the Rolling Stones. And the next time someone tells you something will happen "when pigs fly," you can remind them of this day in 1976.

### December 4th

On this date in 1956, a jam session took place in Memphis, Tennessee. Jam sessions are not uncommon whenever musicians gather. Someone is apt to break out a guitar or sit down at a piano and start noodling aimlessly, only to be joined in by the others. Snippets of songs are often played in between moments of conversation and laughter. It's what musicians do. So this jam session was no different than similar ones that have taken place millions of times through the years. Except for the fact that four of the most famous musicians of the era happened to be the musicians jamming. And since it all took place in a studio, and someone was smart enough to hit the record button, we can listen back to what has become known as the "Million Dollar Quartet."

December 4th, 1956 was a chilly Tuesday in Memphis, Tennessee. Carl Perkins arrived at Sun Studios to do some work for an upcoming release. He'd already scored a hit with his single "Blue Suede Shoes" and he and Sun Studio owner Sam Phillips were hoping to expand his sound a little from his previous sparse, rockabilly recordings by adding some further instrumentation. To that end, Phillips invited a piano player he'd just signed named Jerry Lee Lewis. As the session got underway Elvis Presley stopped in with a girlfriend named Marilyn Evans, to pay a visit to Phillips. A year earlier, Phillips had sold Presley's recording contract to RCA and Presley was already a huge name nationally, but he still lived in Memphis and would often stop by to see his old friend and mentor. As Phillips and Presley chatted they also listened in on Perkins' recording session which Presley was impressed with. During a break in the recording, Presley entered the studio to meet the other two musicians. Then another Sun Studio artist named Johnny Cash happened to stop in as well (in Cash's biography he claims to have been in the studio before Presley but the point seems moot.) After pleasantries and introductions, Presley sat down at the piano and the foursome started singing some gospel tunes they all knew. Phillips and Jack Clement, who was engineering the Perkins' session, hit record. It is unclear whether the four musicians knew they were being recorded although if you listen to the tapes there is a certain looseness that implies they either didn't know or didn't care. For more than an hour the four bounced back and forth between rockabilly, country and gospel. They even played around with one of Presley's hits "Don't Be Cruel." This being weeks before the holidays, they also played some Christmas songs.

At some point in the afternoon, Phillips realized how historic this session could be and he called a local newspaper. They sent a reporter and photographer and covered the session the next day under the headline "Million Dollar Quartet." The article ran with the now iconic picture of Elvis sitting at the piano surrounded by Jerry Lee Lewis, Carl Perkins and Johnny Cash. In the uncropped version Evans sits on the piano to their left looking on admiringly. It's no stretch to say she had the best seat for the most historic gathering of musicians ever.

After the session Phillips inexplicably shelved the tapes and other than the article, the session didn't get much exposure and fell into the obscurity of history. Then, in 1969 Sam Phillips decided to sell Sun Records to Shelby Singleton who started going through over 10,000 hours of tapes to find some old recordings worth releasing. Singleton discovered the tapes from that day and released them. When Presley passed away his estate discovered that he too had a copy of the session that was even more extensive than the tapes from Sun Records and RCA released those. In 2010 a musical called *Million Dollar Quartet* opened on Broadway which retells the story of the jam session. The musical tours to this day.

If you listen to the complete session, you'll hear 47 different segments of mostly incomplete snippets of songs as well as some banter between the artists. It's your typical jam session, only this one featuring four men who would literally change the face and sound of music in the upcoming years. They'd go on to be some of the biggest names in the early days of rock and roll but on this day in 1956, in a small studio that would be so influential to the creation of this fresh new genre, they were just four young men hanging out and having some fun.

### December 5th

On this date in 1992, Whitney Houston's version of Dolly Parton's "I Will Always Love You" began its second week at #1 on the *Billboard* Hot 100 chart. It would remain at the top into March of 1993, an at-the-time record fourteen week run. As with so many stories of success in the music industry a number of twists and turns had to take place for this song to achieve such dominance, most impressively, an actor with no musical background putting his foot down in an argument with an iconic music figure. But when it was all said and down, "I Will Always Love You" became one of the highest-selling singles ever, and *The*

*Bodyguard: Original Soundtrack Album* became the highest selling soundtrack of all time, beating *Purple Rain* and *Saturday Night Fever*.

In 1973 Dolly Parton dissolved her business relationship with Porter Wagoner. Wagoner had been a mentor to Parton as well as songwriting partner, and though she felt she could grow artistically on her own, this was an emotional decision for her. Like so many artists are likely to do, in the midst of her sadness, she wrote a song. "I Will Always Love You," is a unique song because it speaks of a relationship ending but not through bitterness or anger. The song offers nothing but good wishes and of course the promise that the person will always be loved. Or as Parton said later, "Just because I'm going don't mean I won't love you." Parton recorded the song and released it as a single in 1974. It went to #1 on the country chart.

In 1975 Linda Ronstadt recorded a cover version of the song although she left out the last verse (the "I hope life treats you kind" part). Also that year Elvis Presley's manager Colonel Tom Parker contacted Parton telling her his client was interested in recording the song. Parton was thrilled until Parker told her the caveat. Presley wanted half of the publishing rights signed over to him. Not just for the version he'd record but for any future uses of the song. Parton declined and Presley did not release a version of the song. A few years later, Parton re-recorded "I Will Always Love You" for her movie *The Best Little Whorehouse in Texas*. That version reached #1 on the country chart as well, making Parton the first artist ever to reach the top of that chart with the same song twice.

Then the movie *The Bodyguard* came along.

The screenplay for the movie, in which a bodyguard and the famous female singer he's charged with protecting fall in love, had been floating around Hollywood since the mid-seventies. An early attempt to get the movie made had Steve McQueen as the bodyguard and Diana Ross as the singer. A few years later Ryan O'Neal was set to take McQueen's place but the two stars did not get along. Throughout the eighties various combinations of stars were proposed by different production companies. The list of female singers suggested to star in *The Bodyguard* at some point is incredible: Olivia Newton-John, Pat Benatar, Madonna, Cher, Joan Jett, Deborah Harry, Liza Minnelli, Janet Jackson, Donna Summer, Kim Carnes, Crystal Gayle, and, wouldn't you know, even Dolly Parton. Finally Kevin Costner signed on, not just to star in the movie but as a producer. Costner was white-hot in Hollywood at the time, coming off his critical and commercial success with *Dances with Wolves* and once he took interest in the project it was inevitable *The Bodyguard* would finally see the light of day.

Costner had one demand early on. He wanted Whitney Houston in the co-starring role. The problem was Houston wasn't available for over a year. Costner was unfazed. He made *Robin Hood: Prince of Thieves* and *JFK* in 1991 and postponed production for *The Bodyguard* till 1992. Once it was decided that Houston would star in the movie they needed the right song for the bittersweet ending part. Jimmy Ruffin's "What Becomes of the Brokenhearted" was considered until it was discovered that song was about to be used in *Fried Green*

*Tomatoes.* That's when Costner recommended Dolly Parton's "I Will Always Love You." Costner also made another request. He wanted Houston to sing the opening of the song a cappella. Clive Davis, who ran Houston's record label and had served as her mentor throughout her career advised against it. He didn't think the song was right and he thought the a cappella opening would stop it from getting radio play. Costner insisted and eventually his arguments won the day. As Costner has explained: "I said, 'This is a very important song in this movie.' I didn't care if it was ever on the radio. I didn't care. I said, 'We're also going to do this a cappella at the beginning. I need it to be a cappella because it shows a measure of how much she digs this guy - that she sings without music.'"

David Foster was brought in to produce the song. He gave Houston a copy of the Ronstadt version of the song because the arrangement was closer to the one he was planning. He also contacted Parton to get official permission to use her song (and since he wasn't insisting on 50% of the publishing, Parton was happy to grant it). But before they got off the phone Parton informed Foster that Ronstadt had left out that crucial last verse. She sent him the complete lyrics and few would argue it's those final words that really add poignancy to the song. Rumors at the time claimed that Dolly Parton didn't like Houston's version but nothing could be further from the truth, at least from what Parton has said publicly. She told *Q* Magazine that she was "blown away" by Houston's version. And because she had said "no" to Colonel Tom Parker, it's estimated Parton made over $6 million in royalties for the song, instead of splitting that with the Presley estate.

"I Will Always Love You" was released on November 3rd, 1992, a few weeks ahead of the movie and the soundtrack. It did exactly what a lead single is supposed to do, climb the charts and build anticipation. It got to #11 on November 21st (the week the soundtrack came out) and leapt to #1 the following week to coincide with the film's release. Single, soundtrack and film all enjoyed incredible success over the next few months and "I Will Always Love You" has certainly become Whitney Houston's signature song. It also conveys Parton's simple message, "Just because I'm going don't mean I won't love you" better than any "break-up" song ever has.

### December 6th

On this date in 1969, the Altamont Speedway Free Festival was held in Northern California. What began life as "Woodstock West" and was envisioned to continue the feel-good vibes and counter-culture sense of community that began in upstate New York, ended with disorganization, violence, and ultimately death. Just months after Woodstock, which is often regarded as the high water mark for hippie idealism, Altamont officially ended the sixties with tragedy.

There are a number of different accounts of how planning began for a free concert in California. Some say the Jefferson Airplane proposed the idea. Other narratives say it was Mick Jagger who got the ball rolling. The Rolling Stones were touring throughout 1969 and had been criticized for their high-priced tickets and some theorize that Jagger wanted a little feel-good PR to end their year. Playing a free concert that would rival Woodstock's size was just what he envisioned. Plus the Stones had a film crew following them around, hoping to document the tour so a big finale would be perfect for the movie. But whoever got the ball rolling on the concept, it was clear as the date approached that disorganization would be a theme of the day. Various sites were proposed for the concert but nothing was locked in until just two days before. That left no time to set up adequate facilities like portable toilets and medical tents.

Security also became a last minute issue and the ultimate decision was to hire members of the motorcycle club the Hell's Angels. The Grateful Dead and Jefferson Airplane had both used members of the Hell's Angels at shows in the Bay Area for security and when they recommended them to the Rolling Stones the decision was made. Legend has it the deal with the Hell's Angels paid them $500 worth of beer and though some involved dispute that, it's such a ridiculously bad idea, the story has basically become fact. And besides, it fits into everything else that went on that day. Sam Cutler, the Stones' road manager on that tour and the man credited (or blamed) for making the deal explains he was desperate, it was last minute, and he had no other options. Or as he so gently explained it, "In the country of the blind, the one-eyed man is king."

As Altamont Speedway began to fill up prior to Santana kicking off the concert, the differences between this show and Woodstock were already obvious. Where Woodstock was set in bucolic upstate New York and Yasgur's farm was green and lush and surrounded by trees, the speedway was stark and barren and instead of trees the landscape featured trash and abandoned vehicles. Spencer Dryden of the Jefferson Airplane recalled: "It was just a horrible, pink-sky Hieronymus Bosch dustbin, not a tree in sight, just a hellhole. It was the beginning of the end. No, not the beginning, it was the end." The mood was far different from the euphoria of Woodstock as well. There was a sinister vibe in the air that was felt by the artists as well as many of the attendees. And the stage, which had been thrown up at the last minute was only a yard or so off the ground, making access by the concert goers fairly easy. Many Hell's Angels would say afterwards that their lone instruction was to keep people off the stage, which explains why so many of them were positioned at the front of the stage, drinking their beers and looking menacingly out into the crowd of hippies.

Shoving matches and fights broke out all afternoon. During the Jefferson Airplanes' set a brawl broke out between a few Hell's Angels and some of the stage crew, some say over a few motorcycles that had been accidentally toppled over. Marty Balin, the Airplanes' lead singer, attempted to intervene and at one point said, "Fuck you," to one of the Angels who replied back, "You never say fuck you to an Angel." Balin said it again and this time the Angel punched him, knocking the lead singer of the band that was onstage unconscious. Grace Slick recalls, "Our crew had to pull Angels off Marty." When the Grateful Dead heard about the incident they backed out of performing and left the area. Still, the show went on and the Angels continued drinking their beers.

The Rolling Stones took the stage last, after the sun had already set. As soon as they did thousands of concert-goers pressed forward and fights immediately began to break out. Jagger constantly spoke to the crowd, urging for calm and order. His requests of "Just be cool down in the front there, don't push around" went largely ignored. During "Sympathy for the Devil," a large fight broke out between attendees and Angels and the band stopped playing until order could be restored. A few songs later, during "Under My Thumb" an 18 year old named Meredith Hunter and a few Hell's Angel started throwing punches, some say because Hunter had attempted to get on the stage. The film crews taping the concert captured what happened next. Though the low light and grainy film make it impossible to know definitively, it seemed to most that Hunter pulled out a gun at this point and a Hell's Angel named Alan Passaro stabbed him to death. Passaro would later be acquitted of murder based on self-defense so this explanation of the events has at least been accepted legally. An autopsy also showed Hunter to have meth in his system which probably explains why some said he looked like a man possessed as he tried to gain access to the stage. Rock Skully, a member of the Grateful Dead's crew who was watching from backstage recalled: "I saw what he was looking at, that he was crazy, he was on drugs, and that he had murderous intent. There was no doubt in my mind that he intended to do terrible harm to Mick or somebody in the Rolling Stones, or somebody on that stage."

The Stones stopped playing again and Jagger urged the crowd to move back and sit down. They were aware of the skirmish but not that someone had been fatally wounded. As Hunter's body was taken away, the Stones started back up, afraid that if they left the stage abruptly it could cause even more unrest and possibly even a full on riot. They finished their set without any other major interruptions and the band and their crew very quickly boarded a helicopter to whisk them away.

Criticism of the debacle at Altamont was fast and furious, with most laying the blame at the feet of the Rolling Stones. They were the headliners, the de facto organizers and they stood the most to gain if the concert was a success and the film they'd commissioned to capture it was as well. Rock critic Robert Christgau has said, "Altamont became, whether fairly or not, a symbol for the death of the Woodstock Nation" and *Rolling Stone* would write, "Altamont was the product of diabolical egotism, hype, ineptitude, money manipulation, and, at base, a fundamental lack of concern for humanity," in an article whose title ("The Rolling Stones Disaster at Altamont: Let It Bleed") shows just who they held responsible for the tragic events. A year later the Stones released *Gimme Shelter*, a documentary covering their U.S. tour and, of course, Altamont. Many criticized the film for exploiting Hunter's death as well as making the Stones seem both sympathetic and naïve and the Hell's Angels as the true villains. In 2008, an FBI report was leaked that showed some members of the Hell's Angels had planned on killing Mick Jagger as revenge for his lack of public support following the concert, and for how the Angels were portrayed in *Gimme Shelter*. According to a BBC News report a former FBI agent said, "The gang tried to reach Jagger's home in Long Island, New York, by sea, but a storm almost sank their boat." Jagger has refused to comment on the report.

The Woodstock Music & Art Fair took place in August of 1969 and is considered the zenith of the counter-culture's ideals of peace, love and community. Just four months later those ideals lay shattered in a dusty old speedway at a concert that will forever be viewed as the end of an era. The zeitgeist was shattered, the Aquarian dream ended and the sixties were officially over.


### December 7th

On this date in 1980, the Talking Heads' masterwork *Remain in Light* was sitting at its peak position, #19 on the *Billboard* 200 chart. This certainly doesn't qualify it as an all-time great-selling LP, yet the boundaries that the album broke, and the musical changes it foretold, cannot be overstated. All these years later *Remain in Light* is rightfully seen as not only the Talking Heads' greatest album but one of the great artistic achievements of the eighties.

David Byrne, Chris Frantz and Tina Weymouth were all students at the Rhode Island School of Design in the early seventies and first played together in a band called the Artistics. When that band broke up they moved to New York City to be a part of the new music scene that was emerging there. They took the name "Talking Heads" from the term they'd read in *TV Guide* describing a commentator on television and played their first gig together at New York's famed CBGB, opening for the Ramones in 1975. They added Jerry Harrison soon after and they quickly developed an avid following among the punk rock crowd. They signed with Sire Records and released their debut album, *Talking Heads: 77*, in, you guessed it, 1977. David Byrne had quickly emerged as the band's leader, composing every song on their debut except "Psycho Killer" in which he shares writing credit with Frantz and Weymouth. As early as their debut album the Talking Heads were showing that they were more than just punk rockers. Their musicianship was far more advanced than the "three chords and a manic drum beat" crowd and if any single band ushered in the post-punk, new wave sound it was certainly the Talking Heads. Their 1978 LP, *More Songs About Buildings and Food*, began their collaboration with producer Brian Eno who would encourage the band to dive even further into an avant-garde sound. The following year saw the Talking Heads release *Fear of Music*. By this point Byrne's leadership was beginning to chafe the rest of the band. When *Fear of Music* was first released, Byrne was credited with composing every song but one, the opening track "I Zimbra." After complaints from the rest of the band, the credits were changed to reflect their contributions. "Life During Wartime" is one of those songs. Originally credited to just Byrne, the entire band shares in the writing credits now. And rightfully so. The song emerged from a jam session and when Byrne sat down to write lyrics for it, he very neatly wrapped up the seventies. His, "This ain't no party, this ain't no disco," became a common phrase as the decade of polyester pants and platform shoes was ending.

In just a few short years the Talking Heads had gone from unknowns playing in the shittiest clubs in lower Manhattan to worldwide rockstars. But there was trouble in paradise as the rest of the band regretted Byrne's excessive control. Byrne, too, was questioning the future, burnt out from being the main creative force behind the band. After an extensive tour to support *Fear of Music,* in January of 1980 the Talking Heads decided to take a hiatus with their future very much in doubt. Chris Frantz and Tina Weymouth, who were married by this point, took a long Caribbean vacation and wound up buying a place in Nassau, the Bahamas, right above Compass Point Studios. Meanwhile Byrne and Eno collaborated on an experimental album called *My Life in the Bush of Ghosts* which incorporated many African and Middle Eastern rhythms. They were both delving deep into Afro-centric literature. In fact the title of the album is taken from a Nigerian novel of the same name. Eventually Byrne and Harrison joined Frantz and Weymouth in the Bahamas and the four began jamming, still unsure if they were making a record or just trying to find the joy in playing together once again.

Many of the jam sessions began with the lead song off their last LP, "I Zimbra." That song is also steeped in African rhythms and contains non-sensical lyrics. The band would begin with that riff and then, in true jazz-style, head off in whatever musical direction they felt. They were all getting along better - not perfectly, but enough to start thinking they could record another album. Eventually they reached out to Brian Eno who was reluctant to work with Byrne again but when he heard what the band was working on, signed on. When formal recording sessions began, additional percussionists were brought in and Byrne made a conscious effort to not take control. In fact every track is credited to the entire band and Brian Eno (and Byrne didn't need his arm twisted this time to make it happen).

"Once in a Lifetime" was another song that came about as a true collaboration. It began as another rhythm born in a jam session before Byrne added some spoken lyrics, inspired by sermons he'd recorded off the radio. His spoken delivery during the verses has a definite preaching-style. Eno was not a fan of the song at first but then he came up with the chorus ("letting the days go by...") and suddenly he heard the song's potential.

*Remain in Light* was released in October of 1980 and it peaked at #19 this week. It sold modest number and because production costs were so exorbitant the band actually lost money on the record. But it is one of those albums that looks and sounds better all these decades later than it did in the moment (sometimes that happens with groundbreaking art). It is often at or near the top of any list of best albums of the eighties and even included in many lists of greatest albums of all time. Though the Talking Heads would have more successful albums before they eventually called it quits in the early nineties, most point to *Remain in Light* as the high-water mark of their artistry and certainly collaboration.

## December 8th

On this date in 1980, John Lennon woke up in a great mood. His latest album, *Double Fantasy*, which hadn't even been out a month yet, had just been certified gold and the lead single had cracked the Top 10. He had a busy day ahead: a photo shoot with one of the most famous photographers in the world, an interview with a radio station from the West coast and then a recording session in the evening. After a five year hiatus, in which he focused his time on raising his son Sean, he was back and as excited as ever.

After the breakup of the Beatles, John Lennon released music at a furious rate, an album a year from 1970 to 1975. Then, in October of 1975, he and his wife Yoko Ono had a son, Sean Taro Ono Lennon, and Lennon stepped away from the glare of the spotlight and the non-stop travel and activity that comes with being a rock star to be a stay-at-home dad and househusband.

Finally, as a new decade began, Lennon felt it was time to get back into the business. He went into the studio in the late summer of 1980 and began recording. He was so prolific he not only recorded the fourteen tracks that would make up *Double Fantasy* but almost enough for another LP. "(Just Like) Starting Over" was chosen as the lead single, not because Lennon felt it was the best song on the album, but because he felt the message was appropriate after his five year absence. The song was released on October 24th and started to receive immediate airplay and it moved solidly up the charts. *Double Fantasy* was released a month later and while reviews weren't exactly glowing, it too got solid airplay and did well in the record stores. The public had clearly missed John Lennon.

So on Monday, December 8th, Lennon awoke with a full slate of events scheduled. He left the Dakota Building on the upper west side of Manhattan, where he and Ono had been living for seven years, and strolled a few blocks to get a haircut. It was an oddly warm day in New York City for the first week of December and there were few things John Lennon loved more than a stroll through the city he'd adopted as his own. Soon after he returned to the apartment, famed photographer Annie Leibovitz arrived. Lennon had been promised a cover article in *Rolling Stone* magazine and Leibovitz was there to take the shot. They got into a discussion about the picture because Leibovitz was instructed to get a shot of Lennon by himself but he insisted Ono be in it as well. Leibovitz gave in to Lennon and then suggested a picture similar to their *Two Virgins* album cover. But Ono said she wasn't comfortable getting naked. Lennon then stripped naked and cuddled next to his fully clothed wife and Leibovitz took a polaroid so the two could see it. Lennon exclaimed, "You've captured our relationship exactly," and the shoot came to an end.

On her way out, Leibovitz must have passed the two men standing around waiting to get a glimpse of John Lennon. One, Paul Goresh, was a regular outside of the Dakota. He was an amateur photographer and someone Lennon had actually come to recognize after signing so much of his memorabilia and posing for so many pictures for him. The other guy was holding a copy of *Double*

*Fantasy* and wearing an overcoat which the weather did not call for. Goresh had never seen him before so he introduced himself to the man. The guy said he'd flown all the way from Hawaii to get his album signed. Goresh assured him it would happen because Lennon was always so generous with his fans. Lennon had recently said in an interview: "People come and ask for autographs, or say 'Hi', but they don't bug you." Goresh then asked the man where he was staying in New York and the guy got very defensive so the conversation came to an end.

Dave Sholin, a radio DJ from San Francisco, arrived next for an interview. Ono let him and his crew in and as they got settled into the couple's living room Sholin smiled at the beautiful clouds that were painted on the ceiling. Suddenly, the doors from the bedroom flew open and an upbeat and jovial John Lennon jumped out, exclaiming, "Well, here I am, folks, the show's ready to begin." Sholin commenced with an in-depth interview that covered everything from Lennon's latest work to his feelings about Sean. During the interview, Sean and his nanny and bodyguard returned home after spending the weekend on Long Island. Lennon was thrilled to see his son and they spent a few minutes catching up. You can find the interview on the internet and it's worth listening to. You can clearly hear Lennon's excitement about getting back into the business. Sholin would comment later, "In the three-and-a-half hours we were together, he could not have been more upbeat, more excited about what lay ahead – both musically and with Yoko and Sean." Lennon ended the interview by saying, "I consider that my work won't be finished until I'm dead and buried and I hope that's a long, long time."

After the interview Lennon and Ono left their apartment to head to the Record Plant where they were working on one of her songs. Their limousine wasn't out in front of the Dakota so they stood on the sidewalk waiting for it. Lennon then spotted Goresh and engaged him in a conversation, telling him he'd signed a book for him and it was waiting with the doorman in the building. During this conversation the other guy approached with the album in hand but didn't say anything. Finally Lennon asked the stranger if he wanted the album signed and the guy nodded. Lennon obliged and Goresh took a picture of the encounter. Lennon then asked the stranger if he wanted anything else but he just smiled and turned away. Lennon had graciously signed his album without the man even saying a word.

The radio crew's car showed up at this time and Lennon asked if they would mind driving him and Ono to the studio. Sholin was more than happy to do so and on the way he asked Lennon a question he hadn't asked while the tape was rolling: "What's your relationship with Paul McCartney?" Lennon smiled and answered: "Well, he's like a brother. I love him." As the busy streets of New York flashed by outside the car's windows Lennon continued his answer: "Families – we certainly have our ups and downs and our quarrels. But at the end of the day, when it's all said and done, I would do anything for him and I think he would do anything for me."

At the Record Plant John and Yoko worked on her new song, "Walking on Thin Ice." The song includes the lyric: "I may cry some day. But the tears will dry whichever way. And when our hearts return to ashes. It'll be just a story." They finally wrapped up about 10:30 pm and this time their limousine was waiting for them. They got in and started heading uptown. Ono suggested they go to the Stage Deli for a late dinner but Lennon said he'd rather stop home first so they could tuck Sean into bed. It was still unseasonably warm for that time of year so when the limousine turned off Central Park West onto 72nd street it stopped at the curb in front of the Dakota instead of pulling into the building's courtyard. As Yoko and John walked towards the building Lennon saw the guy from earlier who he'd signed the album for. They made eye contact and Lennon passed him by. He'd get two more steps before it happened.

In 1965, Queen Elizabeth presented all four Beatles with one of the highest honors she can bestow on a citizen, making them all Members of the Most Honorable Order of the British Empire. In 1969, Lennon returned his MBE with a note that, in typical Lennon fashion, is equal parts serious and snarky. The note read:

> Your Majesty,
> I am returning my MBE as a protest against Britain's involvement in the Nigeria-Biafra thing, against our support of America in Vietnam and against 'Cold Turkey' slipping down the charts.
> With love. John Lennon of Bag

Later, Lennon would offer another reason for not wanting the MBE: "Neither of us [Yoko or I] want to make the mistake that Gandhi and Martin Luther King did, which is get killed one way or the other. Because people only like dead saints, and I refuse to be a saint or a martyr."

John Lennon was nobody's martyr and certainly nobody's saint. He was a dreamer. A poet. A voice of a generation. He was a rebel and an artist and a provocateur. But most importantly, on this night in 1980, he was a father who just wanted to get home to tuck his son into bed.

### December 9th

On this date in 1989, Billy Joel's "We Didn't Start the Fire" got to the top spot on the *Billboard* Hot 100 chart, knocking Milli Vanilli's "Blame It On the Rain" from #1. Joel's song would enjoy a two week stay before giving way to Phil Collins' "Another Day in Paradise." It was Billy Joel's third chart-topper and to date, it is his last one. Joel was inspired to write the lyrics by a casual conversation with a young man, and also by turning forty. Here's the story:

William Martin Joel was born in 1949 in the Bronx, New York and was raised on Long Island. His mother pushed him to take up piano lessons at a young age but in his teens he was much more interested in boxing. It wasn't until he broke his nose in a fight that he shifted his attention to music. He started playing local bars and missed so many high school classes due to his late nights that he was told he'd have to attend summer school to graduate. His reply: "To hell with it. If I'm not going to Columbia University, I'm going to Columbia Records."

Joel did indeed wind up at Columbia Records where he enjoyed an incredible run of success beginning with 1973's *Piano Man*. By the mid-eighties he'd established himself as one of the most successful artists in music and a rare rocker who had enough pop-savvy to stay relevant during the MTV years. Joel turned 40 years old in May of 1989. He was hard at work at the time writing and recording material for his eleventh studio album. One day Sean Lennon and a friend stopped in to the studio. The friend had just turned 21 and he was complaining that it was a rough time to be that age. Joel told the kid that he too had a tough time growing up, what with the Vietnam war raging and civil rights and drug problems. Then the kid said, "Yeah but at least you grew up in the fifties and everybody knows that nothing happened in the fifties." Joel was confused by this and the fact that the kid obviously thought the fifties were this idyllic, *Happy Days*, kind of time. So he reminded the young man about the Korean War and Suez Canal Crisis and the Cold War.

When the conversation ended Joel was still reminiscent and he started scribbling notes about each year he'd been alive, thinking of some of the headlines from every year. This came naturally to Joel who is a history buff. As the piece shaped up Joel saw there was an underlying malevolence to it. Having lived through the Cold War, that emotion can be innate. When you practice bombing drills in grade school, hiding beneath your desk in case the Russians drop an H-bomb on your town, you find yourself a little jaded sometimes. He mentioned pop cultural events and moments in music history but he intertwined them with political figures and more sinister incidents like "Children of Thalidomide" which refers to pregnant women who took the drug Thalidomide and had babies born with congenital birth defects.

When the lyrics were done he set them to music which is uncommon for Joel. He's usually a musician first, building a melody and then finding words to fit it. But he threw something together and turned his walk through his life into a song. He has since said he hates the melody. "It's terrible," Joel opines, comparing it to, "mosquito buzzing around your head," or worse, "a dentist drill." Joel also complains about performing the song live. It's rapid-fire lyrics leave him no room for error. "If I miss one word," he explains, "it's a train wreck."

Nightmare to perform live with a melody like buzzing insects doesn't sound like the formula for a hit song but "We Didn't Start the Fire" certainly was. Backed by a video that shows the march through the decades in one kitchen setting, and how fashion and furniture changed with the times, "We Didn't Start the Fire" got steady airplay on radio and MTV. In the video Joel is a passive observer in the kitchen, as we all are to historical events, except during the chorus which shows him singing directly to the camera while a fire rages behind him. But even then he is seated while singing (another sign of passivity) until finally, after the line "Rock and roller cola wars" he stands up, flips the table and screams, "I can't take it anymore!" It's a moment similar to the scene in *Network*, when Peter Finch's character Howard Beale, urges his viewers to shout out of their windows: "I'm mad as hell, and I'm not going to take this anymore!" Joel is expressing the same frustration in "We Didn't Start the Fire" and the video is perhaps urging everyone to flip the table and scream. Of course in the coda Joel also remind us that even when we're gone the fire will burn "on and on and on and on..."

Not only did "We Didn't Start the Fire" top the singles' chart but Joel's 1989 LP, *Storm Front,* also hit #1 on the album chart.  His follow-up, 1990's *River of Dreams* was also a #1 album and then, strangely for a guy who had been writing and recording music his entire adult life, he stopped. Since 1990 Joel has released just one album, which was filled with instrumental, classical compositions. When pressed for a reason, Joel told ABC news: "I've had my say. If I put out an album now, it would probably sell pretty well, because of who I am, but that's no reason to do it. I'd want it to be good."

He certainly did have his say and if Joel stands by his promise to never again release new material, he has left his fans and music lovers alike more than enough material to enjoy for years to come. And though he doesn't release new material he still plays live consistently so anyone, young or old can enjoy his piano playing, singing and even watch him struggle through "the nightmare" of singing one of his most successful songs.


## December 10<sup>th</sup>

On this date in 1993, Pearl Jam's second album *Vs* would spend its final day at the top of the *Billboard* 200 chart. Incredibly, the album had debuted at #1 and spent the next five weeks atop the charts. In its first week alone, *Vs* sold nearly a million copies, outselling the rest of the Top 10 albums that week combined. The LP was met with not only commercial success but critical praise as well. Pearl Jam had somehow avoided the sophomore slump that strikes so many bands. In fact, in the eyes (and ears) of many, they had produced a better record than their groundbreaking debut, *Ten*. All this from an album recorded under intense pressure and in a location that the lead singer of the band hated.

Pearl Jam burst onto the musical scene in 1992, the year the grunge movement took a stranglehold on rock radio. Their debut, *Ten,* is often thought to have followed Nirvana's *Nevermind* and sometimes Pearl Jam is even criticized for copying their fellow Seattleites which is wrong on two fronts: *Ten* was released a month before *Nevermind* and Nirvana isn't even from Seattle but rather a neighbor of that fine Northwestern city, Aberdeen, Washington. But most casual music fans don't let facts get in the way of their generalities and since *Nevermind* became the bigger hit first, and radio stations started playing Pearl Jam songs off their debut like "Even Flow" and "Jeremy" after the grunge-gates had opened, Pearl Jam is often thought of as the Rolling Stones if Nirvana is the Beatles.

All that aside, *Ten* eventually became a huge hit, peaking at #2 on the album chart, blocked from reaching the top for four straight weeks by Billy Ray Cyrus' debut album *Some Gave All* (sometimes, there's no explaining musical tastes). Pearl Jam toured relentlessly through most of 1992 and anticipation for their follow-up grew exponentially.

There are many reasons cited for the propensity of sophomore slumps in music, but the two most logical are these: One, material. So many bands spend years and years playing clubs, writing and perfecting their original songs before being signed. They then record the best songs they've crafted and perfected in that time and release a debut album. If the album becomes a hit, their label wants a second LP quickly, so now they have to write and record a bunch of new songs by a deadline. Which also leads to the second reason for sophomore slumps: pressure. When bands are starting out and playing the club circuit there is little expectation for their original work. Sure, the day a record label guy is in the audience might ratchet up the nerves a bit, but they're still playing songs they've played forever. Once a band blows up though, now the spotlight gets white-hot and everyone wants to hear what they come up with next. The rock and roll highway is littered with artists like Hootie and Blowfish and Terence Trent D'Arby who never came close to matching the excellence of their first releases.

Pearl Jam was well aware of all this as they got together in early 1993 to start the recording process. They made a critical decision early on, asking Brendan O'Brien to helm the recording sessions. O'Brien had already made a name for himself by engineering and producing some of the best rock records of the last few years: *Shake Your Money Maker* by the Black Crowes, *Blood Sugar Sex Magik* by Red Hot Chili Peppers and the Stone Temple Pilots' epic debut *Core*. The band also took an "us against them" attitude, defiantly determined to do things their own way. Despite the fact that the video for "Jeremy" had helped break them, they announced that they would not be producing any videos for *Vs.* Plus they tackled topics that were bound to alienate some of their fans, but they were issues the band felt were important enough to write about like gun control and police racism. Their attitude determined the title of the album as well. Initially they were going to name it *Five Against One* (a line from the song "Animal") but they eventually decided on simply *Vs.* Guitarist Stone Gossard would tell *Rolling Stone*, "For me, that title represented a lot of the struggles that you go through to make a record. Your own independence, your own soul, versus everybody else's."

The band rehearsed for a time at Potatohead Studio in Seattle, Washington. When it came time to record, they moved to The Site in tranquil Nicasio in northern California. Lead singer Eddie Vedder had very strong feelings about this area, telling *Rolling Stone* at the time, "I fucking hate it here," and wondering, "How do you make a rock record here?" The pressure and serene surroundings got so bad for Vedder that after a few weeks of recording he began driving down into San Francisco and sleeping in his truck just to get away from all the peace and quiet. Maybe Vedder's angst was part of the magic of the record though as you can hear his passion and, at times, anger come through on almost every track. He'd tell *Spin*: "The second record, that was the one I enjoyed making the least. I just didn't feel comfortable in the place we were at because it was very comfortable. I didn't like that at all."

*Vs* hit the record stores on October 19th, 1993 and went to #1 immediately. The lead single "Go," with no accompanying video, gave notice to the music world that Pearl Jam was still playing hard and fast. Reviews were generally glowing and the band hit the road again to promote the album. It was during this tour, in the spring of 1994, that Kurt Cobain killed himself. Vedder was deeply moved by this. At a concert a few days later he announced from the stage, "I don't think any of us would be in this room tonight if it weren't for Kurt Cobain."

Certainly, Nirvana had opened up the airwaves for the harder, grittier sound of grunge but Pearl Jam should never take a back seat to them artistically. They brought all the same rage to the stage and recording studio as Cobain ever did. And with their second album, they proved they were more than one hit wonders. If recording *Vs* really was them against the world, they won.


## December 11th

On this date in 1968, the Rolling Stones hosted an event meant to be aired at a later date, called The Rolling Stones Rock and Roll Circus. It was designed to help them promote their newest album, *Beggars Banquet*, but after the event was over the band, to a man, was so disappointed in their performance that the tapes sat on the shelves for nearly 30 years. It was an innovative idea for its time but once the videos were finally released most music lovers took one look out of curiosity and never gave it another thought. An event dreamt up by the Stones' lead singer wound up providing some odd and interesting moments, but certainly no promotion.

The Rolling Stones recorded their ninth studio album, *Beggars Banquet*, in the first half of 1968. As they finalized plans for its release at the end of the year, Mick Jagger started thinking of unique ways to promote it. One idea he came up with was a rock concert in a circus tent that would feature other bands and artists but culminate with a Stones' performance featuring some of their new songs. The special would be taped and then aired on television at a later date. Jagger reached out to some of his friends and was able to set up an impressive list of performers. He then set about filling the sound stage with invited guests who all wore brightly colored robes, which he figured would look interesting and eclectic when they cut to crowd shots.

The Rock and Roll Circus began in the mid-afternoon with all the performers as well as acrobats and cowboys on horses entering the stage to circus music. Jagger then opened the show by saying, "You've heard of Oxford Circus, you've heard of Picadilly Circus, well this is the Rolling Stones Rock and Roll Circus!"

Jethro Tull performed first and the only thing notable about their set was that this was during the very brief time that Tony Iommi was with the band. Iommi of course would leave Tull and go on to be a founding member of Black Sabbath. After Tull, Keith Richards, in pirate attire including eye patch, introduced the Who. Their performance of "A Quick One While He's Away" was clearly the show-stealer. This is the only footage in fact that would see the light of day over the next twenty years as the Who showed this in their 1979 rockumentary *The Kids Are Alright* (and included the audio from it on the accompanying soundtrack). Taj Mahal and Marianne Faithfull each performed next before the supergroup Dirty Mac hit the stage. John Lennon put Dirty Mac together (when the other Beatles showed no interest in taking part in the Circus) bringing together Eric Clapton, Mitch Mitchell and Keith Richards. The band played two songs, "Yer Blues" which had just been released on the Beatles' *White Album* and "Whole Lotta Yoko" which is an instrumental blues workout that would have sounded great if Yoko Ono did a little less screaming and wailing during it.

All this was a precursor to the Rolling Stones' performance but because the day was marred with delays and equipment problems, the Stones didn't hit the stage till about 2am. Everybody was exhausted by this point, musicians and audience alike. Still, to look back on it today, the Stones did themselves justice, especially with their romp through the brand new "Sympathy For the Devil" (Jagger is a bit over the top playing to the camera but his vocals are impassioned) and "You Can't Always Get What You Want." Their rendition of "No Expectations" is notable for Brian Jones' impressive slide guitar work. This would turn out to be Jones' last public performance with the band he'd founded. In June of 1969 they fired him and a month later he'd be found dead in his swimming pool.

When the Rock and Roll Circus was over and the band had a chance to review the footage, they were aghast. The Who had clearly blown them away with their incredible, one song performance ("A Quick One" is an eight minute suite of song snippets) and they didn't feel a television show featuring the footage would help them promote their newest album. So they shelved the project and since there was no upcoming tour *Beggars Banquet* was left to its own devices to becoming a hit. Ultimately, it fell a little short of what the Stones were used to. The album peaked in the U.S. at #5 (their previous three albums had all gone to #2) and produced just one single, the commercially disappointing "Street Fighting Man" which failed to crack the Top 40 in the States.

Viewing the footage today is a quaint walk back in time. Sort of a rock and roll time capsule. The performances are inconsistent at best but to see some of the rock stars who left us too soon, alive and young and performing in their element is certainly a treat. And of course those who are still with us, to see them in all their youthful glory. The years since have been kind to some, crueler to others, so it's worth seeking out some of the clips that have been put on Youtube or just purchasing the whole show which was released on DVD in 2004, 36 years after they were originally taped for airing. Some ideas just sound better in theory than they become in reality. You can't blame Jagger for thinking outside the box, or in this case, the circus tent.

On this date in 1957, Jerry Lee Lewis, one of the first generation of rock and rollers whose star was steadily on the rise after releasing back-to-back ground-breaking songs, married his thirteen year old second cousin, Myra Gale Brown. The marriage would remain hush-hush for a number of months but once it became international news, Lewis, who had earned the nickname The Killer because of his relentless energy on stage, had all but torpedoed his own career. It would take decades for Lewis to get back into the good graces of his fans and the media. And the marriage was only one of seven for Lewis.

Jerry Lee Lewis was born a rebel and a rocker in 1935. He learned to play piano at a young age and his parents mortgaged their home to buy him one to practice on. His mother then enrolled him in the Southwest Bible Institute, in Waxahachie, Texas, where he was able to play piano during their church services. One day, in front of a church assembly, Lewis took an old hymn named "My God is Real" and gave it a boogie woogie send-up. He was promptly expelled. After that he traveled to Nashville to try to get in on the country-western scene that was developing but then he heard about this new rock and roll sound emerging from Memphis so he made his way across the state in 1956 to audition for Sun Records. He was signed initially as a studio musician but after playing on some early Sun songs it was clear he needed to be the headliner. In 1957 he released back-to-back songs that would establish him as a unique force in this burgeoning new sound: "Whole Lotta Shakin' Goin' On" and "Great Balls of Fire," which went to #3 and #2 respectively on the pop chart. He was becoming known for his outrageous stage shows, pounding the piano keys with his hands and feet, raking his fingers up and down the keys and even kicking the piano stool over as he played. In early 1958 Hollywood attempted to cash in on the success of rock and roll, and Lewis was cast in *High School Confidential* in which he would demonstrate that outrageous performance style.

Meantime, by 1957, Jerry Lee Lewis, all of 22 years old, had already been married twice. He was seventeen when he took his first trip down the aisle (that marriage lasted twenty months) then, a month before he even divorced his first wife he married again (at aged nineteen). That marriage ended in October of 1957 as Lewis' career was exploding. His next wedding, however, was the dubious one. On this date in 1957 he married his second cousin, Myra Gale Brown. She was thirteen years old at the time.

After the wedding Lewis went right about his business, performing and recording. He and his handlers didn't go out of their way to keep the marriage a secret but they certainly didn't send out a press release either. This was decades before *People* magazine and *TMZ* so there were fewer people prying into celebrities' personal lives. So it wasn't until Lewis arrived in England for a tour in May of 1958 with his new wife that the marriage became an issue. There was a lot of excitement about this trip because Elvis Presley had yet to cross the Atlantic to perform in the U.K. (he actually never would) so this was England's first chance to get a real live view of an American rock and roller. Lewis was met at the airport by Paul Canfield of the *Daily Mail* who started asking him questions about his upcoming shows. When Canfield spotted a young girl in Lewis' entourage he very innocently asked her who she was. When she replied, "I'm Myra. Jerry's wife" Canfield realized he might be writing a very different article than he'd first thought. His next question was about her age and Lewis interrupted and answered "fifteen," which was a lie. She was thirteen. But it didn't matter. Fifteen was still below the age of consent in England.

The next day, Canfield broke the story in the *Daily Mail*. The British press as well as most of its citizens latched on to the scandal quickly. Since its inception, rock and roll was viewed as the devil's music and most adults urged their children to turn away from the temptations that surely awaited. Now, here was proof positive of rock and roll's soul stealing-qualities.

Lewis' first show after the scandal broke was interrupted numerous times by boos and shouts of "cradle snatcher." He was then thrown out of the hotel where he and his crew were staying and brought in for questioning by the police. Lewis' explanation that where he came from in Mississippi, such marriages are common, fell on deaf ears with the police as well as the fans. After only two more shows, both of which were also marred by audience interruptions, Lewis cancelled the rest of the tour and returned back to the States where he hoped to find a more understanding public and press.

He was mistaken. The scandal had actually beaten him home. Lewis was blacklisted on radio stations across the country and from the traveling shows where he'd made his fame. He went from earning up to $10,000 a night at some shows in bigger venues to $250 a night in small bars and clubs. Plus he became a pariah, with former friends and mentors, like Sam Phillips and Dick Clark, turning their backs on him. Though Lewis struggled during the next few years he did have a few bright moments. His 1961 cover of the Ray Charles song, "What'd I Say" went to #25. He also released a live album in 1964, *Live at the Star Club, Hamburg*, which is regarded by many to be the best early live rock and roll record. Due to legal complications the album wasn't released in the U.S. so Lewis remained an outsider in his home country.

Lewis would turn to Nashville (again) for his comeback. A decade after the scandal that sidelined him, Lewis released a cover of "Another Place, Another Time" which made some noise on the country chart. What followed was a string of country hits that salvaged his career and allowed him to continue to record and tour when it looked for all the world that his days as a professional musician were ending. When the Rock and Roll Hall of Fame inducted its charter members in 1986, Jerry Lee Lewis was part of the first group of rock and roll pioneers to be enshrined. At the time he'd just married his sixth wife. In 2012, he'd make it lucky number seven.

On this date in 1984, Leonard Cohen had just released his seventh studio album, *Various Positions*. The LP would include an album track called "Hallelujah" that had little to no impact when it was first released yet somehow, today, is one of the most popularly performed songs (especially if you watch any of the singing shows like *The Voice* or *American Idol*) and it's been covered and released hundreds of times. Here's the remarkable story of "Hallelujah."

Leonard Cohen was a Canadian singer, songwriter, poet and novelist. His recording career began in 1967 with his debut album *Songs of Leonard Cohen* and he quickly became a cult favorite for his mixture of unique poetic writing and his hypnotic, spoken delivery. He was never known to be prolific, taking years between each album and laboring obsessively at times over lyrics. In the early eighties he started working on a song that combined some biblical and erotic imagery. He used the simple chorus of "Hallelujah" to evoke both spiritual as well as sexual euphoria. At one point he became haunted by the process, writing as many as 80 different six-line stanzas, all using the rhyme scheme of A-A-B-C-C-B with the third line ending with a rhyme for "Hallelujah" and the sixth line ending with that word. At one writing session, he sat on the floor in his underwear for hours, banging his head when he got stuck for a word. It was a labor of love that Cohen finally finished and recorded in 1984. When he toured to support *Various Positions* he gave "Hallelujah" a prominent spot in his shows and was disappointed that it didn't resonate with his audience. In the next few years the song became less crucial to his performances and Cohen eventually dropped it from his setlists altogether.

But one person who had seen Cohen perform the song, and was duly impressed, was John Cale, he of Velvet Underground fame. In 1991, when a call went out to musicians for a Leonard Cohen tribute album, Cale asked if he could contribute a version of "Hallelujah." Cohen faxed him fifteen pages of his handwritten lyrics and told him to pick whatever stanzas he wanted. Cale choose the "cheekier" lyrics and his version has two different verses than Cohen's original. Jeff Buckley, a singer-songwriter from California, heard Cale's version of "Hallelujah" and recorded a cover for his debut album, *Grace*, which was released in 1994. Buckley tragically died at just 30 years old the next year, drowning during an evening swim in the Mississippi river, so he wasn't around to see his version of "Hallelujah" start to gain traction and get airplay. Buckley's version became so popular that many people assumed it was his composition. TV shows like *E.R.*, *West Wing* and *House* have used Buckley's version in poignant moments of their shows because the song can convey a wide range of emotions, sadness and elation, all within a few minutes. In 2001, Cale's version of the song appeared in the animated movie *Shrek* which also helped raise its visibility and popularity.

The floodgates were now open. Over 300 cover versions have been released in various languages. The song has become ubiquitous on singing shows and in coffee houses. There are even some small clubs that have a house rule banning "Hallelujah." And even Cohen went back to performing the song live in concert, saving it, once again, for a prominent spot in his shows. When he passed away in November of 2016 the song was used whenever the media did a story or tribute of his life. Somehow this song that had gone completely unnoticed when he released it, had become his signature composition. And what better epitaph for a poet and artist than the final stanza of most versions of the song:

> I did my best it wasn't much
> I couldn't feel, so I tried to touch
> I've told the truth, I didn't come to fool you
> And even though it all went wrong
> I'll stand before the lord of song
> With nothing on my tongue but hallelujah.

### December 14th

On this date in 1976, The Roxy opened in London and a brand new band, Generation X, played their first live gig ever at the new club. The Roxy would become as important to the London-based punk scene as CBGB was to New York's and Generation X would become an early and influential punk band, showing these young rockers that they didn't have to be ugly and angry just to be heard.

1976 saw the emergence of many new bands in London, most falling under the new heading of "punk." The economy in London was in the shitter and a new generation of young people was maturing and realizing their options in life were extremely limited. The anger this produced found an outlet, for many, in music. These bands played aggressive and hard, if unskilled, and they began to get attention, with some even landing recording contracts and, perhaps, a way out of the class system in England that was guaranteed to keep them down. One such band was Chelsea, which featured Gene October on vocals, William Broad on guitar, Tony James on bass and John Towe on drums. In October of 1976, three of the members of Chelsea broke the news to October that they were leaving to form their own band. October would find new bandmates and Chelsea would go on to some success while the other three formed a band they chose to call Generation X. The name came from a book Broad's mother owned. Broad changed his name to Billy Idol, switched from guitar to lead singer and Bob "Derwood" Andrews was brought in to play guitar. The band rehearsed for a number of weeks then scored the coveted spot of opening up the new club called the Roxy in London's Covent Garden section.

Before the band scored a record deal with Chrysalis Records, Towe was replaced on drums by Mark Laff. Generation X released their debut single "Your Generation" ten months after their debut performance. 1977 was the year punk music literally exploded like a geyser after boiling below the surface for a few years. Generation X was in the right place at the right time but when they were selected to appear on the BBC program *Top of the Pops* they started getting some push-back with criticism ranging from, "They're too pretty," to, "They're too clean," to, "They're not angry enough." And indeed, Billy Idol was much more of a frontman than Joey Ramone or Johnny Rotten ever could be. Plus, he and the rest of the band looked like they practiced personal hygiene on a fairly regular basis. If these traits meant they weren't hardcore enough, the band was unfazed. For the first few years of their existence they were selling records and playing to packed houses and that's usually enough to satisfy a few rambunctious young men.

Like so many of the early punk bands, Generation X had a short shelf life. By 1980 internal strife over the direction of the band was pulling the members apart. Of course the genre that they'd cut their teeth on was changing as well, as punk was already morphing into the new wave sound that would sustain it throughout the 1980s. After some personnel changes, they shortened their name to Gen X and released their final album *Kiss Me Deadly*, which included the first version of "Dancing with Myself." When Gen X finally dissolved, Idol moved to New York City to try to launch a solo career. There he started working with former KISS manager Bill Aucoin and continued polishing his sound. He had been a punk pioneer and now, at the advent of the MTV generation, he became a trailblazer in the post-punk era, showing rockers how to maximize the exposure music television offered. Billy Idol would go on to be one of the most recognizable faces and voices of the eighties.

Years later, when Billy Idol's 1993 No Religion Tour made a stop at the Astoria Theatre in London, the original members of the band joined him on stage for a one-off reunion show. None of the others had gone on to the heights of fame that Billy Idol did but for one night, they rewound the clock. They were young and wild and loud young men once again, thrashing through hits like "Ready Steady Go", "Kiss Me Deadly" and of course their first single "Your Generation." Idol, as always was the perfect frontman, snarling, sneering, and yeah, pretty as ever.

### December 15th

On this date in 1921, Albert James Freed was born in a small mining town just east of Pittsburgh. He would go on to popularize the term "rock and roll" and help introduce this new genre of music through his *Moondog House* radio show. And while his career was short-lived and scandal-ridden, in his limited time of influence he helped change the musical landscape like few other non-musicians ever have.

When Freed was twelve years old his family moved to Salem, Ohio. In high school he started a band called the Sultans of Swing and his dream was to become a leader of a big band but an ear infection quashed that dream. After high school he went to Ohio State University where he first became interested in radio. He served during World War II and landed a role as a DJ for Armed Forces Radio. After the war, he pursued this new career, working in smaller markets before landing a job in Cleveland. His shows were known for their eclectic mix of music. He'd go from a pop song to a jazz number to a rhythm and blues song. And he did not segregate like so many disc jockeys of the time. If a song was hot he didn't care if the artist was black, white or purple. He'd play it.

In Cleveland he became friends with Leo Mintz who owned one of the city's biggest record stores, Record Rendezvous. Mintz told Freed about the increase in sales of his rhythm and blues catalog and this encouraged Freed even more to start playing this music. Freed adopted an R&B song called "Moondog Symphony" as his theme song and began incorporating some of the "hipster" lingua franca into his DJ patter. One of those terms was "rock and roll" which Freed started using to describe this new music that was emerging, mixing elements of rhythm and blues with country and even some jazz and gospel. Some say the term rock and roll was a euphemism for sex but it's doubtful Freed was trying to be salacious when using the term. He just thought it sounded good and described these new songs perfectly and soon the term began to grab hold. Some have argued whether or not Freed was the first to coin the phrase and indeed, it may be impossible to prove either way. But there's no doubt that Freed, with the growing popularity of his *Moondog House* radio show, where he proudly served as "The King of the Moondoggers," thrust this term into the lexicon of the day.

Freed also took his radio show to the public and in 1952 he planned something called the Moondog Coronation Ball in which he brought together some of the artists he spun on his radio show to play live. The show was scheduled for the 10,000 seat Cleveland Arena but when twice that number of people showed up, the show had to be cancelled after just one song. Despite this truncation, the Moondog Coronation Ball is often cited as the first major rock and roll concert.

In 1954 Freed was enticed to move his show to New York City which is where he encountered his first in a series of legal troubles. Freed rolled into town with his radio show (that he was now calling the *Moondog Rock and Roll Matinee*) and was promptly sued by a popular street musician and poet who was famous around town and went by the name Moondog. Freed settled with Moondog, cutting a $6,000 check and agreeing to give up the Moondog moniker. He simply called his radio show, which now aired nightly on WINS, the *Rock 'n' Roll Party*. In New York his celebrity grew. He continued organizing live shows and branched into movies, appearing as himself in several films meant to capitalize on the growing popularity of this new music, like 1956's *Rock Around the Clock*, 1957's *Don't Knock the Rock* and 1959's *Go, Johnny Go!*

Freed made plenty of enemies during this time as he bucked the establishment. The bigger record labels despised him for playing and promoting releases from smaller independent labels. And many people thought his radio show and concerts, which encouraged blacks and whites to listen to the same music and even dance together at the live shows, was dangerous to society. America was still very much segregated at this time but Alan Freed was color blind. To him a great song with a driving beat was all you needed for a good time. But parental groups and church leaders vociferously disagreed and many fought to get his radio show off the air and his concerts banned. The *New York Daily News* called rock and roll, "an inciter of juvenile delinquency," and named Freed as a chief offender.

And so his troubles continued. In 1958, at a live show in Boston he announced from the stage, "It looks like the Boston police don't want you to have a good time." As a result, Freed was arrested and charged with inciting a riot. The following year, ABC gave him a weekly television show called *The Big Beat*, then cancelled it after just a few episodes over outrage that Frankie Lymon was seen dancing with a white girl in the studio audience. All this was the precursor to Freed's biggest problems. Those came late in 1959 when the government decided to crack down on payola (the practice where record companies give money or other incentives to radio DJs to get their songs played). Freed had been listed as a cowriter on some songs, most notably Chuck Berry's "Maybellene," which gave him the financial incentive to promote those songs. Freed would plead guilty to two charges of commercial bribery, and he was promptly fired from his radio show.

After leaving New York City, Freed got some jobs on smaller radio stations but no large station would hire him. He died in January of 1965 from uremia and cirrhosis brought on by alcoholism. He was 43 years old.

When the concept of a Rock and Roll Hall of Fame was dreamt up in the early eighties it was decided it would reside in Cleveland because that is the city where Freed had popularize the term "rock and roll." The very first group of inductees is a "Who's Who" of artists who helped shape the early sound of rock and roll: Buddy Holly, Chuck Berry, Fats Domino. They're all there. And so is Alan Freed. The Moondog. He was part of that first class of inductees and deservedly so. He not only gave rock and roll so much promotion early on, enlisting so many new fans by proudly playing and promoting songs that sometimes no one else would, but he literally gave the genre its name.

## December 16th

On this date in 1965, the Byrds were enjoying a three week stay at the top of the pop chart with their version of "Turn! Turn! Turn! (To Everything There is a Season)." It would prove to be their last trip to the top of the charts as folk music was losing favor to harder rock music and within just a few years the band's lineup was changing as various members went their separate ways and pursued other interests. They could seek solace, of course, in the lyrics of their biggest hit, words that had been around for thousands of years.

Pete Seeger, one of America's great folk artists and social activists, started playing music as far back as the early forties. He was in his twenties at the time and, along with fellow folk pioneer Woodie Guthrie, was a member of the Almanac Singers who wrote and sang songs advocating their anti-war, anti-racism and pro-union philosophies. Thus was the beginning of one of the great careers in American folk music. Seeger was never a big bible reader but he did admit to leafing through it occasionally and, as he's remarked: "I'm amazed by the foolishness at times and the wisdom at other times. I call it the greatest book of folklore ever given. Not that there isn't a lot of wisdom in it. You can trace the history of people poetically."

One day while flipping through the bible, Seeger discovered the Book of Ecclesiastes, one of the more philosophical books of the Old Testament. Ecclesiastes was composed around the third century BC so by the time Seeger read it, it was more than two thousand years old. He was inspired by chapter three of Ecclesiastes and put it to music, simply adding the chorus "turn, turn, turn" and changing the sequence of some of the lines.

Seeger began playing this in his live shows and in 1962 the folk group the Limeliters recorded the song under the title "To Everything There Is a Season." Inspired by this, Seeger finally recorded his own version using the same title. One of the Limeliters' backing musicians around this time was Jim McGuinn. In 1963 he worked with Judy Collins and encouraged her to record the song. She did, releasing it on her album *Judy Collins 3*, and using the longer title "Turn! Turn! Turn! (to Everything There Is a Season)." The following year Jim McGuinn changed his named to Roger McGuinn and formed the Byrds along with fellow folkies Gene Clark, and David Crosby. Their 1965 cover version of Bob Dylan's "Mr. Tambourine Man" spent a week at #1 in the summer of 1965, and after this success they searched for a follow-up. That's when McGuinn recommended Pete Seeger's song. Despite the fact that there were already three versions recorded (and none had troubled the charts) McGuinn felt the Byrds could turn the song into a hit. He and Crosby gave the song a whole new arrangement, adding a slightly more "rock" feel to it. The trio took over 50 takes to get it right, and in the end, the Byrds had their biggest hit. There is little doubt that "Turn! Turn! Turn! (To Everything There is a Season)" features the oldest lyrics of any chart-topper.

By 1966 the Byrds were already going through line-up changes. Gene Clark was the first to leave. He'd witnessed a plane crash as a kid, and one day as he was boarding a flight he had a panic attack. He got off the plane and refused to fly. McGuinn told him, "If you can't fly, you can't be a Byrd," and pretty soon Clark had left the band. Crosby was the next to leave and soon enough Roger McGuinn was the sole original member, with the band evolving from folk to psychedelia and even country. The wisdom of the Book of Ecclesiastes was appropriate once again. For the Byrds there was a time to be born. And a time to die. A time to embrace. And time to refrain from embracing.

## December 17<sup>th</sup>

On this date in 1982, Toni Basil's "Mickey" spent its last day at #1 on the *Billboard* Hot 100 chart. A week earlier it had knocked Lionel Richie's "Truly" from the top and the next day it would give way to "Maneater" by Hall and Oates. "Mickey" had been out for almost a year when it peaked at #1, one of the earliest examples of the hit-making ability of MTV.

Toni Basil was a dancer and choreographer whose career began in the mid-sixties on the television show *Shindig!* From there she scored gigs dancing and choreographing for movies like *American Graffiti*, *The Cool Ones* and the Monkees' film *Head*. She also choreographed David Bowie's Diamond Dogs Tour in 1974 and worked with the Talking Heads on the music video for their 1981 song "Once in a Lifetime." It was that experience that inspired her to sing her own song and make her own video. Having been a cheerleader in college she thought a video featuring cheerleaders could be fun. Now, she just needed a song.

She turned to a song called "Kitty" that had been released in 1979 by the English band Racey. The song had been written by Mike Chapman and Nicky Chinn who'd also written "Ballroom Blitz" which Sweet took to #5 in 1975. Basil changed the female name Kitty to the male name Mickey, added the cheerleader chant at the opening of the song and voila! she had the vehicle for her video concept. She released the song and video in early 1982 but MTV didn't pick it up right away. When they finally did the song began to shoot up the charts. MTV had begun broadcasting in the summer of 1981 and a year later the channel wasn't even available in some of the major markets of the U.S., but Basil's rise to the top, was an early example of the promotional power of an eye-catching video in heavy rotation on the music channel.

There has been much speculation through the years about two different aspects of "Mickey" that Toni Basil attempted to clear up in an interview with the pop culture website Vulture a few years ago. First, why the name Mickey? Some have said that Basil became infatuated with Micky Dolenz after meeting him on the set of *Head*. She laughs when she hears that, saying she barely interacted with him during the film shoot. So, again, why Mickey? Basil simply says because it's the closest sounding male name to Kitty. Fair enough. Next up, the question about the line, "I'll take it like a man." Due to Basil's gender swapping of the original song, that line has always made heads turn (and rumors fly). Speculation was that the title character is gay and Basil is saying she would let him give her anal sex. Again, Basil scoffs, saying: "That's ridiculous. Everyone reads shit into everything. It's not about anything dirty. You change the name from boy to girl, i.e., from Kitty to Mickey, and they read anything they want into it! When it's a guy singing about a girl, it's a sweet line. But when a girl sings it, it must mean butt-fucking! This is how the wrong foot gets cut off when the doc wheels you into the E.R. Then it's Micky Dolenz and butt-fucking." If she sounds a bit defensive it's from years and years of answering the same two questions about her one and only hit song.

Though Basil never matched her musical success, she continued right along with her great choreography career. When she's not trying to clear up the rumors about her most successful song, she's working on movies, tours and television shows. And as she proudly says, "There's nothing better than being head cheerleader." And when she says that, she's talking about cheerleading and nothing else. Don't start any rumors.

### December 18th

On this date in 1971, Sly and the Family Stone's long-delayed LP, *There's a Riot Goin' On*, went to #1 on the *Billboard* 200 album chart. The album was a culmination of two years of pressure on the band's artistic visionary, Sly Stone, as well as his increased drug use, which was making him more unpredictable and unreliable. None of these factors boded well for the band's latest work which is why it shocked everyone when *There's a Riot Goin' On* was released. The band (or was it all just Stone?) had produced their most ambitious and groundbreaking album.

Sly and the Family Stone emerged from San Francisco at the height of that city's musical influence. Sly Stone (born Sylvester Stewart) had been in various groups as far back as his childhood. He was also a radio DJ in the Bay Area as well as music producer. In 1966 he formed a band called Sly & the Stoners which would evolve over the next few months to Sly and the Family Stone. The band was remarkable not just for their incredible musicianship and ability to blend seamlessly between multiple genres (rock, funk, soul) but because they were multi-ethnic and multi-gendered (both rare qualities at the time). Their 1967 single, "Dance to the Music," peaked at #8 and introduced America to this exciting new band. They reached the top of the singles' chart a year later with "Everyday People." 1969 would not only see two more hit singles ("Hot Fun in the Summertime" which went to #2 and "Thank You (Falettinme Be Mice Elf Agin)" which made it to #1) but also their critically acclaimed set at Woodstock.

As the decade came to an end, the band's record label, Epic, felt they had a bankable commodity and they wanted more material that was just as commercially accessible as their recent chart-topping singles. But problems inside the band, and outside pressure on Sly Stone, were mounting. The band had moved from San Francisco to Los Angeles and their drug use, which had already been abundant, increased. Stone took to carrying a violin case with him wherever he went. The case was packed with drugs. Plus the Black Panther movement had gotten close to Stone and was pressuring him to produce more socially conscious material (their 1969 LP *Stand!* had included the album track "Don't Call Me Nigger, Whitey" and they wanted more of the same) and also to fire the white band members and replace them with black musicians. When it became obvious that no new material would be forthcoming, Epic re-released their debut album (with all new packaging to make it look new), then put out a *Greatest Hits* album towards the end of 1970. Meanwhile, Stone and the band did some touring in 1970 but with Stone missing almost a third of the performances due to his drug use, it became harder and harder to rely on him. They also recorded some new material in 1970 but nothing that could begin to resemble a new album.

In 1971 Stone began recording more earnestly. Sometimes he would work in the studio alone, using a drum machine (one of the first to do so) and playing most of the instruments himself. He also brought in other artists like Billy Preston, Bobby Womack and Ike Turner to help on some tracks. Clearly the internal band strife had pushed him to the edge and his own unpredictable behavior made it impossible to collaborate. As the album finally took shape he intended to call it, *Africa Talks to You* (one of the songs he was working on was titled "Africa Talks to You 'The Asphalt Jungle'"), but in the spring of 1971 Marvin Gaye released his own groundbreaking LP *What's Going On* and Stone decided to change the title of his latest work to answer Gaye's question.

What Stone produced was a huge departure from anything the band had done earlier. Where most of their work in the sixties was filled with optimism and joy, and was danceable and fun, *There's a Riot Goin' On* is gritty and funky. Idealism is gone, replaced with cynicism and weariness. The music is dense and dark (especially compared to some of their effervescent earlier stuff) and Stone's voice is slurred, almost unintelligible at times. "Africa Talks to You 'The Asphalt Jungle,'" (which was almost the title track) is a nine minute funk jam that is nearly impossible to turn off. "Family Affair," the album's lead single is a somber look at relationships (no doubt influenced by the friction in his own band). On its surface, and often on its first listen, *Riot* seems too dark and dense to dive into. But the album grows on the listener today, as it clearly did upon its release.

*There's a Riot Goin' On* was met with mostly positive reviews. And while it certainly turned off some of Stone's earlier fans, it also won over plenty of new ones. The sixties were over and *Riot* was as much of an introduction to a new decade as anyone would produce. All these years later the album is viewed by critics and musicologists as influential to an entire generation of artists who aimed to produce dark and sultry funk that had no truck for pop sensibility or commercialism. They say it takes intense pressure to turn a stone into a diamond. The same can be said for the 1971 LP *There's a Riot Goin' On.* Intense pressure on Stone produced his most powerful and influential work.

On this date in 1955, Carl Perkins walked into Sun Studios in Memphis, Tennessee and recorded "Blue Suede Shoes," a song he'd written just weeks before. Rock and roll was still in its nascent phase at this point. In fact the term "rock and roll" wasn't even being used yet to describe this amalgamation of country and rhythm and blues. Perkins' song, along with a handful of others, would create the blueprint for this genre.

Carl Lee Perkins was born in 1932 in Tiptonville, Tennessee to a family of sharecroppers. When he was a young child, he asked his parents for a guitar but they were too poor to afford one so his father made him a musical instrument from a cigar box and a broomstick. He mastered that and was playing in local bars by fourteen. One day he heard Elvis Presley's "Blue Moon of Kentucky" on the radio and said: "There's a man in Memphis who understands what we're doing. I need to go see him." That man, of course, was Sun Records' owner Sam Phillips for whom Perkins successfully auditioned. Perkins was quickly added to the early roster of rock and roll pioneers recording and touring together. In the fall of 1955, during one of those tours, Johnny Cash mentioned to Perkins that he knew of a guy who referred to his regulation airmen's footwear as "blue suede shoes," something they both found funny. Weeks later while Perkins was performing he overheard a couple that was dancing in front of the stage. The guy was upset at his date because she'd stepped on his shoes. Perkins heard the guy holler, "Don't step on my suedes!" Sure enough, he was wearing blue suede shoes. Perkins remembers thinking, "Good gracious, a pretty little thing like that and all he can think about is his blue suede shoes."

Back-to-back mentions of blue suede shoes was enough to get Perkins' creative juices flowing. That night he started working on a song, using the nursery rhyme "One For the Money" to get started. He couldn't find any paper so he jotted down the lyrics on a potato sack. Unfamiliar with the word suede, he spelled it "swade."

And so it was on this date in 1955 that Perkins recorded "Blue Suede Shoes," with Sam Phillips at the controls, his brother Jay Perkins on rhythm guitar, his other brother Clayton Perkins playing bass and W.S. "Fluke" Holland on drums. It was Phillips who suggested changing the line, "Go, man, go," to, "Go, cat, go," because he thought it sounded less country and more hip. According to Perkins, the two extra beats between the opening, "One for the money," and, "Two for the show," was an accident and when he played the song live he would sometimes eliminate those beats until it was pointed out that that was a signature of his version. When Elvis Presley recorded the song in the winter of 1956 he eliminated the pause between the lines, which speeds up the opening considerably but eliminates that energy-through-anticipation in Perkins' version.

"Blue Suede Shoes" was released on New Year's Day, 1956 and became a huge success on multiple charts (pop, R&B and country). It also launched Perkins to national fame and he began getting requests for television appearances. His biggest booking came in March when he was scheduled to appear on *The Perry Como Show* on NBC but on the way to New York City he and his band were involved in a bad car accident. Perkins was hospitalized and missed the show. He'd lament later, "I was a poor farm boy, and with 'Shoes' I felt I had a chance but suddenly there I was in the hospital." Meanwhile Presley's version of "Blue Suede Shoes," one of his first recordings for RCA who had purchased his contract from Sun, started climbing the charts and Presley started performing the song during his own television appearances. In fact, the first time Presley performed the song on television was April 3rd, 1956 on *The Milton Berle* show. Carl Perkins watched it from his hospital bed. After a while, Perkins became known more for writing the song than for recording it.

But that perception didn't last forever. Today Perkins is recognized as an early and influential rock and roll artist and "Blue Suede Shoes" makes every list of songs that shaped the genre. He's often called the "King of Rockabilly" and he's been inducted into the Rock and Roll Hall of Fame, the Rockabilly Hall of Fame, the Memphis Music Hall of Fame, and the Nashville Songwriters Hall of Fame. He was also presented with a Grammy Hall of Fame Award. In 1996 he published his autobiography titled *Go Cat Go*. The word "suede" was spelled correctly.


### December 20th

On this date in 1980, AC/DC's *Back in Black* peaked at #4 on *Billboard's* album chart. The LP spent over two years on that chart and has gone on to sell over 50 million copies worldwide. An incredible feat especially considering that months before recording the album, the band lost its lead singer and was on the precipice of disbanding.

AC/DC is an Australian hard rock band that rose to international prominence in the seventies on the strength of their high energy live shows and increasingly successful albums. With their 1979 offering *Highway to Hell,* they finally achieved massive success in the U.S. They set out on a tour from July of 1979 through January of 1980 and then planned to take a few weeks off before hitting the studio to record a follow-up. Then on February 19th, tragedy struck. Lead singer and chief lyricist, Bon Scott, he of the signature raspy voice, died of alcohol poisoning after a night of heavy drinking. The band was devastated and for a while they considered breaking up. It was Bon Scott's father who urged them to continue. They held auditions and very quickly chose Brian Johnson as their new lead singer. Johnson had a distinct advantage in the auditions. The band already knew of him from previous work he'd done in a band called Geordie and he regularly covered a number of AC/DC songs.

In April of 1980, the band and producer Jeff "Mutt" Lange made their way to Nassau in the Bahamas to begin work on their next album. Previously, their writing process had always been that guitarists (and brothers) Malcolm and

Angus Young came up with the riffs and melody, then Bon Scott wrote the lyrics. As recording got underway in Nassau, the Young brothers hoped to continue this tradition. The first thing they handed their new lead singer was a riff and music bed they'd created, telling him they wanted to use the title "You Shook Me All Night Long." For Johnson this was an early test. Could he write lyrics to match what he recognized immediately as a winning riff? He listened to the track a few times, then wandered outside and looked at some of the beautiful women vacationing on the island. Surely the brothers' suggested title echoed in his head as he searched for inspiration. He then dashed off some of the greatest, sexually-urgent, double-entendre-filled lyrics ever written. "She told me to come but I was already there," is both succinct and hilarious in its naïveté. Johnson also wrote the line, "She was a fast machine, she kept her motor clean," thinking of the similarities between cars and women. He later explained, "They both go fast, let you down, but then make you happy again when you see the new model." If "You Shook Me All Night Long" was Johnson's initiation to AC/DC, you'd have to say he passed with flying colors.

During the band's month-long stay in Nassau, the island was clobbered with tropical storms, causing power outages and delaying production. Johnson channeled the weather into the opening of "Hells Bells," writing the now familiar: "I'm rolling thunder, pourin' rain. I'm comin' on like a hurricane." For another song, Malcolm Young came up with a guitar riff from a warm-up he frequently did before playing. The band had decided by this point that they wanted to pay tribute to Bon Scott somehow so Young suggested the title "Back in Black" for this song. Instead of turning the song into a somber tribute though, Johnson made it a defiant statement about going on, featuring lyrics like, "Forget the hearse cause I'll never die." The band loved it and chose the song as the title track.

By the end of May, AC/DC and Lange were mixing the album in New York City and planning for its release. When they submitted it, their original concept for an album cover was all black, as a memorial to Bon Scott. Their record label, Atlantic, insisted they add the grey stencil of their name at the very least. They agreed and the now classic cover was complete.

*Back in Black* was released in July of 1980, less than six months after Bon Scott's death. It went on to achieve unprecedented success and helped make AC/DC an even bigger band than they'd been before. Their momentum continued throughout the eighties and beyond, with album after album going platinum and AC/DC's tours selling out stadiums around the world. They've sold over 200 million records in their decades together and established themselves as one of the most successful hard rock acts ever. Celebrate their career today by blasting *Back in Black* (or just "You Shook Me All Night Long" if you haven't got 42 minutes to spare) and consider for a moment how close they came to disbanding after Bon Scott's death.

On this date in 1964, the Temptations released "My Girl." It's a song they practically had to beg the song's composers to let them record and it turns out they were right to do so. They obviously knew an all-time classic when they heard it.

The Temptations had been with Gordy (a Motown subsidiary) since 1961 and scored some success prior to 1965 but no chart-toppers which at Motown, made them second class citizens. Songs like "The Way You Do the Things You Do" and "Girl (Why You Wanna Make Me Blue)" featured Eddie Kendricks on lead vocals and he'd clearly become the band's de facto lead singer. In 1964, they, along with most other bands in the Motown stable, were on tour as part of the Motortown Revue. When the tour arrived in New York City, it played at the famed Apollo Theater. Before soundcheck, Smokey Robinson and bandmate Ronald White were working out a song called "My Girl" as a mellower follow-up to "My Guy" which Robinson had written and Mary Wells had just had a #1 hit with. As the two composed the song at the piano on the stage of the Apollo, the Temptations listened and were blown away. They approached Robinson later about recording the song but he was hesitant, sensing it could be big and intending it for his own band, the Miracles. After some badgering, Robinson agreed under one condition, he wanted David Ruffin, who'd recently replaced Elbridge Bryant in the band, to take the lead vocal. Robinson, who got to see the Temptations perform every night on the tour, felt Ruffin was a "sleeping giant" in the group and his voice would be perfect for the ballad. The band agreed and when they all returned to Detroit, a recording session was scheduled.

With the song's release right before Christmas, it began a steady climb up the charts and hit #1 in early March of 1965. With the song's success, the sleeping giant was awoken and it was Ruffin who would take the lead on many of the band's next singles: "It's Growing", "Since I Lost My Baby", "My Baby", "Ain't Too Proud to Beg" and "Beauty Is Only Skin Deep." As happens so often in music, success led to an over-inflated ego and soon Ruffin's was out of control. He stopped traveling on the band's bus, insisting instead on a custom limousine with his signature black rimmed glasses painted on the door. After the Supremes changed their name to Diana Ross & the Supremes, Ruffin petitioned Berry Gordy to do the same, demanding the band be renamed David Ruffin & the Temptations. Finally the band had enough and in 1967 they fired him, replacing him with former Contour Dennis Edwards. Ruffin then began showing up at Temptations' concerts and walking out on stage when the band launched into songs he'd sang lead on (which embarrassed the band but delighted the fans). The band actually gave him another shot at joining their ranks but when he showed up late for a performance, they fired him again, this time permanently.

Though it may have been the beginning of an ego run amok, "My Girl" is also seen as the Temptations' signature song as well as some of Smokey Robinson's greatest lyrics (which, considering the breadth of his career, is saying a lot). The song sings lovingly of a woman's charms and, as Robinson predicted, it is perfect for Ruffin's passionate voice. Through the decades "My Girl" has made an indelible mark on pop culture and today is considered one of the greatest love song of all time. Because, really, who among us could hear the opening melody and finger snaps and not launch loudly, into "I've got sunshine . . ."

## December 22nd

On this date in 1978, the duet by Barbra Streisand & Neil Diamond, "You Don't Bring Me Flowers," spent its final day at #1 on the *Billboard* Hot 100 chart. The song had first arrived at the top on December 2nd when it knocked Donna Summer's "MacArthur Park" from that spot. A week later Chic's "Le Freak" would reach #1 only to be bumped off the following week when "You Don't Bring Me Flowers" returned to the top again. After this date "Flowers" would give way to Chic once again. Such was the state of music in 1978 when ballads and dance songs literally fought for chart dominance. But "You Don't Bring Me Flowers" had a very interesting and unique journey to the top. Many hit songs can thank radio DJs for their exposure, helping the song reach the masses through on-air promotion. But "You Don't Bring Me Flowers," the duet version anyway, literally has a radio DJ to thank for its creation.

In 1977 Norman Lear approached Neil Diamond about writing a theme song for a television show he was producing called *All That Glitters*. Diamond, along with Alan Bergman and Marilyn Bergman wrote a short, 45 second piece called "You Don't Bring Me Flowers." When the direction of the TV show changed the song was no longer needed but Diamond felt it had potential so he fleshed it out by adding more lyrics and started playing the song during his concerts. When it was received well, he decided to record it and he included it on his 1977 LP, *I'm Glad You're Here with Me Tonight*, but it wasn't released as a single. The following year Barbra Streisand recorded a cover version which she included on her *Songbird* album but again, the song was not released as a single.

Gary Guthrie, program director at WAKY-AM in Louisville, Kentucky, is the one who created the duet. He and his wife Becky were going through a hard time and when she heard the Neil Diamond version it made her cry. When Guthrie heard the Streisand version he decided to splice the two solo tracks together (an early mash-up, if you will) and give it to his wife as a present. When the project was finished he also played it on air which created quite the stir. First WAKY became deluged with requests and then, very quickly, the national media picked up on the story. *Good Morning America* did a piece about the homemade duet and *People* magazine mentioned it in an article. Though other radio DJs claim to have done the same thing around the same time, it was Guthrie's story that got picked up by the national media and as we all know, the winner is the one who gets the headlines.

Both Diamond and Streisand were signed to Columbia Records at the time and their label promptly brought them together to make a real duet version of the song. The recording session was helmed by Bob Gaudio (songwriter and producer for the Four Seasons) who was nervous about having two major stars in the studio at the same time. He envisioned keeping the melody simple with Diamond and Streisand singing over a simple piano track, but he had a full orchestra standing by in another room should they be needed. But by all accounts everything went smoothly and both singers completed the song "nose to nose" as Gaudio described it. Within a few hours a final version was cut and mixed down. The song was released as a single (finally!) in late October of 1978. Capitalizing on the media around the song, it debuted at #48 and made a quick climb to #1.

Columbia sent Guthrie a Gold Record to thank him for his involvement in the song. Streisand sent a telegram with words of appreciation and Diamond, ironically, sent flowers. Not only was his gift to his wife not enough to save their marriage but apparently Guthrie had channeled the song's message of despair over a crumbling relationship. He became dissatisfied with those tokens of appreciation and filed a $5 million lawsuit against Columbia which the label promptly settled, no doubt singing under their breath as they cut that check, "Used-to-be's don't count anymore."

## December 23rd

On this date in 1979, Rupert Holmes' "Escape (The Pina Colada Song)" had just begun a two week run at #1 on the pop chart by knocking the Styx ballad, "Babe," from the top. In the first week of 1980, "Please Don't Go," KC and the Sunshine Band's final #1, would take over the top spot but "Escape" would return a week later and then give way to Michael Jackson's "Rock with You." Such was the state of music as the seventies came to a close, as disco, in its final throes, battled with soft rock for chart supremacy.

Sometime in early 1979, Rupert Holmes was working on material for his fifth studio album when he realized he needed something a little more uptempo to balance out the mellower tracks he'd already completed. He had a melody in mind but was unhappy with the lyrics so he figured he'd lay down the backing track then come up with the words. He did so with his band, then listened back and was equally unhappy with the instrumentation, except for one section. He found 16 bars of music where everyone was tight and in a nice groove. So he spliced those 16 bars from the master tape and duplicated them over and over, creating a five minute track with over 60 loops. He then sat down to come up with lyrics, knowing the song's focus would have to be on the words because the backing track was so repetitive.

Holmes sat in his apartment wracking his brain to come up with something clever enough to steal the listener's attention from the music. Finally he saw a copy of the *The Village Voice* and picked it up, hoping for some inspiration. He flipped through the entire magazine without getting a spark. Then at the very back he saw the personal ads and read one from a woman who described herself in glowing terms. His first thought was, "If you're so wonderful why do you need to place a personal ad?" Then he had a thought that is equal parts hilarious and scary: what if he replied to the ad only to find out it was his current girlfriend who had placed it because she was bored in their relationship and looking for an escape?

And just like that he had his idea. It was interesting enough to keep the focus on the lyrics and off the music. Once he had the storyline the words came quickly. The only major revision he made was in his first draft the woman asked, "If you like Humphrey Bogart and getting caught in the rain." Rupert already had a number of movie references in his previous albums so he felt like that line needed alteration. He started focusing on the concept of escaping which led to vacationing which led to an exotic drink. He played with Daiquiri, then Mai Tai before coming up with Pina Colada (a drink he claims to have never had before the song).

When Holmes submitted his finished album he wanted to release "Him" as the lead single. His record company, however, felt "Escape" had the best chance to be successful and to convince him they gave it to a radio station to sample. The station played it and the phone lines lit up. The problem was though that all the callers were asking for "The Pina Colada Song." The label in turn wanted to change the title to "Escape (The Pina Colada Song)" and told Rupert it wouldn't sell if they didn't. Rupert replied, "I guess it's The Pina Colada Song."

Rupert Holmes has a very impressive literary resume. He's written Broadway plays and novels, created a television series and composed songs that have been recorded by singers as diverse as Barbara Streisand and Britney Spears. His mantle is adorned with Tony awards and Emmys. Yet, he laments, he will always be known as the guy who wrote "The Pina Colada Song." "I have a feeling," he has said, "that if I saved an entire orphanage from a fire and carried the last child out on my shoulders, as I stood there charred and smoking, they'd say, 'Aren't you the guy who wrote The Pina Colada Song?' It's tough when you have this one thing that pulls focus from all these other things that you've done, yet every songwriter lives to have a song that most everybody knows." And if you're old enough to have listened to the radio in the winter of 1980, you most definitely know his most famous song. To put it bluntly, there was no way to escape from it that year.

On this date in 1984, "Do They Know It's Christmas?" by a charity supergroup called Band Aid made its first appearance on the *Billboard* Hot 100 chart. The song was already #1 in England where most of the members of Band Aid came from and it would go on to raise millions as well as give birth to both a concert that raised even more money and plenty of other copy-cat charity efforts. All of this because one guy saw a news report that moved him to action.

In late October of 1984, Boomtown Rats singer Bob Geldof saw a BBC report about the famine in Ethiopia and he was moved to action. He reached out to his friend Midge Ure (who was currently the frontman for the band Ultravox) who agreed to help. The two met in the beginning of November to talk about what they could do and very quickly they came up with the idea of releasing a Christmas song for charity. Even though it was already November they felt if they worked quickly enough they could have it out by that Christmas. Geldof made two important phone calls at this point to see if he could get high profile figures in the industry involved (which they'd determined was the key to the project's success.) He reached out to Sting and Simon Le Bon (of Duran Duran) and both singers enthusiastically lent their support. Now they had the ball rolling.

Geldof and Ure then had to decide upon which song to record. They talked about covering an existing Christmas carol but decided against it because they'd have to give a portion of the proceeds to the original writers. Composing something new was their best choice. Ure came up with the basic melody track and Geldof took a song he was already working on, called "It's My World," and tweaked some of the lyrics to fit the theme. Within a day they had the basic backing track and lyrics complete. Geldof then asked music producer Trevor Horn if he could helm the project. Horn was a red-hot producer at the time based on his work with Frankie Goes to Hollywood. Unfortunately, Horn's calendar was all booked up through the end of the year so he couldn't personally oversee the session. But he told Geldof his London studio, SARM West, was free on one day, Sunday November 25th, and he'd donate the studio space free of charge to Geldof. Ure decided he could produce the song himself and he set about finishing the backing track while Geldof worked the phones and recruited more musicians. He even contacted newspapers and magazines in the U.K. and many offered free ad space to promote the single. Geldof struck a deal with the *Daily Mirror* giving them exclusive access to the recording studio in exchange for an article that would build anticipation for the song.

When the recording day arrived, musicians started stumbling into the studio as early as 8:30am. There was a feeling of camaraderie in the air (enhanced, no doubt, when Francis Rossi and Rick Parfitt, the two frontmen of rock band Status Quo, produced some cocaine and whiskey) and Geldof and Ure decided to capitalize on that vibe right away so they started the recording session by having everyone sing the big ending, the "Feed the world. Let them know it's Christmas time," refrain over and over. Nobody had heard the song prior to this morning so it took some organizing but before too long everyone was singing heartily and they were all happy with the ending. Then Ure started recording each individual artist for the opening of the song and its bridge. Tony Hadley, lead singer for Spandau Ballet, was selected to go first and he's admitted to more than a few nerves while he sang his line with so many of his industry peers looking on. One after the other, or in combinations of two and threes, artists got up to take their crack at their line. The only singer who hadn't shown by this point was Boy George who was on a Concorde flight from New York City, having performed there the night before. George arrived towards the end of the day and was the last to lay down his vocals (which is why he's not in the group photo that graced the back of the single).

Ure made plenty of great choices in his final edit, none better than allowing U2's frontman, Bono, to sing the impassioned line "Well, tonight thank God it's them instead of you." Other than the huge ending, which has a transcendent, "Hey Jude," feeling to it, that one line, delivered with Bono's gritty passion, rings the truest.

All the hype and anticipation paid off handsomely, especially in the U.K. where the single opened up at #1 on the charts and sold unprecedented numbers, moving over 3 million copies by the end of the year. In the U.S. the song didn't do quite as well, peaking at #13 in early January of 1985 and selling about two and half million copies. Still, it raised approximately $10 million worldwide (back when $10 million actually meant something) but more importantly it helped raise awareness for the famine in Ethiopia and set in motion other charitable events. U.S. artists, perhaps feeling guilty that they hadn't thought of the idea first, hopped on the bandwagon and produced "We Are the World" in March of 1985. That summer the Live Aid concerts took place and in 1985 the telethon *Comic Relief* was held, all to help the starving people in famine torn Ethiopia. It was an incredible moment of charity and giving and it's all because one man saw a news report and was moved to action.

### December 25th

On this date in 1954, Bing Crosby's "White Christmas" re-entered the charts for a record eleventh time. The song had already become an annual holiday favorite and it would remain so for decades. Though many other artists have released their own version of "White Christmas," it will always be Bing Crosby's that is viewed as the quintessential recording. And Crosby will forever be linked to Christmastime in the U.S.

Irving Berlin was composing music for the 1935 film *Top Hat* when he originally came up with the melody and some of the lyrics for what would become "White Christmas." When *Top Hat*'s director passed on the song, Berlin shelved it till a few years later when Paramount hired him to compose music for the motion picture *Holiday Inn*. Berlin was charged with coming up with a song for every holiday in the year and so, along with writing "Easter Parade" and "Let's Start the New Year Right" he handed in a song called "White Christmas." Bing Crosby, who would star in the film and sing most of the songs, was unimpressed when he was first given "White Christmas." Legend has it he simply said, "I don't think we have any problems with that one, Irving." Not exactly a ringing endorsement.

Since Crosby was playing a New Yorker in sunny California around Christmas, Berlin's original lyrics for the movie open with the lines:

> The sun is shining, the grass is green
> The orange and palm trees sway
> There's never been such a day
> In Beverly Hills, LA
> But it's December the 24th
> And I'm longing to be up north

When Crosby set out to record the song for commercial release, it was his record producer, Jack Kapp, who suggested leaving those opening lines out to make the song more universally relatable. This left just eight lines which Crosby then sang twice.

"White Christmas" made its first public appearance on Christmas Day in 1941 when Crosby performed it on his NBC radio show *The Kraft Music Hall*. He recorded his first version of the song in May of 1942 and it was released a few months later as part of an album of six 78-rpm discs from *Holiday Inn*. By the end of October, 1942, with the U.S. embroiled in World War II and the entire country mobilized for the war effort, "White Christmas," a simple yet beautiful song of yearning and hope, made it to #1 on the Your Hit Parade chart, where it would remain throughout the holiday season. The following year, as the holidays of 1943 approached, "White Christmas" re-emerged onto the national charts, a trend that would repeat year after year. Crosby also began doing annual Christmas shows around this time, first on the radio, then moving to television in the early sixties. Crosby's annual Christmas shows would feature other guest stars and a myriad of holiday songs, both religious and secular, yet "White Christmas" was inevitably always performed.

The music industry, like most of the arts, follows trends whenever they spot them, and once everyone realized, "There's gold in them thar Christmas songs," the floodgates were open. In 1944 Nat King Cole released what can be considered the first holiday music album, *Merry Christmas*, which contained his now iconic "The Christmas Song." According to that song's cowriter Mel Torme, "The Christmas Song," with its imagery of, "Chestnuts roasting on an open fire," and, "Jack Frost nipping at your nose," was written as an effort to stay cool on an oppressively hot summer day. Pretty soon just about every songwriter was trying to compose their own holiday anthem and every artist was aiming to release an album that could dominate the December charts. It also became obvious that there was a huge market for secular songs that focused less on the holiness of the night and more on the timeless images we can all relate to at Christmastime.

And by all, it was clear that included everyone. Indeed, Irving Berlin, the composer of the song that got the ball rolling on annual tunes that we hear this time of year, was Jewish. And years after he passed away his daughter, Mary Ellin, told Mark Steyn, author of *A Song for the Season*, which recounts the creation and impact "White Christmas" has had on American pop culture: "My father believed in the secular American Christmas. There's a lot of controversy about that, about whether there should be, apart from the Christian celebration of the birth of Jesus Christ, a general festive celebration that anyone can join in with."  There may have been controversy years ago but clearly, no more. Whether you believe that today is the birth of the Son of God, or just one of the nicest days you can spend with loved ones, and whether you wake up to palm trees swaying or snow falling, clearly, the magic of Christmas is all inclusive. And with a soundtrack of carols both old and new, there's no shortage of music to sing along to. Merry Christmas!


### December 26th

On this date in 1978, Chic's first #1 hit, "Le Freak," returned to the top spot on the charts for a second time. It would slip again at the beginning of 1979 only to return to #1 for two more weeks in January, making "Le Freak" the first song ever to have three separate stays at the top of the pop chart. The fact that it was at #1 on New Year's Eve of 1978 is somehow fitting since it was a misunderstanding exactly one year before that led to the song's creation.

The band Chic came together in 1976, organized by guitarist Niles Rogers and bassist Bernard Edwards just as disco was exploding on the airwaves and in the night clubs. Rogers was as impressed with the popularity of dance music as he was with the fashion sense of English glam rock as well as the band KISS with their makeup and outrageous shows. He and Edwards put together a lineup of musicians and singers that would be a complete entertainment package, producing infectious dance music as well as dressing and acting as glamorous as possible. This was the seventies after all and extravagant fashions were an integral part of the nightclub scene.

Chic signed a record deal with Atlantic and released their eponymous debut album in November of 1977. The album's lead single, "Dance, Dance, Dance (Yowsah, Yowsah, Yowsah)" was released a few months earlier and was already climbing the charts. It would peak at #6 in February of 1978.

So by December of 1977, while Chic were fairly new, they were a band with a name and a growing reputation. About this time Rogers was talking to Grace Jones, another up and coming dance artist, about producing an album for her. So as New Year's Eve 1977 approached, with Jones performing at disco's mecca, Studio 54, it was only natural Rogers and Edwards would be invited. They had a lot to celebrate. Their debut album was out and they had a single on the rise. 1978 promised to be a big year, not just for Chic but for this genre of dance music called disco which just seemed to keep growing and growing in popularity. So why not usher it in in style?

All that had to be on Rogers' and Edwards' minds when they arrived at Studio 54 on December 31st, 1977. The crowd out front was understandably immense with thousands of people hoping to slip past the velvet rope and gain entrance to the disco's temple of debauchery. Rogers and Edwards muscled their way up front and expected to be whisked into the club. But the doormen didn't recognize them. They must be on a list. The doormen checked. Nope. They probably said something to the effect of, "But we're the guys from Chic." The doormen probably heard that kind of thing all the time. Sorry guys. Can't get in.

All dressed up with nowhere to go, and seething with anger, the two went back to Rogers' place and started jamming. They developed an infectious, driving hook which they punctuated from time to time by shouting, "Ahhh, fuck off," as a cathartic way to release their anger. After a while, the two realized what they'd created as an outlet for their vexation may actually have commercial potential. Knowing the expletive would stop it from getting airplay, they changed it to, "Ahh freak out," and came up with the rest of the lyrics. By the time they did, their anger towards the club must have subsided because the song actually includes a shout out to Studio 54 ("Just come on down, to fifty-four. Find a spot out on the floor").

"Le Freak" was released in July of 1978 as the lead single from the band's second LP, *C'est Chic*. The song began a slow and steady climb up the charts, hitting #1 for the first time on December 9th. It would then do a little dance at the top of the charts. Having knocked off the Barbra Streisand and Neil Diamond duet "You Don't Bring Me Flowers," "Le Freak" lasted just one week, before being displaced by that same song. A week later, on this date in 1978, "Le Freak" would get back to #1 where it would stay through the holidays. On January 6th, 1978, the Bee Gees would hit #1 with their R&B ballad, "Too Much Heaven." That song would remain at #1 for two weeks before "Le Freak" returned for a record third stay at the top. In total "Le Freak" spent six weeks at #1, making it, by far, the band's most successful song (although "Good Times," their only other #1, is arguably their signature song).

No one knows what Niles Rogers and Bernard Edwards did on New Years Eve of 1978, but with a song sitting at #1 on the pop chart and the whole world singing, "Ahhhhhhhhh, freak out," you can be sure they got into whatever club they wanted to.

On this date in 1974, Harry Chapin's "Cat's in the Cradle" was spending its final day at #1 on *Billboard*'s Hot 100 chart. A week earlier it had displaced Karl Douglas' early disco hit "Kung Fu Fighting" from the top just in time for Christmas. It would give up the top spot after just one week, surrendering to Helen Reddy's "Angie Baby." A song that began life as a poem would serve forever as a warning to young fathers to get involved with their children. It's a warning that millions heard and hopefully heeded.

Sandra Gaston had always been a poet. During her first marriage, to James John Cashmore, who was the son of John Cashmore, Borough President of Brooklyn, she was saddened by the distance between her husband and his father. They were both busy men and would talk on the phone often but rarely saw each other even though they lived close by. It got to the point that John would communicate with his son through Gaston. Even when they were all in the same room together, he would say to her, "tell Jimmy. . ." Gaston was so moved by this she eventually wrote a poem about it. During her marriage with Cashmore she decided to take guitar lessons. Her instructor was a struggling singer-songwriter named Harry Chapin. The two quickly fell in love. She divorced Cashmore to marry Chapin in November of 1968, something he wrote explicitly about in his song "I Wanna Learn a Love Song."

Sandra and Harry Chapin were not only wife and husband but they would collaborate from time to time on songs. As a poet, she was prone to writing longer pieces and sometimes she'd show them to Chapin and he would rework them into songs. Early on, she showed him the poem she'd written about her first husband and his father but Chapin was uninspired. It wasn't till a few years later when their first son was born, and Chapin missed the birth because he was on the road, that he started working on the poem. Sandra would say later, "I'm assuming he was looking at things differently after Josh was born, but he didn't really talk about it to me."

Harry's genius was not only telling the story in four verses that show the cycle of one father being distant and how that affects his son (who goes on to be just like him) but also in using some imagery from nursery rhymes in the chorus. From the title of the song to the silver spoons, little boy blue and the man in the moon, the chorus of "Cat's in the Cradle" sounds like something a father would sing to their child to get them to fall asleep. If only he were there.

As Chapin was finishing his fourth album, *Verities & Balderdash*, it was his label chief David Geffen, who recommended "Cat's in the Cradle" as the lead single. When Sandra got wind of that she thought it was ridiculous, figuring it would only appeal to, "45 year old men and they don't buy records." She couldn't have been more wrong. The song's message of missed opportunities was universal and there is no doubt that as the holiday season of 1974 approached, "Cat's in the Cradle" became a popular gift to give a young father (or father-to-be). The Chapins had written a compelling song with the underlying message: "Don't be this guy."

One could argue whether or not that message made a difference, certainly as you walk through a park nowadays and see parents glued to their phones while their children play, or sit in a restaurant and see children playing video games while their parents dine, you can wonder if we all haven't become, "just like him." Be that as it may, the Chapins' timeless song still stands as a warning to us all. Children grow up quickly and life moves fast, take some time to be with the ones you love before that time slips away.

## December 28th

On this date in 1973, a new club had just opened in the lower east side section of New York City. The club's owner, Hilly Kristal, would name the place for what he envisioned as the type of music he'd feature, but within months that vision would change. Some of the bands that played at this establishment would go on to be pioneers in a new genre of music, loud, brash and angry music, that would help redefine rock as we know it today. The club is best described by those who were there as a dive. It was dirty, crowded, stuffy and at times disgusting. The perfect place, really, for the birth of punk music.

Hilly Kristal was a New Yorker by birth. He studied music in college and managed the famous Village Vanguard for a while, where he booked jazz greats such as Miles Davis. In 1970 he opened a bar in the Bowery section of New York City that he called "Hilly's on the Bowery." New York City in the seventies was the definition of urban decay and the Bowery section was one of the worst areas of the Big Apple. Streets were graffiti marked, abandoned and often dangerous. "Hilly's" was a dive bar that fit in well with its surrounding neighborhood. Kristal owned another place in New York but when that closed he focused his full attention on his place in the Bowery and decided to rebrand it and start offering live music. He gave the place a very odd new name, calling it "Country, Blue Grass, and Blues and Other Music For Uplifting Gormandizers." Kristal would explain later that though "gormandizer" means a person who eats a lot of food, in his case he meant someone who devours good music. He used the initials for this awkward name, shortening the club to CBGB & OMFUG which he proudly displayed on the bar's now famous awning.

Initially, Kristal booked bands that matched the club's name, but country and blue grass outfits aren't very rampant throughout New York City and their fan base is even more sparse. So by the winter of 1974 he was already rethinking this strategy. The first rock band he booked was in February of that year, a local band called Squeeze (not the new wave band from England that would go on to fame) and though they played traditional rock music (and not the hard-driving punk style) they were a departure from the country thing Kristal envisioned. When his bar tab was up that night, he started looking around for other acts to fill his club.

Kristal instituted two rules early on that he held firm on: bands had to move their own equipment and they had to play mostly original songs. This lent itself to the fresh new sound emanating from the club. Kristal wasn't interested in cover bands. Or anyone big enough to have roadies. He wanted young artists on their way up and he wanted them to play songs they'd written, with voices and messages all their own.

The first historic night at CBGB was March 31st, 1974 when the band Television played their first gig. Legend has it when they approached Kristal about playing at his club he told them he needed a proper stage put in and the band members built it. It's a story both Tom Verlaine and Richard Hell (Television's founders and punk rock pioneers) deny but like most rock and roll legends, it's too good to completely dismiss. Television's sound was new and different, hard and thrashing. They weren't great musicians or intricate songwriters but they played with an anger and abandon that fit this grimy little club, and the city around it, perfectly. There were only a handful of people in the club that night, most of them members of the Third Street Hell's Angels Club who had taken to using CBGB as a home base, and it's doubtful anyone realized they were witnessing the birth of a whole new genre of music that evening, but that's exactly what it was. So much of rock music in the mid-seventies had become big and bloated and even bands who played hard like Led Zeppelin were doing nine minute epic songs with tempo changes and piano solos and lyrics about a "bustle in your hedgerow." Here was a band who wrote in their press kit: "Television's music fulfills the adolescent desire to fuck the girl you've never met because you've just been run over by a car." Whatever that means it probably describes Television, and all the early punk bands, perfectly.

Once Television blew the doors open, CBGB became host to so many new bands. On August 16th, 1974, the Ramones also played their very first gig there. The set lasted just 12 minutes. When they were called back for an encore they just repeated the same songs, not even changing the order. No one in the club seemed to notice or care. The punk pioneers from Queens, New York would play at CBGB more than seventy times over the course of their careers. On January 17th, 1975, Blondie played its first gig at CBGB. A month later the Patti Smith Group made their debut. In June of the year, the Talking Heads took the stage for the first time. And in October of 1978, the Police played their first gig on American soil at CBGB.

Not every night at CBGB was historic and not every band went on to be legendary. But as punk music became a legitimate genre and changed the sound of rock in the late seventies, CBGB became the music's mecca. This dirty little club in filthy little lower Manhattan became the center of the scene. But punk exploded quickly and burnt out even faster. It would evolve into genres like new wave and synth pop and post-punk. CBGB was non-discriminatory in the years after punk flamed out. As long as you played originals and were willing to schlep your own gear, and didn't mind the size and smell of the joint, you could hit that stage and play your heart out.

In 2005 the owners of the building where CBGB resided sued Hilly Kristal for back rent. He'd been paying $19,000 a month but they claimed his rent had gone up and he was in arrears. Kristal said he was never notified of the increase. He won the case but the owners jacked his rent up to $35,000 (and this time they made sure he knew). New York City had changed. It had turned around. You could walk down most streets and feel safe. Even Times Square was family friendly, done over by Disney and Red Lobster and Madame Tussauds. CBGB, which had fit in so well when New York was at its lowest, now stood out like a sore thumb. Kristal announced he'd be closing his club in October of 2006. Patti Smith played an epic last night there and sure enough, the place was shuttered. Less than a year later Hilly Kristal died of lung cancer. He was 75 years old. Both he and his famous club were now gone, but the sites and sounds they enabled will echo on in the annals of rock music for eternity. Punk music was the sound of a generation, a "blank generation" as Richard Hell called it with "no future" as the Sex Pistols so famously yelled. And CBGB was the Petri dish in which it flourished.

### December 29th

On this date in 1974, ten days after it was supposed to take place, the Beatles were officially and legally dissolved as a business entity when John Lennon signed the voluminous documents that would end their existence as a band. They hadn't recorded anything together in five years and each was pursuing their own solo careers. Still the Beatles were legally an entity until Lennon became the last of the four to sign-off. And he did it in Disney World, with Magic Kingdom as a backdrop, because the stars were finally aligned.

By 1969, with the Beatles recording what would become *Let It Be*, the band was at loggerheads. There are a million reasons for it and each have been picked over and analyzed to death, but suffice to say that in their ten years together the Fab Four had gone from no-name kids playing music to drunks and trying to make a buck (or in their case a pound), to four of the most famous people in the world. Along the way, their friendships and working relationships were torn asunder. When Paul McCartney put out his press release on April 17th, 1970, announcing that the Beatles were officially breaking up, nobody within the band or its inner circle were surprised. In fact, John Lennon's only reaction was, "Why didn't I put out a release sooner?"

The next few years, while each Beatle released new music, formed new bands and pursued new interests, they were embroiled in untangling their former business relationships. Negotiations and compromises took years to hash out but finally towards the end of 1974 it looked like everything was ready to be signed and sealed. A meeting was scheduled for December 19th at the Plaza in New York City. This was the hotel the Beatles had stayed in during their famous first trip to America so it seemed only fitting. Ringo Starr was unable to attend so he signed all of the documents beforehand. George Harrison was already in town because he had a concert that night in the city. Paul McCartney flew to New York specifically to be there in person.

As the meeting got underway, Starr was tracked down on the phone to verify that it was indeed his signature on all the documents and that he was still alive. Then Harrison, McCartney and the lawyers waited. John Lennon, who only lived a few blocks away, wasn't there yet. Finally his lawyer made contact via telephone but Lennon wouldn't speak. Instead his secretary/lover May Pang got on the phone. This was during his separation from Yoko Ono, what is popularly referred to as Lennon's "lost weekend," which lasted almost two years. Pang relayed a message: "The stars aren't aligned." Lennon had read his astrological chart that morning and something must have said it wasn't a good day to dissolve a multi-million dollar business entity. Harrison and McCartney were aghast. Harrison, who had invited Lennon to join him onstage that night at Madison Square Garden, told Pang to tell Lennon not to show. Harrison and McCartney both put their signature to the proper documents and then left the Plaza, still unsure if things would ever get resolved (or, in this case, dissolved). Lennon and Pang then left New York for Florida where they planned to spend the holidays at Disney World.

While away, Lennon brought up one clause that he felt would burden him with an unfair tax disadvantage. The contracts were amended and brought to Florida. On this date in 1974, John Lennon signed his name, officially dissolving the Beatles. Pang snapped a quick picture of Lennon just after, looking like he is about to say something. Pang would describe Lennon as being bittersweet about the moment. She would tell *The New York Times:* "John had started this band that changed the world. It changed pop culture. It changed how we live and how we dress. And he knew that. So, when he sat down to sign, he knew that this was it. His was the last signature. As he had started the group, he was the one to end it."

Rumors of a reunion would persist for a while, ending of course when John Lennon was killed six years later. The other three performed together from time to time until Harrison's death in 2001.

There has never been as groundbreaking a band as the Beatles. They invented the whole concept of a rock band, created the whole image of how they should act and perform. And Pang was correct in her assessment. The Beatles not only affected music but fashion and philosophies as well. They altered the zeitgeist of the sixties like no one else and in terms of social norms, many would argue that the sixties were as important a decade as there ever has been. Though the four of them never recorded anything together after the sixties were over, their legacy lives on even today.

On this date in 1961, the Tokens' "The Lion Sleeps Tonight" was in the middle of a three week run at #1 on the *Billboard* Hot 100 chart. The song had already had a decades-old journey from the jungles of South Africa through Europe and eventually to the top of the U.S. pop chart. But the song's saga had only just begun. Along the way, its original composer, or more accurately his descendants, would have to fight very hard just to get a portion of their just due from a song that has earned millions upon millions of dollars.

Solomon Linda was born in 1909, a South African with Zulu ancestry. The Zulus had a hunting chant that went back far before Linda, built around the words, "Mbube zimbe" (Zulu for "Lion, stop"). As a kid Linda worked as a cattle herder and no doubt learned the chant. In his twenties he moved to Johannesburg where he formed an a cappella band called The Evening Birds. Linda's remarkably high soprano voice helped them gain popularity. He worked the Zulu chant into a complete song he simply called "Mbube" and released it on a ten inch, 78 rpm record in 1939. The song became a local hit, becoming the first African record to sell over 100,000 copies. Linda and his band enjoyed a brief period of fame in their homeland.

About a decade later the record somehow made its way to the U.S. where folk singer Pete Seeger fell in love with it. Since no lyrics came along with the disc Seeger transcribed them himself, writing "Wimoweh" for the consistent chant that runs through the song. He worked up a version that his band, the Weavers, released, under the name "Wimoweh," in 1952. That record lists "Paul Cambell" as the composer, a pseudonym for the group. There was no mention of Solomon Linda. According to Seeger he was told the song was in the public domain. When Seeger was told the song wasn't and someone named Solomon Linda had written the original, he sent a $1,000 check to South Africa.

Around this time, Solomon Linda, having fallen on hard times, sold his rights to the song to Gallo Studios, the company that had released the original recording, for ten shillings, less than a dollar. Gallo also generously hired Linda to clean up the studio and serve tea in their packing house.

Back in the U.S., "Wimoweh" had become a popular song for night club acts. Jimmy Dorsey recorded a jazz version in 1952, the Weavers released a live version in 1957 and two years later the Kingston Trio had a minor hit with the song, with their version listing Cambell and Linda as composers (although no royalties were sent overseas to Gallo or Linda himself).

The Tokens were a young doo-wop band at the time and they auditioned for RCA Records using "Wimoweh" to show off their vocal range. Their producers loved the song so much they brought in lyricist and composer George Weiss to come up with some English lyrics to go along with the old Zulu chant. Weiss' genius is that he kept the melody of the original intact, in fact he moved it even further forward by eliminating some of the wild screaming in the other versions, and then came up with the lyrics that puts the listener literally in the jungle, the mighty jungle. Solomon Linda's original composition, though buried under multiple layers of pop reworkings, was still very much the backbone of the song that was now called "The Lion Sleeps Tonight." The Tokens thought the song was a novelty at best (and an embarrassing joke at worst) and didn't even want to release it. Their record company insisted though and so "The Lion Sleeps Tonight" was initially released as the B side to their song "Tina." The single went nowhere till a DJ named Dick Smith, on WORC in Worcester, Massachusetts, started playing the B side. Then the song broke nationally, shooting up the charts and hitting #1 the week of Christmas, 1961.

Gallo Records in South Africa, which now held Linda's original copyright, wasn't receiving anything for any of the versions of the song that were out in the U.S. They made every effort but the American publishing companies insisted they owed nothing since South African copyrights were not valid in the U.S. (because South Africa was not a signatory to U.S. copyright law). Solomon Linda would live long enough to see his song become an international hit but he died of kidney disease in October of 1962. Posthumously, his song and singing style became so influential in South Africa it became known as Mdube music. Years later, Lady Blacksmith Mambazo would send gifts to Linda's family to thank them for Solomon's influence. But presents, adulation and respect don't pay the bills and aside from Seeger's one-time check, there were no other financial gains for Linda or his widow once he passed away. He was buried in a pauper's grave and she sent their children to school barefoot.

Then came *The Lion King.* Disney included lyrics from "The Lion Sleeps Tonight" in a scene in the 1994 movie and the song was included on the second soundtrack the über-successful movie produced. It's estimated "The Lion Sleeps Tonight" generated $15 million in royalties in the nineties alone from its resurgence in popularity in the movie and inclusion on the soundtrack. Still, any money the Lindas received was a mere pittance.

In 2000, South African journalist and author Rian Malan wrote an article for *Rolling Stone* that detailed the plight of Solomon Linda and his ancestors and the article actually seemed to guilt some of the parties involved into finally doing the right thing. Though the Lindas would never receive fair compensation for Solomon's work, a figure that would be near impossible to calculate anyway, they at least were able to emerge from poverty and put a roof over their heads. After all, Solomon Linda had written the most famous African melody ever and his song has evolved and morphed into dozens of iterations that have entertained tens of millions. At the very least they should be able to put shoes on their children's feet.

## December 31st

On this date in 1929, Guy Lombardo and his Royal Canadian Orchestra broadcast their show from the Roosevelt Hotel in New York City, becoming the first nationwide New Year's Eve radio broadcast. Included in their setlist that night was Lombardo's big band take on an old Scottish song called "Auld Lang Syne." The band played the song just after midnight. The broadcast went well and Lombardo became a New Year's Eve staple on radio, and then in the fifties, television, and "Auld Lang Syne" soon became the song that ushered in everyone's new year. Even if very few people understand it.

"Auld Lang Syne" is often credited to the Scottish poet Robert Burns, even though it is commonly accepted that he didn't write the original poem. The original, or at least fragments of it, likely goes back to the 16th century so it was nearly 200 years old when Burns wrote it down and set it to music in 1788. Indeed the phrase itself, "auld lang syne," which strictly translates to "old long since" but is more commonly paraphrased as "days gone by" or even "for old times sake," has made appearances in English literature since before Shakespeare. But Burns did transcribe it and set it to a traditional Scottish folk melody before submitting it to the Scottish Musical Museum with a note that read, "The following song, an old song, of the olden times, and which has never been in print, nor even in manuscript until I took it down from an old man." By the beginning of the 19th century the song was commonly sung by the Scots at funerals, graduations, farewells and, of course, on "Hogmanay," the Scottish word for the last day of the year. The tradition spread through the years to all the people in the British Isles and as they emigrated around the world, they took the song with them.

Gaetano Alberto Lombardo was born in 1902 in Ontario, Canada. His father was a tailor by trade but at heart, he was a performer. He was an amateur singer with a rich baritone voice and he taught all his children to play instruments so they could accompany him. With this early instruction, Gaetano, who soon became known as "Guy," had formed his first orchestra with his brothers by the time he was twelve years old. He would soon dub his orchestra the Royal Canadians and bill them as, "the sweetest music this side of Heaven." He signed his first record deal in his early twenties and was soon a very popular band leader in Canada as well as the States. On this date in 1928, he played his first New Year's Eve show in New York City and a year later he struck a deal with the NBC Radio Network to have the show broadcast live across the country. This became an annual tradition until 1956 when the broadcast became a telecast. An entire generation of people listened to, or watched, Guy Lombardo entertain them as one year drew to a close, and another began, with the Scottish folk song, "Auld Lang Syne." In fact, when Dick Clark started broadcasting on New Year's Eve, it was to grab the younger audience who no longer wanted to watch what their parents and grandparents watched on December 31st. Still, Clark understood tradition and his *New Year's Rockin' Eve* usually played a recording of Lombardo's "Auld Lang Syne" at midnight before returning to the pop music of the day.

Like most standards, there have been too many recorded versions of "Auld Lang Syne" to even count. While Lombardo's is the one that most people think of, there have been others of note. In 1964, the Beach Boys released a Holiday album called *The Beach Boys' Christmas Album* that included a beautiful a cappella version of the song and just in time for the turn of the millennia, Kenny G released a version he called "Auld Lang Syne (The Millennium Mix)" which featured an incredible instrumental version of the song played by G interspersed with famous audio clips from the 20th century. Kenny G became the first artist to take "Auld Lang Syne" into the Top 10 in January of 2000. Ten years later Mariah Carey released a house version called "Auld Lang Syne (The New Year's Anthem)." A year later, in 2011, Lombardo's version peaked at #2.

So what *does* the song mean? What do we mean when a year is just minutes old and we sing: "Should old acquaintance be forgot and never brought to mind? Should old acquaintance be forgot and old lang syne?" Billy Crystal's character in the 1989 rom-com *When Harry Met Sally* wondered just that, when he said: "What does this song mean? My whole life, I don't know what this song means. I mean, 'Should old acquaintance be forgot,' does that mean we should forget old acquaintances or does it mean that if we should happen to forget them, we should remember them which is not possible, because we already forgot?" The answer, of course, can best be summed up the way Meg Ryan's character does: "It's about old friends." That's the reason the poem so intrigued Robert Burns when he first heard it "from an old man" and it's the reason the song is so popular today of all days, as we look back on the year that is ending. It's good to recall the good times we had with our loved ones and raise a "cup of kindness" for old time's sake.

# Acknowledgements

This whole project began with a few Facebook posts. When David Bowie died I told a few stories about his career and got some awesome feedback from some of my social media friends. I started telling other stories with an "On This Date" theme and the feedback continued. I kept going. I'll never forget a day about three months into posting when I was in Las Vegas on business. I woke up and saw that I had two posts on Facebook asking, "Where's my daily music post?" It was morning in Vegas but lunchtime back home and I'd never posted that late. That's when it hit me that people were anticipating these stories and I had to continue. All that encouragement kept me going for 365 straight days: researching, writing and sharing. So first and foremost I want to thank those people I am connected with on Facebook who encouraged me early on. Your comments and shares were awesome motivation for me.

Speaking of research I need to begin by thanking Al Gore for inventing the internet. Without it, this project would have taken five times longer. There's a wealth of knowledge out there on the world wide web (duh!) So many old interviews have been archived, so many documentaries are on Youtube. I'd get an idea of something to write about and after a good Google search and a few clicks, I had my information. There were many sites that helped tremendously but the ones that stand out are Billboard.com, RollingStone.com, SongFacts.com, ThisDayInMusic.com and Wikipedia.com. And of course I referenced many of the books I've read through the years so to authors like Stephen Davis and Jerry Hopkins and Wendy Leigh (just to name a few) I tip my cap and offer my eternal gratitude. As I do to the artists who have written their own memoirs, like Rod Stewart, Paul Stanley and Pete Townsend. Your firsthand accounts have been fascinating reads and invaluable research.

Once I had a completed manuscript I needed it proofread. My brother Mark began the process and helped point out some styling issues that I hadn't thought of. Thank you Mark! I also have to thank my friend Neen James for turning me on to a wonderful woman named Barb. Barb did an amazing job cleaning up my typos and sloppy grammar as did my second proofreader, my dear friend Randy Bartlett. He not only caught the few things Barb hadn't but he saved me from some musical embarrassments as well (Mary G. Blige? Really?) Any mistakes still in the text fall completely on my shoulders and I take full responsibility.

Also, I need to send a huge thanks across the country to Steve Addeo who designed the cover. Steve is an incredible artist and visionary who not only suggested the record shot for the cover but gave me a subtitle when I hadn't even thought of one. Plus he's promised to mention me in his Oscar acceptance speech someday.

And finally, thank you for reading this. It was a long project from start to finish and there were many times I thought to just throw in the towel and leave these essays to my Facebook memories. But I decided to keep going simply because I wanted these stories read and enjoyed. I hope you have done just that.

# Index by Artist or Subject Matter

Disco Demolition Night July 12th
Dolly Parton December 5th
Don Kirshner September 12th, October 5th and 10th
Don McClain January 25th
Donna Summer November 26th
Doobie Brother July 1st
Dr. Dre April 3rd, September 3rd
Duane Allman October 29th

Earth Wind and Fire February 10th
Eddy Grant April 11th
Edgar Winter May 26th
Edison, Thomas February 19th
Edwin Starr September 5th
Elton John January 18th, February 16th, October 26th
Elvis Presley June 26th, July 19th, August 13th , September 10th, October 15th, December 4th
Eminem January 29th, April 3rd
Eric Clapton June 7th, July 30th, September 7th, October 29th, December 11th
Eurythmics September 4th

Faces November 17th
Fifth Dimension May 23rd
Flashdance May 29th
Fleetwood Mac February 4th, August 20th
Foreigner January 4th
Four Seasons March 13th
Francis Scott Key September 11th
Franke Previte December 2nd
Frank Sinatra February 27th, May 14th,  July 2nd
Frank Zappa March 25th, July 9th, August 8th

Gamble & Huff March 29th
Garth Brooks August 6th
Gary Lewis and the Playboys February 26th
Generation X March 27th, December 14th
Genesis May 31st
George Harrison March 15th, September 7th, October 18th, November 27th
George Michael October 30th
Gilbert O'Sullivan March 23rd, July 26th, September 2nd
Giorgio Moroder May 29th, September 4th, November 26th
Gladys Knight October 27th
Glenn Miller September 23rd
Gloria Gaynor March 10th
Grandmaster Flash January 12th
Grateful Dead August 9th, December 6th
Grease June 10th
Green Day September 21st
Guglielmo Marconi  March 2nd
Guess Who May 9th
Guns n Roses July 21st
Guy Lombardo December 31st

Hall and Oates March 26th
Hank Ballard and the Midnighters September 30th
Hanson May 24th
Harry Chapin December 27th
Heart February 14th

Holland-Dozier-Holland January 9th, July 30th, August 22nd
Hootie and the Blowfish May 30th
Hoyt Axton April 17th

Ice-T July 28th
Iggy Pop April 7th
Ike Turner March 3rd
INXS October 19th
Irene Cara May 29th

Jackie Brenston March 3rd
Jackie Wilson August 4th
Jackson Five June 20th and 30th
James Brown September 12th  October 24th
James Taylor June 12th
Janet Jackson February 1st
Janis Joplin January 11th
Jay Z July 18th, October 17th
Jeff Lynne March 15th, October 18th
Jefferson Airplanes December 6th
Jermaine Dupri April 25th
Jerry Garcia August 9th
Jerry Lee Lewis December 4th and 12th
Jesus Christ Superstar May 10th
Jethro Tull January 10th, June 6th, December 11th
Jimi Hendrix August 17th, September  11th and 18th
Jim Morrison  March 1st
Jim Steinman April 18th, October 21st
Jimmy Buffet January 16th
Jimmy Cliff March 11th
Joan Jett March 20th
John Hammond  January 23rd, March 19th, August 25th,
John Lennon June 1st, August 3rd, September 20th, December 8th, 11th and 29th
Johnny Cash January 13th, December 4th
Johnny Nash December 1st
Joni Mitchell July 3rd, November 7th
Journey November 19th
Justin Timberlake February 1st, October 7th

Kansas April 22nd
Kanye West October 1st
KC and the Sunshine Band September 2nd
Keith Richards March 27th and 31st, June 3rd and 4th, July 11th, December 11th
Kenny Loggins April 18th
Kenny Rogers January 28th, November 29th
Kid Rock February 1st
Kim Carnes July 24th
KISS May 20th, October 28th
Kool and the Gang February 7th
Kris Kristofferson January 11th
Kris Kross April 25t
Kurt Cobain April 5th, September 13th

Led Zeppelin January 1st, March 5th, June 21st, July 13th
Lenny Kravitz January 5th
Leonard Cohen December 13th
Linda Ronstadt May 27th, June 28th, December 5th,
Lionel Richie January 28th, August 24th, October 6th, November 29th
Little Richard September 14th

Live Aid July 13th
Los Del Rio November 2nd
Lou Reed August 23rd
Lynyrd Skynyrd June 24th, October 20th

Madonna January 5th and 26th, May 6th, October 6th
Marcia Griffith November 23rd
Marc Bolan March 14th
Mariah Carey June 20th
Mark Ronson  April 24th, July 23rd
Malcolm McLaren May 27th, July 5th, October 12th, November 18th
Marvin Gaye January 9th, August 10th, September 5th and 8th
Maureen McGovern August 12th
Max Martin January 31, September 6th
MC Hammer June 9th
MC5   April 7th and 16th
Meatloaf April 1st, October 21st
Metallica January 10th, September 3rd
Michael Jackson January 28th, April 11th and 21st, May 16th, June 30th, November 8th and 12th
Michael Sembello May 29th
Mick Jagger January 6th, May 25th, June 4th and 29th, December 6th and 11th
Milli Vanilli November 15th
Million Dollar Quartet December 4th
Monkees September 12th, October 10th
Motley Crue January 17th
Motown 25th Anniversary May 16th
Mott the Hoople November 11th
MTV January 26th, April 11th and 23rd, June 20th, August 1st, September 17th, October 8th, December 17th
Mutt Lange January 4th, December 20th

Nancy Sinatra February 27th
Napster September 3rd
Nat King Cole November 5th
Naughty By Nature November 12th
Neil Diamond September 12th and 16th, December 22nd
Neil Young May 4th, June 24th September 19th
Nelly February 1st, July 6th
New York City Blackout July 14th
Niles Rodgers  January 12th and 26th, April 8th and 14th, December 26th
Nirvana April 5th, September 13th
Norman Greenbaum April 20th
Nortorious BIG February 13th, March 9th, June 14th

Otis Day  August 4th
Otis Redding March 16t, June 16th
Ozzie Osbourne January 20th

Pat Benatar February 20th
Patsy Cline August 21st
Pattie Boyd September 7th
Paul Anka May 14th, August 5th and 31st
Paul McCartney May 19th, September 28th, October 9th, December 29th
Paul Simon January 7th, March 11th, October 11th, November 8th
Pearl Jam December 10th
Percy Sledge May 28th

Pete Best August 16th
Pete Seeger June 1st, July 25th, September 16th, November 7th, December 16th and 30th
Peter Frampton April 10th
Peter Gabriel May 31st
Pharrell May 1st, July 6th, August 10th
Phil Collins July 13th
Phil Spector January 30th, February 6th, June 18th, July 16th, August 15th, November 27th
Pink Floyd February 5th, March 22nd, April 28th, December 3rd
Prince January 28th, March 15th, April 2nd, May 11th, August 20th, November 20th
Procol Harem May 12th
Puff Daddy June 14th

Queen June 27th, July 13th, August 28th, October 31st, November 3rd
Quincy Jones January 28th , April 21st, November 8th

Ray Charles January 28th, June 23rd, October 1st
Red Hot Chilli Peppers September 24th
Richard Hell November 18th
Richie Havens August 17th
Richie Valens February 3rd
Rick Rubin March 7th, August 2nd, September 24th and 29th,
Ricky Astley March 12th
Ricky Martin May 17th
Righteous Brothers February 6th, June 18th
Risky Business August 7th
Rob Base and DJ E-Z Rock September 1st
Robert Stigwood January 21st, May 13th,
Robin Thicke May 1st, August 10th
Rock and Roll Hall of Fame January 23rd, March 15th
Rocky Movies  August 28th
Rocky Horror Picture Show April 1st
Rod Stewart October 2nd, November 17th
Rolling Stone Magazine November 9th
Roy Orbison September 26th, October 18th
Run DMC September 29th
Rupert Holmes December 23rd
Rush February 12th
Russell Simmons March 7th, July 14th, September 29th

Sam Phillips January 13th, January 23rd, March 3rd, June 26th, July 19th, September 26th, December 4th and 19th
Santana April 4th October 23rd, December 6th
Saturday Night Fever January 21st
Saturday Night Live May 11th, October 3rd and 11th, November 10th
Sheryl Crow November 14th
Sid and Nancy October 12th
Simon and Garfunkel February 28th , June 8th
Simple Minds May 18th
Sinead O'Connor May 11th, October 3rd
Sir Mix-a- Lot August 2nd
Sister Sledge March 18th
Sly and the Family Stone December 18th
Sonny Bono August 15th
Soulja Boy August 27th
Spice Girls February 22nd
Spinal Tap March 4th

Star Spangled Banner September 11th
Starland Vocal Band July 10th
Steely Dan February 21st
Steve Winwood June 7th, July 30th
Stevie Nicks August 20th
Stevie Ray Vaugh
Stevie Wonder January 18th and 28th May
19th and 21st November 24th
Sting April 29th, June 14th , October 13th
Stone Temple Pilots September 9th
Stooges April 7th
Storm Thorgerson December 3rd
Studio 54 April 26th, May 20th, December
26th
Styx July 7th
Super Bowl Shuffle February 8th
Summer of Love March 28th, May 12th, June
5th, July 8th, September 18th,
Survivor August 28th

T Rex March 14th
Talking Heads December 7th
Taylor Swift September 6th
Tears for Fears August 3rd
Television November 18th, December 28th
The Band November 25th
The Beatles January 1st and 30th, February
11th, 15th and 29th, March 21st, June 25th,
July 8th, August 16th and 29th, September
28th, October 9th, November 27th,
December 29th
The Bee Gees January 21st
The Big Bopper February 3rd
The Bodyguard December 5th
The Byrds December 16th
The Carpenters November 21st
The Cars August 26th
The Chiffons March 30th
The Clash January 22nd, July 5th
The Commodores August 24th
The Doors March 1st, May 5th, June 5th
The Eagles May 7th, June 28th
The Go-Gos March 6th
The Graduate June 8th
The Isley Brothers August 4th
The Kingsmen January 14th
The Kinks January 1th, November 28th
The Knack June 11th
The Lion King December 30th
The Mamas & the Papas July 29th
The O'Jays March 29th
The Police April 29th, June 14th, August 18th
The Poseidon Adventure August 12th
The Ramones July 25th, December 28th
The Rolling Stones March 20th, May 25th,
June 3rd and 4th, July 11th, August 11th
September 22nd, November 1st, December 6th
and 11th
The Runaways March 20th
The Sex Pistols May 27th, July 5th, October
12th
The Sugarhill Gang January 12th
The Supremes August 22nd
The Temptations December 21st
The Tokens March 30th,  December 30th
The Velvet Underground August 23rd
The Walkman March 24th

The Who January 15th, May 2nd, August 15th
and 17th, December 11th
The Yardbirds  May 2nd, June 21st
Three Dog Night April 17th
Tina Turner September 15th
Todd Rundgren October 21st
Tom Kelly January 26th, April 2nd
Tom Petty March 15t,  July 4th,  October 18th
Tommy Edwards November 4th
Tommy James June 15th
Tommy Tutone November 16th
Tone Lōc May 22nd
Toni Basil December 17th
Train April 13th
Traveling Wilbury's October 18th
Tupac February 13th, March 9th
U2 March 17th

Van Halen February 25th
Van Morrison January 27th, March 28th
Vanilla Ice November 3rd
Village People February 17th

Warren Zevon  January 8th
We Are the World January 28th
Wham! October 30th
Whitney Houston April 4th, September 11th,
December 5th
Willie Nelson August 21st
Wiz Khalifa June 19th
Woodstock May 2nd, July 15th, August 17th
Woody Guthrie February 23r, March 19th,
December 16th

Yes February 2nd, April 15th
Young MC May 22nd
Yvonne Elliman May 13th

ZZ Top July 22nd

*Not in this book, but
should be —
Josie James
Theresa Brewer
Patti Page
Jo Stafford*

*over*

## Not in this Book

Teresa Brewer
Joni James
Frankie Laine
Patti Page
Pat Boone
Les Paul & Mary Ford
Jo Stafford
Paul Anka

CPSIA information can be obtained
at www.ICGtesting.com
Printed in the USA
FSHW022120081221
86803FS

9 780692 179796